FINALS
MPRE Exam

CORE CONCEPTS AND KEY QUESTIONS

PUBLISHING

New York

This publication is designed to provide accurate and authoritative information in regard to the subject matter covered. It is sold with the understanding that the publisher is not engaged in rendering legal, accounting, or other professional service. If legal advice or other expert assistance is required, the services of a competent professional should be sought.

Series Editor: Lisa T. McElroy, Associate Professor, Drexel University College of Law
Editorial Director: Jennifer Farthing
Editor: Michael Sprague
Production Editor: Fred Urfer
Cover Designer: Carly Schnur

© 2008 by Kaplan, Inc.

Published by Kaplan Publishing, a division of Kaplan, Inc.
1 Liberty Plaza, 24th floor
New York, NY 10006

All rights reserved. The text of this publication, or any part thereof, may not be reproduced in any manner whatsoever without written permission from the publisher.

Printed in the United States of America

January 2008
10 9 8 7 6 5 4 3 2 1

ISBN13: 978-1-4277-9668-4

Kaplan Publishing books are available at special quantity discounts to use for sales promotions, employee premiums, or educational purposes. Please email our Special Sales Department to order or for more information at kaplanpublishing@kaplan.com, or write to Kaplan Publishing, 1 Liberty Plaza, 24th floor, New York, NY 10006.

TABLE OF CONTENTS

INTRODUCTION	v

I. INTRODUCTION — 1
- A. Purpose of Professional Responsibility — 1
- B. Sources of Professional Responsibility — 1
- C. The Bar Examinations — 1
- D. Purpose and Scope of this Book — 2

II. FORMAT OF THE GUIDELINES — 2
- A. Format of the Model Rules of Professional Conduct (MRPC) — 2
- B. Format of the Code of Professional Responsibility: Disciplinary Rules Versus Ethical Considerations — 3
- C. Neither Code Ascribes Punishment Nor Civil Liability — 3
- D. When are the Rules Mandatory, When are They Discretionary? — 3

III. A SUMMARY OVERVIEW OF THE ABA MODEL RULES OF PROFESSIONAL CONDUCT (MRPC) — 4
- A. General Overview — 4
- B. A Lawyer's Responsibilities (Preamble) — 4
- C. The Duty of Competence (MR 1.1) — 4
- D. Scope of Representation and Allocation of Authority — 5
- E. The Duty of Diligence (MR 1.3) — 5
- F. Responsibilities to the Client (MR 1.4) — 6
- G. Fees (MR 1.5) — 6
- H. The Duty of Confidentiality (MR 1.6) — 7
- I. Conflicts of Interest Should be Avoided (MR 1.7, 1.8, 1.9) — 8
- J. When Disqualification is Necessary (MR 1.10, 1.11, 1.12) — 10
- K. The Business Organization as Client (MR 1.13) — 11
- L. A Lawyer may Seek the Appointment of a Guardian When the Client's Abilities are Impaired (MR 1.14) — 12
- M. Safekeeping Client Property (MR 1.15) — 12
- N. Mandatory and Permissive Withdrawal (MR 1.16) — 12
- O. Sale of a Law Practice — 13
- P. Duties to Prospective Clients — 13
- Q. The Lawyer as Counselor — 14
- R. Ethical Requirements of the Lawyer as Advocate (MR 3.1, 3.2, 3.3, 3.4, 3.5, 3.6, 3.7, 3.9) — 14
- S. Treatment of Third Parties (MR 4.1, 4.2, 4.3, 4.4) — 17
- T. Subordinate Attorneys — 17
- U. Non-Lawyer Assistants — 18
- V. Sharing Legal Fees — 18
- W. Unauthorized Practices — 18
- X. Bettering the Law — 19
- Y. Advertising and Solicitation (MR 7.1, 7.2, 7.3, 7.4, 7.5) — 20
- Z. Integrity and Propriety (MR 8.1, 8.2, 8.3, 8.4) — 21
- AA. Jurisdiction to Discipline (MR 8.5) — 21

IV. THE ABA MODEL CODE OF JUDICIAL CONDUCT (CJC) — 22
- A. Introduction — 22
- B. Preamble — 22

C.	Canon 1: Integrity and Independence	22
D.	Canon 2: Propriety and the Appearance of Impropriety	23
E.	Canon 3: Impartiality and Diligence	23
F.	Canon 4: Extra-Judicial Activities	26
G.	Judges Should File Annual Public Reports as to Their Extra-Judicial Earnings	27
H.	Canon 5: Inappropriate Political Activity	28

V. UNITED STATES SUPREME COURT CASES IMPACTING THE NORMS OF PROFESSIONAL RESPONSIBILITY — 29

A.	Advertising	29
B.	Solicitation	30
C.	Discipline for Extra-Judicial Statements	31
D.	Self-Incrimination and State Bar Investigation of Applicants and Attorneys	31
E.	Residency and Other Requirements for Licensing and Practicing	31
F.	Fee Schedules	32
G.	Corporations	32
H.	Competence of the Criminal Defense Attorney and Related Issues	32
I.	Supreme Court Cases Affecting Judges	33

VI. KEY PROVISIONS OF THE MODEL CODE OF PROFESSIONAL RESPONSIBILITY (CPR) — 33

A.	Bar Admission and Self-Policing (Canon 1)	33
B.	Advertising, Solicitation, Public Access, Fees, and Withdrawal (Canons 2 and 9)	34
C.	Preventing the Unauthorized Practice of Law (Canon 3)	38
D.	Preserving Confidences and Secrets (Canon 4)	39
E.	Perjury and Fraud Problems	40
F.	Avoiding Conflicts of Interest (Canon 5)	40
G.	Competence and Liability (Canon 6)	42
H.	The Limitations Placed on Representation (Canon 7)	43

PROFESSIONAL RESPONSIBILITY EXAM QUESTIONS — 46

PROFESSIONAL RESPONSIBILITY EXPLANATORY ANSWERS — 94

PROFESSIONAL RESPONSIBILITY ESSAY QUESTIONS — 130

PROFESSIONAL RESPONSIBILITY ESSAY ANSWERS — 137

MODEL RULES OF PROFESSIONAL CONDUCT — 157

ABA MODEL CODE OF JUDICIAL CONDUCT — 238

ABA MODEL CODE OF PROFESSIONAL RESPONSIBILITY — 261

INTRODUCTION

FINALS is a new law school preparatory series. It is designed to provide students with all the ammunition needed to succeed on their law school exams. Remember that **FINALS** is not simply another commercial outline series. Rather, each edition consists of several integrated sections. This edition contains a substantive outline; multiple choice questions similar to those that might appear on a law school exam, the bar exam, or the MPRE; essay exam questions; fully detailed explanatory answers; the ABA Model Rules of Professional Conduct; the ABA Code of Judicial Conduct; and the ABA Model Code of Professional Responsibility.

This edition of **FINALS** is designed to be used as a pre-exam study aid for law school exams and the MPRE. You should be aware that most law schools are now implementing objective AND essay questions on their final examinations. In the past, virtually all law school exams were written solely in an essay format. No longer is this the case. Now the modern trend is to test students with objective and subjective types of questions. Why? There are two reasons.

First, objective questions on exams eliminate the subjectivity of essay grading. All too often, students complain about the lack of uniformity in the grading of law school essay exams. There are constant charges of favoritism, unfairness, and lack of uniformity in grading. Obviously, objective exam questions provide a uniform and reliable grading scheme.

Second, law schools are beginning to realize that it is necessary to start exposing students to objective-style questions as early as possible in preparation for the Multistate Bar Examination (commonly referred to as the "MBE") and the Multistate Professional Responsibility Examination (the "MPRE"). The MBE is a uniform, national, 200-question multiple choice exam covering the six subject areas of Torts, Contracts, Real Property/Future Interests, Evidence, Constitutional Law, and Criminal Law/Procedure. The MPRE is a 50-question multiple choice exam that focuses on the Model Rules of Professional Conduct, the Code of Judicial Conduct, and relevant Constitutional Law cases.

Because **FINALS** is designed as an MPRE study aid, all of the questions and answers are based on the Model Rules of Professional Conduct, the Code of Judicial Conduct, and where applicable, the Model Code of Professional Responsibility. Thus, **FINALS** can be used by students all across the country without taking into account regional differences.

This edition of **FINALS** includes two types of simulated exam questions. The multiple-choice questions require knowledge of the black letter law and legal reasoning skills. Therefore, students might want to do a few of these each day during the weeks leading up to final exams and the MPRE. The essay questions require deep thought and extensive legal reasoning. In order to thoroughly prepare for law school exams, students will want to do a number of each type of question. To prepare for the MPRE, students will wish to do all of the multiple choice questions.

Best of luck . . . and we're sure that you will find **FINALS** to be a very valuable study aid in preparation for your law school exams and the MPRE.

I. INTRODUCTION

A. PURPOSE OF PROFESSIONAL RESPONSIBILITY

1. A good lawyer is fundamentally ethical. She may be skilled in several areas of substantive law and expert at legal analysis and oral argument, but her primary responsibility is to serve each client – as well as the profession – in a moral, scrupulous, and conscientious manner. This outline will discuss the written norms of professional ethics, often called "professional responsibility."

2. The most common complaints to state bar associations are that (1) lawyers are not diligent (e.g., do not return phone calls, miss deadlines, etc.); (2) they are incompetent (do not handle cases effectively); and (3) to a lesser degree, they are dishonest (e.g., they commingle or misappropriate funds).

B. SOURCES OF PROFESSIONAL RESPONSIBILITY

1. The regulation and licensing of lawyers is essentially a matter of state, not federal, jurisdiction.

2. Each of the several states has created its own bar examination and has its own case and statutory law, but there is a great deal of uniformity and consistency among the states.

3. Presently there are two major sources of Legal Ethics for practicing attorneys: the Code of Professional Responsibility (CPR) adopted in 1969 by the American Bar Association (ABA), and the Model Rules of Professional Conduct (MRPC), adopted in 1983 as the official ABA Code. Almost all states have adopted some version of the MRPC, although some states still follow the older CPR.

    a. The Code of Professional Responsibility was influenced by the 1908 ABA Canons of Professional Ethics, the 1887 Alabama Code, and the earlier 1854 Sharswood Essay and 1836 Hoffman Resolutions.

    b. The heavy involvement of lawyers in the "Watergate crisis" and repeated criticism by former Chief Justice Warren Burger were responsible for the promulgation of the MRPC.

4. Other sources of professional responsibility include: (1) ABA Formal and Informal Opinions; (2) each of the states' own codes (which are generally close modifications of either the CPR or MRPC); and (3) state case law. The ABA has also promulgated a separate Code of Judicial Conduct (CJC) which, though technically non-binding, is influential in setting standards for judges. Practicing attorneys who are faced with ethical dilemmas should consult the applicable codes and cases and call the local bar for advice prior to acting.

C. THE BAR EXAMINATIONS

1. Most of the states require bar applicants to pass a national multiple choice bar examination on professional responsibility called the Multistate Professional Responsibility Examination ("MPRE"). Most states, however, also include minor or major issues in this area on other parts of their bar examination.

MPRE Exam

2. The MPRE consists of 50 questions. The MPRE tests knowledge and understanding of the ethical standards of the legal profession. Specifically, the MPRE tests the law governing the conduct of lawyers, including the disciplinary rules of professional conduct currently articulated in the ABA Model Rules of Professional Conduct and the ABA Code of Judicial Conduct as well as the controlling constitutional decisions and generally accepted principles established in leading federal and state cases and in the procedural and evidentiary rules.

   a. The difficult debates in professional responsibility occur when two or more fundamental beliefs in the system conflict. For example, the United States legal system is adversarial in nature, and each party is generally represented by a trained lawyer. With such a system, the expectation is that truth will be discernible by the judge and jury. However, because of overzealotry, etc., often an adversary can obscure the truthfinding function of trial. Difficult issues in legal ethics occur when the need for an adversary system conflicts with the need for truth at trial. Difficult ethical dilemmas often occur when the advocate must balance the duties owed to her client against those owed to opposing parties. Similarly, the duties owed to the tribunal, society, and those owed to personal conscience may well conflict. The ABA norms try to balance these conflicts.

D. PURPOSE AND SCOPE OF THIS BOOK

1. Like the other Finals editions, this book not only sets out a capsule outline but also furnishes sample MPRE and law school bar questions and answers. In addition, included are sample Professional Responsibility essay questions intended to help students prepare for law school essay exams.

2. Note that, because the MRPC is the major influence on the Multistate Professional Responsibility Examination (MPRE), the key sections of the MRPC are included in the appendix of this book. However, this volume also covers relevant sections of the Code of Professional Responsibility (CPR). Therefore, they, too, are included here. Many law schools still follow the CPR because it provides such a comprehensive coverage of professional responsibility. It is important to keep in mind that for the most part, the CPR and the MRPC are consistent.

   a. All of the guidelines are very "readable." We therefore recommend that all law students and lawyers read the guidelines at the back of this edition of Finals in their entirety before reading this outline.

II. FORMAT OF THE GUIDELINES

A. FORMAT OF THE MODEL RULES OF PROFESSIONAL CONDUCT (MRPC)

1. The MRPC is divided into Rules and Commentary. There are eight broad headings of rules, with several rules under each heading. Each Rule is followed by several Comments. The MRPC follows the "Restatement" format.

B. **FORMAT OF THE CODE OF PROFESSIONAL RESPONSIBILITY: DISCIPLINARY RULES VERSUS ETHICAL CONSIDERATIONS**

1. There are nine sections or "canons" of the CPR. Each section is divided into binding "Disciplinary Rules" and aspirational "Ethical Considerations."

    a. An attorney generally is not subject to discipline for violating an Ethical Consideration, but is subject to discipline for violating a Disciplinary Rule.

    b. Because of the overlap between Ethical Considerations and Disciplinary Rules, and because some states have disciplined lawyers for violating Ethical Considerations, the drafters of the MRPC abandoned this format.

C. **NEITHER CODE ASCRIBES PUNISHMENT NOR CIVIL LIABILITY**

1. Neither the CPR nor the MRPC ascribes degrees of punishment for violations. However, according to state case law, there are several standard degrees of punishment: private reprimand, public reprimand, suspension, or disbarment. Generally, first time "honest" mistakes are either not disciplined or are handled via private reprimand. The more serious penalties are used for wilful mistreatment of clients.

2. The CPR and MRPC are not intended to impose civil (tort) monetary liability. Thus, attorney malpractice is not addressed in either code. However, the codes do set up an applicable "standard of care" which may be relevant in malpractice suits.

    a. The most common theory of attorney malpractice is "negligence." In order to prove attorney negligence, a plaintiff client must prove a deviation from the controlling standard of care. The test is not "community standards," but is rather reasonable national norms. The applicable code may aid the plaintiff in meeting his standard of proof.

    b. In a malpractice claim, the attorney is civilly liable for the errors of her employees.

    c. As a general rule, if the plaintiff-client's case was a "loser," she will be unable to prove damages. Thus, attorney malpractice cases are generally "trials-within-trials."

3. An attorney's error(s) may give rise to a successful malpractice claim but will not necessarily subject that attorney to discipline (because, e.g., it was a first-time honest mistake). Do not confuse these two distinct issues of discipline and civil liability. Discipline is the focus of this outline and of professional responsibility doctrine.

D. **WHEN ARE THE RULES MANDATORY, WHEN ARE THEY DISCRETIONARY?**

1. The following words and phrases indicate mandatory lawyer behavior: "must," "shall," "subject to discipline," and "disciplinary rule."

2. The following words and phrases indicate aspirational or discretionary lawyer conduct: "should," "may," "proper," and "ethical consideration."

III. A SUMMARY OVERVIEW OF THE ABA MODEL RULES OF PROFESSIONAL CONDUCT (MRPC)

A. GENERAL OVERVIEW

1. As noted, the MRPC has been adopted in most of the states. This outline will follow the order of the MRPC, which is divided into rules (some of which are binding and some of which are not) and non-binding commentary.

B. A LAWYER'S RESPONSIBILITIES (PREAMBLE)

1. The Preamble of the MRPC states that lawyers are officers of the court. Unlike the CPR, the MRPC was written to give guidance not only for the lawyer as advocate, but also for the lawyer as advisor, negotiator, mediator, and evaluator. A practicing lawyer plays all of these roles.

2. The MRPC advises the use of personal conscience and mentions each lawyer's personal responsibility to be ethical because lawyers are members of a self-regulating profession. The MPRC also says that lawyers should do *pro bono* work so that those who cannot afford legal services can still access the legal system. Note that this is discretionary language; the MPRC does not **require** *pro bono* work, but strongly recommends it.

3. Under the MRPC approach, the attorney's duty of confidentiality begins whenever a potential client approaches an attorney for legal advice and the attorney agrees to consider taking the case (even if she does not ultimately take the case). The attorney-client relationship begins after the case has been accepted. The relationship continues until either the attorney or the client informs the other of its termination.

    a. The attorney-client confidentiality privilege exists solely for the benefit of the client. The attorney cannot invoke it for her own personal protection.

C. THE DUTY OF COMPETENCE (MR 1.1)

1. The MRPC requires lawyers be reasonably competent in order to take a case. This requirement is satisfied by either reasonable knowledge, skill, thoroughness, preparation or by associating oneself with a competent attorney.

    a. In some cases, a lawyer need only have the knowledge base of a general practitoner in order to be competent. In others, a lawyer needs special expertise in a particular, specialized field.

    b. In emergencies, a lawyer may give **necessary advice** to clients who need it, even if they lack the skill or knowledge ordinarily needed.

    c. In order to be competent, a lawyer must do factual and legal research into a client's problem.

    d. A lawyer should always keep up to date about changes in the law through continuing legal education and self-education.

Example: John, an estates lawyer, gets a call from a long-standing client who has been arrested for drunk driving. John has no experience in criminal matters, so, he calls his friend, Carl, who handles misdemeanor criminal cases. John and Carl agree to work together on the client's case.

D. **SCOPE OF REPRESENTATION AND ALLOCATION OF AUTHORITY**

1. In criminal cases, lawyers are to follow the client's wishes regarding whether to plead, whether to have a jury, and whether to testify. In civil cases, the lawyer must follow the client's wishes as to whether or not to settle.

    a. Where a client and lawyer disagree, however, about how a client's objectives may be reached, the lawyer should consult with the client to resolve the disagreement. If they cannot resolve it, the lawyer may withdraw or the client may fire her.

    Example: Sara is on trial for attempted murder. Her lawyer, Chris, feels that she will probably be acquitted if the case goes to trial. Sara, however, is very nervous about going to trial. She is a single mom, and she can't afford to go to jail. If she pleads, she will not go to jail. Against Chris' advice, she instructs Chris to accept the prosecution's plea offer. Even though he does not agree with Sara's decision, Chris must accept the plea offer on Sara's behalf.

2. Although a lawyer shall not assist a client in fraud, he should feel free to discuss the legal consequences of actions with the client.

    a. This rule suggests that lawyers should keep the lines of communication open and encourages them to tell clients the consequences of proposed actions.

    Example: Jacob is on trial for spousal battery. He asks his lawyer, Sam, what would happen "hypothetically" if he were to say (untruthfully) on the witness stand that he was out of town when his wife was hurt. Sam should instruct Jacob that to lie on the stand would be an actionable crime, and he should not help Jacob by allowing him to so testify.

3. A lawyer should not decline to represent someone because she cannot afford legal services or because he does not agree with her viewpoint or position.

4. Agreements concerning the scope of representation are acceptable and enforceable.

E. **THE DUTY OF DILIGENCE (MR 1.3)**

1. This rule requires attorneys to be reasonably diligent and prompt. In no way does the rule require attorneys to use standard approaches to problems, however.

    a. The Commentary indicates that attorneys especially need to attend to: (1) controlling work-load; (2) statutes of limitations; (3) procrastination; (4) informing the client that the representation is complete (so that the client knows the attorney is no longer overseeing her affairs).

F. RESPONSIBILITIES TO THE CLIENT (MR 1.4)

1. MR 1.4 indicates that lawyers must: (1) keep clients reasonably informed as to the status of their cases; (2) make sure that the client understands what the attorney is doing; and (3) respond to client inquiries. This rule is designed to allow the client to make informed decisions about her case.

   Example: Sydney's divorce has been pending in the family court for many months. Sydney calls her lawyer, James, to ask what is happening with the case. John should investigate (e.g., call the court, communicate with opposing counsel) and promptly return Sydney's call.

G. FEES (MR 1.5)

1. Fees must not be unreasonable. The MRPC enumerates several factors in deciding whether a fee is reasonable: (1) time required; (2) difficulty of the case; (3) the likelihood that acceptance of this representation will preclude the lawyer from accepting other employment; (4) customary fee for this kind of work; (5) the time limitations for the case; (6) the type of relationship between the lawyer and client; (7) the lawyer's experience; (8) the lawyer's reputation; (9) the lawyer's skill; and (10) whether or not the fee was contingent (which may, of course, yield a higher fee if the lawyer prevails).

2. With new clients, lawyers shall explain the fee and how it is calculated, preferably in writing, before or soon after the representation begins. The lawyer will also promptly communicate fee changes.

3. Contingent fees must be agreed to in writing. Such a writing must include the method of fee calculation and court and other costs (if any) to be borne by the client. Moreover, if there is a recovery, a lawyer must make a written accounting to the client.

   CPR Distinction: The CPR does not require contingency fee agreements to be in writing.

   a. Under the MRPC, contingency fees are prohibited in criminal and domestic relations cases.

   CPR Distinction: The CPR rarely permits contingency fees in domestic relations cases.

   b. Under the MRPC, court costs can be contingent on the outcome and can even be free for the indigent.

   CPR Distinction: The CPR requires court costs to be paid by the client.

4. The MRPC allows attorneys to divide the fee proportionately to actual work done, provided that (1) each lawyer takes proportional responsibility for the case; (2) such division is agreed to in writing by the client; and (3) the total fee is reasonable.

   CPR Distinction: The CPR allows fee splits based on proportionate (actual) work done and does not require written agreement.

   a. The client should be told what percentage of the fee each attorney receives.

5. Lawyers are permitted to receive property instead of money from clients, but such an arrangement is subject to more scrutiny if there is a dispute.

   Example: Susan needs help with a real estate transaction. She is buying a large farm, and she needs a lawyer to handle the closing. However, she is using all of her money to buy the property. Albert Attorney may accept an acre of the land she is buying as payment for his services.

6. In the event of a dispute with the client about the fee, the lawyer should attempt to have the dispute arbitrated, not litigated.

7. Lawyers may accept fee payments from third parties, but they must remain completely independent of those third parties and remember that their loyalty is to the client. Where a third party pays a lawyer's fee, the lawyer must still preserve the client's confidentiality pursuant to MR 1.6. and MR 5.5(c).

H. THE DUTY OF CONFIDENTIALITY (MR 1.6)

1. Lawyers shall keep all information relating to a client's representation confidential unless a client consents to its disclosure. However, they may reveal confidential information (1) to prevent reasonably certain death or substantial bodily harm; (2) to obtain advice about ethics; (3) to defend themselves; or (4) to comply with a court order or the law.

   a. The policy of this rule is to promote trust between the client and lawyer. Moreover, it is noted that clients will usually follow the attorney's advice when they know that the attorney will not reveal confidences.

   b. This rule ***does not require*** attorneys to reveal confidential information even when clients forewarn them of the intent to do a violent crime (the rule uses permissive language, i.e., "may," not mandatory language). Since the weight of authority and ABA Opinions take the opposite stance, this rule is likely still a minority national position.

   Example: Olivia is on trial for murdering three patients at the nursing home where she works. Olivia admits to Gary, her lawyer, that she did kill the patients. Furthermore, she tells Gary that she plans to kill another patient as soon as he is moved onto her floor. Gary may not reveal the fact that she has already killed three people but may tell that she plans to kill in the future. Note that, under the MRPC, Gary does not have to tell that Olivia is planning a future murder, but he may do so if he wants to.

   c. The rule allows disclosure of some confidential information when discussing the case with firm members or when engaging in authorized negotiations.

   Example: Evan, a corporate attorney, wants advice from Larry, a partner in his firm who handles litigation matters, about a corporate client's potential exposure to litigation. Evan may share pertinent confidential information about the client with Larry.

d. The confidentiality requirement of this rule applies also to government lawyers, even when they disagree with the official government policy.

e. Although the attorney-client privilege only applies when the attorney is called to be a witness or produce evidence, the ethical standard of this rule attaches to any information relating to the case, no matter what its source.

f. In no way should this rule be construed as to allow the attorney to help the client defraud a tribunal or commit a crime. Moreover, attorneys must withdraw if their services are to be used to further a crime, and they may disaffirm any opinion or document that the attorney produced based on fraudulent information.

g. MR 1.6 does not prevent an attorney from disclosing confidences to obtain her fee.

h. Attorneys must invoke the attorney-client privilege to protect the client in court, but they must obey the court, even when such obedience compromises the privilege.

Example: Where a client has jumped bail and left the court's jurisdiction, the court may, under the crime-fraud exception, require his attorney to reveal the client's whereabouts if they are known to him.

I. **CONFLICTS OF INTEREST SHOULD BE AVOIDED (MR 1.7, 1.8, 1.9)**

1. Lawyers must not take a case where there is a potential conflict of interest (with another current client, third party, or self) unless the lawyer has a reasonable belief that there is not a problem and each client consents *in writing* to the representation after full consultation.

    a. Certainly this rule precludes representing opposing parties in litigation.

    b. It does not preclude representing multiple parties, provided there is no conflict and each consents to any plea (criminal) or settlement (civil).

    c. It is acceptable to take opposite positions on the same legal question if such is in a different and later case or on behalf of different clients.

    Example: John is an attorney who handles mostly mass tort actions. In 1994, he represents a large class of plaintiffs who are suing an asbestos manufacturer for damages. In this case, he asserts that the asbestos manufacturer knowingly (and illegally) withheld information from the plaintiffs that asbestos was harmful if inhaled. In 2001, John represents a different asbestos manufacturer and argues to the court that the manufacturer had no duty to reveal the risks of asbestos to the plaintiff. John's advocacy, although contradictory, is acceptable in both cases.

    d. As stated previously, payment of the client fee by a third party is acceptable provided there is client consent after disclosure and no interference by the third party.

    e. There is a permissible conflict when the lawyer serves on a legal services organization that represents clients adverse to those represented by the lawyer's firm, provided the lawyer does not adversely affect any particular individual client.

2. Where an attorney enters into a business transaction with a client, (1) the terms must be fair; (2) the attorney's offer must be in writing; (3) the client should be informed of the conflict; and (4) the client must be advised that he should seek the independent advice of another lawyer.

    a. Attorneys must not use information obtained from clients against them unless there is consent after consultation.

    b. Attorneys cannot solicit gifts from clients or prepare documents giving gifts to themselves (except as a favor to a relative).

    c. Attorneys must not obtain book or media rights regarding the retelling of a pending case prior to the completion of the case. However, it is permissible to obtain as a fee a percentage of independent literary material that is the subject of the representation.

3. Where a lawyer represents multiple clients in a civil action, he may not accept a settlement on their behalf without their written consent. Similarly, in a criminal action, he may not accept a plea on behalf of defendant clients without their written consent. The lawyer must relay all material information about any settlement or plea to all of the clients.

4. A lawyer is not permitted to limit his malpractice liability (unless the jurisdiction so allows).

5. In settling a malpractice claim, lawyers must inform the client in writing that she should seek the advice of independent counsel.

6. Except for liens to collect his fee or contingency fees, a lawyer may not obtain a proprietary interest in the subject of a litigation.

7. A lawyer may not have sexual relations with a client if the sexual relationship begins after the attorney-client relationship. Preexisting consensual relationships are permitted.

8. If the opposing counsel is a close relative, the lawyer shall not take the case unless there is consent after consultation. However, if the lawyer is disqualified because of a familial relationship to opposing counsel, the disqualified lawyer's firm is not disqualified provided the disqualified lawyer stays away from the case.

9. It is impermissible for a lawyer or his firm to oppose a former client on a related matter or to use privileged information against a former client unless there is written consent after consultation.

    Example: In 1991, Loretta represented Simone in an action for encroachment against Simone's next door neighbor, Luis. In 1993, Luis approaches Loretta and asks her to sue Simone for trespass, as he still feels that the property she claims as her own actually belongs to him. Loretta may not accept the case unless Simone consents.

J. WHEN DISQUALIFICATION IS NECESSARY (MR 1.10, 1.11, 1.12)

1. As indicated previously, disqualification is necessary where there is either an actual conflict of interest regarding the lawyer's duty of loyalty to the client or where there is a potential conflict and the client, after being so informed, does not accept the arrangement.

2. As a general rule, when one attorney is disqualified, her whole firm is also disqualified unless the conflict is based on a personal interest of the prohibited lawyer that does not materially limit representation by other lawyers in the firm. There is a presumption that all partners and associates know about all cases.

   a. However, if a lawyer leaves a firm, his former firm may represent "a client with interests materially adverse to those of a client represented by the formerly associated lawyer and not currently represented by the firm, unless" it involves the same or a related matter or to do so would violate the confidentiality and loyalty rules.

   b. This rule of imputed conflicts does not apply when the disqualification is due to opposing counsel's being a relative, but it does apply (absent informed written consent) when the disqualification is because a former government attorney has joined a firm representing a party with whom he had contact as a government attorney (unless proper & timely screening is implemented and written permission is obtained from the government agency in question).

   Example: Susie is a lawyer with ABC law firm. Her client, Mabel, asks her to sue Rhonda. However, Rhonda is represented by Susie's sister, Claire. Susie should disqualify herself from the litigation, but she may ask her partner, Amanda, to handle the case.

   Example: Tamika was a U. S. Attorney for many years, but now she practices law with DTC, P.C., a private firm in Utopia. While a U. S. Attorney, Tamika handled an action against Christopher, an alleged drug dealer. DTC now represents Christopher. While Tamika should not work on Christopher's case, the firm may continue the representation.

3. Where a new lawyer in a firm was (1) privy to material privileged information and (2) had an adverse interest to the opposing party, the entire firm is vicariously disqualified, even retroactively.

   a. Note that the Commentary to MR 1.10 softens the rule. Vicarious disqualification is only a presumption; where there is no involvement with the relevant case in the old firm, firm disqualification may not always be necessary.

   b. The client may, of course, waive the disqualification.

4. A lawyer leaving a firm is permitted to oppose former clients unless it is on the same matter or unless he acquired material privileged information.

   Example: Jeanette worked as an attorney for many years at Silver & Smith, P.C. There, she handled cases on behalf of Cable, Inc. Now she works at Christmas & Easter,

L.L.P., who is suing Cable, Inc. on behalf of one of its clients. If she did not acquire material privileged information from Cable, Inc. while at the former firm, there is no conflict.

5. Former government attorneys shall not take clients with whom they were substantially involved when they worked for the government unless the government consents after consultation.

   a. Moreover, in this situation, the entire firm is disqualified unless: (1) the lawyer concerned is screened off the case; (2) the attorney receives no extra fee for this case; and (3) notice of the situation is given to the government.

6. Conversely, new government attorneys must take all reasonable steps to avoid taking cases with which they were involved while in the private sector.

   Example: Jonathan was an attorney with Hale and Farewell, P.C. While there, he handled cases on behalf of Tommy Traitor. Now Jonathan is a District Attorney, and he has been assigned to prosecute Tommy for bank fraud. Jonathan should decline to prosecute Tommy and ask to be assigned to another case.

7. Former judges, arbitrators, and law clerks shall not accept as clients parties who appeared before them unless all involved parties consent after disclosure.

   a. In this situation, even if the attorney is disqualified, the firm is not if (1) this attorney is screened off the case; (2) she receives no fee; and (3) notice is given to the applicable tribunal.

K. **THE BUSINESS ORGANIZATION AS CLIENT (MR 1.13)**

1. When the attorney is representing a business organization, his duty is to the entity itself, not to any of its officers or workers.

   a. Where the attorney learns of illegal or injurious conduct, the attorney should not immediately disrupt the organization ("blow the whistle"). Rather, the attorney should ask his contact within the organization to reconsider his conduct. If this approach fails, the attorney should then request that another attorney's advice be obtained. Where this approach likewise fails, the attorney may "climb the ladder" and ultimately resign.

   b. A lawyer may represent workers of the entity if there is no conflict or if there is informed consent (where required).

   Example: Jennifer represents BigCorp., a software manufacturer, on various corporate and litigation matters. Jason, a software engineer at BigCorp., approaches Jennifer and asks her to represent him on an action against his former wife for child custody. If she is competent to handle such a matter, Jennifer may accept the representation.

   c. Communications to the attorney are privileged insofar as they protect the entity. Thus, the attorney should be careful to apprise workers that the confidentiality rules do not protect them individually.

Example: Alexis represents Shallow Oil, an oil digging company that has been sued for environmental infractions. Joshua, an employee of Shallow Oil, tells Alexis that he dumped oil on the ground in violation of federal law. Joshua's communication to Alexis is not confidential, as Shallow Oil is her client, and she need not keep his admission secret if she chooses not to (especially if it is for the benefit of the client).

L. **A LAWYER MAY SEEK THE APPOINTMENT OF A GUARDIAN WHEN THE CLIENT'S ABILITIES ARE IMPAIRED (MR 1.14).**

M. **SAFEKEEPING CLIENT PROPERTY (MR 1.15)**

1. Client fees are to be kept in separate (trust) accounts in the lawyer's state of residence (unless the client consents to an out-of-state account). Other client property should be similarly safeguarded.

    a. Records of all property must be kept for 5 years.

    b. Notice to the client must be given upon receipt of funds.

    ***MPRE Exam Tip:** Providing client with notice of funds is a frequently tested issue.*

    c. Delivery of funds, when a client is so entitled, is mandated, as is a prompt accounting.

    d. When there is any question of ownership of the property, the property must be kept separate from the attorney's own funds. In the event of a dispute, arbitration should be suggested.

    e. The attorney owes a duty to her client, but also to third parties with legitimate interests (e.g., creditors).

    f. The client trust account must safekeep the client's portion of settlements, disputed funds, and client advances on court costs as yet unused.

    CPR Distinction: The CPR does not require court costs to be so sequestered.

    g. A lawyer may deposit his own funds in a client trust account to pay bank service charges, and shall deposit prepaid legal fees and expenses into the client trust account.

N. **MANDATORY AND PERMISSIVE WITHDRAWAL (MR 1.16)**

1. Withdrawal is mandated when (1) continued representation will result in the attorney violating an ethical norm or the law; (2) when the attorney is so ill as to be impaired; or (3) when the attorney has been fired.

    Example: Sharon represents Clara, a crotchety old lady who has trouble getting along with anyone. One day, after Sharon looks at her in a funny way, Clara tells Sharon, "You're fired!" Even if she does not want to, Sharon must withdraw.

Example: Clara orders Sharon to hide evidence from the prosecution. Sharon refuses, and Clara insists. Sharon should withdraw in order to keep from violating an ethical norm.

2. Withdrawal is permissible if (1) no harm results to the client; (2) if the client irrevocably intends to commit a crime or fraud; (3) if the lawyer finds the case either repugnant or imprudent; (4) if the lawyer's fee has not been paid and the lawyer had forewarned the client that in such instance she would withdraw; or (5) if the case is posing substantial financial hardship on the lawyer.

Example: Jessica represents Keith, who is accused of a hate crime against Ethel, an elderly woman. In the course of representing Keith, Jessica learns that Keith routinely beats up old ladies and steals their money. If Jessica is so repulsed by Keith and his actions that she can no longer zealously defend him, she may withdraw.

Example: Jessica represents Jonathan but learns that his case will come up for trial when she is scheduled to be away on vacation. She may withdraw as long as he has plenty of time to find another lawyer who can adequately represent him.

   a. However, withdrawal is not permissible if the controlling tribunal requires the lawyer to continue with the case.

   b. Upon terminating representation, the lawyer shall give the client notice, relevant client papers, and the unearned parts of the prepaid fee (unless applicable law allows an attorney lien on the papers to guarantee fee payment).

O. **SALE OF A LAW PRACTICE**

1. A lawyer may sell or buy a law practice if (1) the seller will no longer practice law in the same geographical and/or substantive area; (2) the whole practice is sold to one lawyer or group; (3) the seller notifies all clients about the sale, their right to obtain other counsel, and the fact that there is a presumption that they will remain with the practice if they do nothing for 90 days; (4) no greater fees will be charged to clients. If a client cannot be notified, his case will not be transferred to the new owners unless a court so authorizes.

P. **DUTIES TO PROSPECTIVE CLIENTS**

1. Even if he does not ultimately retain the lawyer, a person who interviews a lawyer for the purpose of representation is considered to be a prospective client.

2. Prospective clients are protected by attorney-client privilege and the protections of MR 1.6.

3. Clients are given the same protection when it comes to conflicts of interest with prospective clients. Therefore, an attorney or firm cannot accept representation of a person who has interests materially adverse to those of a current or former client. Of course, if a lawyer is so disqualified, he may nevertheless represent the client if both parties consent or if he did not receive too much information from the prospective client.

Q. THE LAWYER AS COUNSELOR

1. A lawyer should give clients honest, professional advice. In giving advice, a lawyer should take into account a client's non-legal concerns ("such as moral, economic, social and political factors") as well as a client's legal concerns. (MR 2.1).

   a. A lawyer should tell a client the truth, even when the truth is unpleasant.

   b. In explaining legal concepts, a lawyer should try to use layperson language and avoid technical terms (unless the client is legally sophisticated).

   c. A lawyer may refer a client to other types of professionals (such as therapists or social workers) where it is appropriate to do so.

2. A lawyer may prepare an evaluation of a client's case for another professional "if the lawyer reasonably believes that making the evaluation is compatible with other aspects of the lawyer's relationship with the client." If the evaluation will be detrimental to the client, the lawyer must obtain the client's permission for the evaluation. Such an evaluation is confidential. (MR 2.3).

   a. A lawyer should advise the client if the rendering of such an evaluation will create a duty for the lawyer to a third party.

3. A lawyer may serve as a mediator or arbitrator to help non-clients resolve their problems. However, the lawyer should clearly inform the parties to such an intermediation that he is not their lawyer and is serving in a neutral capacity. (MR 2.4).

R. ETHICAL REQUIREMENTS OF THE LAWYER AS ADVOCATE (MR 3.1, 3.2, 3.3, 3.4, 3.5, 3.6, 3.7, 3.8, 3.9)

1. A lawyer shall not bring a frivolous claim unless a good faith argument to change the law exists.

   Example: David does not like his co-worker, Ryan. David asks his lawyer, Samantha, to bring a sexual harassment claim against Ryan, claiming that Ryan laughed at David in a funny way and David was sexually intimidated. In this jurisdiction, laughing at someone is not considered to be sexual harassment. Unless Samantha can come up with a good faith argument that laughing should be considered sexual harassment, she should not accept the case.

   a. However, since the burden of proof and purposes of a criminal proceeding are different, a lawyer should pursue all appeals (even those not particularly promising) for the criminal defendant.

   Example: Ella has been convicted of larceny. Her lawyer, Christopher, wants to appeal the conviction. Christopher may argue that Ella was actually sleepwalking (and was therefore incapacitated) when she stole a radio, even if this defense is not promising.

2. Lawyers should attempt to expedite litigation.

3. A lawyer shall not knowingly lie to a judge regarding the facts or the law or offer evidence the lawyer knows to be false.

   a. Moreover, lawyers must cite adverse relevant law of that jurisdiction, even if opposing counsel misses such law.

   Example: Greg brings a case against Sarah for stalking. His lawyer, Fred, writes a brief in support of his motion for preliminary injunction citing old cases that held that following someone home from work could alone constitute stalking. Fred must also cite a recent precedential case in the jurisdiction that holds that essential elements of stalking are threats and intimidation, even if to cite the case would hurt Greg's chances of prevailing.

4. Lawyers shall take all reasonable remedial measures (including refusal to offer false evidence) to prevent a crime or fraud on the tribunal.

   a. The confidentiality requirements of MR 1.6 are inapplicable in this situation, i.e., when the crime or the fraud is upon the tribunal itself. Therefore, if a client will be fraudulent in a tribunal proceeding, the lawyer should confidentially remonstrate the client and disclose the fraud to the tribunal if the client refuses to cooperate.

   b. Lawyers shall remedy frauds on the court.

      i. This requirement may be satisfied by a request to the judge for withdrawal (with an explanation to the judge as to the reason for the request).

   c. Where the client intends to perjure himself, the lawyer should not assist him in doing so.

   Example: Bully is Sissy's lawyer in a case against Rocky Balboa. Sissy claims that Rocky beat her up on the playground. Sissy confides to Bully that Rocky did not actually beat her up, but that she wants to collect damages from him because he is very rich and can afford to pay. She says that she plans to testify that Rocky broke her nose. Bully cannot ask her questions on the witness stand about Rocky's conduct and possibly may not put her on the stand at all, if he knows that she is going to perjure herself.

5. In *ex parte* proceedings, lawyers shall make material facts known to the tribunal, "whether or not the facts are adverse." MR 3.3(d).

6. Lawyers shall not conceal evidence, destroy evidence, falsify evidence, disobey a court order, make a frivolous discovery request, inject their own personal knowledge or opinion at trial, or instruct another to falsify evidence.

   Example: Paying an expert a contingency fee is behavior reasonably likely to cause evidence to be falsified.

7. Lawyers shall not disrupt judges, nor shall they seek to influence or communicate *ex parte* with judges and/or jurors during the proceeding.

8. **Trial publicity** concerning (1) the identity, character, or credibility of witnesses, (2) a criminal defendant's guilt or innocence, (3) expected testimony, (4) a plea, (5) whether there was a confession, (6) examination results, (7) the fact that a defendant has been criminally charged, and (8) potentially excludable evidence is not allowed.

   CPR Distinction: Unlike the CPR, the MRPC also deems improper revealing evidence which will likely be excluded at trial.

   Example: A prosecutor may not tell the press that the defendant has been convicted on similar charges in the past (if such information is likely to be excluded at trial).

   a. Although it is acceptable to state a charge, such a statement should be prefaced by an explanation that the charge is an **accusation only** and that the defendant is "presumed innocent until and unless proven guilty." MR 3.6 Comment [5(b)].

   Example: A lawyer may state the the defendant "allegedly" trespassed on his neighbor's lawn or that a defendant is charged with criminal trespass. He may not state that the defendant "trespassed."

   b. It is acceptable to reveal (1) a claim or defense; (2) matters that are part of the public record; (3) that an investigation is ongoing; (3) the involved parties; (4) "the scheduling or result of any step in litigation;" (5) and/or a request for help or a warning of danger. Similarly, the accused may be named and the time of arrest (for a criminal case) may be made public. Finally, a lawyer may respond to publicity that may prejudice her client.

   Example: Adam Attorney may state that his client, Polly Plaintiff, is suing Donald Defendant and Darlene Defendant.

   Example: Pauline Prosecutor may ask the public for help in locating a witness who may provide crucial evidence in a murder trial.

9. A lawyer must not serve as an advocate if she is likely to be a witness unless (1) she will testify about an uncontested issue; (2) her testimony will concern the worth of her services; or (3) withdrawal poses a substantial hardship on the client.

   Example: If a matter involves a dispute about the cost of preparing a will, an attorney may testify that she typically charges $175/hour to perform this service even if she acts as an advocate in the matter.

10. Prosecutors have special duties: (1) they must believe there is probable cause of criminality in order to prosecute; (2) they must tell the accused of his right to counsel; (3) they must not attempt to seek from the accused a waiver of fundamental rights; (4) they must disclose all exculpatory evidence; (5) they must not subpoena lawyers to disclose privileged information about clients unless there is no other way to get essential information; and (6) they must control police behavior surrounding the investigation of the case.

11. If a lawyer appears in a non-court proceeding, he must disclose for whom he is lobbying.

S. TREATMENT OF THIRD PARTIES (MR 4.1, 4.2, 4.3, 4.4)

1. When dealing with third parties in their representation of clients, lawyers must not lie. Third parties must be treated with respect. Furthermore, lawyers must disclose material facts to avoid helping a client commit criminal or unethical acts (unless such information is privileged). (MR 4.1).

   Example: Evan Attorney is representing BigCompany, who is being sued by Agnes for environmental pollution. He has a conversation with one of Agnes' neighbors, Grace. When Grace asks him, he acknowledges that he represents BigCompany, but he does not tell Grace that Agnes has sued BigCompany (and Grace does not ask). His behavior is proper.

2. Lawyers shall not communicate with represented parties absent that party's lawyer's consent. (MR 4.2).

   Example: Scott is a witness in a criminal trial. Although he has been granted immunity, he was also involved in the crime in question, and he is represented by counsel. Defense counsel may not contact Scott without his lawyer's permission.

3. When dealing with unrepresented interested parties, the lawyer shall not state that she is disinterested and shall affirmatively correct any misunderstanding this person may have about the lawyer's (opposing or potentially opposing) role. Furthermore, a lawyer should not give legal advice to an unrepresented person whose interests conflict with the client's. (MR 4.3).

4. Lawyers should not harass or embarrass third parties. They should avoid obtaining evidence in ways that violate their rights. (MR 4.4(a)).

5. Lawyers who receive documents (including emails) relating to the representation of their clients and "know[] or reasonably should know that the document was inadvertently sent" should let the sender know. (MR 4.4(b)).

   a. *Note:* The Rules do not address whether the receipt of such a document would waive any privilege attached to it.

   b. Whether or not to return a wrongfully-sent document is a matter reserved for the lawyer's own professional judgment.

T. SUBORDINATE ATTORNEYS

1. Partners or supervising attorneys shall make all reasonable efforts to ensure that all attorneys in their employ comply with the ethical rules and have policies in place to further that goal. Moreover, supervising attorneys are personally responsible for ethical violations if they order or ratify the subordinate's work. (MR 5.1).

   Example: Lois Lawyer is a first-year associate at XYZ, LLP, a large law firm. XYZ is responding to a document request from opposing counsel. Her boss, Peter Partner, tells her only to produce documents with no handwritten notes on them, even though these must properly be produced under the document request. If Lois follows Peter's orders, Peter will be personally responsible.

a. Subordinate attorneys are professionally responsible for all work they do, notwithstanding the fact that they followed a superior's orders. (MR 5.2). When conduct clearly violates the MRPC, they may not engage in it. Where conduct is arguably ethical, however, a subordinate attorney does not violate the MRPC by following her bosses' orders.

Example: Lois Lawyer is a first-year associate at XYZ, LLP, a large law firm. XYZ is responding to a document request from the SEC. Her boss, Peter Partner, tells her only to produce documents with no handwritten notes on them, even though these must properly be produced under the document request. If Lois follows Peter's orders, Lois will also be personally responsible, even though she only did what she was told.

b. Where a subordinate attorney does not know that conduct is unethical, she may not violate the MRPC.

U. NON-LAWYER ASSISTANTS

1. Similarly, lawyers are responsible for overseeing the work of their non-lawyer assistants and are subject to discipline if they order or assent to wrongdoing. (MR 5.3).

Example: Jamie's paralegal, Gail, is working on a document production for one of Jamie's clients. In the course of going through the documents, Gail finds a "smoking gun" that all but sinks Jamie's case. Gail tells Jamie that she is going to conveniently spill grape juice all over the only copy of the document. If Jamie tells Gail to go ahead (or does not stop her), she will be subject to discipline.

V. SHARING LEGAL FEES

1. Lawyers shall not share legal fees with non-lawyers, except that they may pay into the retirement plans of retired lawyers and estates of former partners and may include non-lawyer employees in retirement or compensation plans. (MR 5.4(a)).

Example: Kate, Bonnie and Sally all work together. Kate is a lawyer, and Bonnie and Sally are real estate agents. Kate handles all of the closings for the homes that Bonnie and Sally sell. Kate may not give Bonnie and Sally a portion of the fees she earns for performing legal work, even if it is on homes that Bonnie and Sally sold and if Bonnie and Sally referred their clients to Kate.

W. UNAUTHORIZED PRACTICES

1. Lawyers may not (1) practice law with non-lawyers; (2) practice in jurisdictions where they are not licensed or authorized (or help others to do so); (3) allow third parties to control cases; or (4) restrict another lawyer's right to practice law after termination of a partnership.

Example: Gretchen approaches her friend, Cecelia, an attorney in the state of Camden, and asks her to represent her in a matter in the state of Gulf. If Cecelia is not licensed in Gulf, she may not represent Gretchen there.

Example: June, a criminal defense attorney, knows that July, a former police officer who is not a lawyer, is very knowledgeable about criminal procedure. June proposes to July that they practice together; July will do everything that June does (e.g., draft pleadings, advise clients, do legal research) except appear on behalf of a client in court. They will split all legal fees on a 60%/40% basis. This arrangement would subject June to discipline.

2. Lawyers cannot be part of any partnership or other business association that "restricts [their] right to practice after termination of the relationship," nor can a client settlement be conditioned on the lawyer's right to practice. (MR 5.7).

   a. Note that public policy guides these requirements. If a lawyer is required to cease the practice of law or is not allowed to represent other clients, it limits his own autonomy and narrows the field of lawyers from which a client may choose.

   b. Note also that the sale of a law practice does not apply in this case.

3. When he provides law-related services to clients, a lawyer should ensure that they are distinct from the legal services he also provides. In the course of providing non-legal services, the lawyer should ensure that the client understands that there is no related attorney-client relationship. (MR 5.7).

X. BETTERING THE LAW

1. Lawyers should do some pro bono legal work (50 hours per year is recommended) and should attempt to better the law and legal profession. (MR 6.1, 6.4).

   Note: Pro bono work is not required, only strongly recommended.

2. When a client's interest is bettered by this behavior, the lawyer shall disclose his client's interest in this activity.

   Example: Denver, an attorney who sues landlords on behalf of indigent clients, is asked to serve on the state housing commission. The commission is a volunteer organization committed to helping improve housing in the state. If, as a result of serving on the commission, Denver is in a position to make policy that will help his clients, he should disclose this fact.

   Note: The mere fact that the policy will help his clients does not create a conflict.

3. Where a lawyer is appointed to represent a client, he should accept the appointment unless (1) doing so would cause him to commit an ethical violation; (2) it would cause him an "unreasonable financial burden;" or (3) the lawyer feels that he cannot represent the client well because he is so repulsed by the client or the client's cause. (MR 6.2).

   a. Appointed lawyers have the same duties to clients as do ones retained and chosen by the client.

4. Even if a lawyer has a client with adverse interests, a lawyer may serve as an officer or member of a legal services organization. However, he should not participate in the organization's decisions if to do so would prejudice a client or a client of the organization whose interests are adverse to a client of the lawyer. (MR 6.3).

5. A lawyer may serve as an officer or member of an organization that is involved in legal reform, even if to do so will affect the interests of a client of the lawyer. As noted above, the lawyer should disclose to the organization any benefit a client will receive from a decision of the organization, but he need not reveal the client's identity. (MR 6.4).

6. A lawyer may provide short-term legal representation for a client through a non-profit organization or court. Where he does so, the lawyer may not be able to systematically screen for conflicts of interest and is only required to withdraw where he actually knows of a conflict. (MR 6.5).

Y. **ADVERTISING AND SOLICITATION (MR 7.1, 7.2, 7.3, 7.4, 7.5)**

1. Advertising must be truthful and must not be misleading. That said, a lawyer may advertise "through written, recorded or electronic communication." MR 7.2(a).

   Example: An ad that creates an unjustified expectation in a potential client or that compares the advertising lawyer to other attorneys is misleading.

   Example: An ad must not state that the lawyer will definitely win a case.

2. It is impermissible to accept consideration for referral of clients, and all ads must include the name and office address of at least one attorney.

   Example: Harriet is an attorney in Milltown. Just as she is about to go out on maternity leave, Oliver Warbucks approaches her and asks her to be his attorney on a major case. Harriet sees dollar signs, but she knows that she can't take the case. She therefore refers Mr. Warbucks to her friend, Hilda. Harriet may not accept a referral fee or a percentage of the fees from Hilda, even though Hilda would not have gotten the case were it not for Harriet's referral.

3. However, *solicitation* (lawyer-initiated contact with a specific person for the purpose of representation) is not allowed, unless it is made to a family member, past client, or close personal friend.

   Example: Lisa, while driving her kids home from the mall, sees a major accident off the side of the highway. Lisa is tempted to stop and offer her card; she is an attorney who specializes in personal injury cases, and she can tell that this accident will yield major damages. To do so, however, would subject her to discipline, and Lisa keeps driving.

   a. Advertising circulars sent through the mail are allowed, but they should be labeled "attorney advertisement" and should be a general rather than a target mailing.

      Example: Angela, a medical malpractice attorney, sends out a brochure to everyone in her hometown of Oldtown, population 5000. The brochure reads, "Has a doctor missed a diagnosis? Has a loved one died due to medical malpractice? Call Attorney Angela for a free consultation." At the bottom of the brochure, the words "Attorney Advertisement" appear. Angela will not be subject to discipline for sending out this mailing.

   b. *Note:* The Supreme Court has held that non-misleading, written solicitations are legitimate.

4. In an advertisement, it is acceptable to identify the area of law in which an attorney practices, especially if one practices patent or admiralty law.

   Example: Jim places an ad in his town newspaper. The ad reads, "Jim is an attorney who practices real estate, securities, and estates law." This ad is appropriate and will not subject Jim to discipline.

   a. However, a statement like: "practice is limited to...," absent ABA-approved certification as a specialist, is not allowed.

      CPR Distinction: Unlike the CPR, the MRPC allows an attorney to use a trade name to describe his law practice as long as the trade name is not misleading.

   b. National law firms are permitted to use the same name in every state provided that the ad identifies those partners not licensed to practice in that state.

   c. Occasionally lawyers may share a secretary or a library but are not partners. In this situation, calling the association a partnership is clearly improper.

Z. INTEGRITY AND PROPRIETY (MR 8.1, 8.2, 8.3, 8.4)

1. Lawyers, bar applicants, and those appearing before a disciplinary board shall not lie.

   Example: Susan is applying to become a member of the bar in the state of Charisma. The application asks, "Have you ever been convicted of a misdemeanor?" Susan was convicted of a misdemeanor as a minor, and her record has since been expunged. Nevertheless, Susan may not answer, "No" to this question.

2. Lawyers shall not insult judges or make false or reckless statements about them.

3. When a lawyer has a reasonable belief that another lawyer or judge has acted unprofessionally or unethically, she shall report her suspicion to the appropriate disciplinary authority.

4. Professional misconduct includes not only the several preceding instances of victimization of clients, but also the commission of crimes involving moral turpitude, any dishonesty or the disobedience of any of the preceding professional norms.

   a. Those lawyers holding public office are obligated to follow an even higher standard of honor.

AA. JURISDICTION TO DISCIPLINE (MR 8.5)

1. A lawyer licensed in a state is subject to discipline in that state for all unprofessional or unethical acts committed anywhere.

   Example: Joan is a lawyer in Blueacre. She applies to the state of Whiteacre for a law license, and she lies on her bar application. Blueacre may discipline her even though her unprofessional act occurred in Whiteacre.

Example: Cynthia is a lawyer in the state of Sandville. While on vacation in the state of Wellington, Cynthia steals some money from a fellow traveler and is prosecuted in Wellington for petty theft. Sandville may discipline Cynthia even though her crime occurred in Wellington.

IV. THE ABA MODEL CODE OF JUDICIAL CONDUCT (CJC)

A. INTRODUCTION

1. The CJC was adopted by the ABA in 1972. As noted earlier, none of its provisions necessarily subject judges to discipline. However, as a practical matter, deviation from the standards may well lead to a judge being removed from office (via impeachment, judge panel, or recall depending on the jurisdiction). According to the Preamble, judges are bound by the CJC.

2. Six to ten percent of the MPRE is comprised of questions based on the CJC.

B. PREAMBLE

1. The Preamble reminds judges that the American judicial system is about fairness and justice and that the public must be able to trust it.

2. The Preamble also notes, however, that it is merely a set of guidelines intended to "provide guidance to judges and judicial candidates." It is not a code that imposes civil or criminal liability.

C. CANON 1: INTEGRITY AND INDEPENDENCE

1. Canon 1 indicates that judges should uphold the integrity of the judiciary. Judges "should establish, maintain, and enforce high standards of conduct so that the integrity and independence of the judiciary will be preserved."

    a. According to the Commentary, judges should act without "fear or favor" and always obey the law so that the public will continue to have confidence in the judicial system.

Example: Alexandra is a district court judge. One night, when she is working late, she hears her fellow judge, Andrew, tell his clerks that he plans to do his friend Jennifer a favor by dismissing a case against her, even though the prosecution has adequate evidence to go forward. Alexandra should report Andrew to the disciplinary authorities.

Example: Nellie knows that her fellow judge, Sam, regularly accepts bribes to decide cases in favor of certain big businessmen. One night, she sees Sam out drinking with the CEO of a big company. She sees the CEO pass Sam a wad of bills and hears Sam say, "No problem, buddy, I'll make sure the case goes away." The next day, Nellie investigates and sees that the CEO has been sued and that Sam is the judge presiding over the case. Nellie should report Sam to the disciplinary authorities.

Outline

D. **CANON 2: PROPRIETY AND THE APPEARANCE OF IMPROPRIETY**

   1. Judges should avoid impropriety and the appearance of impropriety. Therefore, not only should judges be honorable, but they should make every effort to appear honorable and impartial to the public. A judge is under constant scrutiny by the public.

      a. Judges should not be influenced in their decisions by third parties and should not appear to have been influenced.

         Example: Henry is a judge on the state Court of Appeals. He is currently hearing a case about a doctor who failed to diagnose a patient with cancer. The patient subsequently died, and her family has sued the doctor for malpractice. If Henry's friend, George, tells Henry that George's wife died due to the same doctor's neglect, Henry must not let that information influence his handling of the case before him.

      b. Judges should not use their name or influence or the prestige of their office to support private or personal causes. Judges also should not allow others to think that they are in a "special position" to influence decisions that judges will make.

      c. Judges should not voluntarily be character witnesses; however, if a judge is subpoenaed, she must testify.

         Example: Allison is on trial for defaming a co-worker. Allison asks her friend, Judge Judy, to testify at trial that Allison is a good, truthful person who would never defame anyone. Judge Judy should decline to testify unless Allison subpoenas her.

      d. Judges should not be members of discriminatory organizations.

E. **CANON 3: IMPARTIALITY AND DILIGENCE**

   1. Canon 3 indicates that judges should be impartial and should require and exhibit order, decorum, and professionalism. Judges should hear matters assigned to them and uphold the law. Judges should also be impartial and should not be "swayed by partisan interests, public clamor or fear of criticism. **Judges should put their judicial duties before all else.**

   2. Canon 3 stresses in several places that judges must act without bias or prejudice and must require all court staff and lawyers before the court to act similarly. A judge should not tolerate discrimination.

   3. Judges should promote equal opportunity to be heard in their court.

      a. Judges should not communicate *ex parte* regarding pending cases except with respect to administrative matters or emergencies where the non-present parties will not be prejudiced by their absence. Where *ex parte* communications do occur, the judge should promptly notify the absent parties of the substance of these communications and allow them an opportunity for input.

         i. Note that a judge may conduct *ex parte* communications when the parties so consent for mediation or settlement purposes.

ii. Judges may also communicate *ex parte* when the law allows them to do so.

Example: Nancy has a case before Judge Hawkins. She approaches him in the hall while court is in recess and asks him to consider a piece of new evidence. Judge Hawkins should refuse to discuss this matter with Nancy until all other counsel are present.

b. However, communication with other judges and law clerks is considered to be completely proper and not *ex parte*.

Example: Judge Louis is a judge on the state Supreme Court. He is very confused about a legal issue in *Smith v. Jones*, a case currently under review by his court. He may discuss the case with his fellow judges and with his law clerks in order to better understand the case and form an opinion about it.

c. In some instances, it may be necessary for a judge to consult with a disinterested legal expert. In such cases, the judge should give all parties notice and an opportunity to respond.

Example: Experts in a particular field may file amicus briefs, and judges may solicit amicus briefs if they so desire.

4. Canon 3 is very specific that a judge should "dispose of all judicial matters promptly, efficiently, and fairly." According to the Commentary, this means that judges should make every effort to contain costs and avoid unnecessary delays. Judges should also be punctual and expeditious.

5. Judges should refrain from public comment about pending proceedings and insure that their staffs similarly so refrain. However, judges may make public statements about court procedures for informational purposes. Of course, judges may make public statements about cases in which they are a party.

6. While judges may thank jurors for their service, judges should not express an opinion about the correctness of the verdict the jurors have reached.

   a. Were a judge to comment on the verdict, jurors would have a difficult time acting fairly and impartially on other occasions.

7. If a judge receives information in his judicial capacity, he may not reveal it for non-judicial purposes.

8. Judges shall administrate fairly and without bias or prejudice. Furthermore, they must require their employees to act accordingly.

9. Judges should cooperate with other judges and, when supervising other judges, ensure that they properly perform their judicial duties.

10. In making administrative appointments, a judge should avoid nepotism, appoint based on merit, and be otherwise fair in his dealings.

    a. The absolute immunity that judges enjoy for their decisions does not attach to their administrative functions.

Example: A state judge who wrongly fired a probation officer could be sued in his personal capacity. *See Forrester v. White*, 108 S. Ct. 538 (1988).

  b. A judge should not appoint a lawyer who is found to have contributed to his campaign in an amount to be determined by the state bar) unless (1) the position is mostly a volunteer one; (2) the lawyer has been chosen through rotation rather than individually; or (3) there is no other qualified and available lawyer for the position.

11. A judge should report reprehensible attorney or judicial conduct to the appropriate disciplinary body. Such reports are absolutely privileged.

  a. Judges may also directly communicate with the offending party.

    Example: Judge Albertson learns that Attorney Christopher has offered a juror in a pending case a bribe to vote in favor of Christopher's client. Judge Albertson should immediately report the attorney to the appropriate authorities.

12. Judges should *disqualify* (recuse) themselves when their impartiality "might reasonably be questioned." Note that the standard for recusal is not whether the judge is actually neutral, but rather whether the judge *appears to be impartial.*

  a. For example, recusal is necessary where: (1) the judge was an involved lawyer in the matter; (2) his prior firm was involved; (3) the judge was or will be a material witness; (4) he or a household member has a financial interest in the case; (5) a close family member is involved in the case as a lawyer, party, or otherwise interested party; (6) he has a personal bias about a party or a lawyer before him; (7) he has knowledge about the case before him; or (8) he learns that a party or a party's lawyer has made a significant contribution (amount to be determined by state bar guidelines) to the judge's campaign.

  b. Disqualification is *not* required where (1) the judge was a government lawyer not involved in the present case; (2) the judge's "financial" interest is only in the ownership of a mutual fund which invests in the company of one of the present parties; (3) the judge's interest is only as an insurance subscriber; or (4) the judge's interest is only as a depositor in a mutual savings association.

    Example: A judge need not disqualify himself because he is a member of the ABA and the suit is against the ABA.

    i. CJC 3(F) further allows a *waiver* of disqualification if the judge discloses *on the record the nature of his interest and if all parties agree that the judge should not be disqualified*. This agreement should be entered into the record.

      (a) Previous versions of the CJC required this agreement/waiver to be in writing and signed by both parties. The current version of the CJC includes no such requirement, but only requires that the agreement of the parties become part of the record. However, the Commentary notes that the judge "may wish to have all of the parties and their lawyers sign the remittal agreement."

(b) Because of the shortage of judges and the delays engendered by recusal (particularly after a case is in progress), disqualification is generally frowned upon.

F. CANON 4: EXTRA-JUDICIAL ACTIVITIES

1. Judges are not required to be islands unto themselves. Thus, judges may participate in ***extra-judicial activities*** provided that these activities do not affect the judge's impartiality or appearance of impartiality or interfere with judicial duties. Furthermore, if the judge makes money from extra-judicial activities, he should report these earnings.

   Example: Judge Samantha enjoys teaching bar review seminars. She teaches about 5 seminars each summer for a bar review company. While she should report the income she makes from these seminars, she may properly teach the seminars if she likes.

2. Judges may teach, write, lecture, and be a member of organizations. Judges may not raise funds for organizations. They may not be members of organizations that are litigious or discriminatory.

3. Although a judge may not properly speak at fundraising functions, he may attend them.

   Example: Judge Ursula is strongly in favor of helping orphans. She regularly attends dinners that raise money for orphans in third world countries. As long as she does not speak at these dinners, her conduct is proper.

4. Judges should not be officers of for-profit businesses except for those held by the judge and her close family. However, they are permitted to manage their own investments and those of family members, including any real estate investments they may hold.

   Example: Judge Jordahl did well in the stock market boom of 2000. He is now quite wealthy and enjoys playing the market. His investment activities are perfectly proper.

5. Judges should not testify at hearings before executive or legislative bodies except about the law and the legal system. Judges may also appear *pro se*.

6. Judges should not hold government positions unless they are law-related.

7. Judges may serve on boards of non-profit or government organizations that are legally related or that promote educational, religious, charitable, fraternal, or civic purposes.

   a. However, judges should not serve as officers or advisors of such organizations if they are likely to be litigious and involved in the judicial system, either before the judge or the appeals court to which the judge's decisions are appealed.

   b. As officers, judges may help plan fundraising, but shall not solicit funds (except from other peer judges). They may make recommendations for grants for legal projects.

c. Judges should not solicit members to the organization if prospective members would feel forced to join because of the judge's prestige or if such solicitation is essentially fundraising. Above all, a judge should avoid using his office to make others feel that they must join an organization or donate funds.

8. Judges should not engage in financial dealings with people who are likely to appear before them in court. Furthermore, judges should not "engage in financial or business dealings" if these will be perceived to be an abuse of the judge's influence.

9. Judges should not engage in financial and business dealings that require them to come in frequent contact with lawyers who will frequently appear before them. Judges should also discourage family members from engaging in such dealings because of the appearance of impropriety.

10. Judges should divest themselves of investments that would require them frequently to disqualify themselves. Of course, judges should do so in a way that would not cause them "serious financial detriment."

11. Judges may accept the following gifts: (1) public testimonials (honoraria); (2) books supplied from publishers; (3) social and family gifts; (4) loans received in the ordinary course of business and not as a result of the judge's influence; (5) complimentary invitations to bar functions; (6) ordinary wedding and engagement gifts; and (7) scholarships, provided they are awarded based on the judge's or judge's family member's merit.

    a. A judge should not accept gifts from a donor who is likely to appear before her in court. The gift requirements apply not only to the judge, but to the close family of the judge.

    b. If the value of the gift exceeds $150, it should be officially reported as per the suggested annual reporting requirements, *infra*.

12. Judges should not be executors unless they serve in this capacity for former family members and there will likely not be a conflict.

13. Similarly, judges should not serve as arbitrators or fiduciaries and should not practice law.

    a. Even if a judge is newly elected (in the state system) or newly appointed (the federal method) to office, she is not permitted to practice law, even to "wrap things up", once she is sworn in.

14. Judges also should avoid governmental appointments except to governmental commissions dedicated to improving the administration of justice.

G. JUDGES SHOULD FILE ANNUAL PUBLIC REPORTS AS TO THEIR EXTRA-JUDICIAL EARNINGS

1. As noted previously, gifts and loans over $150 should be reported on an annual basis.

2. Reimbursement (for actual costs of food, travel, and lodging, including for the spouse when appropriate) need not be included in this report.

3. Compensation for extra-judicial activities should, as a general rule, be reasonable, and should not give the appearance of impropriety. Compensation should be commensurate with that paid to non-judges.

Example: Remember Judge Samantha, who enjoyed teaching bar review seminars? She may accept a fee of $1000 for each seminar she teaches, but she should not accept an excessive fee, e.g., $100,000, even if her name draws prospective students in.

H. CANON 5: INAPPROPRIATE POLITICAL ACTIVITY

1. A judge's political activities should not cast doubt on the judge's impartiality.

2. Thus, *judges should not (1) publicly endorse other candidates; (2) personally solicit funds; (3) campaign for another elected office while sitting as judges; or (4) hold office in a political organization.*

    a. However, judges may vote.

    b. Judges may correct false information about judicial candidates.

    c. Judges may also privately express their views about candidates.

    Example: Judge James is a member of the state Democratic party. If the party wants to name him Parliamentarian, however, he should decline.

    Example: Alice, a candidate for school board, asks Lori, her friend who is a judge, to endorse her candidacy. While Lori may vote for Alice, she should decline to publicly endorse her.

3. *Upon becoming a candidate for a non-judicial office, a judge should resign her judgeship.*

4. Those judges who are elected should campaign with dignity and require their staffs to do the same. They should not make campaign promises (except that they may promise to be impartial) or state their views on disputed legal issues. Finally, they should not lie about their qualifications or those of others.

    Example: Sara is a candidate for a position as judge on the Utopia district court. She tells a reporter that she is against the death penalty and, if elected, would not instruct a jury to consider it. Sara has acted improperly in making this statement.

    a. *Elected judges are permitted to attend and speak to political gatherings*, to identify themselves as members of and contribute to a political party, to establish committees for their election, and to campaign in traditional ways when they are candidates.

    b. Committees for a judge's election may properly solicit campaign contributions. Campaign contributions should not be used for the judge's personal purposes.

    c. If possible, the campaign committee should keep the names and amounts of contributions unavailable to the judge, thus preserving impartiality and its appearance.

d. A judge's campaign committee is permitted to initiate contact with potential lawyer-donees.

5. Judges who are appointed may not accept funds to support their candidacy and may not politically campaign for office. However, they may communicate with appointment and recommending bodies about their qualifications or any other requested information.

   a. Candidates for appointed judgeships who are not already judges may continue to be involved in political activities.

V. UNITED STATES SUPREME COURT CASES IMPACTING THE NORMS OF PROFESSIONAL RESPONSIBILITY

A. ADVERTISING

1. In *Bates v. Arizona State Bar*, 433 U.S. 350 (1977), a newspaper ad in which an attorney advertised routine legal services and fees was held permissible. The state bar had prohibited such advertisements. Notwithstanding the state prohibition, the Supreme Court held that (1) this kind of advertisement improved the public's right to be informed; (2) allowed new attorneys to break in to the practice of law; (3) did not decrease the "professionalism" of the bar; and (4) would likely lower prices, thus benefitting the public. The court also noted that (1) Arizona's own legal services corporation advertised; (2) there was no evidence here whatsoever of attorney incompetence; and (3) in order to reduce prices for the public, volume (and thus ads) were necessary.

   a. The decision was based on the First and Fourteenth Amendments' freedom of speech and due process clauses, respectively. Under the First Amendment's commercial speech protection, when advertising is *lawful and not misleading*, it can be restricted only if necessary to further a *substantial government interest* and if the limitation is *narrowly tailored* to meet that interest.

2. *In re R.M.J.*, 455 U.S. 191 (1982) indicated that the old CPR "laundry list" approach to attorney advertising was invalid because it infringed protected speech. In this case, an attorney did not use the approved language of the state's code of professional responsibility in his ad. For example, the state code required attorneys to use the terms "torts" and "property" and R.M.J. used the more popular language, "personal injury" and "real estate." Moreover, R.M.J. impermissibly listed where he was licensed. *In re R.M.J.* thus stands for the proposition that attorney ads are protected commercial speech which cannot be limited unless they are "misleading." The old CPR laundry list approach became obsolete after this case.

3. In *Zauderer v. Office of Disciplinary Counsel*, 471 U.S. 626 (1985), the attorney placed an ad recruiting women for a lawsuit against the manufacturer of a defective "IUD" birth control device. The ad contained an illustration of the device. Under state law, such illustrations were impermissible. The ad also promised that if the attorney did not recover damages, the plaintiffs would not owe him a legal fee. The Ohio State Supreme Court deemed such a statement to be deceptive because it did not indicate that the client *would* be responsible for paying filing fees and other costs. The U.S.

Supreme Court held that the illustration and most other provisions of Zauderer's ad could not subject Zauderer to discipline because it was protected by the First Amendment commercial speech doctrine.

    a. However, Zauderer could be disciplined for not telling clients they would be liable for filing fees and costs.

    b. Another Zauderer ad, in which he promised no fee if the client were convicted of (criminal) drunken driving (without mention of the likelihood that plea bargaining also subjected him to discipline), subjected the attorney to discipline for several reasons. First, criminal cases cannot be handled on a contingency basis, the effect of Zauderer's promised refund. Second, the ad was deceptive in that it did not tell clients that many drunken driving cases were plea bargained to a lesser offense (in which case Zauderer would be paid).

    c. Therefore, although the IUD illustration was proper, Zauderer violated several other ethical requirements (i.e., he did not state that the client must pay costs, he used a contingency fee in a criminal case, and he did not state that a fee refund was unlikely because of the likelihood of a plea bargain). Zauderer's public reprimand was sustained insofar as it was based on the above three violations.

B. SOLICITATION

1. In *Ohralik v. Ohio State Bar Association*, 436 U.S. 447 (1978) an attorney initiated in-person contact with two 18-year-old automobile accident victims regarding representing them in a personal injury suit. He was uninvited but nevertheless contacted one in the hospital and one at home. Additionally, Ohralik refused to withdraw after being fired by each. The state bar's indefinite suspension of Ohralik was upheld by the U.S. Supreme Court. Such attorney-initiated personal contact for the purpose of representation is not protected by the First Amendment. The lay public needs to be protected from such "ambulance chasing."

2. However, where the solicitation is not for a profit motive and implicates a social interest, it is protected. Thus, an ACLU (American Civil Liberties Union) attorney who solicited women who had been and/or were to be sterilized as a condition of receiving government medical benefits for the purpose of blocking this procedure and penalty was protected under the First Amendment. *In re Primus*, 436 U.S. 412 (1978).

3. In the very important and somewhat surprising case of *Shapero v. Kentucky Bar Association*, 108 S. Ct. 1916 (1988), the Supreme Court held that the First and Fourteenth Amendments' commercial speech doctrines protect an attorney's right to solicit business by mail from named individuals regarding a specific legal problem, provided that the letter solicitation is not misleading. Attorney Shapero wished to send letters to individuals who had a foreclosure suit filed against them. The U.S. Supreme Court held that the public's interest in access to legal services outweighed the potential dangers in written solicitation. *Shapero* stands for the proposition that only in-person solicitation can be constitutionally prohibited.

C. DISCIPLINE FOR EXTRA-JUDICIAL STATEMENTS

1. *In re Snyder*, 472 U.S. 634 (1985), stands for the proposition that attorneys cannot be disciplined for extra-judicial statements critical of the judiciary unless they are gross deviations from propriety. Attorney Snyder, in a private letter, criticized the handling of a case by a judge. The letter, though arguably rude, did not subject Snyder to discipline, and his six-month suspension was therefore overturned.

D. SELF-INCRIMINATION AND STATE BAR INVESTIGATION OF APPLICANTS AND ATTORNEYS

1. In order to effectively license attorneys and maintain the integrity of the profession, state bars are permitted to investigate all aspects of applicants' pasts which may reflect upon their integrity. In *Konigsberg v. Board of Bar Examiners*, 353 U.S. 252 (1957), an applicant who advocated the violent overthrow of the government and who refused to answer whether he was a member of the Communist Party could be denied bar admission on these grounds. Note that the burden is on an applicant to show good moral character.

2. Although an attorney has a duty to cooperate with the licensing authority, she cannot be compelled to incriminate herself. *Spevack v. Klein*, 385 U.S. 511 (1967). Thus, an attorney could not be disbarred solely because she refused to testify and produce subpoenaed financial records (on self-incrimination grounds). The Fifth Amendment self-incrimination clause (as applied to the states by the Fourteenth Amendment due process clause) prohibited such penalty.

E. RESIDENCY AND OTHER REQUIREMENTS FOR LICENSING AND PRACTICING

1. In *New Hampshire v. Piper*, 470 U.S. 274 (1985) New Hampshire's residency requirement that the attorney must have a home address in New Hampshire in order to be licensed was held to violate the Privileges and Immunities Clause of the U.S. Constitution (Article IV §2). The court held that New Hampshire would have to have substantial reasons for refusing to license non-residents.

2. The court used similar reasoning in *Supreme Court of Virginia v. Friedman,* 108 S. Ct. 2260 (1988). Here, Virginia did not require Virginia residents who were members of another bar to take the state bar exam but did require non-resident attorneys to do so. The court struck down this policy, saying that it was a violation of the Privileges and Immunities Clause.

3. In *Frazier v. Heebe*, 107 S. Ct. 2607 (1987), the District Court for the Eastern District of Louisiana was not permitted to restrain non-Louisiana residents from practicing before it. Such restriction was unreasonable and set up an indefensible residency requirement.

4. In *Sperry v. Florida*, 373 U.S. 379 (1963), a federally licensed patent attorney who was not licensed in Florida practiced federal patent law in Florida. The Florida Supreme Court enjoined such practice. However, because patent practice is a federal matter, the Supremacy Clause of the Constitution prohibited Florida from enjoining Sperry's practice.

F. FEE SCHEDULES

1. In *Goldfarb v. Virginia State Bar*, 421 U.S. 773 (1975), a state bar's promulgation of recommended fees was held violative of federal antitrust laws. State bars are not permitted to set attorney fees. This rule allows the public to receive legal services at competitive rates.

G. CORPORATIONS

1. In *Upjohn Corp. v. United States*, 449 U.S. 383 (1981), the court held that communications from all levels of employees are subject to the attorney-client privilege.

2. In *Commodity Futures Trading Commission v. Weintraub*, 471 U.S. 343 (1985), it was held that the trustee of a corporation in bankruptcy has the authority to waive the privilege protecting attorney-corporation confidential communications.

H. COMPETENCE OF THE CRIMINAL DEFENSE ATTORNEY AND RELATED ISSUES

1. ***Incompetence subjects an attorney to discipline***. In several cases, the U.S. Supreme Court has set out what is and is not incompetent in the criminal context. A successful ineffective assistance of counsel claim must show that (1) the attorney's performance was unreasonable under prevailing national norms; and (2) there is a reasonable probability that a different result would have been reached with a competent attorney. *See Strickland v. Washington*, 466 U.S. 668 (1984).

    a. In *Nix v. Whiteside*, 475 U.S. 157 (1986), a lawyer's threat to his client that if he perjured himself the lawyer would (1) seek to withdraw; (2) tell the judge why he was withdrawing; and (3) be available to impeach the defendant's testimony did not constitute ineffective assistance of counsel.

    b. In *Morris v. Slappy*, 461 U.S. 1 (1983), the Supreme Court indicated that although indigents generally have the right to counsel, they do not have the right to a "meaningful relationship" with counsel. Thus, where the appointed counsel is competent, the requirements of the Sixth Amendment are satisfied.

    c. Although a defendant has the right to decline counsel at trial, *Faretta v. California*, 422 U.S. 806 (1975), this right is not compromised when the court appoints standby counsel, provided that the defendant is and appears to be still in control of his case. *See McKastle v. Wiggins*, 465 U.S. 168 (1984).

2. *Anders v. California*, 386 U.S. 738 (1967), discourages appointed defense attorneys from asking to withdraw based on a belief that the case is frivolous. In criminal defense cases, usually, an argument for appeal can be made. Thus, *Anders* requires from those appointed attorneys who wish to withdraw a statement that the appeal is wholly frivolous and a list of possible defense arguments. These requirements are, of course, somewhat contradictory. *See also McCoy v. Wisconsin*, 108 S. Ct. 1895 (1988).

3. *Jones v. Barnes*, 463 U.S. 745 (1983) indicates that appellate defense counsel has the discretion not to brief and argue non-frivolous issues as requested by the defendant. This case indicates that although it is up to the defendant ***whether to appeal***, what

issues should be appealed are within the discretion of the attorney. Disagreement with client-chosen issues does not constitute incompetence (which would subject the attorney to discipline).

I. **SUPREME COURT CASES AFFECTING JUDGES**

1. As set out in the CJC outline, the absolute immunity judges enjoy in decision-making does not attach to their administrative functions. Thus, a state judge could be sued for an allegedly sexually discriminatory firing of a probation officer. See *Forrester v. White*, 108 S. Ct. 538 (1988).

2. In *Aetna Life Insurance Co. v. LaVoie*, 106 S. Ct. 1580 (1986) at issue was the mandatory recusal (disqualification) of a state judge. Here, under Alabama Supreme Court procedures, each judge was to individually decide whether he was or was not to be disqualified. In *Aetna*, the questioned judge wrote the opinion, was involved in a case against the defendant, and had a pecuniary interest in the case (he received $30,000 in settlement). This extensive involvement by the judge was held to violate the due process clause of the Fourteenth Amendment. Disqualification was mandatory and reversal of the decision was therefore appropriate.

    a. This case supports the general rule that when a judge is financially involved in a case, he must disqualify himself.

    b. Although this case does not deal with discipline of the judge, it is likely that the judge — who should have recused himself — would be subject to discipline for this behavior.

3. In *Liljeberg v. Health Services Acquisition Corp.*, 108 S. Ct. 2194 (1988), judicial disqualification because of partiality was again at issue. Here, the judge was a member of a university board of trustees which stood to benefit. Although the evidence indicated the judge was actually unaware of the conflict, he should nevertheless have disqualified himself. Because he did not, reversal of the decision was proper. Judicial disqualification is mandatory when a reasonable person would believe the judge to be biased. The test is solely ***objective***; scienter (knowledge) is not required.

VI. KEY PROVISIONS OF THE MODEL CODE OF PROFESSIONAL RESPONSIBILITY (CPR)

A. **BAR ADMISSION AND SELF-POLICING (CANON 1)**

1. Disciplinary Rule (DR) 1-101 requires applicants to the bar to be truthful on their bar applications.

    a. Although good faith mistakes may be acceptable, intentional falsehoods are not, as they indicate the unfitness of an individual to practice law.

    b. The state bar has a right to investigate all aspects of the applicant's past which reflect upon his integrity. Moreover, short of incriminating himself, the attorney has a duty to cooperate with this investigation.

c. A hearing about an applicant's fitness to practice law can require the potential attorney to prove her fitness. State courts have inherent jurisdiction to license and disbar. Most state bars require all licensed attorneys to be members of their state bar association.

d. DR 1-01 also requires attorneys to further applications for bar admission only of qualified persons.

2. DR 1-102 is a catch-all provision which subjects attorneys to discipline if they disobey any CPR disciplinary rule, act with "moral turpitude," are dishonest, or interfere with the administration of justice. *See also* Canon 9, which requires attorneys to avoid even the appearance of impropriety.

Examples: Felony convictions, willful tax fraud, and direct dealings with individuals an attorney knows to be represented by a lawyer (without opposing counsel's permission) all fall within the rubric of this provision.

3. DR 1-103 *requires attorneys to turn in their delinquent peers (lawyers and judges) provided that their knowledge is unprivileged.*

a. An attorney need not report a peer when she merely "suspects" violation of a disciplinary rule. Only when the attorney is aware of a "clear violation" is reporting necessary. See ABA Informal Opinion 1379.

B. **ADVERTISING, SOLICITATION, PUBLIC ACCESS, FEES, AND WITHDRAWAL (CANONS 2 AND 9)**

1. The CPR positions on *advertising* have been superseded and are discussed in detail in the sections on the MRPC and U.S. Supreme Court pronouncements. It is sufficient to know that *attorney advertising cannot be misleading*.

a. Examples of misleading ads include: (1) calling oneself a partner if one is not; (2) falsely claiming specialization; (3) falsely claiming to hold a license to practice in a foreign jurisdiction; and (4) reneging on an advertised price. Incidentally, patent lawyers need special licensing and are allowed to state this special skill.

i. DR 2-101 requires honoring an advertised price for at least 30 days, or, if in the printed media, until the next issue (with 30 days as a minimum).

ii. DR 2-101(B) requires "dignity" in lawyer advertising. Some jurisdictions in applying this or similar rules have forbidden "jingles" in lawyer ads, testimonials, victory promises, and other such "hoopla."

2. Although the CPR provisions on *solicitation* have not entirely been superseded, U.S. Supreme Court pronouncements comprise the major testable issues.

a. Where advertising is presently generally permissible, *in-person solicitation still is not*.

i. Advertising is general public notice of the availability of legal services.

ii. Solicitation is lawyer-initiated contact with a specific, named potential client, either in-person, through an agent, or in writing.

iii. As U.S. Supreme Court cases indicate, only when there is no profit motive on an attorney's part and when the case implicates a fundamental right is in-person solicitation acceptable. Solicitation by letter, provided it is not misleading, is acceptable.

b. DR 2-103 not only prohibits solicitation but also prohibits giving anything of value to another who "refers" clients to that lawyer. Furthermore, lawyers must not ask others to find clients for them.

i. Only when referrals are state-bar approved or come via a legal services organization are they acceptable.

(a) Legal service organizations are desirable in that they enhance public access to the benefits of the law. However, they should be non-profit, the individual lawyer working for the organization must retain his independent judgment in the best interests of the client, and the organization must file annual reports. See DR 2-103(D)(4).

ii. DR 2-104 also requires that when an attorney gives a layperson unsolicited legal advice, that attorney may not take the case.

(a) There are a few noteworthy exceptions to this rule: attorneys **may** take work from close relatives, from former clients, and from those who will participate in a class action.

(1) In fact, it is likely the attorney's duty to inform a past client of changed law in an area which she did work (e.g., in a will). See ABA Opinions 173, 210, and 229.

(2) Writing a legal article or giving a public lecture on the law is acceptable attorney behavior because these activities help educate the public about the law. They are not considered to be solicitation unless the attorney markets herself in the talk or refers people back to her office for more conversation. However, it is acceptable for clients to approach the attorney of their own volition. (Note that attorneys in such public forums must be careful not to offer simplistic panaceas and must ensure that no audience member in a public forum be allowed to compromise his own confidentiality. Lawyer statements in such forums must be general and hypothetical only.)

3. **The public's right of access to legal services.**

a. Closely linked with advertising and solicitation is the public's right of access to legal services. In fact, both advertising and solicitation likely *increase* access! This is why prohibitions on advertising have been overturned. Nevertheless, as noted above, there are still major prohibitions on in-person solicitation. The above rules on legal services and public lectures indicate the tension between the principles of "professionalism" and "public access."

b. EC 2-26 through 2-28 *suggest lawyers take all cases, even those which are unpopular.* The Code certainly suggests that lawyers should do some free work for the indigent ("pro bono"). However, *pro bono* work is not required.

c. DR 2-109 indicates that lawyers must avoid only those cases that are **totally unsupported** by the law (unless the attorney can argue in good faith for a change in the law) and those cases brought entirely **to harass another**.

4. DR 2-106 requires that attorney fees be reasonable, not excessive.

   a. Among the factors used in evaluating the reasonableness of the fee are (1) the time required to complete the work; (2) the skill necessary; (3) the customary fee for this kind of work; (4) the result; (5) the experience and reputation of the attorney; and (6) whether the fee is contingent. Charging an excessive fee subjects the attorney to discipline.

      i. Contingency fees are those where the attorney receives court costs (investigation and filing fees) from the client and nothing else unless she wins the case. When she wins the case, the lawyer also receives a percent - often 33% of the verdict. Thus, contingency fees, when permissible, will often yield a higher wage than other fees. Incidentally, under the CPR, a client must repay any advanced court costs, even if the lawyer loses the case.

      ii. **Contingency fees are prohibited in criminal cases** - likely because of both an appearance of impropriety and because of an indigent person's right to free counsel when jail time may be imposed.

      iii. Although not outright prohibited, **lawyers should not accept contingency fees in domestic relations cases** or in other types of cases where the client is able to pay. This policy reflects the older position that, in order to remain objective, lawyers should not stir up litigation and should not have a stake in the outcome. These policies have mostly been superseded due to the bar's desire to make legal services more available to more people.

5. DR 2-107 *prohibits lawyers who do not practice together in the same firm from dividing fees unless* three conditions are met: (1) the client consents after full disclosure; (2) the fee division is proportional to the actual work done by each attorney and each attorney remains fully responsible to the client; and (3) the total fee is still reasonable.

   a. This rule in no way prohibits paying retired partners' pensions.

   b. The rule *does prohibit attorneys from giving each other "finders' fees"* and also prevents them from trading off cases without client consent.

6. DR 9-102 lays out other applicable rules regarding attorney fees. Under this rule, attorneys must take all precautions so as to keep inviolate the identity of client funds and property. In short, *attorneys must not commingle funds*. Where commingling occurs, the identity of the client's property is lost and there is a danger that the attorney, a third party, or an attorney's creditor will obtain the client's property.

   a. All unearned funds paid by the client to the attorney and all funds received by the attorney which are in any way disputed must be kept in a separate bank account.

b. ***This separate account is called a client's trust account***, and the CPR requires it be in the same state as the attorney's law office. ***A separate account for each client is not required***.

c. Attorneys must not place their own funds in this account except as necessary to pay the typical (monthly) banking fees.

d. Attorneys may take undisputed funds owed to them from this account, but categorically ***must not*** take disputed funds. Undisputed funds include agreed-upon earned fees as well as court costs and expenses.

e. ***Attorneys must pay to the client all undisputed funds owed to the client***. In the event of a dispute, bar-sponsored mediation is recommended.

f. All funds or property received by the attorney which belong entirely or in part to the client must be correctly labeled and recorded, and the attorney must notify the client that they were received.

7. Attorney withdrawal generally requires judicial approval when the case has a judge assigned to it. In withdrawing, attorneys must be careful not to prejudice the client's interests. An attorney may protect a client's interest by (1) giving notice; (2) allowing time for the client to find another attorney; and (3) by giving the client all papers and property to which he is entitled. Some jurisdictions allow attorneys to retain papers in order to receive their fee. However, the CPR and all states require unearned portions of the fee be returned.

    a. Under DR 2-110, ***an attorney must withdraw*** where (1) a client brings a case solely for the purpose of harassing the opposing party; (2) where a case conflicts with a disciplinary rule (e.g., as when the tribunal is to be defrauded); (3) where the attorney is extremely ill or otherwise incompetent; or (4) where the client fires the attorney.

        i. It is ***completely within the client's discretion*** to terminate the professional relationship. Since the attorney-client relationship is fiduciary in nature and since the power of the attorney generally far exceeds that of the client, undue penalties on a client dissatisfied with his attorney must not be erected. Thus, for example, a dismissed attorney is entitled only to the quantum meruit value of his services. The fee recovered may not exceed the amount of the original contract and, furthermore, where there is a contingency contract, the contingency will not be enforced if it exceeds the quantum meruit value of services. Moreover, if the new attorney loses the contingency case, then the fired attorney receives nothing (not even the quantum meruit).

    b. An attorney ***may withdraw*** if (1) a case is frivolous; (2) the client wants to pursue an illegal or unethical course of action; (3) the client and attorney disagree significantly as to how to handle the case; (4) where the client wilfully does not pay; (5) where there are major disagreements with co-counsel; or (6) where the client concurs and consents in the withdrawal.

i. The attorney **may not withdraw** if the attorney had notice of the client's indigency or if the client becomes indigent after representation has begun and withdrawal will pose a hardship on the client.

C. PREVENTING THE UNAUTHORIZED PRACTICE OF LAW (CANON 3)

1. Although the CPR avoids precisely defining "law practice," certainly such services as appearing in court for another and preparing wills for others fall within this category, particularly if a fee is paid. Because the U.S. legal system is so complicated, people will fare poorly if they attempt to represent themselves or if non-lawyers are allowed to practice.

   a. However, in the ordinary practice of law, lawyers will **delegate** work to non-licensed law clerks, secretaries, etc. **Delegation is permissible provided that all work is adequately supervised and examined by the attorney**. The attorney is fully responsible for all delegated work.

2. DR 3-101 **prohibits lawyers from aiding non-lawyers in the practice of law** and also admonishes lawyers not to practice law in any jurisdiction where they are not licensed.

   a. Not only do the 50 states have independent licensing requirements and independent bar exams, but so do the federal district courts, federal appellate courts, and the U.S. Supreme Court. A lawyer licensed in one state cannot, absent the other state's waiver, practice in another state. On a one-time basis, states will often grant a waiver, "pro hac vice," but the states do not have to permit this practice. Similarly, many states waive in experienced practitioners (e.g., after 8 years), but this is mainly a courtesy. Note that a jurisdiction may not erect an unreasonable residency barrier to obtaining a license.

   b. A group of lawyers may form a multi-state partnership and practice law in each of the states provided that at least one lawyer in the group is licensed in the state of practice and those named attorneys not licensed in that state are so designated and do not practice law therein.

   c. A foreign lawyer may generally practice law in association with a licensed local attorney. Moreover, an attorney may teach law, serve as a law clerk, and practice corporate law in states where she is not licensed.

3. DR 3-102 prohibits lawyers from dividing their legal fees with non-lawyers, unless fees are paid to the estate of a dead former partner or to office workers in the form of a retirement plan.

4. DR 3-103 prohibits lawyers from forming partnerships with non-lawyers if the partnership's activities will include the practice of law.

   a. This rule does not restrict lawyers from entering into business dealings which do not include law practice with non-lawyers.

D. **PRESERVING CONFIDENCES AND SECRETS (CANON 4)**

1. Because of the great trust between lawyer and client and because of the vulnerability of the client, the CPR in several ethical considerations admonishes the lawyer to keep secret anything even potentially embarrassing to the client. This duty continues even after the attorney-client relationship has ended.

    a. Thus, for example, an attorney **must not** accept employment against a former client which **may** require him to reveal secrets of the former client.

    b. This policy encourages the public to seek legal advice without fear and, thus, furthers the rule of law.

    c. Even where attorneys give free legal advice, the confidentiality and secrecy rules apply.

2. DR 4-101(A) delineates two types of client information, both of which are to be held sacrosanct by the attorney.

    a. A *confidence is information learned by the attorney from the client in the attorney-client relationship*. Confidences are protected not only by the state's code of professional responsibility, but also by an evidentiary privilege, the "attorney-client privilege."

    b. A *secret is that information learned indirectly about the client* that the client would or should want kept private.

    c. The attorney-client evidentiary privilege prohibits attorneys from revealing in court communications given in the course of the attorney-client relationship.

3. DR 4-101(B) *generally requires attorneys reveal neither confidences nor secrets —* particularly when to do so would disadvantage the client.

4. Only in a few set instances may confidences and secrets be revealed: (1) after consent and disclosure; (2) if a disciplinary rule allows; (3) if the jurisdiction permits or requires; (4) if the client intends to commit a future crime; (5) to collect a fee; or (6) to defend oneself. See DR 4-101(C).

    a. The language of the CPR in these instances is discretionary ("may"), not mandatory. Nevertheless, ABA Opinion 314 indicates attorneys must reveal confidences if the attorney is virtually certain that a client will otherwise commit a crime in the future.

    b. An attorney must give a court requested information, even if to do so would reveal a client's confidence or secret.

    c. When an attorney must reveal confidential or secret information to protect himself or to obtain a fee, the revelation must be limited only to that which is necessary to fulfill that justifiable purpose.

    d. The attorney may reveal confidential information to respond to a charge of wrongful conduct. This charge need not have come directly from his client.

e. Attorneys must use reasonable care to assure that their employees either keep confidences and secrets or that they cannot access client files. When an attorney must keep matters confidential, her employees are also so bound.

E. PERJURY AND FRAUD PROBLEMS

1. An attorney must not use perjured testimony. See DR 7-102(A)(4).

   a. Under the CPR, an attorney must instruct a client not to perjure himself. Furthermore, an attorney must refrain from using perjured testimony. However, the attorney is not to "blow the whistle" on the client. Note that, where a client threatens to perjure himself or actually does so, the attorney may properly withdraw.

   b. An attorney should withdraw where she learns that a client has already perjured himself.

   c. Traditionally, where the client intended to perjure himself and ignored advice from the attorney not to do so, the attorney was advised either to withdraw or to allow his client to testify on the witness stand without aid or questioning by the attorney. According to *Nix v. Whiteside* and the MRPC, this practice is now considered questionable.

2. Where an attorney finds himself in possession of **material evidence**, e.g., when the attorney is furnished the "smoking gun," the attorney is not permitted to keep and hide it. See DR 7-109(A). In this situation, the proper course is to furnish the evidence to the prosecution and detail the manner in which it came into the attorney's custody.

   a. If an attorney hides or disposes of material evidence, he will be subject to discipline.

   b. However, if the attorney simply witnesses material evidence, but does not possess it, then he has no duty to disclose its existence to the prosecution. In fact, doing so would subject the attorney to discipline. Only when the attorney (or his worker) interferes with the evidence must the attorney furnish it to the prosecution.

   c. Where the client shows material evidence to the attorney or requests advice as to what to do with it, the attorney **must** counsel the client to give it to the authorities, but **must not** "blow the whistle" if the client does not do so.

   d. When an attorney comes into possession of material evidence from a third party **independent** of client communication, he must give it to the prosecution.

   e. Notwithstanding any of the above, when the legal requirements of various jurisdictions differ, the attorney must follow the law of the appropriate jurisdiction.

F. AVOIDING CONFLICTS OF INTEREST (CANON 5)

1. The attorney as "champion" of the client owes a strong duty of loyalty. Certainly, the attorney's own personal interests should never be permitted to outweigh the interests of the client. Likewise, even the *appearance of impropriety should be avoided*. For example, opposing a present client on an unrelated matter is improper. Likewise,

influencing a client to name the attorney in a will or to give the attorney a gift is also improper.

    a. If the client wishes to name an attorney as beneficiary in his will, the lawyer should insist that another attorney prepare the will.

2. DR 5-101(A) requires lawyers not accept cases where there is a potential conflict of interest unless the client gives an informed consent. Section B prohibits lawyers from accepting cases in which they are to be witnesses, except when their testimony is on an uncontested matter or about their fee.

    a. ABA Opinions 49 and 72 indicate that when one lawyer in a firm is disqualified for any reason, ***the entire firm*** is also disqualified from taking the case.

    b. If, after the trial begins, a lawyer learns she is to be a witness on a contested matter, she must withdraw unless to do so would cause the client to suffer a substantial hardship.

        i. Certainly if the testimony is noninjurious to the client but is contested, the attorney should not make reference to her own testimony, as to do so would appear unprofessional.

3. DR 5-103 mandates that attorneys obtain no monetary interest in the litigation. To do so compromises the attorney's neutrality and duties as an officer of the court and essentially renders the attorney an interested party.

    a. However, contingency fees are allowed except as outlined above. Furthermore, obtaining a lien to receive the fee is generally acceptable.

    b. In contingency cases, attorneys are permitted to advance trial preparation costs (research, medical exams, and payments to witnesses) and court costs (filing fees) provided that, even if the case loses, the client must repay such costs to the attorney.

    c. Attorneys are not permitted to loan or give money to the client for living expenses.

4. DR 5-104 prohibits attorneys from entering into business deals with their clients if there are even potentially opposing interests. However, an attorney may do so where there is consent after disclosure.

    Example: An attorney receives publication rights for a book about a case during the course of representation. To accept such rights would subject the attorney to discipline. DR 5-104(B).

5. Disciplinary Rules 5-105 and 5-106 address the situation where one attorney has multiple clients, a situation considered undesirable in both the civil and criminal contexts. However, unless there is an actual conflict which adversely affects the attorney's performance, the arrangement is acceptable.

a. When representing multiple clients, the attorney must, prior to accepting employment, *advise each client of the pitfalls* of such multiple representation *and obtain consent from each* prior to proceeding.

b. If the lawyer does have to withdraw because an actual conflict develops, he must withdraw from representing *all of the clients*, if *any* confidences or secrets were learned. Otherwise, confidences and secrets of the others might be compromised.

c. Multiple defendant representation in the criminal setting is inadvisable, though permissible. It is inadvisable because defendants may be culpable to differing extents. One may have incriminating evidence on the other(s) which is exculpating for him, and the favorable opportunity of a plea bargain for one may be declined so as to protect the others.

d. In the civil setting, it is improper for an attorney to make a settlement absent consent and disclosure *from each client*. For example, an attorney may not agree to settle a case for four clients for $100,000 unless each client consents and each agrees as to how to divide the $100,000. Were the attorney to divide the settlement without client consent, he would be subject to discipline. DR 5-106.

6. DR 5-107 prohibits attorneys from being influenced by third parties.

   a. If the attorney is to be paid not by the client but by a third party (even if the third party is a relative), the client must be informed and must give consent to this arrangement in advance. In this situation, the attorney must remain fully loyal to the client. The third party has no right to discuss the case with the attorney and has no right to control the case.

   b. Even where an attorney is working for a non-profit legal services corporation, supervisors may not control cases once the attorney-client relationship has attached.

   c. If the attorney receives a commission for referring the client to a business service, the attorney must either (1) give this money to the client or (2) obtain a voluntary consent from the client after disclosure.

      i. *Attorneys may not accept finder's fees from lawyers.*

   d. *When the attorney is representing a corporation, the lawyer owes a duty of loyalty to the corporation, not to its individual employees* (e.g., directors or other workers).

G. COMPETENCE AND LIABILITY (CANON 6)

1. The Disciplinary Rules of this section simply require competence (either by preparation or association), admonish attorneys not to neglect cases, and prohibit attorneys from trying to escape or limit their personal liabilities in the case of malpractice.

   Example: An attorney may not require a client to sign a malpractice waiver agreement. DR 6-102.

2. To be competent, a lawyer need not be an expert. ***The standard of care is that of a reasonably competent attorney, and national norms are applied***. To be competent, a lawyer must know where to look and how to find the law, but need not have actual knowledge about that law at the time that he accepts a case. Therefore, where an attorney is inexpert in an area, he can take a case if he can become expert with timely preparation.

   a. An attorney may not bill a client for the preparation needed to become competent.

   b. Inexperienced attorneys may associate with another, more experienced attorney, provided that the client consents.

   c. All attorneys ***should*** keep up on the literature, help train new attorneys, and strive to better their own and the system's abilities.

H. **THE LIMITATIONS PLACED ON REPRESENTATION (CANON 7)**

   1. Canon 7 requires attorneys "zealously" to represent their clients. It also suggests that attorneys are not simply "hired guns;" they owe duties to opposing counsel, opposing and third parties, and the system of justice as well. Harassment is therefore prohibited.

      a. Previously discussed was the limitation placed on the use of perjured testimony.

      b. Attorneys are also prohibited from offering into evidence law or facts that they know are incorrect.

      c. An attorney must make available to the court law which goes against her case.

         i. Thus, where the opposing counsel has missed a case and the case is relevant but highly damaging to the attorney's case, she must bring the case to the court's attention.

         ii. However, only that law from the relevant jurisdiction or U.S. Supreme Court case law must be furnished. Therefore, if an attorney is trying a case in State C, she need not cite a highly relevant case from State D. However, if there is a controlling case from State C or a U.S. Supreme Court case which sets a minimum constitutional standard for all states, she must cite the case.

         iii. If the attorney does not cite damaging relevant cases because she is unaware of them, she is not subject to discipline. However, her competence may be lacking in this situation.

         iv. After making available damaging precedent, the attorney is permitted to (and truly should) attempt to distinguish such precedent and/or argue for a change in the law. This is good advocacy.

      d. Attorneys should not perform questionable actions for their clients.

2. DR 7-103, among other things, delineates the special duties of prosecuting attorneys and other government attorneys. Where the defense attorney must do everything permitted by law to acquit his client, the prosecutorial duty is to advocate instead for justice. Therefore, a prosecutor shall not bring a case unless there is probable cause. Prosecutors have a duty not to prosecute the innocent. Moreover, prosecutors must make exculpatory evidence available to the defense.

3. Canon 7 also dictates the manner in which an attorney should handle a case. EC 7-7 (which is likely misplaced because it is mandatory), requires attorneys to follow the client's wishes in civil cases regarding settlement and whether to waive a defense. In criminal cases, the attorney must inform the client and follow the client's wishes regarding what *plea* to enter and whether to file an appeal. Finally, a defense attorney must allow a defendant to testify if he so desires.

4. Miscellaneous other disciplinary rules in this section prohibit attorneys from (1) threatening criminal prosecution so as to gain civil advantage (a practice which approaches extortion); (2) arguing facts that they cannot prove; (3) offering their own personal opinions; and (4) hiding the identity of their client (unless that information is privileged).

5. As mentioned previously, attorneys may not communicate either directly or indirectly with represented parties unless the opposing counsel so allows.

    a. This rule is in force even if it is the opposing party who initiates the discussion.

    b. The rule is also in force when the opposing party is a business entity.

    c. Furthermore, attorneys are prohibited from communicating with a third party whose interests are likely to conflict with the represented client (except that the attorney can advise such an individual to obtain an attorney).

6. DR 7-107 concerns the acceptable parameters of trial publicity. This area is highly debated. The First Amendment rights of an attorney and the press may conflict with the rights of the defendant to a fair trial (guaranteed under the Sixth Amendment).

    a. The following are acceptable pre-trial publicity items in a criminal case: (1) stating that which is already public information; (2) indicating that the government is investigating the case; (3) identifying the offense charged; (4) identifying the victim; (5) requesting help to capture the suspect (and the dangers therein involved); and (6) revealing any discovered tangible evidence.

    b. The following items are **unacceptable pre-trial publicity in a criminal case** and would, if offered, subject the offending attorney to discipline: (1) offering statements about a party's character; (2) revealing the existence of a past criminal record; (3) revealing whether there has been a guilty plea or confession; and (4) revealing examination results, the identities of witnesses, or personal opinion. See DR 7-107(B).

    c. The above trial publicity provisions are equally applicable to juvenile, administrative, and disciplinary proceedings.

    d. As to *civil* proceedings, similar prohibitions, as well as the CPR's prohibitions on harassment and offering false evidence, would control.

7. DR 7-108 sets out rules governing the attorney's behavior with jurors. Although an attorney certainly may investigate a potential juror's background, this investigation must be discreet. Harassment is clearly prohibited.

    a. Attorneys must avoid personal contact with potential and actual jurors and the families of jurors.

    b. Moreover, if an attorney learns that another attorney has contacted a juror, she must report this.

    c. **After the trial, an attorney is permitted to contact jurors**, but he must do so in a dignified way.

8. Attorneys must not counsel witnesses as to how to avoid process. Although expert witnesses may be paid an expert witness fee and traveling expenses, they may not be paid on a contingency basis. Other witnesses may be paid lost wages and traveling expenses. See DR 7-109.

9. DR 7-110 sets out the rules governing contact with judges and other court employees.

    a. As a general rule, attorneys should not give gifts to judges unless they are token and have been customary based on a personal friendship. Under no circumstances should the gifts be based on the judge's position or a desire to influence the judge.

    b. In those jurisdictions where judges run for office, campaign gifts are acceptable if given to the judge's campaign committee (not given directly to the judge).

    c. Attorneys generally should not communicate out of court with the judge before whom the case is to be or is presently being tried. However, when such communication is deemed necessary by the attorney, then it may be acceptable if he promptly delivers a copy of the communication to the opposing party.

    d. Former judges must not accept cases in which they were involved as judges. See DR 9-101(A).

10. In related sections of Canon 8, the Disciplinary Rules indicate that judges must not try to influence governmental decisions for personal or client gain and that attorneys must not knowingly make false statements about individuals who are seeking judicial office. Furthermore, lawyers who hold public office must not use their influence as public officials for personal or client gain, nor should they accept bribes.

11. In an analogous provision of DR 9-101(B), former government attorneys are precluded from accepting private cases in which they were privy to privileged information while working for the government.

    a. This provision is interpreted to mean that if the former government attorney is screened from the case and receives no extra fee for the case, then the entire firm need not be disqualified.

EXAM QUESTIONS

Question 1

Alicia Attorney is trying a major personal injury case involving an auto accident. The defendant's auto was a Ford Fiasco which hit the plaintiff's car when the Fiasco's brakes failed. Eleven people in nearby cars witnessed the accident, which took place in Surfer City.

Alicia wants to call ten of the people who witnessed the accident to testify at trial. She also wishes to retain an expert to state that Ford Fiasco brakes often fail.

Alicia's retention agreement with Paul Plaintiff states, *inter alia*, that Paul will reimburse all reasonable expenses.

Which of the following is permissible?

(A) Alicia may pay the plane fare for one lay witness who lives 2000 miles away and was in Surfer City on business on the day of the accident.
(B) Alicia may pay a witness the documented pay that the witness lost by missing work in order to come to court to testify.
(C) Alicia may agree to pay an expert $500 if she loses the case and $1000 if she wins the case.
(D) A and B.

Question 2

Ernie has served as Burt's attorney for ten years. His excellent advice has contributed to the success of Burt's financial investments. As a token of appreciation, Burt offers Ernie a very valuable gift.

Which of the following statements is/are correct?

I. Ernie must refuse the gift.
II. Ernie should not urge a client to give him a gift, but will not be subject to discipline for accepting Burt's voluntary offer.
III. Ernie must first urge his client to seek the advice of an outsider.
IV. Ernie should not accept the gift without urging Burt to seek an outsider's advice.

(A) I only.
(B) II and III.
(C) II and IV.
(D) IV only.

Question 3

Judge Busy participates in many law-related activities. She teaches, speaks and writes on legal topics. She also appears at public legislative hearings on legal subjects and consults with administrators on matters relating to the administration of justice. She also serves on an organization devoted to penal reform, where she personally participates in both public fundraising and fund management.

Which of the above activities are permitted?

(A) Judge Busy may participate in all of the above activities, including the penal reform organization, however she may not participate in their fund management.
(B) Judge Busy is not permitted to participate in public fundraising for such groups as the penal reform organization, but she may participate in their fund management, in addition to the other above-mentioned activities which are permitted.
(C) Judge Busy may speak, teach and write on legal topics, but her other law-related activities are not permitted.
(D) All of Judge Busy's law-related activities are permitted.

Question 4

Dean hires Attorney Frank to defend him in a case involving drunk driving. Dean admits to his attorney, that he was drunk on the night in question. When Frank makes his own investigation of the incident, a third party, Foster, tells Frank that Dean gets drunk every night.

Which of the following statements are correct?

I. Dean's communication to Attorney Frank is covered by the attorney-client privilege, as is the communication made by Foster.
II. Only Dean's communication to Frank is covered by the attorney-client privilege.
III. Foster's communication to Frank is a secret covered by the ethical duty, because Frank heard it in the course of acting for Dean and its disclosure would likely harm or embarrass Dean.
IV. Neither Dean's nor Foster's communication to Frank are covered by the attorney-client privilege, but Frank has an ethical duty not to disclose either.

(A) I only.
(B) II only.
(C) II and III.
(D) III and IV.

Question 5

Lauren Lawyer is a member of the Business Law Committee of the Dodge City Bar Association. The committee is considering whether to recommend a change in the state's statutes that would allow board meetings to be held via video conferencing. One of Lauren's clients, who is a member of the board of Camera Corp., has a home in Dodge City but also lives for much of the year in Barbados. If the law is passed, Lauren's client will not have to return to Dodge City several times a year for board meetings but will be able to stay in Barbados and video conference in whenever there's a board meeting. Lauren's client faxes her a note that says, "Lauren, be sure to support the recommendation of the change in law the next time you have a committee meeting!"

Lauren is in a quandary. Now that she knows that her client wants her to vote for the recommendation, she isn't sure whether she may properly do so. As her attorney, what do you advise?

(A) Lauren should decide on her own how she feels about the proposed recommendation. If she supports it, she should vote for it, but she should also disclose that she has a client who would benefit from it.
(B) Lauren should vote for the ordinance because her ethical duty as an attorney requires her to act in the best interests of her clients.
(C) Lauren should vote against the ordinance, because she has a conflict of interest in the situation.
(D) Lauren should abstain from voting in order to avoid the appearance of impropriety.

Question 6

Attorney Alpha represents Exco Oil, Inc., a large conglomerate that has publically expressed support of a tax exemption that affects big business. Alpha is personally opposed to the exemption to such an extent that he wishes to express his views in public.

Alpha's ethical obligation is to:

I. Abstain from taking an open position contrary to that of a client which he represents.
II. First, Alpha must obtain Exco's permission before expressing publically views that are in opposition to those of Exco.
III. Alpha must make it clear that he speaks on his own behalf and not on behalf of Exco.
IV. Alpha may take a public position contrary to his client's interest, but he must present the speech in such a way so as not to prejudice Exco.

(A) I only.
(B) II and IV.
(C) II, III and IV.
(D) III and IV.

Question 7

Mr. McCoy intensely dislikes his neighbor, Mr. Hatfield. Tired of feuding, Mr. McCoy decides to try a new method of harassment. Mr. McCoy directs his attorney, Ms. Montigue, to file a baseless tort claim against Mr. Hatfield.

If Ms. Montigue knows or should know that the action is solely for an ulterior purpose, is she subject to discipline if she files the suit on Mr. McCoy's behalf?

(A) No, because she is acting on her client's behalf.
(B) No, she is only subject to tort liability for abuse of process.
(C) No, she has a duty to zealously represent her client and carry out his wishes.
(D) Yes, she must not file the suit.

Question 8

What is the difference between the position of the Model Rules and the Model Code on mandatory and aspirational conduct?

(A) There is no difference.
(B) The Model Code recognizes no distinction.
(C) The Model Rules recognize no distinction.
(D) The Model Rules focus only on mandatory conduct.

Question 9

During the course of a complex trial, a juror named Cathy Curious was confused about a crucial point of law. During an afternoon recess, she phoned her own private lawyer to question him about the point of law which perplexed her.

If Cathy's attorney, knowing she's a juror, answers her questions about the case, is he subject to discipline?

I. No, only lawyers connected with the case must refrain from communication with a member of the jury about any subject during trial.
II. No, although Cathy's attorney should not answer her question, in doing so he merely violated an ethical consideration.
III. No, because the conversation took place outside the courtroom and falls within the attorney-client privilege.
IV. Yes, although Cathy's attorney is not connected with the case, he must refuse to discuss the matter with her.

(A) IV only.
(B) I and III.
(C) II only.
(D) I only.

Question 10

Peter Plaintiff really hates Donald Defendant, whom he is suing, alleging that Donald has encroached on Peter's land. Donald has filed a counterclaim against Peter, saying that Peter has been trespassing on Donald's land for years. Peter tells Leslie, his lawyer, not to grant Donald any courtesies in the litigation. He tells her that, when Donald wants continuances, extensions, or other favors, she is not to grant them. If Leslie acts according to Peter's instructions, she:

(A) Will act improperly, because attorneys have an ethical obligation to grant each other professional courtesies.
(B) Will act improperly, because she, as attorney, may make routine decisions concerning matters that do not affect the merits of the case.
(C) Will act properly, as long as she does not violate any procedural rules.
(D) Will act properly, because litigation should be as adversarial as possible.

Question 11

Judge Smith from California is invited as a guest speaker to give a speech on penal reform. The invitation is extended by the Community Service Club of Arizona.

Which of the following statements are correct?

I. Judge Smith may give the speech but should decline to be paid for such outside activities.
II. Judge Smith may give the speech and may accept an amount of pay equal to that which a lay-person would receive.
III. Judge Smith may be reimbursed by the Club for actual travel, lodging and meal expenses incurred while participating in this outside activity.
IV. If appropriate to the occasion, Judge Smith may be reimbursed by the Club for travel, lodging and meal expenses incurred by his wife.

(A) I only.
(B) I and III.
(C) II and III.
(D) II, III and IV.

Question 12

Attorney Rich is a well-known art dealer as well as a practicing attorney. He keeps both businesses completely separate and maintains two separate offices. While in his gallery, negotiating the sale of a painting, he deliberately defrauds Mr. Naive. Attorney Straight hears of the fraud from a third party, Mr. Snoop, who was present at the gallery when the fraud took place. After conducting his own investigation, Attorney Straight substantiates that Attorney Rich did indeed defraud Mr. Naive.

Which of the following statements is the proper course of action for Attorney Straight to take?

I. Attorney Straight should report Attorney Rich to the appropriate attorney tribunal for running an art gallery at the same time he has an active law practice.
II. Attorney Straight should report the fraud to the appropriate attorney tribunal, even though the fraud was not connected with Rich's law practice.
III. Attorney Straight must report the fraud to the appropriate attorney disciplinary tribunal, even though the fraud was not committed in the course of practicing law.
IV. Attorney Straight must not volunteer legal advice to Mr. Naive.

(A) I and II.
(B) III only.
(C) II only.
(D) III and IV.

Question 13

Mr. Hood walks into Attorney James's office, places a gun on the attorney's desk and says, "I just used this gun to rob the First National Bank."

Which of the following is correct?

(A) Both Hood's communication and the gun are covered by the attorney-client privilege.
(B) Only the communication but not the gun is covered by the attorney-client privilege.
(C) Neither the communication nor the gun is covered by the attorney-client privilege.
(D) The communication is only subject to the attorney-client privilege if Attorney James accepts the case or offers Mr. Hood advice.

Question 14

Angus Attorney is a real estate and trusts and estates lawyer who wants to provide a full range of services to his clients. He therefore enters into an arrangement with a real estate agent, Ron, and a funeral director, Frank, to form a partnership. The three share offices, secretaries, phone lines, and necessary equipment. They also share a bank account and split all revenues equally.

If the Board of Bar Overseers learns of this arrangement, will Angus be disciplined?

(A) No, because Angus can split fees with the other two.
(B) No, because Angus' First Amendment right to free association allows him to partner with the other two.
(C) Yes, but if Angus stops splitting fees with the others, the partnership may stand and Angus will no longer be subject to discipline.
(D) Yes, both because of the fee-splitting and the partnership arrangement.

Question 15

Attorney Young is asked to represent a client in a complex tax matter. Because Attorney Young is inexperienced in complex tax laws, his conduct will be considered proper if he does which of the following?

I. Refuses to handle the matter.
II. Accepts the case and associates competent co-counsel.
III. Accepts the matter and associates co-counsel who is competent, but first obtains his client's consent to do so.
IV. Accept the matter because he expects, in good faith, to be competent through study and believes that such research would not cause the client undue delay or expense.

(A) I, III and IV.
(B) I, II and IV.
(C) I only.
(D) III and IV.

Question 16

Attorney Splitter represents W on a 25% contingent fee basis. If Attorney Splitter receives a check in the amount of $2,000.00 in settlement on W's claim:

(A) She must promptly send 75% (seventy-five per cent) to W and deposit $500.00 in her personal account.
(B) She must deposit the entire $2,000.00 in her client's trust account and, when W agrees that she is entitled to $500.00, she must promptly withdraw $500.00 from her client's trust account.
(C) She should deposit the entire $2,000.00 in her client's trust account, but must promptly withdraw her 25% fee.
(D) She must deposit the entire amount in her personal account, but must immediately send a check in the amount of $1,500.00 to W.

Question 17

Darryl District Attorney asks the grand jury to indict Carrie Criminal for bribery and racketeering. Darryl doesn't have any evidence that Carrie committed these crimes, but he wants to use the indictment as a carrot to try to get Carrie to testify against her friends, Carlos and Cressida.

Will Darryl be disciplined for this conduct?

(A) No, because getting Carlos and Cressida is in the interests of justice.
(B) No, as long as he doesn't intend to actually prosecute Carrie for bribery and racketeering.
(C) Yes, because he is trying to put one over on the grand jury.
(D) Yes, because he doesn't have any evidence to support an indictment.

Question 18

Mr. Pain and Ms. Suffering are co-plaintiffs in a personal injury suit resulting from an automobile accident. Attorney Sleuth represents Mr. Pain only but calls Ms. Suffering as a witness. If, during the course of the trial, Attorney Sleuth discovers that Ms. Suffering perjured herself in testifying about the nature and extent of her injuries, which of the following statements are correct?

(A) He must reveal Ms. Suffering's perjury to the court.
(B) He must seek Mr. Pain's consent before revealing the perjury to the court.
(C) He should promptly reveal the fraud to the trier of fact.
(D) He must urge Ms. Suffering to rectify the fraud, but may not reveal the fraud himself because of possible prejudice to his client.

Question 19

Five-year-old Maggie is in a coma following a car crash which claimed the lives of both her parents. Maggie's guardian hires Attorney Sharp to bring a wrongful death and personal injury action on Maggie's behalf. The defendant's insurance company proposes a settlement offer of $500,000.00, which is far less than Attorney Sharp believes he can recover.

Which of the following statements is/are correct?

I. Attorney Sharp must convey any settlement offer to Maggie's guardian.
II. Attorney Sharp should refuse the settlement offer because it would be to Maggie's benefit if the case went to trial.
III. Attorney Sharp must accept the settlement offer if Maggie's guardian directs him to do so.
IV. Attorney Sharp need not accept the settlement offer because he represents Maggie, who lacks capacity. In this situation, the attorney must protect the child's best interest.

(A) I and III.
(B) II and IV.
(C) I only.
(D) III only.

Question 20

Susan is a member of the Utopia bar, but she has not practiced for many years. She now works for an insurance company. In 1999, Agnes, Susan's best friend, experienced a house fire, and all of her belongings were lost. Susan herself examined the damage and, hoping that Agnes would give her a piece of the action, intentionally overestimated Agnes' loss. Agnes refused to give Susan a kickback.

Will Susan be disciplined?

(A) No, because Susan was acting as an insurance adjuster, not as a lawyer.
(B) No, because Agnes didn't give Susan a piece of the action.
(C) Yes, because in submitting a fraudulent assessment, she acted dishonestly.
(D) Yes, because she should have sent another adjustor to assess the damage to Agnes' house.

Question 21

Mr. Builder tells his attorney, Ms. Investor, about his confidential plans to build a shopping center on Meadow Oak Lane. Ms. Investor, based on her client's confidence, purchased a piece of property on Meadow Oak Lane, which will greatly increase in value after the shopping center is built.

Is Attorney Investor subject to discipline?

(A) No, unless the purchase was disadvantageous to Mr. Builder.
(B) No, but she should abstain from using information confidentially obtained from a client for her own advantage.
(C) Yes, if her purchase causes some harm or difficulty for her client.
(D) Yes, even if her purchase does no harm at all to her client.

Question 22

Partners Penelope and Petra went to Anna Attorney's office together to talk about how to end their business partnership. They told Anna that they both wanted to dissolve the partnership but could not agree on the terms and an equitable split of the partnership's assets. They asked Anna to help resolve these issues by mediating a discussion between them.

The three women sat down and talked for two hours. At the end of that time, with Anna's help, Penelope and Petra came to an agreement. Anna drew up a simple document outlining the terms of the agreement, Penelope and Petra signed it, and the matter seemed resolved.

Two months later, however, Penelope decided that she didn't like the terms of the agreement, after all. She hired Luna Lawyer to sue Petra for all of the assets of the partnership. Petra called Anna, and Anna — without asking Penelope's permission — filed an answer in the action on Petra's behalf.

Did Anna act properly?

(A) No, because she mediated the dispute between both Penelope and Petra.
(B) No, but she is not subject to discipline.
(C) Yes, because Penelope had hired a new attorney, Luna.
(D) Yes, because she was already representing Petra.

Question 23

Attorney Baker is hired to represent Client X in a personal injury case, resulting from an automobile accident. Attorney Baker agreed to accept the case on a 33% contingent fee arrangement. Before the case got to trial, Client X fired Attorney Baker and retained Attorney Jones, who eventually lost the case at the trial and on appeal.

What amount is Attorney Baker entitled to?

(A) The reasonable value of her services rendered up to the time of the discharge.
(B) Nothing.
(C) 33% of any fee actually paid to Attorney Jones.
(D) A flat hourly rate for the time she invested in the case.

Question 24

Attorney Ali practices securities law and also teaches a course in securities regulation at Utopia State Law School. She is one of three adjunct professors at USLS. At a faculty meeting, she requests that the course description for her course read as follows:

"This course will cover securities regulation issues under the 1933 and 1934 Acts. Professor Ali is a practicing attorney in the area of securities law."

Does this statement violate ethical standards for attorney advertising?

(A) No, if Ali practices securities law.
(B) No, if Ali is rated the top securities lawyer in Utopia.
(C) Yes, because the statement will appear in a course catalog, a publication that will be read by non-lawyers.
(D) Yes, unless Ali is a certified specialist in the area of securities law.

Question 25

Attorney Swift successfully defended Schemers Unlimited, in a suit involving misrepresentation. Schemers Unlimited, in confidence, told Attorney Swift about the company's internal policies regarding sales and warranties. Two years later, Mr. Mark asks Attorney Swift to represent him in a law suit against Schemers Unlimited for intentional misrepresentation. Because the internal policies regarding sales and warranties are in issue, under which circumstances may Attorney Swift properly accept the case?

I. If Schemers Unlimited gives informed written consent.
II. If Mr. Mark knows of the circumstances and gives informed written consent.
III. If both Schemers Unlimited and Mr. Mark give their informed written consent.

(A) I only.
(B) II only.
(C) III only.
(D) None of the above.

Question 26

During the course of a personal injury trial in which Attorney Scott represents the plaintiff, he will call Dr. Famous, an expert witness from out of state, to testify as to the extent and lasting effects of the plaintiff's injuries.

Attorney Scott can properly pay which of the following?

I. The doctor's expenses incurred in attending the trial, including travel, hotel and meals.
II. A reasonable flat fee for his services for testifying at trial and in pre-trial preparation.
III. If agreed upon by the witness, an amount of compensation contingent on the outcome of the trial.
IV. Travel expenses and loss of income only.

(A) I only.
(B) I and II.
(C) I and III.
(D) IV only.

Question 27

Judge Old is in the process of campaigning for re-election as Judge of the Superior Court. Running in opposition on the ballot is Attorney New. Which of the following may Judge Old and Attorney New do during the campaign?

I. Attend political gatherings.
II. Speak at political gatherings in support of their own candidacy.
III. Identify themselves as members of a political party.
IV. Contribute money to a political party or organization.

(A) I, II, III and IV.
(B) I and II.
(C) I, II and III.
(D) I, II and IV.

Question 28

Louisa Lawyer is a partner in a business which is having trouble collecting its receivables. Therefore, Louisa, who is very busy with her law practice, has hired Carla to attempt to collect all outstanding amounts owed. Under their arrangement, Carla is to call each debtor and ask for the money owed. If the money is not forthcoming within 30 days, Carla may, at her own discretion, write a letter to the debtor telling the debtor that Louisa Lawyer will sue unless the debt is satisfied within a week. The letters should go out on Louisa's stationery and under Louisa's name, which Carla should sign. Louisa trusts Carla's judgment and does not see the letters unless it becomes necessary to file suit.

Is Louisa acting properly in handling the collections in this way?

(A) No, because she should not threaten suit to help collect a debt.
(B) No, because she should not allow a non-lawyer to collect debts for her business.
(C) No, because her business, through Carla, is practicing law without authorization.
(D) Yes, because Carla is simply helping Louisa.

Question 29

Attorney Smith made an oral informal agreement to prepare a contract for Client A for a flat fee of $100.00 an hour. Is Attorney Smith subject to discipline?

I. Yes, for failing to reduce the fee arrangement to writing.
II. Yes, if the fee charged is found to be clearly excessive.
III. Yes, if the fee falls far below the minimum established by the state bar association and the case is not *pro bono*.

(A) I only.
(B) I and II.
(C) I and III.
(D) II only.

Question 30

Attorney Bright witnesses a serious automobile accident in which the injured party is her close friend Ted. If Attorney Bright visits Ted at the hospital and offers him legal advice, is she subject to discipline if she then proceeds to accept the case?

(A) Yes, she would be subject to discipline for solicitation.
(B) Yes, unless Ted is a previous client.
(C) Yes, because Ted is not a relative or family friend.
(D) No, because Ted is a close friend.

Question 31

Amanda Attorney gets a call one day from her erstwhile client, Flaky Frivolous. Flaky is extremely upset because he was not invited to Malibu Bob's 4th of July beach party. He demands that Amanda sue Bob for $1,000,000 for humiliation and suffering and to "do whatever it takes" to make Bob's life miserable in court. Amanda initially tells Flaky that she will not take the case because his claim is frivolous, but Flaky — who is a dot.com zillionaire — eventually convinces Amanda to accept the case for a fee of $100,000.

Should Amanda be disciplined for accepting the case?

(A) Yes, because Amanda hadn't even worked on the case when she accepted the $100,000.
(B) Yes, because knowingly to bring a frivolous claim is unethical; a claim must have a basis in existing law or contest existing law in some way.
(C) No, because Amanda told Flaky that his claim was baseless and he said that he wanted to bring the case anyway.
(D) No, because her fee is reasonable given the amount in controversy.

Question 32

Attorney is in the private practice of law, conducting a general practice. Psy is licensed by the state as a clinical psychologist and maintains a private practice as a marriage counselor. In his practice Psy sees many individuals whose marriages are, in Psy's judgment, irretrievably broken. Psy has many clients who are unable to pay any fee. Psy has been represented by Attorney in both his business and personal affairs, and Psy has confidence in Attorney's ability.

Attorney proposed to Psy that Psy refer all of his clients who want a divorce to Attorney and Attorney will represent them for a reasonable hourly rate.

Is Attorney subject to discipline if Attorney enters into this agreement?

- (A) Yes, because Attorney requested that Psy recommend the use of Attorney's legal services.
- (B) Yes, unless Psy agrees not to attempt to influence the exercise of Attorney's independent professional judgment.
- (C) No, if Psy is not compensated in any way for referring cases to Attorney.
- (D) No, if Psy's clients are fully informed of Psy's arrangements with Attorney and are given an opportunity to consult other lawyers.

Question 33

Attorney Famous has received a great deal of publicity due to his successful spectacular defense in a controversial rape case. Which of the following would constitute proper conduct on the part of Attorney Famous?

I. It would be proper for him to author a legal publication in which he is identified as an attorney as well as by name.
II. It would be proper to appear as a guest on a national television program and discuss penal reform and the justice system.
III. It would be proper to send an expensive gift to the editor of the Los Angeles Times in appreciation for its excellent coverage of his brilliant defense in the above mentioned case.

- (A) I and II.
- (B) I only.
- (C) II only.
- (D) None of the above.

Question 34

Lenny Lawyer has worked for 9 years on a major asbestos lawsuit, representing the 39 plaintiffs. The asbestos company has finally offered a favorable settlement, agreeing to pay each plaintiff or estate $10,000 to $100,000, depending on the level of injury suffered. However, the asbestos company wants to be done with this case, and part of the settlement offer states that it will not settle with any individual plaintiff unless all of the plaintiffs agree to settle at this time. Lenny does not want to tell each individual plaintiff the terms of the entire settlement, as those who will receive less may balk, but he doesn't know how he can avoid doing so.

If Lenny does reveal the terms to all of the plaintiffs, is he subject to discipline?

(A) No, but he would not be acting very ethically.
(B) Yes, because he might not manage to settle the case.
(C) Yes, because to do so would violate the attorney-client privilege held by each plaintiff.
(D) No, because under the doctrine of informed consent, he must tell each plaintiff that others are participating in the settlement.

Question 35

Which of the following may Attorney Helpfulsen assist her friends with without aiding in the unauthorized practice of law?

I. She may assist her friend who is drafting his own will.
II. She can assist her friend who is drafting a will for his uncle who in return gives the friend an Oriental rug.
III. She can provide a real estate broker with statutes that he wishes to read, which correspond to the lawyer-prepared form which he uses.
IV. She can give advice to a housewife who plans to file a suit in small claims court.

(A) I and III.
(B) II and III.
(C) III only.
(D) I, III and IV.

Question 36

In violation of new state and federal laws which provide for criminal as well as civil sanctions for undue harassment and coercive tactics used by collection agencies, the Brass Knuckle Agency continues to harass Mr. Weak. If Mr. Weak consults Attorney Strong, which of the following actions may Attorney Strong take?

I. He may inform Brass Knuckle Agency that if the harassment continues he will file criminal charges against them.
II. He may inform Brass Knuckle Agency of his intention to file a civil suit if harassment continues.
III. He may inform them that he will file both criminal and civil charges as provided for under the new state and federal laws, if their tactics toward his client do not improve.

(A) I only.
(B) II only.
(C) III only.
(D) None of the above.

Question 37

A prosecuting attorney in a criminal case is subject to discipline in which of the following situations?

I. If he institutes a criminal proceeding without probable cause.
II. If he fails to promptly notify defense counsel of any evidence which tends to negate guilt or mitigate the degree of the offense.
III. If he fails to pursue evidence just because it appears to be harmful to the prosecution and/or favorable to the defense.

(A) I and II.
(B) I, II and III.
(C) I only.
(D) II only.

Question 38

Governor Grant is on trial in State Green for sexual harassment. His attorney advises him that he needs character witnesses to testify on his behalf. Governor therefore asks his old friend Sam, who is a Supreme Court Justice in State Green, to testify to Governor's good character.

Should Sam do so?

(A) No, if Governor appointed Sam to the bench.
(B) No, unless Governor subpoenas him.
(C) Yes, because he knows a great deal about Governor's character.
(D) No, even if Governor subpoenas him.

Question 39

The Parents' Association of Ourtown, Yourstate regularly sponsors lectures appropriate for parents of minor children. This month, the topic to be covered is "Planning for Your Children's Future," and the speaker is Larissa Lawyer, a trusts and estates lawyer. Larissa plans to stress in her talk that every parent should consult with an attorney about estate planning for his/her children.

When Larissa gives her talk, she does not discuss her own credentials. She does not accept one-on-one questions after the lecture.

According to the Rules and the Code, is Larissa's talk proper?

(A) No, because lawyers should not recommend to non-lawyers that they seek legal advice.
(B) No, unless Larissa declines to professionally represent any person who attends her lecture.
(C) Yes, and she may accept as clients people who attend the lecture.
(D) Yes, because Larissa has a right to freedom of speech under the First Amendment.

Question 40

Delton is negotiating a service contract for Lucas with Maestro Systems. In the process of negotiation, Delton lies, berates, threatens criminal prosecution, and physically assaults Maestro's manager Thomas. Delton is subject to discipline by the Columbia State Supreme Court if:

(A) He is licensed as a lawyer in Columbia.
(B) This negotiation is akin to practicing law.
(C) He is licensed as a lawyer in any state.
(D) What he did is considered unethical.

Question 41

Larry, a licensed attorney in the state of C, loves hot tub bathing. One afternoon, at the local health club, he strikes up a conversation with Linda while bathing. Larry, in response to a question as to his occupation, tells Linda that he is a general practitioner lawyer. Linda says in response, "What luck. I've got a little problem...I was bitten last week by a dog. But I was teasing the dog. Do I have a case?" Larry does not take Linda's case. Larry is subpoenaed to testify against Linda's $25,000 claim against the owner of the dog.

(A) Larry may testify because he is not Linda's attorney.
(B) Larry may testify because there was never an attorney-client relationship.
(C) Larry must not testify because the attorney-client evidentiary privilege had attached.
(D) Larry must not testify because Linda spoke to him in confidence.

Questions 42–44 are based on the following fact pattern.

Donna is a defense attorney who handled Ned's case. Her research and arguments are found to fall below reasonably prevailing norms and also found to prejudice Ned's case. Thus, Ned is awarded a new trial.

Question 42

Ned's subsequent civil suit against Donna will:

(A) Prevail, because Donna was incompetent.
(B) Prevail, if Donna is actually incompetent.
(C) Prevail, if damages are proven.
(D) Not prevail, because incompetence is a different issue from malpractice.

Question 43

In Ned's subsequent civil suit, Donna refuses to testify based on the attorney-client evidentiary privilege. This refusal is:

(A) Proper, because there is a reasonable likelihood that she would have to reveal confidences.
(B) Proper, because testifying would compromise the fiduciary nature of the relationship.
(C) Improper, because there can be no civil damages arising out of criminal malpractice.
(D) Improper, because the attorney-client privilege is solely for the benefit of the client and Ned did not want the benefit.

Question 44

In order to defend herself in Ned's civil suit against her, Donna reveals several damaging admissions of Ned. Donna is:

(A) Subject to discipline for compromising the attorney-client relationship.
(B) Subject to discipline if she revealed a confidence.
(C) Subject to discipline if she revealed a secret.
(D) Not subject to discipline because she was defending herself.

Question 45

Which of the following statements, if made during trial, would subject Arthur Attorney to discipline?

I. "As you can see from the evidence, Wanda Witness did not testify truthfully."
II. "The dog bit the plaintiff, and I know for a fact that this is true."
III. "In my humble opinion, the defendant is accountable for the damage done to my client's lawn."

(A) I only.
(B) II only.
(C) I and III.
(D) II and III.

Question 46

Loretta Lawyer was disbarred in 1998 for embezzling client funds. After rehabilitating herself, she applied to be readmitted to practice, and her application is in the process of being approved. Larry Litigator would like to hire Loretta to be a lawyer in his firm because he likes her personally, believes that she is a skilled lawyer, and agrees that she has truly reformed. Larry is worried, however, about others' perception of him and his firm if he hires Loretta. He is concerned that important leaders in the community will question Larry's ethics or look at him suspiciously.

According to the Model Code, Larry should:

(A) assist Loretta in being readmitted to the bar.
(B) decline to hire Loretta in order to impress the important leaders in the community.
(C) hire Loretta today as a law clerk, then name her to be an associate attorney as soon as she is readmitted to the bar.
(D) Decline to hire Loretta because she has been previously disciplined.

Question 47

Todd just passed the state bar exam. Client walks into his office, querying regarding a complex land use planning problem. Todd never took land use planning in law school and knows nothing about it. Nevertheless, Todd takes the case. Which of the following are acceptable for Todd?

(A) Associate himself with a land use planning expert after receiving the consent to do so by client.
(B) Purchase a practice manual on land use planning, study this, and not charge client for his initial preparation.
(C) Withdraw from the case and not charge client.
(D) All of the above.

Question 48

Judge Jones was assigned the case of *Polly v. Daniel*, a personal injury case in the state of Euphoria. Upon seeing the parties in the courtroom, Judge Jones realized that he was acquainted with Polly's mother. He informed the parties of the nature of his personal connection to one of the parties and that he was willing to recuse himself unless the parties were satisfied that there was no problem with his hearing the case. Polly and Daniel both stated that they felt that his acquaintance with Polly's mother was immaterial. Judge Jones therefore heard the case.

Under the Code of Judicial Conduct, did Judge Jones act properly?

(A) No, because the CJC requires the waiver to be in writing and signed by both parties.
(B) No, because he had a conflict of interest which created an appearance of impropriety.
(C) Yes, because the parties consented to his presiding over the case.
(D) Yes, because Polly's mother was only an acquaintance, not a close friend.

Question 49

Joel is a licensed attorney in the state of Eastcoast. His client, Doe, is involved in "high tech" marketing. Joel believes some of Doe's activities to infringe on copyright protection. Joel tells Doe this and also tells him how he can avoid detection. Joel is subject to discipline because:

(A) Once an attorney knows of crime he must withdraw.
(B) A lawyer can never counsel how to perpetrate a crime.
(C) A lawyer can never counsel how to avoid criminal prosecution.
(D) Once an attorney knows of crime he must counsel his client how to rectify the crime.

Questions 50 and 51 are based on the following facts.

Badman was represented by Altman. Badman, although not an attorney, had some very strong views about the law. Badman was being prosecuted for the crime of false pretenses. Badman had a long criminal record of fraud. Badman also had "sleazy" mannerisms. Altman thus counseled Badman to waive jury trial and not take the stand in his own defense (thereby to avoid damaging impeachment). Badman, however, insisted that he knew best. Against Badman's wishes, Altman waived jury trial and did not call on Badman to testify. Badman was found not guilty.

Question 50

(A) Altman is subject to discipline because he did not allow Badman to testify.
(B) Altman is subject to discipline because he disobeyed his client's wishes as to strategy.
(C) Altman is not subject to discipline because an attorney can choose the trial strategy.
(D) Altman is not subject to discipline because Badman was found "not guilty."

Question 51

Assume that Badman was found guilty:

(A) Altman is subject to discipline because he disobeyed Badman's desire to have a jury.
(B) Altman is subject to discipline because he disobeyed Badman's legitimate desires.
(C) Altman is subject to discipline because he contravened Badman's control of the case.
(D) Altman is subject to discipline because Badman lost, i.e., his errors were not harmless.

Question 52

Several years ago, Albert was an Assistant District Attorney. One of the cases then being handled by the DA's office was the case of *State v. Susan*, a murder case. However, while Albert was working in the office, the case was still a long way from trial, and it was not tried until two years after Albert left the office.

While Albert was working in the DA's office, however, Susan's attorney called the office to request some documents. Albert took the call, as the ADA handling the case was on vacation, and asked an intern to copy the requested documents and send them to Susan's attorney. Albert did not look at the documents or at any other documents in the case file at any time.

Three months after Susan's attorney called, Albert went to work for ABC law firm and began specializing in criminal defense work. Last week, Susan, who was convicted of murder, called Albert and asked him to handle her appeal. May Albert do so?

(A) No, because Albert arranged for the documents to be copied and sent to Susan's attorney.
(B) No, because Albert may not take a case against his former office.
(C) Yes, unless Albert learned confidential facts about the case while he was an ADA.
(D) Yes, unless Albert dealt with the case substantially while he was an ADA.

Question 53

Abigail, Zoe, Nina and Sarah are all in-house lawyers for SuperSaver Corp. All four women gave up traditional law firm practice when they had children and now work exclusively for SuperSaver, which offers them flex time and child care benefits.

Peter President, the CEO of SuperSaver, has told Abigail, Zoe, Nina and Sarah that they should correspond with non-SuperSaver entities on stationery that does not include the SuperSaver logo or address. A great deal of the correspondence that the four lawyers draft constitutes demand and collections letters, and Peter wants the letters to pack a punch — one that he feels will be more convincing if the letters seem to come from an outside firm. The stationery would simply have the names and contact information for the four attorneys on its letterhead.

Abigail and Sarah feel that to send letters on this stationery would be improper, but they're afraid to say anything to Peter for fear of losing their very convenient jobs. Nina and Zoe don't see a problem. Who is correct, and why?

(A) Nina and Zoe, because the stationery does identify the attorneys.
(B) Nina and Zoe, because the four women share the same office.
(C) Abigail and Sarah, because the stationery constitutes prohibited advertising.
(D) Abigail and Sarah, because the four women are not law partners, as the stationery seems to suggest.

Question 54

Lawson's client Rick tells Lawson to settle his insurance claim if Insurer offers $10,000. Insurer offers $15,000 and Lawson does not settle, eventually going to trial and gaining a $100,000 verdict. Lawson is:

(A) Subject to discipline for taking the case to trial.
(B) Subject to discipline for not obeying Rick's instructions as to settlement.
(C) Not subject to discipline because Rick gained much more money.
(D) Not subject to discipline because the attorney has the right to control the strategy of the case.

Question 55

Attorney Delmarter created a trust for Client Chuck. Four years later the trust laws changed dramatically. Chuck was unaware of this. Delmarter did not speak to Chuck about the changes in law. Delmarter is:

(A) Subject to discipline because he did not tell Chuck of the change in law.
(B) Subject to discipline if Chuck is damaged by the error.
(C) Subject to discipline if he did not tell Chuck the attorney-client relationship had ended earlier.
(D) Not subject to discipline if Chuck is no longer his client.

Question 56

Lawyer Lincoln was a government attorney for the Environmental Protection Agency from 2000-2003. While employed there in 2001, Lincoln was the lead attorney on a case against a local conglomerate, BigCorp. In 2003, Lincoln left the EPA office and returned to his home state of Jefferson, where he opened a private law practice.

Last week, the Jefferson State Environmental Board contacted Lincoln and asked him to bring a lawsuit - on a contingency basis - against BigCorp. The case involves facts and allegations that are nearly identical to those in the 2001 case Lincoln handled against BigCorp. This case would be only one among many that Lincoln would handle in his private practice.

May Lincoln properly accept the case?

(A) Yes, unless his position in this matter would be adverse to that of the EPA.
(B) Yes, if BigCorp. knows about it and doesn't have a problem with it.
(C) No, because of the appearance of impropriety.
(D) No, because he had significant responsibility in the 2001 case, when he worked for the government.

Question 57

Client, a new client of Attorney, has asked Attorney to write a letter recommending Client's nephew for admission to the bar. Client has told Attorney that he has no direct contact with the nephew, but that Client's sister (nephew's mother) has assured Client that the nephew is industrious and honest.

Which of the following is (are) proper for Attorney?

I. Write the letter on the basis of Client's assurance.
II. Write the letter on the basis of Client's assurance if Attorney has no unfavorable information about the nephew.
III. Make an independent investigation and write the letter only if Attorney is thereafter satisfied that the nephew is qualified.

(A) III only.
(B) I and II, but not III.
(C) I and III, but not II.
(D) I, II, and III.

Question 58

Attorney Albert was trying a murder case in Fairhaven. The trial was well underway when, one afternoon, Attorney Angus saw Albert eating lunch in Uglyhaven with one of the jurors on the case. Angus recognized Albert and the juror because Angus had attended one morning of the trial to hear the testimony of an expert that Angus was considering retaining for one of his upcoming trials.

What should Angus do?

(A) Tell the judge presiding over the case.
(B) Call the disciplinary arm of the local bar association and let them handle it.
(C) Nothing; Albert was doing nothing wrong.
(D) Wait until the juror leaves, then tell Albert that he thinks Albert's conduct is inappropriate.

Questions 59–61 are based on the following fact situation.

Client retained Attorney to institute an action against Deft for breach of contract. The retainer agreement provided for a nonrefundable retainer fee of $1,000, which Client paid, and a charge of $50 per hour for services rendered in connection with the matter. Attorney spent eight hours preparing a complaint for filing, reviewing Client's files, and making an independent investigation of some facts in Client's case. Attorney became convinced that Client's recollection of the facts was faulty and that Client would not prevail in a lawsuit. The statute of limitations will run on Client's claim in one week. Attorney wishes to withdraw without filing suit. Client insists that Attorney at least file the complaint in the matter before withdrawing.

Question 59

Is Attorney subject to discipline if she files the complaint for Client?

(A) Yes, because Attorney was convinced that Client would not prevail in a lawsuit.
(B) Yes, if Client's story to Attorney was, in fact, untrue.
(C) No, unless the action was filed merely to harass the defendant.
(D) No, because Attorney had accepted a retainer before she was convinced that Client would not prevail in a lawsuit.

Question 60

Is it proper for Attorney to withdraw without filing the suit?

(A) Yes, if Attorney reasonably believes that Client's recollection is faulty.
(B) Yes, because the matter is not yet pending before a tribunal.
(C) No, because Attorney has accepted a retainer to represent Client.
(D) No, unless Client's rights are adequately protected.

Question 61

If Client admits that his story was untrue and Attorney withdraws with Client's consent, is it proper for Attorney to keep all or any part of the $1,000 retainer that Client paid?

(A) Yes, the entire $1,000, if $1,000 was a reasonable nonrefundable retainer.
(B) Yes, but no more than $400 for the eight hours of her services.
(C) No, if Attorney withdraws without filing suit.
(D) No, because Attorney withdrew from further representation of Client.

Question 62

Julia is an attorney admitted to practice in the state of Whiteacre. She is currently trying a case, however, in Blueacre, where she has been admitted *pro hac vice*. Unfortunately, opposing counsel in this case has accused her of destroying evidence. The judge in the case, horrified by the possibility that Julia has indeed destroyed evidence, tells her, "I would recommend your disbarment if you were an attorney in Blueacre and this accusation were true."

If Julia is destroying evidence, may Whiteacre discipline her?

(A) No, because her misconduct occurred in Blueacre.
(B) No, because Blueacre must take action against her first.
(C) Yes, because she is improperly practicing law in Blueacre.
(D) Yes, because the discipline authorities in Whiteacre may discipline her even for her actions in other jurisdictions.

Questions 63–67 are based on the following facts.

Shawn is being represented by Nora on a charge of murder in the first degree. One afternoon Shawn walks into Nora's office and throws a gun on her desk. Shawn says, "This is the murder weapon." Shawn then tells Nora he is going to kill Beth, one of the witnesses to the charged crime.

Shawn continues and tells Nora that there are some of her belongings at the scene of the homicide and that he removed, them.

Nora puts the gun in a safe place and Shawn goes to trial. Shawn is convicted of voluntary manslaughter then claims Nora was incompetent. In a civil suit by Shawn against Nora, Nora takes the stand in her own defense and, after relevant questioning, states that Shawn admitted to the killing.

Question 63

If Nora took no action to protect Beth after Shawn's threat, Nora is:

(A) Not subject to discipline because the attorney-client confidentiality privilege had attached.
(B) Not subject to discipline because Shawn may have been lying.
(C) Subject to discipline because there was a reasonable likelihood Shawn was telling the truth.
(D) Subject to discipline because an attorney should prevent a future dangerous crime.

Question 64

Nora's suppression of the gun was:

(A) Proper because Shawn was her client.
(B) Proper because the attorney-client evidentiary privilege had attached.
(C) Proper because the gun was a direct product of the attorney-client relationship.
(D) Not proper.

Question 65

Nora should have told the prosecution that Shawn removed evidence from the scene of the crime.

(A) True, because the evidence was probative.
(B) False, because Nora's knowledge was obtained through the attorney-client relationship.
(C) True, because Shawn's removal of evidence was not testimonial.
(D) False, because the evidence was prejudicial.

Question 66

Nora's taking the stand in her own defense and offering privileged information was:

(A) Improper, because the attorney-client relationship had attached.
(B) Improper, because Nora could have defended herself without damaging Shawn.
(C) Proper, because an attorney has the right to defend herself against a client, even if that means revealing a confidence.
(D) Proper, because since Shawn was convicted, no further harm could befall her.

Question 67

Bob prepares a contract for Larry. Many months later Bob learns that the contract was fraudulent. Bob tells Larry to rectify the problem. Larry does not. Bob then writes the other party and disaffirms the contract. Bob's actions were:

(A) Necessary.
(B) Permissible.
(C) Impermissible.
(D) None of the above.

Question 68

Linda Lawyer is a practicing attorney in the state of Narnia in the field of landlord tenant law. Linda is also a member of a Narnia commission to improve upon statutory language and content.

Tessa Tenant asks Linda to represent her in an action against Landlord. When Linda researches the relevant law, she realizes that the law on point is extremely biased and unfair to tenants. Upon reading some publications of the Narnia bar, she also finds that many experts in the field agree with her assessment of the law. She therefore recommends to the commission that they recommend to the legislature that the law be overturned. She does explain to the commission that she discovered this particular unfair provision through her representation of Tessa, who has granted her consent for Linda to disclose their attorney-client relationship.

Given that a change in the law would help Tessa, has Linda acted improperly?

(A) Yes, because she took advantage of her position on the commission to help a client in her private practice.
(B) Yes, because not all experts feel that the law is unfairly biased in favor of landlords.
(C) No, because Linda was not acting against the public interest in making her recommendation to the commission.
(D) No, because she had to make the recommendation in order to satisfy her duty zealously to represent Tessa.

Question 69

John Judge has been a judge for years. Before going on the bench, John was an associate for 6 years with the firm of Alpha, Beta and Gamma. While at ABG, when he was a first-year associate, John did some legal research on jurisdiction issues; this research was used by senior associates and partners in preparing the case of *Palmer v. Dodge*. John did no other work on *Palmer v. Dodge*, never met the client, and was not privy to any confidential conversations concerning the case.

Now, 8 years later, the case is finally going to trial, and the random docket selection has assigned the case to John. May John properly hear the case?

(A) No, because John obtained substantial knowledge of the case while an associate at ABG.
(B) No, because John worked on the case while he was at ABG.
(C) Yes, because John learned no confidential information about the case while he was at ABG.
(D) Yes, if both parties consent in writing.

Question 70

Sarah and Stanley are both attorneys in State X. They are also executives in Alphabet Corp., a lending institution that owns a nine-story building in City Y in State X. Alphabet's offices are in the building.

Outside of the hours that they work at Alphabet, Sarah and Stanley work together as law partners with a corporate law practice. For efficiency's sake, they maintain an office in the building where Alphabet is located. Many other businesses, law firms, and medical practices also have offices in the building. Sarah and Stanley's firm does not represent Alphabet and has never solicited business from it.

Are Sarah and Stanley acting within the framework of the disciplinary rules?

(A) No, because their law office is in the same building as Alphabet.
(B) No, because they work for Alphabet, and practicing corporate law is a conflict of interest.
(C) Yes, as long as they keep their law practice a secret from Alphabet.
(D) Yes.

Questions 71–74 are based on the following facts.

Lucien has handled a high price tag insurance case for Mitchell. A verdict of $6,000,000 has been awarded. The contingency contract provided that Lucien would receive 33 1/3%. Mitchell refuses to pay up. Lucien then pays Mitchell the uncontested $4,000,000 and sues him for his fee, which he left in his client trust account. Lucien takes the stand and testifies as to the difficulty of the case, the hours he spent working on it, and further indicates that, because Mitchell has a severe drug and alcohol problem, his work was more difficult. This later response was objected to and the court ruled such response relevant and admissible.

Question 71

Lucien is subject to discipline for:

I. Charging a clearly excessive fee.
II. Suing Mitchell for his fee.

(A) I only.
(B) II only.
(C) I and II.
(D) Neither I nor II.

Question 72

Lucien is subject to discipline for:

I. Revealing a confidence when he sued Mitchell.
II. Suing Mitchell.
III. Revealing a secret when he sued Mitchell.

(A) I only.
(B) II only.
(C) III only.
(D) None of the above.

Question 73

Lucien's placing the $2,000,000 in his client trust account was:

(A) Proper, because this was the contested amount.
(B) Proper, because under the circumstances, this was his legitimate fee.
(C) Proper, because all of the money could have been put there, so certainly 1/3 of it was not a violation.
(D) Not proper.

Question 74

Assume for the purposes of this question only that the bar procedures for this jurisdiction require an attorney to submit all fee disputes first to the bar, then to binding arbitration. In this instance, Lucien's actions were:

I. Improper, because he disobeyed a local rule.
II. Improper, because he should not have sued anyway.
III. Proper, because local bar rules are secondary to the national standard.

(A) I only.
(B) II only.
(C) I and II only.
(D) III only.

Question 75

Judge Jonas is celebrating his engagement to the lovely Jessica. He and his fiancée are throwing a party and inviting all of their friends, including Lonnie Lawyer, a close friend of Jonas. Lonnie is a litigator who occasionally appears before Jonas. Lonnie buys a Waterford crystal ice bucket for $250 and gives it to Jonas and his fiancée at the engagement party.

Jonas is not sure whether he may accept the gift. He asks your legal advice. What should you tell him?

(A) He may not accept the gift because Lonnie appears before him on occasion.
(B) He may not accept the gift because the gift cost a great deal.
(C) He may accept the gift because it is an engagement present.
(D) He may accept the gift because there are no limitations on what gifts judges may receive.

Question 76

Baxter with informed consent represents both Harry and his wife Wanda in a contested divorce litigation. His fee is to be calculated based on 5% of the total settlement. Baxter is subject to discipline for:

I. Representing both sides of the same case.
II. Representing both sides in litigation.
III. Handling a divorce case on a contingency basis.

(A) I and III only.
(B) II and III only.
(C) I and II only.
(D) III only.

Question 77

David Defendant has been charged with embezzling $500,000 from his employer. He contacts Anna Attorney and asks her to represent him in his criminal trial. Anna, a trusts and estates attorney, declines to represent David but refers him to her friend Abigail, who regularly represents white collar criminal defendants. After Anna refuses to represent David, but during the same conversation, David brags to Anna that he's sure he'll be acquitted because the plan he used to embezzle the money was so clever that no prosecutor would ever be able to figure the whole thing out. Anna tells David that he may want to think about using consent as an affirmative defense, then terminates the conversation. She never hears from David again and does not charge him a fee.

If the prosecutor wants to call Anna as a witness against David, may she testify as to his admission?

(A) Yes, because David was never Anna's client.
(B) Yes, because David did not pay Anna any money.
(C) No, David may become Anna's client, and she may not disclose his confidences and/or secrets.
(D) No, she would not be allowed to testify as to his admission, as it is hearsay.

Question 78

Kirk represented Will 5 months ago and argued to the appellate court that an arcane aspect of the state's laws be overruled. Today Kirk argues the opposite side of that legal question to the very same appellate court, but for a different client and against a different party. Kirk's behavior is:

(A) Impermissible.
(B) Permissible.
(C) Fully proper.
(D) Dependent on whether the jurisdiction follows the Code of Professional Responsibility or the Model Rules of Professional Conduct.

Question 79

Tommy is arrested on a charge of "joyriding." Tommy's father hires his friend Amanda to handle Tommy's case. Since Tommy's father is a lawyer, he has firm ideas how to handle Tommy's defense. Amanda should:

(A) Not take the case because there is an inherent conflict of interest.
(B) Take the case because Tommy's father is a licensed lawyer.
(C) Not take the case because Tommy's father will continue to interfere.
(D) Take the case, but make sure that she not be influenced by Tommy's father.

Question 80

The test concerning the appearance of impropriety is:

(A) Part of both the Model Rules and the Model Code.
(B) Part of only in the Model Rules.
(C) Part of only the Model Code, because the drafters of the Model Rules found it to be overly vague.
(D) Commentary in the Model Rules.

Question 81

Voren runs a busy inexpensive-fee law firm. In order to charge low fees Voren advertises and requires all of his clients to sign a contract waiving all possible malpractice claims. Voren is subject to discipline because:

I. He advertises.
II. He requires a waiver of liability.
III. His fees are too low.

(A) I and II only.
(B) I and III only.
(C) II and III only.
(D) None of the above.

Question 82

Fawn walks into Lori's office. She is charged with grand theft auto. As it turns out, Fawn is to be prosecuted by Lori's sister Dawn. Lori advised Fawn that the prosecutor is her sister and then says, "Okay, Fawn, let's hear your side." Lori does not talk to her sister during the course of the prosecution. Lori is:

(A) Not subject to discipline because there was no breach of trust.
(B) Subject to discipline because there was no consent.
(C) Not subject to discipline because there was a full disclosure.
(D) Subject to discipline because there was an inherent conflict of interest.

Question 83

Liam Lawyer has been practicing criminal law in New City for 20 years. Last year, he was voted the best criminal lawyer in New City by the New City Bar Association.

Last week, the New City District Court called Liam and asked him to represent, *pro bono*, a young man who has been accused of a hate crime.

Should Liam accept the representation?

(A) No, if he has heard about the case and is already convinced of the young man's guilt.
(B) No, if he feels that taking the case would lower his status as an attorney in the eyes of his colleagues.
(C) No, if he has such strong negative feelings towards the young man and his actions that his feelings would interfere with his ability to zealously defend his client.
(D) Yes, because every lawyer must do a certain amount of *pro bono* work a year.

Question 84

Ralph, a licensed attorney, works for Widget Industries, Inc. of the state of Columbia. Ralph is general counsel, but Ralph is not licensed to practice law in Columbia. Ralph learns that Widget's CEO is planning to defraud the shareholders. Ralph speaks to the CEO who does nothing. Ralph also does nothing. Ralph is:

I. Subject to discipline for practicing law without a license.
II. Subject to discipline for not speaking to the board of directors.
III. Not subject to discipline.

(A) I only.
(B) I and II only.
(C) III only.
(D) None of the above.

Question 85

Mike works for Acme corporation, as a staff attorney. One afternoon Ed, an employee of Acme, approaches Mike. Ed says, "Mike, I'm in a lot of trouble." He pauses then continues, "I've got this bad drug problem. I think it may be affecting my work." Mike says, "Please go on." Ed does and Mike makes a formal note to Ed's superior indicating Ed may be a liability to Acme. Mike is:

(A) Subject to discipline for divulging Ed's confidence.
(B) Subject to discipline for not telling Ed he was not his lawyer.
(C) Not subject to discipline because he was Acme's lawyer only.
(D) Not subject to discipline because nothing he revealed was confidential.

Question 86

Andrew Attorney has a general law practice in a medium-sized city. For about three months, he has been assisting Polly Plaintiff with a minor contract claim. The case is due to go to trial in three months. Last week, Nerdy Ned asked Andrew to assist him in suing Polly for running into and damaging her car two years, 11 months ago. The statute of limitations on such claims is 3 years.

May Andrew represent Ned against Polly?

(A) No.
(B) No, but he may refer the case to another firm and receive a referral fee or ask his law partner to handle the matter.
(C) Yes, if Ned knows that Andrew represents Polly in another matter and does not have a problem with it.
(D) Yes, but he shouldn't do so for appearance's sake.

Question 87

Rhonda works for Cuestick Pooltables, Inc. as their general counsel. Rhonda has been doing a very fine job handling customer complaints, contracts, and employer-employee disputes. The management of Cuestick, however, has changed. Rhonda has worked for Cuestick for 10 years and has decided to make a life with the company. The new management, however, fires Rhonda on the spot. Rhonda asks why and the C.E.O. replies, "I don't believe a woman can handle the male billiard business." Against Cuestick's wishes, Rhonda continues to litigate the one case in court for Cuestick Pooltables, Inc. and simultaneously files an employment discrimination suit on her own behalf.

(A) Not subject to discipline because her discharge was wrongful.
(B) Not subject to discipline because she has an equal protection claim.
(C) Not subject to discipline because an attorney should see a case to its conclusion.
(D) Subject to discipline.

Question 88

Anna Attorney knows Judge Jeremy and has seen him drink to excess on a number of occasions, including one time when he was on the bench and took a swig from a silver flask. Anna reasonably believes that Jeremy's drinking interferes with his judgely duties and causes him to lack the proper "judicial temperament." When Jeremy runs for reelection, Anna, in an interview, tells a reporter that Jeremy is a drunk and that his drinking interferes with his work.

Will Anna be disciplined for her statement?

(A) Yes, because Anna has made the judicial system look bad.
(B) No, but she may not support the candidate who is running against Jeremy.
(C) Yes, because she made the statement when Jeremy was running for reelection.
(D) No, because she reasonably believed her statement to be true.

Questions 89 and 90 are based on the following fact pattern.

Glen is representing Cal in an appeal in the State of X. Glen comes across four cases apparently on point. One case is from a lower court in State X, another is from State X's supreme court, the third case is from sister State Y, and the fourth case is from the federal circuit court of appeals. The judge whom Glen is before is patently incompetent. Thus, Glen takes a calculated risk, after consultation with Cal, and does not cite any of the above four cases.

Question 89

Glen is not subject to discipline for:

(A) Not citing State X's lower court case.
(B) Not citing State X's supreme court case.
(C) Not citing sister State Y's case.
(D) All of the above.

Question 90

Glen is subject to discipline for:

I. Not citing State X's lower court case.
II. Not citing State X's supreme court case.
III. Not citing sister State Y's case.
IV. Not citing the federal circuit court case.

(A) I only.
(B) I and II only.
(C) III only.
(D) I, II, and IV only.

Questions 91 and 92 refer to the following fact pattern.

Loni Lawyer is very pleased when a case in which she represents Carrie Client is settled to Carrie's benefit. Donald Defendant pays up and sends Loni a check for $100,000. The check is made out to Loni, not to Carrie. Carrie has agreed to pay Loni 40% of any settlement, and Carrie is so happy with the result of the case that she has no interest in disputing Loni's fee at this time.

Question 91

What is Loni permitted to do with the money?

(A) Deposit the check in Carrie's trust fund account and send her a check for $60,000.
(B) Endorse the check and send it to Carrie along with a bill for $40,000.
(C) Deposit the check in her personal bank account and send Carrie a check for $60,000.
(D) A and B.

Question 92

Assume for the purposes of this question only that Loni deposits the money in Carrie's trust fund account, where it earns $600 in interest before it is disbursed. Who is entitled to keep this interest?

(A) Carrie.
(B) Loni.
(C) They should split it evenly.
(D) Carrie should get $400, and Loni should get $200.

Question 93

In closing argument, Prosecutor Alamo alludes to the crimes of the so-called "Night Molester." He closes, saying, "I've never prosecuted a more despicable human." No objection is made. Night Molester is acquitted. Alamo is:

(A) Not subject to discipline because Night Molester was acquitted and there was thus harmless error.
(B) Not subject to discipline because no objection was made.
(C) Subject to discipline only if Alamo was lying.
(D) Subject to discipline for injecting his own views.

Questions 94 and 95 refer to the following fact pattern.

Jag is assigned the prosecution of Edward. Edward was apprehended based on an unlawful arrest. Evidence which is likely to be suppressed was discovered pursuant to that arrest. The principal witness against Edward is Susanne. The charge is sexual assault. Medical tests have indicated that scrapings from the fingernails of Susanne (while fighting her assailant) match Edward's skin and blood-type.

Jag is interviewed by the press and states the following: "On May 7 at 2:00 A.M. Edward was arrested. The charge is sexual assault. We have a witness, Ms. Susanne. We also have a good amount of evidence. We've matched the blood of the assailant to Edward. Edward has a long history of crime and we feel the public is now much safer. We expect Susanne to give us the testimony we need. However, should any other person recognize Edward, their testimony would be very helpful. Incidentally, Edward has confessed to not only this crime but to two other related episodes."

In response to a question by Reporter Night, Jag replied, "Yes, Ms. Night, I believe we will be able to meet the legal standard of proof beyond a reasonable doubt."

Questions 94

Jag is subject to discipline for:

I. Stating that Edward confessed.
II. Stating his own opinion as to the case.
III. Stating Edward's past criminal convictions.

(A) I only.
(B) I and II only.
(C) I, II, and III.
(D) None of the above.

Questions 95

In analyzing what is permissible to say by way of pretrial publicity, Jag should consider:

I. Whether there is a substantial likelihood that what he says will prejudice the trial.
II. Whether the public has a right to know certain things.
III. Whether the press has a right to know certain things.

(A) I only.
(B) II and III only.
(C) I and III only.
(D) All of the above.

Question 96

Judge Julia is a sitting judge on the Appeals Court of the state of Madison. However, her lifelong dream is to represent Madison in the U.S. House of Representatives. When her local Congressman retires, Julia decides to throw her hat into the ring and run for the office.

Julia wants to continue working as a judge for as long as possible; the job constitutes her only source of income, and she doesn't want to have a gap in her employment. Furthermore, if she loses the election, she'd like to remain on the court. What should she do?

(A) Resign immediately.
(B) Resign as soon as she announces her candidacy for the office.
(C) Resign after the primary election, if she continues on to the general election.
(D) Resign after she is sworn in to the U.S. House of Representatives.

Question 97

Attorney, who represented Plaintiff, received a check from Deft payable to Attorney's order in the sum of $10,000 in settlement of Plaintiff's claim against Deft.

Which of the following is (are) proper?

I. Endorse the check and send it to Plaintiff.
II. Deposit the check in Attorney's own personal bank account and send Attorney's personal check for $10,000 to Plaintiff.
III. Deposit the check in a client trust account, advise Plaintiff, and forward a check drawn on that account to Plaintiff.

(A) I only.
(B) III only.
(C) I and III, but not II.
(D) I, II, and III.

Question 98

Albert Attorney is a member of the Bar of Blackacre and has been actively practicing law for over 20 years. Last week, he was retained by a new client, Sarah Sisterhood. Sarah is looking for legal advice because her previous lawyer, Inlaw, stole money from her, causing her great financial hardship. Sarah says, "I want to invoke attorney-client privilege!" and tells Albert that he can not tell anyone about Inlaw's actions, as Inlaw is married to Sarah's brother, who is dying of cancer and who has never been able to see Inlaw in her true light. Albert explains to Sarah that he can't help her unless he can reveal the information, but promises to keep the secret nevertheless.

Will Albert get in trouble with the disciplinary authorities if he doesn't report Inlaw's conduct?

(A) Yes, because he is ethically required to report attorney misconduct to the disciplinary authorities.
(B) No, unless Inlaw stole a lot of money.
(C) Yes, if Sarah doesn't really need to worry about her brother.
(D) No, because the information is subject to the attorney-client privilege.

Question 99

Able is a member of the bar. He does not practice law, but operates a licensed investment counseling business. Investor consults Able, who persuades investor to invest $10,000 in a business venture. Able does not reveal to Investor that he, Able, owns 100% of the business venture.

Is Able subject to discipline?

(A) Yes, because a lawyer cannot have an interest in a business.
(B) Yes, because Able's nondisclosure of his interest is a form of fraud.
(C) No, because Investor did not consult Able as an attorney.
(D) No, because Able does not practice law.

Question 100

Attorney Alpha has tried many contested cases before Judge Gamma. Alpha believes the judge is lacking in both knowledge of the law and in good judgment and that Attorney Beta would make an excellent judge. Alpha wishes to defeat Judge Gamma and assist Beta in getting elected.

Alpha intends to contribute $5,000 to Beta's campaign.

Is it proper for Alpha to do so?

(A) Yes, Alpha may give $5,000 to Beta personally for his campaign.
(B) Yes, if Alpha's contribution to Beta is made anonymously.
(C) No, because Alpha is practicing before the court to which Beta seeks election.
(D) No, unless Alpha gives the $5,000 to a committee formed to further Beta's election.

Question 101

Lara Lawyer has always stressed the importance of client confidentiality to her employees, and each of her staff members has been with her for many years without incident. One day, however, Shannon Secretary is on the elevator in her office building and talks with Marvin Mail Boy in a loud voice about one of Lara's clients, thus revealing confidential information. Shannon does not realize that Ernie Eavesdropper is in the elevator and has overheard the conversation.

May Lara, as Shannon's boss, be disciplined for breaching confidentiality?

- (A) No, because she has always stressed the importance of confidentiality and supervised her employees.
- (B) No, because Shannon's actions are her own.
- (C) Yes, because she is vicariously liable for the acts of her employees.
- (D) Yes, because the confidence was broken when Ernie overheard Shannon.

Questions 102–104 are based on the following fact pattern.

David works for a large law firm. He works under the supervision of Holtz. In the course of David's work, Holtz requests David to "not understate your billable hours regarding Beta Corporation's business. They have a healthy legal budget. With the help of your secretary, I am sure you can bill 70 hours this week. That means David, 50 hours work. I'd like to see you as partner."

David delegates all of the work, which includes review of contracts; drafting of settlement letters, and an employment discrimination claim to his secretary (who does excellent legal work). David scans most of this work before mailing it to Beta. He bills them for 70 hours.

Question 102

Regarding the billing, David is:

- (A) Subject to discipline for overbilling.
- (B) Not subject to discipline because he was acting under Holtz's orders.
- (C) Not subject to discipline if the bill was reasonable.
- (D) Subject to reprimand, but not to discipline because this was not a major infraction.

Question 103

Regarding David's secretary:

- (A) The secretary is subject to discipline for practicing law without a license.
- (B) David is subject to discipline for not adequately supervising the secretary's work.
- (C) Holtz is subject to discipline for ordering David to utilize his secretary in this manner.
- (D) No one is subject to discipline because the procedure utilized was standard.

Question 104

David is subject to discipline for:

- (A) Continuing to work for the Holtz firm.
- (B) Not telling Beta of the fraud.
- (C) Aiding the secretary in the unauthorized practice of law.
- (D) None of the above.

Question 105

Cathy Client dies suddenly at the age of 73, leaving a sister, Rudie, and a brother, Greedy. Cathy's husband is dead, and she had no children, so Rudie and Greedy are her only living relatives.

Cathy's will leaves all of her estate to Lenny, the little boy who mows her lawn. Rudie and Greedy are horrified by this and have decided to contest the will.

If Artie Attorney, Cathy's lawyer, is contacted by the press, which of the following statements may he properly make?

I. "It is a proven fact that Rudie and Greedy haven't even seen their sister in over 30 years!"
II. "Rudie and Greedy allege that the will was written under duress, but our answer details several conversations that Cathy had with neighbors and friends in which she firmly stated that she wanted to leave her estate to Lenny because he was such a sweet boy."
III. "I definitely believe that Rudie and Greedy's claim to the estate is stupid and baseless."
IV. "I choose to say nothing at this time."

(A) II and IV.
(B) I and III.
(C) III only.
(D) II only.

Question 106

Plager has just passed the bar exam of State Z. He has been appointed to represent Defendant George in a bigamy prosecution. Plager feels incompetent to handle the case - he did not understand criminal procedure and also believes bigamy should be a capital offense. Plager asks the court to appoint another attorney for this particular case. In so requesting:

I. Plager is subject to discipline because court appointments cannot be refused.
II. Plager is not subject to discipline if he was actually incompetent.
III. Plager is not subject to discipline if his distaste for the case would have impaired his performance.

(A) I only
(B) II only
(C) II and III only
(D) III only

Question 107

Lawyer Harr runs a television spot in order to secure legal business. He appears in a three-piece suit (which he never wears); surrounds himself with law books (that he never uses - he does his research at the library); and proceeds to give the following 20-second speech.

"My name is Harr. I'm a licensed attorney. I believe my fees are fair and very low. Further, almost all of my clients are satisfied by my work."

In fact, Harr's fees are low, and, based on client questionnaires, most of Harr's clients are pleased with his work. Harr's advertisement:

(A) Violates prevailing ethical standards by promising a result.
(B) Violates prevailing ethical standards by misleading the public.
(C) Does not violate prevailing ethical standards because advertising is unrestricted.
(D) Does not violate prevailing ethical standards because the advertisement was basically truthful.

Question 108

Agatha Attorney is representing Deirdre Defendant, who has been indicted for murder. Deirdre tells Agatha that she testified before the grand jury that Dastardly killed Veronica Victim. Deirdre also tells Agatha that this testimony was a lie; actually, Deirdre herself pulled the trigger on the gun that killed Veronica.

Which of the following actions would subject Agatha to discipline?

(A) Privately telling Deirdre that she should not have lied to the grand jury.
(B) Continuing to serve as Deirdre's attorney.
(C) Calling the DA and telling him that Deirdre perjured herself before the grand jury.
(D) Declining to call the DA to tell him that Deirdre perjured herself before the grand jury.

Question 109

Lloyd Lawyer has asked his friend Aloysius Attorney to serve on the Attorney Conduct Committee of State X. The ACC regulates and monitors the conduct of attorneys in the state and sanctions them when appropriate. If Aloysius accepts, the board will consist of Lloyd, Aloysius, and Susie Secretary, who is not a lawyer. All three would volunteer their services.

Should Aloysius accept Lloyd's invitation?

(A) Yes, because in serving on the ACC he can help improve the practice of law in State X, but he doesn't have to serve.
(B) Yes, because he has an obligation to serve on some state bar committee.
(C) No, because the fact that he will be unpaid would subject him to temptation if he's offered bribes.
(D) No, because attorneys cannot serve on committees with laypeople.

Question 110

Attorney, an expert in securities law, has represented Exco for several years. Each time Exco has issued new debentures, Attorney has written an opinion letter on whether the debenture issue requires prior approval by the state public utilities commission.

Attorney was recently asked to write an opinion letter for a new Exco debenture issue of $10,000,000. In doing so, Attorney spent approximately twenty-five minutes checking to make sure the law had not changed since her last opinion letter and five minutes dictating to her secretary some minor changes from her last opinion letter to Exco. Attorney's normal hourly billing rate for handling any securities matter is $100 per hour, which is the hourly rate generally charged in the locality for similar services.

In arriving at a fee of $1,500 for the opinion letter, is it proper for Attorney to consider that:

I. Most lawyers in the area would charge a fee of $2,000 for such an opinion letter.
II. The security issue is for $10,000,000.
III. Attorney has represented Exco for a long period of time and is familiar with governmental regulations applicable to it.

(A) I only
(B) I and II, but not III
(C) I and III, but not II
(D) I, II, and III

Question 111

Heather is a licensed attorney in the town of Guile. She is the only attorney in the town. In the yellow pages she takes out a small ad which reads "Guile Legal Clinic...operated by Attorney Heather...Guile is not affiliated with any public agency." Heather is:

(A) Subject to discipline for soliciting clients.
(B) Subject to discipline for advertising.
(C) Not subject to discipline because the solicitation was not misleading.
(D) Not subject to discipline.

Question 112

Milton Mineworker, along with about 500 co-workers, was improperly exposed to fumes and dangerous chemicals over a 20-year period. He and the other miners have developed health problems which are attributable to the conditions in the mines. The owners have admitted liability and have settled claims with many of the miners for amounts ranging from $500,000 to $550,000. The owners have also stated that it is willing to settle with miners who have lung problems (as Milton does) for $540,000.

Milton asks Lisa Lawyer to represent him in obtaining a settlement from the mine owners. Milton offers Lisa a generous hourly fee to do so, but Lisa insists on a contingency fee of 40%. If Milton pays Lisa the 40%, may Lisa properly accept it?

(A) Yes, because Milton could have just hired a different attorney if he didn't want to pay Lisa's fee.
(B) No, unless a 40% contingency fee is normal in this kind of case in Lisa's community.
(C) No, if an hourly fee would have provided Milton with more of the money from the settlement.
(D) Yes, unless an hourly fee would have yielded a larger fee for Lisa than a contingency fee would have.

Question 113

Luto argues a case before Judge Skeet. Luto notices that the opposing counsel paid Skeet $500 before the case. Luto is convinced that the payment was a bribe. Luto confronts Skeet, who denies the charge. Luto argues the case, loses, appeals, loses the appeal, then moves on to other work. Luto is:

(A) Subject to discipline for insulting the judge.
(B) Subject to discipline for not reporting the judge to the bar.
(C) Not subject to discipline because he was not sure Skeet was bribed.
(D) Not subject to discipline because it was Skeet and not Luto who acted improperly.

Question 114

Alaric is licensed to practice in the State of Montana. He moves to New York and proceeds to practice law there without a license. Alaric:

I. Can be disciplined under the New York code of legal ethics.
II. Can be disciplined under the Montana code of legal ethics.
III. Cannot be disciplined.

(A) I only
(B) II only
(C) I and II only
(D) III only

Question 115

Attorney Anderson is a very conscientious attorney. She practices business law and regularly incorporates small businesses.

Several years ago, Anderson incorporated a gift shop, Bella Bella, for Client Christine. The incorporation was relatively routine, and, although Anderson knows that the shop is still in business, she has not heard from Christine since. Recently, Anderson learned of some new business regulations that she believes would affect Christine's business organization. Is she subject to discipline if she contacts Christine to advise her of the new regulations?

(A) No, unless Anderson is trying to drum up some business.
(B) No, because good lawyers advise their clients, active and inactive, of relevant new developments in the law.
(C) Yes, because Christine has concluded her business with Anderson and is no longer a client.
(D) Yes, because such contact would constitute solicitation.

Question 116

Deft retained Attorney to appeal Deft's criminal conviction and to seek bail pending appeal. The agreed fee for the appearance on the bail hearing was $50 per hour. Attorney received $800 from Deft, of which $300 was a deposit to secure Attorney's fee and $500 was for bail costs in the event that bail was obtained. Attorney maintained two office bank accounts: a "Fee Account," in which all fees were deposited and from which all office expenses were paid, and a "Clients' Fund Account." Attorney deposited the $800 in the "Clients' Fund Account" the week before the bail hearing. Attorney expended six hours of time on the bail hearing. The effort to obtain bail was unsuccessful. Dissatisfied, Deft immediately demanded return of the $800.

Is it proper for Attorney to:

(A) Transfer the $800 to the "Fee Account."
(B) Transfer $300 to the "Fee Account" and leave $500 in the "Clients' Fund Account" until Attorney's fee for the final appeal is determined.
(C) Transfer $300 to the "Fee Account" and send Deft a $500 check on the "Clients' Fund Account."
(D) Send Deft a $500 check and leave $300 in the "Clients' Fund Account" until the matter is resolved with Deft.

Question 117

Alpha is an attorney licensed to practice law in State A. After ten years of practicing law, Alpha moved to Europe and opened a successful restaurant. The restaurant was very popular among individuals suspected of being involved in organized crime. After a police undercover operation, several suspects were arrested while dining in Alpha's restaurant. One of the suspects told the police that Alpha had offered to assist them in any smuggling and money laundering activities. Alpha returned to State A before the authorities determined whether there was sufficient evidence to prosecute Alpha. Assuming that Alpha did offer to assist in the commission of a crime, is Alpha *subject to discipline* in State A?

(A) Yes, because Alpha has engaged in conduct demonstrating unfitness to be a lawyer.
(B) Yes, because Alpha has returned to State A and may attempt to engage in the practice of law.
(C) No, because Alpha did not engage in any criminal conduct in State A while acting as an attorney.
(D) No, because Alpha was never prosecuted for any crime.

Question 118

Judge Jessica is a District Court judge in Fair City. She has been on the bench for three years, and in that time, she has become known for her very strict sentencing of convicted criminals. In fact, in local legal circles, she is known as "Lock-Em-Up-and-Throw-Away-The-Key" Jessica. In Fair City, judges serve four-year terms and then must run for reelection.

As Jessica is about to run for reelection, she is often asked by the press to comment on her judicial practices and philosophy. What may Jessica properly say?

I. "I will always try to promote the interests of justice."
II. "I believe that criminals should be locked up and we should throw away the key. I've always thought that and I'll stand by it, so the people should reelect me."
III. "My sentencing decisions to date have been correct, and I'll make similar decisions whenever criminals are brought before me for sentencing."

(A) II only.
(B) II and III.
(C) III only.
(D) I only.

Question 119

Lawyer is a private practitioner who represented Client in a personal injury action against Grocer. Client alleged that she suffered a serious back injury when she slipped and fell in the defendant's grocery store. During the course of seeking legal advice, Client disclosed to Lawyer that she had previously injured her back in an automobile accident and had sought the assistance of Beta, another attorney in the community, but Beta had failed to file the claim before the statute of limitations had run and had not returned any of the funds she deposited with Beta to represent her. Client asked Lawyer not to reveal any part of this information because she did not want Grocer to find out about the prior accident or that she had been so foolish as to trust that Beta would protect her interests in the prior action. Lawyer told Client that she would have to reveal the existence of any pre-existing back injury but that he could only reveal the information about Beta's misconduct if Client agreed.

If Client refuses to allow Attorney to reveal Beta's misconduct, will Attorney be *subject to discipline* if Attorney does not reveal the misconduct to the disciplinary authorities?

(A) No, unless Lawyer determines that Beta's conduct amounted to malpractice.
(B) No, because Attorney cannot reveal Beta's misconduct without violating the duty of confidentiality owed to Client.
(C) Yes, Client's embarrassment is insufficient to override the duty to report unethical conduct.
(D) Yes, if Beta's conduct amounts to a crime.

Question 120

Attorney was a well-known litigation attorney who had recently been involved in a televised trial that was closely followed by the public. The judge at the trial was Judge X. After the trial was over, a television reporter asked Attorney about a controversial ruling made by Judge X to exclude the testimony of one of Attorney's witnesses. In response, Attorney told the interviewer that "I'm glad the trial was televised...now you all can see the unjust rulings Judge X hands down all the time."

Will Attorney be *subject to discipline* for making this statement?

(A) Yes, even if Judge X actually did hand down unjust rulings.
(B) Yes, because Attorney has violated the ethical duty to defend the judicial system and refrain from engaging in personal attacks on the members of the judiciary.
(C) No, as long as Attorney did not make a knowingly false statement or act with reckless disregard for the truth or falsity of the statement.
(D) No, if Attorney is a candidate for the same judicial office as Judge X.

Question 121

Judge Judy is a District Court Judge in State Purple. She is one of five judges on the District Court. She employs, among others, Catherine Clerk.

On Monday, Judge Judy heard a case between Pauline Plaintiff and David Defendant, and she's having a lot of trouble reconciling conflicting case law on the key legal issue in the case. She asks Catherine and three of the other District Court judges for their opinion on the matter (identifying the case at issue and the conflicting common law). She does not tell Pauline and David (or their attorneys) about these consultations.

Did Judge Judy act properly?

(A) Yes, because she may consult with other members of the court and court personnel on this issue.
(B) No, because she did not tell the parties of her conversations.
(C) No, because she is prohibited from talking with anyone about matters before the court.
(D) Yes, because she may freely communicate with experts on the law.

Question 122

Able was injured while operating some heavy machinery manufactured by Conco. As a result of the injury, Able experienced frequent unpredictable loss of consciousness. When Conco refused to pay for Able's medical bills and loss of future wages, Able retained Lawyer to represent him in the action. Able successfully negotiated a settlement of all claims, and Able received payment from Conco. Three years later, Able was driving his vehicle when he suffered a loss of consciousness and struck Baker, a pedestrian. Baker approached Lawyer and asked Lawyer to represent Baker in a personal injury action against Able. Lawyer reasonably determined that the suit against Baker would involve substantial reliance on the facts regarding Able's medical condition that Lawyer learned during confidential attorney-client discussions with Able.

Which of the following statements is most accurate?

(A) It is *proper* for Lawyer to represent Baker, but only if Lawyer fully discloses all relevant facts to Baker and Able.
(B) It is *proper* for Lawyer to decline to represent Baker.
(C) It is *proper* for Lawyer to refer the case to Attorney, an attorney in Lawyer's firm who was not a member of the firm when Attorney represented Able.
(D) It is *proper* for Lawyer to refer the case to Barrister, an attorney who in another law firm, in exchange for Barrister's promise to refer Barrister's next conflict of interest client to Lawyer.

Question 123

Client was injured when struck by a Driver who failed to stop at a red light. Client retained Lawyer for legal representation and signed a contingent fee agreement that would provide that Attorney would receive one-third of any settlement agreement. Subsequently, Client authorized Lawyer to settle the case for $60,000. When Lawyer received the $60,000 payment from the defendant, Lawyer promptly told Client that Lawyer had a check for $40,000 available for Client. Client became angry and stated that Lawyer was only entitled to $5,000, because the case settled so quickly.

It is *proper* for Lawyer to

I. Deposit the $60,000 check in Client's trust fund account, send Client a check for $40,000 and write a check to Lawyer's personal account in the amount of $20,000.
II. Deposit the $60,000 check in Client's trust fund account, send Client a check for $60,000 with a note requesting that Client send $20,000 to Lawyer.
III. Deposit the $60,000 check in Client's trust fund account, send Client a check for $55,000 and write a check to Lawyer's personal account for $5,000.
IV. Deposit the $60,000 check in Client's trust fund account but refuse to disburse any funds to client until the fee dispute can be resolved by arbitration or mediation.

(A) I and III only.
(B) I, II and III only.
(C) II and III only.
(D) I, II, III and IV.

Question 124

Client was injured when a bus (operated by Defendant) overturned on the road. All of the other passengers were injured and the Defendant, to expedite matters, admitted liability and thus each passenger only had to prove damages in order to recover. Client hired Attorney to represent her in obtaining a settlement of her claim against Defendant. Several other passengers who had suffered substantially the same type and extent of injury as Client had received settlements of $100,000 each. Based on this knowledge, Client asked Attorney to work for an hourly fee. Attorney refused claiming that in personal injury actions it was customary for attorneys to be paid on a contingency basis at a rate of one-third of any recovery. After more discussion, Client agreed and signed a contingent fee agreement.

Was Attorney's insistence on being paid a one-third contingent fee *proper*?

(A) Yes, the use of a contingent fee in personal injury actions is customary and proper.
(B) Yes, because Client agreed to execute the written contingent fee agreement after consultation and negotiation.
(C) No, if the contingent fee was not reasonable under the circumstances.
(D) No, unless the one-third contingent fee is customary in personal injury cases in the community where Lawyer practices.

Question 125

Arnold Attorney was driving home from the office late one night when he got a traffic ticket for running a red light. In Arnold's state, getting a traffic ticket is considered a criminal misdemeanor. Will Arnold be disciplined by the bar?

(A) No, because Arnold was not acting as a lawyer at the time.
(B) No, because the crime of running a red light is not one of moral turpitude.
(C) Yes, because he was driving recklessly.
(D) Yes, because any criminal conviction warrants disciplinary action.

Question 126

Alice Attorney is a litigator in State Blue. She often tries cases before Judge Dingbat, among others. Alice believes that Judge Dingbat is not a very good judge and that he is very stupid. She also feels that Sam Smart would be a much better judge than Judge Dingbat.

Will Alice be subject to discipline if she tells the Blue Blaze, the state legal paper, that she supports Smart as a candidate for judge because she believes that Dingbat is stupid?

(A) Yes, because Alice often tries cases before Dingbat.
(B) Yes, because Dingbat is currently on the bench.
(C) No, because Alice believes her statement to be true.
(D) No, unless she bases her right to say so on the First Amendment.

Questions 127 and 128 are based on the following fact situation.

Tom was a high school classmate of Attorney. One afternoon, Tom came to visit Attorney in Attorney's office to "discuss a legal situation." When Tom sat down, he pulled a pistol from his pocket and told Attorney, "I shot my wife this morning." Attorney quickly told Tom to put the gun back in his pocket and to say nothing more. Attorney then told Tom that his practice was limited to tax and real estate matters, that he was not qualified to represent Tom or give competent legal advice and that Tom should seek representation from a good criminal defense attorney. Attorney handed Tom a list of competent criminal defense attorneys and told him to leave. Tom was subsequently arrested and charged with murder. Attorney was called to testify as to the substance of Attorney's conversation with Tom in Attorney's office.

Question 127

Is it *proper* for Attorney to testify as to the statement made by Tom?

(A) Yes, because Attorney declined to represent Tom.
(B) Yes, because Attorney has assisted in the suppression of evidence.
(C) No, because Tom's statement is protected by the duty to protect client confidences and secrets.
(D) No, because the statement was detrimental to Tom's interests.

Question 128

Assume for purposes of this question only that Attorney is prosecuted for evidence tampering after Tom told the police that Attorney told him to hide the gun. Is Attorney subject to discipline if Attorney reveals that he told Tom to put the gun back in his pocket?

(A) Yes, Attorney must preserve the confidences and secrets of Tom.
(B) Yes, if the disclosure would be detrimental to Tom's interests.
(C) No, if the disclosure is necessary to defend against the evidence tampering charge.
(D) No, the gun is tangible evidence that is not within the testimonial attorney-client privilege.

Question 129

Louise Lawyer is representing Dawn Defendant in a tort case in State Orange. Petrova Plaintiff, while trespassing on Louise's yard, fell into a ditch there and broke her leg, which later had to be amputated.

Louise plans to argue that Dawn should not be liable because Petrova was trespassing on Louise's property when she fell. She will offer as precedent two cases from the Supreme Courts of neighboring states, Yellow and Red. The Orange Supreme Court has held in two recent decisions that property owners are liable for injuries caused to trespassers by dangerous conditions on the owners' property.

Is Louise subject to discipline for offering this defense?

(A) Yes, if she knows that the Orange Supreme Court has held that the property owner is liable in such cases.
(B) Yes, unless she can find some case law from lower courts in Orange that would support her case.
(C) No, because she must zealously defend her client.
(D) No, as long as she has a good faith belief that her defense has merit.

Question 130

Deft was charged with murder. The victim was Deft's brother. Lawyer was a deputy district attorney who was assigned to lead the prosecution of Deft. Ultimately, Deft was convicted of murder. The charge was later overturned on appeal when it was determined that the arresting officers had fabricated evidence to support the prosecution's case against Deft. Disillusioned, Lawyer resigned from the district attorney's office and entered private law practice. Spouse, the widow of Deft's deceased brother, approached Lawyer and asked Lawyer to represent her in filing a wrongful death claim against Deft.

Is it *proper* for Lawyer to represent Spouse in the wrongful death action?

- (A) No, because Lawyer had substantial responsibility for the criminal prosecution of Deft.
- (B) No, because Lawyer may have continuing ties with members of law enforcement and the district attorney's office.
- (C) Yes, because Spouse's interests are not adverse to Lawyer's former employer's interests.
- (D) Yes, unless Attorney uses confidential information gained while prosecuting Deft in the representation of Spouse.

Question 131

Attorney, a former compliance officer with the Internal Revenue Service, developed a practice assisting taxpayers in preparing tax returns and representing them when their returns were audited by the Internal Revenue Service. As the practice grew, Attorney had to turn away new clients in order to properly serve existing clients. In order to accept more clients, Attorney hired Preparer, a licensed tax preparer, to assist Attorney in the preparation of client tax returns. In exchange for Preparer's assistance, Attorney will pay Preparer ten percent of all profits received from Attorney's tax practice.

Is Attorney subject to discipline for entering into this relationship with Preparer?

- (A) No, a lawyer may compensate nonlawyer employees in a profit-sharing compensation plan.
- (B) No, if Attorney fully disclosed the relationship and obtained consent from all affected clients.
- (C) Yes, because some of Preparer's compensation will be derived from fees derived from Attorney's law practice.
- (D) Yes, because Attorney is assisting in the unauthorized practice of law.

Question 132

Susie is a lawyer in the state of Despair. She is applying for a food vendor's license in the state of Euphoria. A question on the application for the food vendor's license asks, "Have you ever been charged with a crime?" Susie answers no, and, in doing so, fails to disclose that she has recently been charged with criminal fraud.

May Despair discipline her for this conduct?

(A) No, because she was acting as an applicant for the food vendor's license, not as an attorney.
(B) No, because her conduct did not take place in Despair.
(C) Yes, because she lied on her application.
(D) Yes, because a lawyer may not hold a food vendor's license.

Question 133

Attorney hired Paralegal to assist Attorney in the preparation of documents for Client. Attorney and Paralegal have worked together for three years and Attorney has carefully reviewed all of Paralegal's work for Attorney before submitting any such work to a client or the court. On one occasion, Attorney left one of Client's documents with Paralegal with specific written instructions to file the document in Court A. Paralegal carelessly misread the instructions and filed Client's document with Court B instead. Court B had no jurisdiction to review the document, and the statute of limitations expired before Attorney discovered the misfiling. Court A refused to allow Attorney to file Client's document because it was not timely.

Which of the following statements most accurately summarizes Attorney's legal and professional responsibility?

(A) Attorney is subject to liability for malpractice and for violation of the disciplinary rules.
(B) Attorney is subject to liability for malpractice but is NOT subject to discipline unless Attorney failed to reasonably supervise Paralegal.
(C) Attorney is subject to discipline but is NOT subject to malpractice liability.
(D) Attorney is NOT subject to discipline or for malpractice.

Question 134

A talk radio station hired Attorney to produce and host a one-hour weekly radio program discussing legal topics and answering questions presented by callers to the radio program. During the program, a caller asked whether she should represent herself in an eviction proceeding instituted against her by her landlord. Attorney responded that an eviction case could involve multiple legal issues that could require the assistance of a lawyer to properly protect the tenant's legal rights. The next day, the same caller appeared at Attorney's office and offered to retain Attorney to defend her in the eviction action filed by her landlord.

Is it *proper* for Attorney to accept representation of the caller for the eviction case?

(A) No, if Attorney accepts client, Attorney will violate the rule against direct solicitation of clients.
(B) No, but another Attorney in Attorney's firm may accept the case.
(C) Yes, Attorney may accept the caller as a client because Attorney's statement was not false, fraudulent, misleading, deceptive, self-laudatory or unfair.
(D) Yes, Attorney may accept the caller as a client because the client initiated the contact with Attorney.

Question 135

Attorney is a district attorney in a small town in State A who has aspirations of running for Attorney-General in State A. A local individual, D, was reputed to be a drug smuggler responsible for importing vast quantities of illegal narcotics into State A for sale to schoolchildren. Thus far, D had evaded arrest because of the inability of the police to find sufficient evidence to prove D's involvement in drug smuggling activities. Attorney believed that if D could be indicted and convicted, the public would be rid of a dangerous criminal, not to mention the publicity that would be generated by the prosecution of such a dangerous criminal. Knowing of Attorney's desire to prosecute D, Informant approached Attorney and offered to work undercover for Attorney to infiltrate and obtain incriminating evidence against D. Attorney eagerly agreed and Informant began to gather information. After several weeks, Informant gave Attorney a videotape that purported to show D loading bundles of cocaine into the trunk of D's car. Attorney immediately had D arrested and sought a grand jury indictment against D. Prior to the indictment, Attorney discovered that the videotape was skillfully edited to make it appear that D was loading cocaine into a car when in fact it was Informant disguised as D who was depicted in the videotape. Attorney knew that a skillful defense attorney would probably discover that videotape was not genuine, but honestly believed that if D was indicted, he would no longer be able to continue smuggling drugs because of the publicity an indictment would bring. Attorney proceeded to obtain an indictment against D.

Is Attorney *subject to discipline*?

(A) No, because a prosecutor is charged with the duty to prosecute zealously and the grand jury must determine whether there is sufficient evidence to indict.
(B) No, because Attorney honestly believed that a grand jury indictment would result in a reduction in D's criminal activities.
(C) Yes, because Attorney did not have probable cause to arrest or indict D.
(D) Yes, because Attorney was motivated by personal ambition rather than public protection.

Question 136

Andrea Attorney handles large tort reform cases on behalf of plaintiffs. When she wishes to make a settlement offer, she always does so in writing, sending a copy of the settlement offer to opposing counsel and also to the defendant. Such a letter generally states that the plaintiffs will consent to a dismissal of the lawsuit if defendants agree to pay a stated sum of money and to reform their business practices.

Is Andrea acting properly?

(A) Yes, because she has an ethical duty to try to settle cases.
(B) Yes, if she genuinely believes that the defendants' counsel will not inform them of the settlement offer.
(C) No, unless the defense attorney knows that she is sending the letter to the defendants and consents to her doing so.
(D) No, unless she keeps a copy of the settlement letter to show that she made a settlement offer.

Question 137

Attorney was a member of the state legislature of State B. Attorney also represented Landowner who was seeking an exemption from a State B regulation requiring Landowner and other owners of similar type properties to set aside ten percent of their land for open space requirements. At Landowner's insistence, Attorney researched the regulation and determined that it was, in Attorney's view, an unworkable regulation that imposed an excessive burden on State B landowners. Attorney introduced a bill in the State B legislature to repeal the land use regulation and publicly disclosed Attorney's relationship with Landowner. Other State B legislators were not convinced and defeated the bill by a majority vote.

Is Attorney *subject to discipline*?

(A) No, because an Attorney must act zealously in the representation of a client.
(B) No, because Attorney did not seek a special advantage for Landowner where Attorney knew or where it was obvious the legislation was not in the public interest.
(C) Yes, because Attorney used a public position on behalf of a private client to obtain a special advantage.
(D) Yes, because the fact that the bill was defeated is proof that Attorney was not acting for the public benefit.

Questions 138 and 139 are based on the following fact situation.

Attorney was retained by Husband to represent him in a divorce action filed by Wife, who was represented by Lawyer. Pending a final dissolution of the marriage, Wife retained custody of their minor children. Husband was very concerned about the welfare of the children and urged Attorney to negotiate with Lawyer to resolve the property and financial issues as quickly as possible because Husband wanted to make sure he would receive joint custody of the children. Attorney was aware of Lawyer's reputation as a skilled negotiator who would not want to quickly resolve any issues because Lawyer believed it was always best to "wear down the opponent" with protracted negotiations until the opposing party gave in to all Lawyer's client's demands. Husband assured Attorney that Wife had only hired Lawyer based on the fact that Husband, Wife and Lawyer were casual acquaintances (because they all belonged to the same civic organization) and that Wife was not interested in harming the children with a bitter custody fight. Wife had made this same representation at several depositions attended by the parties and their attorneys. Based on this information, Attorney drafted a letter which Husband signed, stating that Attorney and Husband were prepared to give in to wife on all her property and financial demands if she would agree to joint custody of the children. Attorney mailed the letter to Wife.

Question 138

Was Attorney's action in mailing the letter to Wife *proper*?

(A) No, because Lawyer never consented to the communication.
(B) No, unless Attorney reasonably believes that Lawyer would not inform Wife about the contents of the letter.
(C) Yes, because in a divorce action the interests of the children may be considered when determining the proper strategy and tactics.
(D) Yes, because Attorney was merely the conduit of a communication between Husband and Wife.

Question 139

Assume for purposes of this question only that instead of mailing the letter, Attorney told X, the minister at Husband and Wife's church, to call on Wife and tell her that all parties would benefit from a quick resolution and that Husband would be willing to accede to all her property and financial demands in exchange for joint custody of the children.

Is this conduct by Attorney *proper*?

(A) Yes, parties to a matter may directly communicate with one another.
(B) Yes, because there is no risk of undue influence or overreaching when someone other than the opposing counsel communicates the message.
(C) No, the substance of a settlement offer must always be first communicated to the attorney for a represented party.
(D) No, a lawyer may not use an intermediary to communicate with a represented party without the prior consent of that party's attorney.

Question 140

Larry Lawyer represents Loan Shark, a lending institution that offers consolidation, home equity, mortgage, and other types of loans. LoanShark hires Larry to look over some of its old home equity loans in order to update its files and improve on the language in future loan documents. When he reviews the loans, however, Larry realizes that the terms of the documents on the outstanding loans allow LoanShark to raise rates on the loans if the borrowers miss any payments. Larry realizes that many of the loans he is reviewing may fall within that category, but he also realizes that LoanShark, who has a problem with customer perception anyway, may rank low on customer service ratings if it actually raises the rates on the loans where it is entitled to do so. Incredibly, LoanShark doesn't seem to understand the terms of its own loans.

Should Larry tell LoanShark's officers about the provision that would allow it to raise rates?

(A) It's up to Larry — he doesn't have to tell LoanShark (unless they ask him directly about the relevant provision), but he can if he wants to.
(B) He really has to tell LoanShark about the relevant provision while also advising it about the possible customer relations problems.
(C) He has to tell LoanShark about the relevant provision but shouldn't mention the possible ramifications — that's up to the bank's officers to figure out.
(D) Given the possible bad customer relations that might ensue, he should not tell LoanShark about the provision.

Question 141

In a medical malpractice trial, Client alleges that Defendant (the surgeon who performed the operation) negligently failed to remove a cancerous tumor. Attorney will be calling three witnesses to testify on behalf of Client. Witness A will testify that she was in the operating room and heard Defendant state that Defendant was in a hurry to complete Client's operation because Defendant had an important meeting with a business partner. Witness B will testify that Client suffered a slow lingering death following the operation. Witness C is a surgeon who will testify that based on C's expert opinion, a competent surgeon would have discovered and removed Client's tumor. Witnesses A and B request that Attorney reimburse them for the costs of travel and lost wages incurred as a result of their trial testimony. Witness C has requested a flat fee of $1,000 or, in the alternative, a $5,000 fee if Client prevails in the suit or no fee if Client is unsuccessful. It would be *proper* for Attorney to pay the following expenses:

(A) The reasonable travel and loss of wages expenses incurred by Witnesses A and B and a fee to Witness C under either formula proposed by Witness C.
(B) The reasonable travel and loss of wages expenses incurred by Witnesses A and B and the $1,000 flat fee to Witness C.
(C) The reasonable travel expenses incurred by Witnesses A and B (but not the loss of wages expenses) and the $1,000 flat fee to Witness C.
(D) Only the $1,000 flat fee to Witness C because Witness A and Witness B are lay witnesses who cannot be compensated for providing testimony about events they witnessed.

Question 142

Attorney represented Client in a breach of contract case against Defendant. At a pre-trial hearing, the judge ruled that Defendant's wife could not testify for Client in the case because she was barred by the spousal incompetency privilege from testifying against Defendant. After the first day of trial, Attorney was asked by a reporter to comment about the case. Attorney made several statements. Assuming that each statement is true, which of the following statements were *proper*?

I. "My client stands by the allegations in the complaint; Defendant never delivered the goods as promised."
II. "I do not believe the Defendant's testimony today was credible, and I trust that the jury shared this belief."
III. "When the Defendant's own wife told my Client that Defendant admitted to breaching the contract, I believe that jury will make the right decision in this case."

(A) I only.
(B) I and II only.
(C) I, II and III.
(D) Neither I nor II nor III.

Question 143

Bank was undergoing an internal audit when it discovered that there were several hundred savings accounts that had been inactive for over 10 years. None of the accounts contained more than $1,000. Bank called Counsel, an in-house attorney, to ask Counsel to research the law and give Bank a legal opinion as to what to do with the inactive accounts. Counsel researched the applicable state and federal banking laws and discovered that Bank was not required to locate or notify the owners or the inactive accounts and that, after 10 years of non-activity, a bank was entitled to close the accounts and retain any funds. Counsel did some other research and determined that over 90% of the account owners could be located at minor expense. In Counsel's judgment, it would be in the best interests of justice and could increase Bank's good will in the community if Bank would pay the expenses to locate and contact the account owners and ask them to close or reactivate their accounts with Bank. What are Counsel's responsibilites in this situation?

(A) Counsel *may* inform Bank that it may close the accounts but *must* recommend that Bank attempt to contact the account owners and Counsel *must* withdraw from representation if Bank refuses to follow the recommendation.
(B) Counsel *may* inform Bank that it may close the accounts but *must* recommend that Bank attempt to contact the account owners and Counsel *may* continue the representation even if Bank refuses to follow the recommendation.
(C) Counsel *must* inform Bank that it may close the accounts but *may* recommend that Bank attempt to contact the account owners and Counsel *may* continue the representation even if Bank refuses to follow the recommendation.
(D) Counsel *must* inform Bank that it may close the accounts but *may not* recommend that Bank attempt to contact the account owners because Counsel was only asked to provide a legal opinion, not business advice.

Question 144

Able and Baker approached Attorney and asked Attorney to represent them in formation of a business partnership. Attorney agreed, and, after meeting with both Able and Baker to determine their goals and concerns, Attorney drafted a partnership agreement that was executed by Able and Baker. Several years later, the partnership began to experience financial difficulties, and Able and Baker began to argue about their individual right to compensation under the partnership agreement. Both partners consulted Attorney and asked Attorney to mediate their dispute. After he consulted with Able and Baker concerning the advantages and risks of mediation, both parties consented to the mediation by Attorney. After a two-hour session, Able and Baker executed an amendment to the original partnership agreement expressing their new agreement as to individual compensation. Two weeks later, Able called Counsel, a litigation attorney, and asked Counsel to represent him in a breach of contract suit against Baker. Able claimed that Baker had withdrawn partnership funds in breach of both the original and amended partnership agreement. Baker contacted Attorney and asked Attorney to represent Baker in the breach of contract suit.

May Attorney represent Baker in this suit?

(A) No, because Attorney had represented both Able and Baker in the creation and amendment of the partnership agreement currently in dispute.
(B) No, because Attorney cannot act as an objective intermediary for a dispute resulting from the interpretation of a document drafted by Attorney.
(C) Yes, because Able voluntarily withdrew from mediation and retained independent counsel.
(D) Yes, if Able knowingly violated the partnership agreement.

Question 145

Jennifer represented Alison in an important litigation in 1995 and has not represented or even spoken with her since. Lauren had no involvement in the 1995 litigation. In 2005, Lauren asks Jennifer to represent her in an action against Alison. This present action involves some of the same facts and circumstances — including confidential ones — as did Alison's 1995 litigation.

Jennifer should:

(A) Tell Lauren that she cannot represent her in this action.
(B) Tell Lauren she can represent her but cannot reveal any confidential information from the prior litigation.
(C) Tell Lauren she can represent her but must notify Alison before accepting the case.
(D) Refer the case to another attorney in her firm as long as Jennifer does not actively participate in the representation.

Question 146

Alpha is a criminal defense attorney who voluntarily submitted his name for inclusion on a list of attorneys willing to serve as appointed counsel for indigent criminal defendants. Alpha is also quite active in local community efforts on behalf of underprivileged and abused children and takes on many cases on a *pro bono* basis for children needing protection from abusive homes or help from government social service agencies. The clerk of the local criminal court contacted Alpha and told Alpha that his name was next on the list for appointed counsel and the next case involved Deft. Alpha had read about the case in the newspapers and believes that Deft was guilty of the crimes charged—that Deft committed a series of murders involving children and torture. Personally revolted by the prospect of defending someone who victimized innocent children and fearing that the negative publicity from the trial would jeopardize his standing with the various community groups he belonged to, Alpha falsely told the clerk that he was going on an extended business trip and would be unable to represent any new clients for the next two weeks. He asked the clerk to skip over his name for this appointment and stated truthfully that he (Alpha) would be happy to take the next indigent defendant case available upon his return.

Was it *proper* for Alpha to seek to avoid appointment to represent Deft?

(A) Yes, an attorney should not agree to represent a criminal defendant if the attorney has already formed an opinion that the client is guilty.
(B) Yes, an attorney should not take a case to represent a client if the attorney's personal feelings are so strong that the representation of the client is likely to be impaired.
(C) No, an attorney must not allow his or her personal feelings to interfere with the professional obligation to zealously defend a client.
(D) No, an attorney cannot allow the views of third parties to override the attorney's professional judgment.

Question 147

Judge was appointed to the bench by the governor after working as a partner at a law firm. Partner was also a partner in the same law firm and was recently indicted for criminal tax evasion. The attorney representing Partner is planning to call Judge as a character witness to testify on behalf of Partner.

Is it *proper* for Judge to provide testimony on behalf of Partner?

(A) No, because Judge will be called to testify on a collateral matter and is not a percipient witness to any acts or events essential to the elements of the charge.
(B) No, a judge cannot appear voluntarily as a character witness.
(C) Yes, but only if Judge receives an official summons compelling Judge to appear.
(D) Yes, regardless of whether Judge receives an official summons compelling Judge to appear.

Question 148

Judge A was appointed to the bench after a lengthy career as a prosecutor in a small community. Judge A had little experience with civil cases and was concerned that the issues in a wrongful termination suit filed in Judge A's court would be novel and complex. To gain further knowledge and expertise, Judge A called a well-respected employment law professor at a local law school and asked for some assistance and guidance as to what literature was available on the topic of wrongful termination. The law professor answered all of Judge A's substantive questions and told Judge A about three law review articles relevant to the topic and questions discussed. After Judge A finished the conversation and had read the law review articles, Judge A informed counsel for both parties about the communication with the law professor and the citations for the three law review articles consulted.

Has Judge A acted in a *proper* manner?

(A) No, a judge cannot initiate an *ex parte* communication with respect to a pending matter.
(B) No, unless Judge asked the parties' permission before he called the law professor.
(C) Yes, because a judge is entitled to communicate *ex parte* whenever s/he wishes, based on his/her good judgment.
(D) Yes, because the law professor was a disinterested legal expert.

Question 149

Judge has many friends and acquaintances in the local legal community. After many years on the bench, Judge decided to run for Attorney-General of the state. For financial reasons, Judge could not afford to immediately resign from the bench.

At what point *must* Judge resign?

(A) As soon as Judge publicly announces that Judge is a candidate for Attorney-General.
(B) Only after Judge signs the necessary papers officially entering Judge's name on the ballot as a candidate for Attorney-General.
(C) Only after Judge prevails in the election for Attorney-General.
(D) Only after the Judge is sworn in as Attorney-General.

Question 150

Prior to becoming a trial judge, Judge was a member of a civil law firm that specialized in civil litigation. Judge worked primarily on family law cases while a member of the firm. One of Judge's cases involves a securities law dispute between Corp and three dissatisfied Corp shareholders that had been filed when Judge worked for the law firm. Corp was originally and continues to be represented by Partner, a law partner who had practiced law with Judge at the same law firm. Judge had never worked on any case involving Corp or the three shareholders, but one of the shareholders had previously been a plaintiff in an unrelated personal injury action and was represented in the personal injury action by Associate, a lawyer who had also practiced law with Judge while both were members of the same firm.

Is it *proper* for Judge to hear this case?

(A) No, because Judge practiced law with Partner and Associate.
(B) No, because Judge practiced law with Partner when the present case was filed.
(C) Yes, because Judge did not personally participate in any prior case involving Corp or the three shareholders.
(D) Yes, but only if Judge obtains a waiver of disqualification from all of the parties after full disclosure of the potential conflicts of interest.

EXPLANATORY ANSWERS

1. **(D)** According to DR 7-109(C), a lawyer "may advance, guarantee, or acquiesce in the payment of...expenses reasonably incurred by a witness in attending or testifying...reasonable compensation to a witness for his loss of time in attending or testifying...[and] a reasonable fee for the professional services of an expert witness." Therefore, (A) and (B) are permissible. (C) is incorrect because DR 7-109(C) also states that "[a] lawyer shall not pay, offer to pay, or acquiesce in the payment of compensation to a witness contingent upon the content of his testimony or the outcome of the case." The only mention in the Model Rules appears in section 3 of the Comment to Model Rule 3.4, which states that it is not improper to pay a witness' expenses or to pay a fee to an expert witness; (A) and (B) would therefore be appropriate under the Model Rules, as well.

2. **(C)** In accordance with EC 5-5, "a lawyer should not suggest to his client that a gift be made to himself or for his benefit." Moreover, if a client voluntarily offers to make a gift to his lawyer, the lawyer may accept the gift, but, before doing so, he should urge that his client secure disinterested advice from an independent, competent person who is cognizant of all of the circumstances. Thus, Answer (C) provides the most correct statements concerning Ernie's acceptance of a voluntary gift from his client Burt. *See also* MR 1.8(c) ("A lawyer shall not solicit any substantial gift from a client...").

3. **(B)** Choice (B) provides that the best answer concerning the outside law-related activities in which Judge Busy may participate. Canon 4 of the Code of Judicial Conduct ("CJC") provides that a judge may participate in the following law-related outside activities: (A) a judge may speak write, lecture, teach, and participate in other activities concerning the law, the legal system, the administration of justice, and non-legal subjects, (B) a judge may appear at public legislative or administrative hearings on legal subjects, (C) a judge may consult with legislators or administrators on matters relating to the administration of justice, (D) a judge may serve in organizations devoted to law reform and may participate in their fund management (NOTE: a judge may not personally participate in public fund-raising for the group), and (E) a judge may make recommendations to foundations and related funding groups on law reform projects. In reference to our hypothetical, Judge Busy may not actively participate in public fund-raising for the penal reform group. However, she may offer assistance in the group's fund management.

4. **(C)** Statements II and III are correct. Dean's communication to Frank is protected by the evidentiary attorney-client privilege. This privilege applies to confidential communications made by an individual to an attorney who is sought out for the purpose of obtaining legal advice or counsel. Note that Dean's statement was made to Frank in confidence after Dean hired Frank as his attorney. Secondly, Foster's statement to Frank is a secret which Frank has an ethical duty not to disclose to other third persons. Frank obtained the information from Foster during the attorney-client relationship with Dean. Their professional relationship would prohibit the disclosure of this secret which would be embarrassing or detrimental to Dean. It is important to note that DR 4-101(B) provides that "except when permitted under DR 4-101(C) a lawyer shall not knowingly: (1) Reveal a confidence or secret of a client." Examples of what an attorney may reveal in accordance with the aforementioned section (C) are as follows: (1) confidences or secrets with the consent of the client, but only after a full disclosure has been made to the client, (2) confidences

or secrets when permitted under the Disciplinary Rules or required by law or court order, (3) the intention of a client to commit a crime and the information necessary to prevent its commission and (4) confidences and secrets necessary to establish or collect his fee or to defend himself or his employees against accusations of wrongful conduct. *See also* MR 1.6(a) ("A lawyer shall not reveal information relating to the representation of a client unless the client gives informed consent...[or] the disclosure is impliedly authorized in order to carry out the representation...") and MR 1.8(b) ("A lawyer shall not use information relating to representation of a client to the disadvantage of the client.").

5. **(A)** Model Rule 6.4 is directly on point, stating that "[a] lawyer may serve as a director, officer or member of an organization involved in reform of the law or its administration notwithstanding that the reform may affect the interests of a client of the lawyer. When the lawyer knows that the interests of a client may be materially benefitted by a decision in which the lawyer participates, the lawyer shall disclose that fact but need not identify the client." Therefore, Lauren should support the recommendation if she so desires but disclose that she has an interested client. EC 8-1 and 8-4 are consistent with the Model Rules. (B) is wrong because Lauren must act in the public interest, even if it conflicts with that of her client. However, (C) and (D) are wrong because, under the Model Rules, Lauren has no conflict here and will not act improperly by voting on the issue.

6. **(D)** EC 5-1 provides that "professional judgment of a lawyer should be exercised within the bounds of the law solely for the benefit of his client and free of compromising influences and loyalties. Neither his personal interests, the interests of other clients, nor the desires of third persons should be permitted to dilute his loyalty to his client." *See also* MR 1.7(a)(2) ("[A] lawyer shall not represent a client if the representation involves a concurrent conflict of interest. A concurrent conflict of interest exists if:...there is a significant risk that the representation of one or more clients will be materially limited by...a personal interest of the lawyer."). Thus, a lawyer's own interests, personal or business, should not be permitted to have an adverse effect on representation of a client. By the same token, representing a client does not constitute approval of the client's views or activities. In our case, Alpha may personally oppose a position taken by his client, Exco Oil Co. However, Alpha must act in such a manner as not to prejudice Exco or in any way adversely affect his obligations of loyalty to his corporate client. Choice (D) correctly provides the statements relating to Alpha's ethical obligation to his client Exco.

7. **(D)** Ms. Montigue would be subject to discipline under the CPR and the MRPC if she filed the lawsuit for Mr. McCoy. In accordance with DR 2-109(A)(1) "a lawyer shall not accept employment on behalf of a person if he knows or it is obvious that such person wishes to: (1) bring an action, conduct a defense, or assert a position in litigation, or otherwise have steps taken for him, merely for the purpose of harassing or maliciously injuring any person." *See also* MR 1.16(a)(1) ("[A] lawyer shall not represent a client...if: (1) the representation will result in violation of the rules of professional conduct...") and MR 3.1 ("A lawyer shall not bring or defend a proceeding, or assert or controvert an issue therein, unless there is a basis in law and fact for doing so that is not frivolous..."). Consequently, an attorney should reject employment if he or she has actual knowledge or obvious belief that the proposed client wishes to institute a lawsuit solely for the purpose of harassment of another person, as in our case.

MPRE Exam

8. **(A)** (A) is the best answer because both the Model Rules and the Model Code provide guidance for attorneys as to proper and desirable conduct. While there is certainly a difference in the exact wording and approach, the Model Rules and Model Code are mostly consistent. (B), (C) and (D) are therefore incorrect.

9. **(A)** Cathy's attorney would be subject to discipline if he answered her questions with the knowledge that she is a member of an impaneled jury. The CPR prohibits an attorney (except within the course of the official court proceedings), whether or not connected with the case, from communicating directly or indirectly with a juror concerning the case itself. DR 7-108(B)(2) explicitly provides that "during the trial of a case: [a] lawyer who is not connected therewith shall not communicate with or cause another to communicate with a juror concerning the case." The Code thus forbids improper contact with members of a jury in order to preserve the fairness of the legal system. So do the MRPC. *See* MR 3.5(a) and (b) ("A lawyer shall not: (a) seek to influence a...juror...by means prohibited by law; [or] (b) communicate *ex parte* with [a juror] during the proceeding unless authorized to do so...").

10. **(B)** According to EC 7-7, "In certain areas of litigation not affecting the merits of the cause or substantially prejudicing the rights of a client, a lawyer is entitled to make decisions on his own." Furthermore, EC 7-8 states that "the lawyer should always remember that the decision whether to forego legally available objectives or methods because of non-legal factors is ultimately for the client and not for himself." Similarly, the Commentary for Model Rule 1.2 states that "[c]lients normally defer to the special knowledge and skill of their lawyer with respect to the means to be used to accomplish their objectives, particularly with respect to technical, legal, and tactical matters." Therefore, while lawyers do not necessarily have an ethical obligation to grant each other professional courtesies, as stated in (A), Leslie may make the decision regarding professional courtesies such as continuances and extensions. (C) and (D) are therefore incorrect.

11. **(D)** Choice (D) includes the three accurate statements (II, III, and IV) relating to the payment for Judge Smith's services and the reimbursement for expenses incurred by Judge Smith and his wife for attending the function in Arizona. According to CJC Canon 4(H)(1)(a) and 4(H)(1)(b), a judge is entitled to be: (1) paid for outside activities if the amount of pay is no more than a lay person would receive and there is otherwise no appearance of impropriety and (2) reimbursed for actual travel, lodging and meal expenses incurred in outside activities. In regard to such travel, lodging and meal expenses, a judge may even be reimbursed for these expenses incurred by his wife, if they are appropriate under the circumstances.

12. **(B)** Only III is correct. Therefore, Attorney Straight has the obligation to report the fraud perpetrated by Attorney Rich to the appropriate attorney tribunal in the jurisdiction in which they practice law. Every attorney has an affirmative obligation to disclose actions by other attorneys which the attorney believes to be in violation of the Disciplinary Rules listed in the Code of Professional Responsibility. In regard to an attorney's misconduct, DR 1-102(A)(4) specifically provides that "a lawyer shall not engage in conduct involving dishonesty, fraud, deceit, or misrepresentation." Furthermore, DR 1-103(A) states that "a lawyer possessing unprivileged knowledge of a violation of DR 1-102 shall report such knowledge to a tribunal or other authority empowered to investigate or act upon such violation." The MRPC agree. *See* MR 8.3(a) ("A lawyer who knows that another lawyer has committed a violation

of the Rules of Professional Conduct that raises a substantial question as to that lawyer's honesty, trustworthiness or fitness as a lawyer in other respects, shall inform the appropriate authority.").

13. **(B)** The attorney-client privilege is limited exclusively to confidential communications between the attorney and client. The privilege relates solely to information received by the attorney during the attorney-client relationship. Consequently, the gun used by client Hood to commit the crime would not be protected by the privilege. If an attorney knowingly takes possession of and attempts to secret the fruits and/or instrumentalities of a crime, the attorney would be subject to discipline. In the case of *In Re Ryder*, 381 F.2d 713 (1967), attorney Ryder transferred his client's stolen money and gun to his own safe deposit box with the purpose of avoiding the presumption of guilt which would arise, if the money and the weapon were found in the client's possession. The court concluded that Ryder's acts were not protected by the attorney-client privilege and that he became an active participant in a criminal act while ostensibly portraying the loyal advocate.

14. **(D)** Model Rule 5.4(b) prohibits a lawyer from entering into a partnership with a non-lawyer if any of the partnership's business constitutes the practice of law. Furthermore, MR 5.4(a) prohibits fee-splitting by a lawyer with a non-lawyer except under very limited circumstances. DR 3-102 and DR 3-103 contain language very similar to that in the Model Rules. Because Angus is practicing law (and this practice is part of the business of the partnership) as well as splitting fees with Ron and Frank, he is in violation of both the Rules and the Code. (A) and (C) are therefore incorrect. Note that (B) is incorrect because the right to free association does not extend to partnerships between lawyers and non-lawyers.

15. **(A)** The actions described in I, III, and IV would be considered proper conduct by Attorney Young. Attorney Young may properly refuse to handle the case, decide to handle the case and associate competent co-counsel with the client's initial consent, or accept the case and in good faith proceed to acquire the necessary competence by study and diligent research. Two sections in the CPR specifically relate to an attorney's obligation to provide adequate representation for his clients. EC 2-30 provides that "employment should not be accepted by a lawyer when he is unable to render competent service." Secondly, DR 6-101(A)(1) states that "a lawyer shall not handle a legal matter which he knows or should know that he is not competent to handle, without associating with him a lawyer who is competent to handle it." The Model Rules also emphasize competence. *See* MR 1.1 ("A lawyer shall provide competent representation to a client. Competent representation requires the legal knowledge, skill, thoroughness and preparation reasonably necessary for the representation."). The Commentary to MR 1.1 notes that competence may be established through "necessary study" or "through the association of a lawyer of established competence in the field in question." Furthermore, it notes that "[a] lawyer may accept representation where the requisite level of competence can be achieved by reasonable preparation." Of particular relevance to Attorney Young is the statement in the Commentary that "A newly admitted lawyer can be as competent as a practitioner with long experience."

16. **(B)** In accordance with DR 9-102, Attorney Splitter is under the ethical obligation to deposit the check for the entire $2000 in her client's trust account. She may withdraw the sum of $500 as per the contingency fee arrangement when W agrees that she is entitled to be compensated under the said agreement for services rendered on his behalf. MR 1.15 discusses a lawyer's obligations to safekeep the property of clients and requires that lawyers set up a separate account for client funds. However, the Commentary states that "[l]awyers often received funds from which the lawyer's fee will be paid. The lawyer is not required to remit to the client funds that the lawyer reasonably believes represent fees owed." The Commentary goes on to say that disputed funds should remain in the account until the dispute is resolved. The Model Code agrees. DR 9-102(A)(2) states that "all funds of clients paid to a lawyer or law firm, other than advances for costs and expenses, shall be deposited in one or more identifiable bank accounts maintained in the state in which the law office is situated and no funds belonging to the lawyer or law firm shall be deposited therein except as follows: funds belonging in part to a client and in part presently or potentially to the lawyer or law firm must be deposited therein, but the portion belonging to the lawyer or law firm may be withdrawn when due, unless the right of the lawyer or law firm to receive it is disputed by the client." NOTE: If a dispute exists concerning the amounts due the attorney for services, the disputed portion must remain in the client's trust account pending resolution of the controversy.

17. **(D)** Model Rule 3.8 deals with the special duties of prosecutors. According to the rule, "The prosecutor in a criminal case shall...refrain from prosecuting a charge that the prosecutor knows is not supported by probable cause." DR 7-103 contains similar language. Therefore, Darryl is completely out of line here! Whether or not getting Carlos and Cressida is in the interests of justice, and even if he doesn't intend to actually prosecute Carrie, his behavior is sanctionable because he has no evidence to support an indictment.

18. **(A)** The Model Rules and Model Code would compel Attorney Sleuth to reveal Ms. Suffering's perjury to the court. MR 3.3(a)(3) states that "a lawyer shall not knowingly...offer evidence that the lawyer knows to be false. If a lawyer, the lawyer's client, or a witness called by the lawyer, has offered material evidence and the lawyer comes to know of its falsity, the lawyer shall take reasonable remedial measures, including, if necessary, disclosure to the tribunal." DR 7-102(A)(4) provides that "in his representation of a client, a lawyer shall not...[k]nowingly use perjured testimony or false evidence." Any lawyer who knowingly participates in the introduction of fraudulent, false or perjured testimony or evidence would thus be subject to discipline. Consequently, Attorney Sleuth would be obligated to disclose his knowledge of Ms. Suffering's perjury to the court in which the case is being tried.

19. **(A)** Statements I and III are correct. Therefore, (A) is the best answer. The Code and the Rules mandate that a lawyer is to exercise his independent professional judgment throughout all the various stages of the attorney-client relationship. However, the client has the ultimate control or "upper hand" in most decisions that must be made in connection with the case. MR 1.2 states that "a lawyer shall abide by a client's decisions concerning the objectives of representation...A lawyer shall abide

Explanatory Answers

by a client's decision whether to settle a matter." EC 7-7 states that "[i]n certain areas of legal representation not affecting the merits of the cause or substantially prejudicing the rights of a client, a lawyer is entitled to make decisions on his own. But otherwise the authority to make decisions is exclusively that of the client and, if made within the framework of the law, such decisions are binding on his attorney." A typical example of such a decision in a civil case would be the client's right to decide whether or not to accept a settlement offer. In our hypothetical, Attorney Sharp's client is Maggie's guardian, who would have the sole decision as to whether or not the settlement offer is to be accepted. The guardian is acting in Maggie's behalf and has the obligation to protect her best interests. Therefore, Attorney Sharp has a duty to notify Maggie's guardian of the settlement offer. Secondly, if Maggie's guardian chooses to accept the settlement offer, Attorney Sharp must abide by his client's decision, as such a decision would substantially prejudice the rights of the client.

20. **(C)** Both the Model Rules and the Model Code have provisions addressing fraudulent conduct. According to DR 1-102(A)(4), "[a] lawyer shall not...[e]ngage in conduct involving dishonesty, fraud, deceit, or misrepresentation." Similarly, Model Rule 8.4(c) states that "[i]t is professional misconduct for a lawyer to...engage in conduct involving dishonesty, fraud, deceit or misrepresentation." There is no requirement that the fraud or dishonesty be committed in a lawyer's professional capacity. Therefore, (A) is incorrect. (B) is incorrect because Susan's submission of a false insurance appraisal was in violation of the Rules and the Code. Whether or not she actually received a kickback is immaterial. (D) is incorrect because it is the fraudulent behavior that is at issue, not any potential conflict of interest.

21. **(D)** Attorney Investor would be subject to discipline even if her purchase of the property on Meadow Oak Lane does no harm at all to her client, Mr. Builder. Attorney Investor's actions would be a breach of the fiduciary relationship which exists between the attorney and the client. In accordance with DR 4-101(B)(3) "a lawyer shall not knowingly use a confidence or secret of his client for the advantage of himself or of a third person, unless the client consents after full disclosure." Students should note that it is irrelevant under DR 4-101 whether the client suffers any harm as a result of the attorney's conduct.

22. **(A)** EC 5-20 states unequivocally that "[a]fter a lawyer has undertaken to act as an impartial arbitrator or mediator, he should not thereafter represent in the dispute any of the parties involved." The Model Rules agree. According to MR 1.12(a), a lawyer "shall not represent anyone in connection with a matter in which the lawyer participated personally and substantially...as an arbitrator, mediator, or other third-party neutral, unless all parties to the proceeding give informed consent, confirmed in writing." Penelope has not given written consent to Anna's representation of Petra. Therefore, Anna may not represent Petra in this litigation and may be subject to discipline.

23. **(B)** Attorney Baker would not be entitled to anything. In a contingency fee arrangement, which is permissible in civil cases, a lawyer assumes the risk of no recovery. Since the fee is contingent on the successful outcome of the client's case and payable from the proceeds of the judgment, the lawyer may not even be recompensated for his expenses incurred on behalf of the client. Moreover, the client retains the right

to discharge his attorney hired on a contingency fee basis at anytime during the proceedings. Therefore, Client X had the authority to discharge Attorney Baker and retain Attorney Jones. Furthermore, Client X would not be obligated to pay Attorney Baker for services rendered. Students should note, however, that in some cases the lawyer will be entitled to be compensated for the reasonable value of services rendered up to the time of the discharge.

24. **(A)** Model Rule 7.4 states that "[a] lawyer may communicate the fact that the lawyer does or does not practice in particular fields of law." It does not require that an attorney be the top attorney in his/her field or that the attorney limit such statements to attorney audiences. (B) and (C) are therefore incorrect. It also does not require the attorney to be a specialist (unless the attorney holds herself out as such; *see* MR 7.4(d) and DR 2-105(A)). (D) is therefore incorrect.

25. **(C)** Attorney Swift may properly accept the case if he obtains the consent of both Schemers Unlimited and Mr. Marks. Therefore, statement III provides the correct answer. The lawyer's duty is not only to preserve confidences of a client (even beyond the actual representation of a client), but also to exercise professional judgment on behalf of a client. Consequently, a lawyer may not (without the consent of the affected prior client) represent a new client where any substantial relationship can be shown between the subject matter contained in the former case and that of the subsequent representation for the new client. Thus, the informed consent of both Schemers Unlimited and Mr. Mark must be given. Model Rule 1.9(a) governs this situation ("A lawyer who has formerly represented a client in a matter shall not thereafter represent another person in the same or a substantially related matter in which that person's interests are materially adverse to the interests of the former client unless the former client gives informed consent, confirmed in writing."). EC 4-6 provides that "the obligation of a lawyer to preserve the confidences and secrets of his client continues after the termination of employment."

26. **(B)** I is correct since Attorney Scott can properly pay the travel, hotel and meal expenses incurred by Dr. Famous. II is also correct as Attorney Scott may pay Dr. Famous a reasonable flat fee for his services as an expert witness in pre-trial preparation and for testifying at trial. Both III and IV are incorrect statements. Model Rule 3.4(b) states that "[a] lawyer shall not...offer an inducement to a witness that is prohibited by law." However, the Commentary to the rule states that "it is not improper to pay a witness's expenses or to compensate an expert witness...it is improper to pay an expert witness a contingent fee." Furthermore, DR 7-109(C) specifically states that "a lawyer shall not pay, offer to pay or acquiesce in the payments of compensation to a witness contingent upon the content of his testimony or the outcome of the case. But a lawyer may advance, guarantee, or acquiesce in the payment of: (1) Expenses reasonably incurred by a witness in attending or testifying, (2) reasonable compensation to a witness for his loss of time in attending or testifying, and (3) a reasonable fee for the professional services of an expert witness."

27. **(A)** Statements I, II, III and IV are all correct in regard to the proper conduct of both Attorney New and Judge Old during the political campaign for judge of the Superior

Court. The Code of Judicial Conduct permits an opposed candidate for judicial office to (1) attend political gatherings and speak there on the candidate's own behalf, (2) identify himself publicly as a member of a political party and (3) contribute to a political party. CJC Canon 5(c). Students should note that the CJC prohibits a judge from engaging in any political activity or conduct except (1) where he is campaigning for reelection to the judicial office or (2) where he is acting on behalf of measures to improve the legal system or the administration of justice.

28. **(C)** Model Rule 5.5(b) instructs that "a lawyer shall not...assist a person who is not a member of the bar in the performance of activity that constitutes the unauthorized practice of law." DR 3-101 is nearly identical to Model Rule 5.5(b), and EC 3-5 states that there are certain matters where a lawyer's judgment is required. Because Carla is making a judgment about whether or not to threaten suit, and Louisa is not supervising these decisions, Louisa is violating both the Model Rules and the Code. (A) is incorrect because there is no rule stating that one may not threaten suit in order to collect a debt. (B) is not correct; many lawyers use collection agencies. (D) is incorrect because, while Carla may help Louisa, she may not render professional legal judgment.

29. **(D)** Attorney Smith would be subject to discipline under both the Model Rules and the Model Code, if the fee charged Client A is found to be clearly excessive. In accordance with DR 2-106(A) "a lawyer shall not enter into an agreement for, charge or collect an illegal or clearly excessive fee." This Disciplinary Rule furthermore, defines "clearly excessive" as a fee that a lawyer of ordinary prudence would determine was in excess of a reasonable fee. DR 2-106(B) delineates the following factors to be considered as guidelines in determining the reasonableness of a fee: (1) the time and labor required, the novelty and difficulty of the question involved, and the skill requisite to perform the legal service properly, (2) the likelihood, if apparent to the client, that the acceptance of the particular employment will preclude other employment by the lawyer, (3) the fee customarily charged in the locality for similar legal services, (4) the amount involved and the results obtained, (5) the time limitations imposed by the client or circumstances, (6) the nature and length of the professional relationship with the client, (7) the experience, reputation and ability of the lawyer performing the services and (8) whether the fee is fixed or contingent. The Model Rules (MR 1.5(a)) contain identical language.

30. **(D)** In accordance with the Disciplinary Rules, Attorney Bright would not be subject to discipline for offering legal advice and then accepting Ted's case because he is a close friend. DR 2-104(A)(1) specifically provides that "a lawyer who has given unsolicited advice to a layman that he should obtain counsel or take legal action shall not accept employment resulting from that advice, except that a lawyer may accept employment by a close friend, relative, former client (if the advice is germane to the former employment) or one who the lawyer reasonably believes to be a client." In the MRPC, MR 7.3(a)(2) most closely addresses this situation, stating that a lawyer shall not "solicit employment from a prospective client when a significant motive for the lawyer's doing so is the lawyer's pecuniary gain, unless the person contacted...has a family [or] close personal...relationship with the lawyer." Thus, Choice (D) provides the best answer.

31. **(B)** Model Rule 3.1 states: "A lawyer shall not bring or defend a proceeding, or assert or controvert an issue therein, unless there is a basis in law or fact for doing so that is not frivolous, which includes a good faith argument for an extension, modification, or reversal of existing law." DR 7-102(A)(2) includes almost identical language. Furthermore, DR 7-102(A)(1) asserts that "a lawyer shall not...file a suit... on behalf of his client when it is obvious that such action would serve merely to harass or maliciously injure another." DR 2-109(A) is similar to DR 7-102(A)(1). Therefore, Amanda should not take the case; it is clear that Flaky is merely trying to harass Bob. (A) is immaterial here; Amanda accepts the case and presumably will file a claim on Flaky's behalf. (C) is incorrect; in situations where a claim is baseless, the lawyer may not bring it, even if the client wants to. (D) is incorrect because the amount of her fee doesn't matter here; it's her accepting the case that's the problem.

32. **(A)** An attorney must not request a layperson to refer business to him. (A) is the correct answer. *See* MR 7.3; DR 2-103; *Ohralik v. Ohio State Bar Association*, 436 U.S. 447 (1978). In requesting that Psy recommend the use of Attorney's legal services, Attorney is asking Psy to solicit potential clients for him. Lawyers are prohibited from soliciting business in-person for a pecuniary gain to prevent the potential harm to prospective clients. It does not matter whether the solicitation is performed personally by Attorney or by his agent; both will subject Attorney to discipline, provided the solicitation is in-person. *Shapero v. Kentucky Bar Association*, 108 S. Ct. 1916 (1988). (B) is incorrect. The issue is not whether Psy may attempt to influence the exercise of Attorney's judgment. The issue is whether Attorney may enter into this referral agreement. As discussed, he may not. (C) is incorrect. It is true that a lawyer must not compensate a person for referring a client. Nevertheless, a lawyer must not request such a referral even in the absence of compensation. (D) is incorrect. Due to the nature of solicitation, there is an inherent potential for abuse. The reasoning capacity of prospective clients is often impaired. As a result, a full disclosure will not adequately protect the interests of prospective clients. Therefore there is no mitigation of the solicitation.

33. **(A)** The conduct described in statements I and II would constitute proper conduct for Attorney Famous under the Model Code and the Model Rules. Under DR 2-101(B), a lawyer is permitted to be identified as a lawyer as well as by name in and on legal textbooks, treatises and other legal publications. Therefore, Attorney Famous may author a legal publication in which he is both identified and mentioned by name. EC 8-1 states that "by reason of education and experience, lawyers are especially qualified to recognize deficiencies in the legal system and to initiate corrective measures therein. Thus, they should participate in programs to improve the system, without regard to the general interests or desires of a client or former client." Consequently, Attorney Famous would be acting in accordance with this ethical consideration by appearing as a guest on a national television program to discuss penal reform and the justice system. Please note that statement III is incorrect since DR 2-101(C) precludes a lawyer from compensating or giving anything of value to representatives of the press, radio or television in return for professional publicity in a news item. *See also* MR 7.1.

Explanatory Answers

34. **(D)** Model Rule 1.8(g) is directly on point here, saying that "[a] lawyer who represents two or more clients shall not participate in making an aggregate settlement of the claims of or against the clients...unless each client gives informed consent, in a writing signed by the client. The disclosure shall include the existence and nature of all the claims or pleas involved and of the participation of each person in the settlement." DR 5-106(A) is almost identical to the Model Rule but also requires the attorney to inform each client of the total amount of the settlement. Therefore, (A), (B) and (C) must all be incorrect.

35. **(D)** Model Rule 5.5(b) states that "[a] lawyer shall not . . . assist a person who is not a member of the bar in the performance of activity that constitutes the unauthorized practice of law." Similarly, DR 3-101(A) provides that "a lawyer shall not aid a non-lawyer in the unauthorized practice of law." In regard to this Disciplinary Rule, the Code of Professional Responsibility does not attempt to set forth a specific definition of what actually constitutes the practice of law. However, EC 3-5 states that "functionally, the practice of law relates to the rendition of services for others that call for the professional judgment of a lawyer." Therefore, Attorney Helpfulsen may assist her friends only in the activities described in statements I and III without aiding in the unauthorized practice of law. With respect to statement I, Attorney Helpfulsen may assist her friend in drafting his own will, since it does not constitute unauthorized practice for a lay person to do something for himself, such as in drafting his own will. Secondly, Attorney Helpfulsen may provide a real estate broker with statutes he wishes to read, which correspond to the lawyer-prepared form which he uses. In this matter she is not aiding or encouraging him to practice law. A real estate broker may educate himself by reading statutes pertaining to related matters. However, a real estate broker may not draft contracts, deeds, mortgages, etc., as that activity would constitute the unauthorized practice of law. See *Chicago Bar Association v. Quinlan and Tyson, Inc.*, 34 Ill. 2nd 116 (1966). Please note that statement II would constitute the unauthorized practice of law since the friend is being remunerated for services in drafting the uncle's will. Also, statement IV is correct because in accordance with EC 7-18, "a lawyer should not undertake to give advice to the person who is attempting to represent himself." However, this provision appears to apply only when the unrepresented person is on the other side of a matter in which the lawyer is participating.

36. **(B)** Attorney Strong may take the action described in statement II, thus informing the Brass Knuckles Agency of his intention to file suit if the harassment against his client continues. In communicating with an adverse party that does not have counsel, a lawyer representing a client may contact such adverse party directly. In accordance with DR 7-104(A)(2) "during the course of his representation of a client, a lawyer shall not give advice to a person who is not represented by a lawyer, other than the advice to secure counsel, if the interests of such person are or have a reasonable possibility of being in conflict with the interests of his client." MR 4.3 contains language identical to DR 7-104(A)(2). Therefore, Attorney Strong may notify the collection agency of his intention to sue if the harassment continues. Students should note that the conduct described in statements I and II is improper under the Disciplinary Rules. DR 7-105 specifically states that "a lawyer shall not present, participate in presenting, or threaten to present criminal charges solely to obtain an advantage in a civil matter." However, the Model Rules do not address this issue.

MPRE Exam

37. **(A)** Choice (A) is the best answer since statements I and II describe the particular conduct of a public prosecutor which is prohibited under the Model Rules and Model Code. DR 7-103(A) states that "a public prosecutor or other government lawyer shall not institute or cause to be instituted criminal charges when he knows or it is obvious that the charges are not supported by probable cause." Moreover, DR 7-103(B) provides that "a public prosecutor or other government lawyer in criminal litigation shall make timely disclosure to the counsel for the defendant, or to the defendant if he has no counsel, of the existence of evidence, known to the prosecutor or other government lawyer, that tends to negate the guilt of the accused, mitigate the degree of the offense, or reduce the punishment." Model Rules 3.8(a) and 3.8(d) contain very similar language.

38. **(B)** If he is subpoenaed, Sam must testify. See CJC Canon 2B ("[A judge] shall not testify voluntarily as a character witness.") *Cf.* Commentary: "A judge may, however, testify when properly summoned." (D) is therefore incorrect. (C) is incorrect because, according to the canon, he must not testify unless subpoenaed. (A) is incorrect because he may testify if subpoenaed, even if Grant did appoint Sam to the bench.

39. **(C)** DR 2-104(A)(4) states that a lawyer may speak publicly about legal matters without affecting his right to accept employment as long as "he does not emphasize his own professional experience or reputation and does not undertake to give legal advice." Since Larissa does not discuss her own credentials or take one-on-one questions, she may accept as clients people who attend the lecture (assuming that they approach her).

40. **(A)** *Negotiation is considered to be part of the practice of law; therefore a lawyer who is in the process of negotiation must obey the professional ethics requirements. However, to be subject to professional discipline, a lawyer must be licensed in the state which means to discipline him.* (A) is the correct answer. Clearly Delton's conduct of lying, threatening and assaulting an opposing party is improper. *See* MR 4.1, 4.4; DR 7-105(A); 7-102(A). Further, negotiation is considered to be legal practice. MRPC Preamble. However, to discipline an attorney, the attorney must be licensed in that state. MRPC 8.5. Therefore, (A) is the best answer. (B) is incorrect because there is no question — negotiating *is* part of the practice of law. (C) is incorrect because although Delton's home state could discipline him for acts done outside that state, again, in-state "attorney" discipline requires an in-state license. (Of course, there are other remedies, e.g., contempt of court, criminal prosecution, etc., for those who practice law without a license). (D) is incorrect, because, as set out above, clearly what Delton did *is* unethical.

41. **(C)** *The attorney-client evidentiary privilege generally precludes an attorney from compelled testimony when a client or potential client reveals confidential information either in the course of the attorney-client relationship; or prior to the relationship if the client is seeking to have that lawyer become her attorney.* (C) is the correct answer. Here, although Larry did not become Linda's attorney, Linda did ask him legal advice with the knowledge that he was an attorney; and with the hope that he would help her. Thus, the possibly incriminating statement she made about teasing the dog is privileged. The privilege attaches not based only on actual representation, but also when there is a subjective belief on the client's part that

the relationship has begun when the client is seeking legal advice. Issue: Was it a confidential communication? (A) is incorrect because the attorney-client privilege does not require that the attorney be *presently* representing that client. For example, the relationship may have been terminated — but still prior confidences are protected. (B) is incorrect because although there was never an attorney-client relationship (Larry did not consent to be Linda's attorney); nevertheless, the evidentiary privilege attaches when a potential client consults with a known lawyer for the purpose of obtaining legal advice. (D), though correct, is not the best answer. Linda's admission is confidential. However, the reason why Larry cannot *testify* is because of the applicability of the attorney-client privilege.

42. **(C)** The issues of attorney incompetence and attorney malpractice are legally distinct. Each requires different proof in a different forum. (C) is the correct answer. The facts state essentially that Donna handled Ned's criminal case in an incompetent manner. Her unreasonable and damaging performance satisfy the right to competent counsel test of *Strickland v. Washington*, 466 U.S. 668 (1984). However, although an attorney is subject to discipline for incompetence (MR 1.1, DR 6-101(A)); incompetence does not, *per se*, prove malpractice. Further, not always does an ethical violation result in actual damages. That is a separate inquiry. Thus, (C), which states that damages must be proven independently, is the correct answer. *See* MRPC Preamble. (A) is incorrect because it implies that malpractice and discipline does not prove damages. (D) is legally correct; but is an incorrect answer because Ned might prevail if he shows damages.

43. **(D)** The attorney-client evidentiary privilege (which protects against attorney disclosure of client confidences) is solely for the benefit of the client. (D) is the correct answer. Donna is not permitted to use the privilege for her own benefit. It is not a shield against malpractice suit. The privilege is solely for Ned and Ned did not want it. *See* MR Preamble; MR 1.6(a); Comment to MR 1.6. (A) is incorrect because, again, when Ned sues in malpractice he takes the risk that confidences will be relevant to his case. (B) is incorrect because, although the attorney-client relationship is fiduciary in nature, it has already been compromised by Donna's incompetence and Ned's subsequent suit. Incidentally, Donna is not permitted to go beyond the needs of relevance when she testifies in her own defense. Furthermore, even if Ned did not want her to disclose his secrets, she would be allowed to do so in the context of this lawsuit under MR 1.6(b)(3) ("A lawyer may reveal information relating to the representation of a client to the extent the lawyer reasonably believes necessary...to establish a claim or defense of the lawyer in a controversy between the lawyer and the client, to establish a defense to a criminal charge or civil claim against the lawyer based upon conduct in which the client was involved, or to respond to allegations in any proceeding concerning the lawyer's representation of the client."). She cannot simply "smear" Ned at will. (C) is incorrect because there can be civil damages in both civil and criminal malpractices.

44. **(D)** An attorney may reveal confidences or secrets in order to defend herself from a malpractice claim, provided the admissions are limited to that which is relevant to the claim. (D) is the correct answer. Donna was simply defending herself. See MR 1.6(b)(3); DR 4-101(c)(4). Any other rule would place unreasonable hardship on the attorney and would eventually dilute the attorney-client relationship. (A) is incorrect for the same reason that (D) is correct. (B) and (C) are incorrect because,

while Donna would normally have a duty under the Model Rules and Model Code to keep the confidences and secrets of her client, she does not have to in this case because Ned is suing her. Note that that Model Rules do not use the term "secrets" but simply refer to "confidences" and "information relating to the representation." Preamble; MR 1.6(a). The Model Code distinguishes between secrets and confidences, saying that "'[c]onfidence' refers to information protected by the attorney-client privilege under applicable law, and 'secret' refers to other information gained in the professional relationship that the client has requested be held inviolate or the disclosure of which would be embarrassing or would likely be detrimental to the client." DR 4-101(A).

45. **(D)** Model Rule 3.4(e) states, *inter alia*, that a lawyer shall not "assert personal knowledge of facts in issue except when testifying as a witness, or state a personal opinion as to...the culpability of a civil litigant..." DR 7-106(C)(3) and (4) contain similar language and specifically state that a lawyer may not make such assertions or state such opinions when "appearing in his professional capacity before a tribunal." Therefore, statements II (asserting a fact) and III (giving a personal opinion) are improper. Statement I is permissible as a summing up of evidence, something trial lawyers do all the time!

46. **(A)** According to Canon 1 of the Model Code, section E-6, "[w]hen the disqualification [of an attorney] has terminated, members of the bar should assist such person in being licensed, or, if licensed, in being restored to his full right to practice." Therefore, under the Model Code, Larry has an ethical obligation to help Loretta. (B) and (D), however tempting, are not options for Larry because they would require him to act unethically. (C) is incorrect because Larry should help Loretta get her license back in addition to giving her a job. The Model Rules do not appear to directly address this issue.

47. **(D)** *A lawyer must be reasonably competent in order to ethically accept a case.* (D) is the correct answer. New lawyers can be competent — even when they are unfamiliar with the area of dispute. MR 1.1. One is "competent" not only when one is an expert, but also when reasonable preparation will lead to competence. (A) is correct because it is a viable alternative to associate oneself with an attorney who is expert in the area – provided the client is told and consents. *See* DR 6-101(A)(1). (B) is correct because, again, an attorney is allowed to prepare himself for a case – provided he does not charge for that which merely brings him up to the level of reasonable competence. (C) is correct because incompetence is a legitimate reason to withdraw from a case, although, of course, it would have been better not to have taken the case at all. Since (D) includes each of the correct options of (A), (B), and (C), it is the best answer.

48. **(C)** Although previous versions of the CJC required parties to execute a signed writing waiving a judge's need to disqualify herself, the current version does not. According to CJC Canon 4(F), the parties must simply agree that the judge should not be disqualified. Then, if the judge agrees to participate, the parties' agreement is entered into the record. No writing is required, but the Commentary does suggest one ("[a]s a practical matter, a judge may wish to have all parties and their lawyers sign the remittal agreement.") (A) is therefore incorrect. Note that the conflict is waiveable under Canon 4(F), and (B) is therefore incorrect. (D) is correct so far as

it goes, in that the judge did not have a material relationship with Polly's mother, but it does not address the adequacy of the waiver.

49. **(B)** A lawyer must not assist his client in perpetrating a crime. (B) is the correct answer. The facts indicate that Joel counseled Doe how to conceal his unlawful activities. As such, the lawyer becomes a mere aider and abettor to crime. This is clearly proscribed conduct. See MR 1.2(d); DR 7-102(A)(7); EC 7-5. (A) is incorrect because attorneys often represent guilty defendants and this is a legitimate part of our adversary system. Each person should have the right to effective assistance of counsel. (A) is overly broad. (C) is incorrect because good lawyers counsel on how to avoid criminal prosecution by counseling how to obey the law. (C) ignores this legitimate aspect of law work. (D) is incorrect because it is an incomplete statement of the law. If the client refuses to rectify, then counsel should reveal the crime "except when protected by the privilege," which is nearly always the case. DR 7-102(B)(1); MR 1.2(d).

50. **(A)** *In a criminal case, a lawyer must abide by a client's decision whether the client will testify.* (A) is the correct answer. *See* MR 1.2(a); EC 7-7. Although an attorney can and should make reasonable strategic choices throughout trial, the decision whether or not to testify is so fundamental to one's defense that an attorney cannot contravene the client's wishes. This would impinge too severely on the client's autonomy - one value which our adversary system means to protect. (B) is incorrect because, as a general rule, the attorney should make the trial strategy (subject to few exceptions - one of which being that stated in answer (A)). (C) is incorrect, because although an attorney should choose the trial strategy, whether or not the client testifies is one thing which the attorney is not allowed to choose. (D) is incorrect because it is irrelevant whether Badman won or lost. The issue is not the verdict, but the attorney's obedience or disobedience to the standards of professional responsibility.

51. **(A)** *In a criminal case, the lawyer shall abide by the client's decision, after consultation with the lawyer, as to whether to waive jury trial.* (A) is the correct answer. See MR 1.2(a); EC 7-7. Although Altman was likely correct that the jury would likely have been unimpressed by Badman, nevertheless, whether or not to have a jury is a client decision. (B) is incorrect because an attorney can disobey a client's legitimate desires when it comes to *strategy. See, eg.*, Jones v. Barnes, 463 U.S. 745 (1983). (C), in different language, states approximately the same position as (B) and is therefore also incorrect. (D) is incorrect because it confuses the procedural "harmless error" rule with disciplinary proceedings. In fact, the two issues, harmless error and attorney discipline, are legally distinct. An attorney can be disciplined even when his client wins. Discipline is based on violation of a rule of conduct. The attorney's duties are not only to the client, but also to the system of justice.

52. **(C)** Model Rule 1.11(a) requires an attorney to decline representation of a client in connection with a case in which the lawyer participated personally and substantially as a public employee (unless the government gives informed written consent). Similarly, DR 9-101(B) states that "[a] lawyer shall not accept private employment in a matter in which he had substantial responsibility while he was a public employee." Here, the facts make clear that Albert did not have substantial responsibility on the case when he was an ADA, but if he had, he would have to decline

the representation. (D) is therefore incorrect. (A) is incorrect because copying the documents does not constitute "substantial responsibility" under either the Code or the Rules. (B) is incorrect. He would only be disallowed from accepting the case if he had had personal and substantial responsibility on the case.

53. **(D)** Model Rule 7.5(d), which deals with letterheads and firm names, states that "[l]awyers may state or imply that they practice in a partnership or other organization only when that is the fact." Similarly, DR 2-102(C) states that "[a] lawyer shall not hold himself out as having a partnership with one or more other lawyers or professional corporations unless they are in fact partners." Therefore, because the stationery here seems to suggest that the four women are law partners, Abigail and Sarah are correct that to send letters on it would be improper. Note that the letterhead is not prohibited advertising; most attorneys use letterhead stationery properly.

54. **(B)** *In a civil case, an attorney must abide by his client's decision whether to settle a matter.* (B) is the correct answer. Settlement, like plea and jury in criminal cases, is solely up to the client. See MR 1.2(a); EC 7-7. Lawson unequivocally disobeyed Rick's instruction to settle. The error is even more grievous because Insurer offered more than Rick's expressed minimum. (A) is incorrect only because it is ambiguous. Lawson would not be subject to discipline had Insurer not made a good offer above his minimum. That is, merely taking a case to trial is not, *per se*, unethical. (C) is incorrect because the test for attorney discipline is not the attorney's performance with regards to the trial result, but rather whether the attorney contravened professional norms. Although Rick gained more money for Lawson, his error in disobeying an express instruction to settle was grievous. (D) is incorrect because settlement is one of the few things in which a client has the ultimate responsibility of choice.

55. **(C)** *An attorney must tell a client when the attorney-client relationship has ended.* See Comment [4] to MR 1.3 ("so that the client will not mistakenly suppose the lawyer is looking after the client's affairs when the lawyer has ceased to do so..."); EC 2-32. (C) is the correct answer. The situation in this question is not atypical. Whenever there is a reasonable possibility that a client believes he is still being represented, the duty is on the attorney to tell the client otherwise - preferably in writing. Otherwise, the client might be damaged believing his legal affairs are being taken care of. (A) is incorrect because, once the attorney-client relationship has properly been terminated, there is no duty on the part of the attorney to tell the client of changes in the law. (B) is incorrect because it confuses the issue of malpractice damages with the issue of ethical violations. Whether or not a client was damaged, an attorney can be *disciplined*. In fact, some attorney actions leading to discipline (*eg.*, aiding a client in fraud) are *helpful* for the client. (D) is incorrect because if Chuck incorrectly but reasonably believes that Delmarter is still representing him, then Delmarter is subject to discipline.

56. **(D)** Model Rule 1.11(a) requires an attorney to decline representation of a private client in connection with a case in which the lawyer participated personally and substantially as a public employee (unless the government consents). Similarly, DR 9-101(B) states that "[a] lawyer shall not accept private employment in a matter in which he had substantial responsibility while he was a public employee."

Here, Lincoln was the lead attorney in the 1991 case and certainly had substantial responsibility. Therefore, he may not accept this representation. Note that (B) is incorrect because the EPA, not BigCorp, would have to consent under Model Rule 1.11(a).

57. **(A)** *An attorney should write a letter recommending an applicant's admission to the bar only if such recommendation is based upon the attorney's personal knowledge of the applicant's fitness.* (A) is the correct answer. *See* EC 1-2; EC 1-3; DR 1-101(B); DR 1-102(A)(4); MR 8.1. An attorney should aid in preventing admission to the bar of candidates unfit or unqualified because deficient in either moral character or education. An assessment by an attorney recommending an applicant for admission is relied on in evaluating the professional or personal fitness of the applicant. Therefore, honest and candid opinions on such matters are necessary. Attorney has been asked by a new client to write a letter recommending Client's nephew for admission to the bar. A letter of recommendation implicitly represents that such recommendation is based upon *personal knowledge.* However, in the present case, Attorney has no personal knowledge of nephew's fitness to practice law. In fact, even his new client who is requesting the letter does not have personal knowledge but rather is relying on the assurance of nephew's mother! If Attorney were to write the recommendation based on another's assurance, he would be misleading the persons to whom the letter is addressed. It would therefore be improper for Attorney to recommend the nephew unless he investigated the nephew and wrote the letter only if he is thereafter satisfied that the nephew is qualified. It should be noted, however, that an investigation is not necessary in all circumstances, but is necessary in cases such as this to form a basis to support the recommendation. Therefore, response number III is correct. Likewise, response numbers I and II are incorrect because such recommendations would be based on the mere assurances of a third party and not on Attorney's personal knowledge. (B), (C), and (D) are incorrect because they indicated that response numbers I or II would be proper.

58. **(A)** Model Rule 8.3 requires Angus to report Albert's conduct to the judge. That Rule states: "A lawyer who knows that another lawyer has committed a violation of the rules of professional conduct that raises a substantial question as to that lawyer's honesty, trustworthiness or fitness as a lawyer in other respects, shall inform the appropriate professional authority." In this situation, Albert is behaving improperly by eating lunch with a juror on a pending case. *See* Model Rule 3.5(b) ("A lawyer shall not...communicate *ex parte* with [a judge or juror]....") and DR 7-108(B)(1) ("During the trial of a case,...[a] lawyer connected therewith shall not communicate with or cause another to communicate with a juror concerning the case." The appropriate authority here is the judge presiding over the case, and Angus has a duty to report Albert, as Angus doesn't know what Albert is discussing with the juror.

59. **(C)** An attorney is not subject to discipline if she files a complaint which she does not think will prevail so long as such complaint is legally warranted. *See* MR 3.1; DR 2-109(A)(2). (C) is the correct answer. Even if Attorney believes Client's recollection of the facts are faulty and that Client would not prevail in a lawsuit, she will not be subject to discipline unless the action was filed merely to harass the defendant. If the complaint can be supported by a good faith legal argument, then its filing is

proper regardless of Attorney's belief as to whether the suit would be successful. (A) is incorrect. It does not matter whether Attorney believes Client will prevail. It is the legal validity of the complaint which is determinative. If the complaint is warranted under existing law or can be supported by a good faith argument for an extension, modification, or reversal of existing law then it may be properly filed. (B) is incorrect. It is true that if Attorney knowingly filed a false complaint she would be subject to discipline. However, answer (B) does not state that Attorney knew that Client's story was untrue. If Attorney in good faith believed the story were true, she would not be subject to discipline for filing the complaint, even if Client's story was found to be untrue. (D) is incorrect. It is immaterial whether Attorney has accepted a retainer. If an attorney accepts a retainer and then discovers there is no legally warranted action her first duty is to the law. Therefore, in such instance, she must not bring such an unwarranted action. In addition, it is not Attorney's belief regarding the outcome of the suit which is determinative but rather the legal validity of the action.

60. **(D)** An attorney shall not withdraw from employment until she has taken reasonable steps to avoid foreseeable prejudice to the rights of her client. (D) is the correct answer. *See* DR 2-110; MR 1.16. Upon withdrawing from employment, Attorney must take all reasonable steps to mitigate the consequences to Client. The statute of limitations will run on Client's claim in one week. Attorney must take all reasonable steps to insure that Client's claim will not be foreclosed by the expiration of the statute of limitations. Thus, it is improper for Attorney to withdraw without filing the suit unless Attorney insures that Client's rights are adequately protected. (A) is incorrect. If Client wishes to assert a legally supportable claim, then Client has the right to expect his attorney to assert such claim. It would be improper for Attorney to withdraw without filing the action merely because she believes Client's recollection to be faulty. (B) is incorrect. Once Attorney accepts employment, there are certain obligations created as to Client, the most important being that Attorney protect the interests of Client. This obligation may not be dispensed with merely because the matter is not yet pending before a tribunal. There is only one week remaining under the statute of limitations in which Client can assert his claim. The issue is whether Attorney owes less of a duty to Client if the matter is not yet pending before a tribunal. She does not, and she must adequately protect Client's interests regardless of what stage litigation is in. (C) is incorrect. It is not because Attorney had accepted a retainer to represent Client that it is improper for her to withdraw from the case without filing the suit. Rather, upon accepting employment from Client, Attorney became the representative of Client, and if it is improper for her to withdraw without filing the suit, it is because the rights of Client would not be adequately protected, not because Attorney accepted a retainer.

61. **(A)** *An attorney may retain fees which are determined to be reasonable under the circumstances.* (A) is the correct answer. *See* DR 2-106; MR 1.5. It is proper for Attorney to retain all fees which are reasonable. Attorney and Client specifically agreed that Client would pay a nonrefundable retainer fee of $1,000 which Client paid. This was to be in addition to the per hour charge of $50. Attorney is withdrawing with Client's consent. (A) expressly provides that $1,000 was a reasonable and non-refundable retainer; it is therefore proper for Attorney to keep the entire $1,000. (B) is incorrect. It is true that $400 is the proper amount earned according to the per hour charge. However, the per hour charge was separate and distinct

from the $1,000 retainer, and both Attorney and Client specifically agreed that the retainer was to be nonrefundable. Thus, provided the retainer was reasonable, Attorney may keep the entire amount. (C) is incorrect. Attorney is not required to file a suit before he is entitled to keep the retainer. A retainer is for the purpose of initially hiring an attorney. Attorney did represent, and is now only withdrawing with Client's consent after Client has admitted his allegations are untrue. Incidentally, if Attorney were to file a suit he would be subject to discipline for filing a fraudulent claim. (D) is incorrect. Attorney has represented Client to the completion of this case. Client has admitted that his story was false. Therefore, there is no further legal action to be taken on behalf of Client. Thus, it is proper for Attorney to keep the retainer.

62. **(D)** According to DR 1-102(A)(4), "[a] lawyer shall not...[e]ngage in conduct involving dishonesty, fraud, deceit, or misrepresentation." Furthermore, under Model Rule 8.5, "[a] lawyer admitted to practice in this jurisdiction is subject to the disciplinary authority of this jurisdiction regardless of where the lawyer's conduct occurs." If Julia has destroyed evidence, she has acted dishonestly, and Whiteacre may discipline her even if her conduct occurred in Blueacre. (A) is therefore wrong. (B) is incorrect because Whiteacre may act independently of Blueacre; it need not wait for Blueacre to act first. (C) is incorrect because attorneys may practice in other jurisdictions if they are admitted *pro hac vice*, as Julia was here.

63. **(D)** *A lawyer may reveal information the lawyer reasonably believes necessary to prevent reasonably certain death or substantial bodily harm.* (D) is the correct answer. Although the language of MR 1.6(b)(1) and DR 4-101(C)(3) indicates that an attorney "may" reveal such confidence, the weight of authority is that the attorney must reveal this kind of confidence. Although the attorney-client privilege is generally sacrosanct, in this instance the privilege must fall to protect human life. (A) is not the best answer for the same reason that (D) is the best answer. (B) is incorrect because it misses the point, i.e., whether the attorney-client privilege should be compromised. (B) is also incorrect because no facts indicate Shawn to have been lying. (C) is incorrect because it, like (B), misses the all-important legal issue regarding the extent of the confidentiality privilege.

64. **(D)** *Material evidence in the attorney's possession must be surrendered to the prosecution.* (D) is the correct answer. Although testimonial evidence is almost always protected by the attorney-client confidentiality privilege, material evidence is not. Certainly an attorney's observations and work-product are protected. But, when the attorney changes the evidence so that the prosecution cannot find it, a different situation occurs. The attorney then should surrender the evidence to the prosecution, with a stipulation that such was found in the defendant's possession. See DR 7-109(A); MR 3.4(a). (A) is incorrect because the attorney-client privilege, though strong, is not absolute. (B) is incorrect for the same reason that (A) is incorrect and also because, technically, since this question did not deal with Nora's in-court testimony, labeling the issue "evidentiary" was improper. (C) is incorrect for the same reason that (D) is correct.

65. **(B)** *Communications to an attorney from her client during the course of the attorney-client relationship are privileged and should not be revealed.* (B) is the correct answer. See DR 4-101(A) and (B); MR 1.6(a). The policy of the United States adversarial

system is to promote candor between the attorney and client. Were "whistleblowing" the rule — and not a limited exception — this candor would not be possible. Thus, were Nora to tell the prosecution that Shawn removed evidence, this would be improper. As other answers indicate, a different response is necessary if the attorney has the material evidence in her possession. Furthermore, and incidental to this answer, it would not be improper for Nora to have *counseled* Shawn to turn in the evidence. But such is not a requirement. (A) is incorrect because, although the evidence was certainly probative, the issue here is not in evidence law, but in whether the attorney-client privilege prohibits disclosure. It does. (C) is incorrect because although Shawn's removal of evidence was *not* testimonial, her telling Nora was testimonial and thus protected. (D) is incorrect because the mere fact that the evidence is prejudicial is legally irrelevant.

66. **(C)** *An attorney has a right to defend herself against a client, even if to do do requires the attorney to reveal confidential information*. (C) is the correct answer. *See* DR 4-101(C)(4); MR 1.6(b)(3). Of course the attorney should reveal such confidence only as a last resort, but the weight of authority clearly so allows. It should also be noted that only that amount of information necessary for the attorney's defense may be revealed. (A) is incorrect because, in this particular situation, the attorney-client relationship does not protect against revealing a confidence. (B) is incorrect because the facts state that Nora's revealing of the confidence was "after relevant questioning." (D) is incorrect because the standards for disciplining an attorney are not whether the client was prejudiced nor whether the attorney committed only "harmless error," but rather whether the attorney breached the ethical standards of the profession. The former two inquiries are more relevant to the constitutional right to effective counsel and to civil malpractice suits.

67. **(B)** *An attorney may disaffirm a document he prepared based on client-proffered fraudulent information*. (B) is the correct answer. *See* MR 1.6 Comment [14] ("The lawyer *may* also withdraw or disaffirm any opinion, document, affirmation or the like"). Although Bob does not have to disaffirm the contract, it is certainly permissible for him to do so. By allowing the decision to rest on the attorney and by limiting the admission to merely disaffirmation, the competing professional values of maximizing truth and justice while also giving to each accused a zealous advocate are effectively balanced. (A) is incorrect because no ethical standard *requires* Bob to disaffirm. (C) is incorrect because no ethical standard requires Bob to do nothing. (D) is incorrect because (B) is correct.

68. **(C)** DR 8-101(A)(1) states that "[a] lawyer who holds public office shall not...use his public position to obtain, or attempt to obtain, a special advantage in legislative matters for himself or for a client under circumstances where he knows or it is obvious that such action is not in the public interest." *See also* MR 8.4 Comment [5]. Here, Linda is not acting against the public interest, because the law is very biased and unfair to tenants. Therefore, she is not violating the Code or the Rules.

69. **(B)** Under CJC Canon 3(E)(1)(b), a judge should disqualify himself from hearing cases on which he worked as a lawyer when he practiced law. (A) and (C) are incorrect because it doesn't matter whether or not John learned confidential matters or had substantial knowledge of the case when at ABG; all that matters is that he worked on the case. Furthermore, consent should not be an option here, because his relationship to the case cannot be considered immaterial.

Explanatory Answers

70. **(D)** There is no conflict of interest here. Sarah and Stanley keep their business and legal jobs completely separate, and the fact that their law practice is located in the same building as Alphabet is not a problem. Therefore, they are acting within the framework of the disciplinary rules.

71. **(D)** *A lawyer shall not make an agreement for, charge, or collect an unreasonable fee or an unreasonable amount for expenses*. The lawyer is permitted to sue a client for the fee if a dispute arises. (D) is the correct answer. Although a lawyer's fee must be reasonable, it can also be large. *See* MR 1.5(a); DR 2-106(A) and (B). A 33 1/3% contingency fee is clearly reasonable. Thus, answers (A) and (C), which state the converse, are incorrect. Further, although it is not preferred to have a lawyer sue a client over his fee, it is clearly permissible. MR 1.5 Comment; DR 4-101(C)(4); MR 1.6(b)(3). Thus, answers (B) and (C), which state the converse, are incorrect.

72. **(D)** *An attorney may reveal a secret in order to prove a fee was owed*. (D) is the correct answer. *See* MR 1.6(b)(3); DR 4-101(C)(4). Again, lawyers suing clients for fees is not preferred — but it is acceptable. A lawyer simply does not have to accept not being paid for work done. Of course, in this suit, the lawyer should reveal only that which is necessary to make his claim. The lawsuit must not be an opportunity to "tell all" and thus, as it were, "extort" the client to pay the fee. In the case at hand, Lucien seems to have revealed only one piece of embarrassing evidence — that Mitchell has a drug and alcohol problem. It is arguable that this was or was not relevant. However, since the context was the difficulty of Lucien's job, it appears that dealing with such a person *would* make the job more difficult. Thus, Lucien's revelation was not improper. (A) is incorrect for the above reasons and also because the above revelation was likely not a "confidence." Rather, since it was likely not gained via attorney-client consultation — but instead was likely just noticed by Lucien — it is better categorized as a "secret." (B) is incorrect because, as indicated, an attorney *can* sue a client for a fee. (C) is incorrect because, although secrets should be kept inviolate, an exception (when suing for a fee) is applicable here. Note, of course, that the MRPC do not distinguish between secrets and confidences.

73. **(A)** *An attorney should maintain a client trust account and should place in it all funds which are in dispute*. (A) is the correct answer. Lucien's actions were quite proper here. *See* MR 1.15(a) and (c) and Comment ("The disputed portion of the funds should be kept in trust account..."); DR 9-102(A)(2). Lucien paid the undisputed part ($4,000,000) and put the disputed part, unused, in his trust account. (B) is incorrect, because the issue is not whether the fee was correct but whether there was a legitimate dispute over the fee. The argued fee could be found excessive, and yet there would not be discipline for putting it into a trust account. (C) is incorrect because the undisputed amount — the $4,000,000 owed Mitchell — could not have been retained in the trust account; it was to be paid promptly to Mitchell. MR 1.15(d). (D) is incorrect for the same reason that (A) is correct.

74. **(A)** *A lawyer must obey all local rules of professional conduct*. MR 8.4(a); DR 1-102(a)(1). (A) is the correct answer. Neither the Model Code nor the Model Rules

are binding in state proceedings; rather, the state rules for attorney conduct apply. Note, however, that most states have adopted either the Model Rules or the Model Code. Thus, (D) is an incorrect answer. (B) and (C) are incorrect because an attorney is permitted to sue to recover a fee. MR 1.6; DR 4-101(C)(4).

75. **(C)** According to CJC Canon 4(D)(5)(d), a judge may accept gifts for special occasions. (A) is incorrect because, for a special occasion gift, it does not matter that Lonnie appears before him. Similarly, for special occasion gifts, the standard is whether the gift is fairly commensurate with the occasion and the relationship, and (B) is therefore wrong. Lonnie is a close friend, and the gift is not outrageously expensive. (D) is incorrect because Canon 3(C)(4) contains many restrictions on the types of gifts a judge may accept and under what circumstances he may accept them.

76. **(B)** *An attorney is not permitted to handle both sides of a litigated case and is also not permitted to handle a domestic relations case on a contingency fee basis.* (B) is the correct answer. *See* EC 5-16; EC 5-17; DR 5-105(A)(B)(C); MR 1.7(a) and Comment; MR 1.5(d)(1); EC 2-20. Were an attorney to handle both sides of a litigated case, there would be an inevitable and glaring conflict of interest. However, on occasion, an attorney is permitted to represent multiple parties in a case that is not going to court as, for example, in an insurance settlement case. Thus (A) and (C) are incorrect answers. Although the CPR does not absolutely prohibit handling divorce cases on a contingency basis ("contingency fee arrangements in domestic relations are rarely justified"; EC 2-20), and the Model Rules allow contingency fees to be collected for "the recovery of post-judgment balance due under support, alimony or other financial orders…"; MR 1.5 Comment [b], the best rule is that to do so is impermissible.

77. **(C)** Canon 4 of the Model Code requires a lawyer to keep the confidences and secrets of a client. DR 4-101(A) and MR 1.6(a) expound upon this responsibility. Because David approaches Anna seeking representation, his communications with her are privileged. (A) is therefore incorrect. (B) is incorrect because an attorney-client relationship is not determined by the payment or non-payment of a fee (consider *pro bono* representations!). (D) is incorrect because, if Anna could reveal David's statement, it would be an admission and would not be hearsay.

78. **(A)** Kirk's conduct is probably impermissible. While the Model Rules do allow lawyer to argue different sides of the same legal issue in subsequent cases, they are specific that "[a] conflict of interest exists…if there is a significant risk that a lawyer's action on behalf of one client will materially limit the lawyer's effectiveness in representing another client in a different case; for example, when a decision favoring one client will create a precedent likely to seriously weaken the position taken on behalf of the other client." MR 1.7 Comment [24]. Here, if Kirk prevails in the second action, it will seriously weaken the position of his client in the first action. (B) and (C) are incorrect for this reason. (D) is incorrect because, although the CPR is not as direct on this point, the result is clearly implied.

Explanatory Answers

79. **(D)** ***An attorney's fee may be paid by another, but the attorney must make sure that her loyalties are solely to the client.*** See MR 1.7 Comment [13]; MR 1.8(f); DR 5-107(A) and (B). (D) is the correct answer. Certainly Amanda can take the case — otherwise no dependents could ever be represented by private counsel! However, Amanda must make sure that her loyalties are solely to Tommy. The fact that Tommy's father is an attorney does not change that requirement. (A) is incorrect because this is not one of the situations where the conflict of interest is so severe as to preclude the attorney from taking the case. (B) is incorrect because whether or not Tommy's father is an attorney is irrelevant to the issue. Amanda must be loyal to Tommy, only. (C) is incorrect because no facts indicate that Tommy's father has or will interfere.

80. **(C)** While the Model Code focused a great deal on the appearance of impropriety, the drafters of the Model Rules found this term to be vague and therefore of little use. (A) is incorrect because only the Model Code employs the "appearance of impropriety" test. (B) and (D) are incorrect for the same reason.

81. **(D)** ***An attorney must not prospectively limit his own liability for malpractice.*** See MR 1.8(h)(1); DR 6-102(A). (D) is the correct answer. Only "II" was correct. Such a waiver, aside from being contrary to codal provisions, is also against public policy. Since choices "I" and "III" are incorrect, (D) is the best answer. (A) is incorrect because "I" is incorrect. Advertising, provided it is not misleading, is clearly now permissible. MR 7.2(a); DR 2-101(B). (B) is incorrect because "III" is incorrect. It is not an ethical violation to charge low fees. (C) is incorrect for the same reasons that (A) and (B) are incorrect.

82. **(B)** ***A lawyer who learns that opposing counsel is a close relative must not take the case unless there is consent after consultation.*** See DR 5-101(A); *see also* MR 1.7. (B) is the correct answer. Here, although Lori told Fawn of the potential conflict, she did not ask for Fawn's consent to proceed. This was her fundamental error. (A) is incorrect, because whether or not there is a breach of trust, the preceding is a clear ethical violation. Of course, the rule is based on protecting against breaches of trust, but the rule, itself, is "bright line," and thus allows for no harmless errors. (C) is incorrect because the facts indicate that there was a full disclosure of the potential sibling conflict of interest. (D) is incorrect because the conflict was not "inherent."

83. **(C)** Model Rule 6.2(c) states that "[a] lawyer shall not seek to avoid appointments by a tribunal to represent a person except for good cause, such as...the client or the cause is so repugnant to the lawyer as to be likely to impair the client-lawyer relationship or the lawyer's ability to represent the client." EC 2-30 contains a similar provision. However, according to EC 2-27, a lawyer should not decline to represent someone because of the community's perception of the client and/or his cause. (B) is therefore incorrect. EC 2-29 states, *inter alia*, that a lawyer should not refuse representation because he believes his client is guilty. (A) is therefore wrong. (D) is incorrect because neither the Model Rules nor the Code requires *pro bono* representation (although MR 6.1 states that every lawyer should do *pro bono* work).

84. **(D)** ***An attorney working for a corporation represents the organization, not any of its personnel.*** (D) is the correct answer. *See* MR 1.13(a), (d), and (e); EC 5-18. In such a fact pattern, the attorney should ask the CEO to reconsider his action; then, if this fails, the attorney should climb the corporate ladder, eventually speaking to the board of directors, MR 1.13(b). (A) is incorrect because, generally, an in-house corporate counsel need be licensed only in one jurisdiction (but see MR 5.5(a))—not necessarily the jurisdiction of the corporation. (B) is incorrect for this same reason. (C) is incorrect because choice "II" is correct. Although MR 1.13(b) is only phrased in optional terms, "may" is in regard to speaking to the Board of Directors. Since none of the answers included only choice "II," (D) is the best answer.

85. **(B)** ***A staff attorney represents the business organization only and must take precautions to insure that employees are aware that this attorney is not their attorney.*** (B) is the correct answer. *See* MR 1.13(a) and (d) and Comment; EC 5-18. Mike works for Acme. Acme, only, is his client. Thus, when Ed approached Mike for legal advice, Mike should have told Ed he could not be his attorney were there to be a conflict of interest between Ed and Acme. Instead, Mike just listened and used the information *against* Ed. This was totally unprofessional and contrary to the stated ethical standard. (A) is partially correct — Mike should not have revealed Ed's confidence — but (A) misses the key point regarding conflicts of interest. (C) is also only partially correct. Mike was Acme's lawyer. However, when an attorney listens to one who states that he needs legal advice, that attorney has allowed himself to become embroiled in a conflict of interest unnecessarily. Answer (C) misses that issue. (D) is incorrect because Ed's damaging admission is ***clearly confidential***.

86. **(A)** According to Model Rules 1.7(a)(1) and (b)(1), "A lawyer shall not represent a client...if the representation of one client will be directly adverse to another client...[unless] the lawyer reasonably believes [he] will be able to provide competent and diligent representation to each affected client". The Model Code is also clear on this point (*see* DR 5-105). Here, Ned needs to find another attorney, as it would be difficult, if not impossible, for Andrew to represent Ned without adversely affecting his relationship with Polly.

87. **(D)** ***An attorney shall withdraw when discharged by her client.*** See DR 2-110(B)(4); MR 1.16(a)(3). (D) is the correct answer. The standards leave no room for discretion. Even were the discharge wrongful — as this discharge certainly appears to be—an attorney staying on is impermissible. The client's desires, in this fiduciary relationship, are virtually inviolate. (A) is incorrect because, as above noted, the client has a near-absolute right to discharge the attorney. (B) is incorrect because, again, even a constitutional infraction on the employer's part (directed to the attorney-employee) cannot require that the attorney retain her position. Of course, the point is, there are other remedies for such employer wrongdoings, e.g., civil suit for wrongful discharge. (C) is incorrect because although an attorney, generally, *should* see a case through to its end, a client's desires should be kept at the forefront. Although, of course, were the court to require the attorney to stay on, so as not to disrupt the litigation process, such would take precedence over the client's desires. Otherwise, however, the attorney must withdraw. Since no facts indicated the *court* required Rhonda to stay on, (C) is incorrect.

Explanatory Answers

88. **(D)** According to Model Rule 8.2(a), "[a] lawyer shall not make a statement that the lawyer knows to be false or with reckless disregard as to its truth or falsity concerning the qualifications or integrity of judge, adjudicatory officer or public legal officer or of a candidate for election or appointment to judicial or legal office." Similarly, DR 8-102(A) states, "A lawyer shall not knowingly make false statements of fact concerning the qualifications of a candidate for election or appointment to a judicial office." Here, Anna believes her statement to be true. Since she is not making a statement that she knows to be false and is not speaking with reckless disregard for the truth, her conduct will not be disciplined. (A) is incorrect because Anna has not made any statements about the judicial system as a whole. (B) is incorrect because the identity of the candidate that Anna supports is immaterial; what matters is the truth or falsity of her statements and her knowledge thereof. (C) is entirely irrelevant.

89. **(C)** *An attorney need not cite a sister state case directly on point.* See DR 7-106(B)(1); EC 7-23; MR 3.3(a)(2). (C) is the correct answer. Although, of course, an attorney is better off to cite, and then distinguish, all contrary case law, there is no ethical violation for either intentionally or unintentionally failing to cite a sister state's case "on point." (A) is incorrect, because the ethical standards are quite clear: an attorney must cite cases directly on point in that jurisdiction. (B) is incorrect for the same reason that (A) is incorrect. Obviously if it is unprofessional to fail to cite a lower court case which is "on all fours," the same is true for a supreme court case. (D) is incorrect because (A) and (B) are incorrect.

90. **(B)** *A lawyer shall not knowingly fail to disclose to the tribunal legal authority in the controlling jurisdiction known to the lawyer to be directly adverse to the position of the client and not disclosed by opposing counsel.* See DR 7-106(B)(1); EC 7-23; MR 3.3(a)(2). It is a breach of an attorney's duties — as an officer of the court — to fail to make known to the court "legal authority in the controlling jurisdiction." Thus, both the state X lower and supreme court cases are on point and implicated. Therefore, (B) is the correct answer. (A) is an incorrect answer only because *both the lower court and the higher court cases should have been revealed*. (A), unlike (B), is only partially correct. (C) is incorrect because an attorney has *no ethical obligation* to cite the law of other jurisdictions. (D) is incorrect for the same reason that (C) is incorrect.

91. **(D)** Both (A) and (B) are proper actions. See Model Rule 1.15 ("A lawyer shall promptly deliver to the client or third person any funds or other property that the client or third person is entitled to receive...") and DR 9-102(A)(2) ("All funds of clients paid to a lawyer or law firm, other than advances for costs or expenses, shall be deposited in one or more identifiable bank accounts maintained in the state in which the law office is situated and no funds belonging to the lawyer or law firm shall be deposited therein except...[f]unds belonging in part to a client and in part presently or potentially to the lawyer or law firm must be deposited therein, but the portion belonging to the lawyer or law firm may be withdrawn when due..."). There is no dispute that Loni is due the fee, so Loni may send Carrie her percentage of the settlement and leave the rest in the account. Under the Rules and the Code, Loni may not put the funds in her personal bank account, and (C) is therefore incorrect.

92. **(A)** Any interest earned is due to the client. *See* DR 9-102(A) and Model Rule 1.15(a).

93. **(D)** *An attorney is not permitted to inject his personal opinions as to the facts or a party into the record. See* MR 3.4(e); DR 7-106(C)(4). (D) is the correct answer. Although Alamo's error was a typical one, it is nevertheless a serious error. Were attorneys permitted to inject their personal views, much would be lost: the professionalism of trial; the impartiality of the court; and eventually, such would require *all* advocates to lie regarding the case. Otherwise, silence would be considered as disbelief in this particular case. (A) is incorrect, because the test is not harmless error (which is the test for reversal of criminal verdict) but instead whether this attorney violated a disciplinary rule. (B) is incorrect, because an attorney can be disciplined whether or not his adversary points out the error. (C) is incorrect because the standards of prosecutorial professional advocacy do not depend on the culpability of the accused.

94. **(C)** *A prosecuting attorney is subject to discipline for stating pretrial that the accused confessed, stating his own opinion, and for stating the prior criminal record of the accused.* (C) is the correct answer. See DR 7-107(B); MR 3.6 Comment [5]. I, II, and III would all subject Jag to discipline. (A) is incorrect because I is incorrect: relaying to the public that there was a confession is highly prejudicial and clearly precluded. (B) is incorrect for the above reason and also because an attorney should not state his own opinion as to the merits of a case. Jag did this in response to Night's query. (D) is incorrect for the same reasons as above, and also because stating a prior record is highly prejudicial, not particularly probative, and in any case, clearly proscribed.

95. **(D)** *By way of trial publicity, an attorney should balance the following factors: prejudice to the trial, public right to information, and freedom of the press. See* MR 3.6(a) and Comment; DR 7-107. (D) is the correct answer. Thus, answers (A), (B), and (C) are only partially correct — for each includes only one of the above three factors. Although prejudice to the accused is the most important factor, the other First Amendment values are also of legal import. Both the public and the press have a right to know.

96. **(B)** CJC Canon 5(A)(2) states that "[a] judge shall resign [from judicial] office upon becoming a candidate for a non-judicial office either in a primary or in a general election...". Therefore, Judge Julia will have to resign her judgeship as soon as she announces her candidacy.

97. **(C)** *An attorney should handle funds or other property of a client with the care required of a professional fiduciary.* (C) is the correct answer. See DR 9-102; MR 1.15. Alternative I is proper. The check is for the settlement of Plaintiff's claim. It is proper for Attorney to promptly deliver to the client the funds by endorsing the check and sending it to her. Alternative II is not proper. To preserve the identity of funds of a client, all funds received by Attorney belonging in part or whole to Client must be deposited and maintained in a client's trust account and thus be kept completely separate from Attorney's personal funds. Commingling of client funds with an attorney's personal funds is not allowed. Thus, it is improper for Attorney to deposit the check in his personal bank account and send a personal check. Alternative III is proper. The check is properly deposited in the trust account, Client

is advised promptly of its receipt, which is required, and the check forwarded to Client is properly drawn from the trust account. Thus (C) is the correct answer. (A), (B) and (D) are incorrect as they improperly include II or exclude I or III.

98. **(D)** According to both the Model Code and the Model Rules, a lawyer must report any unprivileged knowledge of a violation of the Code or the Rules to the proper authorities. *See* Model Rule 8.3(a) and (c); DR 1-103(A). However, privileged information is protected. Here, Sarah is Albert's client and tells him about Inlaw's actions in the context of the attorney-client relationship, rendering the information privileged. Therefore Albert may not report Inlaw without Sarah's permission (unless he comes across the information in an independent, non-privileged way). (A) is therefore wrong. (B) and (C) are immaterial because the information about Inlaw is privileged and cannot be revealed under any circumstances.

99. **(B)** *An attorney should not engage in conduct involving dishonesty, fraud, deceit or misrepresentation*. (B) is the correct answer. See DR 1-102(A)(3),(4); MR 8.4(c). An attorney should maintain high standards of professional conduct, and should refrain from all illegal and dishonest conduct. Such standard should be maintained not only when rendering legal services but at all times. Able persuaded Investor to invest $10,000 in a business venture. However, Able did not inform Investor that he owned 100% of the business venture. Such information is material and, had Investor been aware of this fact, he may have decided to invest his money differently. Such an omission by Able is tantamount to fraud. Therefore, Able is subject to discipline. (A) is incorrect. It is not that an attorney is prohibited from owning an interest in a business, it is that he may not fraudulently conceal such interest. (C) is incorrect. Dishonesty adversely reflects upon one's fitness to be a member of the bar, regardless of whether the dishonesty occurred while rendering legal services. Accordingly, any dishonest act will subject a member of the bar to discipline. (D) is incorrect. Though Able does not practice law, he is still a member of the bar and is subject to the code.

100. **(D)** *An attorney may make a contribution to the fund of candidate for judicial office, providing the contribution is given to the candidate's campaign committee*. (D) is the correct answer. See DR 7-110(A); CJC 5(C)(2); MR 8.4(f). So as not to impair the impartiality of the judges in our legal system, campaign contributions may be made to a candidate only if such contribution is given to the candidate's campaign committee. Thus, it is not proper for Alpha to contribute $5,000 to Beta, unless Alpha gives the $5,000 to a committee formed to further Beta's election. (A) is incorrect. It is improper for Alpha to give $5,000 to Beta personally for his campaign. This may be construed as an attempt to gain special consideration or favors from Beta. At the least, it appears improper. (B) is incorrect. Even if the contribution is anonymous, it must be given to the campaign committee. Otherwise it may appear that Beta is dishonestly and improperly profiting from his own campaign. (C) is incorrect. Provided the contribution is given in the appropriate manner, it is irrelevant whether Alpha practices before the court to which Beta seeks election.

101. **(A)** Model Rule 5.3(a) stresses that lawyers must carefully supervise non-lawyer employees "to ensure that the firm has in effect measures giving reasonable assurance that . . . conduct is compatible with the professional obligations of the

lawyer." Furthermore, DR 4-101(D) states that "[a] lawyer shall exercise reasonable care to prevent his employees, associates, and others whose services are utilized by him from disclosing or using confidences or secrets of a client...". Here, Shannon has wrongly, if inadvertently, revealed client confidences, but Lara is not responsible because she has always supervised her employees carefully. (C) and (D) are therefore wrong. (B) is incorrect because Lara could be responsible if she had not properly supervised Shannon.

102. **(A)** *A lawyer shall not make an agreement for, charge, or collect an unreasonable fee or an unreasonable amount for expenses*. See MR 1.5(a); DR 2-106(B). (A) is the correct answer. The reasonable implication from the facts is that David billed Beta for more hours than he spent. His superior told him to bill for 70 hours and also indicated that such should take him only 50 hours. Further, it seems David did not even spend that. He only "scanned" the work which his secretary prepared. (B) is incorrect because although he was apparently acting under Holtz' orders regarding billing, each licensed attorney is *personally* responsible for obeying the standards of the profession. See MR 5.2(a) ("A lawyer is bound by the Rules of Professional Conduct notwithstanding that the lawyer acted at the direction of another person"). That is, under the Model Rules, David has no defense in arguing he was merely obeying his superior's orders. The Model Code contains no similar provision. (C) is incorrect because it begs the question. If one is billing by *hours*, it is *per se* unreasonable to overstate the hours spent - as here. (D) is incorrect because it confuses the fact that a reprimand *is* a type of discipline. Attorney discipline can be in the form of private reprimand, public reprimand, suspension, or disbarment. Although David would likely not be disbarred for this overbilling, he should be reprimanded.

103. **(B)** *An attorney is personally responsible for and must oversee the legal work drafted by his non-lawyer assistants*. See MR 5.3(b) and (c); *Cf.* DR 4-101(D); MR 5.5(b); EC 3-5, EC 3-6, DR 3-101(A). (B) is the correct answer. The facts indicated that David gave all of the Beta work to his secretary and that he merely scanned "most" of the secretary's end product. This is clearly unsatisfactory. The attorney must oversee and read *all* of the legal work. He clearly abrogated this requirement. (A) is incorrect because although, essentially, the secretary did practice law without a license, the phrase in (A), "subject to discipline," is inapposite. A layperson who practices law without a license is not subject to discipline. *Attorneys* are subject to discipline. Such a person, instead, is likely guilty of a crime or perhaps would be found in contempt of court. Moreover, this secretary likely did nothing wrong. The work was given back to David. The secretary's obligations were fulfilled. (C) is incorrect because although Holtz' billing instructions were improper, *supra*, his instructions to David regarding using his secretary were permissible. He merely told David to enlist his secretary's "help." There is nothing wrong with utilizing assistants if their work is overseen. (D) is incorrect for the same reason that (B) is correct.

104. **(C)** *A lawyer shall not aid another in the unauthorized practice of law*. (C) is the correct answer. See DR 3-101(A); MR 5.5(b). Although it was not necessarily the secretary's intent to practice law, because David delegated all of the work and more fundamentally because he did not oversee and examine this work, in the last analysis, he was aiding this secretary in the unauthorized practice of law. (A) is

incorrect because the extreme measure of quitting one's job is not yet necessary for David. He should have spoken to Holtz and perhaps the other partners about Holtz' request to inflate the bill. Withdrawal is necessary only if, by continuing employment, he will be forced to disobey professional responsibility guidelines. *See* DR 2-110(B)(2); MR 1.16(a). (B) is an incorrect answer, because, as he was the perpetrator of the billing "fraud," it is redundant to require him to tell Beta. More fundamentally, he should not have inflated the bill. Because of this, (C) is the better answer. (D) is incorrect because (C) is correct, and also because (B) is partially correct.

105. **(A)** According to MR 3.6, a lawyer may state information that is in the official record of the case (Statement II) but may not make statements that will prejudice the proceeding. A statement is likely to prejudice the proceeding (among other ways) if it speaks to a party's character or credibility (Statement III), or if it contains information that the lawyer knows will come up at trial (Statement I). Of course, a lawyer may refuse to comment if she wishes. *See also* DR 7-107(G).

106. **(C)** *An attorney may seek to avoid a court appointment if he is incompetent in the area of the case or if he finds the case so repugnant as to interfere with his competent handling of the case.* (C) is the correct answer. Although a lawyer, generally, should not refuse court appointments, there are exceptions to this rule. Thus, answer (A) is incorrect. It states the rule as an absolute, which it is not. (B), which incorporates choice II, is a correct answer. If an attorney is actually incompetent (which can be inferred from his poor academic record in criminal procedure) the attorney can seek to avoid court appointment. *See* MR 6.2(a) and Comment; *Cf.* MR 1.1; EC 2-29, EC 2-30. (D) is also a correct answer. When the repugnance to a case is so extreme as to likely impair the lawyer's performance, refusing an appointment is acceptable. *See* MR 6.2(c); EC 2-30. In the case at hand, because Plager believes bigamists should be given the death sentence — an extreme view — his repugnance may reach this extreme level. Choice (C), the correct answer, incorporated both the correct aspects of answers (B) and (D), and is thus the best answer.

107. **(D)** *A lawyer is permitted to advertise his legal services provided that the ad is not misleading.* See MR 7.1; MR 7.2; DR 2-101. (D) is the correct answer. Ever since *Bates v. State Bar of Arizona*, 433 U.S. 350 (1977), a blanket ban on lawyer advertising has not been permitted. The present standard for lawyer advertising is best stated in the above-cited Model Rule. Essentially that standard requires the ad be truthful, not misleading. Although Harr dressed uncharacteristically for the ad, and although he surrounded himself with books he did not use, this is more like wearing make-up for a TV appearance. It is not misleading. Promising low fees and stating that his clients are generally satisfied is more problematic. However, since it was given that his fees are low and since it was also given that he did client surveys which proved satisfaction, his ad was not misleading. That is, he can substantiate his claims. MR 7.2(a); MR 7.1; DR 2.101(B) and (E). *See* MR 7.1 Comment [3]. (A) is incorrect for the same reason that (D) is correct. (B) is incorrect because the ad was not misleading, as set out above. (C) is incorrect because there certainly are still restrictions on lawyer advertising.

108. **(C)** Model Rule 1.6 and its Commentary make clear that a lawyer must keep client communications confidential, even if the subject matter involves past crimes such

as murder or perjury. DR 4-101(B)(2) is even stronger, stating that "a lawyer shall not knowingly...[u]se a confidence or secret of his client to the disadvantage of the client." Clearly, calling the DA would be to Deirdre's disadvantage, and Agatha may not do so. Note that Agatha would not be required to (and should not) assist Deirdre in lying under oath again.

109. **(A)** Under MR 6.1, a lawyer should do work in the public interest, and serving on the Committee would satisfy that goal for Aloysius. However, he will not be disciplined if he refuses, and (B) is therefore incorrect. Furthermore, EC 1-4 states that "[a] lawyer should, upon request, serve on and assist committees and boards having responsibility for the administration of the Disciplinary Rules." Aloysius should definitely serve, therefore, if he is able. Note that the fact that a layperson serves on the committee is not a problem, and (D) is therefore incorrect.

110. **(D)** *In setting a fee, it is proper for Attorney to consider the fee customarily charged for similar legal services, the amount involved, the results obtained, and the nature and length of the professional relationship with Client.* (D) is the correct answer. See DR 2-106; MR 1.5(a). The threshold requirement of setting a fee is that it be reasonable. In determining the reasonableness of a fee DR 2-106 and MR 1.5(a) specifically provide that the factors listed above may be considered when setting a fee. Attorney may take into consideration the length of the professional relationship. Here, Attorney represented Exco for a long period of time and is familiar with the particular governmental regulations, applicable to issuing new debentures. Therefore, Attorney has a higher level of skill in the area and is able to complete the work much more quickly than other attorneys. It is also proper for Attorney to consider the amount of money involved and what most other lawyers would charge for such an opinion letter. The amount of money involved is great, $10,000,000, and most attorneys would charge $2,000 for such an opinion letter. Accordingly, it was proper for Attorney to consider all of the factors listed in I, II and III. (A), (B), and (C) are incorrect as each leave out a factor which is proper to consider.

111. **(D)** *Use of a trade name is permissible, if it is not misleading.* See MR 7.5(a) and Comment; *cf.* EC 2-11; DR 2-102(B). Although it has been impermissible in the past, the position of the Model Rules is the best approach. Thus, (D) is the correct answer. Since Heather was the only attorney in Guile and since she noted that her clinic was not run by the government, her ad was not misleading. (A) is incorrect because Heather was not soliciting clients. The ad was not aimed at named people. (B) is incorrect because some ads are permissible. The rule of (B) is therefore incorrect. (C) is incorrect because, again, Heather was not soliciting. It was an ad. Thus, even were such trade names held impermissible in Heather's state, (D) is still the best answer.

112. **(C)** According to EC 5-7, "a lawyer, because he is in a better position to evaluate a cause of action, should enter into a contingent fee arrangement only in those circumstances where the arrangement will be beneficial to the client." Furthermore, EC 2-20 explains that a contingent fee arrangement will be desirable where the client needs to enter into such an arrangement in order to finance the litigation. Similarly, Comment 3 to MR 1.5 tells us that "Contingent fees, like any other fees, are subject to [a] reasonableness standard." Therefore, Lisa should have looked to Milton's best interests and allowed Milton to pay her on an hourly basis, if he so

desired, especially as he appears from the facts of the question to be financially able to do so. (A) is wrong because Lisa has the responsibility here, not Milton. (B) is incorrect, because, according to both the Code and the Model Rules, custom is immaterial in this situation. (D) is clearly wrong, because both the Code and the Model Rules instruct the attorney to benefit the client in lieu of self-benefit.

113. **(B)** *An attorney who possesses knowledge of another attorney's or judge's impermissible conduct must inform the proper authorities.* MR 8.3 and Comment; DR 1-103(A). (B) is the correct answer. A judge accepting a sizeable cash payment is clearly impermissible because it is likely to appear to be a bribe. Luto had to report this. (A) is incorrect because Luto did not insult the judge by simply asking what happened. This was, in fact, the best first step. (C) is incorrect because the facts indicated he was "convinced" Skeet was bribed. (D) is incorrect because an attorney is acting improperly for not reporting errant judges. Note that Luto should also report opposing counsel to the disciplinary authority for bribing a judge.

114. **(B)** *A lawyer admitted to practice in one jurisdiction is subject to discipline in that jurisdiction for ethical violations committed outside that jurisdiction.* See MR 8.5. (B) is the correct answer. Since Alaric was practicing law without a license, he is aiding in the unauthorized practice of law, which is a disciplinary problem. See MR 5.5(a) and (b); DR 3-101(B). Thus, Montana can discipline him for practicing in New York without a license. (A) is incorrect because, since he does not have a New York law license, the remedy for his impermissible practice is New York prosecution, New York contempt, and/or Montana discipline. New York does not have professional jurisdiction over him. (C) is incorrect because I, above, is incorrect. (D) is incorrect for the same reason that (B) is correct.

115. **(B)** DR 2-104(A)(1) is directly on point, stating that solicitation is generally inappropriate but that "[a] lawyer may accept employment by a...former client (if the advice is germane to the former employment...")". Here, (B) is the best answer because the other three are clearly wrong. However, note that, according to the Code, Anderson may only contact Christine if the advice is germane to a matter on which Anderson had formerly advised her. *Cf.* MR 7.3(a)(2) (allowing attorneys to solicit professional employment from people with whom they have had past professional relationships).

116. **(D)** *An attorney must return any unearned fee to a client. However, if the amount due the attorney is disputed, the disputed portion shall remain in the client's fund account until the dispute is resolved.* (D) is the correct answer. See DR 9-102; MR 1.15. Attorney is obligated to return any unearned fees. However, if there is a dispute as to the fee, the disputed portion shall remain in the client's fund account until the dispute is resolved. Deft has demanded return of the entire $800 he gave to Attorney. Attorney believes he has earned $300, as per the agreement, in that he expended six hours attempting to obtain bail. Attorney must immediately send Deft a $500 check, and the disputed $300 is to remain in the client's fund account, until the dispute is resolved. (A) is incorrect. It is improper to transfer any portion of the funds to the fee account until the dispute is resolved. Furthermore, Attorney has only earned $300 to date, and thus the remaining $500 must be returned to Deft, while the disputed $300 is to remain in the client's fund account until the dispute is resolved. (B) is incorrect. The $300 fee is in dispute and must remain in

the client's fund account until the dispute is resolved. At this time, the $500 has yet to be earned and must be returned to Deft upon request. (C) is incorrect. While it is proper to send Deft a check for $500, Attorney may not transfer the $300 to the fee account until the dispute is resolved.

117. **(A)** (A) is correct because under DR 1-102(A)(3), a lawyer shall not engage in illegal conduct involving moral turpitude, and, under MR 8.4(b), a lawyer must not commit a criminal act. (C) is incorrect because, under MR 8.5, the rules of professional conduct apply to a lawyer regardless of where the misconduct occurs or whether the lawyer was practicing law at the time of the misconduct. (D) is incorrect because a criminal conviction is not essential. If a lawyer has engaged in criminal conduct or any conduct involving dishonesty, fraud, deceit or misrepresentation, the lawyer will be subject to discipline. DR 1-102(A)(3) and (4).

118. **(D)** CJC Canon 5(A)(3)(d)(i) and 5(A)(3)(d)(ii) states that a candidate for judicial office "shall (i) not make pledges or promises of conduct in office other than the faithful and impartial performance of the duties of the office [or] (ii) make statements that commit or appear to commit the candidate with respect to cases, controversies or issues that are likely to come before the court...". Under this guideline, Statement I is permissible, as it is in line with the faithful and impartial performance of the duties of the office. Statement II is impermissible, as it announces Jessica's views on a disputed legal or political issue: sentencing. Statement III is impermissible because it is not in line with Jessica's impartial performance of her duties; it would seem that she already has her mind made up about how she's going to decide future sentencing issues!

119. **(B)** (B) is correct because, under the Code and Model Rules, an attorney who knows that another attorney has engaged in misconduct that violates the rules of professional conduct raising a substantial question as to that attorney's honesty, trustworthiness, or fitness to practice law must inform the disciplinary authorities, unless such a report would violate the attorney's obligation to preserve client confidences. DR 1-103(A) and MR 8.3(a).

120. **(C)** (C) is correct because, under DR 8-102(A) and MR 8.2(A), a lawyer is prohibited from making statements about the qualifications of a judge if the lawyer knows the statement is false or makes the statement with reckless disregard as to its truth or falsity.

121. **(A)** The Commentary to CJC Canon 3(B)(7)(c) allows a judge to discuss pending cases with other judges and court personnel "whose function it is to aid the judge in carrying out [her] adjudicative responsibilities." Therefore, (B) and (C) are incorrect. (D) is incorrect because Judy need not consult only with experts; if she does so, she must give the parties notice thereof. *See* Canon 3(B)(7)(b).

122. **(B)** (B) is correct because a lawyer cannot represent a new client in a matter adverse to a former client if the subject matter of the two representations are **substantially related** or **if confidential information relating to the former representation is used in the present representation**. MR 1.9(a). Here, the two representations will be substantially related because both involve Able's medical condition that would (possibly) preclude him from safely operating an automobile. Note that Lawyer could

not refer the case to a lawyer in the same firm (vicarious disqualification under DR 5-105(D) and MR 1.10(a)) or to a different firm if the referring attorney expects payment for the referral (referral fees or giving anything of value in exchange for the recommendation prohibited by DR 2-103(B) and MR 7.2(b)).

123. **(C)** (C) is correct because, when a lawyer receives property in which the client has an interest, the lawyer must promptly notify the client and give the client any and all property to which the client is entitled. DR 9-102(B)(1) and (4); MR 1.15(d). However, if a dispute develops between the client and lawyer regarding right to the property, the disputed amount must be kept separate and the amount which both parties agree belongs to the client must be given promptly to the client. DR 9-102(A)(2) and MR 1.15(d) and (e). Thus, Lawyer was obligated promptly to send at least $40,000 to Client and could only immediately keep $5,000 or less. I is incorrect because, as noted above, while the funds are in dispute, Lawyer may not pay himself more than the amount Client has authorized. In I, Lawyer pays himself $20,000 when the client has only authorized $5,000. IV is incorrect because, as also noted above, Lawyer must give Client any funds to which he is entitled. In IV, Lawyer tries to retain the whole amount. II and III are correct because, in each, Lawyer gives Client all of the money to which he is entitled and only withholds (if anything) the amount that Client has authorized.

124. **(C)** (C) is correct because, under MR 1.5(a) and DR 2-106(A) and (B), a lawyer's fee must not be unreasonable. This reasonableness requirement overrides all other considerations. Thus, even if a contingent fee is customary and the client has agreed to a contingent fee in writing, the fee agreement will still be improper if the overall fee is not reasonable.

125. **(B)** According to both the Model Code and the Model Rules, in order to be grounds for discipline, a crime must be connected to a lawyer's capacity to be trustworthy. *See, e.g.*, MR 8.4(b) ("It is professional misconduct for a lawyer to...commit a criminal act that reflects adversely on the lawyer's honesty, trustworthiness or fitness as a lawyer in other respects..."). *See also* DR 1-102(A)(3); *cf.* DR 7-101(A) and (B). (D) is therefore incorrect. (A) is incorrect because a lawyer may be disciplined for dishonest acts even if they are not committed in his professional capacity. (C) is incorrect because a lack of respect for traffic laws does not necessarily warrant professional discipline.

126. **(C)** According to MR 8.2(a), "[a] lawyer shall not make a statement that the lawyer knows to be false or with reckless disregard as to its truth or falsity concerning the qualifications or integrity of judge, adjudicatory officer or public legal officer, or of a candidate for election or appointment to judicial or legal office." Similarly, DR 8-102(A) states, "A lawyer shall not knowingly make false statements of fact concerning the qualifications of a candidate for election or appointment to a judicial office." Here, Alice believes her statement to be true. The facts that she often practices before Dingbat or that Dingbat is currently on the bench are irrelevant; (A) and (B) are therefore wrong.

127. **(C)** (C) is correct because a person who engages in a confidential communication with an attorney while seeking legal representation is entitled to the protection of any

confidential information disclosed, even if no attorney-client relationship results from the consultation. DR 4-101; EC 4-1; MR 1.6 and 1.18.

128. **(C)** (C) is correct because, under DR 4-101(C)(4) and MR 1.6(b)(3), a lawyer may reveal confidential client communications if necessary to respond to accusations of wrongful conduct. The lawyer should only reveal such portions of any confidential client communication that are necessary to establish the defense to the accusation of wrongdoing.

129. **(D)** Under DR 7-102(A)(2) and MR 3.1, Louise may argue the defense as long as she believes it has merit and argues for a reversal of the recent Orange Supreme Court holdings. Note that, under MR 3.3(a)(2) and DR 7-106(B)(1), she must cite the adverse recent holdings in her brief and oral argument.

130. **(A)** (A) is correct because under DR 9-101(B), EC 9-3, and MR 1.11(a)(2), a lawyer shall not represent a client in a matter in which the lawyer had *substantial responsibility* while employed as a public employee. Here, Lawyer was the government lawyer assigned to lead the criminal prosecution of Deft while employed by the government and cannot now take on the civil wrongful death suit against Deft on behalf of a private client.

131. **(A)** (A) is correct because, while there is a general prohibition against the sharing of legal fees with nonlawyers, an exception exists under MR 5.4(a)(3) that permits a lawyer or law firm to include nonlawyer employees in a compensation or retirement plan, even though the plan is based in whole or in part on a profit-sharing arrangement. Note that DR 3-102(A)(3) only allows participation by non-lawyers in a profit-sharing retirement plan.

132. **(C)** Again, according to DR 1-102(A)(4), "[a] lawyer shall not...[e]ngage in conduct involving dishonesty, fraud, deceit, or misrepresentation." Furthermore, under Model Rule 8.4(c) "[i]t is professional misconduct for a lawyer to...engage in conduct involving dishonesty, fraud, deceit or misrepresentation...", and under MR 8.5, "[a] lawyer admitted to practice in this jurisdiction is subject to the disciplinary authority of this jurisdiction, regardless of where the lawyer's conduct occurs." Susie has acted dishonestly here by declining to report the fact that she has been charged with criminal fraud. Furthermore, under MR 8.5, the fact that her application was in Euphoria doesn't matter, as Despair may discipline her for dishonest conduct even if it occurred in another jurisdiction. (B) is therefore incorrect. (A) is incorrect because there is no requirement under the Code or the Rules that dishonest conduct take place in one's capacity as a lawyer. (D) is incorrect because neither the Rules nor the Code restrict a lawyer from obtaining other types of licenses.

133. **(B)** (B) is correct because, under EC 3-6 and MR 5.1 and 5.3, a lawyer must make reasonable efforts to supervise the actions of any lawyers he or she may have supervisory authority over and must reasonably supervise all non-lawyer employees. Even if properly supervised, under tort law concepts of vicarious responsibility (e.g., *respondeat superior*), a lawyer is liable for malpractice if the negligence of one of lawyer's employees results in harm to a client's case.

Explanatory Answers

134. **(C)** (C) is correct because, under DR 2-101(A), truthful advertising that does not involve "false, fraudulent, misleading, deceptive, self-laudatory or unfair statements or claims" is not prohibited. *See also* MR 7.2. The fact that the caller initiated the contact by going to Attorney's office is not relevant because Attorney's radio program would be considered a form of advertising which can be regulated under the Code and Rules.

135. **(C)** (C) is correct because, under DR 7-103(A) and MR 3.8(a), a prosecutor cannot bring charges against a defendant unless the charge is supported by probable cause. In addition, the prosecutor has an ethical obligation to inform the defense about the existence of any evidence which tends to negate the guilt of the accused or reduce the potential punishment. DR 7-103(B); MR 3.8(d).

136. **(C)** The Model Rules are clear that a lawyer may not communicate with a party that the lawyer knows to be represented by an attorney without the other lawyer's permission or a court order. *See* MR 4.2. The Model Code provision is nearly identical. *See* DR 7-104(A)(1). (A) is wrong because Andrea must try to settle cases through the defendants' attorneys, not by communicating with them directly. (B) is incorrect because Andrea must monitor her own conduct, not that of the other attorneys. (D) is incorrect; her keeping of copies is entirely irrelevant.

137. **(B)** (B) is correct because DR 8-101(A)(1) allows a lawyer-legislator to represent private clients so long as the lawyer-legislator does not use the lawyer's position as a legislator to obtain a "special advantage in legislative matters for himself or for a client" in cases "where he knows or it is obvious that such action is not in the public interest." *See also* MR 8.5 Comment [5]. Thus, Attorney is not subject to discipline for offering a bill to repeal the regulation because Attorney determined that the regulation was unworkable and unfair to State B landowners, not just Attorney's client.

138. **(A)** (A) is correct because, under DR 7-104(A) and MR 4.2, an attorney may not communicate directly with a represented party unless the other party's legal representative consents to the communication. The fact that the communication would be beneficial to the represented party or that the interests of third parties (e.g., the children) might be benefitted is not sufficient to override the fear that any direct communication may result in overreaching by the attorney attempting the direct communication.

139. **(D)** (D) is correct because, under MR 4.2 and DR 7-104(A), a lawyer cannot communicate with a represented party about the subject of the representation unless the lawyer has the consent of the other lawyer or is authorized by a court order to do so. In addition, Model Rule 8.4(a) provides that "[i]t is professional misconduct for a lawyer to violate or attempt to violate the Rules of Professional Conduct...or to do so through the acts of another." *See also* DR 1-102(A)(2). Consequently, it was improper for Attorney to ask X to communicate the settlement offer to Wife.

140. **(B)** According to Comment [1] to MR 2.1, a lawyer should give straightforward advice to a client, whether or not it is palatable. Furthermore, a lawyer may give a client advice before being asked for it if it appears to be in the client's interest. *See* Comment 5. Furthermore, EC 7-8 tells us that "[a] lawyer should advise his client

of the possible effect of each legal alternative." Therefore, (B) is the best answer, although it would be even better if it said that Larry may tell Loanshark about the customer relations problems. (Remember that you're looking for the best, not always a perfect answer!).

141. **(B)** (B) is correct because, under DR 7-109(C) and MR 3.4(b) Comment [3], a lawyer may reimburse (or advance) a witness the reasonable costs associated with traveling, appearing and testifying, including reasonable compensation to a witness for his loss of time in testifying or attending trial. However, a lawyer shall not pay a witness contingent on the content of his testimony or the outcome of the case.

142. **(A)** (A) is correct because, under DR 7-107(G) and MR 3.6 (b)(2) and (c), a lawyer may make statements about the general nature of the claim or defense or other information contained in a public record. However, a lawyer may not make statements concerning the credibility or character of a party or witness (Statement II) or that contain information the lawyer knows or reasonably should know are likely to be inadmissible at trial.

143. **(C)** (C) is correct because, under MR 2.1, when rendering advice, a lawyer may refer to moral, economic, social and political factors as well as the law. *See also* EC 7-8 ("Advice of a lawyer need not be confined to purely legal considerations..."). Ultimately, it is up to the client whether to follow the lawyer's advice or not as to the ultimate objective or outcome of the representation. Here, it was up to the Bank to decide whether to exercise the legal right to close the accounts or take Counsel's advice and attempt to increase its good will by contacting the account owners. Mandatory withdrawal is not required simply because a client fails to follow a lawyer's advice as to which of two legal objectives is most just.

144. **(B)** (B) is correct because, under MR 2.4, a lawyer may act as a third-party neutral between clients (after full disclosure of the risks and benefits and consent from both clients). *See also* EC 5-20. However, an attorney who has acted as an intermediary between clients cannot represent one of the clients in a dispute between the clients as to the matter that was the subject of the intermediation.

145. **(A)** Several provisions of the Code and Model Rules apply here. Most importantly, MR 1.9(a) states that "[a] lawyer who has formerly represented a client in a matter shall not thereafter represent another person in the same or a substantially related matter in which that person's interests are materially adverse to the interests of the former client unless the former client gives informed consent, confirmed in writing." *See also* DR 5-105. Therefore, Jennifer probably should not represent Lauren, because the confidential facts and circumstances she knows about would be used to Alison's disadvantage in this new litigation. *See* MR 1.9(c)(1). (C) is wrong because mere notification is not enough; both Alison and Lauren would have to consent to the representation and waive any conflict.

146. **(B)** (B) is correct because, under EC 2-29 and 2-30 and MR 6.2, a lawyer may seek to avoid representation for good cause. An example of "good cause" includes representation of a "client or cause which is so repugnant to the lawyer as to be likely to impair the client-lawyer relationship or the lawyer's ability to represent the client."

Explanatory Answers

147. **(C)** (C) is correct because, under the CJC Canon 2(B), a judge shall not testify voluntarily as a character witness. However, the Commentary to Canon 2(B) states that a judge may testify when properly summoned and offers no immunity which would excuse a judge from testifying if summoned, even if the summons was invited or welcomed by the judge.

148. **(D)** (D) is correct because, under CJC Canon 3(B)(7)(a), a judge may not initiate or consider an *ex parte* communication concerning a pending or impending proceeding unless the communication involves scheduling, administrative matters, or an emergency unrelated to substantive issues. **Exceptions to this rule (thus allowing a judge to initiate or consider ex parte communications of a substantive nature regarding a pending or impending proceeding) exist for discussions with court personnel or a disinterested expert on the law** Canon 3(B)(7)(b). In all cases of an *ex parte* communication, the judge must notify the parties and afford them a reasonable opportunity to respond.

149. **(A)** (A) is correct because, under CJC Canon 5(A)(2), a judge shall resign from judicial office upon becoming a candidate for non-judicial office, either in the primary or in the general election. A person becomes a "candidate" as soon as he or she declares, files or makes a public announcement of candidacy for judicial or non-judicial office.

150. **(B)** (B) is correct because, under CJC Canon 3(E)(1)(b), a judge shall disqualify himself or herself in a proceeding in which the judge's impartiality might reasonably be questioned, including (but not limited to) instances where the judge served as a lawyer in the matter in controversy or *a lawyer with whom the judge previously practiced law* served during the association as a lawyer concerning the matter. The fact that a lawyer with whom the judge previously practiced law has previously represented one of the parties is not sufficient, absent other facts, to disqualify a judge.

ESSAY QUESTIONS

Essay Question 1

Courtney was in prison, doing time for "insider trading." One day he was having lunch with Melbelle, the local so-called "jailhouse attorney." Melbelle had done a habeas petition for Courtney some time back, after Courtney had exhausted his direct appeals and his money. Melbelle handled cases for many of the inmates and seemed to have a surprisingly good mastery of the law.

During this lunch, Courtney bragged to Melbelle, "Sure, they got me for insider trading, but what they don't know is, number 1, where I stashed the money, and number 2, that I have got $250,000 coming from Stan Fillings of Excorp, who was in on the trades from day one."

Melbelle decided to contact the authorities and revealed the preceding information to them. Melbelle testified, over objection, against Courtney and Fillings. Both are convicted. What claims does Courtney have?

Essay Question 2

Wanda walks into Zelda's office. Zelda is a general practice lawyer. Wanda tells Zelda that she has a legal problem having to do with property law. Zelda takes excellent notes and tells Wanda that she will look into the problem further. As a retainer fee, Zelda asks for $500, which Wanda pays.

Wanda calls Zelda five times in the next six months. Zelda returns two of those calls and tells Wanda that she is "looking into the problem."

After six months, Zelda, in fact, looks into the problem. She sees that she has no expertise in the area whatsoever. She spends twelve hours trying to gain the expertise, then realizes she simply does not understand this area of the law.

Zelda then calls up the law firm of Smith & Jones, property law experts. She speaks to Smith, who says his firm would be glad to take the case. Smith offers Zelda $1,000 as a referral fee and 10% of whatever other fees are collected. Zelda accepts.

Zelda then writes Wanda the following: "Dear Wanda: I have spent an additional 12 hours on your case. My hourly fee is $100. Thus, please send a check for $1,200. You will be pleased to know that I have referred your case to the leading firm in this area of the law, Smith & Jones. They will handle the remaining aspects of the case. Sincerely, Zelda."

Is Zelda subject to discipline? Why?

Essay Question 3

Attorney was licensed to practice law in State A. At one point in his career, he had impermissibly commingled funds, for which he was suspended from practice for one year. He resumed practice and became a leading lawyer in State A.

In order to be near his grandchildren and to be active during his retirement, Attorney moves to State B. On his bar application to State B, Attorney purposely omits the fact that he was suspended many years ago.

Attorney's application is pending in State B. Is Attorney subject to discipline?

Essay Question 4

Ronson burst into his attorney Donna's office. He said, "I've just killed a man!"

Donna said, "Okay, Ronson, tell me all about it."

Ronson replied, "We got into a fight about money. I pulled out my gun and shot him." Donna asked whether anyone had seen the fight. Ronson said, "I don't think so." Ronson then asked, "What should I do about the gun?"

Donna replied, "As an officer of the court, I must counsel you to turn it in to the police. If you do not, however, I cannot testify as to what you have told me. If you give the gun to me, I will turn it over to the police."

130

Abruptly Ronson threw the gun on Donna's desk and said, "Get rid of it for me." He ran out.

Donna picked up the gun with a tissue, put it into a brown paper bag and left it in a phone booth. She called the local police and said, "There's a gun in the phone booth at the corner of Main and Williams." She hung up and left. No charges have been brought against Ronson.

Did Donna handle her ethical obligations properly?

Essay Question 5

Talvo is a fine trial attorney and part-time law professor. Because he has gained much notoriety for taking on big-name cases, he is a frequent recipient of offers to appear on television. This afternoon, he accepts one such offer and appears on the "Don't Take It From Anyone" television show.

The format of the show allows the host, "Brim," to ask questions to his guest. A certain part of the show allows studio guests to ask questions and offer comments. During this segment, Dott tells Talvo the following: "I believe I was harassed at my work place. Although I did date my supervisor, after I broke off our relationship, I found other people were being promoted and I was not. My supervisor then suggested we start going out again. I know what he meant by that and I don't like it one bit."

Dott stops and the crowd claps. Brim says, "Well, Talvo, does she have a claim?"

Talvo responds, "Yes, Dott, I believe you have a claim. I suggest you come to my office, if you like, and we can discuss it in more detail."

Is Talvo subject to discipline?

Essay Question 6

Lawyer Lori works for Linton Corporation, a manufacturer of potentially toxic chemicals. Pursuant to company policy, all employees are given an employment contract. One clause of the contract reads, "Linton agrees the responsibility for any work done with reasonable diligence, in the scope of employment by employee, which causes injury to Linton or any of its customers, shall be borne by Linton." Lori signed such a contract.

Discuss the relevant professional standards and whether Lori has done anything wrong.

Essay Question 7

Marty has just graduated from a joint J.D. - M.B.A. program. He is going into solo law practice. Realizing the difficulty of "going it alone," after passing the state's bar, Marty decides to advertise. In order to make his ads work, he utilizes techniques he learned in business school. For one, he purchases twenty 30-second slots which are to air on television during a popular law show.

In the ad, Marty appears well-dressed with six scantily clad high school cheerleader girls. They sing a little tune with Marty's name and telephone number. The ad closes with an old, white-haired man saying, "Marty handled my law case, quickly, inexpensively and fairly." The man was a professional actor who had never used Marty as his lawyer.

Is Marty subject to discipline?

Essay Question 8

Neil gets into a car accident. The accident is obviously the fault of Richard. Neil hires Fred to be his attorney. Neil amasses $3,000 in medical bills.

Neil and Fred agree to a contingency fee agreement whereby Fred will advance all costs and Neil will pay nothing until the settlement is received. If no money is recovered, Neil will not have to pay Fred the court costs. Whatever sum is recovered, Fred is authorized to deduct his court costs from that amount. Neil authorizes Fred to settle for anything over $9,000. The contingency agreement awards Fred 1/3 of the net sum (after costs are deducted).

Fred devotes approximately two hours total to the case. In a phone conversation with the opposing party's insurer, Fred articulately and forcefully underscores the merits in Neil's case. The insurer then calls back and offers a sum of $12,000, which is objectively a generous settlement for Neil's case.

Fred places the entire $12,000 in his client trust account. He then writes Neil the following letter:

> Dear Neil:
>
> I have settled your case pursuant to your directions. You will be pleased to learn I have received $12,000. Of that, no money is owed me for costs in preparation of litigation. Therefore, pursuant to our agreement, my fee is $4,000 and the remaining $8,000 is your settlement. Enclosed is a copy of the settlement by the insurer and a check drawn from my client trust account in the amount of $8,000 made out to you. I will call in a few days.
>
> Sincerely,
> Fred
> Attorney at Law

Fred calls Neil a few days later. Neil says he received the check and asks how much time Fred spent on the case. Fred replies, "Only a few hours – which is not atypical."

After hearing this, Neil becomes very angry and calls Fred a typical "lawyer crook." Fred suggests Neil hire a lawyer if he believes this fee to be unfair. Neil then says, "Oh, keep it. I can't do anything."

Fred writes Neil another letter explaining how contingency contracts work and closes the letter by telling Neil it is his understanding that his $4,000 fee is acceptable; and if not, then Neil should hire another attorney or complain to the state bar.

Fred writes himself a check for $4,000 out of his client trust account.

Has Fred violated any disciplinary rules?

Essay Question 9

Mary and Jeff are undergoing severe financial difficulties. In part due to their financial stress, but also because they have "had it" with married life, they decide to get a divorce.

In order to save money, they go to Fawn, who placed an ad in the newspaper advertising that she will obtain a no-fault divorce for any couple for a $175 fee plus court costs.

Fawn takes the case and interviews both Mary and Jeff separately so as to discover whether there truly is a potential conflict between them. In her talk with Jeff, she discovers he has stashed away $50,000 that Mary does not know about.

In the interview with Mary, Fawn learns that the couple would like to pay Fawn, as her fee, the first month's child support.

What should Fawn do?

Essay Question 10

Nix is defending Olly on a charge of kidnapping in State X. In Nix's research, he finds six cases on point to the key issue of concealment. Three of those cases are from State X. Case 1 is an unpublished opinion. Case 2 is an older case, helpful to Olly. Case 3 is a more recent case, relevant, but likely damaging.

Of the three other cases, one is a federal case and two are from sister states. They are all relevant, but all are damaging.

Nix neglects to discover two State Y cases, right on point, which are helpful.

In briefing his legal arguments to the court, Nix cites only Case 2 and the unpublished opinion.

Is Nix subject to discipline? Why?

Essay Question 11

Tim and Tom are twins arrested on a charge of grand theft auto. They are 18 years old. Their mother, Tawny, enters your law office and asks you to take their case. She states she will pay all attorney fees. Before leaving she adds, "I have only one requirement: I must be told everything about the case and be allowed an active voice."

May you take the case?

Essay Question 12

Cindy is corporate legal counsel for Inlet Corporation, a manufacturer of Cajun cuisine. A purchaser of Inlet hot sauce, Don, is hospitalized for food poisoning. Don sues Inlet.

Ellen, the Vice President of Inlet, and Cindy's supervisor, tells Cindy to "wear down" Don. "Stall him, and, remember, we don't need any bad publicity. Don is not a wealthy man and I hear he's got no stomach for a fight. Make him feel us."

Cindy believes Don has a case and also that she should not "wear Don down." She thus approaches the President of Inlet, Fred. Fred says he is too busy to talk to her. Cindy then writes the board of directors.

Has Cindy subjected herself to discipline? What should she do?

Essay Question 13

Ned and Sheila are attorneys. Ned is representing Norco, an insurer. Sheila is representing Sharon, who was injured in a car accident. Norco is Sharon's insurer. Because this is a "no-fault" jurisdiction, and because the given accident falls within the category of those where it is unnecessary to adjudicate fault, Ned and Sheila quite quickly come to a settlement.

Ned is to prepare the settlement agreement in accordance with the terms to which he and Sheila agreed. However, Ned, instead of writing in $20,000 as the amount of the settlement, writes in $25,000. He mails the agreement to Sheila so that Sharon may sign it.

Sheila notes that Ned has offered $5,000 too much. Can she allow Sharon to sign it anyway?

Essay Question 14

Dove is indigent and is charged with arranging sexual liaisons for public figures with prostitutes. Dove is charged with several vice counts. A competent public defender is appointed as Dove's counsel. However, Dove is displeased with this appointment.

Instead, Dove wants Ghost, a private practitioner, to take his case. Ghost is a first-rate criminal defense attorney. Dove calls Ghost. Because Dove is indigent, Ghost suggests a novel way of paying him: Dove will give Ghost literary and cinematic rights to Dove's story. Dove likes this idea, but suggests they split all profits 50-50. After some haggling, Ghost agrees.

Prosecutor moves to disqualify Ghost on the ground that he may be a witness. In fact, Ghost was a client of Dove's "escort" service.

Is Ghost subject to discipline? Should the court grant Prosecutor's motion to disqualify Ghost?

Essay Question 15

Quint drafts a will for Lort. Quint represented Lort for many years. Lort dies. Lort's son, Mort, wishes to attack the will. Because he knew Quint from his father's association with him, and because he respected Quint, he asks Quint to take the case.

1. Can Quint take the case?

2. Can Quint's partner, Brent, take the case?

3. What should Quint say to Mort?

4. When Mort made an appointment with Quint, he made it through Quint's secretary. The secretary advised Mort that there was a $50 fee for the first consultation. Can Quint bill Mort for this?

Essay Question 16

Foster is a plaintiff's personal injury attorney. He is representing Amster in a suit against Artel. Artel's counsel, Ken, requests production of certain records. Foster digs up these records but instructs his secretary to set the office photocopy machine on a very light setting. The copies are thus extremely difficult to read.

In order to help Amster, Foster contacts Artel. He says, "Sir, you ought to settle. I don't know if you've been sued before or not, but life becomes very difficult."

At trial, Foster calls Artel a "crook," over sustained objection. A large sum is awarded Amster by the jury.

Is Foster subject to discipline? Why?

Essay Question 17

May lives in a jurisdiction where judges are elected. May is an attorney. She believes June, a fellow attorney who is running for the state Supreme Court, will make an excellent judge. She therefore gives $10,000 to June's campaign committee. May, it might be noted, is primarily an appellate attorney who argues many cases yearly at the state Supreme Court.

May and June are also friends. They give each other Christmas presents and work out at the local health club together.

June is elected.

1. Has May behaved improperly?

2. Is May precluded from arguing cases before June?

3. June, after being sworn in, would like to wrap up one big case before the U.S. Supreme Court. Is such permissible?

Essay Question 18

Murry asks his longtime friend, Wharton, a federal District Court judge, to be a reference for Muffy at the bank where he is applying for a loan. Wharton writes out a truthful letter to the bank, using District Court stationery. Wharton is a bit slow in writing the letter because he is presiding over a case where a classical musician is suing his record company, which he complains defrauded him. Muffy is neither an attorney nor business partner of Wharton.

Wharton and Muffy are both members of the local chamber orchestra. Wharton, in fact, is on the Board of Directors of this non-profit organization. Wharton and Muffy, like all members of the orchestra, receive $2,000 yearly as a sort of honorarium.

The loan is granted.

Has Wharton violated any of the norms applicable to judges?

Essay Question 19

No complaints have been filed against Attorney Ella. However, there is a rumor floating around the local bar that Ella is addicted to heroin, and has been for some time.

In this state, the disciplinary committee can look into the conduct of an attorney, under its own motion.

Ella is subpoenaed and is asked if she has ever used controlled substances. She refuses to answer the question on the ground that such answer may tend to incriminate her. On this basis, the committee recommends Ella be suspended. She is.

Was the action of the disciplinary committee proper?

Essay Question 20

Mirage, in her application to the bar of State X, leaves blank a question asking whether she is a member of any group wishing to violently overthrow the state or federal government. She is allowed to take the bar exam, but her file is asterisked, so that if she passes, her reasons for refusing to answer the question will be investigated. Mirage does pass the bar exam.

In her letter of acceptance, the bar states that it will be necessary for her to come before them to explain why she left blank the above query. The letter also states that Mirage should send along her $150 induction fee, which includes $75 as her first year's dues.

Mirage writes the bar back, saying that she refuses to be "harassed" regarding her political views and thus refuses to agree to the "sham proceeding." She writes that she will not appear before the bar. However, she encloses a check for $75. Mirage adds, "I have enclosed a check for $75, my induction fee. I am not obligated to pay the other $75 because it is used to further the communist/fascist activities of the state bar."

Mirage is refused induction into the State X bar. She appeals federally. What will be the result of that appeal?

Essay Question 21

Andrew is a licensed lawyer and a licensed medical doctor. His law license is in State A, while his medical license is in State B.

Andrew opens up a clinic in State B, entitled "Personal Injury Medicine." At the desk is a book, written by Andrew discussing how to file your own personal injury claim. The book is free.

Andrew's procedure is to examine the patient, then interview him/her to ascertain whether there is a legal claim. If Andrew believes there is, he outlines, orally, to the patient how to litigate that claim. Andrew offers to be an expert medical witness.

Andrew charges $500 per visit or, at the patient's discretion, 40% of all settlement money obtained.

Is Andrew subject to discipline in State B?

Is Andrew subject to discipline in State A?

Essay Question 22

Attorney is hired by Client to sue Driver, who damaged Client's automobile. The fee arrangement is 33% contingency. Through no fault of Attorney, Client becomes dissatisfied with Attorney and fires her. Attorney spends 30 hours on the case. Attorney bills Client for $6,000, based on her usual $200 per hour rate. Client refuses to pay. Client's new attorney, Sly, contacts Attorney, who informs Sly that she is owed $6,000 and intends to assert a lien on the papers Client furnished. Sly says to Attorney that a check will be coming.

A check for $6,000 is received, but the cover letter states that the payment is under protest. Before depositing the check, Attorney writes back that the $6,000 is only "partial compensation." Sly and Attorney co-sign an agreement whereby each side preserves its rights. Attorney gives Sly Client's papers.

Client's case is brought to trial, and Client is awarded $25,000,000. Attorney sues Client for one-third of the net, something over $8,000,000. What result? Is Attorney subject to discipline? Is Sly?

Essay Question 23

Leigh is a partner in the large multi-state law firm of James, Ellingson and DeNormluc. John is represented by Leigh at a wrongful termination trial. DeNormluc, a fellow partner, represented West, the opposing party, on a different but related matter some time ago.

John's case comes out well, and John is pleased with Leigh's work. Nevertheless, Leigh decides to see how she can improve. Thus, she invites all of the jurors to an expensive lunch and queries them as to her style.

Is Leigh subject to discipline?

Essay Question 24

Attorney and Earl are partners in a joint business venture. Attorney has served as Earl's attorney for many years. Earl has a reputation as a good businessman. That is why Attorney tried to include Earl in this venture.

In fact, the venture goes poorly. Even worse, Attorney is investigated by a grand jury. Attorney refuses to answer questions about the deal, invoking the attorney-client privilege. Attorney also refuses to give the name of his partner, Earl, on those grounds.

Attorney is found in contempt of court and is suspended by the state bar. Are such results proper?

Essay Question 25

Attorney is representing A, B, and C (all multi-millionaires) in a wrongful termination case against D Corp. D Corp offers Attorney $1,000,000. Attorney evaluates the claim of A, B, and C and then offers A $500,000, B $300,000, and C $200,000. Attorney does not tell A, B, and C that the specifics of the settlement was up to him. They each consent.

Attorney also accepts an additional $100,000 for himself, without telling A, B, or C. From A, B, and C he requests and is paid a 50% contingency fee: $250,000 from A, $150,000 from B, and $100,000 from C.

That year Attorney donates $600,000 (the amount received in the above case) to the local non-profit legal aid society.

Is Attorney subject to discipline?

ESSAY ANSWERS

Essay Answer 1

1. Courtney's best claim is that Melbelle could not testify against him because of the attorney-client evidentiary privilege.

This privilege requires that an attorney cannot reveal in a judicial proceeding confidences received in the attorney-client relationship. *See* DR 4-101(B); MR 1.6. It was given that Melbelle had done legal work for Courtney before and that Courtney may have been talking to him in the scope of this relationship. The problem, of course, is that Melbelle is only a jailhouse attorney, *not* a licensed attorney. Attorney licensing is within the jurisdiction of the locality, and Melbelle is not licensed in this locality. However, the U.S. Supreme Court has held that jailhouse attorneys do have somewhat of a protected status. *See, e.g., Johnson v. Avery*, 393 U.S. 483 (1969). Prisoners must be given law books and lawyers, or must be allowed to use "jailhouse lawyers." Thus, Courtney may make a claim that the sacrosanct attorney-client privilege was contravened by allowing Melbelle to testify. The best answer, however, is likely that the privilege does not attach because, in the last analysis, Melbelle is not a licensed attorney, not an officer of the court. Moreover, a factual argument can be made that the luncheon where Courtney revealed the information was not an attorney-client meeting. It was not in association with or for the purpose of any litigation.

Essay Answer 2

1. Is Zelda subject to discipline for taking Wanda's case when she was not an expert in this area of the law?

The norms of the profession require "reasonable" competence. *See* MR 1.1; DR 6-101(A). At issue here is whether Zelda fell below this standard because she was not then an expert in this area of the law. It is quite clear that an attorney can take a case even though ignorant (or incompetent) in that area of the law *if reasonable preparation will make the attorney competent in that area. See* MR 1.1 Comment [4]. Thus, Zelda is *not* subject to discipline for taking Wanda's case.

2. Was the $500 retainer fee excessive?

Excessive fees subject an attorney to discipline. *See* DR 2-106(A); MR 1.5(a). However, it is unlikely that $500 is excessive, particularly in light of the given fact that this was a complex case. *See* DR 2-106(B)(1); MR 1.5(a)(1).

3. Is Zelda subject to discipline for not returning three of Wanda's calls and for not researching the case for six months?

DR 6-101(A)(3) states that a lawyer is subject to discipline for *neglecting* a legal matter. See also MR 1.3; MR 1.3 Comment [3]; MR 1.4. In the case at hand, we have a classic example of neglect. Not returning calls and just letting the case gather dust for six months definitely subjects Zelda to discipline. Although the facts are unclear as to whether Wanda was damaged by this neglect, there does *not* have to be damage to a client for the attorney to be disciplined.

4. Is Zelda subject to discipline for engaging the firm of Smith & Jones without Wanda's consent?

It was improper for Zelda to assign the case to Smith & Jones without Wanda's informed consent. *See* DR 2-107(A); MR 1.5(e). Because the attorney-client relationship is fiduciary in nature, attorneys cannot "trade off" without fully apprising the client of the situation. Zelda did not apprise Wanda of her intention to contact Smith & Jones. It may be argued that her after-the-fact notification to Wanda was enough. It was not. Moreover, Zelda's letter to Wanda gave Wanda no choice in who would represent her. Wanda was simply *told* that Smith & Jones would be handling the case. This is clearly improper. Wanda had no opportunity to object and enter into this decision.

5. Is Zelda subject to discipline for billing Wanda $1,200 and for keeping the $500 retainer?

Fees must be reasonable. *See* MR 1.5; DR 2-106. As a general rule, attorneys should not bill clients for the time they spend that merely elevates them to the level of competence. Because the facts state that Zelda spent the 12 hours only trying to get up to speed, it is likely improper for Zelda to have billed Wanda $1,200. She is subject to discipline for that bill. As for the $500, this is a more difficult issue. Zelda spent some time with Wanda taking down the facts of the case, returning the phone calls, and looking into options. Therefore, at least some of the $500 may be retained by Zelda. The facts are unclear as to just how much. Zelda is not necessarily subject to discipline for keeping the retainer.

6. Is Zelda subject to discipline for accepting the $1,000 referral fee and 10% of whatever else is received?

The CPR position is that a fee split must be *proportional* to the work actually done, that the total fee be reasonable and that the client consent to the split. *See* DR 2-107(A); MR 1.5(e). In the case at hand, the split was disproportional, the total fee was likely unreasonable, and as mentioned previously, there was no client consent. Zelda is subject to discipline for this as well. Even under the MR position, because Wanda was not apprised of the split and because there was likely not *equal* responsibility for the case, there was a clear ethical violation. *See* MR 1.5(e); MR 7.2(b) ("A lawyer shall not give anything of value to a person for recommending the lawyer's services..."); DR 2-107(A); DR 2-103(B).

7. Although the call of this question asked only for Zelda's disciplinary rule violations, those of Smith & Jones are also somewhat relevant. DR 1-103(B) and MR 8.3(a) require attorneys to turn in other delinquent attorneys.

Smith violated several of the same norms: unconsented-to fee-split, disproportional fee split, referral fee. Further, as a general rule, partners in a law firm are responsible for the work of their co-partners. If Jones had knowledge of Smith's practice, he, too, is subject to discipline.

Essay Answer 3

1. The commingling of client funds is a "classic" error. *See* DR 9-102(A); MR 1.15(a). It is thus of no surprise whatsoever that Attorney was suspended for this practice.

2. At issue in this fact pattern, however, is not this prior commingling of funds, but Attorney's wilful omission of this prior suspension on his new bar application to State B. Does this subject Attorney to discipline?

In fact, it clearly does subject Attorney to discipline. *See* DR 1-101(A); MR 8.1(a) and (b). These rules mandate that an attorney be forthright on his bar application. Violation of these rules will clearly subject Attorney to discipline. The facts establish that his was a wilful violation, so Attorney will be disciplined — be it by suspension, disbarment, public or private reprimand. (Incidentally, because of his stellar legal career, the punishment will likely be no worse than a suspension.)

3. The next issue is whether State A, State B or both states can discipline Attorney for this malfeasance.

Since it is B's bar application, and since DR 1-101 and MR 8.1 are right on point, there is no doubt whatsoever that State B can (and will) discipline Attorney. The more interesting issue is whether State A can discipline Attorney for acts done outside its jurisdiction. MR 8.5(a) is right on point. *See also* DR 1-102. It essentially states that an attorney is subject to discipline for doing conduct involving dishonesty anywhere. Because Attorney made a "misrepresentation" on State B's bar application, he has violated DR 1-102(A)(4), DR 1-101(A), MR 8.1(a) and (b), and MR 8.4(c). Thus, he is subject to discipline in State A, as well. Incidentally, State B has a duty to disclose Attorney's fraud to State A. *See* DR 1-103; MR 8.3(a).

Essay Answer 4

1. Should Donna have told the police that Ronson did the killing?

The attorney-client privilege prohibits an attorney from revealing client confidences gained in the attorney-client relationship. *See* DR 4-101(B); MR 1.6(a). Because Ronson's confession to Donna was clearly a confidential communication, and because he went to see her *as his attorney*, there is no doubt that Donna was correct in *not* revealing the confession to the police.

2. Was Donna's counsel to Ronson ethical?

Donna told Ronson to turn in the gun. She also told him that, if he gave it to her, she could not keep it; she would have to turn it in. Again, Donna's advice was quite professional. Only when there is a future danger of reasonably certain death or substantial bodily harm may the lawyer reveal the client's confidences. *See* DR 4-101(c)(3); MR 1.6(b)(1). These factors did not seem to be present here.

3. Was Donna's leaving the gun in a phone booth, with a tip to the police about where it was — but not whose it was — proper?

This issue is the most problematic. As set out above, certainly communications to the attorney are privileged, but tangible evidence is not. Thus, as Donna correctly told Ronson, if he gave her the gun, she could not keep it. She did not. However, at issue is whether her retention of the fingerprints and anonymous tip to the police were enough. This issue is by no means clear-cut. However, by accepting Ronson's gun, she *did interfere* with the prosecution's chance of ever finding the gun on Ronson. In this sense, she did alter or change the evidence. Thus, her better behavior would have been to simply give the gun to the police, saying only that Ronson gave it to her. Nevertheless, because she did go part way to fulfilling her obligation to opposing counsel (the prosecution), it is unlikely severe discipline would result from this "murky" case. *Cf.* MR 3.4(a); DR 7-109(A); EC 7-6; EC 7-27.

Essay Answer 5

1. Talvo's appearance on the talk show is acceptable. There is a strong policy favoring the public's right to know about the law. CPR Preamble; *Bates v. Arizona State Bar*, 433 U.S. 350 (1977).

    However, this does not give the lawyer a "carte blanche" to be self-laudatory, nor does it allow the lawyer to use this platform to try to attract clients. *See* EC 2-4; MR 7.3.

2. The issue here is whether Talvo solicited Dott's business.

    Advertising is permissible, provided it is not misleading. *See* MR 7.1 and 7.2; DR 2-101. However, in-person solicitation is generally impermissible. *See* MR 7.3; DR 2-103. The difference between advertising and solicitation is as follows: Solicitation is attorney-initiated contact with a specific person who is not the attorney's client. Advertising is simply letting the general public know of the availability and price of an attorney's services. Although an argument can be made that it was Dott who initiated the conversation with Talvo, this argument should fail. More truly, Talvo initiated it by offering his own availability on the TV show to answer the audience's questions. Talvo might argue that his in-person solicitation here was protected free speech. *Cf. In Re Primus*, 436 U.S. 412 (1978). However, since Talvo would likely receive a fee from Dott if she went to his office, this is not the kind of attorney solicitation permitted. Talvo was embarked upon a money-making proposition, and his conduct is *not* protected. Were Dott to have been indigent and Talvo to have foregone any fee, he might then fall under the exception. Note that *written* solicitation is also acceptable, provided it is not misleading. *See Shapero v. Kentucky Bar Association*, 108 S. Ct. 1916 (1988).

3. Talvo, as a general proposition, should refrain from giving panaceas over the air. *See* EC 2-5. Although no facts clearly indicate Talvo did this, he was leading in that direction.

4. In conclusion, Talvo would be subject to discipline for his in-person solicitation.

Essay Answer 6

1. An in-house staff attorney for a corporation is still bound by the ethical norms of the profession. Thus, here Lori is bound. The main issue in this case is whether Lori could sign such a contract that limits all employees' liabilities.

    DR 6-102(A) and MR 1.8(h)(1) could not be more clear: lawyers *must* not try to limit their own liability against malpractice. This is precisely what this contract from Linton did. Although we may infer that Linton included this clause because of the nature of its business (i.e., there is a great potential for lawsuits when manufacturing toxic substances and as a result of this, good employees might be afraid to work for such a corporation absent the corporation's assurance that it would accept all responsibilities), nevertheless Lori should not have signed this contract. Lori, even though a corporate attorney, is bound by the Rules and the Code. Limiting malpractice liability is prohibited.

2. There is a minor issue here as well. Not only did Lori disobey DR 6-102(A) and MR 1.8(h)(1), but in not recognizing the issue, she was likely incompetent. See MR 1.1; DR 6-101(A). Incompetence is another ethical violation.

3. This question brings to the forefront the difficult area of staff attorney norms. As a general rule, in-house counsel is *not* given the same protection as other employees. The employer's right to discharge, etc. are balanced in the direction of the client (the corporation) far more than for the typical non-attorney worker. The reason for this is that the attorney fills a very special *fiduciary* relationship, and is therefore bound by this higher standard.

Essay Answer 7

1. The issue in this case is whether Marty's advertisement violated the rules of the profession.

The American Bar Association and the states have seesawed quite a bit on the issue of lawyer advertising. After *Bates v. State Bar of Arizona,* 433 U.S. 350 (1970), it became quite clear that there could not be an outright ban on lawyer advertising. Moreover, as *Bates* and other cases have made clear, attorney advertising is protected "commercial speech." It cannot be prevented unless there is a substantial government interest and the limitation is no greater than necessary. *See, eg., In Re R.M.J,* 455 U.S. 191 (1982). Nevertheless, the state of the law is not that "anything goes." The MRPC require that attorney ads not be "misleading." *See* MR 7.1; 7.2; *see also* DR 2-101(A). In the case at hand, we can easily answer the threshold issue of whether it is permissible for Marty to do 30 TV ads. It clearly is. The next issue is whether it was acceptable to use six cheerleaders as a marketing technique. Using the standard of the Model Rules, in no way was such use untruthful or misleading. Thus, on its face, it would seem to be permissible. However, a counter-argument can be made. That is, such a "sex sells" technique reduces the dignity of the legal profession and therefore undermines the respect necessary for the profession to effectively function. Several lower courts have taken this approach and dicta in Supreme Court opinions also supports this argument. Nevertheless, the better conclusion is that the mere using of the girls does not subject Marty to discipline.

The next sub-issue is whether Marty is subject to discipline for having the girls sing a lyric. Again, the key inquiry is whether the lyric was misleading. Since it only stated his telephone number and name, it was not. However, it can be counter-argued that Marty's ad violated the requirements of professional dignity. The key issue is whether the public is better-informed by this ad. Certainly, some restrictions *can be* made by the state bar. *Cf. Zauderer v. Disciplinary Counsel of Ohio,* 471 U.S. 626 (1985). In fact, some states have required attorney ads to be *only* informational, and have precluded the use of this kind of lyric. Nevertheless, on balance, although this is a close call, we can conclude that Marty is not subject to discipline for using a lyric.

The final sub-issue is whether the "testimonial" by the actor subjects Marty to discipline. The use of testimonials is itself suspect. They tend to mislead, and many states prohibit their use. Like lyrics, however, the best rule is that such do *not* subject an attorney to discipline unless they are misleading. Thus, the issue is whether this testimonial is misleading or untruthful. Because it was a fake, and the actor was not a former client of Marty, this testimonial is clearly misleading. Because the testimonial was misleading, Marty *is* subject to discipline.

Under all of the circumstances, this discipline seems warranted. In sum, not only did Marty clearly contravene a required norm, but he also "walked the line" several times.

Essay Answer 8

1. Fred *should* have committed the initial contingency fee agreement to writing, but such omission does *not* subject him to discipline under the CPR. *See* EC 2-19. However, the MRPC requires contingency fee contracts be committed to writing and signed by the client. MR 1.5(c). Thus, this answer depends on what rule the jurisdiction follows.

2. The contingency contract itself is acceptable.

   A contingency fee of one-third of any settlement or recovery to the attorney is somewhat typical. Contingency fees are customarily higher than ordinary fees because the attorney is required to bear risk of loss and is required to advance the costs. *Cf.* DR 2-106; MR 1.5(a). Fred's advancing of court costs, with Neil being ultimately responsible to repay these, is also fully acceptable. *See* DR 5-103(B); *cf.* MR 1.8(e).

3. Fred's settling the claim for $12,000 after just two hours work is acceptable.

   Attorneys must be diligent. *See* MR 1.1; MR 1.3; DR 6-101(A); DR 7-101(A). The fact that this case took so little time does not disprove Fred's competence. In fact, the facts state that Fred did a good job and received a greater-than-average settlement. As a rule of thumb, with such a case, the pre-trial settlement is three times the medical expenses. Fred therefore did do well for Neil. Attorneys should not settle cases absent client approval. *See* MR 1.2(a); EC 7-7. Here, Neil gave Fred the okay to settle for anything over $9,000. Thus, Fred's settling the case was proper.

4. Fred's placing the $12,000 into his client trust account and then paying Neil the uncontested amount was also fully proper. *See* DR 9-102(A); MR 1.15.

   Fred's immediate payment to Neil of the $8,000 (uncontested amount) was proper. Further, his giving to Neil an accounting of the method of fee calculation was also fully proper.

5. Although it is clear that Neil was upset by the fee, nevertheless it appears he consented. Therefore, Fred's writing himself a $4,000 check was acceptable.

   This is particularly true because Fred told Neil he should seek another lawyer's advice — or complain to the bar — if he was unhappy. This procedure is recommended. *See* MR 1.15 Comment.

6. Fred is *not* subject to discipline.

Essay Answer 9

1. As a threshold issue, Fawn's advertisement was acceptable, since it was not misleading. *See* MR 7.1.

2. Can Fawn represent both sides in a no-fault divorce?

Particularly when there is a potential for litigation, an attorney should avoid representing multiple clients. *See* EC 5-15; DR 5-105(B); MR 1.7(a). In this situation, taking opposing sides in a single case is highly risky. At the very least, Fawn *must* tell both Mary and Jeff of the potential dangers in this multiple representation and must obtain informed consent if they are to proceed. Nevertheless, such an arrangement is unwise.

3. Fawn must withdraw from the case after learning that Jeff has unrevealed assets.

Once Fawn learns that Jeff has $50,000 Mary does not know about, she must withdraw. Her representation of Mary obviously would *not* be zealous if Fawn were to keep Jeff's secret from her. *See* DR 7-101; MR 1.3. Moreover, Fawn cannot reveal to Mary Jeff's *confidential* communication. *See* DR 4-101(B); MR 1.6(a). Thus, Fawn is in a no-win situation. She must keep Jeff's confidence *and* must withdraw from representing either Jeff or Mary. She cannot represent *either* party without compromising either the zealous representation or confidentiality requirements of the ethical guidelines.

4. As a remaining threshold issue, even if Fawn could stay on (which she cannot), the one-month child support fee is improper.

This fee proposal is essentially a contingency fee. Contingency fees are improper in domestic relations cases. *See* MR 1.5(d); EC 2-20.

5. Fawn should withdraw from her representation of Mary and Jeff. Were she to continue, she would be subject to discipline.

Essay Answer 10

1. An attorney owes a duty of candor to the tribunal. The first issue here is Nix's purposeful non-citation of Case 3 and of the three cases outside State X.

Although an attorney is free to distinguish contrary cases, he *must* cite to the court cases directly on point *in that jurisdiction*. *See* EC 7-23; DR 7-106(B)(1); MR 3.3(a)(2). The facts state that Case 3 was a State X case and relevant to the case. The facts also state that Nix was aware of this case. Under the prevailing standards, that ends the inquiry on Nix's obligations. An attorney simply *must* make known to the court all in-state cases on point. Although an attorney owes a duty to his client to zealously defend him (DR 7-101 and MR 1.3), the attorney also owes certain duties to the court. Attorneys, as officers of the court, can never defraud the tribunal. Further, all relevant *law* must be cited, even if to do so will hurt the client's case. Therefore, the attorney is subject to discipline for not making the court aware of Case 3. In passing, it should be noted that this kind of infraction very rarely leads to *actual* discipline, although perhaps it should.

Nix had *no* obligation to make reference to the three relevant cases outside of State X. Although a court would find highly useful other jurisdictions' cases which are similar, an attorney does not have to cite them. The ethical rules *mandate* citation only to in-state (in jurisdiction) cases. Nix is not subject to discipline for omitting these three. However, as a practical matter, most often courts discover relevant authority, even if an attorney does not cite to it. Thus, aside from the disciplinary gamble an attorney takes by not citing, there is likely a strategic error as well. The best strategy is to cite "contrary" cases, then *distinguish* them. This is fully acceptable. EC 7-23; MR 3.3 Comment [4]. When the attorney completely ignores contrary cases, this is essentially *conceding* the opposing counsel's point.

2. Was Nix's citation to an unpublished opinion improper?

Most jurisdictions make it clear that unpublished opinions are not given precedential weight. Many jurisdictions also state that such opinions should not be cited. If State X is one such jurisdiction, then Nix's citing of Case 1 was improper.

3. Is attorney incompetence a ground for discipline?

Here it is given that Nix missed two cases on point. Incompetence can subject an attorney to discipline. *See* DR 6-101(A)(2); MR 1.1. Again, however, perhaps improperly, attorneys are generally not disciplined for missing cases on point, although technically they could be. Note, of course, that Nix's failure to find the cases may be malpractice.

4. Thus, Nix is subject to discipline for not citing Case 3 and for failing to find and cite the two cases in State X on point. He is likely subject to discipline for citing an unpublished opinion. However, it is unlikely Nix will actually be disciplined for these infractions.

Essay Answer 11

1. There are several professional problems in this case. The first is whether it is permissible to represent multiple clients.

As a general rule, it is not wise to represent multiple defendants in a criminal trial. *See* DR 5-105(B); MR 1.7(a). The potential problem is that the interests of the multiple defendants may differ. What if here it was Tim who instigated the theft? What if Tom used duress on Tim? What if the prosecutor wants to strike a deal with one co-defendant and not the other? In all of these circumstances, the attorney cannot serve both clients well. The interests of one may be sacrificed to those of the other. However, if the clients give informed consent and if the attorney reasonably believes there is no potential for conflict, then he may take the case.

2. Of course, the attorney would not accept the case without the *clients'* approval. Here, it was Tawny, not Tim and Tom, who requested legal aid. Tim and Tom would have to approve the representation, which, as of yet, they have not done. *Cf.* DR 7-101(A)(1); MR 1.2(a).

3. Is it permissible for a third party to pay the legal fees?

It is permissible for a third party to pay the legal fees. *See* DR 5-107(A)(1); MR 1.8(f). However, the clients must consent to such an arrangement after being apprised of the situation. More importantly, the third party *cannot* be allowed to influence the handling of the case. Tawny's condition that she be allowed "an active voice" is clearly in conflict with the professional rules. The attorney should explain to Tawny that the attorney-client relationship is personal and that Tawny cannot have an active role unless Tim and Tom give their informed consent.

4. Moreover, Tawny's condition that she be told "everything about the case" is highly problematic. Aside from the problem of interference by a third party just discussed, there is another major problem.

Such arrangement would cause the attorney to breach the *confidentiality* required between attorney and client. *See* DR 4-101(B); MR 1.6. This requirement is, *per se,* improper.

Essay Answer 12

1. Cindy should not harass Don.

   When Cindy's supervisor, Ellen, told Cindy to wear down Don, she was basically telling Cindy to abuse the legal process. Such abuse can take the form of intimidation, excessive discovery orders, etc. As an attorney, Cindy would potentially be subject to discipline if she were to follow Ellen's orders. *See* DR 7-102(A)(1); MR 3.4(d); MR 3.1; MR 4.4. However, because there is some ambiguity in Ellen's instructions, Cindy likely does not have to withdraw. Were Ellen to unequivocally demand Cindy harass Don, then Cindy would *have* to withdraw from the case, or be subject to discipline. *See* DR 2-109(A); DR 2-110(B)(1); MR 1.16(a); MR 1.4(a)(5). In such a case, Cindy's staying on the case would essentially be assisting a client in fraudulent/illegal conduct. *See* DR 7-102(A); MR 1.2(d). Moreover, in this situation, an attorney who harassed another would also be subject to discipline on the ground that such conduct involved moral turpitude. *See* DR 1-102; MR 8.4(a).

2. If, however, Ellen's orders are merely to put up a good fight, then Cindy may and should follow them. Provided that a reasonable argument can be made for a client's case, an attorney is not subject to discipline for pursuing it — even if the attorney disagrees with the course of action. The attorney should seek all lawful objectives of his client. *See* DR 7-101(A)(1); MR 1.2(a). If, because of personal repugnance to the case, the attorney is unable to so proceed, then the attorney should withdraw. *See* MR 1.16(b)(4); EC 2-30; *cf.* EC 2-29.

3. Should Cindy have gone over Ellen's head?

   The facts are unclear about whether Cindy voiced her disagreements to Ellen. If she did not, then she is possibly subject to discipline. An attorney should "minimize disruption" of the corporation. *See* MR 1.13(b). By going over Ellen's head unnecessarily, Cindy did not do so. However, when an attorney acts in good conscience, as here, and also where the facts are ambiguous, it is extremely unlikely that she is subject to discipline for approaching the President and the board of directors. Moreover, a corporate counsel represents the corporation as a whole, *not* any one individual. *See* MR 1.13(a); EC 5-18. Thus, Cindy represents not Ellen, but Inlet. Therefore, if she believes Ellen is asking her to pursue an unlawful course of legal conduct, it is fully proper for her to climb the corporate ladder, as she did. *See* MR 1.13(b). Note, however, that Cindy's preferred course is to explain her point of view to Ellen, ask Ellen to reconsider, suggest that another outside legal opinion be obtained, and then, finally, as a last resort, climb the corporate ladder. *See* MR 1.13(b).

4. Here, although it appears Cindy did not follow the preferred procedure, nevertheless her deviation was not so significant as to subject her to discipline.

Essay Answer 13

1. The difficulty in this case centers around Sheila's possible conflicting duties to her client and those she owes to her fellow lawyers.

   An attorney owes a duty of "zealous" representation to her client. *See* DR 7-101; MR 1.3. However, an attorney also owes a duty of honesty to fellow attorneys. *Cf.* MR 8.4(c). In the case at hand, especially since the case was settled, were Sheila to allow Sharon to sign the erroneous settlement, this would be a fraud. It was a clear error. Further, it was not a legal or factual misunderstanding. It was just a "typo." Sheila must correct this prior to signing. Moreover, were Sheila to allow the error she caught to go uncorrected, her conduct would likely be *criminal*. One can commit a crime by *omission* when there is a duty to act. This crime might be a form of theft. As such, were Sheila not to correct it, she would clearly be subject to discipline. *See* DR 1-102(A)(3); MR 8.4(b).

2. The next issue is *how* Sheila should correct the problem.

Does Sheila have to consult with Sharon prior to telling Ned of the error? Although Sheila may want to tell Sharon because Sharon apparently agreed to the $20,000, Sharon does not have to be consulted. There is certainly no confidentiality requirement attached to this information. *Cf.* MR 1.6. Sheila should tell Ned of the error and suggest he send another corrected copy for signature. *Cf.* MR 4. 1(b); EC 9-2.

Essay Answer 14

1. Ghost is subject to discipline for his fee contract with Dove.

An attorney is clearly not permitted to accept as his fee literary and cinematic rights regarding the subject matter of the litigation. *See* DR 5-104(B); MR 1.8(d). The problem here is that there is an impermissible conflict of interest; Ghost's and Dove's interests now may be divergent. *See* EC 5-4. For example, Ghost would like a "flashy" trial, with many big-name people involved. Moreover, it may even help Ghost's interests if Dove is found guilty. The more revelations in the trial, the more likely it is that Ghost will obtain a publisher/producer for the book/movie. The spicier the trial, the more public interest there will be in the lawyer's account of it. The problem with this is that, *legally* speaking, Dove's best defense strategy may be to plea bargain, or just to let the prosecution try to meet its heavy burden of proof (beyond a reasonable doubt). The best legal strategy may therefore be to run a *dull* trial. This conflict is why this kind of fee arrangement is forbidden. *See* EC 5-4. It could be argued that the client's interest in choosing the attorney of his choice outweighs the considerations in the above ethical rules. This position is bolstered by the fact that it is given Ghost is a "first-rate" attorney. However, because the U.S. Supreme Court has held that an indigent defendant only has a right to *competent* counsel, *not* to the right to counsel of his choice, the above argument will fail. *See Morris v. Slappy*, 461 U.S. 1 (1983). The best conclusion is that Ghost is subject to discipline for arranging this fee agreement.

2. Moreover, Ghost may also be subject to discipline for accepting a case in which he is perhaps *criminally* involved.

The facts stipulated that Ghost was a client of Dove's likely unlawful escort service. Since there is a reasonable possibility that Ghost will be a witness, he should not have taken the case in the first place. The reasons for this are twofold: First, again, his interests may conflict with those of Dove. *See* DR 5-101; MR 1.7(a)(2). Second, when a lawyer is to be a witness in a case, on a likely-to-be contested issue, he should not take the case. *See* DR 5-101(B); MR 3.7(a). The reasons for precluding lawyers who are to be witnesses are that such a lawyer may compromise his client's interests to his own and that the jury may perceive this lawyer not to be a professional advocate, but instead, just a party. In such a circumstance, the lawyer loses credibility and may injure the client's case.

3. Ghost, if involved in illegal prostitution, may also be subject to discipline for conduct involving moral turpitude. *See* DR 1-102(A)(3); MR 8.4(b). However, unless Ghost were a co-proprietor, it is unlikely he would be disciplined for this alone.

4. Prosecutor's motion to disqualify Ghost should be granted.

In light of Ghost's involvement with Dove's escort service and the reasonable possibility that he is to be a witness, Prosecutor's motion to disqualify should be granted. *See* DR 5-101; DR 5-102; MR 3.7. Allowing Ghost to defend Dove could make a "farce and mockery" of justice.

Essay Answer 15

1. Quint cannot take the case.

There is an impermissible conflict of interest between two actual or potential clients: Lort (now deceased) and Mort. Because Quint drafted the will which Mort wants to attack, it is totally inappropriate for him to attack that will. Were he to do so, he would be disloyal to his client Lort and his wishes. *See* DR 5-105(B); MR 1.9(a). Although the professional standards allow for client waiver, because Lort is dead, there can be no informed waiver here. *See* DR 5-105(B) and (C); MR 1.9(a).

2. Quint's partner Brent cannot represent Mort.

The general rule is that if one attorney in a firm is disqualified, all attorneys in that firm are, unless the prohibition is based on a personal interest of the prohibited lawyer and does not present a significant risk of materially limiting the representation of the client by the remaining lawyer in the firm. *See* DR 5-105(D); MR 1.10(a). The case at hand fits squarely within the general prohibition. Brent is Quint's partner. He is therefore disqualified. The reasons for this rule are twofold. First, partners generally have access to each other's files and often talk to each other regarding their cases. Second, even if they do not talk or see the confidential files, there is an appearance of impropriety. It *looks* like they are. Under the Model Code, the appearance of impropriety should also be avoided. *See* DR 9-101. (Note that the Model Rules do not specifically deal with the appearance of impropriety).

3. Quint should explain to Mort that he drafted his father's will. Therefore, by the rules of the profession, he cannot attack that will for an adverse party. He should say this quickly, and insure that Mort not tell him things which are privileged. *Cf.* MR 1.6; DR 4-101(B). Quint must make it clear to Mort that he is not and cannot be his lawyer.

4. Quint should not charge Mort for the consultation.

The touchstone for attorney fees is reasonableness. *See* DR 2-106(A); MR 1.5(a). Although a $50 consultation fee is reasonable, in the case at hand it is not. This consultation was solely to tell Mort that Quint could not be his lawyer. Thus, no "legal services" were given. It follows, if no services are given, no fee should be charged. It might be argued that Mort in fact received some legal advice, i.e., that lawyers can't be involved in both sides of the same case. However, this begs the question. Were Quint to take money, there would be, at the least, an appearance of impropriety. *See* DR 9-101.

Essay Answer 16

1. Foster is subject to discipline for several instances of unprofessional conduct. Although an attorney should zealously represent his client, he must do so within the boundaries of the law. DR 7-101; MR 1.3. Foster went outside those boundaries.

It was improper for Foster to make Ken's work more difficult by purposely sending bad photocopies. *See* DR 7-102(A)(1); MR 3.4(d). Essentially, Foster played a "dirty trick" on Ken. Attorneys, as officers of the court, are forbidden from treating the tribunal or other attorneys in an unfair or discourteous manner. Although Foster's ploy might have slightly helped Amster, this is not the kind of attorney behavior which is acceptable. Foster is subject to discipline — and should be disciplined — for this behavior. In passing, and incidental to the call of this question, were Ken aware of Foster's dirty trick, he should let the state bar know of Foster's unprofessional conduct. *See* DR 1-103; MR 8.3(a).

It was impermissible for Foster to directly contact Artel because Artel was a represented party and no facts indicate Artel's lawyer, Ken, consented to opposing counsel's contact. *See* DR 7-104(A); MR 4.2.

The facts also indicate that Foster tried to intimidate Artel into settling the case out of court. Laypersons are generally susceptible to intimidation from lawyers. It is for this reason that the above-cited ethical rules preclude lawyer contact with represented clients. Foster deviated from this requirement. Moreover, not only did Foster contact Artel impermissibly, but this contact took the form of a near extortion. Foster is therefore subject to discipline on an additional count, i.e., engaging in "conduct involving moral turpitude." *See* DR 1-102(A)(3); MR 8.4(b).

Although the facts are again sparse, it seems that Foster's calling Artel a crook also subjects him to discipline. Attorneys are precluded from harassing opposing parties. *See* DR 7-102(A)(1); MR 3.4(e); MR 4.4(a). Calling a man a crook is such a harassment. It doesn't matter that Foster did well for his client, Amster. "Success" at trial is but one of many factors in judging whether an attorney is subject to discipline.

Essay Answer 17

In states with elected judiciaries, lawyers are free to donate money to their chosen candidate's campaign. *See* DR 7-110(A). Such donation, however, must be to a properly constituted campaign committee — not to the judge herself. *See* CJC Canon 5(C)(2). The facts here indicate May did give to the campaign committee — so she did nothing wrong. As a general rule, it is *lawyers* who are in the best position to evaluate the fitness of judges. *See* EC 8-6. Thus, there is simply nothing wrong with May's (who believes June will "make an excellent judge") donation of money to June's campaign. In fact, this is exemplary behavior. As for May's friendship with June, the exchange of presents, the fact that they exercise together, and the inchoate potential of arguing cases before the newly elected judge do not consitute any wrongdoing whatsoever. There is no implication of trying to "buy" influence. Were there, there would be a problem with dishonesty. *See* DR 1-102; MR 8.4.

2. The phrasing of question 2 is somewhat misleading. Read literally, of course, May can argue cases before June. May, an attorney, is not required to disqualify herself from a case just because she knows the judge. Even were the relationship intimate, it is not *May's* responsibility to recuse herself. Rather, the responsibility is *June's*. *Cf.* DR 5-101(A).

As discussed above, there is no implication that the $10,000 campaign contribution was anything but proper. Therefore, it does not require June to recuse herself. However, there are two other factors which must be discussed. At issue is whether exercising together requires June to recuse herself from cases in which May argues. CJC Canon 3(E)(1) and 3(E)(1)(a) counsel judges to avoid activities which may give rise to a conflict of interest. A judge, like any lawyer, should avoid the appearance of impropriety. However, judges are not required to be recluses. Judges should not be required to give up all of their lawyer friends. Thus, if June is not influenced by her friendship with May, there is no reason for her to recuse herself from hearing cases just because they work out together.

June's giving and receiving Christmas presents from May is more problematic. Whenever there is an exchange of a thing of value, influence is more easily — and more *tangibly* — questionable. Although the common sense reading of the facts does not indicate their gifts to be of value, nevertheless a disinterested party's suspicions could be aroused. Certainly were the gifts June received worth over $150, she would *have* to report them. *See* CJC Canon 4(D)(5)(h). The best course of conduct for June is to discontinue this practice of gift exchange. Nevertheless, were she to continue, although a somewhat close call, she probably would not have to recuse herself. *See* CJC Canon 3(E). Christmas gifts could probably be characterized as "ordinary social hospitality," and would probably be acceptable. CJC Canon 4(D)(5)(c). *Cf. Li1jeberg v. Health Services Acquisition Corp.*, 108 S. Ct. 2194 (1988).

3. After June is sworn in, she is *not* permitted to practice law, period. *See* CJC Canon 4(G). Wrapping up one big case, especially before the U.S. Supreme Court, is very tempting. However, the rules could not be more clear. After accession to the bench, law practice is precluded. Finishing a case is obviously law practice.

The reason for the rule is that for a judge to practice law appears improper — from many angles. First, the opposing party will feel at a disadvantage. That is, he/she might believe the court will favor the judge-advocate's side. Second, when such a judge returns to her bench, it may appear that instead of an impartial arbiter, she is just another advocate. These conclusions, even if factually incorrect, will damage the *appearance* of justice and are therefore to be avoided.

Essay Answer 18

As a federal judge, Wharton should comply with both the spirit and the letter of the American Bar Association Code of Judicial Conduct, (CJC). It appears from these facts that Wharton has behaved acceptably except for his use of the stationery. The several instances where his conduct may be questioned will be discussed chronologically.

Wharton's letter of reference for Muffy was acceptable. *See* Commentary to CJC Canon 2(B). However, Wharton should not have used the District Court stationery because it may give the impression that the letter is *official* business. *See* Commentary to CJC Canon 2(B). Wharton had no financial stake in Muffy's receiving the loan. He was not paid to write it. Muffy was not a business partner or even a lawyer. Certainly, Wharton should have stated in the letter that the letter was not official business of the court, and that he was writing the bank as a private individual. *Id.* However, the facts are silent on the actual substance of the letter. The mere fact that Muffy and Wharton are both on the board and play for the local chamber orchestra reinforces the conclusion that Wharton wrote for Muffy simply because he knew and respected him.

Wharton's membership on the board of directors of the orchestra is itself proper, aside from his relationship with Muffy. A judge does not have to ostracize himself from society. He may "serve as an officer, director...of...a civic organization not conducted for profit." *See* CJC Canon 4(C)(3). This is what Wharton was doing.

It may be argued that his being a *director* is improper. However, provided that he does not personally solicit funds for the organization and provided that this organization is not litigious, such position is proper. *See* CJC Canon 4(C)(3) and 4(C)(3)(a)(i) and (ii). A different rule would apply were this organization a "for-profit" type business. Further, a chamber orchestra hardly seems litigious.

Wharton is permitted to accept $2,000 in compensation from the chamber orchestra, provided that he reports it. Judges can be compensated for non-judicial activities provided that such activities do not interfere with their judicial duties. *See* CJC Canon 4(H)(1). Another factor regarding whether a judge can be paid for non-law activities is whether such reflects adversely on his appearance of impartiality. *Id.* Finally, Wharton is paid the same amount as the other directors, a fact which supports the acceptability of the honorarium. CJC Canon 4(H)(1)(a). Certainly, playing for a chamber orchestra, if anything, reflects well on the judge. It is proper. However, Wharton should file an annual report of this earning. *See* CJC Canon 4(H)(2).

It is proper for Wharton to preside over the classical musician/record company case. A judge should disqualify himself when his impartiality might reasonably be questioned. *See* CJC Canon 3(E)(1). The only bias which could possibly be alleged against Wharton is that he is a classical music buff and therefore will favor the musician. No facts indicate such a bias. A classical musician buff could just as well favor the record company which makes classical music available! Moreover, were judges to disqualify themselves when there was no true problem, the system of justice would be gravely injured. Thus,, in a case like this,, there is a strong policy against recusal. *Cf. Brody v. Harvard*, 664 F.2d 10 (1st Cir. 1981) (where a Harvard alumni judge was not required to withdraw in a case in which Harvard was a party).

Except for his use of the stationery, Wharton has behaved acceptably.

Essay Answer 19

1. This problem brings to light a very real circumstance: attorney incompetence waiting to happen. The facts stipulate that there have been no complaints against Ella. Although this does not mean she has not committed any ethical violations, the question is, should the disciplinary committee look into her case?

    Both sets of guidelines for attorney ethics preclude attorneys from committing crimes "that reflect[] adversely on [their] honesty, trustworthiness or fitness as a lawyer in other respects..." or doing anything involving moral turpitude. *See* DR 1-102(3); MR 8.4(b). Illegal drug use would be covered by these provisions. However, ours is a system of law, and attorneys do not give up their basic legal rights just because they are attorneys. The mere speculation that an attorney is an addict should not give rise to a suspension. More concrete evidence should be required. Otherwise, disciplinary committees, instead of being fair investigatory bodies, would turn into "witch hunts," perhaps more guided by political motives than by justice. Nevertheless, it seems proper for the committee to *question* Ella.

2. The next question is whether Ella's suspension for failing to answer questions asked her is acceptable. It is not. *See Spevack v. Klein*, 385 US. 511 (1967).

In *Spevack v. Klein,* a New York attorney refused to honor a subpoena duces tecum to produce his financial records. He also refused to testify at a disciplinary inquiry regarding the charge that he solicited clients. He claimed the Fifth Amendment self-incrimination clause (as applicable to the states via the Fourteenth Amendment) allowed him to refuse to so answer. The Appellate Division of the New York Supreme Court disagreed and disbarred the attorney. However, the U.S. Supreme Court overruled the disbarment, holding that the Constitution's self-incrimination clause was applicable to such a proceeding. The case at hand is similar. Were Ella to admit using drugs, DR 1-102 and MR 8.4 would be violated. She would thus be subject to discipline. Ella should not be penalized for the assertion of a constitutional right. A state disciplinary committee action satisfies the state action requirement necessary to invoke the Fifth Amendment privilege. Therefore, Ella's suspension was improper. For Ella to be suspended, the committee must not rely on Ella to furnish the case against herself. They must find their own evidence.

Essay Answer 20

1. Although it might be argued that the question Mirage refused to answer is 1) irrelevant to the practice of law and 2) infringes on her First Amendment expression rights, nevertheless the bar can refuse admission on this ground. *See Law Students v. Wadmond*, 401 U.S. 154 (1971).

Since Mirage has not (yet) been refused admission to the bar, her only argument is that the query "chills" First Amendment rights. However, such a question actually merely asks whether the applicant will support the constitution of State X and the federal constitution. This is acceptable. Attorneys, as officers of the court, can be required to swear to uphold the law. *See* DR 1-101(A); MR 8.1. The language is neither vague nor overbroad.

2. Even if Mirage disagrees with the bar's right to query her, she should appear at the hearing to argue her case. By not appearing, she is circumventing legitimate court process. *See* DR 1-102(A)(5); MR 8.4(d).

Her unwillingness to appear before the tribunal casts doubt on her fitness to practice law. Although this should not be grounds to refuse her bar admission, nevertheless it should be a factor in deciding her fitness. It evidences a total disregard for court process. As a general rule, to preserve a claim, one must contest it. Mirage did not do so. This may indicate *incompetence! See* MR 1.1; DR 6-101(A)(1).

3. Mirage should not have called the proceeding "sham," and should not have characterized it as "harassment." Attorneys should treat tribunals (here the bar admission committee) with respect. *Cf.* DR 1-102; MR 8.4.

Referring to the state bar in such a way evidences only disrespect. Although the case might be different were the bar to have acted inappropriately, no facts indicate this. Even were the "dice to be loaded," Mirage should have treated the tribunal more respectfully. Her present treatment evidences only a disrespect for the administration of justice and a misunderstanding as to how to appeal a case. Again, Mirage's conduct indicates an unfitness to practice law.

4. Mirage should have paid the full $150 to the State X bar.

Although the facts are unclear, it is clear that State X is a so-called "integrated bar." Were it shown that State X used its fees for *political* purposes (which Mirage disagreed with), it might be proper for Mirage to withhold the $75; no such facts are shown here. As a general rule, states use the collected fees for educating lawyers, educating the public, and for disciplining attorneys. Fee gathering for this purpose is *fully* appropriate. *See Lathrop v. Donahue*, 367 U.S. 820 (1961).

5. In sum, the federal appeal will likely fail. Mirage should have answered the question, should have appeared for the hearing, should not have questioned the integrity of the hearing examiners, and should have paid the $75.

A just federal decree will allow Mirage to pursue her application if she complies with the bar's legitimate procedures.

Essay Answer 21

1. Andrew is not subject to discipline in State B.

To be subject to discipline in a state, an individual must be licensed to practice law in that state. Because Andrew is not licensed to practice law in State B, he is not subject to discipline by the State B bar. This is not to say, however, that he cannot be disciplined by State A. Furthermore, if, in fact, he is practicing law in State B, then State B can likely find him guilty of a statutory crime (e.g., impersonating a lawyer, practicing law without a license). Moreover, it is even possible he could be found in contempt of court by his behavior.

2. Andrew is subject to discipline, on several grounds, in State A (where he is licensed). The issues will be discussed in the order they appeared in the fact pattern.

The obvious and first issue is that Andrew was practicing law in State B, where he was not licensed. His post-exam interview, where he "ascertain(s) whether there is a legal claim" is certainly legal practice. He is giving legal advice about whether or not to pursue a PI case. Because he is not licensed in State B, he is practicing law there without a license. This is proscribed conduct. *See* DR 3-101(B); MR 5.5(a). Although Andrew's conduct takes place outside the borders of State A, State A still has jurisdiction over him. *See* MR 8.5. State A has good cause to discipline Andrew for practicing law elsewhere without a license. Further, such conduct evidences dishonesty and poor character, which is also grounds for discipline. *See* DR 1-102; MR 8.4.

Although Andrew's office name, "Personal Injury Medicine," is unusual and may well subject Andrew to discipline by the medical society or by the State B Attorney General, such naming will not subject Andrew to additional discipline in State A. Under the MRPC, trade names for firms are now acceptable, provided they are not misleading. *See* MR 7.1; MR 7.5(a). Andrew's trade name aptly described what he was practicing and should not itself give rise to additional discipline.

Andrew's "how-to" book on filing a personal injury claim is, itself, acceptable and, standing alone, does not subject Andrew to additional discipline. Attorneys should not aid in the unauthorized practice of law. *See* DR 3-101(A); MR 5.5(b). However, attorneys should do

their best to make the public aware of their legal rights and to educate the public about the law. *See* EC 1-1; EC 1-2; MR Preamble; MR 7.2. Comment; *cf.* MR 6.1. Although Andrew has violated several disciplinary rules, he should not be punished for giving away a how-to book. Not only should the balance be struck in favor of increasing the public's information regarding the law, but there are First Amendment issues involved as well.

Andrew's *combined* medical/legal exam is impermissible. Although lawyers who possess skills necessary to practice another profession as well may practice these two professions in *one office*, such individuals are not permitted to "commingle" these two occupations. A potential client's freedom to choose an attorney of his/her liking must be preserved. Andrew, by funneling his patients into a legal consultation, reduces the client's freedom to choose an attorney s/he truly wants.

Moreover, in a very real sense, Andrew is impermissibly soliciting business. Although advertising is permissible, if not misleading, in-person solicitation is not. *See* MR 7.3; DR 2-103(A); *Ohralik v. Ohio Bar Association*, 436 U.S. 447 (1978). The name of Andrew's clinic, "Personal Injury Medicine," is predominantly *medical*, and Andrew is likely listed in State B as a doctor. Once patients come in his door, however, they are given a legal pitch. This is probably an in-person solicitation (attorney initiated personal contact with a specific client) and subjects Andrew to discipline. The reason why in-person solicitation is prohibited is because, again, the client is subject to abuse by the attorney. His free will in deciding what is his best legal avenue is diminished.

In the case at hand, many, if not most, of Andrew's clients would be better served by having a State B licensed attorney handle their case. Andrew's plan precludes that. Andrew's quasi-contingency fee agreement is an impermissible entanglement with his medical practice and gives the appearance that a fraud on the opposing party is underway. As to the fraud, it appears that Andrew is willing to rack up the bill so his patient/client can get more. This is dishonest. *See* DR 1-102(A)(4); MR 8.4(c). Moreover, such a fee is unreasonable and is thus precluded. *See* MR 1.5; DR 2-106(A). Finally, Andrew's arrangement has the strong appearance of impropriety. *See* DR 9-101. Andrew should have severed his law practice entirely.

3. Andrew should be disciplined.

Essay Answer 22

1. Is Attorney entitled to more than $6,000 for her work for Client?

The general rule is that an attorney discharged, *without cause*, is entitled to her fees based on quantum meruit, provided that the fees do not exceed what the attorney would have received had she stayed on the case. Although different jurisdictions have differing variations of the above rule, the basic policy is that the client should be allowed the freedom to choose who is to handle his case. In order to effectuate this policy, undue penalties must not be levied on the client who discharges his/her attorney. The quantum meruit or actual value basis is thus the fair and majority way to handle the problem. In the case at hand, Attorney was paid $6,000, the figure she herself gave as the actual value of her services (30 hours at $200 per hour). Thus, Attorney should *not* prevail in her $8,000,000 lawsuit against Client.

2. Attorney is not subject to discipline.

Provided that this jurisdiction allows attorney's liens, Attorney's actions are permissible if intended to secure payment of attorney fees. *See* DR 5-103(A)(1); MR 1.8(i)(1). The facts do not state the law of this jurisdiction, but liens are probably acceptable. A lien which holds work-product and papers given by the client in the course of the representation is somewhat typical. Attorney is not likely to be subjected to discipline for asserting the lien. Attorney's and Sly's haggling over the reservation of rights implicates no question of unprofessional conduct. Attorney had a right to try to be paid. Attorneys may sue clients for fees. At issue in this case was whether the suit was a form of *harassment*, because it was Attorney who set the $6,000 as fair compensation. Harassment, of course is a disciplinary violation. *See* DR 7-102(A)(1); MR 3.1; MR 4.4(a). Attorney must have a good faith argument that she is entitled to more than $6,000. The general rule is that there is a right to sue when the argument can be made that the law should be changed. Thus, although a close call, Attorney is probably not subject to discipline for suing Client.

3. No facts indicate that Sly behaved improperly. No facts indicate he was unprofessional in his behavior to Attorney. Attorneys can take clients who fire other attorneys! Thus, Sly is not subject to discipline.

Essay Answer 23

1. Since DeNormluc represented the opposing party on a different but related matter, it is improper for Leigh to have represented John.

The facts are unclear about whether Leigh knew of this impermissible conflict of interest. If she did not know, then she lacked diligence and evidenced neglect for not having routinely apprised fellow partners of her cases. *See* DR 6-101(A)(3); MR 1.1; MR 1.3. If Leigh did know of this conflict, then she has violated the spirit of several disciplinary rules. It should be noted, of course, that the general confidentiality rules do not apply to fellow partners. That is, partners are free to discuss cases amongst themselves and, in fact, it is presumed that they do. Thus, there is imputed automatic disqualification to fellow partners. *See* DR 5-105(D); MR 1.10. Here, DeNormluc represented the opposing party, West, on a related matter. The query is: could DeNormluc represent John in his case against West? The answer is, under these facts, no. To do so would appear improper because the attorney would be taking both sides of the same suit. *See* CPR Canon 9. Moreover, in such a situation, DeNormluc might use confidences revealed to her by West against John. This betrayal of confidences is prohibited. *See* DR 4-101(B); MR 1.6(a). Because DeNormluc is precluded from taking this case, Leigh is, as well. DR 5-105(D); MR 1.10. Thus, it is clear Leigh is subject to discipline for taking the cases. The harshness of the imposed sanction depends on her knowledge of the conflict.

2. Although Leigh's inviting the jurors out to lunch was unusual and probably inappropriate, because it was after the verdict and implicated no wrongful intent, she should not be disciplined for this under the ethical guidelines. Note that some states do prohibit contact with jurors even after the trial. *See* MR 3.5(c).

Pre-trial and trial contact with jurors, out-of-court, is precluded. *See* MR 3.5(b); DR 7-108(A) and (B)(1); DR 7-110(B). However, Leigh's contact with the jurors occurred *after* the trial was over. Although it might be argued such contact gave the appearance of impropriety, because the facts stipulated that this was to improve her demeanor, it was likely proper. *Cf.* CPR Canon 9. One's performance would be improved by feedback from jurors. Competence is obviously extremely important. *See* MR 1.1; DR 6-101(A). Thus, although Leigh's behavior was unusual, it should not be disciplined.

Essay Answer 24

1. The finding of contempt against Attorney is proper.

A tribunal has the inherent power of contempt. Traditionally, refusal to comply with a tribunal's legitimate requests will support a contempt finding. Refusal to give the name of Earl was improper. Although attorneys should protect the confidences of their clients, the mere giving of a name is not likely to be such a confidence. *See, eg., In Re Grand Jury Proceedings*, 517 F. 2d 666 (5th Cir. 1975); *cf.* DR 4-101(B); MR 1.6(a). Moreover, in the case at hand, Attorney's invocation of the attorney-client privilege was probably not supported by the facts. Although he *was* Earl's attorney, the facts here seem to indicate that in this instance, he was involved with Earl in only a business relationship— not a legal relationship. Thus, again, the contempt finding was likely justified. Finally, although Attorney attempted not to answer based on professional norms, in truth the rules were against him. Attorneys, when directed to do something by a tribunal, should obey that order and preserve their argument by obeying the order under formal protest. *Cf.* DR 4-101(C)(2); MR 1.6(b)(4). Although the phrasing of the above disciplinary rule does not make such a revelation mandatory, it is generally believed that such a course is proper. Thus, for all of the above reasons, the contempt finding was probably proper.

2. Attorney's suspension by the state bar was probably proper.

Although the facts are sparse, Attorney did clearly make two errors. Together, these errors subject Attorney to discipline. As for whether a suspension (as opposed to a public or private reprimand) is too severe a penalty, we would have to refer to the jurisprudence of this state. However, it is probably acceptable. The finding of contempt reflects adversely on Attorney's fitness to practice law. It evidences moral turpitude and conduct prejudicial to the administration of justice. *See* DR 1-102(A)(3), (5); MR 8.4(a), (c), (d). Discipline is in order. Secondly, Attorney likely skirted professional norms by entering into a business deal with a client absent informed consent. *See* DR 5-104(A); MR 1.8. Although the facts neither prove nor refute that there was not *informed* consent, the reasonable reading of the facts indicates that there was probably consent but not disclosure. That is, obviously Earl *consented* to the deal. However, was he made aware by Attorney of the dangers involved? Attorneys owe a fiduciary duty to their clients. They know the law and the client does not. Thus, attorney-client business deals are always suspect. They are a kind of conflict of interest. The ethical guidelines, in fact, require a signed writing proving the consent and disclosure. *See* MR 1.8(a)(3); DR 5-104(A). Although the facts do not consciously show there was not disclosure to Earl, Attorney did likely violate DR 5-104(A) and MR 1.8(a)(3) and thus is subject to discipline on this count as well. The suspension was likely proper.

Essay Answer 25

1. Attorney is subject to discipline.

The decision whether to settle or not is up to each client. In the multiple client situation, each client must be fully apprised of the offer of settlement. Only then can an informed consent be given. *See* DR 5-106; MR 1.8(g). In the case at hand Attorney did not tell A, B, and C all of the facts. D Corp. offered $1,000,000 to A, B, and C. D Corp. did not offer A $500,000, B $300,000, and C $200,000. That was *Attorney's* calculation. This case illustrates the potential for conflict of interest when there are multiple clients. Had A, B, and C known what was really offered, they might not have been willing to settle as they did. Attorney's behavior, in not telling A, B, and C the *actual* settlement offer, violated the letter of the above-cited rules.

Moreover, in lying to his clients, Attorney evidenced dishonesty and is, therefore, also subject to discipline. *See* DR 1-102(4); MR 8.4(c). Honesty is integral to the practice of law. Because clients are in a fiduciary relationship, honesty becomes all the more important. Here, A, B, and C likely had no idea that Attorney was lying regarding the offer.

Attorney's accepting of $100,000 "under the table" from D Corp. violated the standards of the profession. An attorney is not allowed to accept compensation from anyone other than his client, for services performed for that client, unless there is consent and disclosure. *See* DR 5-107(A)(1); MR 1.8(f)(1). Here, D Corp. paid him $100,000 ostensibly for A, B, and C's case. This is clearly proscribed. Moreover, the appearance is that Attorney was bribed by D Corp. to accept a too-low offer. Such might also be characterized as an *embezzlement* from A, B, and C. Therefore, Attorney may have also violated DR 1-102 and MR 8.4. It is certainly improper and will subject Attorney to discipline.

Attorney's 50% contingency fee and $100,000 on the side is too high a fee and subjects Attorney to discipline. *See* DR 2-106(A); MR 1.5; MR 1.5 Comment [3]. Contingency fee contracts should generally be in writing, and this was not. *See* MR 1.5(c); EC 2-19. Most importantly, although quite a bit of variance is acceptable in attorneys fees, although attorneys are expected to make a good living, and although contingency fees are generally higher than others, this fee is too high. The wealth of a client can be a factor in setting the fee, but it cannot allow the attorney to steal, as here, from the client. These fees were simply too much. Attorney is therefore subject to discipline for excessive fees, as well.

2. Although Attorney's donation of $600,000 to the non-profit legal aid society is a mitigating factor, it does not relieve him of responsibility for his other ethical violations.

Making legal services available to the poor should be undertaken by all attorneys. *See* MR 6.1; EC 2-16; EC 2-24; EC 2-25. However, stealing from some clients to give to others is not a proper means of serving the poor. Attorney could have set high but reasonable fees for A, B, and C. He is not permitted to wash out what he did to A, B, and C by being generous.

AMERICAN BAR ASSOCIATION
MODEL RULES OF PROFESSIONAL CONDUCT (2002 Version)

TABLE OF CONTENTS

Preamble: A Lawyer's Responsibilities, and Scope

Rule

1.0	Terminology
1.1	Competence
1.2	Scope of Representation and Allocation of Authority Between Client and Lawyer
1.3	Diligence
1.4	Communication
1.5	Fees
1.6	Confidentiality of Information
1.7	Conflict of Interest: Current Clients
1.8	Conflict of Interest: Current Clients: Specific Rules
1.9	Duties to Former Client
1.10	Imputation of Conflicts of Interest: General Rule
1.11	Special Conflicts of Interest for Former and Current Officers and Government Employees
1.12	Former Judge, Arbitrator, Mediator, or Other Third-Party Neutral
1.13	Organization as Client
1.14	Client with Diminished Capacity
1.15	Safekeeping Property
1.16	Declining or Terminating Representation
1.17	Sale of Law Practice
1.18	Duties to Prospective Client
2.1	Advisor
2.2	[Deleted]
2.3	Evaluation for Use by Third Persons
2.4	Lawyer Serving as Third-Party Neutral
3.1	Meritorious Claims and Contentions
3.2	Expediting Litigation
3.3	Candor toward the Tribunal
3.4	Fairness to Opposing Party and Counsel
3.5	Impartiality and Decorum of the Tribunal
3.6	Trial Publicity
3.7	Lawyer as Witness
3.8	Special Responsibilities of a Prosecutor
3.9	Advocate in Nonadjudicative Proceedings
4.1	Truthfulness in Statements to Others
4.2	Communication with Person Represented by Counsel
4.3	Dealing with Unrepresented Persons
4.4	Respect for Rights of Third Persons

Model Rules of Professional Conduct

5.1	Responsibilities of Supervisory Lawyers or Law Firms
5.2	Responsibilities of a Subordinate Lawyer
5.3	Responsibilities Regarding Nonlawyer Assistants
5.4	Professional Independence of a Lawyer
5.5	Unauthorized Practice of Law
5.6	Restrictions on Right to Practice
5.7	Restrictions Regarding Law-related Services
6.1	Voluntary Pro Bono Publico Service
6.2	Accepting Appointments
6.3	Membership in Legal Services Organization
6.4	Law Reform Activities Affecting Client Interests
6.5	Non-Profit and Court-Annexed Limited Legal-Service Programs
7.1	Communications Concerning a Lawyer's Services
7.2	Advertising
7.3	Direct Contact with Prospective Clients
7.4	Communication of Fields of Practice and Specialization
7.5	Firm Names and Letterheads
7.6	Political Contributions to Obtain Government Legal Engagements or Appointments by Judges
8.1	Bar Admission and Disciplinary Matters
8.2	Judicial and Legal Officials
8.3	Reporting Professional Misconduct
8.4	Misconduct
8.5	Disciplinary Authority; Choice of Law

Model Rules of Professional Conduct

PREAMBLE: A LAWYER'S RESPONSIBILITIES

[1] A lawyer, as a member of the legal profession, is a representative of clients, an officer of the legal system and a public citizen having special responsibility for the quality of justice.

[2] As a representative of clients, a lawyer performs various functions. As advisor, a lawyer provides a client with an informed understanding of the client's legal rights and obligations and explains their practical implications. As advocate, a lawyer zealously asserts the client's position under the rules of the adversary system. As negotiator, a lawyer seeks a result advantageous to the client but consistent with requirements of honest dealings with others. As an evaluator, a lawyer acts by examining a client's legal affairs and reporting about them to the client or to others.

[3] In addition to these representational functions, a lawyer may serve as a third-party neutral, a nonrepresentational role helping the parties to resolve a dispute or other matter. Some of these Rules apply directly to lawyers who are or have served as third-party neutrals. See, e.g., Rules 1.12 and 2.4. In addition, there are Rules that apply to lawyers who are not active in the practice of law or to practicing lawyers even when they are acting in a nonprofessional capacity. For example, a lawyer who commits fraud in the conduct of a business is subject to discipline for engaging in conduct involving dishonesty, fraud, deceit or misrepresentation. See Rule 8.4.

[4] In all professional functions a lawyer should be competent, prompt and diligent. A lawyer should maintain communication with a client concerning the representation. A lawyer should keep in confidence information relating to representation of a client except so far as disclosure is required or permitted by the Rules of Professional Conduct or other law.

[5] A lawyer's conduct should conform to the requirements of the law, both in professional service to clients and in the lawyer's business and personal affairs. A lawyer should use the law's procedures only for legitimate purposes and not to harass or intimidate others. A lawyer should demonstrate respect for the legal system and for those who serve it, including judges, other lawyers and public officials. While it is a lawyer's duty, when necessary, to challenge the rectitude of official action, it is also a lawyer's duty to uphold legal process.

[6] As a public citizen, a lawyer should seek improvement of the law, access to the legal system, the administration of justice and the quality of service rendered by the legal profession. As a member of a learned profession, a lawyer should cultivate knowledge of the law beyond its use for clients, employ that knowledge in reform of the law and work to strengthen legal education. In addition, a lawyer should further the public's understanding of and confidence in the rule of law and the justice system because legal institutions in a constitutional democracy depend on popular participation and support to maintain their authority. A lawyer should be mindful of deficiencies in the administration of justice and of the fact that the poor, and sometimes persons who are not poor, cannot afford adequate legal assistance. Therefore, all lawyers should devote professional time and resources and use civic influence to ensure equal access to our system of justice for all those who because of economic or social barriers cannot afford or secure adequate legal counsel. A lawyer should aid the legal profession in pursuing these objectives and should help the bar regulate itself in the public interest.

[7] Many of a lawyer's professional responsibilities are prescribed in the Rules of Professional Conduct, as well as substantive and procedural law. However, a lawyer is also guided by personal conscience and the approbation of professional peers. A lawyer should strive to attain the highest level of skill, to improve the law and the legal profession and to exemplify the legal profession's ideals of public service.

[8] A lawyer's responsibilities as a representative of clients, an officer of the legal system and a public citizen are usually harmonious. Thus, when an opposing party is well represented, a lawyer can be a zealous advocate on behalf of a client and at the same time assume that justice is being done. So also, a lawyer can be sure that preserving client confidences ordinarily serves the public interest because people are more likely to seek legal advice, and thereby heed their legal obligations, when they know their communications will be private.

[9] In the nature of law practice, however, conflicting responsibilities are encountered. Virtually all difficult ethical problems arise from conflict between a lawyer's responsibilities to clients, to the legal system and to the lawyer's own interest in remaining an ethical person while earning a satisfactory living. The Rules of Professional Conduct often prescribe terms for resolving such conflicts. Within the framework of these Rules, however, many difficult issues of professional discretion can arise. Such issues must be resolved through the exercise of sensitive professional and moral judgment guided by the basic principles underlying the Rules. These principles include the lawyer's obligation zealously to protect and pursue a client's legitimate interests, within the bounds of the law, while maintaining a professional, courteous and civil attitude toward all persons involved in the legal system.

[10] The legal profession is largely self-governing. Although other professions also have been granted powers of self-government, the legal profession is unique in this respect because of the close relationship between the profession and the processes of government and law enforcement. This connection is manifested in the fact that ultimate authority over the legal profession is vested largely in the courts.

[11] To the extent that lawyers meet the obligations of their professional calling, the occasion for government regulation is obviated. Self-regulation also helps maintain the legal profession's independence from government domination. An independent legal profession is an important force in preserving government under law, for abuse of legal authority is more readily challenged by a profession whose members are not dependent on government for the right to practice.

[12] The legal profession's relative autonomy carries with it special responsibilities of self-government. The profession has a responsibility to assure that its regulations are conceived in the public interest and not in furtherance of parochial or self-interested concerns of the bar. Every lawyer is responsible for observance of the Rules of Professional Conduct. A lawyer should also aid in securing their observance by other lawyers. Neglect of these responsibilities compromises the independence of the profession and the public interest which it serves.

[13] Lawyers play a vital role in the preservation of society. The fulfillment of this role requires an understanding by lawyers of their relationship to our legal system. The Rules of Professional Conduct, when properly applied, serve to define that relationship.

SCOPE

[14] The Rules of Professional Conduct are rules of reason. They should be interpreted with reference to the purposes of legal representation and of the law itself. Some of the Rules are imperatives, cast in the terms "shall" or "shall not." These define proper conduct for purposes of professional discipline. Others, generally cast in the term "may," are permissive and define areas under the Rules in which the lawyer has discretion to exercise professional judgment. No disciplinary action should be taken when the lawyer chooses not to act or acts within the bounds of such discretion. Other Rules define the nature of relationships between the lawyer and others. The Rules are thus partly obligatory and disciplinary and partly constitutive and descriptive in that they define a lawyer's professional role. Many of the Comments use the term "should." Comments do not add obligations to the Rules but provide guidance for practicing in compliance with the Rules.

[15] The Rules presuppose a larger legal context shaping the lawyer's role. That context includes court rules and statutes relating to matters of licensure, laws defining specific obligations of lawyers and substantive and procedural law in general. The Comments are sometimes used to alert lawyers to their responsibilities under such other law.

[16] Compliance with the Rules, as with all law in an open society, depends primarily upon understanding and voluntary compliance, secondarily upon reinforcement by peer and public opinion and finally, when necessary, upon enforcement through disciplinary proceedings. The Rules do not, however, exhaust the moral and ethical considerations that should inform a lawyer, for no worthwhile human activity can be completely defined by legal rules. The Rules simply provide a framework for the ethical practice of law.

[17] Furthermore, for purposes of determining the lawyer's authority and responsibility, principles of substantive law external to these Rules determine whether a client-lawyer relationship exists. Most of the duties flowing from the client-lawyer relationship attach only after the client has requested the lawyer to render legal services and the lawyer has agreed to do so. But there are some duties, such as that of confidentiality under Rule 1.6, that attach when the lawyer agrees to consider whether a client-lawyer relationship shall be established. See Rule 1.18. Whether a client-lawyer relationship exists for any specific purpose can depend on the circumstances and may be a question of fact.

[18] Under various legal provisions, including constitutional, statutory and common law, the responsibilities of government lawyers may include authority concerning legal matters that ordinarily reposes in the client in private client-lawyer relationships. For example, a lawyer for a government agency may have authority on behalf of the government to decide upon settlement or whether to appeal from an adverse judgment. Such authority in various respects is generally vested in the attorney general and the state's attorney in state government, and their federal counterparts, and the same may be true of other government law officers. Also, lawyers under the supervision of these officers may be authorized to represent several government agencies in intragovernmental legal controversies in circumstances where a private lawyer could not represent multiple private clients. These Rules do not abrogate any such authority.

[19] Failure to comply with an obligation or prohibition imposed by a Rule is a basis for invoking the disciplinary process. The Rules presuppose that disciplinary assessment of a lawyer's conduct will be made on the basis of the facts and circumstances as they existed at the time of the conduct in question and in recognition of the fact that a lawyer often has to act upon uncertain or incomplete evidence of the situation. Moreover, the Rules presuppose that whether or not discipline should be imposed for a violation, and the severity of a sanction, depend on all the circumstances, such as the willfulness and seriousness of the violation, extenuating factors and whether there have been previous violations.

[20] Violation of a Rule should not itself give rise to a cause of action against a lawyer nor should it create any presumption in such a case that a legal duty has been breached. In addition, violation of a Rule does not necessarily warrant any other nondisciplinary remedy, such as disqualification of a lawyer in pending litigation. The Rules are designed to provide guidance to lawyers and to provide a structure for regulating conduct through disciplinary agencies. They are not designed to be a basis for civil liability. Furthermore, the purpose of the Rules can be subverted when they are invoked by opposing parties as procedural weapons. The fact that a Rule is a just basis for a lawyer's self-assessment, or for sanctioning a lawyer under the administration of a disciplinary authority, does not imply that an antagonist in a collateral proceeding or transaction has standing to seek enforcement of the Rule. Nevertheless, since the Rules do establish standards of conduct by lawyers, a lawyer's violation of a Rule may be evidence of breach of the applicable standard of conduct.

[21] The Comment accompanying each Rule explains and illustrates the meaning and purpose of the Rule. The Preamble and this note on Scope provide general orientation. The Comments are intended as guides to interpretation, but the text of each Rule is authoritative.

RULE 1.0: TERMINOLOGY

(a) "Belief" or "believes" denotes that the person involved actually supposed the fact in question to be true. A person's belief may be inferred from circumstances.

(b) "Confirmed in writing," when used in reference to the informed consent of a person, denotes informed consent that is given in writing by the person or a writing that a lawyer promptly transmits to the person confirming an oral informed consent. See paragraph (e) for the definition of "informed consent." If it is not feasible to obtain or transmit the writing at the time the person gives informed consent, then the lawyer must obtain or transmit it within a reasonable time thereafter.

(c) "Firm" or "law firm" denotes a lawyer or lawyers in a law partnership, professional

Model Rules of Professional Conduct

corporation, sole proprietorship or other association authorized to practice law; or lawyers employed in a legal services organization or the legal department of a corporation or other organization.

(d) "Fraud" or "fraudulent" denotes conduct that is fraudulent under the substantive or procedural law of the applicable jurisdiction and has a purpose to deceive.

(e) "Informed consent" denotes the agreement by a person to a proposed course of conduct after the lawyer has communicated adequate information and explanation about the material risks of and reasonably available alternatives to the proposed course of conduct.

(f) "Knowingly," "known," or "knows" denotes actual knowledge of the fact in question. A person's knowledge may be inferred from circumstances.

(g) "Partner" denotes a member of a partnership, a shareholder in a law firm organized as a professional corporation, or a member of an association authorized to practice law.

(h) "Reasonable" or "reasonably" when used in relation to conduct by a lawyer denotes the conduct of a reasonably prudent and competent lawyer.

(i) "Reasonable belief" or "reasonably believes" when used in reference to a lawyer denotes that the lawyer believes the matter in question and that the circumstances are such that the belief is reasonable.

(j) "Reasonably should know" when used in reference to a lawyer denotes that a lawyer of reasonable prudence and competence would ascertain the matter in question.

(k) "Screened" denotes the isolation of a lawyer from any participation in a matter through the timely imposition of procedures within a firm that are reasonably adequate under the circumstances to protect information that the isolated lawyer is obligated to protect under these Rules or other law.

(l) "Substantial" when used in reference to degree or extent denotes a material matter of clear and weighty importance.

(m) "Tribunal" denotes a court, an arbitrator in a binding arbitration proceeding or a legislative body, administrative agency or other body acting in an adjudicative capacity. A legislative body, administrative agency or other body acts in an adjudicative capacity when neutral official, after the presentation of evidence or legal argument by party or parties, will render a binding legal judgment directly affecting party's interests in a particular matter.

(n) "Writing" or "written" denotes a tangible or electronic record of a communication or representation, including handwriting, typewriting, printing, photostating, photography, audio or videorecording and e-mail. A "signed" writing includes an electronic sound, symbol or process attached to or logically associated with a writing and executed or adopted by a person with the intent to sign the writing.

COMMENT

Confirmed in Writing

[1] If it is not feasible to obtain or transmit a written confirmation at the time the client gives informed consent, then the lawyer must obtain or transmit it within a reasonable time thereafter. If a lawyer has obtained a client's informed consent, the lawyer may act in reliance on that consent so long as it is confirmed in writing within a reasonable time thereafter.

Firm

[2] Whether two or more lawyers constitute a firm within paragraph (c) can depend on the specific facts. For example, two practitioners who share office space and occasionally consult or assist each other ordinarily would not be regarded as constituting a firm. However, if they present themselves to the public in a way that suggests that they are a firm or conduct themselves as a firm, they should be regarded as a firm for purposes of the Rules. The terms of any formal agreement between associated lawyers are relevant in determining whether they are a firm, as is the fact that they have mutual access to information concerning the clients they serve. Furthermore, it is relevant in doubtful cases to consider the underlying purpose of the Rule that is involved. A group of lawyers could be regarded as a firm for purposes of the Rule that the same lawyer should not represent opposing parties in litigation, while it might not be so regarded for purposes of the Rule that information acquired by one lawyer is attributed to another.

[3] With respect to the law department of an organization, including the government, there is ordinarily no question that the members of the department constitute a firm within the meaning of the Rules of Professional Conduct. There can be uncertainty, however, as to the identity of the client. For example, it may not be clear whether the law department of a corporation represents a subsidiary or an affiliated corporation, as well as the corporation by which the members of the department are directly employed. A similar question can arise concerning an unincorporated association and its local affiliates.

[4] Similar questions can also arise with respect to lawyers in legal aid and legal services organizations. Depending upon the structure of the organization, the entire organization or different components of it may constitute a firm or firms for purposes of these Rules.

Fraud

[5] When used in these Rules, the terms "fraud" or "fraudulent" refer to conduct that is characterized as such under the substantive or procedural law of the applicable jurisdiction and has a purpose to deceive. This does not include merely negligent misrepresentation or negligent failure to apprise another of relevant information. For purposes of these Rules, it is not necessary that anyone has suffered damages or relied on the misrepresentation or failure to inform.

Informed Consent

[6] Many of the Rules of Professional Conduct require the lawyer to obtain the informed consent of a client or other person (e.g., a former client or, under certain circumstances, a prospective client) before accepting or continuing representation or pursuing a course of conduct. See, e.g., Rules 1.2(c), 1.6(a) and 1.7(b). The communication necessary to obtain such consent will vary according to the Rule involved and the circumstances giving rise to the need to obtain informed consent. The lawyer must make reasonable efforts to ensure that the client or other person possesses information reasonably adequate to make an informed decision. Ordinarily, this will require communication that includes a disclosure of the facts and circumstances giving rise to the situation, any explanation reasonably necessary to inform the client or other person of the material advantages and disadvantages of the proposed course of conduct and a discussion of the client's or other person's options and alternatives. In some circumstances it may be appropriate for a lawyer to advise a client or other person to seek the advice of other counsel. A lawyer need not inform a client or other person of facts or implications already known to the client or other person; nevertheless, a lawyer who does not personally inform the client or other person assumes the risk that the client or other person is inadequately informed and the consent is invalid. In determining whether the information and explanation provided are reasonably adequate, relevant factors include whether the client or other person is experienced in legal matters generally and in making decisions of the type involved, and whether the client or other person is independently represented by other counsel in giving the consent. Normally, such persons need less information and explanation than others, and generally a client or other person who is independently represented by other counsel in giving the consent should be assumed to have given informed consent.

[7] Obtaining informed consent will usually require an affirmative response by the client or other person. In general, a lawyer may not assume consent from a client's or other person's silence. Consent may be inferred, however, from the conduct of a client or other person who has reasonably adequate information about the matter. A number of Rules require that a person's consent be confirmed in writing. See Rules 1.7(b) and 1.9(a). For a definition of "writing" and "confirmed in writing," see paragraphs (n) and (b). Other Rules require that a client's consent be obtained in a writing signed by the client. See, e.g., Rules 1.8(a) and (g). For a definition of "signed," see paragraph (n).

Screened

[8] This definition applies to situations where screening of a personally disqualified lawyer is permitted to remove imputation of a conflict of interest under Rules 1.11, 1.12 or 1.18.

[9] The purpose of screening is to assure the affected parties that confidential information

known by the personally disqualified lawyer remains protected. The personally disqualified lawyer should acknowledge the obligation not to communicate with any of the other lawyers in the firm with respect to the matter. Similarly, other lawyers in the firm who are working on the matter should be informed that the screening is in place and that they may not communicate with the personally disqualified lawyer with respect to the matter. Additional screening measures that are appropriate for the particular matter will depend on the circumstances. To implement, reinforce and remind all affected lawyers of the presence of the screening, it may be appropriate for the firm to undertake such procedures as a written undertaking by the screened lawyer to avoid any communication with other firm personnel and any contact with any firm files or other materials relating to the matter, written notice and instructions to all other firm personnel forbidding any communication with the screened lawyer relating to the matter, denial of access by the screened lawyer to firm files or other materials relating to the matter and periodic reminders of the screen to the screened lawyer and all other firm personnel.

[10] In order to be effective, screening measures must be implemented as soon as practical after a lawyer or law firm knows or reasonably should know that there is a need for screening.

RULE 1.1: COMPETENCE

A lawyer shall provide competent representation to a client. Competent representation requires the legal knowledge, skill, thoroughness and preparation reasonably necessary for the representation.

COMMENT

Legal Knowledge and Skill

[1] In determining whether a lawyer employs the requisite knowledge and skill in a particular matter, relevant factors include the relative complexity and specialized nature of the matter, the lawyer's general experience, the lawyer's training and experience in the field in question, the preparation and study the lawyer is able to give the matter and whether it is feasible to refer the matter to, or associate or consult with, a lawyer of established competence in the field in question. In many instances, the required proficiency is that of a general practitioner. Expertise in a particular field of law may be required in some circumstances.

[2] A lawyer need not necessarily have special training or prior experience to handle legal problems of a type with which the lawyer is unfamiliar. A newly admitted lawyer can be as competent as a practitioner with long experience. Some important legal skills, such as the analysis of precedent, the evaluation of evidence and legal drafting, are required in all legal problems. Perhaps the most fundamental legal skill consists of determining what kind of legal problems a situation may involve, a skill that necessarily transcends any particular specialized knowledge. A lawyer can provide adequate representation in a wholly novel field through necessary study. Competent representation can also be provided through the association of a lawyer of established competence in the field in question.

[3] In an emergency a lawyer may give advice or assistance in a matter in which the lawyer does not have the skill ordinarily required where referral to or consultation or association with another lawyer would be impractical. Even in an emergency, however, assistance should be limited to that reasonably necessary in the circumstances, for ill-considered action under emergency conditions can jeopardize the client's interest.

[4] A lawyer may accept representation where the requisite level of competence can be achieved by reasonable preparation. This applies as well to a lawyer who is appointed as counsel for an unrepresented person. See also Rule 6.2.

Thoroughness and Preparation

[5] Competent handling of a particular matter includes inquiry into and analysis of the factual and legal elements of the problem, and use of methods and procedures meeting the standards of competent practitioners. It also includes adequate preparation. The required attention and preparation are determined in part by what is at stake; major litigation and complex transactions ordinarily require more

extensive treatment than matters of lesser complexity and consequence. An agreement between the lawyer and the client regarding the scope of the representation may limit the matters for which the lawyer is responsible. See Rule 1.2(c).

Maintaining Competence

[6] To maintain the requisite knowledge and skill, a lawyer should keep abreast of changes in the law and its practice, engage in continuing study and education and comply with all continuing legal education requirements to which the lawyer is subject.

RULE 1.2: SCOPE OF REPRESENTATION AND ALLOCATION OF AUTHORITY BETWEEN CLIENT AND LAWYER

(a) Subject to paragraphs (c) and (d), a lawyer shall abide by a client's decisions concerning the objectives of representation and, as required by Rule 1.4, shall consult with the client as to the means by which they are to be pursued. A lawyer may take such action on behalf of the client as is impliedly authorized to carry out the representation. A lawyer shall abide by a client's decision whether to settle a matter. In a criminal case, the lawyer shall abide by the client's decision, after consultation with the lawyer, as to a plea to be entered, whether to waive jury trial and whether the client will testify.

(b) A lawyer's representation of a client, including representation by appointment, does not constitute an endorsement of the client's political, economic, social or moral views or activities.

(c) A lawyer may limit the scope of the representation if the limitation is reasonable under the circumstances and the client gives informed consent.

(d) A lawyer shall not counsel a client to engage, or assist a client, in conduct that the lawyer knows is criminal or fraudulent, but a lawyer may discuss the legal consequences of any proposed course of conduct with a client and may counsel or assist a client to make a good faith effort to determine the validity, scope, meaning or application of the law.

COMMENT

Allocation of Authority between Client and Lawyer

[1] Paragraph (a) confers upon the client the ultimate authority to determine the purposes to be served by legal representation, within the limits imposed by law and the lawyer's professional obligations. The decisions specified in paragraph (a), such as whether to settle a civil matter, must also be made by the client. See Rule 1.4(a)(1) for the lawyer's duty to communicate with the client about such decisions. With respect to the means by which the client's objectives are to be pursued, the lawyer shall consult with the client as required by Rule 1.4(a)(2) and may take such action as is impliedly authorized to carry out the representation.

[2] On occasion, however, a lawyer and a client may disagree about the means to be used to accomplish the client's objectives. Clients normally defer to the special knowledge and skill of their lawyer with respect to the means to be used to accomplish their objectives, particularly with respect to technical, legal and tactical matters. Conversely, lawyers usually defer to the client regarding such questions as the expense to be incurred and concern for third persons who might be adversely affected. Because of the varied nature of the matters about which a lawyer and client might disagree and because the actions in question may implicate the interests of a tribunal or other persons, this Rule does not prescribe how such disagreements are to be resolved. Other law, however, may be applicable and should be consulted by the lawyer. The lawyer should also consult with the client and seek a mutually acceptable resolution of the disagreement. If such efforts are unavailing and the lawyer has a fundamental disagreement with the client, the lawyer may withdraw from the representation. See Rule 1.16(b)(4). Conversely, the client may resolve the disagreement by discharging the lawyer. See Rule 1.16(a)(3).

[3] At the outset of a representation, the client may authorize the lawyer to take specific action on the client's behalf without further consultation. Absent a material change in circumstances and subject to Rule 1.4, a lawyer may rely on

such an advance authorization. The client may, however, revoke such authority at any time.

[4] In a case in which the client appears to be suffering diminished capacity, the lawyer's duty to abide by the client's decisions is to be guided by reference to Rule 1.14.

Independence from Client's Views or Activities

[5] Legal representation should not be denied to people who are unable to afford legal services, or whose cause is controversial or the subject of popular disapproval. By the same token, representing a client does not constitute approval of the client's views or activities.

Agreements Limiting Scope of Representation

[6] The scope of services to be provided by a lawyer may be limited by agreement with the client or by the terms under which the lawyer's services are made available to the client. When a lawyer has been retained by an insurer to represent an insured, for example, the representation may be limited to matters related to the insurance coverage. A limited representation may be appropriate because the client has limited objectives for the representation. In addition, the terms upon which representation is undertaken may exclude specific means that might otherwise be used to accomplish the client's objectives. Such limitations may exclude actions that the client thinks are too costly or that the lawyer regards as repugnant or imprudent.

[7] Although this Rule affords the lawyer and client substantial latitude to limit the representation, the limitation must be reasonable under the circumstances. If, for example, a client's objective is limited to securing general information about the law the client needs in order to handle a common and typically uncomplicated legal problem, the lawyer and client may agree that the lawyer's services will be limited to a brief telephone consultation. Such a limitation, however, would not be reasonable if the time allotted was not sufficient to yield advice upon which the client could rely. Although an agreement for a limited representation does not exempt a lawyer from the duty to provide competent representation, the limitation is a factor to be considered when determining the legal knowledge, skill, thoroughness and preparation reasonably necessary for the representation. See Rule 1.1.

[8] All agreements concerning a lawyer's representation of a client must accord with the Rules of Professional Conduct and other law. See, e.g., Rules 1.1, 1.8 and 5.6.

Criminal, Fraudulent and Prohibited Transactions

[9] Paragraph (d) prohibits a lawyer from knowingly counseling or assisting a client to commit a crime or fraud. This prohibition, however, does not preclude the lawyer from giving an honest opinion about the actual consequences that appear likely to result from a client's conduct. Nor does the fact that a client uses advice in a course of action that is criminal or fraudulent of itself make a lawyer a party to the course of action. There is a critical distinction between presenting an analysis of legal aspects of questionable conduct and recommending the means by which a crime or fraud might be committed with impunity.

[10] When the client's course of action has already begun and is continuing, the lawyer's responsibility is especially delicate. The lawyer is required to avoid assisting the client, for example, by drafting or delivering documents that the lawyer knows are fraudulent or by suggesting how the wrongdoing might be concealed. A lawyer may not continue assisting a client in conduct that the lawyer originally supposed was legally proper but then discovers is criminal or fraudulent. The lawyer must, therefore, withdraw from the representation of the client in the matter. See Rule 1.16(a). In some cases, withdrawal alone might be insufficient. It may be necessary for the lawyer to give notice of the fact of withdrawal and to disaffirm any opinion, document, affirmation or the like. See Rule 4.1.

[11] Where the client is a fiduciary, the lawyer may be charged with special obligations in dealings with a beneficiary.

[12] Paragraph (d) applies whether or not the defrauded party is a party to the transaction. Hence, a lawyer must not participate in a transaction to effectuate criminal or fraudulent avoidance of tax liability. Paragraph (d) does not preclude undertaking a criminal defense incident to a general retainer for legal services to a lawful enterprise. The last clause of paragraph (d) recognizes that determining the validity or

interpretation of a statute or regulation may require a course of action involving disobedience of the statute or regulation or of the interpretation placed upon it by governmental authorities.

[13] If a lawyer comes to know or reasonably should know that a client expects assistance not permitted by the Rules of Professional Conduct or other law or if the lawyer intends to act contrary to the client's instructions, the lawyer must consult with the client regarding the limitations on the lawyer's conduct. See Rule 1.4(a)(5).

RULE 1.3: DILIGENCE

A lawyer shall act with reasonable diligence and promptness in representing a client.

COMMENT

[1] A lawyer should pursue a matter on behalf of a client despite opposition, obstruction or personal inconvenience to the lawyer, and take whatever lawful and ethical measures are required to vindicate a client's cause or endeavor. A lawyer must also act with commitment and dedication to the interests of the client and with zeal in advocacy upon the client's behalf. A lawyer is not bound, however, to press for every advantage that might be realized for a client. For example, a lawyer may have authority to exercise professional discretion in determining the means by which a matter should be pursued. See Rule 1.2. The lawyer's duty to act with reasonable diligence does not require the use of offensive tactics or preclude the treating of all persons involved in the legal process with courtesy and respect.

[2] A lawyer's work load must be controlled so that each matter can be handled competently.

[3] Perhaps no professional shortcoming is more widely resented than procrastination. A client's interests often can be adversely affected by the passage of time or the change of conditions; in extreme instances, as when a lawyer overlooks a statute of limitations, the client's legal position may be destroyed. Even when the client's interests are not affected in substance, however, unreasonable delay can cause a client needless anxiety and undermine confidence in the lawyer's trustworthiness. A lawyer's duty to act with reasonable promptness, however, does not preclude the lawyer from agreeing to a reasonable request for a postponement that will not prejudice the lawyer's client.

[4] Unless the relationship is terminated as provided in Rule 1.16, a lawyer should carry through to conclusion all matters undertaken for a client. If a lawyer's employment is limited to a specific matter, the relationship terminates when the matter has been resolved. If a lawyer has served a client over a substantial period in a variety of matters, the client sometimes may assume that the lawyer will continue to serve on a continuing basis unless the lawyer gives notice of withdrawal. Doubt about whether a client-lawyer relationship still exists should be clarified by the lawyer, preferably in writing, so that the client will not mistakenly suppose the lawyer is looking after the client's affairs when the lawyer has ceased to do so. For example, if a lawyer has handled a judicial or administrative proceeding that produced a result adverse to the client and the lawyer and the client have not agreed that the lawyer will handle the matter on appeal, the lawyer must consult with the client about the possibility of appeal before relinquishing responsibility for the matter. See Rule 1.4(a)(2). Whether the lawyer is obligated to prosecute the appeal for the client depends on the scope of the representation the lawyer has agreed to provide to the client. See Rule 1.2.

[5] To prevent neglect of client matters in the event of a sole practitioner's death or disability, the duty of diligence may require that each sole practitioner prepare a plan, in conformity with applicable rules, that designates another competent lawyer to review client files, notify each client of the lawyer's death or disability, and determine whether there is a need for immediate protective action. Cf. Rule 28 of the American Bar Association Model Rules for Lawyer Disciplinary Enforcement (providing for court appointment of a lawyer to inventory files and take other protective action in absence of a plan providing for another lawyer to protect the interests of the clients of a deceased or disabled lawyer).

RULE 1.4: COMMUNICATION

(a) A lawyer shall:
(1) promptly inform the client of any decision or circumstance with respect to which the

client's informed consent, as defined in Rule 1.0(e), is required by these Rules;

(2) reasonably consult with the client about the means by which the client's objectives are to be accomplished;

(3) keep the client reasonably informed about the status of the matter;

(4) promptly comply with reasonable requests for information; and

(5) consult with the client about any relevant limitation on the lawyer's conduct when the lawyer knows that the client expects assistance not permitted by the Rules of Professional Conduct or other law.

(b) A lawyer shall explain a matter to the extent reasonably necessary to permit the client to make informed decisions regarding the representation.

COMMENT

[1] Reasonable communication between the lawyer and the client is necessary for the client effectively to participate in the representation.

Communicating with Client

[2] If these Rules require that a particular decision about the representation be made by the client, paragraph (a)(1) requires that the lawyer promptly consult with and secure the client's consent prior to taking action unless prior discussions with the client have resolved what action the client wants the lawyer to take. For example, a lawyer who receives from opposing counsel an offer of settlement in a civil controversy or a proffered plea bargain in a criminal case must promptly inform the client of its substance unless the client has previously indicated that the proposal will be acceptable or unacceptable or has authorized the lawyer to accept or to reject the offer. See Rule 1.2(a).

[3] Paragraph (a)(2) requires the lawyer to reasonably consult with the client about the means to be used to accomplish the client's objectives. In some situations—depending on both the importance of the action under consideration and the feasibility of consulting with the client—this duty will require consultation prior to taking action. In other circumstances, such as during a trial when an immediate decision must be made, the exigency of the situation may require the lawyer to act without prior consultation. In such cases the lawyer must nonetheless act reasonably to inform the client of actions the lawyer has taken on the client's behalf. Additionally, paragraph (a)(3) requires that the lawyer keep the client reasonably informed about the status of the matter, such as significant developments affecting the timing or the substance of the representation.

[4] A lawyer's regular communication with clients will minimize the occasions on which a client will need to request information concerning the representation. When a client makes a reasonable request for information, however, paragraph (a)(4) requires prompt compliance with the request, or if a prompt response is not feasible, that the lawyer, or a member of the lawyer's staff, acknowledge receipt of the request and advise the client when a response may be expected. Client telephone calls should be promptly returned or acknowledged.

Explaining Matters

[5] The client should have sufficient information to participate intelligently in decisions concerning the objectives of the representation and the means by which they are to be pursued, to the extent the client is willing and able to do so. Adequacy of communication depends in part on the kind of advice or assistance that is involved. For example, when there is time to explain a proposal made in a negotiation, the lawyer should review all important provisions with the client before proceeding to an agreement. In litigation a lawyer should explain the general strategy and prospects of success and ordinarily should consult the client on tactics that are likely to result in significant expense or to injure or coerce others. On the other hand, a lawyer ordinarily will not be expected to describe trial or negotiation strategy in detail. The guiding principle is that the lawyer should fulfill reasonable client expectations for information consistent with the duty to act in the client's best interests, and the client's overall requirements as to the character of representation. In certain circumstances, such as when a lawyer asks a client to consent to a representation affected by a conflict of interest, the client must give informed consent, as defined in Rule 1.0(e).

[6] Ordinarily, the information to be provided is that appropriate for a client who is a comprehending and responsible adult. However, fully informing the client according to this standard may be impracticable, for example, where the client is a child or suffers from diminished capacity. See Rule 1.14. When the client is an organization or group, it is often impossible or inappropriate to inform every one of its members about its legal affairs; ordinarily, the lawyer should address communications to the appropriate officials of the organization. See Rule 1.13. Where many routine matters are involved, a system of limited or occasional reporting may be arranged with the client.

Withholding Information

[7] In some circumstances, a lawyer may be justified in delaying transmission of information when the client would be likely to react imprudently to an immediate communication. Thus, a lawyer might withhold a psychiatric diagnosis of a client when the examining psychiatrist indicates that disclosure would harm the client. A lawyer may not withhold information to serve the lawyer's own interest or convenience or the interests or convenience of another person. Rules or court orders governing litigation may provide that information supplied to a lawyer may not be disclosed to the client. Rule 3.4(c) directs compliance with such rules or orders.

RULE 1.5: FEES

(a) A lawyer shall not make an agreement for, charge, or collect an unreasonable fee or an unreasonable amount for expenses. The factors to be considered in determining the reasonableness of a fee include the following:

(1) the time and labor required, the novelty and difficulty of the questions involved, and the skill requisite to perform the legal service properly;

(2) the likelihood, if apparent to the client, that the acceptance of the particular employment will preclude other employment by the lawyer;

(3) the fee customarily charged in the locality for similar legal services;

(4) the amount involved and the results obtained;

(5) the time limitations imposed by the client or by the circumstances;

(6) the nature and length of the professional relationship with the client;

(7) the experience, reputation, and ability of the lawyer or lawyers performing the services; and

(8) whether the fee is fixed or contingent.

(b) The scope of the representation and the basis or rate of the fee and expenses for which the client will be responsible shall be communicated to the client, preferably in writing, before or within a reasonable time after commencing the representation, except when the lawyer will charge a regularly represented client on the same basis or rate. Any changes in the basis or rate of the fee or expenses shall also be communicated to the client.

(c) A fee may be contingent on the outcome of the matter for which the service is rendered, except in a matter in which a contingent fee is prohibited by paragraph (d) or other law. A contingent fee agreement shall be in a writing signed by the client and shall state the method by which the fee is to be determined, including the percentage or percentages that shall accrue to the lawyer in the event of settlement, trial or appeal; litigation and other expenses to be deducted from the recovery; and whether such expenses are to be deducted before or after the contingent fee is calculated. The agreement must clearly notify the client of any expenses for which the client will be liable whether or not the client is the prevailing party. Upon conclusion of a contingent fee matter, the lawyer shall provide the client with a written statement stating the outcome of the matter and, if there is a recovery, showing the remittance to the client and the method of its determination.

(d) A lawyer shall not enter into an arrangement for, charge, or collect:

(1) any fee in a domestic relations matter, the payment or amount of which is contingent upon the securing of a divorce or upon the amount of alimony or support, or property settlement in lieu thereof, or

(2) a contingent fee for representing a defendant in a criminal case.

(e) A division of a fee between lawyers who are not in the same firm may be made only if:

(1) the division is in proportion to the services performed by each lawyer or each lawyer assumes joint responsibility for the representation;

(2) the client agrees to the arrangement, including the share each lawyer will receive, and the agreement is confirmed in writing; and

(3) the total fee is reasonable.

COMMENT

Reasonableness of Fee and Expenses

[1] Paragraph (a) requires that lawyers charge fees that are reasonable under the circumstances. The factors specified in (1) through (8) are not exclusive. Nor will each factor be relevant in each instance. Paragraph (a) also requires that expenses for which the client will be charged must be reasonable. A lawyer may seek reimbursement for the cost of services performed in-house, such as copying, or for other expenses incurred in-house, such as telephone charges, either by charging a reasonable amount to which the client has agreed in advance or by charging an amount that reasonably reflects the cost incurred by the lawyer.

Basis or Rate of Fee

[2] When the lawyer has regularly represented a client, they ordinarily will have evolved an understanding concerning the basis or rate of the fee and the expenses for which the client will be responsible. In a new client-lawyer relationship, however, an understanding as to fees and expenses must be promptly established. Generally, it is desirable to furnish the client with at least a simple memorandum or copy of the lawyer's customary fee arrangements that states the general nature of the legal services to be provided, the basis, rate or total amount of the fee and whether and to what extent the client will be responsible for any costs, expenses or disbursements in the course of the representation. A written statement concerning the terms of the engagement reduces the possibility of misunderstanding.

[3] Contingent fees, like any other fees, are subject to the reasonableness standard of paragraph (a) of this Rule. In determining whether a particular contingent fee is reasonable, or whether it is reasonable to charge any form of contingent fee, a lawyer must consider the factors that are relevant under the circumstances. Applicable law may impose limitations on contingent fees, such as a ceiling on the percentage allowable, or may require a lawyer to offer clients an alternative basis for the fee. Applicable law also may apply to situations other than a contingent fee, for example, government regulations regarding fees in certain tax matters.

Terms of Payment

[4] A lawyer may require advance payment of a fee, but is obliged to return any unearned portion. See Rule 1.16(d). A lawyer may accept property in payment for services, such as an ownership interest in an enterprise, providing this does not involve acquisition of a proprietary interest in the cause of action or subject matter of the litigation contrary to Rule 1.8(i). However, a fee paid in property instead of money may be subject to the requirements of Rule 1.8(a) because such fees often have the essential qualities of a business transaction with the client.

[5] An agreement may not be made whose terms might induce the lawyer improperly to curtail services for the client or perform them in a way contrary to the client's interest. For example, a lawyer should not enter into an agreement whereby services are to be provided only up to a stated amount when it is foreseeable that more extensive services probably will be required, unless the situation is adequately explained to the client. Otherwise, the client might have to bargain for further assistance in the midst of a proceeding or transaction. However, it is proper to define the extent of services in light of the client's ability to pay. A lawyer should not exploit a fee arrangement based primarily on hourly charges by using wasteful procedures.

Prohibited Contingent Fees

[6] Paragraph (d) prohibits a lawyer from charging a contingent fee in a domestic relations matter when payment is contingent upon the securing of a divorce or upon the amount of alimony or support or property settlement to be obtained. This provision does not preclude a contract for a contingent fee for legal representation

in connection with the recovery of post-judgment balances due under support, alimony or other financial orders because such contracts do not implicate the same policy concerns.

Division of Fee

[7] A division of fee is a single billing to a client covering the fee of two or more lawyers who are not in the same firm. A division of fee facilitates association of more than one lawyer in a matter in which neither alone could serve the client as well, and most often is used when the fee is contingent and the division is between a referring lawyer and a trial specialist. Paragraph (e) permits the lawyers to divide a fee either on the basis of the proportion of services they render or if each lawyer assumes responsibility for the representation as a whole. In addition, the client must agree to the arrangement, including the share that each lawyer is to receive, and the agreement must be confirmed in writing. Contingent fee agreements must be in a writing signed by the client and must otherwise comply with paragraph (c) of this Rule. Joint responsibility for the representation entails financial and ethical responsibility for the representation as if the lawyers were associated in a partnership. A lawyer should only refer a matter to a lawyer whom the referring lawyer reasonably believes is competent to handle the matter. See Rule 1.1.

[8] Paragraph (e) does not prohibit or regulate division of fees to be received in the future for work done when lawyers were previously associated in a law firm.

Disputes over Fees

[9] If a procedure has been established for resolution of fee disputes, such as an arbitration or mediation procedure established by the bar, the lawyer must comply with the procedure when it is mandatory, and, even when it is voluntary, the lawyer should conscientiously consider submitting to it. Law may prescribe a procedure for determining a lawyer's fee, for example, in representation of an executor or administrator, a class or a person entitled to a reasonable fee as part of the measure of damages. The lawyer entitled to such a fee and a lawyer representing another party concerned with the fee should comply with the prescribed procedure.

RULE 1.6: CONFIDENTIALITY OF INFORMATION

(a) A lawyer shall not reveal information relating to the representation of a client unless the client gives informed consent, the disclosure is impliedly authorized in order to carry out the representation or the disclosure is permitted by paragraph (b).

(b) A lawyer may reveal information relating to the representation of a client to the extent the lawyer reasonably believes necessary:

(1) to prevent reasonably certain death or substantial bodily harm;

(2) to secure legal advice about the lawyer's compliance with these Rules;

(3) to establish a claim or defense on behalf of the lawyer in a controversy between the lawyer and the client, to establish a defense to a criminal charge or civil claim against the lawyer based upon conduct in which the client was involved, or to respond to allegations in any proceeding concerning the lawyer's representation of the client; or

(4) to comply with other law or a court order.

COMMENT

[1] This Rule governs the disclosure by a lawyer of information relating to the representation of a client during the lawyer's representation of the client. See Rule 1.18 for the lawyer's duties with respect to information provided to the lawyer by a prospective client, Rule 1.9(c)(2) for the lawyer's duty not to reveal information relating to the lawyer's prior representation of a former client and Rules 1.8(b) and 1.9(c)(1) for the lawyer's duties with respect to the use of such information to the disadvantage of clients and former clients.

[2] A fundamental principle in the client-lawyer relationship is that, in the absence of the client's informed consent, the lawyer must not reveal information relating to the representation. See Rule 1.0(e) for the definition of informed consent. This contributes to the trust that is the hallmark of the client-lawyer relationship. The client is thereby encouraged to seek legal assistance and to communicate fully and frankly with the lawyer even as to embarrassing or legally damaging subject matter. The lawyer needs this information

to represent the client effectively and, if necessary, to advise the client to refrain from wrongful conduct. Almost without exception, clients come to lawyers in order to determine their rights and what is, in the complex of laws and regulations, deemed to be legal and correct. Based upon experience, lawyers know that almost all clients follow the advice given, and the law is upheld.

[3] The principle of client-lawyer confidentiality is given effect by related bodies of law: the attorney-client privilege, the work product doctrine and the rule of confidentiality established in professional ethics. The attorney-client privilege and work-product doctrine apply in judicial and other proceedings in which a lawyer may be called as a witness or otherwise required to produce evidence concerning a client. The rule of client-lawyer confidentiality applies in situations other than those where evidence is sought from the lawyer through compulsion of law. The confidentiality rule, for example, applies not only to matters communicated in confidence by the client but also to all information relating to the representation, whatever its source. A lawyer may not disclose such information except as authorized or required by the Rules of Professional Conduct or other law. See also Scope.

[4] Paragraph (a) prohibits a lawyer from revealing information relating to the representation of a client. This prohibition also applies to disclosures by a lawyer that do not in themselves reveal protected information but could reasonably lead to the discovery of such information by a third person. A lawyer's use of a hypothetical to discuss issues relating to the representation is permissible so long as there is no reasonable likelihood that the listener will be able to ascertain the identity of the client or the situation involved.

Authorized Disclosure

[5] Except to the extent that the client's instructions or special circumstances limit that authority, a lawyer is impliedly authorized to make disclosures about a client when appropriate in carrying out the representation. In some situations, for example, a lawyer may be impliedly authorized to admit a fact that cannot properly be disputed or to make a disclosure that facilitates a satisfactory conclusion to a matter. Lawyers in a firm may, in the course of the firm's practice, disclose to each other information relating to a client of the firm, unless the client has instructed that particular information be confined to specified lawyers.

Disclosure Adverse to Client

[6] Although the public interest is usually best served by a strict rule requiring lawyers to preserve the confidentiality of information relating to the representation of their clients, the confidentiality rule is subject to limited exceptions. Paragraph (b)(1) recognizes the overriding value of life and physical integrity and permits disclosure reasonably necessary to prevent reasonably certain death or substantial bodily harm. Such harm is reasonably certain to occur if it will be suffered imminently or if there is a present and substantial threat that a person will suffer such harm at a later date if the lawyer fails to take action necessary to eliminate the threat. Thus, a lawyer who knows that a client has accidentally discharged toxic waste into a town's water supply may reveal this information to the authorities if there is a present and substantial risk that a person who drinks the water will contract a life-threatening or debilitating disease and the lawyer's disclosure is necessary to eliminate the threat or reduce the number of victims.

[7] A lawyer's confidentiality obligations do not preclude a lawyer from securing confidential legal advice about the lawyer's personal responsibility to comply with these Rules. In most situations, disclosing information to secure such advice will be impliedly authorized for the lawyer to carry out the representation. Even when the disclosure is not impliedly authorized, paragraph (b)(2) permits such disclosure because of the importance of a lawyer's compliance with the Rules of Professional Conduct.

[8] Where a legal claim or disciplinary charge alleges complicity of the lawyer in a client's conduct or other misconduct of the lawyer involving representation of the client, the lawyer may respond to the extent the lawyer reasonably believes necessary to establish a defense. The same is true with respect to a claim involving the conduct or representation of a former client. Such a charge can arise in a civil, criminal, disciplinary or other proceeding and can be based on a wrong allegedly committed by the lawyer against the client or on

a wrong alleged by a third person, for example, a person claiming to have been defrauded by the lawyer and client acting together. The lawyer's right to respond arises when an assertion of such complicity has been made. Paragraph (b)(3) does not require the lawyer to await the commencement of an action or proceeding that charges such complicity, so that the defense may be established by responding directly to a third party who has made such an assertion. The right to defend also applies, of course, where a proceeding has been commenced.

[9] A lawyer entitled to a fee is permitted by paragraph (b)(3) to prove the services rendered in an action to collect it. This aspect of the rule expresses the principle that the beneficiary of a fiduciary relationship may not exploit it to the detriment of the fiduciary.

[10] Other law may require that a lawyer disclose information about a client. Whether such a law supersedes Rule 1.6 is a question of law beyond the scope of these Rules. When disclosure of information relating to the representation appears to be required by other law, the lawyer must discuss the matter with the client to the extent required by Rule 1.4. If, however, the other law supersedes this Rule and requires disclosure, paragraph (b)(4) permits the lawyer to make such disclosures as are necessary to comply with the law.

[11] A lawyer may be ordered to reveal information relating to the representation of a client by a court or by another tribunal or governmental entity claiming authority pursuant to other law to compel the disclosure. Absent informed consent of the client to do otherwise, the lawyer should assert on behalf of the client all nonfrivolous claims that the order is not authorized by other law or that the information sought is protected against disclosure by the attorney-client privilege or other applicable law. In the event of an adverse ruling, the lawyer must consult with the client about the possibility of appeal to the extent required by Rule 1.4. Unless review is sought, however, paragraph (b)(4) permits the lawyer to comply with the court's order.

[12] Paragraph (b) permits disclosure only to the extent the lawyer reasonably believes the disclosure is necessary to accomplish one of the purposes specified. Where practicable, the lawyer should first seek to persuade the client to take suitable action to obviate the need for disclosure. In any case, a disclosure adverse to the client's interest should be no greater than the lawyer reasonably believes necessary to accomplish the purpose. If the disclosure will be made in connection with a judicial proceeding, the disclosure should be made in a manner that limits access to the information to the tribunal or other persons having a need to know it and appropriate protective orders or other arrangements should be sought by the lawyer to the fullest extent practicable.

[13] Paragraph (b) permits but does not require the disclosure of information relating to a client's representation to accomplish the purposes specified in paragraphs (b)(1) through (b)(4). In exercising the discretion conferred by this Rule, the lawyer may consider such factors as the nature of the lawyer's relationship with the client and with those who might be injured by the client, the lawyer's own involvement in the transaction and factors that may extenuate the conduct in question. A lawyer's decision not to disclose as permitted by paragraph (b) does not violate this Rule. Disclosure may be required, however, by other Rules. Some Rules require disclosure only if such disclosure would be permitted by paragraph (b). See Rules 1.2(d), 4.1(b), 8.1 and 8.3. Rule 3.3, on the other hand, requires disclosure in some circumstances regardless of whether such disclosure is permitted by this Rule. See Rule 3.3(c).

Withdrawal

[14] If the lawyer's services will be used by the client in materially furthering a course of criminal or fraudulent conduct, the lawyer must withdraw, as stated in Rule 1.16(a)(1). After withdrawal the lawyer is required to refrain from making disclosure of the client's confidences, except as otherwise permitted by Rule 1.6. Neither this Rule nor Rule 1.8(b) nor Rule 1.16(d) prevents the lawyer from giving notice of the fact of withdrawal, and the lawyer may also withdraw or disaffirm any opinion, document, affirmation, or the like. Where the client is an organization, the lawyer may be in doubt whether contemplated conduct will actually be carried out by the organization. Where necessary to guide conduct in connection

Model Rules of Professional Conduct

with this Rule, the lawyer may make inquiry within the organization as indicated in Rule 1.13(b).

Acting Competently to Preserve Confidentiality

[15] A lawyer must act competently to safeguard information relating to the representation of a client against inadvertent or unauthorized disclosure by the lawyer or other persons who are participating in the representation of the client or who are subject to the lawyer's supervision. See Rules 1.1, 5.1 and 5.3.

[16] When transmitting a communication that includes information relating to the representation of a client, the lawyer must take reasonable precautions to prevent the information from coming into the hands of unintended recipients. This duty, however, does not require that the lawyer use special security measures if the method of communication affords a reasonable expectation of privacy. Special circumstances, however, may warrant special precautions. Factors to be considered in determining the reasonableness of the lawyer's expectation of confidentiality include the sensitivity of the information and the extent to which the privacy of the communication is protected by law or by a confidentiality agreement. A client may require the lawyer to implement special security measures not required by this Rule or may give informed consent to the use of a means of communication that would otherwise be prohibited by this Rule.

Former Client

[17] The duty of confidentiality continues after the client-lawyer relationship has terminated. See Rule 1.9(c)(2). See Rule 1.9(c)(1) for the prohibition against using such information to the disadvantage of the former client.

RULE 1.7: CONFLICT OF INTEREST: CURRENT CLIENTS

(a) Except as provided in paragraph (b), a lawyer shall not represent a client if the representation involves a concurrent conflict of interest. A concurrent conflict of interest exists if:

(1) the representation of one client will be directly adverse to another client; or

(2) there is a significant risk that the representation of one or more clients will be materially limited by the lawyer's responsibilities to another client, a former client or a third person or by a personal interest of the lawyer.

(b) Notwithstanding the existence of a concurrent conflict of interest under paragraph (a), a lawyer may represent a client if:

(1) the lawyer reasonably believes that the lawyer will be able to provide competent and diligent representation to each affected client;

(2) the representation is not prohibited by law;

(3) the representation does not involve the assertion of a claim by one client against another client represented by the lawyer in the same litigation or other proceeding before a tribunal; and

(4) each affected client gives informed consent, confirmed in writing.

COMMENT

General Principles

[1] Loyalty and independent judgment are essential elements in the lawyer's relationship to a client. Concurrent conflicts of interest can arise from the lawyer's responsibilities to another client, a former client or a third person or from the lawyer's own interests. For specific Rules regarding certain concurrent conflicts of interest, see Rule 1.8. For former client conflicts of interest, see Rule 1.9. For conflicts of interest involving prospective clients, see Rule 1. 18. For definitions of "informed consent" and "confirmed in writing," see Rule 1.0(e) and (b).

[2] Resolution of a conflict of interest problem under this Rule requires the lawyer to: 1) clearly identify the client or clients; 2) determine whether a conflict of interest exists; 3) decide whether the representation may be undertaken despite the existence of a conflict, i.e., whether the conflict is consentable; and 4) if so, consult with the clients affected under paragraph (a) and obtain their informed consent, confirmed in writing. The clients affected under paragraph (a) include both of the clients referred to in paragraph (a)(1) and the one or more clients whose representation might be materially limited under paragraph (a)(2).

[3] A conflict of interest may exist before representation is undertaken, in which event the

representation must be declined, unless the lawyer obtains the informed consent of each client under the conditions of paragraph (b). To determine whether a conflict of interest exists, a lawyer should adopt reasonable procedures, appropriate for the size and type of firm and practice, to determine in both litigation and non-litigation matters the persons and issues involved. See also Comment to Rule 5.1. Ignorance caused by a failure to institute such procedures will not excuse a lawyer's violation of this Rule. As to whether a client-lawyer relationship exists or, having once been established, is continuing, see Comment to Rule 1.3 and Scope.

[4] If a conflict arises after representation has been undertaken, the lawyer ordinarily must withdraw from the representation, unless the lawyer has obtained the informed consent of the client under the conditions of paragraph (b). See Rule 1.16. Where more than one client is involved, whether the lawyer may continue to represent any of the clients is determined both by the lawyer's ability to comply with duties owed to the former client and by the lawyer's ability to represent adequately the remaining client or clients, given the lawyer's duties to the former client. See Rule 1.9. See also Comments [5] and [29].

[5] Unforeseeable developments, such as changes in corporate and other organizational affiliations or the addition or realignment of parties in litigation, might create conflicts in the midst of a representation, as when a company sued by the lawyer on behalf of one client is bought by another client represented by the lawyer in an unrelated matter. Depending on the circumstances, the lawyer may have the option to withdraw from one of the representations in order to avoid the conflict. The lawyer must seek court approval where necessary and take steps to minimize harm to the clients. See Rule 1.16. The lawyer must continue to protect the confidences of the client from whose representation the lawyer has withdrawn. See Rule 1.9(c).

Identifying Conflicts of Interest: Directly Adverse

[6] Loyalty to a current client prohibits undertaking representation directly adverse to that client without that client's informed consent. Thus, absent consent, a lawyer may not act as an advocate in one matter against a person the lawyer represents in some other matter, even when the matters are wholly unrelated. The client as to whom the representation is directly adverse is likely to feel betrayed, and the resulting damage to the client-lawyer relationship is likely to impair the lawyer's ability to represent the client effectively. In addition, the client on whose behalf the adverse representation is undertaken reasonably may fear that the lawyer will pursue that client's case less effectively out of deference to the other client, i.e., that the representation may be materially limited by the lawyer's interest in retaining the current client. Similarly, a directly adverse conflict may arise when a lawyer is required to cross-examine a client who appears as a witness in a lawsuit involving another client, as when the testimony will be damaging to the client who is represented in the lawsuit. On the other hand, simultaneous representation in unrelated matters of clients whose interests are only economically adverse, such as representation of competing economic enterprises in unrelated litigation, does not ordinarily constitute a conflict of interest and thus may not require consent of the respective clients.

[7] Directly adverse conflicts can also arise in transactional matters. For example, if a lawyer is asked to represent the seller of a business in negotiations with a buyer represented by the lawyer, not in the same transaction but in another, unrelated matter, the lawyer could not undertake the representation without the informed consent of each client.

Identifying Conflicts of Interest: Material Limitation

[8] Even where there is no direct adverseness, a conflict of interest exists if there is a significant risk that a lawyer's ability to consider, recommend or carry out an appropriate course of action for the client will be materially limited as a result of the lawyer's other responsibilities or interests. For example, a lawyer asked to represent several individuals seeking to form a joint venture is likely to be materially limited in the lawyer's ability to recommend or advocate all possible positions that each might take because of the lawyer's duty of loyalty to the others. The conflict in effect forecloses alternatives that

would otherwise be available to the client. The mere possibility of subsequent harm does not itself require disclosure and consent. The critical questions are the likelihood that a difference in interests will eventuate and, if it does, whether it will materially interfere with the lawyer's independent professional judgment in considering alternatives or foreclose courses of action that reasonably should be pursued on behalf of the client.

Lawyer's Responsibilities to Former Clients and Other Third Persons

[9] In addition to conflicts with other current clients, a lawyer's duties of loyalty and independence may be materially limited by responsibilities to former clients under Rule 1.9 or by the lawyer's responsibilities to other persons, such as fiduciary duties arising from a lawyer's service as a trustee, executor or corporate director.

Personal Interest Conflicts

[10] The lawyer's own interests should not be permitted to have an adverse effect on representation of a client. For example, if the probity of a lawyer's own conduct in a transaction is in serious question, it may be difficult or impossible for the lawyer to give a client detached advice. Similarly, when a lawyer has discussions concerning possible employment with an opponent of the lawyer's client, or with a law firm representing the opponent, such discussions could materially limit the lawyer's representation of the client. In addition, a lawyer may not allow related business interests to affect representation, for example, by referring clients to an enterprise in which the lawyer has an undisclosed financial interest. See Rule 1.8 for specific Rules pertaining to a number of personal interest conflicts, including business transactions with clients. See also Rule 1.10 (personal interest conflicts under Rule 1.7 ordinarily are not imputed to other lawyers in a law firm).

[11] When lawyers representing different clients in the same matter or in substantially related matters are closely related by blood or marriage, there may be a significant risk that client confidences will be revealed and that the lawyer's family relationship will interfere with both loyalty and independent professional judgment. As a result, each client is entitled to know of the existence and implications of the relationship between the lawyers before the lawyer agrees to undertake the representation. Thus, a lawyer related to another lawyer, e.g., as parent, child, sibling or spouse, ordinarily may not represent a client in a matter where that lawyer is representing another party, unless each client gives informed consent. The disqualification arising from a close family relationship is personal and ordinarily is not imputed to members of firms with whom the lawyers are associated. See Rule 1.10.

[12] A lawyer is prohibited from engaging in sexual relationships with a client unless the sexual relationship predates the formation of the client-lawyer relationship. See Rule 1.80).

Interest of Person Paying for a Lawyer's Service

[13] A lawyer may be paid from a source other than the client, including a co-client, if the client is informed of that fact and consents and the arrangement does not compromise the lawyer's duty of loyalty or independent judgment to the client. See Rule 1.8(f). If acceptance of the payment from any other source presents a significant risk that the lawyer's representation of the client will be materially limited by the lawyer's own interest in accommodating the person paying the lawyer's fee or by the lawyer's responsibilities to a payer who is also a co-client, then the lawyer must comply with the requirements of paragraph (b) before accepting the representation, including determining whether the conflict is consentable and, if so, that the client has adequate information about the material risks of the representation.

Prohibited Representations

[14] Ordinarily, clients may consent to representation notwithstanding a conflict. However, as indicated in paragraph (b), some conflicts are nonconsentable, meaning that the lawyer involved cannot properly ask for such agreement or provide representation on the basis of the client's consent. When the lawyer is representing more than one client, the question of consentability must be resolved as to each client.

[15] Consentability is typically determined by considering whether the interests of the clients will

be adequately protected if the clients are permitted to give their informed consent to representation burdened by a conflict of interest. Thus, under paragraph (b)(1), representation is prohibited if in the circumstances the lawyer cannot reasonably conclude that the lawyer will be able to provide competent and diligent representation. See Rule 1.1 (competence) and Rule 1.3 (diligence).

[16] Paragraph (b)(2) describes conflicts that are nonconsentable because the representation is prohibited by applicable law. For example, in some states substantive law provides that the same lawyer may not represent more than one defendant in a capital case, even with the consent of the clients, and under federal criminal statutes certain representations by a former government lawyer are prohibited, despite the informed consent of the former client. In addition, decisional law in some states limits the ability of a governmental client, such as a municipality, to consent to a conflict of interest.

[17] Paragraph (b)(3) describes conflicts that are nonconsentable because of the institutional interest in vigorous development of each client's position when the clients are aligned directly against each other in the same litigation or other proceeding before a tribunal. Whether clients are aligned directly against each other within the meaning of this paragraph requires examination of the context of the proceeding. Although this paragraph does not preclude a lawyer's multiple representation of adverse parties to a mediation (because mediation is not a proceeding before a "tribunal" under Rule 1.0(m)), such representation may be precluded by paragraph (b)(1).

Informed Consent

[18] Informed consent requires that each affected client be aware of the relevant circumstances and of the material and reasonably foreseeable ways that the conflict could have adverse effects on the interests of that client. See Rule 1.0(e) (informed consent). The information required depends on the nature of the conflict and the nature of the risks involved. When representation of multiple clients in a single matter is undertaken, the information must include the implications of the common representation, including possible effects on loyalty, confidentiality and the attorney-client privilege and the advantages and risks involved. See Comments [30] and [31] (effect of common representation on confidentiality).

[19] Under some circumstances it may be impossible to make the disclosure necessary to obtain consent. For example, when the lawyer represents different clients in related matters and one of the clients refuses to consent to the disclosure necessary to permit the other client to make an informed decision, the lawyer cannot properly ask the latter to consent. In some cases the alternative to common representation can be that each party may have to obtain separate representation with the possibility of incurring additional costs. These costs, along with the benefits of securing separate representation, are factors that may be considered by the affected client in determining whether common representation is in the client's interests.

Consent Confirmed in Writing

[20] Paragraph (b) requires the lawyer to obtain the informed consent of the client, confirmed in writing. Such a writing may consist of a document executed by the client or one that the lawyer promptly records and transmits to the client following an oral consent. See Rule 1.0(b). See also Rule 1.0(n) (writing includes electronic transmission). If it is not feasible to obtain or transmit the writing at the time the client gives informed consent, then the lawyer must obtain or transmit it within a reasonable time thereafter. See Rule 1.0(b). The requirement of a writing does not supplant the need in most cases for the lawyer to talk with the client, to explain the risks and advantages, if any, of representation burdened with a conflict of interest, as well as reasonably available alternatives, and to afford the client a reasonable opportunity to consider the risks and alternatives and to raise questions and concerns. Rather, the writing is required in order to impress upon clients the seriousness of the decision the client is being asked to make and to avoid disputes or ambiguities that might later occur in the absence of a writing.

Revoking Consent

[21] A client who has given consent to a conflict may revoke the consent and, like any other client,

may terminate the lawyer's representation at any time. Whether revoking consent to the client's own representation precludes the lawyer from continuing to represent other clients depends on the circumstances, including the nature of the conflict, whether the client revoked consent because of a material change in circumstances, the reasonable expectations of the other client and whether material detriment to the other clients or the lawyer would result.

Consent to Future Conflict

[22] Whether a lawyer may properly request a client to waive conflicts that might arise in the future is subject to the test of paragraph (b). The effectiveness of such waivers is generally determined by the extent to which the client reasonably understands the material risks that the waiver entails. The more comprehensive the explanation of the types of future representations that might arise and the actual and reasonably foreseeable adverse consequences of those representations, the greater the likelihood that the client will have the requisite understanding. Thus, if the client agrees to consent to a particular type of conflict with which the client is already familiar, then the consent ordinarily will be effective with regard to that type of conflict. If the consent is general and open-ended, then the consent ordinarily will be ineffective, because it is not reasonably likely that the client will have understood the material risks involved. On the other hand, if the client is an experienced user of the legal services involved and is reasonably informed regarding the risk that a conflict may arise, such consent is more likely to be effective, particularly if, e.g., the client is independently represented by other counsel in giving consent and the consent is limited to future conflicts unrelated to the subject of the representation. In any case, advance consent cannot be effective if the circumstances that materialize in the ftiure are such as would make the conflict nonconsentable under paragraph (b).

Conflicts in Litigation

[23] Paragraph (b)(3) prohibits representation of opposing parties in the same litigation, regardless of the clients' consent. On the other hand, simultaneous representation of parties whose interests in litigation may conflict, such as coplaintiffs or codefendants, is governed by paragraph (a)(2). A conflict may exist by reason of substantial discrepancy in the parties' testimony, incompatibility in positions in relation to an opposing party or the fact that there are substantially different possibilities of settlement of the claims or liabilities in question. Such conflicts can arise in criminal cases as well as civil. The potential for conflict of interest in representing multiple defendants in a criminal case is so grave that ordinarily a lawyer should decline to represent more than one codefendant. On the other hand, common representation of persons having similar interests in civil litigation is proper if the requirements of paragraph (b) are met.

[24] Ordinarily a lawyer may take inconsistent legal positions in different tribunals at different times on behalf of different clients. The mere fact that advocating a legal position on behalf of one client might create precedent adverse to the interests of a client represented by the lawyer in an unrelated matter does not create a conflict of interest. A conflict of interest exists, however, if there is a significant risk that a lawyer's action on behalf of one client will materially limit the lawyer's effectiveness in representing another client in a different case; for example, when a decision favoring one client will create a precedent likely to seriously weaken the position taken on behalf of the other client. Factors relevant in determining whether the clients need to be advised of the risk include: where the cases are pending, whether the issue is substantive or procedural, the temporal relationship between the matters, the significance of the issue to the immediate and long-term interests of the clients involved and the clients' reasonable expectations in retaining the lawyer. If there is significant risk of material limitation, then absent informed consent of the affected clients, the lawyer must refuse one of the representations or withdraw from one or both matters.

[25] When a lawyer represents or seeks to represent a class of plaintiffs or defendants in a class-action lawsuit, unnamed members of the class are ordinarily not considered to be clients of the lawyer for purposes of applying paragraph (a)(1) of this Rule. Thus, the lawyer does not typically need to get the consent of such a person

before representing a client suing the person in an unrelated matter. Similarly, a lawyer seeking to represent an opponent in a class action does not typically need the consent of an unnamed member of the class whom the lawyer represents in an unrelated matter.

Nonlitigation Conflicts

[26] Conflicts of interest under paragraphs (a)(1) and (a)(2) arise in contexts other than litigation. For a discussion of directly adverse conflicts in transactional matters, see Comment [7]. Relevant factors in determining whether there is significant potential for material limitation include the duration and intimacy of the lawyer's relationship with the client or clients involved, the functions being performed by the lawyer, the likelihood that disagreements will arise and the likely prejudice to the client from the conflict. The question is often one of proximity and degree. See Comment [8].

[27] For example, conflict questions may arise in estate planning and estate administration. A lawyer may be called upon to prepare wills for several family members, such as husband and wife, and, depending upon the circumstances, a conflict of interest may be present. In estate administration the identity of the client may be unclear under the law of a particular jurisdiction. Under one view, the client is the fiduciary; under another view the client is the estate or trust, including its beneficiaries. In order to comply with conflict of interest rules, the lawyer should make clear the lawyer's relationship to the parties involved.

[28] Whether a conflict is consentable depends on the circumstances. For example, a lawyer may not represent multiple parties to a negotiation whose interests are fundamentally antagonistic to each other, but common representation is permissible where the clients are generally aligned in interest even though there is some difference in interest among them. Thus, a lawyer may seek to establish or adjust a relationship between clients on an amicable and mutually advantageous basis; for example, in helping to organize a business in which two or more clients are entrepreneurs, working out the financial reorganization of an enterprise in which two or more clients have an interest or arranging a property distribution in settlement of an estate. The lawyer seeks to resolve potentially adverse interests by developing the parties' mutual interests. Otherwise, each party might have to obtain separate representation, with the possibility of incurring additional cost, complication or even litigation. Given these and other relevant factors, the clients may prefer that the lawyer act for all of them.

Special Considerations in Common Representation

[29] In considering whether to represent multiple clients in the same matter, a lawyer should be mindful that if the common representation fails because the potentially adverse interests cannot be reconciled, the result can be additional cost, embarrassment and recrimination. Ordinarily, the lawyer will be forced to withdraw from representing all of the clients if the common representation fails. In some situations, the risk of failure is so great that multiple representation is plainly impossible. For example, a lawyer cannot undertake common representation of clients where contentious litigation or negotiations between them are imminent or contemplated. Moreover, because the lawyer is required to be impartial between commonly represented clients, representation of multiple clients is improper when it is unlikely that impartiality can be maintained. Generally, if the relationship between the parties has already assumed antagonism, the possibility that the clients' interests can be adequately served by common representation is not very good. Other relevant factors are whether the lawyer subsequently will represent both parties on a continuing basis and whether the situation involves creating or terminating a relationship between the parties.

[30] A particularly important factor in determining the appropriateness of common representation is the effect on client-lawyer confidentiality and the attorney-client privilege. With regard to the attorney-client privilege, the prevailing rule is that, as between commonly represented clients, the privilege does not attach. Hence, it must be assumed that if litigation eventuates between the clients, the privilege will not protect any such communications, and the clients should be so advised.

[31] As to the duty of confidentiality, continued common representation will almost certainly be inadequate if one client asks the lawyer not to disclose to the other client information relevant to the common representation. This is so because the lawyer has an equal duty of loyalty to each client, and each client has the right to be informed of anything bearing on the representation that might affect that client's interests and the right to expect that the lawyer will use that information to that client's benefit. See Rule 1.4. The lawyer should, -at the outset of the common representation and as part of the process of obtaining each client's informed consent, advise each client that information will be shared and that the lawyer will have to withdraw if one client decides that some matter material to the representation should be kept from the other. In limited circumstances, it may be appropriate for the lawyer to proceed with the representation when the clients have agreed, after being properly informed, that the lawyer will keep certain information confidential. For example, the lawyer may reasonably conclude that failure to disclose one client's trade secrets to another client will not adversely affect representation involving a joint venture between the clients and agree to keep that information confidential with the informed consent of both clients.

[32] When seeking to establish or adjust a relationship between clients, the lawyer should make clear that the lawyer's role is not that of partisanship normally expected in other circumstances and, thus, that the clients may be required to assume greater responsibility for decisions than when each client is separately represented. Any limitations on the scope of the representation made necessary as a result of the common representation should be fully explained to the clients at the outset of the representation. See Rule 1.2(c).

[33] Subject to the above limitations, each client in the common representation has the right to loyal and diligent representation and the protection of Rule 1.9 concerning the obligations to a former client. The client also has the right to discharge the lawyer as stated in Rule 1.16.

Organizational Clients

[34] A lawyer who represents a corporation or other organization does not, by virtue of that representation, necessarily represent any constituent or affiliated organization, such as a parent or subsidiary. See Rule 1.13(a). Thus, the lawyer for an organization is not barred from accepting representation adverse to an affiliate in an unrelated matter, unless the circumstances are such that the affiliate should also be considered a client of the lawyer, there is an understanding between the lawyer and the organizational client that the lawyer will avoid representation adverse to the client's affiliates, or the lawyer's obligations to either the organizational client or the new client are likely to limit materially the lawyer's representation of the other client.

[35] A lawyer for a corporation or other organization who is also a member of its board of directors should determine whether the responsibilities of the two roles may conflict. The lawyer may be called on to advise the corporation in matters involving actions of the directors. Consideration should be given to the frequency with which such situations may arise, the potential intensity of the conflict, the effect of the lawyer's resignation from the board and the possibility of the corporation's obtaining legal advice from another lawyer in such situations. If there is material risk that the dual role will compromise the lawyer's independence of professional judgment, the lawyer should not serve as a director or should cease to act as the corporation's lawyer when conflicts of interest arise. The lawyer should advise the other members of the board that in some circumstances matters discussed at board meetings while the lawyer is present in the capacity of director might not be protected by the attorney-client privilege and that conflict of interest considerations might require the lawyer's recusal as a director or might require the lawyer and the lawyer's firm to decline representation of the corporation in a matter.

RULE 1.8: CONFLICT OF INTEREST: CURRENT CLIENTS: SPECIFIC RULES

(a) A lawyer shall not enter into a business transaction with a client or knowingly acquire an ownership, possessory, security or other pecuniary interest adverse to a client unless:

(1) the transaction and terms on which the lawyer acquires the interest are fair and reasonable to the client and are fully disclosed

and transmitted in writing in a manner that can be reasonably understood by the client;

(2) the client is advised in writing of the desirability of seeking and is given a reasonable opportunity to seek the advice of independent legal counsel on the transaction; and

(3) the client gives informed consent, in a writing signed by the client, to the essential terms of the transaction and the lawyer's role in the transaction, including whether the lawyer is representing the client in the transaction.

(b) A lawyer shall not use information relating to representation of a client to the disadvantage of the client unless the client gives informed consent, except as permitted or required by these Rules.

(c) A lawyer shall not solicit any substantial gift from a client, including a testamentary gift, or prepare on behalf of a client an instrument giving the lawyer or a person related to the lawyer any substantial gift unless the lawyer or other recipient of the gift is related to the client. For purposes of this paragraph, related persons include a spouse, child, grandchild, parent, grandparent or other relative or individual with whom the lawyer or the client maintains a close, familial relationship.

(d) Prior to the conclusion of representation of a client, a lawyer shall not make or negotiate an agreement giving the lawyer literary or media rights to a portrayal or account based in substantial part on information relating to the representation.

(e) A lawyer shall not provide financial assistance to a client in connection with pending or contemplated litigation, except that:

(1) a lawyer may advance court costs and expenses of litigation, the repayment of which may be contingent on the outcome of the matter; and

(2) a lawyer representing an indigent client may pay court costs and expenses of litigation on behalf of the client.

(f) A lawyer shall not accept compensation for representing a client from one other than the client unless:

(1) the client gives informed consent;

(2) there is no interference with the lawyer's independence of professional judgment or with the client-lawyer relationship; and

(3) information relating to representation of a client is protected as required by Rule 1.6.

(g) A lawyer who represents two or more clients shall not participate in making an aggregate settlement of the claims of or against the clients, or in a criminal case an aggregated agreement as to guilty or nolo contendere pleas, unless each client gives informed consent, in a writing signed by the client. The lawyer's disclosure shall include the existence and nature of all the claims or pleas involved and of the participation of each person in the settlement.

(h) A lawyer shall not:

(1) make an agreement prospectively limiting the lawyer's liability to a client for malpractice unless the client is independently represented in making the agreement; or

(2) settle a claim or potential claim for such liability with an unrepresented client or former client unless that person is advised in writing of the desirability of seeking and is given a reasonable opportunity to seek the advice of independent legal counsel in connection therewith.

(i) A lawyer shall not acquire a proprietary interest in the cause of action or subject matter of litigation the lawyer is conducting for a client, except that the lawyer may:

(1) acquire a lien authorized by law to secure the lawyer's fee or expenses; and

(2) contract with a client for a reasonable contingent fee in a civil case.

(j) A lawyer shall not have sexual relations with a client unless a consensual sexual relationship existed between them when the client-lawyer relationship commenced.

(k) While lawyers are associated in a firm, a prohibition in the foregoing paragraphs (a) through (i) that applies to any one of them shall apply to all of them.

COMMENT

Business Transactions Between Client and Lawyer

[1] A lawyer's legal skill and training, together with the relationship of trust and confidence between lawyer and client, create the possibility of overreaching when the lawyer participates in a business, property or financial transaction with

a client, for example, a loan or sales transaction or a lawyer investment on behalf of a client. The requirements of paragraph (a) must be met even when the transaction is not closely related to the subject matter of the representation, as when a lawyer drafting a will for a client learns that the client needs money for unrelated expenses and offers to make a loan to the client. The Rule applies to lawyers engaged in the sale of goods or services related to the practice of law, for example, the sale of title insurance or investment services to existing clients of the lawyer's legal practice. See Rule 5.7. It also applies to lawyers purchasing property from estates they represent. It does not apply to ordinary fee arrangements between client and lawyer, which are governed by Rule 1.5, although its requirements must be met when the lawyer accepts an interest in the client's business or other nonmonetary property as payment of all or part of a fee. In addition, the Rule does not apply to standard commercial transactions between the lawyer and the client for products or services that the client generally markets to others, for example, banking or brokerage services, medical services, products manufactured or distributed by the client, and utilities' services. In such transactions, the lawyer has no advantage in dealing with the client, and the restrictions in paragraph (a) are unnecessary and impracticable.

[2] Paragraph (a)(1) requires that the transaction itself be fair to the client and that its essential terms be communicated to the client, in writing, in a manner that can be reasonably understood. Paragraph (a)(2) requires that the client also be advised, in writing, of the desirability of seeking the advice of independent legal counsel. It also requires that the client be given a reasonable opportunity to obtain such advice. Paragraph (a)(3) requires that the lawyer obtain the client's informed consent, in a writing signed by the client, both to the essential terms of the transaction and to the lawyer's role. When necessary, the lawyer should discuss both the material risks of the proposed transaction, including any risk presented by the lawyer's involvement, and the existence of reasonably available alternatives and should explain why the advice of independent legal counsel is desirable. See Rule 1.0(e) (definition of informed consent).

[3] The risk to a client is greatest when the client expects the lawyer to represent the client in the transaction itself or when the lawyer's financial interest otherwise poses a significant risk that the lawyer's representation of the client will be materially limited by the lawyer's financial interest in the transaction. Here the lawyer's role requires that the lawyer must comply, not only with the requirements of paragraph (a), but also with the requirements of Rule 1.7. Under that Rule, the lawyer must disclose the risks associated with the lawyer's dual role as both legal adviser and participant in the transaction, such as the risk that the lawyer will structure the transaction or give legal advice in a way that favors the lawyer's interests at the expense of the client. Moreover, the lawyer must obtain the client's informed consent. In some cases, the lawyer's interest may be such that Rule 1.7 will preclude the lawyer from seeking the client's consent to the transaction.

[4] If the client is independently represented in the transaction, paragraph (a)(2) of this Rule is inapplicable, and the paragraph (a)(1) requirement for full disclosure is satisfied either by a written disclosure by the lawyer involved in the transaction or by the client's independent counsel. The fact that the client was independently represented in the transaction is relevant in determining whether the agreement was fair and reasonable to the client as paragraph (a)(1) further requires.

Use of Information Related to Representation

[5] Use of information relating to the representation to the disadvantage of the client violates the lawyer's duty of loyalty. Paragraph (b) applies when the information is used to benefit either the lawyer or a third person, such as another client or business associate of the lawyer. For example, if a lawyer learns that a client intends to purchase and develop several parcels of land, the lawyer may not use that information to purchase one of the parcels in competition with the client or to recommend that another client make such a purchase. The Rule does not prohibit uses that do not disadvantage the client. For example, a lawyer who learns a government agency's interpretation of trade legislation during the representation of one client may

properly use that information to benefit other clients. Paragraph (b) prohibits disadvantageous use of client information unless the client gives informed consent, except as permitted or required by these Rules. See Rules 1.2(d), 1.6, 1.9(c), 3.3, 4.1(b), 8.1 and 8.3.

Gifts to Lawyers

[6] A lawyer may accept a gift from a client, if the transaction meets general standards of fairness. For example, a simple gift such as a present given at a holiday or as a token of appreciation is permitted. If a client offers the lawyer a more substantial gift, paragraph (c) does not prohibit the lawyer from accepting it, although such a gift may be voidable by the client under the doctrine of undue influence, which treats client gifts as presumptively fraudulent. In any event, due to concerns about overreaching and imposition on clients, a lawyer may not suggest that a substantial gift be made to the lawyer or for the lawyer's benefit, except where the lawyer is related to the client as set forth in paragraph (c).

[7] If effectuation of a substantial gift requires preparing a legal instrument such as a will or conveyance the client should have the detached advice that another lawyer can provide. The sole exception to this Rule is where the client is a relative of the donee.

[8] This Rule does not prohibit a lawyer from seeking to have the lawyer or a partner or associate of the lawyer named as executor of the client's estate or to another potentially lucrative fiduciary position. Nevertheless, such appointments will be subject to the general conflict of interest provision in Rule 1.7 when there is a significant risk that the lawyer's interest in obtaining the appointment will materially limit the lawyer's independent professional judgment in advising the client concerning the choice of an executor or other fiduciary. In obtaining the client's informed consent to the conflict, the lawyer should advise the client concerning the nature and extent of the lawyer's financial interest in the appointment, as well as the availability of alternative candidates for the position.

Literary Rights

[9] An agreement by which a lawyer acquires literary or media rights concerning the conduct of the representation creates a conflict between the interests of the client and the personal interests of the lawyer. Measures suitable in the representation of the client may detract from the publication value of an account of the representation. Paragraph (d) does not prohibit a lawyer representing a client in a transaction concerning literary property from agreeing that the lawyer's fee shall consist of a share in ownership in the property, if the arrangement conforms to Rule 1.5 and paragraphs (a) and (i).

Financial Assistance

[10] Lawyers may not subsidize lawsuits or administrative proceedings brought on behalf of their clients, including making or guaranteeing loans to their clients for living expenses, because to do so would encourage clients to pursue lawsuits that might not otherwise be brought and because such assistance gives lawyers too great a financial stake in the litigation. These dangers do not warrant a prohibition on a lawyer lending a client court costs and litigation expenses, including the expenses of medical examination and the costs of obtaining and presenting evidence, because these advances are virtually indistinguishable from contingent fees and help ensure access to the courts. Similarly, an exception allowing lawyers representing indigent clients to pay court costs and litigation expenses regardless of whether these funds will be repaid is warranted.

Person Paying for a Lawyer's Services

[11] Lawyers are frequently asked to represent a client under circumstances in which a third person will compensate the lawyer, in whole or in part. The third person might be a relative or friend, an indemnitor (such as a liability insurance company) or a co-client (such as a corporation sued along with one or more of its employees). Because third-party payers frequently have interests that differ from those of the client, including interests in minimizing the amount spent on the representation and in learning how the representation is progressing, lawyers are prohibited from accepting or continuing such representations unless the lawyer determines that there will be no interference with the lawyer's independent professional judgment and there is

informed consent from the client. See also Rule 5.4(c) (prohibiting interference with a lawyer's professional judgment by one who recommends, employs or pays the lawyer to render legal services for another).

[12] Sometimes, it will be sufficient for the lawyer to obtain the client's informed consent regarding the fact of the payment and the identity of the third-party payer. If, however, the fee arrangement creates a conflict of interest for the lawyer, then the lawyer must comply with Rule. 1.7. The lawyer must also conform to the requirements of Rule 1.6 concerning confidentiality. Under Rule 1.7(a), a conflict of interest exists if there is significant risk that the lawyer's representation of the client will be materially limited by the lawyer's own interest in the fee arrangement or by the lawyer's responsibilities to the third-party payer (for example, when the third-party payer is a co-client). Under Rule 1.7(b), the lawyer may accept or continue the representation with the informed consent of each affected client, unless the conflict is nonconsentable under that paragraph. Under Rule 1.7(b), the informed consent must be confirmed in writing.

Aggregate Settlements

[13] Differences in willingness to make or accept an offer of settlement are among the risks of common representation of multiple clients by a single lawyer. Under Rule 1.7, this is one of the risks that should be discussed before undertaking the representation, as part of the process of obtaining the clients' informed consent. In addition, Rule 1.2(a) protects each client's right to have the final say in deciding whether to accept or reject an offer of settlement and in deciding whether to enter a guilty or nolo contendere plea in a criminal case. The rule stated in this paragraph is a corollary of both these Rules and provides that, before any settlement offer or plea bargain is made or accepted on behalf of multiple clients, the lawyer must inform each of them about all the material terms of the settlement, including what the other clients will receive or pay if the settlement or plea offer is accepted. See also Rule 1.0(e) (definition of informed consent). Lawyers representing a class of plaintiffs or defendants, or those proceeding derivatively, may not have a full client-lawyer relationship with each member of the class; nevertheless, such lawyers must comply with applicable rules regulating notification of class members and other procedural requirements designed to ensure adequate protection of the entire class.

Limiting Liability and Settling Malpractice Claims

[14] Agreements prospectively limiting a lawyer's liability for malpractice are prohibited unless the client is independently represented in making the agreement because they are likely to undermine competent and diligent representation. Also, many clients are unable to evaluate the desirability of making such an agreement before a dispute has arisen, particularly if they are then represented by the lawyer seeking the agreement. This paragraph does not, however, prohibit a lawyer from entering into an agreement with the client to arbitrate legal malpractice claims, provided such agreements are enforceable and the client is fully informed of the scope and effect of the agreement. Nor does this paragraph limit the ability of lawyers to practice in the form of a limited-liability entity, where permitted by law, provided that each lawyer remains personally liable to the client for his or her own conduct and the firm complies with any conditions required by law, such as provisions requiring client notification or maintenance of adequate liability insurance. Nor does it prohibit an agreement in accordance with Rule 1.2 that defines the scope of the representation, although a definition of scope that makes the obligations of representation illusory will amount to an attempt to limit liability.

[15] Agreements settling a claim or a potential claim for malpractice are not prohibited by this Rule. Nevertheless, in view of the danger that a lawyer will take unfair advantage of an unrepresented client or former client, the lawyer must first advise such a person in writing of the appropriateness of independent representation in connection with such a settlement. In addition, the lawyer must give the client or former client a reasonable opportunity to find and consult independent counsel.

Acquiring Proprietary Interest in Litigation

[16] Paragraph (i) states the traditional general rule that lawyers are prohibited from acquiring a proprietary interest in litigation. Like paragraph (e), the general rule has its basis in common law champerty and maintenance and is designed to avoid giving the lawyer too great an interest in the representation. In addition, when the lawyer acquires an ownership interest in the subject of the representation, it will be more difficult for a client to discharge the lawyer if the client so desires. The Rule is subject to specific exceptions developed in decisional law and continued in these Rules. The exception for certain advances of the costs of litigation is set forth in paragraph (e). In addition, paragraph (i) sets forth exceptions for liens authorized by law to secure the lawyer's fees or expenses and contracts for reasonable contingent fees. The law of each jurisdiction determines which liens are authorized by law. These may include liens granted by statute, liens originating in common law and liens acquired by contract with the client. When a lawyer acquires by contract a security interest in property other than that recovered through the lawyer's efforts in the litigation, such an acquisition is a business or financial transaction with a client and is governed by the requirements of paragraph (a). Contracts for contingent fees in civil cases are governed by Rule 1.5.

Client-Lawyer Sexual Relationships

[17] The relationship between lawyer and client is a fiduciary one in which the lawyer occupies the highest position of trust and confidence. The relationship is almost always unequal; thus, a sexual relationship between lawyer and client can involve unfair exploitation of the lawyer's fiduciary role, in violation of the lawyer's basic ethical obligation not to use the trust of the client to the client's disadvantage. In addition, such a relationship presents a significant danger that, because of the lawyer's emotional involvement, the lawyer will be unable to represent the client without impairment of the exercise of independent professional judgment. Moreover, a bluffed line between the professional and personal relationships may make it difficult to predict to what extent client confidences will be protected by the attorney-client evidentiary privilege, since client confidences are protected by privilege only when they are imparted in the context of the client-lawyer relationship. Because of the significant danger of harm to client interests and because the client's own emotional involvement renders it unlikely that the client could give adequate informed consent, this Rule prohibits the lawyer from having sexual relations with a client regardless of whether the relationship is consensual and regardless of the absence of prejudice to the client.

[18] Sexual relationships that predate the client-lawyer relationship are not prohibited. Issues relating to the exploitation of the fiduciary relationship and client dependency are diminished when the sexual relationship existed prior to the commencement of the client-lawyer relationship. However, before proceeding with the representation in these circumstances, the lawyer should consider whether the lawyer's ability to represent the client will be materially limited by the relationship. See Rule 13(a)(2).

[19] When the client is an organization, paragraph (j) of this Rule prohibits a lawyer for the organization (whether inside counsel or outside counsel) from having a sexual relationship with a constituent of the organization who supervises, directs or regularly consults with that lawyer concerning the organization's legal matters.

Imputation of Prohibitions

[20] Under paragraph (k), a prohibition on conduct by an individual lawyer in paragraphs (a) through (i) also applies to all lawyers associated in a firm with the personally prohibited lawyer. For example, one lawyer in a firm may not enter into a business transaction with a client of another member of the firm without complying with paragraph (a), even if the first lawyer is not personally involved in the representation of the client. The prohibition set forth in paragraph (j) is personal and is not applied to associated lawyers.

RULE 1.9: DUTIES TO FORMER CLIENTS

(a) A lawyer who has formerly represented a client in a matter shall not thereafter represent another person in the same or a substantially related matter in which that person's interests are materially adverse to the interests of

the former client unless the former client gives informed consent, confirmed in writing.

(b) A lawyer shall not knowingly represent a person in the same or a substantially related matter in which a firm with which the lawyer formerly was associated had previously represented a client

(1) whose interests are materially adverse to that person; and

(2) about whom the lawyer had acquired information protected by Rules 1.6 and 1.9(c) that is material to the matter; unless the former client gives informed consent, confirmed in writing.

(c) A lawyer who has formerly represented a client in a matter or whose present or former firm has formerly represented a client in a matter shall not thereafter:

(1) use information relating to the representation to the disadvantage of the former client except as these Rules would permit or require with respect to a client, or when the information has become generally known; or

(2) reveal information relating to the representation except as these Rules would permit or require with respect to a client.

COMMENT

[1] After termination of a client-lawyer relationship, a lawyer has certain continuing duties with respect to confidentiality and conflicts of interest and thus may not represent another client except in conformity with this Rule. Under this Rule, for example, a lawyer could not properly seek to rescind on behalf of a new client a contract drafted on behalf of the former client. So also a lawyer who has prosecuted an accused person could not properly represent the accused in a subsequent civil action against the government concerning the same transaction. Nor could a lawyer who has represented multiple clients in a matter represent one of the clients against the others in the same or a substantially related matter after a dispute arose among the clients in that matter, unless all affected clients give informed consent. See Comment [9]. Current and former government lawyers must comply with this Rule to the extent required by Rule 1.11.

[2] The scope of a "matter" for purposes of this Rule depends on the facts of a particular situation or transaction. The lawyer's involvement in a matter can also be a question of degree. When a lawyer has been directly involved in a specific transaction, subsequent representation of other clients with materially adverse interests in that transaction clearly is prohibited. On the other hand, a lawyer who recurrently handled a type of problem for a former client is not precluded from later representing another client in a factually distinct problem of that type even though the subsequent representation involves a position adverse to the prior client. Similar considerations can apply to the reassignment of military lawyers between defense and prosecution functions within the same military jurisdictions. The underlying question is whether the lawyer was so involved in the matter that the subsequent representation can be justly regarded as a changing of sides in the matter in question.

[3] Matters are "substantially related" for purposes of this Rule if they involve the same transaction or legal dispute or if there otherwise is a substantial risk that confidential factual information as would normally have been obtained in the prior representation would materially advance the client's position in the subsequent matter. For example, a lawyer who has represented a businessperson and learned extensive private financial information about that person may not then represent that person's spouse in seeking a divorce. Similarly, a lawyer who has previously represented a client in securing environmental permits to build a shopping center would be precluded from representing neighbors seeking to oppose rezoning of the property on the basis of environmental considerations; however, the lawyer would not be precluded, on the grounds of substantial relationship, from defending a tenant of the completed shopping center in resisting eviction for nonpayment of rent. Information that has been disclosed to the public or to other parties adverse to the former client ordinarily will not be disqualifying. Information acquired in a prior representation may have been rendered obsolete by the passage of time, a circumstance that may be relevant in determining whether two representations are substantially related.

In the case of an organizational client, general knowledge of the client's policies and practices ordinarily will not preclude a subsequent representation; on the other hand, knowledge of specific facts gained in a prior representation that are relevant to the matter in question ordinarily will preclude such a representation. A former client is not required to reveal the confidential information learned by the lawyer in order to establish a substantial risk that the lawyer has confidential information to use in the subsequent matter. A conclusion about the possession of such information may be based on the nature of the services the lawyer provided the former client and information that would in ordinary practice be learned by a lawyer providing such services.

Lawyers Moving Between Firms

[4] When lawyers have been associated within a firm but then end their association, the question of whether a lawyer should undertake representation is more complicated. There are several competing considerations. First, the client previously represented by the former firm must be reasonably assured that the principle of loyalty to the client is not compromised. Second, the rule should not be so broadly cast as to preclude other persons from having reasonable choice of legal counsel. Third, the rule should not unreasonably hamper lawyers from forming new associations and taking on new clients after having left a previous association. In this connection, it should be recognized that today many lawyers practice in firms, that many lawyers to some degree limit their practice to one field or another, and that many move from one association to another several times in their careers. If the concept of imputation were applied with unqualified rigor, the result would be radical curtailment of the opportunity of lawyers to move from one practice setting to another and of the opportunity of clients to change counsel.

[5] Paragraph (b) operates to disqualify the lawyer only when the lawyer involved has actual knowledge of information protected by Rules 1.6 and 1.9(c). Thus, if a lawyer while with one firm acquired no knowledge or information relating to a particular client of the firm, and that lawyer later joined another firm, neither the lawyer individually nor the second firm is disqualified from representing another client in the same or a related matter even though the interests of the two clients conflict. See Rule 1.10(b) for the restrictions on a firm once a lawyer has terminated association with the firm.

[6] Application of paragraph (b) depends on a situation's particular facts, aided by inferences, deductions or working presumptions that reasonably may be made about the way in which lawyers work together. A lawyer may have general access to files of all clients of a law firm and may regularly participate in discussions of their affairs; it should be inferred that such a lawyer in fact is privy to all information about all the firm's clients. In contrast, another lawyer may have access to the files of only a limited number of clients and participate in discussions of the affairs of no other clients; in the absence of information to the contrary, it should be inferred that such a lawyer in fact is privy to information about the clients actually served but not those of other clients. In such an inquiry, the burden of proof should rest upon the firm whose disqualification is sought.

[7] Independent of the question of disqualification of a firm, a lawyer changing professional association has a continuing duty to preserve confidentiality of information about a client formerly represented. See Rules 1.6 and 1.9(c).

[8] Paragraph (c) provides that information acquired by the lawyer in the course of representing a client may not subsequently be used or revealed by the lawyer to the disadvantage of the client. However, the fact that a lawyer has once served a client does not preclude the lawyer from using generally known information about that client when later representing another client.

[9] The provisions of this Rule are for the protection of former clients and can be waived if the client gives informed consent, which consent must be confirmed in writing under paragraphs (a) and (b). See Rule 1.0(e). With regard to the effectiveness of an advance waiver, see Comment [22] to Rule 1.7. With regard to disqualification of a firm with which a lawyer is or was formerly associated, see Rule 1.10.

RULE 1.10: IMPUTATION OF CONFLICTS OF INTEREST: GENERAL RULE

(a) While lawyers are associated in a firm, none of them shall knowingly represent a client when any one of them practicing alone would be prohibited from doing so by Rules 1.7 or 1.9, unless the prohibition is based on a personal interest of the prohibited lawyer and does not present a significant risk of materially limiting the representation of the client by the remaining lawyers in the firm.

(b) When a lawyer has terminated an association with a firm, the firm is not prohibited from thereafter representing a person with interests materially adverse to those of a client represented by the formerly associated lawyer and not currently represented by the firm, unless:

   (1) the matter is the same or substantially related to that in which the formerly associated lawyer represented the client; and

   (2) any lawyer remaining in the firm has information protected by Rules 1.6 and 1.9(c) that is material to the matter.

(c) A disqualification prescribed by this rule may be waived by the affected client under the conditions stated in Rule 1.7.

(d) The disqualification of lawyers associated in a firm with former or current government lawyers is governed by Rule 1.11.

COMMENT

Definition of "Firm"

[1] For purposes of the Rules of Professional Conduct, the term "firm" denotes lawyers in a law partnership, professional corporation, sole proprietorship or other association authorized to practice law; or lawyers employed in a legal services organization or the legal department of a corporation or other organization. See Rule 1.0(c). Whether two or more lawyers constitute a firm within this definition can depend on the specific facts. See Rule 1.0, Comments [2]–[4].

Principles of Imputed Disqualification

[2] The rule of imputed disqualification stated in paragraph (a) gives effect to the principle of loyalty to the client as it applies to lawyers who practice in a law firm. Such situations can be considered from the premise that a firm of lawyers is essentially one lawyer for purposes of the rules governing loyalty to the client, or from the premise that each lawyer is vicariously bound by the obligation of loyalty owed by each lawyer with whom the lawyer is associated. Paragraph (a) operates only among the lawyers currently associated in a firm. When a lawyer moves from one firm to another, the situation is governed by Rules 1.9(b) and 1.10(b).

[3] The rule in paragraph (a) does not prohibit representation where neither questions of client loyalty nor protection of confidential information are presented. Where one lawyer in a firm could not effectively represent a given client because of strong political beliefs, for example, but that lawyer will do no work on the case and the personal beliefs of the lawyer will not materially limit the representation by others in the firm, the firm should not be disqualified. On the other hand, if an opposing party in a case were owned by a lawyer in the law firm, and others in the firm would be materially limited in pursuing the matter because of loyalty to that lawyer, the personal disqualification of the lawyer would be imputed to all others in the firm.

[4] The rule in paragraph (a) also does not prohibit representation by others in the law firm where the person prohibited from involvement in a matter is a nonlawyer, such as a paralegal or legal secretary. Nor does paragraph (a) prohibit representation if the lawyer is prohibited from acting because of events before the person became a lawyer, for example, work that the person did while a law student. Such persons, however, ordinarily must be screened from any personal participation in the matter to avoid communication to others in the firm of confidential information that both the nonlawyers and the firm have a legal duty to protect. See Rules 1.0(k) and 5.3.

[5] Rule 1.10(b) operates to permit a law firm, under certain circumstances, to represent a person with interests directly adverse to those of a client represented by a lawyer who formerly was associated with the firm. The Rule applies regardless of when the formerly associated lawyer represented the client. However, the law firm may not represent a person with interests adverse to those of a present client of the firm, which would violate Rule 1.7. Moreover, the firm may not represent the person where the matter is the same or substantially

related to that in which the formerly associated lawyer represented the client and any other lawyer currently in the firm has material information protected by Rules 1.6 and 1.9(c).

[6] Rule 1.10(c) removes imputation with the informed consent of the affected client or former client under the conditions stated in Rule 1.7. The conditions stated in Rule 1.7 require the lawyer to determine that the representation is not prohibited by Rule 1.7(b) and that each affected client or former client has given informed consent to the representation, confirmed in writing. In some cases, the risk may be so severe that the conflict may not be cured by client consent. For a discussion of the effectiveness of client waivers of conflicts that might arise in the future, see Rule 1.7, Comment [22]. For a definition of informed consent, see Rule 1.0(e).

[7] Where a lawyer has joined a private firm after having represented the government, imputation is governed by Rule 1.11(b) and (c), not this Rule. Under Rule 1.11(d), where a lawyer represents the government after having served clients in private practice, nongovernmental employment or in another government agency, former-client conflicts are not imputed to government lawyers associated with the individually disqualified lawyer.

[8] Where a lawyer is prohibited from engaging in certain transactions under Rule 1.8, paragraph (k) of that Rule, and not this Rule, determines whether that prohibition also applies to other lawyers associated in a firm with the personally prohibited lawyer.

RULE 1.11: SPECIAL CONFLICTS OF INTEREST FOR FORMER AND CURRENT GOVERNMENT OFFICERS AND EMPLOYEES

(a) Except as law may otherwise expressly permit, a lawyer who has formerly served as a public officer or employee of the government:

(1) is subject to Rule 1.9(c); and

(2) shall not otherwise represent a client in connection with a matter in which the lawyer participated personally and substantially as a public officer or employee, unless the appropriate government agency gives its informed consent, confirmed in writing, to the representation.

(b) When a lawyer is disqualified from representation under paragraph (a), no lawyer in a firm with which that lawyer is associated may knowingly undertake or continue representation in such a matter unless:

(1) the disqualified lawyer is timely screened from any participation in the matter and is apportioned no part of the fee therefrom; and

(2) written notice is promptly given to the appropriate government agency to enable it to ascertain compliance with the provisions of this rule.

(c) Except as law may otherwise expressly permit, a lawyer having information that the lawyer knows is confidential government information about a person acquired when the lawyer was a public officer or employee, may not represent a private client whose interests are adverse to that person in a matter in which the information could be used to the material disadvantage of that person. As used in this Rule, the term "confidential government information" means information that has been obtained under governmental authority and which, at the time this Rule is applied, the government is prohibited by law from disclosing to the public or has a legal privilege not to disclose and which is not otherwise available to the public. A firm with which that lawyer is associated may undertake or continue representation in the matter only if the disqualified lawyer is timely screened from any participation in the matter and is apportioned no part of the fee therefrom.

(d) Except as law may otherwise expressly permit,, a lawyer currently serving as a public officer or employee:

(1) is subject to Rules 1.7 and 1.9; and

(2) shall not:

(i) participate in a matter in which the lawyer participated personally and substantially while in private practice or nongovernmental employment, unless the appropriate government agency gives its informed consent, confirmed in writing; or

(ii) negotiate for private employment with any person who is involved as a party or as lawyer for a party in a matter in which the lawyer is participating personally and substantially, except that a lawyer serving as a law clerk to a judge, other adjudicative officer or arbitrator may negotiate for private employment as permitted by Rule 1.12(b) and subject to the conditions stated in Rule 1.12(b).

(e) As used in this Rule, the term "matter" includes:

(1) any judicial or other proceeding, application, request for a ruling or other determination, contract, claim, controversy, investigation, charge, accusation, arrest or other particular matter involving a specific party or parties, and

(2) any other matter covered by the conflict of interest rules of the appropriate government agency.

COMMENT

[1] A lawyer who has served or is currently serving as a public officer or employee is personally subject to the Rules of Professional Conduct, including the prohibition against concurrent conflicts of interest stated in Rule 1.7. In addition, such a lawyer may be subject to statutes and government regulations regarding conflict of interest. Such statutes and regulations may circumscribe the extent to which the government agency may give consent under this Rule. See Rule 1.0(e) for the definition of informed consent.

[2] Paragraphs (a)(1), (a)(2) and (d)(1) restate the obligations of an individual lawyer who has served or is currently serving as an officer or employee of the government toward a former government or private client. Rule 1.10 is not applicable to the conflicts of interest addressed by this Rule. Rather, paragraph (b) sets forth a special imputation rule for former government lawyers that provides for screening and notice. Because of the special problems raised by imputation within a government agency, paragraph (d) does not impute the conflicts of a lawyer currently serving as an officer or employee of the government to other associated government officers or employees, although ordinarily it will be prudent to screen such lawyers.

[3] Paragraphs (a)(2) and (d)(2) apply regardless of whether a lawyer is adverse to a former client and are thus designed not only to protect the former client, but also to prevent a lawyer from exploiting public office for the advantage of another client. For example, a lawyer who has pursued a claim on behalf of the government may not pursue the same claim on behalf of a later private client after the lawyer has left government service, except when authorized to do so by the government agency under paragraph (a). Similarly, a lawyer who has pursued a claim on behalf of a private client may not pursue the claim on behalf of the government, except when authorized to do so by paragraph (d). As with paragraphs (a)(1) and (d)(1), Rule 1.10 is not applicable to the conflicts of interest addressed by these paragraphs.

[4] This Rule represents a balancing of interests. On the one hand, where the successive clients are a government agency and another client, public or private, the risk exists that power or discretion vested in that agency might be used for the special benefit of the other client. A lawyer should not be in a position where benefit to the other client might affect performance of the lawyer's professional ftinctions on behalf of the government. Also, unfair advantage could accrue to the other client by reason of access to confidential government information about the client's adversary obtainable only through the lawyer's government service. On the other hand, the rules governing lawyers presently or formerly employed by a government agency should not be so restrictive as to inhibit transfer of employment to and from the government. The government has a legitimate need to attract qualified lawyers as well as to maintain high ethical standards. Thus a former government lawyer is disqualified only from particular matters in which the lawyer participated personally and substantially. The provisions for screening and waiver in paragraph (b) are necessary to prevent the disqualification rule from imposing too severe a deterrent against entering public service. The limitation of disqualification in paragraphs (a)(2) and (d)(2) to matters involving a specific party or parties, rather than extending disqualification to all substantive issues on which the lawyer worked, serves a similar function.

[5] When a lawyer has been employed by one government agency and then moves to a second government agency, it may be appropriate to treat that second agency as another client for purposes of this Rule, as when a lawyer is employed by a

city and subsequently is employed by a federal agency. However, because the conflict of interest is governed by paragraph (d), the latter agency is not required to screen the lawyer as paragraph (b) requires a law firm to do. The question of whether two government agencies should be regarded as the same or different clients for conflict of interest purposes is beyond the scope of these Rules. See Rule 1.13 Comment [6].

[6] Paragraphs (b) and (c) contemplate a screening arrangement. See Rule 1.0(k) (requirements for screening procedures). These paragraphs do not prohibit a lawyer from receiving a salary or partnership share established by prior independent agreement, but that lawyer may not receive compensation directly relating the lawyer's compensation to the fee in the matter in which the lawyer is disqualified.

[7] Notice, including a description of the screened lawyer's prior representation and of the screening procedures employed, generally should be given as soon as practicable after the need for screening becomes apparent.

[8] Paragraph (c) operates only when the lawyer in question has knowledge of the information, which means actual knowledge; it does not operate with respect to information that merely could be imputed to the lawyer.

[9] Paragraphs (a) and (d) do not prohibit a lawyer from jointly representing a private party and a government agency when doing so is permitted by Rule 1.7 and is not otherwise prohibited by law.

[10] For purposes of paragraph (e) of this Rule, a "matter" may continue in another form. In determining whether two particular matters are the same, the lawyer should consider the extent to which the matters involve the same basic facts, the same or related parties, and the time elapsed.

RULE 1.12: FORMER JUDGE, ARBITRATOR, MEDIATOR OR OTHER THIRD-PARTY NEUTRAL

(a) Except as stated in paragraph (d), a lawyer shall not represent anyone in connection with a matter in which the lawyer participated personally and substantially as a judge or other adjudicative officer or law clerk to such a person or as an arbitrator, mediator or other third-party neutral, unless all parties to the proceeding give informed consent, confirmed in writing.

(b) A lawyer shall not negotiate for employment with any person who is involved as a party or as lawyer for a party in a matter in which the lawyer is participating personally and substantially as a judge or other adjudicative officer or as an arbitrator, mediator or other third party neutral. A lawyer serving as a law clerk to a judge or other adjudicative officer may negotiate for employment with a party or lawyer involved in a matter in which the clerk is participating personally and substantially, but only after the lawyer has notified the judge or other adjudicative officer.

(c) If a lawyer is disqualified by paragraph (a), no lawyer in a firm with which that lawyer is associated may knowingly undertake or continue representation in the matter unless:

(1) the disqualified lawyer is timely screened from any participation in the matter and is apportioned no part of the fee therefrom; and

(2) written notice is promptly given to the parties and any appropriate tribunal to enable them to ascertain compliance with the provisions of this rule.

(d) An arbitrator selected as a partisan of a party in a multimember arbitration panel is not prohibited from subsequently representing that party.

COMMENT

[1] This Rule generally parallels Rule 1.11. The term "personally and substantially" signifies that a judge who was a member of a multimember court, and thereafter left judicial office to practice law, is not prohibited from representing a client in a matter pending in the court, but in which the former judge did not participate. So also the fact that a former judge exercised administrative responsibility in a court does not prevent the former judge from acting as a lawyer in a matter where the judge had previously exercised remote or incidental administrative responsibility that did not affect the merits. Compare the Comment to Rule 1.11. The term "adjudicative officer" includes such officials as judges pro tempore, referees, special masters, hearing officers and other parajudicial officers, and also lawyers who

serve as part-time judges. Compliance Canons A(2), B(2) and C of the Model Code of Judicial Conduct provide that a part-time judge, judge pro tempore or retired judge recalled to active service, may not "act as a lawyer in any proceeding in which he served as a judge or in any other proceeding related thereto." Although phrased differently from this Rule, those Rules correspond in meaning.

[2] Like former judges, lawyers who have served as arbitrators, mediators or other third-party neutrals may be asked to represent a client in a matter in which the lawyer participated personally and substantially. This Rule forbids such representation unless all of the parties to the proceedings give their informed consent, confirmed in writing. See Rule 1.0(e) and (b). Other law or codes of ethics governing third-party neutrals may impose more stringent standards of personal or imputed disqualification. See Rule 2.4.

[3] Although lawyers who serve as third-party neutrals do not have information concerning the parties that is protected under Rule 1.6, they typically owe the parties an obligation of confidentiality under law or codes of ethics governing third-party neutrals. Thus, paragraph (c) provides that conflicts of the personally disqualified lawyer will be imputed to other lawyers in a law firm unless the conditions of this paragraph are met.

[4] Requirements for screening procedures are stated in Rule 1.0(k). Paragraph (c)(1) does not prohibit the screened lawyer from receiving a salary or partnership share established by prior independent agreement, but that lawyer may not receive compensation directly related to the matter in which the lawyer is disqualified.

[5] Notice, including a description of the screened lawyer's prior representation and of the screening procedures employed, generally should be given as soon as practicable after the need for screening becomes apparent.

RULE 1.13: ORGANIZATION AS CLIENT

(a) A lawyer employed or retained by an organization represents the organization acting through its duly authorized constituents.

(b) If a lawyer for an organization knows that an officer, employee or other person associated with the organization is engaged in action, intends to act or refuses to act in a matter related to the representation that is a violation of a legal obligation to the organization, or a violation of law which reasonably might be imputed to the organization, and is likely to result in substantial injury to the organization, the lawyer shall proceed as is reasonably necessary in the best interest of the organization. In determining how to proceed, the lawyer shall give due consideration to the seriousness of the violation and its consequences, the scope and nature of the lawyer's representation, the responsibility in the organization and the apparent motivation of the person involved, the policies of the organization concerning such matters and any other relevant considerations. Any measures taken shall be designed to minimize disruption of the organization and the risk of revealing information relating to the representation to persons outside the organization. Such measures may include among others:

(1) asking for reconsideration of the matter;

(2) advising that a separate legal opinion on the matter be sought for presentation to appropriate authority in the organization; and

(3) referring the matter to higher authority in the organization, including, if warranted by the seriousness of the matter, referral to the highest authority that can act on behalf of the organization as determined by applicable law.

(c) If, despite the lawyer's efforts in accordance with paragraph (b), the highest authority that can act on behalf of the organization insists upon action, or a refusal to act, that is clearly a violation of law and is likely to result in substantial injury to the organization, the lawyer may resign in accordance with Rule 1.16.

(d) In dealing with an organization's directors, officers, employees, members, shareholders or other constituents, a lawyer shall explain the identity of the client when the lawyer knows or reasonably should know that the organization's interests are adverse to those of the constituents with whom the lawyer is dealing.

(e) A lawyer representing an organization may also represent any of its directors, officers, employees, members, shareholders or other constituents, subject to the provisions of Rule 1.7. If the organization's consent to the dual representation is required by Rule 1.7, the consent shall be given by an appropriate official of the organization other than the individual who is to be represented, or by the shareholders.

COMMENT

The Entity as the Client

[1] An organizational client is a legal entity, but it cannot act except through its officers, directors, employees, shareholders and other constituents. Officers, directors, employees and shareholders are the constituents of the corporate organizational client. The duties defined in this Comment apply equally to unincorporated associations. "Other constituents" as used in this Comment means the positions equivalent to officers, directors, employees and shareholders held by persons acting for organizational clients that are not corporations.

[2] When one of the constituents of an organizational client communicates with the organization's lawyer in that person's organizational capacity, the communication is protected by Rule 1.6. Thus, by way of example, if an organizational client requests its lawyer to investigate allegations of wrongdoing, interviews made in the course of that investigation between the lawyer and the client's employees or other constituents are covered by Rule 1.6. This does not mean, however, that constituents of an organizational client are the clients of the lawyer. The lawyer may not disclose to such constituents information relating to the representation except for disclosures explicitly or impliedly authorized by the organizational client in order to carry out the representation or as otherwise permitted by Rule 1.6.

[3] When constituents of the organization make decisions for it, the decisions ordinarily must be accepted by the lawyer even if their utility or prudence is doubtful. Decisions concerning policy and operations, including ones entailing serious risk, are not as such in the lawyer's province. However, different considerations arise when the lawyer knows that the organization may be substantially injured by action of a constituent that is in violation of law. In such a circumstance, it may be reasonably necessary for the lawyer to ask the constituent to reconsider the matter. If that fails, or if the matter is of sufficient seriousness and importance to the organization, it may be reasonably necessary for the lawyer to take steps to have the matter reviewed by a higher authority in the organization. Clear justification should exist for seeking review over the head of the constituent normally responsible for it. The stated policy of the organization may define circumstances and prescribe channels for such review, and a lawyer should encourage the formulation of such a policy. Even in the absence of organization policy, however, the lawyer may have an obligation to refer a matter to higher authority, depending on the seriousness of the matter and whether the constituent in question has apparent motives to act at variance with the organization's interest. Review by the chief executive officer or by the board of directors may be required when the matter is of importance commensurate with their authority. At some point it may be useful or essential to obtain an independent legal opinion.

[4] The organization's highest authority to whom a matter may be referred ordinarily will be the board of directors or similar governing body. However, applicable law may prescribe that under certain conditions the highest authority reposes elsewhere, for example, in the independent directors of a corporation.

Relation to Other Rules

[5] The authority and responsibility provided in this Rule are concurrent with the authority and responsibility provided in other Rules. In particular, this Rule does not limit or expand the lawyer's responsibility under Rule 1.6, 1.8, 1.16, 3.3 or 4.1. If the lawyer's services are being used by an organization to further a crime or fraud by the organization, Rule 1.2(d) can be applicable.

Government Agency

[6] The duty defined in this Rule applies to governmental organizations. Defining precisely the identity of the client and prescribing the resulting obligations of such lawyers may be more difficult in the government context and is a matter beyond the scope of these Rules. See Scope [18]. Although in some circumstances the client may be a specific agency, it may also

be a branch of government, such as the executive branch, or the government as a whole. For example, if the action or failure to act involves the head of a bureau, either the department of which the bureau is a part or the relevant branch of government may be the client for purposes of this Rule. Moreover, in a matter involving the conduct of government officials, a government lawyer may have authority under applicable law to question such conduct more extensively than that of a lawyer for a private organization in similar circumstances. Thus, when the client is a governmental organization, a different balance may be appropriate between maintaining confidentiality and assuring that the wrongful act is prevented or rectified, for public business is involved. In addition, duties of lawyers employed by the government or lawyers in military service may be defined by statutes and regulation. This Rule does not limit that authority. See Scope.

Clarifying the Lawyer's Role

[7] There are times when the organization's interest may be or become adverse to those of one or more of its constituents. In such circumstances the lawyer should advise any constituent, whose interest the lawyer finds adverse to that of the organization of the conflict or potential conflict of interest, that the lawyer cannot represent such constituent, and that such person may wish to obtain independent representation. Care must be taken to assure that the individual understands that, when there is such adversity of interest, the lawyer for the organization cannot provide legal representation for that constituent individual, and that discussions between the lawyer for the organization and the individual may not be privileged.

[8] Whether such a warning should be given by the lawyer for the organization to any constituent individual may turn on the facts of each case.

Dual Representation

[9] Paragraph (e) recognizes that a lawyer for an organization may also represent a principal officer or major shareholder.

Derivative Actions

[10] Under generally prevailing law, the shareholders or members of a corporation may bring suit to compel the directors to perform their legal obligations in the supervision of the organization. Members of unincorporated associations have essentially the same right. Such an action may be brought nominally by the organization, but usually is, in fact, a legal controversy over management of the organization.

[11] The question can arise whether counsel for the organization may defend such an action. The proposition that the organization is the lawyer's client does not alone resolve the issue. Most derivative actions are a normal incident of an organization's affairs, to be defended by the organization's lawyer like any other suit. However, if the claim involves serious charges of wrongdoing by those in control of the organization, a conflict may arise between the lawyer's duty to the organization and the lawyer's relationship with the board. In those circumstances, Rule 1.7 governs who should represent the directors and the organization.

RULE 1.14: CLIENT WITH DIMINISHED CAPACITY

(a) When a client's capacity to make adequately considered decisions in connection with a representation is diminished, whether because of minority, mental impairment or for some other reason, the lawyer shall, as far as reasonably possible, maintain a normal client-lawyer relationship with the client.

(b) When the lawyer reasonably believes that the client has diminished capacity, is at risk of substantial physical, financial or other harm unless action is taken and cannot adequately act in the client's own interest, the lawyer may take reasonably necessary protective action, including consulting with individuals or entities that have the ability to take action to protect the client and, in appropriate cases, seeking the appointment of a guardian ad litem, conservator or guardian.

(c) Information relating to the representation of a client with diminished capacity is protected by Rule 1.6. When taking protective action pursuant to paragraph (b), the lawyer is impliedly authorized under Rule 1.6(a) to reveal information about the client, but only to the extent reasonably necessary to protect the client's interests.

COMMENT

[1] The normal client-lawyer relationship is based on the assumption that the client, when properly advised and assisted, is capable of making decisions about important matters. When the client is a minor or suffers from a diminished mental capacity, however, maintaining the ordinary client-lawyer relationship may not be possible in all respects. In particular, a severely incapacitated person may have no power to make legally binding decisions. Nevertheless, a client with diminished capacity often has the ability to understand, deliberate upon, and reach conclusions about matters affecting the client's own well-being. For example, children as young as five or six years of age, and certainly those of ten or twelve, are regarded as having opinions that are entitled to weight in legal proceedings concerning their custody. So also, it is recognized that some persons of advanced age can be quite capable of handling routine financial matters while needing special legal protection concerning major transactions.

[2] The fact that a client suffers a disability does not diminish the lawyer's obligation to treat the client with attention and respect. Even if the person has a legal representative, the lawyer should as far as possible accord the represented person the status of client, particularly in maintaining communication.

[3] The client may wish to have family members or other persons participate in discussions with the lawyer. When necessary to assist in the representation, the presence of such persons generally does not affect the applicability of the attorney-client evidentiary privilege. Nevertheless, the lawyer must keep the client's interests foremost and, except for protective action authorized under paragraph (b), must to look to the client, and not family members, to make decisions on the client's behalf.

[4] If a legal representative has already been appointed for the client, the lawyer should ordinarily look to the representative for decisions on behalf of the client. In matters involving a minor, whether the lawyer should look to the parents as natural guardians may depend on the type of proceeding or matter in which the lawyer is representing the minor. If the lawyer represents the guardian as distinct from the ward, and is aware that the guardian is acting adversely to the ward's interest, the lawyer may have an obligation to prevent or rectify the guardian's misconduct. See Rule 1.2(d).

Taking Protective Action

[5] If a lawyer reasonably believes that a client is at risk of substantial physical, financial or other harm unless action is taken, and that a normal client-lawyer relationship cannot be maintained as provided in paragraph (a) because the client lacks sufficient capacity to communicate or to make adequately considered decisions in connection with the representation, then paragraph (b) permits the lawyer to take protective measures deemed necessary. Such measures could include: consulting with family members, using a reconsideration period to permit clarification or improvement of circumstances, using voluntary surrogate decisionmaking tools such as durable powers of attorney or consulting with support groups, professional services, adult-protective agencies or other individuals or entities that have the ability to protect the client. In taking any protective action, the lawyer should be guided by such factors as the wishes and values of the client to the extent known, the client's best interests and the goals of intruding into the client's decisionmaking autonomy to the least extent feasible, maximizing client capacities and respecting the client's family and social connections.

[6] In determining the extent of the client's diminished capacity, the lawyer should consider and balance such factors as: the client's ability to articulate reasoning leading to a decision, variability of state of mind and ability to appreciate consequences of a decision; the substantive fairness of a decision; and the consistency of a decision with the known long-term commitments and values of the client. In appropriate circumstances, the lawyer may seek guidance from an appropriate diagnostician.

[7] If a legal representative has not been appointed, the lawyer should consider whether appointment of a guardian ad litem, conservator or guardian is necessary to protect the client's interests. Thus, if a client with diminished capacity has substantial property that should be sold

for the client's benefit, effective completion of the transaction may require appointment of a legal representative. In addition, rules of procedure in litigation sometimes provide that minors or persons with diminished capacity must be represented by a guardian or next friend if they do not have a general guardian. In many circumstances, however, appointment of a legal representative may be more expensive or traumatic for the client than circumstances in fact require. Evaluation of such circumstances is a matter entrusted to the professional judgment of the lawyer. In considering alternatives, however, the lawyer should be aware of any law that requires the lawyer to advocate the least restrictive action on behalf of the client.

Disclosure of the Client's Condition

[8] Disclosure of the client's diminished capacity could adversely affect the client's interests. For example, raising the question of diminished capacity could, in some circumstances, lead to proceedings for involuntary commitment. Information relating to the representation is protected by Rule 1.6. Therefore, unless authorized to do so, the lawyer may not disclose such information. When taking protective action pursuant to paragraph (b), the lawyer is impliedly authorized to make the necessary disclosures, even when the client directs the lawyer to the contrary. Nevertheless, given the risks of disclosure, paragraph (c) limits what the lawyer may disclose in consulting with other individuals or entities or seeking the appointment of a legal representative. At the very least, the lawyer should determine whether it is likely that the person or entity consulted with will act adversely to the client's interests before discussing matters related to the client. The lawyer's position in such cases is an unavoidably difficult one.

Emergency Legal Assistance

[9] In an emergency where the health, safety or a financial interest of a person with seriously diminished capacity is threatened with imminent and irreparable harm, a lawyer may take legal action on behalf of such a person even though the person is unable to establish a client-lawyer relationship or to make or express considered judgments about the matter, when the person or another acting in good faith on that person's behalf has consulted with the lawyer. Even in such an emergency, however, the lawyer should not act unless the lawyer reasonably believes that the person has no other lawyer, agent or other representative available. The lawyer should take legal action on behalf of the person only to the extent reasonably necessary to maintain the status quo or otherwise avoid imminent and irreparable harm. A lawyer who undertakes to represent a person in such an exigent situation has the same duties under these Rules as the lawyer would with respect to a client.

[10] A lawyer who acts on behalf of a person with seriously diminished capacity in an emergency should keep the confidences of the person as if dealing with a client, disclosing them only to the extent necessary to accomplish the intended protective action. The lawyer should disclose to any tribunal involved and to any other counsel involved the nature of his or her relationship with the person. The lawyer should take steps to regularize the relationship or implement other protective solutions as soon as possible. Normally, a lawyer would not seek compensation for such emergency actions taken.

RULE 1.15: SAFEKEEPING PROPERTY

(a) A lawyer shall hold property of clients or third persons that is in a lawyer's possession in connection with a representation separate from the lawyer's own property. Funds shall be kept in a separate account maintained in the state where the lawyer's office is situated, or elsewhere with the consent of the client or third person. Other property shall be identified as such and appropriately safeguarded. Complete records of such account funds and other property shall be kept by the lawyer and shall be preserved for a period of [five years] after termination of the representation.

(b) A lawyer may deposit the lawyer's own funds in a client trust account for the sole purpose of paying bank service charges on that account, but only in an amount necessary for that purpose.

(c) A lawyer shall deposit into a client trust account legal fees and expenses that have been paid in advance, to be withdrawn by the lawyer only as fees are earned or expenses incurred.

(d) Upon receiving funds or other property in which a client or third person has an interest, a lawyer shall promptly notify the client or third person. Except as stated in this rule or otherwise permitted by law or by agreement with the client, a lawyer shall promptly deliver to the client or third person any funds or other property that the client or third person is entitled to receive and, upon request by the client or third person, shall promptly render a full accounting regarding such property.

(e) When in the course of representation a lawyer is in possession of property in which two or more persons (one of whom may be the lawyer) claim interests, the property shall be kept separate by the lawyer the dispute is resolved. The lawyer shall promptly distribute a portions of the property as to which the interests are not in dispute.

COMMENT

[1] A lawyer should hold property of others with the care required of a professional fiduciary. Securities should be kept in a safe deposit box, except when some other form of safekeeping is warranted by special circumstances. All property that is the property of clients or third persons, including prospective clients, must be kept separate from the lawyer's business and personal property and, if monies, in one or more trust accounts. Separate trust accounts may be warranted when administering estate monies or acting in similar fiduciary capacities. A lawyer should maintain on a current basis books and records in accordance with generally accepted accounting practice and comply with any recordkeeping rules established by law or court order. See, e.g., ABA Model Financial Recordkeeping Rule.

[2] While normally it is impermissible to commingle the lawyer's own funds with client funds, paragraph (b) provides that it is permissible when necessary to pay bank service charges on that account. Accurate records must be kept regarding which part of the funds are the lawyer's.

[3] Lawyers often receive funds from which the lawyer's fee will be paid. The lawyer is not required to remit to the client funds that the lawyer reasonably believes represent fees owed. However, a lawyer may not hold funds to coerce a client into accepting the lawyer's contention. The disputed portion of the funds must be kept in a trust account and the lawyer should suggest means for prompt resolution of the dispute, such as arbitration. The undisputed portion of the funds shall be promptly distributed.

[4] Paragraph (e) also recognizes that third parties may have lawful claims against specific funds or other property in a lawyer's custody, such as a client's creditor who has a lien on funds recovered in a personal injury action. A lawyer may have a duty under applicable law to protect such third-party claims against wrongful interference by the client. In such cases, when the third-party claim is not frivolous under applicable law, the lawyer must refuse to surrender the property to the client until the claims are resolved. A lawyer should not unilaterally assume to arbitrate a dispute between the client and the third party, but, when there are substantial grounds for dispute as to the person entitled to the funds, the lawyer may file an action to have a court resolve the dispute.

[5] The obligations of a lawyer under this Rule are independent of those arising from activity other than rendering legal services. For example, a lawyer who serves only as an escrow agent is governed by the applicable law relating to fiduciaries even though the lawyer does not render legal services in the transaction and is not governed by this Rule.

[6] A lawyers' fund for client protection provides a means through the collective efforts of the bar to reimburse persons who have lost money or property as a result of dishonest conduct of a lawyer. Where such a fund has been established, a lawyer must participate where it is mandatory, and, even when it is voluntary, the lawyer should participate.

RULE 1.16: DECLINING OR TERMINATING REPRESENTATION

(a) Except as stated in paragraph (c), a lawyer shall not represent a client or, where representation has commenced, shall withdraw from the representation of a client if:

(1) the representation will result in violation of the rules of professional conduct or other law;

(2) the lawyer's physical or mental condition materially impairs the lawyer's ability to represent the client; or

(3) the lawyer is discharged.

(b) Except as stated in paragraph (c), a lawyer may withdraw from representing a client if

(1) withdrawal can be accomplished without material adverse effect on the interests of the client;

(2) the client persists in a course of action involving the lawyer's services that the lawyer reasonably believes is criminal or fraudulent;

(3) the client has used the lawyer's services to perpetrate a crime or fraud;

(4) the client insists upon taking action that the lawyer considers repugnant or with which the lawyer has a fundamental disagreement;

(5) the client fails substantially to fulfill an obligation to the lawyer regarding the lawyer's services and has been given reasonable warning that the lawyer will withdraw unless the obligation is fulfilled;

(6) the representation will result in an unreasonable financial burden on the lawyer or has been rendered unreasonably difficult by the client; or

(7) other good cause for withdrawal exists.

(c) A lawyer must comply with applicable law requiring notice to or permission of a tribunal when terminating a representation. When ordered to do so by a tribunal, a lawyer shall continue representation notwithstanding good cause for terminating the representation.

(d) Upon termination of representation, a lawyer shall take steps to the extent reasonably practicable to protect a client's interests, such as giving reasonable notice to the client, allowing time for employment of other counsel, surrendering papers and property to which the client is entitled and refunding any advance payment of fee or expense that has not been earned or incurred. The lawyer may retain papers relating to the client to the extent permitted by other law.

COMMENT

[1] A lawyer should not accept representation in a matter unless it can be performed competently, promptly, without improper conflict of interest and to completion. Ordinarily, a representation in a matter is completed when the agreed-upon assistance has been concluded. See Rules 1.2(c) and 6.5. See also Rule 1.3, Comment [4].

Mandatory Withdrawal

[2] A lawyer ordinarily must decline or withdraw from representation if the client demands that the lawyer engage in conduct that is illegal or violates the Rules of Professional Conduct or other law. The lawyer is not obliged to decline or withdraw simply because the client suggests such a course of conduct; a client may make such a suggestion in the hope that a lawyer will not be constrained by a professional obligation.

[3] When a lawyer has been appointed to represent a client, withdrawal ordinarily requires approval of the appointing authority. See also Rule 6.2. Similarly, court approval or notice to the court is often required by applicable law before a lawyer withdraws from pending litigation. Difficulty may be encountered if withdrawal is based on the client's demand that the lawyer engage in unprofessional conduct. The court may request an explanation for the withdrawal, while the lawyer may be bound to keep confidential the facts that would constitute such an explanation. The lawyer's statement that professional considerations require termination of the representation ordinarily should be accepted as sufficient. Lawyers should be mindful of their obligations to both clients and the court under Rules 1.6 and 3.3.

Discharge

[4] A client has a right to discharge a lawyer at any time, with or without cause, subject to liability for payment for the lawyer's services. Where future dispute about the withdrawal may be anticipated, it may be advisable to prepare a written statement reciting the circumstances.

[5] Whether a client can discharge appointed counsel may depend on applicable law. A client seeking to do so should be given a full explanation of the consequences. These consequences may include a decision by the appointing authority that appointment of successor counsel is unjustified, thus requiring self-representation by the client.

[6] If the client has severely diminished capacity, the client may lack the legal capacity to discharge the lawyer, and in any event the discharge may be seriously adverse to the client's interests. The lawyer should make special effort to help the client consider the consequences and may take

reasonably necessary protective action as provided in Rule 1.14.

Optional Withdrawal

[7] A lawyer may withdraw from representation in some circumstances. The lawyer has the option to withdraw if it can be accomplished without material adverse effect on the client's interests. Withdrawal is also justified if the client persists in a course of action that the lawyer reasonably believes is criminal or fraudulent, for a lawyer is not required to be associated with such conduct even if the lawyer does not further it. Withdrawal is also permitted if the lawyer's services were misused in the past even if that would materially prejudice the client. The lawyer may also withdraw where the client insists on taking action that the lawyer considers repugnant or with which the lawyer has a fundamental disagreement.

[8] A lawyer may withdraw if the client refuses to abide by the terms of an agreement relating to the representation, such as an agreement concerning fees or court costs or an agreement limiting the objectives of the representation.

Assisting the Client upon Withdrawal

[9] Even if the lawyer has been unfairly discharged by the client, a lawyer must take all reasonable steps to mitigate the consequences to the client. The lawyer may retain papers as security for a fee only to the extent permitted by law. See Rule 1.15.

RULE 1.17: SALE OF LAW PRACTICE

A lawyer or a law firm may sell or purchase a law practice, or an area of law practice, including good will, if the following conditions are satisfied:

(a) The seller ceases to engage in the private practice of law, or in the area of practice that has been sold, [in the geographic area] [in the jurisdiction] (a jurisdiction may elect either version) in which the practice has been conducted;

(b) The entire practice, or the entire area of practice, is sold to one or more lawyers or law firms;

(c) The seller gives written notice to each of the seller's clients regarding:

(1) the proposed sale;

(2) the client's right to retain other counsel or to take possession of the file; and

(3) the fact that the client's consent to the transfer of the client's files will be presumed if the client does not take any action or does not otherwise object within ninety (90) days of receipt of the notice. If a client cannot be given notice, the representation of that client may be transferred to the purchaser only upon entry of an order so authorizing by a court having jurisdiction. The seller may disclose to the court in camera information relating to the representation only to the extent necessary to obtain an order authorizing the transfer of a file.

(d) The fees charged clients shall not be increased by reason of the sale.

COMMENT

[1] The practice of law is a profession, not merely a business. Clients are not commodities that can be purchased and sold at will. Pursuant to this Rule, when a lawyer or an entire firm ceases to practice, or ceases to practice in an area of law, and other lawyers or firms take over the representation, the selling lawyer or firm may obtain compensation for the reasonable value of the practice as may withdrawing partners of law firms. See Rules 5.4 and 5.6.

Termination of Practice by the Seller

[2] The requirement that all of the private practice, or all of an area of practice, be sold is satisfied if the seller in good faith makes the entire practice, or the area of practice, available for sale to the purchasers. The fact that a number of the seller's clients decide not to be represented by the purchasers but take their matters elsewhere, therefore, does not result in a violation. Return to private practice as a result of an unanticipated change in circumstances does not necessarily result in a violation. For example, a lawyer who has sold the practice to accept an appointment to judicial office does not violate the requirement that the sale be attendant to cessation of practice if the lawyer later resumes private practice upon being defeated in a contested or a retention election for the office or resigns from a judiciary position.

Model Rules of Professional Conduct

[3] The requirement that the seller cease to engage in the private practice of law does not prohibit employment as a lawyer on the staff of a public agency or a legal services entity that provides legal services to the poor, or as in-house counsel to a business.

[4] The Rule permits a sale of an entire practice attendant upon retirement from the private practice of law within the jurisdiction. Its provisions, therefore, accommodate the lawyer who sells the practice on the occasion of moving to another state. Some states are so large that a move from one locale therein to another is tantamount to leaving the jurisdiction in which the lawyer has engaged in the practice of law. To also accommodate lawyers so situated, states may permit the sale of the practice when the lawyer leaves the geographical area rather than the jurisdiction. The alternative desired should be indicated by selecting one of the two provided for in Rule 1.17(a).

[5] This Rule also permits a lawyer or law firm to sell an area of practice. If an area of practice is sold and the lawyer remains in the active practice of law, the lawyer must cease accepting any matters in the area of practice that has been sold, either as counsel or co-counsel or by assuming joint responsibility for a matter in connection with the division of a fee with another lawyer as would otherwise be permitted by Rule 1.5(e). For example, a lawyer with a substantial number of estate planning matters and a substantial number of probate administration cases may sell the estate planning portion of the practice but remain in the practice of law by concentrating on probate administration; however, that practitioner may not thereafter accept any estate planning matters. Although a lawyer who leaves a jurisdiction or geographical area typically would sell the entire practice, this Rule permits the lawyer to limit the sale to one or more areas of the practice, thereby preserving the lawyer's right to continue practice in the areas of the practice that were not sold.

Sale of Entire Practice or Entire Area of Practice

[6] The Rule requires that the seller's entire practice, or an entire area of practice, be sold. The prohibition against sale of less than an entire practice area protects those clients whose matters are less lucrative and who might find it difficult to secure other counsel if a sale could be limited to substantial fee-generating matters. The purchasers are required to undertake all client matters in the practice or practice area, subject to client consent. This requirement is satisfied, however, even if a purchaser is unable to undertake a particular client matter because of a conflict of interest.

Client Confidences, Consent and Notice

[7] Negotiations between seller and prospective purchaser prior to disclosure of information relating to a specific representation of an identifiable client no more violate the confidentiality provisions of Model Rule 1.6 than do preliminary discussions concerning the possible association of another lawyer or mergers between firms, with respect to which client consent is not required. Providing the purchaser access to client-specific information relating to the representation and to the file, however, requires client consent. The Rule provides that before such information can be disclosed by the seller to the purchaser the client must be given actual written notice of the contemplated sale, including the identity of the purchaser, and must be told that the decision to consent or make other arrangements must be made within 90 days. If nothing is heard from the client within that time, consent to the sale is presumed.

[8] A lawyer or law firm ceasing to practice cannot be required to remain in practice because some clients cannot be given actual notice of the proposed purchase. Since these clients cannot themselves consent to the purchase or direct any other disposition of their files, the Rule requires an order from a court having jurisdiction authorizing their transfer or other disposition. The Court can be expected to determine whether reasonable efforts to locate the client have been exhausted, and whether the absent client's legitimate interests will be served by authorizing the transfer of the file so that the purchaser may continue the representation. Preservation of client confidences requires that the petition for a court order be considered in camera. (A procedure by which such an order can be obtained needs to be established in jurisdictions in which it presently does not exist).

[9] All elements of client autonomy, including the client's absolute right to discharge a lawyer and transfer the representation to another, survive the sale of the practice or area of practice.

Fee Arrangements Between Client and Purchaser

[10] The sale may not be financed by increases in fees charged the clients of the practice. Existing arrangements between the seller and the client as to fees and the scope of the work must be honored by the purchaser.

Other Applicable Ethical Standards

[11] Lawyers participating in the sale of a law practice or a practice area are subject to the ethical standards applicable to involving another lawyer in the representation of a client. These include, for example, the seller's obligation to exercise competence in identifying a purchaser qualified to assume the practice and the purchaser's obligation to undertake the representation competently (see Rule 1.1); the obligation to avoid disqualifying conflicts, and to secure the client's informed consent for those conflicts that can be agreed to (see Rule 1.7 regarding conflicts and Rule 1.0(e) for the definition of informed consent); and the obligation to protect information relating to the representation (see Rules 1.6 and 1.9).

[12] If approval of the substitution of the purchasing lawyer for the selling lawyer is required by the rules of any tribunal in which a matter is pending, such approval must be obtained before the matter can be included in the sale (see Rule 1.16).

Applicability of the Rule

[13] This Rule applies to the sale of a law practice of a deceased, disabled or disappeared lawyer. Thus, the seller may be represented by a non-lawyer representative not subject to these Rules. Since, however, no lawyer may participate in a sale of a law practice which does not conform to the requirements of this Rule, the representatives of the seller as well as the purchasing lawyer can be expected to see to it that they are met.

[14] Admission to or retirement from a law partnership or professional association, retirement plans and similar arrangements, and a sale of tangible assets of a law practice, do not constitute a sale or purchase governed by this Rule.

[15] This Rule does not apply to the transfers of legal representation between lawyers when such transfers are unrelated to the sale of a practice or an area of practice.

RULE 1.18: DUTIES TO PROSPECTIVE CLIENT

(a) A person who discusses with a lawyer the possibility of forming a client-lawyer relationship with respect to a matter is a prospective client.

(b) Even when no client-lawyer relationship ensues, a lawyer who has had discussions with a prospective client shall not use or reveal information learned in the consultation, except as Rule 1.9 would permit with respect to information of a former client.

(c) A lawyer subject to paragraph (b) shall not represent a client with interests materially adverse to those of a prospective client in the same or a substantially related matter if the lawyer received information from the prospective client that could be significantly harmful to that person in the matter, except as provided in paragraph (d). If a lawyer is disqualified from representation under this paragraph, no lawyer in a firm with which that lawyer is associated may knowingly undertake or continue representation in such a matter, except as provided in paragraph (d).

(d) When the lawyer has received disqualifying information as defined in paragraph (c), representation is permissible if

(1) both the affected client and the prospective client have given informed consent, confirmed in writing, or:

(2) the lawyer who received the information took reasonable measures to avoid exposure to more disqualifying information than was reasonably necessary to determine whether to represent the prospective client; and

(i) the disqualified lawyer is timely screened from any participation in the matter and is apportioned no part of the fee therefrom; and

(ii) written notice is promptly given to the prospective client.

Model Rules of Professional Conduct

COMMENT

[1] Prospective clients, like clients, may disclose information to a lawyer, place documents or other property in the lawyer's custody, or rely on the lawyer's advice. A lawyer's discussions with a prospective client usually are limited in time and depth and leave both the prospective client and the lawyer free (and sometimes required) to proceed no further. Hence, prospective clients should receive some but not all of the protection afforded clients.

[2] Not all persons who communicate information to a lawyer are entitled to protection under this Rule. A person who communicates information unilaterally to a lawyer, without any reasonable expectation that the lawyer is willing to discuss the possibility of forming a client-lawyer relationship, is not a "prospective client" within the meaning of paragraph (a).

[3] It is often necessary for a prospective client to reveal information to the lawyer during an initial consultation prior to the decision about formation of a client-lawyer relationship. The lawyer often must learn such information to determine whether there is a conflict of interest with an existing client and whether the matter is one that the lawyer is willing to undertake. Paragraph (b) prohibits the lawyer from using or revealing that information, except as permitted by Rule 1.9, even if the client or lawyer decides not to proceed with the representation. The duty exists regardless of how brief the initial conference may be.

[4] In order to avoid acquiring disqualifying information from a prospective client, a lawyer considering whether or not to undertake a new matter should limit the initial interview to only such information as reasonably appears necessary for that purpose. Where the information indicates that a conflict of interest or other reason for non-representation exists, the lawyer should so inform the prospective client or decline the representation. If the prospective client wishes to retain the lawyer, and if consent is possible under Rule 1.7, then consent from all affected present or former clients must be obtained before accepting the representation.

[5] A lawyer may condition conversations with a prospective client on the person's informed consent that no information disclosed during the consultation will prohibit the lawyer from representing a different client in the matter. See Rule 1.0(e) for the definition of informed consent. If the agreement expressly so provides, the prospective client may also consent to the lawyer's subsequent use of information received from the prospective client.

[6] Even in the absence of an agreement, under paragraph (c), the lawyer is not prohibited from representing a client with interests adverse to those of the prospective client in the same or a substantially related matter unless the lawyer has received from the prospective client information that could be significantly harmful if used in the matter.

[7] Under paragraph (c), the prohibition in this Rule is imputed to other lawyers as provided in Rule 1.10, but, under paragraph (d)(1), imputation may be avoided if the lawyer obtains the informed consent, confirmed in writing, of both the prospective and affected clients. In the alternative, imputation may be avoided if the conditions of paragraph (d)(2) are met and all disqualified lawyers are timely screened and written notice is promptly given to the prospective client. See Rule 1.0(k) (requirements for screening procedures). Paragraph (d)(2)(i) does not prohibit the screened lawyer from receiving a salary or partnership share established by prior independent agreement, but that lawyer may not receive compensation directly related to the matter in which the lawyer is disqualified.

[8] Notice, including a general description of the subject matter about which the lawyer was consulted, and of the screening procedures employed, generally should be given as soon as practicable after the need for screening becomes apparent.

[9] For the duty of competence of a lawyer who gives assistance on the merits of a matter to a prospective client, see Rule 1.1. For a lawyer's duties when a prospective client entrusts valuables or papers to the lawyer's care, see Rule 1.15.

RULE 2.1: ADVISOR

In representing a client, a lawyer shall exercise independent professional judgment and render candid advice. In rendering advice, a lawyer may refer not only to law but to other considerations such as moral, economic, social and political factors, that may be relevant to the client's situation.

COMMENT

Scope of Advice

[1] A client is entitled to straightforward advice expressing the lawyer's honest assessment. Legal advice often involves unpleasant facts and alternatives that a client may be disinclined to confront. In presenting advice, a lawyer endeavors to sustain the client's morale and may put advice in as acceptable a form as honesty permits. However, a lawyer should not be deterred from giving candid advice by the prospect that the advice will be unpalatable to the client.

[2] Advice couched in narrow legal terms may be of little value to a client, especially where practical considerations, such as cost or effects on other people, are predominant. Purely technical legal advice, therefore, can sometimes be inadequate. It is proper for a lawyer to refer to relevant moral and ethical considerations in giving advice. Although a lawyer is not a moral advisor as such, moral and ethical considerations impinge upon most legal questions and may decisively influence how the law will be applied.

[3] A client may expressly or impliedly ask the lawyer for purely technical advice. When such a request is made by a client experienced in legal matters, the lawyer may accept it at face value. When such a request is made by a client inexperienced in legal matters, however, the lawyer's responsibility as advisor may include indicating that more may be involved than strictly legal considerations.

[4] Matters that go beyond strictly legal questions may also be in the domain of another profession. Family matters can involve problems within the professional competence of psychiatry, clinical psychology or social work; business matters can involve problems within the competence of the accounting profession or of financial specialists. Where consultation with a professional in another field is itself something a competent lawyer would recommend, the lawyer should make such a recommendation. At the same time, a lawyer's advice at its best often consists of recommending a course of action in the face of conflicting recommendations of experts.

Offering Advice

[5] In general, a lawyer is not expected to give advice until asked by the client. However, when a lawyer knows that a client proposes a course of action that is likely to result in substantial adverse legal consequences to the client, the lawyer's duty to the client under Rule 1.4 may require that the lawyer offer advice if the client's course of action is related to the representation. Similarly, when a matter is likely to involve litigation, it may be necessary under Rule 1.4 to inform the client of forms of dispute resolution that might constitute reasonable alternatives to litigation. A lawyer ordinarily has no duty to initiate investigation of a client's affairs or to give advice that the client has indicated is unwanted, but a lawyer may initiate advice to a client when doing so appears to be in the client's interest.

RULE 2.2 (DELETED)

RULE 2.3: EVALUATION FOR USE BY THIRD PERSONS

(a) A lawyer may provide an evaluation of a matter affecting a client for the use of someone other than the client if the lawyer reasonably believes that making the evaluation is compatible with other aspects of the lawyer's relationship with the client.

(b) When the lawyer knows or reasonably should know that the evaluation is likely to affect the client's interests materially and adversely, the lawyer shall not provide the evaluation unless the client gives informed consent.

(c) Except as disclosure is authorized in connection with a report of an evaluation, information relating to the evaluation is otherwise protected by Rule 1.6.

COMMENT

Definition

[1] An evaluation may be performed at the client's direction or when impliedly authorized in order to carry out the representation. See

Model Rules of Professional Conduct

Rule 1.2. Such an evaluation may be for the primary purpose of establishing information for the benefit of third parties; for example, an opinion concerning the title of property rendered at the behest of a vendor for the information of a prospective purchaser, or at the behest of a borrower for the information of a prospective lender. In some situations, the evaluation may be required by a government agency; for example, an opinion concerning the legality of the securities registered for sale under the securities laws. In other instances, the evaluation may be required by a third person, such as a purchaser of a business.

[2] A legal evaluation should be distinguished from an investigation of a person with whom the lawyer does not have a client-lawyer relationship. For example, a lawyer retained by a purchaser to analyze a vendor's title to property does not have a client-lawyer relationship with the vendor. So also, an investigation into a person's affairs by a government lawyer, or by special counsel by a government lawyer, or by special counsel employed by the government, is not an evaluation as that term is used in this Rule. The question is whether the lawyer is retained by the person whose affairs are being examined. When the lawyer is retained by that person, the general rules concerning loyalty to client and preservation of confidences apply, which is not the case if the lawyer is retained by someone else. For this reason, it is essential to identify the person by whom the lawyer is retained. This should be made clear not only to the person under examination, but also to others to whom the results are to be made available.

Duties Owed to Third Person and Client

[3] When the evaluation is intended for the information or use of a third person, a legal duty to that person may or may not arise. That legal question is beyond the scope of this Rule. However, since such an evaluation involves a departure from the normal client-lawyer relationship, careful analysis of the situation is required. The lawyer must be satisfied as a matter of professional judgment that making the evaluation is compatible with other functions undertaken in behalf of the client. For example, if the lawyer is acting as advocate in defending the client against charges of fraud, it would normally be incompatible with that responsibility for the lawyer to perform an evaluation for others concerning the same or a related transaction. Assuming no such impediment is apparent, however, the lawyer should advise the client of the implications of the evaluation, particularly the lawyer's responsibilities to third persons and the duty to disseminate the findings.

Access to and Disclosure of Information

[4] The quality of an evaluation depends on the freedom and extent of the investigation upon which it is based. Ordinarily a lawyer should have whatever latitude of investigation seems necessary as a matter of professional judgment. Under some circumstances, however, the terms of the evaluation may be limited. For example, certain issues or sources may be categorically excluded, or the scope of search may be limited by time constraints or the noncooperation of persons having relevant information. Any such limitations that are material to the evaluation should be described in the report. If after a lawyer has commenced an evaluation, the client refuses to comply with the terms upon which it was understood the evaluation was to have been made, the lawyer's obligations are determined by law, having reference to the terms of the client's agreement and the surrounding circumstances. In no circumstances is the lawyer permitted to knowingly make a false statement of material fact or law in providing an evaluation under this Rule. See Rule 4.1.

Obtaining Client's Informed Consent

[5] Information relating to an evaluation is protected by Rule 1.6. In many situations, providing an evaluation to a third party poses no significant risk to the client; thus, the lawyer may be impliedly authorized to disclose information to carry out the representation. See Rule 1.6(a). Where, however, it is reasonably likely that providing the evaluation will affect the client's interests materially and adversely, the lawyer must first obtain the client's consent after the client has been adequately informed concerning the important possible effects on the client's interests. See Rules 1.6(a) and 1.0(e).

Financial Auditors' Requests for Information

[6] When a question concerning the legal situation of a client arises at the instance of the client's financial auditor and the question is referred to the lawyer, the lawyer's response may be made in accordance with procedures recognized in the legal profession. Such a procedure is set forth in the American Bar Association Statement of Policy Regarding Lawyers' Responses to Auditors' Requests for Information, adopted in 1975.

RULE 2.4: LAWYER SERVING AS THIRD-PARTY NEUTRAL

(a) A lawyer serves as a third-party neutral when the lawyer assists two or more persons who are not clients of the lawyer to reach a resolution of a dispute or other matter that has arisen between them. Service as a third-party neutral may include service as an arbitrator, a mediator or in such other capacity as will enable the lawyer to assist the parties to resolve the matter.

(b) A lawyer serving as a third-party neutral shall inform unrepresented parties that the lawyer is not representing them. When the lawyer knows or reasonably should know that a party does not understand the lawyer's role in the matter, the lawyer shall explain the difference between the lawyer's role as a third-party neutral and a lawyer's role as one who represents a client.

COMMENT

[1] Alternative dispute resolution has become a substantial part of the civil justice system. Aside from representing clients in disputeresolution processes, lawyers often serve as third-party neutrals. A thirdparty neutral is a person, such as a mediator, arbitrator, conciliator or evaluator, who assists the parties, represented or unrepresented, in the resolution of a dispute or in the arrangement of a transaction. Whether a third-party neutral serves primarily as a facilitator, evaluator or decisionmaker depends on the particular process that is either selected by the parties or mandated by a court.

[2] The role of a third-party neutral is not unique to lawyers, although, in some court-connected contexts, only lawyers are allowed to serve in this role or to handle certain types of cases. In performing this role, the lawyer may be subject to court rules or other law that apply either to third-party neutrals generally or to lawyers serving as third-party neutrals. Lawyer-neutrals may also be subject to various codes of ethics, such as the Code of Ethics for Arbitration in Commercial Disputes prepared by a joint committee of the American Bar Association and the American Arbitration Association or the Model Standards of Conduct for Mediators jointly prepared by the American Bar Association, the American Arbitration Association and the Society of Professionals in Dispute Resolution.

[3] Unlike nonlawyers who serve as third-party neutrals, lawyers serving in this role may experience unique problems as a result of differences between the role of a third-party neutral and a lawyer's service as a client representative. The potential for confusion is significant when the parties are unrepresented in the process. Thus, paragraph (b) requires a lawyerneutral to inform unrepresented parties that the lawyer is not representing them. For some parties, particularly parties who frequently use disputeresolution processes, this information will be sufficient. For others, particularly those who are using the process for the first time, more information will be required. Where appropriate, the lawyer should inform unrepresented parties of the important differences between the lawyer's role as third-party neutral and a lawyer's role as a client representative, including the inapplicability of the attorney-client evidentiary privilege. The extent of disclosure required under this paragraph will depend on the particular parties involved and the subject matter of the proceeding, as well as the particular features of the dispute-resolution process selected.

[4] A lawyer who serves as a third-party neutral subsequently may be asked to serve as a lawyer representing a client in the same matter. The conflicts of interest that arise for both the individual lawyer and the lawyer's law firm are addressed in Rule 1.12.

[5] Lawyers who represent clients in alternative disputeresolution processes are governed by the Rules of Professional Conduct. When the dispute-resolution process takes place before a tribunal, as in binding arbitration (see Rule 1.0(m)), the

lawyer's duty of candor is governed by Rule 3.3. Otherwise, the lawyer's duty of candor toward both the third-party neutral and other parties is governed by Rule 4.1.

RULE 3.1: MERITORIOUS CLAIMS AND CONTENTIONS

A lawyer shall not bring or defend a proceeding, or assert or controvert an issue therein, unless there is a basis in law and fact for doing so that is not frivolous, which includes a good faith argument for an extension, modification or reversal of existing law. A lawyer for the defendant in a criminal proceeding, or the respondent in a proceeding that could result in incarceration, may nevertheless so defend the proceeding as to require that every element of the case be established.

COMMENT

[1] The advocate has a duty to use legal procedure for the fullest benefit of the client's cause, but also a duty not to abuse legal procedure. The law, both procedural and substantive, establishes the limits within which an advocate may proceed. However, the law is not always clear and never is static. Accordingly, in determining the proper scope of advocacy, account must be taken of the law's ambiguities and potential for change.

[2] The filing of an action or defense or similar action taken for a client is not frivolous merely because the facts have not first been fully substantiated or because the lawyer expects to develop vital evidence only by discovery. What is required of lawyers, however, is that they inform themselves about the facts of their clients' cases and the applicable law and determine that they can make good faith arguments in support of their clients' positions. Such action is not frivolous even though the lawyer believes that the client's position ultimately will not prevail. The action is frivolous, however, if the lawyer is unable either to make a good faith argument on the merits of the action taken or to support the action taken by a good faith argument for an extension, modification or reversal of existing law.

[3] The lawyer's obligations under this Rule are subordinate to federal or state constitutional law that entitles a defendant in a criminal matter to the assistance of counsel in presenting a claim or contention that otherwise would be prohibited by this Rule.

RULE 3.2: EXPEDITING LITIGATION

A lawyer shall make reasonable efforts to expedite litigation consistent with the interests of the client.

COMMENT

[1] Dilatory practices bring the administration of justice into disrepute. Although there will be occasions when a lawyer may properly seek a postponement for personal reasons, it is not proper for a lawyer to routinely fail to expedite litigation solely for the convenience of the advocates. Nor will a failure to expedite be reasonable if done for the purpose of frustrating an opposing party's attempt to obtain rightful redress or repose. It is not a justification that similar conduct is often tolerated by the bench and bar. The question is whether a competent lawyer acting in good faith would regard the course of action as having some substantial purpose other than delay. Realizing financial or other benefit from otherwise improper delay in litigation is not a legitimate interest of the client.

RULE 3.3: CANDOR TOWARD THE TRIBUNAL

(a) A lawyer shall not knowingly:
(1) make a false statement of fact or law to a tribunal or fail to correct a false statement of material fact or law previously made to the tribunal by the lawyer;
(2) fail to disclose to the tribunal legal authority in the controlling jurisdiction known to the lawyer to be directly adverse to the position of the client and not disclosed by opposing counsel; or
(3) offer evidence that the lawyer knows to be false. If a lawyer, the lawyer's client, or a witness called by the lawyer, has offered material evidence and the lawyer comes to know of its falsity, the lawyer shall take reasonable remedial measures, including, if necessary, disclosure to the tribunal. A lawyer may refuse

to offer evidence, other than the testimony of a defendant in a criminal matter, that the lawyer reasonably believes is false.

(b) A lawyer who represents a client in an adjudicative proceeding and who knows that a person intends to engage, is engaging or has engaged in criminal or fraudulent conduct related to the proceeding shall take reasonable remedial measures, including, if necessary, disclosure to the tribunal.

(c) The duties stated in paragraphs (a) and (b) continue to the conclusion of the proceeding, and apply even if compliance requires disclosure of information otherwise protected by Rule 1.6.

(d) In an ex parte proceeding, a lawyer shall inform the tribunal of all material facts known to the lawyer that will enable the tribunal to make an informed decision, whether or not the facts are adverse.

COMMENT

[1] This Rule governs the conduct of a lawyer who is representing a client in the proceedings of a tribunal. See Rule 1.0(m) for the definition of "tribunal." It also applies when the lawyer is representing a client in an ancillary proceeding conducted pursuant to the tribunal's adjudicative authority, such as a deposition. Thus, for example, paragraph (a)(3) requires a lawyer to take reasonable remedial measures if the lawyer comes to know that a client who is testifying in a deposition has offered evidence that is false.

[2] This Rule sets forth the special duties of lawyers as officers of the court to avoid conduct that undermines the integrity of the adjudicative process. A lawyer acting as an advocate in an adjudicative proceeding has an obligation to present the client's case with persuasive force. Performance of that duty while maintaining confidences of the client, however, is qualified by the advocate's duty of candor to the tribunal. Consequently, although a lawyer in an adversary proceeding is not required to present an impartial exposition of the law or to vouch for the evidence submitted in a cause, the lawyer must not allow the tribunal to be misled by false statements of law or fact or evidence that the lawyer knows to be false.

Representations by a Lawyer

[3] An advocate is responsible for pleadings and other documents prepared for litigation, but is usually not required to have personal knowledge of matters asserted therein, for litigation documents ordinarily present assertions by the client, or by someone on the client's behalf, and not assertions by the lawyer. Compare Rule 3.1. However, an assertion purporting to be on the lawyer's own knowledge, as in an affidavit by the lawyer or in a statement in open court, may properly be made only when the lawyer knows the assertion is true or believes it to be true on the basis of a reasonably diligent inquiry. There are circumstances where failure to make a disclosure is the equivalent of an affirmative misrepresentation. The obligation prescribed in Rule 1.2(d) not to counsel a client to commit or assist the client in committing a fraud applies in litigation. Regarding compliance with Rule 1.2(d), see the Comment to that Rule. See also the Comment to Rule 8.4(b).

Legal Argument

[4] Legal argument based on a knowingly false representation of law constitutes dishonesty toward the tribunal. A lawyer is not required to make a disinterested exposition of the law, but must recognize the existence of pertinent legal authorities. Furthermore, as stated in paragraph (a)(2), an advocate has a duty to disclose directly adverse authority in the controlling jurisdiction that has not been disclosed by the opposing party. The underlying concept is that legal argument is a discussion seeking to determine the legal premises properly applicable to the case.

Offering Evidence

[5] Paragraph (a)(3) requires that the lawyer refuse to offer evidence that the lawyer knows to be false, regardless of the client's wishes. This duty is premised on the lawyer's obligation as an officer of the court to prevent the trier of fact from being misled by false evidence. A lawyer does not violate this Rule if the lawyer offers the evidence for the purpose of establishing its falsity.

[6] If a lawyer knows that the client intends to testify falsely or wants the lawyer to introduce false evidence, the lawyer should seek to persuade the client that the evidence should not

be offered. If the persuasion is ineffective and the lawyer continues to represent the client, the lawyer must refuse to offer the false evidence. If only a portion of a witness's testimony will be false, the lawyer may call the witness to testify but may not elicit or otherwise permit the witness to present the testimony that the lawyer knows is false.

[7] The duties stated in paragraphs (a) and (b) apply to all lawyers, including defense counsel in criminal cases. In some jurisdictions, however, courts have required counsel to present the accused as a witness or to give a narrative statement if the accused so desires, even if counsel knows that the testimony or statement will be false. The obligation of the advocate under the Rules of Professional Conduct is subordinate to such requirements. See also Comment [9].

[8] The prohibition against offering false evidence only applies if the lawyer knows that the evidence is false. A lawyer's reasonable belief that evidence is false does not preclude its presentation to the trier of fact. A lawyer's knowledge that evidence is false, however, can be inferred from the circumstances. See Rule 1.0(f). Thus, although a lawyer should resolve doubts about the veracity of testimony or other evidence in favor of the client, the lawyer cannot ignore an obvious falsehood.

[9] Although paragraph (a)(3) only prohibits a lawyer from offering evidence the lawyer knows to be false, it permits the lawyer to refuse to offer testimony or other proof that the lawyer reasonably believes is false. Offering such proof may reflect adversely on the lawyer's ability to discriminate in the quality of evidence and thus impair the lawyer's effectiveness as an advocate. Because of the special protections historically provided criminal defendants, however, this Rule does not permit a lawyer to refuse to offer the testimony of such a client where the lawyer reasonably believes but does not know that the testimony will be false. Unless the lawyer knows the testimony will be false, the lawyer must honor the client's decision to testify. See also Comment [7].

Remedial Measures

[10] Having offered material evidence in the belief that it was true, a lawyer may subsequently come to know that the evidence is false. Or, a lawyer may be surprised when the lawyer's client, or another witness called by the lawyer, offers testimony the lawyer knows to be false, either during the lawyer's direct examination or in response to cross-examination by the opposing lawyer. In such situations or if the lawyer knows of the falsity of testimony elicited from the client during a deposition, the lawyer must take reasonable remedial measures. In such situations, the advocate's proper course is to remonstrate with the client confidentially, advise the client of the lawyer's duty of candor to the tribunal and seek the client's cooperation with respect to the withdrawal or correction of the false statements or evidence. If that fails, the advocate must take further remedial action. If withdrawal from the representation is not permitted or will not undo the effect of the false evidence, the advocate must make such disclosure to the tribunal as is reasonably necessary to remedy the situation, even if doing so requires the lawyer to reveal information that otherwise would be protected by Rule 1.6. It is for the tribunal then to determine what should be done -making a statement about the matter to the trier of fact, ordering a mistrial or perhaps nothing.

[11] The disclosure of a client's false testimony can result in grave consequences to the client, including not only a sense of betrayal but also loss of the case and perhaps a prosecution for perjury. But the alternative is that the lawyer cooperate in deceiving the court, thereby subverting the truth-finding process which the adversary system is designed to implement. See Rule 1.2(d). Furthermore, unless it is clearly understood that the lawyer will act upon the duty to disclose the existence of false evidence, the client can simply reject the lawyer's advice to reveal the false evidence and insist that the lawyer keep silent. Thus the client could in effect coerce the lawyer into being a party to fraud on the court.

Preserving Integrity of Adjudicative Process

[12] Lawyers have a special obligation to protect a tribunal against criminal or fraudulent conduct that undermines the integrity of the adjudicative process, such as bribing, intimidating or otherwise unlawfully communicating with a witness, juror, court official or other participant in the

proceeding, unlawfully destroying or concealing documents or other evidence or failing to disclose information to the tribunal when required by law to do so. Thus, paragraph (b) requires a lawyer to take reasonable remedial measures, including disclosure if necessary, whenever the lawyer knows that a person, including the lawyer's client, intends to engage, is engaging or has engaged in criminal or fraudulent conduct related to the proceeding.

Duration of Obligation

[13] A practical time limit on the obligation to rectify false evidence or false statements of law and fact has to be established. The conclusion of the proceeding is a reasonably definite point for the termination of the obligation. A proceeding has concluded within the meaning of this Rule when a final judgment in the proceeding has been affirmed on appeal or the time for review has passed.

Ex Parte Proceedings

[14] Ordinarily, an advocate has the limited responsibility of presenting one side of the matters that a tribunal should consider in reaching a decision; the conflicting position is expected to be presented by the opposing party. However, in any ex parte proceeding, such as an application for a temporary restraining order, there is no balance of presentation by opposing advocates. The object of an ex parte proceeding is nevertheless to yield a substantially just result. The judge has an affirmative responsibility to accord the absent party just consideration. The lawyer for the represented party has the correlative duty to make disclosures of material facts known to the lawyer and that the lawyer reasonably believes are necessary to an informed decision.

Withdrawal

[15] Normally, a lawyer's compliance with the duty of candor imposed by this Rule does not require that the lawyer withdraw from the representation of a client whose interests will be or have been adversely affected by the lawyer's disclosure. The lawyer may, however, be required by Rule 1.16(a) to seek permission of the tribunal to withdraw if the lawyer's compliance with this Rule's duty of candor results in such an extreme deterioration of the client-lawyer relationship that the lawyer can no longer competently represent the client. Also see Rule 1.16(b) for the circumstances in which a lawyer will be permitted to seek a tribunal's permission to withdraw. In connection with a request for permission to withdraw that is premised on a client's misconduct, a lawyer may reveal information relating to the representation only to the extent reasonably necessary to comply with this Rule or as otherwise permitted by Rule 1.6.

RULE 3.4: FAIRNESS TO OPPOSING PARTY AND COUNSEL

A lawyer shall not:

(a) unlawfully obstruct another party's access to evidence or unlawfully alter, destroy or conceal a document or other material having potential evidentiary value. A lawyer shall not counsel or assist another person to do any such act;

(b) falsify evidence, counsel or assist a witness to testify falsely, or offer an inducement to a witness that is prohibited by law;

(c) knowingly disobey an obligation under the rules of a tribunal, except for an open refusal based on an assertion that no valid obligation exists;

(d) in pretrial procedure, make a frivolous discovery request or fail to make reasonably diligent effort to comply with a legally proper discovery request by an opposing party;

(e) in trial, allude to any matter that the lawyer does not reasonably believe is relevant or that win not be supported by admissible evidence, assert personal knowledge of facts in issue except when testifying as a witness, or state a personal opinion as to the justness of a cause, the credibility of a witness, the culpability of a civil litigant or the guilt or innocence of an accused; or

(f) request a person other than a client to refrain from voluntarily giving relevant information to another party unless:

(1) the person is a relative or an employee or other agent of a client; and

(2) the lawyer reasonably believes that the person's interests will not be adversely affected by refraining from giving such information.

Model Rules of Professional Conduct

COMMENT

[1] The procedure of the adversary system contemplates that the evidence in a case is to be marshalled competitively by the contending parties. Fair competition in the adversary system is secured by prohibitions against destruction or concealment of evidence, improperly influencing witnesses, obstructive tactics in discovery procedure, and the like.

[2] Documents and other items of evidence are often essential to establish a claim or defense. Subject to evidentiary privileges, the right of an opposing party, including the government, to obtain evidence through discovery or subpoena is an important procedural right. The exercise of that right can be frustrated if relevant material is altered, concealed or destroyed. Applicable law in many jurisdictions makes it an offense to destroy material for purpose of impairing its availability in a pending proceeding or one whose commencement can be foreseen. Falsifying evidence is also generally a criminal offense. Paragraph (a) applies to evidentiary material generally, including computerized information. Applicable law may permit a lawyer to take temporary possession of physical evidence of client crimes for the purpose of conducting a limited examination that will not alter or destroy material characteristics of the evidence. In such a case, applicable law may require the lawyer to turn the evidence over to the police or other prosecuting authority, depending on the circumstances.

[3] With regard to paragraph (b), it is not improper to pay a witness's expenses or to compensate an expert witness on terms permitted by law. The common law rule in most jurisdictions is that it is improper to pay an occurrence witness any fee for testifying and that it is improper to pay an expert witness a contingent fee.

[4] Paragraph (f) permits a lawyer to advise employees of a client to refrain from giving information to another party, for the employees may identify their interests with those of the client. See also Rule 4.2.

RULE 3.5: IMPARTIALITY AND DECORUM OF THE TRIBUNAL

A lawyer shall not:

(a) seek to influence a judge, juror, prospective juror or other official by means prohibited by law;

(b) communicate ex parte with such a person during the proceeding unless authorized to do so by law or court order;

(c) communicate with a juror or prospective juror after discharge of the jury if:

(1) the communication is prohibited by law or court order;

(2) the juror has made known to the lawyer a desire not to communicate; or

(3) the communication involves misrepresentation, coercion, duress or harassment; or

(d) engage in conduct intended to disrupt a tribunal.

COMMENT

[1] Many forms of improper influence upon a tribunal are proscribed by criminal law. Others are specified in the ABA Model Code of Judicial Conduct, with which an advocate should be familiar. A lawyer is required to avoid contributing to a violation of such provisions.

[2] During a proceeding a lawyer may not communicate ex parte with persons serving in an official capacity in the proceeding, such as judges, masters or jurors, unless authorized to do so by law or court order.

[3] A lawyer may on occasion want to communicate with a juror or prospective juror after the jury has been discharged. The lawyer may do so unless the communication is prohibited by law or a court order but must respect the desire of the juror not to talk with the lawyer. The lawyer may not engage in improper conduct during the communication.

[4] The advocate's function is to present evidence and argument so that the cause may be decided according to law. Refraining from abusive or obstreperous conduct is a corollary of the advocate's right to speak on behalf of litigants. A lawyer may stand firm against abuse by a judge but should avoid reciprocation; the judge's default is no justification for similar dereliction by an advocate. An advocate can present the cause, protect the record for subsequent review and preserve professional integrity by patient firmness no less effectively than by belligerence or theatrics.

[5] The duty to refrain from disruptive conduct applies to any proceeding of a tribunal, including a deposition. See Rule 1.0(m).

RULE 3.6: TRIAL PUBLICITY

(a) A lawyer who is participating or has participated in the investigation or litigation of a matter shall not make an extrajudicial statement that the lawyer knows or reasonably should know will be disseminated by means of public communication and will have a substantial likelihood of materially prejudicing an adjudicative proceeding in the matter.

(b) Notwithstanding paragraph (a), a lawyer may state:

(1) the claim, offense or defense involved and, except when prohibited by law, the identity of the Persons involved;

(2) information contained in a public record;

(3) that an investigation of a matter is in progress;

(4) the scheduling or result of any step in litigation;

(5) a request for assistance in obtaining evidence and information necessary thereto;

(6) a warning of danger concerning the behavior of a person involved, when there is reason to believe that there exists the likelihood of substantial harm to an individual or to the public interest; and

(7) in a criminal case, in addition to subparagraphs (1) through (6):

(i) the identity, residence, occupation and family status of the accused;

(ii) if the accused has not been apprehended, information necessary to aid in apprehension of that person;

(iii) the fact, time and place of arrest; and

(iv) the identity of investigating and arresting officers or agencies and the length of the investigation.

(c) Notwithstanding paragraph (a), a lawyer may make a statement that a reasonable lawyer would believe is required to protect a client from the substantial undue prejudicial effect of recent publicity not initiated by the lawyer or the lawyer's client. A statement made pursuant to this paragraph shall be limited to such information as is necessary to mitigate the recent adverse publicity.

(d) No lawyer associated in a firm or government agency with a lawyer subject to paragraph (a) shall make a statement prohibited by paragraph (a).

COMMENT

[1] It is difficult to strike a balance between protecting the right to a fair trial and safeguarding the right of free expression. Preserving the right to a fair trial necessarily entails some curtailment of the information that may be disseminated about a party prior to trial, particularly where trial by jury is involved. If there were no such limits, the result would be the practical nullification of the protective effect of the rules of forensic decorum and the exclusionary rules of evidence. On the other hand, there are vital social interests served by the free dissemination of information about events having legal consequences and about legal proceedings themselves. The public has a right to know about threats to its safety and measures aimed at assuring its security. It also has a legitimate interest in the conduct of judicial proceedings, particularly in matters of general public concern. Furthermore, the subject matter of legal proceedings is often of direct significance in debate and deliberation over questions of public policy.

[2] Special rules of confidentiality may validly govern proceedings in juvenile, domestic relations and mental disability proceedings, and perhaps other types of litigation. Rule 3.4(c) requires compliance with such rules.

[3] The Rule sets forth a basic general prohibition against a lawyer's making statements that the lawyer knows or should know will have a substantial likelihood of materially prejudicing an adjudicative proceeding. Recognizing that the public value of informed commentary is great and the likelihood of prejudice to a proceeding by the commentary of a lawyer who is not involved in the proceeding is small, the rule applies only to lawyers who are, or who have been involved in the investigation or litigation of a case, and their associates.

[4] Paragraph (b) identifies specific matters about which a lawyer's statements would not ordinarily be considered to present a substantial likelihood of material prejudice, and should not in any event be considered prohibited by the general prohibition of paragraph (a). Paragraph

(b) is not intended to be an exhaustive listing of the subjects upon which a lawyer may make a statement, but statements on other matters may be subject to paragraph (a).

[5] There are, on the other hand, certain subjects that are more likely than not to have a material prejudicial effect on a proceeding, particularly when they refer to a civil matter triable to a jury, a criminal matter, or any other proceeding that could result in incarceration. These subjects relate to:

(1) the character, credibility, reputation or criminal record of a party, suspect in a criminal investigation or witness, or the identity of a witness, or the expected testimony of a party or witness;

(2) in a criminal case or proceeding that could result in incarceration, the possibility of a plea of guilty to the offense or the existence or contents of any confession, admission, or statement given by a defendant or suspect or that person's refusal or failure to make a statement;

(3) the performance or results of any examination or test or the refusal or failure of a person to submit to an examination or test, or the identity or nature of physical evidence expected to be presented;

(4) any opinion as to the guilt or innocence of a defendant or suspect in a criminal case or proceeding that could result in incarceration;

(5) information that the lawyer knows or reasonably should know is likely to be inadmissible as evidence in a trial and that would, if disclosed, create a substantial risk of prejudicing an impartial trial; or

(6) the fact that a defendant has been charged with a crime, unless there is included therein a statement explaining that the charge is merely an accusation and that the defendant is presumed innocent until and unless proven guilty.

[6] Another relevant factor in determining prejudice is the nature of the proceeding involved. Criminal jury trials will be most sensitive to extrajudicial speech. Civil trials may be less sensitive. Non-jury hearings and arbitration proceedings may be even less affected. The Rule will still place limitations on prejudicial comments in these cases, but the likelihood of prejudice may be different depending on the type of proceeding.

[7] Finally, extrajudicial statements that might otherwise raise a question under this Rule may be permissible when they are made in response to statements made publicly by another party, another party's lawyer, or third persons, where a reasonable lawyer would believe a public response is required in order to avoid prejudice to the lawyer's client. When prejudicial statements have been publicly made by others, responsive statements may have the salutary effect of lessening any resulting adverse impact on the adjudicative proceeding. Such responsive statements should be limited to contain only such information as is necessary to mitigate undue prejudice created by the statements made by others.

[8] See Rule 3.8(f) for additional duties of prosecutors in connection with extrajudicial statements about criminal proceedings.

RULE 3.7: LAWYER AS WITNESS

(a) A lawyer shall not act as advocate at a trial in which the lawyer is likely to be a necessary witness unless:

(1) the testimony relates to an uncontested issue;

(2) the testimony relates to the nature and value of legal services rendered in the case; or

(3) disqualification of the lawyer would work substantial hardship on the client.

(b) A lawyer may act as advocate in a trial in which another lawyer in the lawyer's firm is likely to be called as a witness unless precluded from doing so by Rule 1.7 or Rule 1.9.

COMMENT

[1] Combining the roles of advocate and witness can prejudice the tribunal and the opposing party and can also involve a conflict of interest between the lawyer and client.

Advocate-Witness Rule

[2] The tribunal has proper objection when the trier of fact may be confused or misled by a lawyer serving as both advocate and witness. The opposing party has proper objection where the combination of roles may prejudice that party's rights in the litigation. A witness is required to testify on the basis of personal knowledge, while an advocate is expected to explain and comment

on evidence given by others. It may not be clear whether a statement by an advocate-witness should be taken as proof or as an analysis of the proof.

[3] To protect the tribunal, paragraph (a) prohibits a lawyer from simultaneously serving as advocate and necessary witness except in those circumstances specified in paragraphs (a)(1) through (a)(3). Paragraph (a)(1) recognizes that if the testimony will be uncontested, the ambiguities in the dual role are purely theoretical. Paragraph (a)(2) recognizes that where the testimony concerns the extent and value of legal services rendered in the action in which the testimony is offered, permitting the lawyers to testify avoids the need for a second trial with new counsel to resolve that issue. Moreover, in such a situation the judge has firsthand knowledge of the matter in issue; hence, there is less dependence on the adversary process to test the credibility of the testimony.

[4] Apart from these two exceptions, paragraph (a)(3) recognizes that a balancing is required between the interests of the client and those of the tribunal and the opposing party. Whether the tribunal is likely to be misled or the opposing party is likely to suffer prejudice depends on the nature of the case, the importance and probable tenor of the lawyer's testimony, and the probability that the lawyer's testimony will conflict with that of other witnesses. Even if there is risk of such prejudice, in determining whether the lawyer should be disqualified, due regard must be given to the effect of disqualification on the lawyer's client. It is relevant that one or both parties could reasonably foresee that the lawyer would probably be a witness. The conflict of interest principles stated in Rules 1.7, 1.9 and 1.10 have no application to this aspect of the problem.

[5] Because the tribunal is not likely to be misled when a lawyer acts as advocate in a trial in which another lawyer in the lawyer's firm will testify as a necessary witness, paragraph (b) permits the lawyer to do so except in situations involving a conflict of interest.

Conflict of Interest

[6] In determining if it is permissible to act as advocate in a trial in which the lawyer will be a necessary witness, the lawyer must also consider that the dual role may give rise to a conflict of interest that will require compliance with Rules 1.7 or 1.9. For example, if there is likely to be substantial conflict between the testimony of the client and that of the lawyer the representation involves a conflict of interest that requires compliance with Rule 1.7. This would be true even though the lawyer might not be prohibited by paragraph (a) from simultaneously serving as advocate and witness because the lawyer's disqualification would work a substantial hardship on the client. Similarly, a lawyer who might be permitted to simultaneously serve as an advocate and a witness by paragraph (a)(3) might be precluded from doing so by Rule 1.9. The problem can arise whether the lawyer is called as a witness on behalf of the client or is called by the opposing party. Determining whether or not such a conflict exists is primarily the responsibility of the lawyer involved. If there is a conflict of interest, the lawyer must secure the client's informed consent, confirmed in writing. In some cases, the lawyer will be precluded from seeking the client's consent. See Rule 1.7. See Rule 1.0(b) for the definition of "confirmed in writing" and Rule 1.0(e) for the definition of "informed consent."

[7] Paragraph (b) provides that a lawyer is not disqualified from serving as an advocate because a lawyer with whom the lawyer is associated in a firm is precluded from doing so by paragraph (a). If, however, the testifying lawyer would also be disqualified by Rule 1.7 or Rule 1.9 from representing the client in the matter, other lawyers in the firm will be precluded from representing the client by Rule 1.10 unless the client gives informed consent under the conditions stated in Rule 1.7.

RULE 3.8: SPECIAL RESPONSIBILITIES OF A PROSECUTOR

The prosecutor in a criminal case shall:

(a) refrain from prosecuting a charge that the prosecutor knows is not supported by probable cause;

(b) make reasonable efforts to assure that the accused has been advised of the right to, and the procedure for obtaining, counsel and has been given reasonable opportunity to obtain counsel;

(c) not seek to obtain from an unrepresented accused a waiver of important pretrial rights, such as the right to a preliminary hearing;

(d) make timely disclosure to the defense of all evidence or information known to the prosecutor that tends to negate the guilt of the accused or mitigates the offense, and, in connection with sentencing, disclose to the defense and to the tribunal all unprivileged mitigating information known to the prosecutor, except when the prosecutor is relieved of this responsibility by a protective order of the tribunal;

(e) not subpoena a lawyer in a grand jury or other criminal proceeding to present evidence about a past or present client unless the prosecutor reasonably believes:

(1) the information sought is not protected from disclosure by any applicable privilege;

(2) the evidence sought is essential to the successful completion of an ongoing investigation or prosecution; and

(3) there is no other feasible alternative to obtain the information;

(f) except for statements that are necessary to inform the public of the nature and extent of the prosecutor's action and that serve a legitimate law enforcement purpose, refrain from making extrajudicial comments that have a substantial likelihood of heightening public condemnation of the accused and exercise reasonable care to prevent investigators, law enforcement personnel, employees or other persons assisting or associated with the prosecutor in a criminal case from making an extrajudicial statement that the prosecutor would be prohibited from making under Rule 3.6 or this Rule.

COMMENT

[1] A prosecutor has the responsibility of a minister of justice and not simply that of an advocate. This responsibility carries with it specific obligations to see that the defendant is accorded procedural justice and that guilt is decided upon the basis of sufficient evidence. Precisely how far the prosecutor is required to go in this direction is a matter of debate and varies in different jurisdictions. Many jurisdictions have adopted the ABA Standards of Criminal Justice Relating to the Prosecution Function, which in turn are the product of prolonged and careful deliberation by lawyers experienced in both criminal prosecution and defense. Applicable law may require other measures by the prosecutor and knowing disregard of those obligations or a systematic abuse of prosecutorial discretion could constitute a violation of Rule 8.4.

[2] In some jurisdictions, a defendant may waive a preliminary hearing and thereby lose a valuable opportunity to challenge probable cause. Accordingly, prosecutors should not seek to obtain waivers of preliminary hearings or other important pretrial rights from unrepresented accused persons. Paragraph (c) does not apply, however, to an accused appearing pro se with the approval of the tribunal. Nor does it forbid the lawful questioning of an uncharged suspect who has knowingly waived the rights to counsel and silence.

[3] The exception in paragraph (d) recognizes that a prosecutor may seek an appropriate protective order from the tribunal if disclosure of information to the defense could result in substantial harm to an individual or to the public interest.

[4] Paragraph (e) is intended to limit the issuance of lawyer subpoenas in grand jury and other criminal proceedings to those situations in which there is a genuine need to intrude into the client-lawyer relationship.

[5] Paragraph (f) supplements Rule 3.6, which prohibits extrajudicial statements that have a substantial likelihood of prejudicing an adjudicatory proceeding. In the context of a criminal prosecution, a prosecutor's extrajudicial statement can create the additional problem of increasing public condemnation of the accused. Although the announcement of an indictment, for example, will necessarily have severe consequences for the accused, a prosecutor can, and should, avoid comments which have no legitimate law enforcement purpose and have a substantial likelihood of increasing public opprobrium of the accused. Nothing in this Comment is intended to restrict the statements which a prosecutor may make which comply with Rule 3.6(b) or 3.6(c).

[6] Like other lawyers, prosecutors are subject to Rules 5.1 and 5.3, which, relate to

responsibilities regarding lawyers and nonlawyers who work for or are associated with the lawyer's office. Paragraph (f) reminds the prosecutor of the importance of these obligations in connection with the unique dangers of improper extrajudicial statements in a criminal case. In addition, paragraph (f) requires a prosecutor to exercise reasonable care to prevent persons assisting or associated with the prosecutor from making improper extrajudicial statements, even when such persons are not under the direct supervision of the prosecutor. Ordinarily, the reasonable care standard will be satisfied if the prosecutor issues the appropriate cautions to law- enforcement personnel and other relevant individuals.

RULE 3.9: ADVOCATE IN NONADJUDICATIVE PROCEEDINGS

A lawyer representing a client before a legislative body or administrative agency in a nonadjudicative proceeding shall disclose that the appearance is in a representative capacity and shall conform to the provisions of Rules 3.3(a) through (c), 3.4(a) through (c), and 3.5.

COMMENT

[1] In representation before bodies such as legislatures, municipal councils, and executive and administrative agencies acting in a rulemaking or policy-making capacity, lawyers present facts, formulate issues and advance argument in the matters under consideration. The decision-making body, like a court, should be able to rely on the integrity of the submissions made to it. A lawyer appearing before such a body must deal with it honestly and in conformity with applicable rules of procedure. See Rules 3.3(a) through (c), 3.4(a) through (c) and 3.5.

[2] Lawyers have no exclusive right to appear before nonadjudicative bodies, as they do before a court. The requirements of this Rule therefore may subject lawyers to regulations inapplicable to advocates who are not lawyers. However, legislatures and administrative agencies have a right to expect lawyers to deal with them as they deal with courts.

[3] This Rule only applies when a lawyer represents a client in connection with an official hearing or meeting of a governmental agency or a legislative body to which the lawyer or the lawyer's client is presenting evidence or argument. It does not apply to representation of a client in a negotiation or other bilateral transaction with a governmental agency or in connection with an application for a license or other privilege or the client's compliance with generally applicable reporting requirements, such as the filing of income-tax returns. Nor does it apply to the representation of a client in connection with an investigation or examination of the client's affairs conducted by government investigators or examiners. Representation in such matters is governed by Rules 4.1 through 4.4.

RULE 4.1: TRUTHFULNESS IN STATEMENTS TO OTHERS

In the course of representing a client a lawyer shall not knowingly:

(a) make a false statement of material fact or law to a third person; or

(b) fail to disclose a material fact when disclosure is necessary to avoid assisting a criminal or fraudulent act by a client, unless disclosure is prohibited by Rule 1.6.

COMMENT

Misrepresentation

[1] A lawyer is required to be truthful when dealing with others on a client's behalf, but generally has no affirmative duty to inform an opposing party of relevant facts. A misrepresentation can occur if the lawyer incorporates or affirms a statement of another person that the lawyer knows is false. Misrepresentations can also occur by partially true but misleading statements or omissions that are the equivalent of affirmative false statements. For dishonest conduct that does not amount to a false statement or for misrepresentations by a lawyer other than in the course of representing a client, see Rule 8.4.

Statements of Fact

[2] This Rule refers to statements of fact. Whether a particular statement should be regarded as one of fact can depend on the circumstances. Under generally accepted conventions in negotiation, certain types of statements ordinarily are not taken as statements of material fact. Estimates of

price or value placed on the subject of a transaction and a party's intentions as to an acceptable settlement of a claim are ordinarily in this category, and so is the existence of an undisclosed principal except where nondisclosure of the principal would constitute fraud. Lawyers should be mindful of their obligations under applicable law to avoid criminal and tortious misrepresentation.

Crime or Fraud by Client

[3] Under Rule 1.2(d), a lawyer is prohibited from counseling or assisting a client in conduct that the lawyer knows is criminal or fraudulent. Paragraph (b) states a specific application of the principle set forth in Rule 1.2(d) and addresses the situation where a client's crime or fraud takes the form of a lie or misrepresentation. Ordinarily, a lawyer can avoid assisting a client's crime or fraud by withdrawing from the representation. Sometimes it may be necessary for the lawyer to give notice of the fact of withdrawal and to disaffirm an opinion, document, affirmation or the like. In extreme cases, substantive law may require a lawyer to disclose information relating to the representation to avoid being deemed to have assisted the client's crime or fraud. If the lawyer can avoid assisting a client's crime or fraud only by disclosing this information, then under paragraph (b) the lawyer is required to do so, unless the disclosure is prohibited by Rule 1.6.

RULE 4.2: COMMUNICATION WITH PERSON REPRESENTED BY COUNSEL

In representing a client, a lawyer shall not communicate about the subject of the representation with a person the lawyer knows to be represented by another lawyer in the matter, unless the lawyer has the consent of the other lawyer or is authorized to do so by law or a court order.

COMMENT

[1] This Rule contributes to the proper functioning of the legal system by protecting a person who has chosen to be represented by a lawyer in a matter against possible overreaching by other lawyers who are participating in the matter, interference by those lawyers with the client-lawyer relationship and the uncounselled disclosure of information relating to the representation.

[2] This Rule applies to communications with any person who is represented by counsel concerning the matter to which the communication relates.

[3] The Rule applies even though the represented person initiates or consents to the communication. A lawyer must immediately terminate communication with a person if, after commencing communication, the lawyer learns that the person is one with whom communication is not permitted by this Rule.

[4] This Rule does not prohibit communication with a represented person, or an employee or agent of such a person, concerning matters outside the representation. For example, the existence of a controversy between a government agency and a private party, or between two organizations, does not prohibit a lawyer for either from communicating with nonlawyer representatives of the other regarding a separate matter. Nor does this Rule preclude communication with a represented person who is seeking advice from a lawyer who is not otherwise representing a client in the matter. A lawyer may not make a communication prohibited by this Rule through the acts of another. See Rule 8.4(a). Parties to a matter may communicate directly with each other, and a lawyer is not prohibited from advising a client concerning a communication that the client is legally entitled to make. Also, a lawyer having independent justification or legal authorization for communicating with a represented person is permitted to do so.

[5] Communications authorized by law may include communications by a lawyer on behalf of a client who is exercising a constitutional or other legal right to communicate with the government. Communications authorized by law may also include investigative activities of lawyers representing governmental entities, directly or through investigative agents, prior to the commencement of criminal or civil enforcement proceedings. When communicating with the accused in a criminal matter, a government lawyer must comply with this Rule in addition to honoring the constitutional rights of the accused. The fact that a communication does not violate a state or federal constitutional right is insufficient to establish that the communication is permissible under this Rule.

[6] A lawyer who is uncertain whether a communication with a represented person is permissible may seek a court order. A lawyer may also seek a court order in exceptional circumstances to authorize a communication that would otherwise be prohibited by this Rule, for example, where communication with a person represented by counsel is necessary to avoid reasonably certain injury.

[7] In the case of a represented organization, this Rule prohibits communications with a constituent of the organization who supervises, directs or regularly consults with the organization's lawyer concerning the matter or has authority to obligate the organization with respect to the matter or whose act or omission in connection with the matter may be imputed to the organization for purposes of civil or criminal liability. Consent of the organization's lawyer is not required for communication with a former constituent. If a constituent of the organization is represented in the matter by his or her own counsel, the consent by that counsel to a communication will be sufficient for purposes of this Rule. Compare Rule 3.4(f). In communicating with a current or former constituent of an organization, a lawyer must not use methods of obtaining evidence that violate the legal rights of the organization. See Rule 4.4.

[8] The prohibition on communications with a represented person only applies in circumstances where the lawyer knows that the person is in fact represented in the matter to be discussed. This means that the lawyer has actual knowledge of the fact of the representation; but such actual knowledge may be inferred from the circumstances. See Rule 1.0(f). Thus, the lawyer cannot evade the requirement of obtaining the consent of counsel by closing eyes to the obvious.

[9] In the event the person with whom the lawyer communicates is not known to be represented by counsel in the matter, the lawyer's communications are subject to Rule 4.3.

RULE 4.3: DEALING WITH UNREPRESENTED PERSON

In dealing on behalf of a client with a person who is not represented by counsel, a lawyer shall not state or imply that the lawyer is disinterested. When the lawyer knows or reasonably should know that the unrepresented person misunderstands the lawyer's role in the matter, the lawyer shall make reasonable efforts to correct the misunderstanding. The lawyer shall not give legal advice to an unrepresented person, other than the advice to secure counsel, if the lawyer knows or reasonably should know that the interests of such a person are or have a reasonable possibility of being in conflict with the interests of the client.

COMMENT

[1] An unrepresented person, particularly one not experienced in dealing with legal matters, might assume that a lawyer is disinterested in loyalties or is a disinterested authority on the law even when the lawyer represents a client. In order to avoid a misunderstanding, a lawyer will typically need to identify the lawyer's client and, where necessary, explain that the client has interests opposed to those of the unrepresented person. For misunderstandings that sometimes arise when a lawyer for an organization deals with an unrepresented constituent, see Rule 1.13(d).

[2] The Rule distinguishes between situations involving unrepresented persons whose interests may be adverse to those of the lawyer's client and those in which the person's interests are not in conflict with the client's. In the former situation, the possibility that the lawyer will compromise the unrepresented person's interests is so great that the Rule prohibits the giving of any advice, apart from the advice to obtain counsel. Whether a lawyer is giving impermissible advice may depend on the experience and sophistication of the unrepresented person, as well as the setting in which the behavior and comments occur. This Rule does not prohibit a lawyer from negotiating the terms of a transaction or settling a dispute with an unrepresented person. So long as the lawyer has explained that the lawyer represents an adverse party and is not representing the person, the lawyer may inform the person of the terms on which the lawyer's client will enter into an agreement or settle a matter, prepare documents that require the person's signature and explain the lawyer's own view of the meaning of

the document or the lawyer's view of the underlying legal obligations.

RULE 4.4: RESPECT FOR RIGHTS OF THIRD PERSONS

(a) In representing a client, a lawyer shall not use means that have no substantial purpose other than to embarrass, delay, or burden a third person, or use methods of obtaining evidence that violate the legal rights of such a person.

(b) A lawyer who receives a document relating to the representation of the lawyer's client and knows or reasonably should know that the document was inadvertently sent shall promptly notify the sender.

COMMENT

[1] Responsibility to a client requires a lawyer to subordinate the interests of others to those of the client, but that responsibility does not imply that a lawyer may disregard the rights of third persons. It is impractical to catalogue all such rights, but they include legal restrictions on methods of obtaining evidence from third persons and unwarranted intrusions into privileged relationships, such as the client-lawyer relationship.

[2] Paragraph (b) recognizes that lawyers sometimes receive documents that were mistakenly sent or produced by opposing parties or their lawyers. If a lawyer knows or reasonably should know that such a document was sent inadvertently, then this Rule requires the lawyer to promptly notify the sender in order to permit that person to take protective measures. Whether the lawyer is required to take additional steps, such as returning the original document, is a matter of law beyond the scope of these Rules, as is the question of whether the privileged status of a document has been waived. Similarly, this Rule does not address the legal duties of a lawyer who receives a document that the lawyer knows or reasonably should know may have been wrongfully obtained by the sending person. For purposes of this Rule, "document" includes e-mail or other electronic modes of transmission subject to being read or put into readable form.

[3] Some lawyers may choose to return a document unread, for example, when the lawyer learns before receiving the document that it was inadvertently sent to the wrong address. Where a lawyer is not required by applicable law to do so, the decision to voluntarily return such a document is a matter of professional judgment ordinarily reserved to the lawyer. See Rules 1.2 and 1.4.

RULE 5.1: RESPONSIBILITIES OF PARTNERS, MANAGERS, AND SUPERVISORY LAWYERS

(a) A partner in a law firm, and a lawyer who individually or together with other lawyers possesses comparable managerial authority in a law firm, shall make reasonable efforts to ensure that the firm has in effect measures giving reasonable assurance that all lawyers in the firm conform to the Rules of Professional Conduct.

(b) A lawyer having direct supervisory authority over another lawyer shall make reasonable efforts to ensure that the other lawyer conforms to the Rules of Professional Conduct.

(c) A lawyer shall be responsible for another lawyer's violation of the Rules of Professional Conduct if:

(1) the lawyer orders or, with knowledge of the specific conduct, raffles the conduct involved; or

(2) the lawyer is a partner or has comparable managerial authority in the law firm in which the other lawyer practices, or has direct supervisory authority over the other lawyer, and knows of the conduct at a time when its consequences can be avoided or mitigated but fails to take reasonable remedial action.

COMMENT

[1] Paragraph (a) applies to lawyers who have managerial authority over the professional work of a firm. See Rule 1.0(c). This includes members of a partnership, the shareholders in a law firm organized as a professional corporation, and members of other associations authorized to practice law; lawyers having comparable managerial authority in a legal services organization or a law department of an enterprise or government agency; and lawyers who have intermediate managerial responsibilities in a firm. Paragraph (b) applies to lawyers who have supervisory authority over the work of other lawyers in a firm.

[2] Paragraph (a) requires lawyers with managerial authority within a firm to make reasonable efforts to establish internal policies and procedures designed to provide reasonable assurance that all lawyers in the firm will conform to the Rules of Professional Conduct. Such policies and procedures include those designed to detect and resolve conflicts of interest, identify dates by which actions must be taken in pending matters, account for client funds and property and ensure that inexperienced lawyers are properly supervised.

[3] Other measures that may be required to fulfill the responsibility prescribed in paragraph (a) can depend on the firm's structure and the nature of its practice. In a small firm of experienced lawyers, informal supervision and periodic review of compliance with the required systems ordinarily will suffice. In a large firm, or in practice situations in which difficult ethical problems frequently arise, more elaborate measures may be necessary. Some firms, for example, have a procedure whereby junior lawyers can make confidential referral of ethical problems directly to a designated senior partner or special committee. See Rule 5.2. Firms, whether large or small, may also rely on continuing legal education in professional ethics. In any event, the ethical atmosphere of a firm can influence the conduct of all its members the partners may not assume that all lawyers associated with the firm will inevitably conform to the Rules.

[4] Paragraph (c) expresses a general principle of personal responsibility for acts of another. See also Rule 8.4(a).

[5] Paragraph (c)(2) defines the duty of a partner or other lawyer having comparable managerial authority in a law firm, as well as a lawyer who has direct supervisory authority over performance of specific legal work by another lawyer. Whether a lawyer has supervisory authority in particular circumstances is a question of fact. Partners and lawyers with comparable authority have at least indirect responsibility for all work being done by the firm, while a partner or manager in charge of a particular matter ordinarily also has supervisory responsibility for the work of other firm lawyers engaged in the matter. Appropriate remedial action by a partner or managing lawyer would depend on the immediacy of that lawyer's involvement and the seriousness of the misconduct. A supervisor is required to intervene to prevent avoidable consequences of misconduct if the supervisor knows that the misconduct occurred. Thus, if a supervising lawyer knows that a subordinate misrepresented a matter to an opposing party in negotiation, the supervisor as well as the subordinate has a duty to correct the resulting misapprehension.

[6] Professional misconduct by a lawyer under supervision could reveal a violation of paragraph (b) on the part of the supervisory lawyer even though it does not entail a violation of paragraph (c) because there was no direction, ratification or knowledge of the violation.

[7] Apart from this Rule and Rule 8.4(a), a lawyer does not have disciplinary liability for the conduct of a partner, associate or subordinate. Whether a lawyer may be liable civilly or criminally for another lawyer's conduct is a question of law beyond the scope of these Rules.

[8] The duties imposed by this Rule on managing and supervising lawyers do not alter the personal duty of each lawyer in a firm to abide by the Rules of Professional Conduct. See Rule 5.2(a).

RULE 5.2: RESPONSIBILITIES OF A SUBORDINATE LAWYER

(a) A lawyer is bound by the Rules of Professional Conduct notwithstanding that the lawyer acted at the direction of another person.

(b) A subordinate lawyer does not violate the Rules of Professional Conduct if that lawyer acts in accordance with a supervisory lawyer's reasonable resolution of an arguable question of professional duty.

COMMENT

[1] Although a lawyer is not relieved of responsibility for a violation by the fact that the lawyer acted at the direction of a supervisor, that fact may be relevant in determining whether a lawyer had the knowledge required to render conduct a violation of the Rules. For example, if a subordinate filed a frivolous pleading at the direction of a supervisor, the subordinate would not be guilty of a professional violation unless the subordinate knew of the document's frivolous character.

[2] When lawyers in a supervisor-subordinate relationship encounter a matter involving professional judgment as to ethical duty, the supervisor may assume responsibility for making the judgment. Otherwise a consistent course of action or position could not be taken. If the question can reasonably be answered only one way, the duty of both lawyers is clear and they are equally responsible for fulfilling it. However, if the question is reasonably arguable, someone has to decide upon the course of action. That authority ordinarily reposes in the supervisor, and a subordinate may be guided accordingly. For example, if a question arises whether the interests of two clients conflict under Rule 1.7, the supervisor's reasonable resolution of the question should protect the subordinate professionally if the resolution is subsequently challenged.

RULE 5.3: RESPONSIBILITIES REGARDING NONLAWYER ASSISTANTS

With respect to a nonlawyer employed or retained by or associated with a lawyer:

(a) a partner, and a lawyer who individually or together with other lawyers possesses comparable managerial authority in a law firm shall make reasonable efforts to ensure that the firm has in effect measures giving reasonable assurance that the person's conduct is compatible with the professional obligations of the lawyer;

(b) a lawyer having direct supervisory authority over the nonlawyer shall make reasonable efforts to ensure that the person's conduct is compatible with the professional obligations of the lawyer; and

(c) a lawyer shall be responsible for conduct of such a person that would be a violation of the Rules of Professional Conduct if engaged in by a lawyer if:

(1) the lawyer orders or, with the knowledge of the specific conduct, ratifies the conduct involved; or

(2) the lawyer is a partner or has comparable managerial authority in the law firm in which the person is employed, or has direct supervisory authority over the person, and knows of the conduct at a time when its consequences can be avoided or mitigated but fails to take reasonable remedial action.

COMMENT

[1] Lawyers generally employ assistants in their practice, including secretaries, investigators, law student interns, and paraprofessionals. Such assistants, whether employees or independent contractors, act for the lawyer in rendition of the lawyer's professional services. A lawyer must give such assistants appropriate instruction and supervision concerning the ethical aspects of their employment, particularly regarding the obligation not to disclose information relating to representation of the client, and should be responsible for their work product. The measures employed in supervising nonlawyers should take account of the fact that they do not have legal training and are not subject to professional discipline.

[2] Paragraph (a) requires lawyers with managerial authority within a law firm to make reasonable efforts to establish internal policies and procedures designed to provide reasonable assurance that nonlawyers in the firm will act in a way compatible with the Rules of Professional Conduct. See Comment [1] to Rule 5.1. Paragraph (b) applies to lawyers who have supervisory authority over the work of a nonlawyer. Paragraph (c) specifies the circumstances in which a lawyer is responsible for conduct of a nonlawyer that would be a violation of the Rules of Professional Conduct if engaged in by a lawyer.

RULE 5.4: PROFESSIONAL INDEPENDENCE OF A LAWYER

(a) A lawyer or law firm shall not share legal fees with a nonlawyer, except that:

(1) an agreement by a lawyer with the lawyer's firm, partner, or associate may provide for the payment of money, over a reasonable period of time after the lawyer's death, to the lawyer's estate or to one or more specified persons;

(2) a lawyer who purchases the practice of a deceased, disabled, or disappeared lawyer may, pursuant to the provisions of Rule 1.17, pay to the estate or other representative of that lawyer the agreed-upon purchase price;

(3) a lawyer or law firm may include non lawyer employees in a compensation

or retirement plan, even though the plan is based in whole or in part on a profit-sharing arrangement; and

(4) a lawyer may share court-awarded legal fees with a nonprofit organization that employed, retained or recommended. employment of the lawyer in the matter.

(b) A lawyer shall not form a partnership with a nonlawyer if any of the activities of the partnership consist of the practice of law.

(c) A lawyer shall not permit a person who recommends, employs, or pays the lawyer to render legal services for another to direct or regulate the lawyer's professional judgment in rendering such legal services.

(d) A lawyer shall not practice with or in the form of a professional corporation or association authorized to practice law for a profit, if:

(1) a nonlawyer owns any interest therein, except that a fiduciary representative of the estate of a lawyer may hold the stock or interest of the lawyer for a reasonable time during administration;

(2) a nonlawyer is a corporate director or officer thereof or occupies the position of similar responsibility in any form of association other than a corporation; or

(3) a nonlawyer has the right to direct or control the professional judgment of a lawyer.

COMMENT

[1] The provisions of this Rule express traditional limitations on sharing fees. These limitations are to protect the lawyer's professional independence of judgment. Where someone other than the client pays the lawyer's fee or salary, or recommends employment of the lawyer, that arrangement does not modify the lawyer's obligation to the client. As stated in paragraph (c), such arrangements should not interfere with the lawyer's professional judgment.

[2] This Rule also expresses traditional limitations on permitting a third party to direct or regulate the lawyer's professional judgment in rendering legal services to another. See also Rule 1.8(f) (lawyer may accept compensation from a third party as long as there is no interference with the lawyer's independent professional judgment and the client gives informed consent).

RULE 5.5: UNAUTHORIZED PRACTICE OF LAW; MULTIJURISDICTIONAL PRACTICE OF LAW

(a) A lawyer shall not practice law in a jurisdiction in violation of the regulation of the legal profession in that jurisdiction, or assist another in doing so.

(b) A lawyer who is not admitted to practice in this jurisdiction shall not:

(1) except as authorized by these Rules or other law, establish an office or other systematic and continuous presence in this jurisdiction for the practice of law; or

(2) hold out to the public or otherwise represent that the lawyer is admitted to practice law in this jurisdiction.

(c) A lawyer admitted in another United States jurisdiction, and not disbarred or suspended from practice in any jurisdiction, may provide legal services on a temporary basis in this jurisdiction that:

(1) are undertaken in association with a lawyer who is admitted to practice in this jurisdiction and who actively participates in the matter;

(2) are in or reasonably related to a pending or potential proceeding before a tribunal in this or another jurisdiction, if the lawyer, or a person the lawyer is assisting, is authorized by law or order to appear in such proceeding or reasonably expects to be so authorized;

(3) are in or reasonably related to a pending or potential arbitration, mediation, or other alternative dispute resolution proceeding in this or another jurisdiction, if the services arise out of or are reasonably related to the lawyer's practice in a jurisdiction in which the lawyer is admitted to practice and are not services for which the forum requires pro hac vice admission; or

(4) are not within paragraphs (c)(2) or (c)(3) and arise out of or are reasonably related to the lawyer's practice in a jurisdiction in which the lawyer is admitted to practice.

(d) A lawyer admitted in another United States jurisdiction, and not disbarred or suspended from practice in any jurisdiction, may provide legal services in this jurisdiction that:

(1) are provided to the lawyer's employer or its organizational affiliates and are not

Model Rules of Professional Conduct

services for which the forum requires pro hac vice admission; or

(2) are services that the lawyer is authorized to provide by federal law or other law of this jurisdiction.

COMMENT

[1] The definition of the practice of law is established by law and varies from one jurisdiction to another. Whatever the definition, limiting the practice of law to members of the bar protects the public against rendition of legal services by unqualified persons. Paragraph (b) does not prohibit a lawyer from employing the services of paraprofessionals and delegating functions to them, so long as the lawyer supervises the delegated work and retains responsibility for their work. See Rule 5.3. Likewise, it does not prohibit lawyers from providing professional advice and instruction to nonlawyers whose employment requires knowledge of law; for example, claims adjusters, employees of financial or commercial institutions, social workers, accountants and persons employed in government agencies. In addition, a lawyer may counsel nonlawyers who wish to proceed pro se.

RULE 5.6: RESTRICTIONS ON RIGHT TO PRACTICE

A lawyer shall not participate in offering or making:

(a) a partnership, shareholders, operating, employment, or other similar type of agreement that restricts the right of a lawyer to practice after termination of the relationship, except an agreement concerning benefits upon retirement; or

(b) an agreement in which a restriction on the lawyer's right to practice is part of the settlement of a client controversy.

COMMENT

[1] An agreement restricting the right of lawyers to practice after leaving a firm not only limits their professional autonomy but also limits the freedom of clients to choose a lawyer. Paragraph (a) prohibits such agreements except for restrictions incident to provisions concerning retirement benefits for service with the firm.

[2] Paragraph (b) prohibits a lawyer from agreeing not to represent other persons in connection with settling a claim on behalf of a client.

[3] This Rule does not apply to prohibit restrictions that may be included in the terms of the sale of a law practice pursuant to Rule 1.17.

RULE 5.7: RESPONSIBILITIES REGARDING LAW-RELATED SERVICES

(a) A lawyer shall be subject to the Rules of Professional Conduct with respect to the provision of law-related services, as defined in paragraph (b), if the law-related services are provided:

(1) by the lawyer in circumstances that are not distinct from the lawyer's provision of legal services to clients; or

(2) in other circumstances by an entity controlled by the lawyer individually or with others if the lawyer fails to take reasonable measures to assure that a person obtaining the law related services knows that the services are not legal services and that the protections of the client-lawyer relationship do not exist.

(b) The term "law-related services" denotes services that might reasonably be performed in conjunction with and in substance are related to the provision of legal services, and that are not prohibited as unauthorized practice of law when provided by a nonlawyer.

COMMENT

[1] When a lawyer performs law-related services or controls an organization that does so, there exists the potential for ethical problems. Principal among these is the possibility that the person for whom the law-related services are performed fails to understand that the services may not carry with them the protections normally afforded as part of the client-lawyer relationship. The recipient of the law-related services may expect, for example, that the protection of client confidences, prohibitions against representation of persons with conflicting interests, and obligations of a lawyer to maintain professional independence apply to the provision of law-related services when that may not be the case.

[2] Rule 5.7 applies to the provision of law-related services by a lawyer even when the lawyer

does not provide any legal services to the person for whom the law-related services are performed and whether the lawrelated services are performed through a law firm or a separate entity. The Rule identifies the circumstances in which all of the Rules of Professional Conduct apply to the provision of law-related services. Even when those circumstances do not exist, however, the conduct of a lawyer involved in the provision of law-related services is subject to those Rules that apply generally to lawyer conduct, regardless of whether the conduct involves the provision of legal services. See, e.g., Rule 8.4.

[3] When law-related services are provided by a lawyer under circumstances that are not distinct from the lawyer's provision of legal services to clients, the lawyer in providing the law-related services must adhere to the requirements of the Rules of Professional Conduct as provided in paragraph (a)(1). Even when the law-related and legal services are provided in circumstances that are distinct from each other, for example through separate entities or different support staff within the law firm, the Rules of Professional Conduct apply to the lawyer as provided in paragraph (a)(2) unless the lawyer takes reasonable measures to assure that the recipient of the law-related services knows that the services are not legal services and that the protections of the client-lawyer relationship do not apply.

[4] Law-related services also may be provided through an entity that is distinct from that through which the lawyer provides legal services. If the lawyer individually or with others has control of such an entity's operations, the Rule requires the lawyer to take reasonable measures to assure that each person using the services of the entity knows that the services provided by the entity are not legal services and that the Rules of Professional Conduct that relate to the client-lawyer relationship do not apply. A lawyer's control of an entity extends to the ability to direct its operation. Whether a lawyer has such control will depend upon the circumstances of the particular case.

[5] When a client-lawyer relationship exists with a person who is referred by a lawyer to a separate law-related service entity controlled by the lawyer, individually or with others, the lawyer must comply with Rule 1.8(a).

[6] In taking the reasonable measures referred to in paragraph (a)(2) to assure that a person using law-related services understands the practical effect or significance of the inapplicability of the Rules of Professional Conduct, the lawyer should communicate to the person receiving the law-related services, in a manner sufficient to assure that the person understands the significance of the fact, that the relationship of the person to the business entity will not be a client-lawyer relationship. The communication should be made before entering into an agreement for provision of or providing law-related services, and preferably should be in writing.

[7] The burden is upon the lawyer to show that the lawyer has taken reasonable measures under the circumstances to communicate the desired understanding. For instance, a sophisticated user of law-related services, such as a publicly held corporation, may require a lesser explanation than someone unaccustomed to making distinctions between legal services and law-related services, such as an individual seeking tax advice from a lawyer-accountant or investigative services in connection with a lawsuit.

[8] Regardless of the sophistication of potential recipients of law-related services, a lawyer should take special care to keep separate the provision of law-related and legal services in order to minimize the risk that the recipient will assume that the law-related services are legal services. The risk of such confusion is especially acute when the lawyer renders both types of services with respect to the same matter. Under some circumstances the legal and law-related services may be so closely entwined that they cannot be distinguished from each other, and the requirement of disclosure and consultation imposed by paragraph (a)(2) of the Rule cannot be met. In such a case a lawyer will be responsible for assuring that both the lawyer's conduct and, to the extent required by Rule 5.3, that of nonlawyer employees in the distinct entity that the lawyer controls complies in all respects with the Rules of Professional Conduct.

[9] A broad range of economic and other interests of clients may be served by lawyers' engaging in the delivery of law-related services. Examples of law-related services include providing title insurance, financial planning,

accounting, trust services, real estate counseling, legislative lobbying, economic analysis, social work, psychological counseling, tax preparation, and patent, medical or environmental consulting.

[10] When a lawyer is obliged to accord the recipients of such services the protections of those Rules that apply to the client-lawyer relationship, the lawyer must take special care to heed the proscriptions of the Rules addressing conflict of interest (Rules 1.7 through 1.11, especially Rules 1.7(a)(2) and 1.8(a), (b) and (f)), and to scrupulously adhere to the requirements of Rule 1.6 relating to disclosure of confidential information. The promotion of the law-related services must also in all respects comply with Rules 7.1 through 7.3, dealing with advertising and solicitation. In that regard, lawyers should take special care to identify the obligations that may be imposed as a result of a jurisdiction's decisional law.

[11] When the full protections of all of the Rules of Professional Conduct do not apply to the provision of law-related services, principles of law external to the Rules, for example, the law of principal and agent, govern the legal duties owed to those receiving the services. Those other legal principles may establish a different degree of protection for the recipient with respect to confidentiality of information, conflicts of interest and permissible business relationships with clients. See also Rule 8.4 (Misconduct).

RULE 6.1: VOLUNTARY PRO BONO PUBLICO SERVICE

Every lawyer has a professional responsibility to provide legal services to those unable to pay. A lawyer should aspire to render at least (50) hours of pro bono publico legal services per year. In fulfilling this responsibility, the lawyer should:

(a) provide a substantial majority of the (50) hours of legal services without fee or expectation of fee to:

(1) persons of limited means or

(2) charitable, religious, civic, community, governmental and educational organizations in matters that are designed primarily to address the needs of persons of limited means; and

(b) provide any additional services through:

(1) delivery of legal services at no fee or substantially reduced fee to individuals, groups or organizations seeking to secure or protect civil rights, civil liberties or public rights, or charitable, religious, civic, community, governmental and educational organizations in matters in furtherance of their organizational purposes, where the payment of standard legal fees would significantly deplete the organization's economic resources or would be otherwise inappropriate;

(2) delivery of legal services at a substantially reduced fee to persons of limited means; or

(3) participation in activities for improving the law, the legal system or the legal profession.

In addition, a lawyer should voluntarily contribute financial support to organizations that provide legal services to persons of limited means.

COMMENT

[1] Every lawyer, regardless of professional prominence or professional work load, has a responsibility to provide legal services to those unable to pay, and personal involvement in the problems of the disadvantaged can be one of the most rewarding experiences in the life of a lawyer. The American Bar Association urges all lawyers to provide a minimum of 50 hours of pro bono services annually. States, however, may decide to choose a higher or lower number of hours of annual service (which may be expressed as a percentage of a lawyer's professional time) depending upon local needs and local conditions. It is recognized that in some years a lawyer may render greater or fewer hours than the annual standard specified, but during the course of his or her legal career, each lawyer should render on average per year, the number of hours set forth in this Rule. Services can be performed in civil matters or in criminal or quasi-criminal matters for which there is no government obligation to provide funds for legal representation, such as post-conviction death penalty appeal cases.

[2] Paragraphs (a)(1) and (2) recognize the critical need for legal services that exists among

persons of limited means by providing that a substantial majority of the legal services rendered annually to the disadvantaged be furnished without fee or expectation of fee. Legal services under these paragraphs consist of a full range of activities, including individual and class representation, the provision of legal advice, legislative lobbying, administrative rule making and the provision of free training or mentoring to those who represent persons of limited means. The variety of these activities should facilitate participation by government lawyers, even when restrictions exist on their engaging in the outside practice of law.

[3] Persons eligible for legal services under paragraphs (a)(1) and (2) are those who qualify for participation in programs funded by the Legal Services Corporation and those whose incomes and financial resources are slightly above the guidelines utilized by such programs but nevertheless, cannot afford counsel. Legal services can be rendered to individuals or to organizations such as homeless shelters, battered women's centers and food pantries that serve those of limited means. The term "governmental organizations" includes, but is not limited to, public protection programs and sections of governmental or public sector agencies.

[4] Because service must be provided without fee or expectation of fee, the intent of the lawyer to render free legal services is essential for the work performed to fall within the meaning of paragraphs (a)(1) and (2). Accordingly, services rendered cannot be considered pro bono if an anticipated fee is uncollected, but the award of statutory attorneys' fees in a case originally accepted as pro bono would not disqualify such services from inclusion under this section. Lawyers who do receive fees in such cases are encouraged to contribute an appropriate portion of such fees to organizations or projects that benefit persons of limited means.

[5] While it is possible for a lawyer to fulfill the annual responsibility to perform pro bono services exclusively through activities described in paragraphs (a)(1) and (2), to the extent that any hours of service remained unfulfilled, the remaining commitment can be met in a variety of ways as set forth in paragraph (b). Constitutional, statutory or regulatory restrictions may prohibit or impede government and public sector lawyers and judges from performing the pro bono services outlined in paragraphs (a)(1) and (2). Accordingly, where those restrictions apply, government and public sector lawyers and judges may fulfill their pro bono responsibility by performing services outlined in paragraph (b).

[6] Paragraph (b)(1) includes the provision of certain types of legal services to those whose incomes and financial resources place them above limited means. It also permits the pro bono lawyer to accept a substantially reduced fee for services. Examples of the types of issues that may be addressed under this paragraph include First Amendment claims, Title VII claims and environmental protection claims. Additionally, a wide range of organizations may be represented, including social service, medical research, cultural and religious groups.

[7] Paragraph (b)(2) covers instances in which lawyers agree to and receive a modest fee for furnishing legal services to persons of limited means. Participation in judicare programs and acceptance of court appointments in which the fee is substantially below a lawyer's usual rate are encouraged under this section.

[8] Paragraph (b)(3) recognizes the value of lawyers engaging in activities that improve the law, the legal system or the legal profession. Serving on bar association committees, serving on boards of pro bono, or legal services programs, taking part in Law Day activities, acting as a continuing legal education instructor, a mediator or an arbitrator and engaging in legislative lobbying to improve the law, the legal system or the profession are a few examples of the many activities that fall within this paragraph.

[9] Because the provision of pro bono services is a professional responsibility, it is the individual ethical commitment of each lawyer. Nevertheless, there may be times when it is not feasible for a lawyer to engage in pro bono services. At such times a lawyer may discharge the pro bono responsibility by providing financial support to organizations providing free legal services to persons of limited means. Such financial support should be reasonably equivalent to the value of the hours of service that would have otherwise been provided. In addition, at times it may

be more feasible to satisfy the pro bono responsibility collectively, as by a firm's aggregate pro bono activities.

[10] Because the efforts of individual lawyers are not enough to meet the need for free legal services that exists among persons of limited means, the government and the profession have instituted additional programs to provide those services. Every lawyer should financially support such programs, in addition to either providing direct pro bono services or making financial contributions when pro bono service is not feasible.

[11] Law firms should act reasonably to enable and encourage all lawyers in the firm to provide the pro bono legal services called for by this Rule.

[12] The responsibility set forth in this Rule is not intended to be enforced through disciplinary process.

RULE 6.2: ACCEPTING APPOINTMENTS

A lawyer shall not seek to avoid appointment by a tribunal to represent a person except for good cause, such as:

(a) representing the client is likely to result in violation of the Rules of Professional Conduct or other law;

(b) representing the client is likely to result in an unreasonable financial burden on the lawyer; or

(c) the client or the cause is so repugnant to the lawyer as to be likely to impair the client-lawyer relationship or the lawyer's ability to represent the client.

COMMENT

[1] A lawyer ordinarily is not obliged to accept a client whose character or cause the lawyer regards as repugnant. The lawyer's freedom to select clients is, however, qualified. All lawyers have a responsibility to assist in providing pro bono publico service. See Rule 6.1. An individual lawyer fulfills this responsibility by accepting a fair share of unpopular matters or indigent or unpopular clients. A lawyer may also be subject to appointment by a court to serve unpopular clients or persons unable to afford legal services.

Appointed Counsel

[2] For good cause a lawyer may seek to decline an appointment to represent a person who cannot afford to retain counsel or whose cause is unpopular. Good cause exists if the lawyer could not handle the matter competently, see Rule 1.1, or if undertaking the representation would result in an improper conflict of interest, for example, when the client or the cause is so repugnant to the lawyer as to be likely to impair the client-lawyer relationship or the lawyer's ability to represent the client. A lawyer may also seek to decline an appointment if acceptance would be unreasonably burdensome, for example, when it would impose a financial sacrifice so great as to be unjust.

[3] An appointed lawyer has the same obligations to the client as retained counsel, including the obligations of loyalty and confidentiality, and is subject to the same limitations on the client-lawyer relationship, such as the obligation to refrain from assisting the client in violation of the Rules.

RULE 6.3: MEMBERSHIP IN LEGAL SERVICES ORGANIZATION

A lawyer may serve as a director, officer or member of a legal services organization, apart from the law firm in which the lawyer practices, notwithstanding that the organization serves persons having interests adverse to a client of the lawyer. The lawyer shall not knowingly participate in a decision or action of the organization:

(a) if participating in the decision or action would be incompatible with the lawyer's obligations to a client under Rule 1.7; or

(b) where the decision or action could have a material adverse effect on the representation of a client of the organization whose interests are adverse to a client of the lawyer.

COMMENT

[1] Lawyers should be encouraged to support and participate in legal service organizations. A lawyer who is an officer or a member of such an organization does not thereby have a client-lawyer relationship with persons served by the organization. However, there is potential conflict between the interests of such persons and the

interests of the lawyer's clients. If the possibility of such conflict disqualified a lawyer from serving on the board of a legal services organization, the profession's involvement in such organizations would be severely curtailed.

[2] It may be necessary in appropriate cases to reassure a client of the organization that the representation will not be affected by conflicting loyalties of a member of the board. Established, written policies in this respect can enhance the credibility of such assurances.

RULE 6.4: LAW REFORM ACTIVITIES AFFECTING CLIENT INTERESTS

A lawyer may serve as a director, officer or member of an organization involved in reform of the law or its administration notwithstanding that the reform may affect the interests of a client of the lawyer. When the lawyer knows that the interests of a client may be materially benefitted by a decision in which the lawyer participates, the lawyer shall disclose that fact but need not identify the client.

COMMENT

[1] Lawyers involved in organizations seeking law reform generally do not have a client-lawyer relationship with the organization. Otherwise, it might follow that a lawyer could not be involved in a bar association law reform program that might indirectly affect a client. See also Rule 1.2(b). For example, a lawyer specializing in antitrust litigation might be regarded as disqualified from participating in drafting revisions of rules governing that subject. In determining the nature and scope of participation in such activities, a lawyer should be mindful of obligations to clients under other Rules, particularly Rule 1.7. A lawyer is professionally obligated to protect the integrity of the program by making an appropriate disclosure within the organization when the lawyer knows a private client might be materially benefitted.

RULE 6.5: NONPROFIT AND COURT-ANNEXED LIMITED LEGAL SERVICES PROGRAMS

(a) A lawyer who, under the auspices of a program sponsored by a nonprofit organization or court, provides short-term limited legal services to a client without expectation by either the lawyer or the client that the lawyer will provide continuing representation in the matter:

(1) is subject to Rules 1.7 and 1.9(a) only if the lawyer knows that the representation of the client involves a conflict of interest; and

(2) is subject to Rule 1.10 only if the lawyer knows that another lawyer associated with the lawyer in a law firm is disqualified by Rule 1.7 or 1.9(a) with respect to the matter.

(b) Except as provided in paragraph (a)(2), Rule 1.10 is inapplicable to a representation governed by this Rule.

COMMENT

[1] Legal services organizations, courts and various nonprofit organizations have established programs through which lawyers provide short-term limited legal services —such as advice or the completion of legal forms —that will assist persons to address their legal problems without further representation by a lawyer. In these programs, such as legal-advice hotlines, advice-only clinics or pro se counseling programs, a client-lawyer relationship is established, but there is no expectation that the lawyer's representation of the client will continue beyond the limited consultation. Such programs are normally operated under circumstances in which it is not feasible for a lawyer to systematically screen for conflicts of interest as is generally required before undertaking a representation. See, e.g., Rules 1.7, 1.9 and 1.10.

[2] A lawyer who provides short-term limited legal services pursuant to this Rule must secure the client's informed consent to the limited scope of the representation. See Rule 1.2(c). If a short-term limited representation would not be reasonable under the circumstances, the lawyer may offer advice to the client but must also advise the client of the need for further assistance of counsel. Except as provided in this Rule, the Rules of Professional Conduct, including Rules 1.6 and 1.9(c), are applicable to the limited representation.

[3] Because a lawyer who is representing a client in the circumstances addressed by this Rule ordinarily is not able to check systematically for

Model Rules of Professional Conduct

conflicts of interest, paragraph (a) requires compliance with Rules 1.7 or 1.9(a) only if the lawyer knows that the representation presents a conflict of interest for the lawyer, and with Rule 1.10 only if the lawyer knows that another lawyer in the lawyer's firm is disqualified by Rules 1.7 or 1.9(a) in the matter.

[4] Because the limited nature of the services significantly reduces the risk of conflicts of interest with other matters being handled by the lawyer's firm, paragraph (b) provides that Rule 1.10 is inapplicable to a representation governed by this Rule except as provided by paragraph (a)(2). Paragraph (a)(2) requires the participating lawyer to comply with Rule 1.10 when the lawyer knows that the lawyer's firm is disqualified by Rules 1.7 or 1.9(a). By virtue of paragraph (b), however, a lawyer's participation in a short-term limited legal services program will not preclude the lawyer's firm from undertaking or continuing the representation of a client with interests adverse to a client being represented under the program's auspices. Nor will the personal disqualification of a lawyer participating in the program be imputed to other lawyers participating in the program.

[5] If, after commencing a short-term limited representation in accordance with this Rule, a lawyer undertakes to represent the client in the matter on an ongoing basis, Rules 1.7, 1.9(a) and 1.10 become applicable.

RULE 7.1: COMMUNICATIONS CONCERNING A LAWYER'S SERVICES

A lawyer shall not make a false or misleading communication about the lawyer or the lawyer's services. A communication is false or misleading if it contains a material misrepresentation of fact or law, or omits a fact necessary to make the statement considered as a whole not materially misleading.

COMMENT

[1] This Rule governs all communications about a lawyer's services, including advertising permitted by Rule 7.2. Whatever means are used to make known a lawyer's services, statements about them must be truthful.

[2] Truthful statements that are misleading are also prohibited by this Rule. A truthful statement is misleading if it omits a fact necessary to make the lawyer's communication considered as a whole not materially misleading. A truthful statement is also misleading if there is a substantial likelihood that it will lead a reasonable person to formulate a specific conclusion about the lawyer or the lawyer's services for which there is no reasonable factual foundation.

[3] An advertisement that truthfully reports a lawyer's achievements on behalf of clients or former clients may be misleading if presented so as to lead a reasonable person to form an unjustified expectation that the same results could be obtained for other clients in similar matters without reference to the specific factual and legal circumstances of each client's case. Similarly, an unsubstantiated comparison of the lawyer's services or fees with the services or fees of other lawyers may be misleading if presented with such specificity as would lead a reasonable person to conclude that the comparison can be substantiated. The inclusion of an appropriate disclaimer or qualifying language may preclude a finding that a statement is likely to create unjustified expectations or otherwise mislead a prospective client.

[4] See also Rule 8.4(e) for the prohibition against stating or implying an ability to influence improperly a government agency or official or to achieve results by means that violate the Rules of Professional Conduct or other law.

RULE 7.2: ADVERTISING

(a) Subject to the requirements of Rules 7.1 and 7.3, a lawyer may advertise services through written, recorded or electronic communication, including public media.

(b) A lawyer shall not give anything of value to a person for recommending the lawyer's services except that a lawyer may

(1) pay the reasonable costs of advertisements or communications permitted by this Rule;

(2) pay the usual charges of a legal service plan or a not-for-profit or qualified lawyer referral service. A qualified lawyer referral service is a lawyer referral service that has been approved by an appropriate regulatory authority; and

(3) pay for a law practice in accordance with Rule

(c) Any communication made pursuant to this rule shall include the name and office address of at least one lawyer or law firm. responsible for its content.

COMMENT

[1] To assist the public in obtaining legal services, lawyers should be allowed to make known their services not only through reputation but also through organized information campaigns in the form of advertising. Advertising involves an active quest for clients, contrary to the tradition that a lawyer should not seek clientele. However, the public's need to know about legal services can be fulfilled in part through advertising. Ibis need is particularly acute in the case of persons of moderate means who have not made extensive use of legal services. The interest in expanding public information about legal services ought to prevail over considerations of tradition. Nevertheless, advertising by lawyers entails the risk of practices that are misleading or overreaching.

[2] This Rule permits public dissemination of information concerning a lawyer's name or firm name, address and telephone number; the kinds of services the lawyer will undertake; the basis on which the lawyer's fees are determined, including prices for specific services and payment and credit arrangements; a lawyer's foreign language ability; names of references and, with their consent, names of clients regularly represented; and other information that might invite the attention of those seeking legal assistance.

[3] Questions of effectiveness and taste in advertising are matters of speculation and subjective judgment. Some jurisdictions have had extensive prohibitions against television advertising, against advertising going beyond specified facts about a lawyer, or against "undignified" advertising. Television is now one of the most powerful media for getting information to the public, particularly persons of low and moderate income; prohibiting television advertising, therefore, would impede the flow of information about legal services to many sectors of the public. Limiting the information that may be advertised has a similar effect and assumes that the bar can accurately forecast the kind of information that the public would regard as relevant. Similarly, electronic media, such as the Internet, can be an important source of information about legal services, and lawful communication by electronic mail is permitted by this Rule. But see Rule 7.3(a) for the prohibition against the solicitation of a prospective client through a real-time electronic exchange that is not initiated by the prospective client.

[4] Neither this Rule nor Rule 7.3 prohibits communications authorized by law, such as notice to members of a class in class action litigation.

Paying Others to Recommend a Lawyer

[5] Lawyers are not permitted to pay others for channeling professional work. Paragraph (b)(1), however, allows a lawyer to pay for advertising and communications permitted by this Rule, including the costs of print directory listings, on-line directory listings, newspaper ads, television and radio airtime, domain-name registrations, sponsorship fees, banner ads, and group advertising. A lawyer may compensate employees, agents and vendors who are engaged to provide marketing or client-development services, such as publicists, public-relations personnel, business-development staff and website designers. See Rule 5.3 for the duties of lawyers and law firms with respect to the conduct of nonlawyers who prepare marketing materials for them.

[6] A lawyer may pay the usual charges of a legal service plan or a not-for-profit or qualified lawyer referral service. A legal service plan is a prepaid or group legal service plan or a similar delivery system that assists prospective clients to secure legal representation. A lawyer referral service, on the other hand, is any organization that holds itself out to the public as a lawyer referral service. Such referral services are understood by laypersons to be consumer-oriented organizations that provide unbiased referrals to lawyers with appropriate experience in the subject matter of the representation and afford other client protections, such as complaint procedures or malpractice insurance requirements. Consequently, this Rule only permits a lawyer to pay the usual charges of a not-for-profit or qualified lawyer referral service. A qualified

lawyer referral service is one that is approved by an appropriate regulatory authority as affording adequate protections for prospective clients. See, e.g., the American Bar Association's Model Supreme Court Rules Governing Lawyer Referral Services and Model Lawyer Referral and Information Service Quality Assurance Act (requiring that organizations that are identified as lawyer referral services (i) permit the participation of all lawyers who are licensed and eligible to practice in the jurisdiction and who meet reasonable objective eligibility requirements as may be established by the referral service for the protection of prospective clients; (ii) require each participating lawyer to carry reasonably adequate malpractice insurance; (iii) act reasonably to assess client satisfaction and address client complaints; and (iv) do not refer prospective clients to lawyers who own, operate or are employed by the referral service.)

[7] A lawyer who accepts assignments or referrals from a legal service plan or referrals from a lawyer referral service must act reasonably to assure that the activities of the plan or service are compatible with the lawyer's professional obligations. See Rule 5.3. Legal service plans and lawyer referral services may communicate with prospective clients, but such communication must be in conformity with these Rules. Thus, advertising must not be false or misleading, as would be the case if the communications of a group advertising program or a group legal services plan would mislead prospective clients to think that it was a lawyer referral service sponsored by a state agency or bar association. Nor could the lawyer allow in-person, telephonic, or real-time contacts that would violate Rule 7.3.

RULE 7.3: DIRECT CONTACT WITH PROSPECTIVE CLIENTS

(a) A lawyer shall not by in-person, live telephone or realtime electronic contact solicit professional employment from a prospective client when a significant motive for the lawyer's doing so is the lawyer's pecuniary gain, unless the person contacted:

(1) is a lawyer; or

(2) has a family, close personal, or prior professional relationship with the lawyer.

(b) A lawyer shall not solicit professional employment from a prospective client by written, recorded or electronic communication or by in-person, telephone or real-time electronic contact even when not otherwise prohibited by paragraph (a), if

(1) the prospective client has made known to the lawyer a desire not to be solicited by the lawyer; or

(2) the solicitation involves coercion, duress or harassment.

(c) Every written, recorded or electronic communication from a lawyer soliciting professional employment from a prospective client known to be in need of legal services in a particular matter shall include the words "Advertising Material" on the outside envelope, if any, and at the beginning and ending of any recorded or electronic communication, unless the recipient of the communication is a person specified in paragraphs (a)(1) or (a)(2).

(d) Notwithstanding the prohibitions in paragraph (a), a lawyer may participate with a prepaid or group legal service plan operated by an organization not owned or directed by the lawyer that uses in-person or telephone contact to solicit memberships or subscriptions for the plan from persons who are not known to need legal services in a particular matter covered by the plan.

COMMENT

[1] There is a potential for abuse inherent in direct in-person, live telephone or real-time electronic contact by a lawyer with a prospective client known to need legal services. These forms of contact between a lawyer and a prospective client subject the layperson to the private importuning of the trained advocate in a direct interpersonal encounter. The prospective client, who may already feel overwhelmed by the circumstances giving rise to the need for legal services, may find it difficult fully to evaluate all available alternatives with reasoned judgment and appropriate self-interest in the face of the lawyer's presence and insistence upon being retained immediately. The situation is fraught with the possibility of undue influence, intimidation, and over-reaching.

[2] This potential for abuse inherent in direct in-person, live telephone or real-time electronic solicitation of prospective clients justifies its prohibition, particularly since lawyer advertising and written and recorded communication permitted under Rule 7.2 offer alternative means of conveying necessary information to those who may be in need of legal services. Advertising and written and recorded communications which may be mailed or autodialed make it possible for a prospective client to be informed about the need for legal services, and about the qualifications of available lawyers and law firms, without subjecting the prospective client to direct in-person, telephone or real-time electronic persuasion that may overwhelm the client's judgment.

[3] The use of general advertising and written, recorded or electronic communications to transmit information from lawyer to prospective client, rather than direct in-person, live telephone or real-time electronic contact, will help to assure that the information flows cleanly as well as freely. The contents of advertisements and communications permitted under Rule 7.2 can be permanently recorded so that they cannot be disputed and may be shared with others who know the lawyer. This potential for informal review is itself likely to help guard against statements and claims that might constitute false and misleading communications, in violation of Rule 7.1. The contents of direct in-person, live telephone or real-time electronic conversations between a lawyer and a prospective client can be disputed and may not be subject to third-party scrutiny. Consequently, they are much more likely to approach (and occasionally cross) the dividing line between accurate representations and those that are false and misleading.

[4] There is far less likelihood that a lawyer would engage in abusive practices against an individual who is a former client, or with whom the lawyer has close personal or family relationship, or in situations in which the lawyer is motivated by considerations other than the lawyer's pecuniary gain. Nor is there a serious potential for abuse when the person contacted is a lawyer. Consequently, the general prohibition in Rule 7.3(a) and the requirements of Rule 7.3(c) are not applicable in those situations. Also, paragraph (a) is not intended to prohibit a lawyer from participating in constitutionally protected activities of public or charitable legal-service organizations or bona fide political, social, civic, fraternal, employee or trade organizations whose purposes include providing or recommending legal services to its members or beneficiaries.

[5] But even permitted forms of solicitation can be abused. Thus, any solicitation which contains information which is false or misleading within the meaning of Rule 7.1, which involves coercion, duress or harassment within the meaning of Rule 7.3(b)(2), or which involves contact with a prospective client who has made known to the lawyer a desire not to be solicited by the lawyer within the meaning of Rule 7.3(b)(1) is prohibited. Moreover, if after sending a letter or other communication to a client as permitted by Rule 7.2 the lawyer receives no response, any further effort to communicate with the prospective client may violate the provisions of Rule 7.3(b).

[6] This Rule is not intended to prohibit a lawyer from contacting representatives of organizations or groups that may be interested in establishing a group or prepaid legal plan for their members, insureds, beneficiaries or other third parties for the purpose of informing such entities of the availability of and details concerning the plan or arrangement which the lawyer or lawyer's firm is willing to offer. This form of communication is not directed to a prospective client. Rather, it is usually addressed to an individual acting in a fiduciary capacity seeking a supplier of legal services for others who may, if they choose, become prospective clients of the lawyer. Under these circumstances, the activity which the lawyer undertakes in communicating with such representatives and the type of information transmitted to the individual are functionally similar to and serve the same purpose as advertising permitted under Rule 7.2.

[7] The requirement in Rule 7.3(c) that certain communications; be marked "Advertising Material" does not apply to communications sent in response to requests of potential clients or their spokespersons or sponsors. General announcements by lawyers, including changes in personnel or office location, do not constitute communications soliciting professional employment from a client known to be in need of legal services within the meaning of this Rule.

[8] Paragraph (d) of this Rule permits a lawyer to participate with an organization which uses personal contact to solicit members for its group or prepaid legal service plan, provided that the personal contact is not undertaken by any lawyer who would be a provider of legal services through the plan. The organization must not be owned by or directed (whether as manager or otherwise) by any lawyer or law firm that participates in the plan. For example, paragraph (d) would not permit a lawyer to create an organization controlled directly or indirectly by the lawyer and use the organization for the in-person or telephone solicitation of legal employment of the lawyer through memberships in the plan or otherwise. The communication permitted by these organizations also must not be directed to a person known to need legal services in a particular matter, but is to be designed to inform potential plan members generally of another means of affordable legal services. Lawyers who participate in a legal service plan must reasonably assure that the plan sponsors are in compliance with Rules 7.1, 7.2 and 7.3(b). See 8.4(a).

RULE 7.4: COMMUNICATION OF FIELDS OF PRACTICE AND SPECIALIZATION

(a) A lawyer may communicate the fact that the lawyer does or does not practice in particular fields of law.

(b) A lawyer admitted to engage in patent practice before the United States Patent and Trademark Office may use the designation "Patent Attorney" or a substantially similar designation.

(c) A lawyer engaged in Admiralty practice may use the designation "Admiralty," "Proctor in Admiralty" or a substantially similar designation.

(d) A lawyer shall not state or imply that a lawyer is certified as a specialist in a particular field of law, unless:

(1) the lawyer has been certified as a specialist by an organization that has been approved by an appropriate state authority or that has been accredited by the American Bar Association; and

(2) the name of the certifying organization is clearly identified in the communication.

COMMENT

[1] Paragraph (a) of this Rule permits a lawyer to indicate areas of practice in communications about the lawyer's services. If a lawyer practices only in certain fields, or will not accept matters except in a specified field or fields, the lawyer is permitted to so indicate. A lawyer is generally permitted to state that the lawyer is a "specialist," practices a "specialty," or "specializes in" particular fields, but such communications are subject to the "false and misleading" standard applied in Rule 7.1 to communications concerning a lawyer's services.

[2] Paragraph (b) recognizes the long-established policy of the Patent and Trademark Office for the designation of lawyers practicing before the Office. Paragraph (c) recognizes that designation of Admiralty practice has a long historical tradition associated with maritime commerce and the federal courts.

[3] Paragraph (d) permits a lawyer to state that the lawyer is certified as a specialist in a field of law if such certification is granted by an organization approved by an appropriate state authority or accredited by the American Bar Association or another organization, such as a state bar association, that has been approved by the state authority to accredit organizations that certify lawyers as specialists. Certification signifies that an objective entity has recognized an advanced degree of knowledge and experience in the specialty area greater than is suggested by general licensure to practice law. Certifying organizations may be expected to apply standards of experience, knowledge and proficiency to insure that a lawyer's recognition as a specialist is meaningful and reliable. In order to insure that consumers can obtain access to useful information about an organization granting certification, the name of the certifying organization must be included in any communication regarding the certification.

RULE 7.5: FIRM NAMES AND LETTERHEADS

(a) A lawyer shall not use a firm name, letterhead or other professional designation that violates Rule 7.1. A trade name may be used by a lawyer in private practice if it does not imply a connection with a government agency or with a public or charitable legal services organization and is not otherwise in violation of Rule 7.1.

(b) A law firm with offices in more than one jurisdiction may use the same name or other professional designation in each jurisdiction, but identification of the lawyers in an office of the firm shall indicate the jurisdictional limitations on those not licensed to practice in the jurisdiction where the office is located.

(c) The name of a lawyer holding a public office shall not be used in the name of a law firm, or in communications on its behalf, during any substantial period in which the lawyer is not actively and regularly practicing with the firm.

(d) Lawyers may state or imply that they practice in a partnership or other organization only when that is the fact.

COMMENT

[1] A firm may be designated by the names of all or some of its members, by the names of deceased members where there has been a continuing succession in the firm's identity or by a trade name such as the "ABC Legal Clinic." A lawyer or law firm may also be designated by a distinctive website address or comparable professional designation. Although the United States Supreme Court has held that legislation may prohibit the use of trade names in professional practice, use of such names in law practice is acceptable so long as it is not misleading. If a private firm uses a trade name that includes a geographical name such as "Springfield Legal Clinic," an express disclaimer that it is a public legal aid agency may be required to avoid a misleading implication. It may be observed that any firm name including the name of a deceased partner is, strictly speaking, a trade name. The use of such names to designate law firms has proven a useful means of identification. However, it is misleading to use the name of a lawyer not associated with the firm or a predecessor of the firm.

[2] With regard to paragraph (d), lawyers sharing office facilities, but who are not in fact associated with each other in a law firm, may not denominate themselves as, for example, "Smith and Jones," for that title suggests that they are practicing law together in a firm.

RULE 7.6: POLITICAL CONTRIBUTIONS TO OBTAIN GOVERNMENT LEGAL ENGAGEMENTS OR APPOINTMENTS BY JUDGES

A lawyer or law firm shall not accept a government legal engagement or an appointment by a judge if the lawyer or law firm makes a political contribution or solicits political contributions for the purpose of obtaining or being considered for that type of legal engagement or appointment.

COMMENT

[1] Lawyers have a right to participate fully in the political process, which includes making and soliciting political contributions to candidates for judicial and other public office. Nevertheless, when lawyers make or solicit political contributions in order to obtain an engagement for legal work awarded by a government agency, or to obtain appointment by a judge, the public may legitimately question whether the lawyers engaged to perform the work are selected on the basis of competence and merit. In such a circumstance, the integrity of the profession is undermined.

[2] The term "political contribution" denotes any gift, subscription, loan, advance or deposit of anything of value made directly or indirectly to a candidate, incumbent, political party or campaign committee to influence or provide financial support for election to or retention in judicial or other government office. Political contributions in initiative and referendum elections are not included. For purposes of this Rule, the term "political contribution" does not include uncompensated services.

[3] Subject to the exceptions below, (i) the term "government legal engagement" denotes any engagement to provide legal services that a public official has the direct or indirect power to award; and (ii) the term "appointment by a judge" denotes an appointment to a position such as referee, commissioner, special master, receiver, guardian or other similar position that is made by a judge. Those terms do not, however, include (a) substantially uncompensated services; (b) engagements or appointments made on the basis of experience, expertise, professional qualifications and cost following a request

for proposal or other process that is free from influence based upon political contributions; and (c) engagements or appointments made on a rotational basis from a list compiled without regard to political contributions.

[4] The term "lawyer or law firm" includes a political action committee or other entity owned or controlled by a lawyer or law firm.

[5] Political contributions are for the purpose of obtaining or being considered for a government legal engagement or appointment by a judge if, but for the desire to be considered for the legal engagement or appointment, the lawyer or law firm would not have made or solicited the contributions. The purpose may be determined by an examination of the circumstances in which the contributions occur. For example, one or more contributions that in the aggregate are substantial in relation to other contributions by lawyers or law firms, made for the benefit of an official in a position to influence award of a government legal engagement, and followed by an award of the legal engagement to the contributing or soliciting lawyer or the lawyer's firm would support an inference that the purpose of the contributions was to obtain the engagement, absent other factors that weigh against existence of the proscribed purpose. Those factors may include among others that the contribution or solicitation was made to further a political, social, or economic interest or because of an existing personal, family, or professional relationship with a candidate.

[6] If a lawyer makes or solicits a political contribution under circumstances that constitute bribery or another crime, Rule 8.4(b) is implicated.

RULE 8.1: BAR ADMISSION AND DISCIPLINARY MATTERS

An applicant for admission to the bar, or a lawyer in connection with a bar admission application or in connection with a disciplinary matter, shall not:

(a) knowingly make a false statement of material fact; or

(b) fail to disclose a fact necessary to correct a misapprehension known by the person to have arisen in the matter, or knowingly fail to respond to a lawful demand for information from an admissions or disciplinary authority, except that this rule does not require disclosure of information otherwise protected by Rule 1.6.

COMMENT

[1] The duty imposed by this Rule extends to persons seeking admission to the bar as well as to lawyers. Hence, if a person makes a material false statement in connection with an application for admission, it may be the basis for subsequent disciplinary action if the person is admitted, and in any event may be relevant in a subsequent admission application. The duty imposed by this Rule applies to a lawyer's own admission or discipline as well as that of others. Thus, it is a separate professional offense for a lawyer to knowingly make a misrepresentation or omission in connection with a disciplinary investigation of the lawyer's own conduct. Paragraph (b) of this Rule also requires correction of any prior misstatement in the matter that the applicant or lawyer may have made and affirmative clarification of any misunderstanding on the part of the admissions or disciplinary authority of which the person involved becomes aware.

[2] This Rule is subject to the provisions of the fifth amendment of the United States Constitution and corresponding provisions of state constitutions. A person relying on such a provision in response to a question, however, should do so openly and not use the right of nondisclosure as a justification for failure to comply with this Rule.

[3] A lawyer representing an applicant for admission to the bar, or representing a lawyer who is the subject of a disciplinary inquiry or proceeding, is governed by the rules applicable to the client-lawyer relationship, including Rule 1.6 and, in some cases, Rule 3.3.

RULE 8.2: JUDICIAL AND LEGAL OFFICIALS

(a) A lawyer shall not make a statement that the lawyer knows to be false or with reckless disregard as to its truth or falsity concerning the qualifications or integrity of a judge, adjudicatory officer or public legal officer, or of a candidate for election or appointment to judicial or legal office.

(b) A lawyer who is a candidate for judicial office shall comply with the applicable provisions of the Code of Judicial Conduct.

COMMENT

[1] Assessments by lawyers are relied on in evaluating the professional or personal fitness of persons being considered for election or appointment to judicial office and to public legal offices, such as attorney general, prosecuting attorney and public defender. Expressing honest and candid opinions on such matters contributes to improving the administration of justice. Conversely, false statements by a lawyer can unfairly undermine public confidence in the administration of justice.

[2] When a lawyer seeks judicial office, the lawyer should be bound by applicable limitations on political activity.

[3] To maintain the fair and independent administration of justice, lawyers are encouraged to continue traditional efforts to defend judges and courts unjustly criticized.

RULE 8.3: REPORTING PROFESSIONAL MISCONDUCT

(a) A lawyer who knows that another lawyer has committed a violation of the Rules of Professional Conduct that raises a substantial question as to that lawyer's honesty, trustworthiness or fitness as a lawyer in other respects, shall inform the appropriate professional authority.

(b) A lawyer who knows that a judge has committed a violation of applicable rules of judicial conduct that raises a substantial question as to the judge's ritness for office shall inform the appropriate authority.

(c) This Rule does not require disclosure of information otherwise protected by Rule 1.6 or information gained by a lawyer or judge while participating in an approved lawyers assistance program.

COMMENT

[1] Self-regulation of the legal profession requires that members of the profession initiate disciplinary investigation when they know of a violation of the Rules of Professional Conduct. Lawyers have a similar obligation with respect to judicial misconduct. An apparently isolated violation may indicate a pattern of misconduct that only a disciplinary investigation can uncover. Reporting a violation is especially important where the victim is unlikely to discover the offense.

[2] A report about misconduct is not required where it would involve violation of Rule 1.6. However, a lawyer should encourage a client to consent to disclosure where prosecution would not substantially prejudice the client's interests.

[3] If a lawyer were obliged to report every violation of the Rules, the failure to report any violation would itself be a professional offense. Such a requirement existed in many jurisdictions but proved to be unenforceable. This Rule limits the reporting obligation to those offenses that a self-regulating profession must vigorously endeavor to prevent. A measure of judgment is, therefore, required in complying with the provisions of this Rule. The term "substantial" refers to the seriousness of the possible offense and not the quantum of evidence of which the lawyer is aware. A report should be made to the bar disciplinary agency unless some other agency, such as a peer review agency, is more appropriate in the circumstances. Similar considerations apply to the reporting of judicial misconduct.

[4] The duty to report professional misconduct does not apply to a lawyer retained to represent a lawyer whose professional conduct is in question. Such a situation is governed by the Rules applicable to the clientlawyer relationship.

[5] Information about a lawyer's or judge's misconduct or fitness may be received by a lawyer in the course of that lawyer's participation in an approved lawyers or judges assistance program. In that circumstance, providing for an exception to the reporting requirements of paragraphs (a) and (b) of this Rule encourages lawyers and judges to seek treatment through such a program. Conversely, without such an exception, lawyers and judges may hesitate to seek assistance from these programs, which may then result in additional harm to their professional careers and additional injury to the welfare of clients and the public. These Rules do not otherwise address the confidentiality of information received by a lawyer or judge participating in an approved lawyers assistance program; such

an obligation, however, may be imposed by the rules of the program or other law.

RULE 8.4: MISCONDUCT

It is professional misconduct for a lawyer to:

(a) violate or attempt to violate the Rules of Professional Conduct, knowingly assist or induce another to do so, or do so through the acts of another;

(b) commit a criminal act that reflects adversely on the lawyer's honesty, trustworthiness or fitness as a lawyer in other respects;

(c) engage in conduct involving dishonesty, fraud, deceit or misrepresentation;

(d) engage in conduct that is prejudicial to the administration of justice;

(e) state or imply an ability to influence improperly a government agency or official or to achieve results by means that violate the Rules of Professional Conduct or other law; or

(f) knowingly assist a judge or judicial officer in conduct that is a violation of applicable rules of judicial conduct or other law.

COMMENT

[1] Lawyers are subject to discipline when they violate or attempt to violate the Rules of Professional Conduct, knowingly assist or induce another to do so or do so through the acts of another, as when they request or instruct an agent to do so on the lawyer's behalf. Paragraph (a), however, does not prohibit a lawyer from advising a client concerning action the client is legally entitled to take.

[2] Many kinds of illegal conduct reflect adversely on fitness to practice law, such as offenses involving fraud and the offense of willful failure to file an income tax return. However, some kinds of offenses carry no such implication. Traditionally, the distinction was drawn in terms of offenses involving "moral turpitude." That concept can be construed to include offenses concerning some matters of personal morality, such as adultery and comparable offenses, that have no specific connection to fitness for the practice of law. Although a lawyer is personally answerable to the entire criminal law, a lawyer should be professionally answerable only for offenses that indicate lack of those characteristics relevant to law practice. Offenses involving violence, dishonesty, breach of trust, or serious interference with the administration of justice are in that category. A pattern of repeated offenses, even ones of minor significance when considered separately, can indicate indifference to legal obligation.

[3] A lawyer who, in the course of representing a client, knowingly manifests by words or conduct, bias or prejudice based upon race, sex, religion, national origin, disability, age, sexual orientation or socioeconomic status, violates paragraph (d) when such actions are prejudicial to the administration of justice. Legitimate advocacy respecting the foregoing factors does not violate paragraph (d). A trial judge's finding that peremptory challenges were exercised on a discriminatory basis does not alone establish a violation of this rule.

[4] A lawyer may refuse to comply with an obligation imposed by law upon a good faith belief that no valid obligation exists. The provisions of Rule 1.2(d) concerning a good faith challenge to the validity, scope, meaning or application of the law apply to challenges of legal regulation of the practice of law.

[5] Lawyers holding public office assume legal responsibilities going beyond those of other citizens. A lawyer's abuse of public office can suggest an inability to fulfill the professional role of lawyers. The same is true of abuse of positions of private trust such as trustee, executor, administrator, guardian, agent and officer, director or manager of a corporation or other organization.

RULE 8.5: DISCIPLINARY AUTHORITY; CHOICE OF LAW

(a) Disciplinary Authority. A lawyer admitted to practice in this jurisdiction is subject to the disciplinary authority of this jurisdiction, regardless of where the lawyer's conduct occurs. A lawyer not admitted in this jurisdiction is also subject to the disciplinary authority of this jurisdiction if the lawyer provides or offers to provide any legal services in this jurisdiction. A lawyer may be subject to the disciplinary authority of both this jurisdiction and another jurisdiction for the same conduct.

(b) **Choice of Law.** In any exercise of the disciplinary authority of this jurisdiction, the rules of professional conduct to be applied shall be as follows:

(1) for conduct in connection with a matter pending before a tribunal, the rules of the jurisdiction in which the tribunal sits, unless the rules of the tribunal provide otherwise; and

(2) for any other conduct, the rules of the jurisdiction in which the lawyer's conduct occurred, or, if the predominant effect of the conduct is in a different jurisdiction, the rules of that jurisdiction shall be applied to the conduct. A lawyer shall not be subject to discipline if the lawyer's conduct conforms to the rules of a jurisdiction in which the lawyer reasonably believes the predominant effect of the lawyer's conduct will occur.

COMMENT

Disciplinary Authority

[1] Paragraph (a) restates longstanding law.

Choice of Law

[2] A lawyer may be potentially subject to more than one set of rules of professional conduct which impose different obligations. The lawyer may be licensed to practice in more than one jurisdiction with differing rules, or may be admitted to practice before a particular court with rules that differ from those of the jurisdiction or jurisdictions in which the lawyer is licensed to practice. In the past, decisions have not developed clear or consistent guidance as to which rules apply in such circumstances.

[3] Paragraph (b) seeks to resolve such potential conflicts. Its premise is that minimizing conflicts between rules, as well as uncertainty about which rules are applicable, is in the best interest of both clients and the profession (as well as the bodies having authority to regulate the profession). Accordingly, it takes the approach of (i) providing that any particular conduct of a lawyer shall be subject to only one set of rules of professional conduct, and (ii) making the determination of which set of rules applies to particular conduct as straightforward as possible, consistent with recognition of appropriate regulatory interests of relevant jurisdictions.

[4] Paragraph (b) provides that as to a lawyer's conduct relating to a proceeding in a court before which the lawyer is admitted to practice (either generally or pro hac vice), the lawyer shall be subject only to the rules of professional conduct of that court. As to all other conduct, paragraph (b) provides that a lawyer licensed to practice only in this jurisdiction shall be subject to the rules of professional conduct of this jurisdiction, and that a lawyer licensed in multiple jurisdictions shall be subject only to the rules of the jurisdiction where he or she (as an individual, not his or her firm) principally practices, but with one exception: if particular conduct clearly has its predominant effect in another admitting jurisdiction, then only the rules of that jurisdiction shall apply. The intention is for the latter exception to be a narrow one. It would be appropriately applied, for example, to a situation in which a lawyer admitted in, and principally practicing in, State A, but also admitted in State B, handled an acquisition by a company whose headquarters and operations were in State B of another, similar such company. The exception would not appropriately be applied, on the other hand, if the lawyer handled an acquisition by a company whose headquarters and operations were in State A of a company whose headquarters and main operations were in State A, but which also had some operations in State B.

[5] If two admitting jurisdictions were to proceed against a lawyer for the same conduct, they should, applying this rule, identify the same governing ethics rules. They should take all appropriate steps to see that they do apply the same rule to the same conduct, and in all events should avoid proceeding against a lawyer on the basis of two inconsistent rules.

[6] The choice of law provision is not intended to apply to transnational practice. Choice of law in this context should be the subject of agreements between jurisdictions or of appropriate international law.

ABA MODEL CODE OF JUDICIAL CONDUCT

PREAMBLE

Our legal system is based on the principle that an independent, fair and competent judiciary will interpret and apply the laws that govern us. The role of the judiciary is central to American concepts of justice and the rule of law. Intrinsic to all sections of this Code are the precepts that judges, individually and collectively, must respect and honor the judicial office as a public trust and strive to enhance and maintain confidence in our legal system. The judge is an arbiter of facts and law for the resolution of disputes and a highly visible symbol of government under the rule of law.

The Code of Judicial Conduct is intended to establish standards for ethical conduct of judges. It consists of broad statements called Canons, specific rules set forth in Sections under each Canon, a Terminology Section, an Application Section and Commentary. The text of the Canons and the Sections, including the Terminology and Application Sections, is authoritative. The Commentary, by explanation and example, provides guidance with respect to the purpose and meaning of the Canons and Sections. The Commentary is not intended as a statement of additional rules. When the text uses "shall" or "shall not," it is intended to impose binding obligations the violation of which can result in disciplinary action. When "should" or "should not" is used, the text is intended as hortatory and as a statement of what is or is not appropriate conduct but not as a binding rule under which a judge may be disciplined. When "may" is used, it denotes permissible discretion or, depending on the context, it refers to action that is not covered by specific proscriptions.

The Canons and Sections are rules of reason. They should be applied consistent with constitutional requirements, statutes, other court rules and decisional law and in the context of all relevant circumstances. The Code is to be construed so as not to impinge on the essential independence of judges in making judicial decisions.

The Code is designed to provide guidance to judges and candidates for judicial office and to provide a structure for regulating conduct through disciplinary agencies. It is not designed or intended as a basis for civil liability or criminal prosecution. Furthermore, the purpose of the Code would be subverted if the Code were invoked by lawyers for mere tactical advantage in a proceeding.

The text of the Canons and Sections is intended to govern conduct of judges and to be binding upon them. It is not intended, however, that every transgression will result in disciplinary action. Whether disciplinary action is appropriate, and the degree of discipline to be imposed, should be determined through a reasonable and reasoned application of the text and should depend on such factors as the seriousness of the transgression, whether there is a pattern of improper activity and the effect of the improper activity on others or on the judicial system. See ABA Standards Relating to judicial Discipline and Disability Retirement.*

The Code of Judicial Conduct is not intended as an exhaustive guide for the conduct of judges. They should also be governed in their judicial and personal conduct by general ethical standards. The Code is intended, however, to state basic standards which should govern the conduct of all judges and to provide guidance to assist judges in establishing and maintaining high standards of judicial and personal conduct.

---

*Judicial disciplinary procedures adopted in the jurisdictions should comport with the requirements of due process. The ABA Standards Relating to judicial Discipline and Disability Retirement are cited as an example of how these due process requirements may be satisfied.

TERMINOLOGY

Terms explained below are noted with an asterisk (*) in the Sections where they appear. In addition, the Sections where terms appear are referred to after the explanation of each term below.

"Aggregate" in relation to contributions for a candidate under Sections 3E(1)(e) and 5C(3) and (4) denotes not only contributions in cash or in kind made directly to a candidate's committee or treasurer, but also, except in retention elections, all contributions made indirectly with the understanding that they will be used to support the election of the candidate or to oppose the election of the candidate's opponent. See sections 3E(1)(e), 5C(3) and 5C(4).

"Appropriate authority" denotes the authority with responsibility for initiation of disciplinary process with respect to the violation to be reported. See Sections 3D(1) and 3D(2).

"Candidate." A candidate is a person seeking selection for or retention in judicial office by election or appointment. A person becomes a candidate for judicial office as soon as he or she makes a public announcement of candidacy, declares or files as a candidate with the election or appointment authority, or authorizes solicitation or acceptance of contributions or support, The term "candidate" has the same meaning when applied to a judge seeking election or appointment to non-judicial office. See Preamble and Sections 5A, 5B, 5C and 5E.

"Continuing part-time judge." A continuing part-time judge is a judge who serves repeatedly on a part-time basis by election or under a continuing appointment, including a retired judge subject to recall who is permitted to practice law. See Application Section C.

"Court personnel" does not include the lawyers in a proceeding before a judge. See Sections 3B(7)(c) and 3B(9).

"De minimis" denotes an insignificant interest that could not raise reasonable question as to a judge's impartiality See Sections 3E(1)(c) and 3E(1)(d).

"Economic interest" denotes ownership of a more than de minimis legal or equitable interest, or a relationship as officer, director, advisor or other active participant in the affairs of a party, except that:

(i) ownership of an interest in a mutual or common investment fund that holds securities is not an economic interest in such securities unless the judge participates in the management of the fund or a proceeding pending or impending before the judge could substantially affect the value of the interest;

(ii) service by a judge as an officer, director, advisor or other active participant in an educational, religious, charitable, fraternal or civic organization, or service by a judge's spouse, parent or child as an officer, director, advisor or other active participant in any organization does not create an economic interest in securities held by that organization;

(iii) a deposit in a financial institution, the proprietary interest of a policy holder in a mutual insurance company, of a depositor in a mutual savings association or of a member in a credit union, or a similar proprietary interest, is not an economic interest in the organization unless a proceeding pending or impending before the judge could substantially affect the value of the interest;

(iv) ownership of government securities is not an economic interest in the issuer unless a proceeding pending or impending before the judge could substantially affect the value of the securities.

See Sections 3E(1)(c) and 3E(2).

"Fiduciary" includes such relationships as executor, administrator, trustee, and guardian. See Sections 3E(2) and 4E.

"Knowingly," "knowledge," "known" or "knows" denotes actual knowledge of the fact in question. A person's knowledge may be inferred from circumstances. See Sections 3D, 3E(1) and 5A(3).

"Law" denotes court rules as well as statutes, constitutional provisions and decisional law. See Sections 2A, 3A, 3B(2), 3B(6), 4B, 4C, 4D(5), 4F, 4I, 5A(2), 5A(3), 5B(2), 5C(1), 5C(3) and 5D.

"Member of the candidate's family" denotes a spouse, child, grandchild, parent, grandparent or other relative or person with whom the candidate maintains a close familial relationship. See Section 5A(3)(a).

"Member of the judge's family" denotes a spouse, child, grandchild, parent, grandparent, or other relative or person with whom the judge maintains a close familial relationship. See Sections 4D(3), 4E and 4G.

"Member of the judge's family residing in the judge's household" denotes any relative of a judge by blood or marriage, or a person treated by a judge as a member of the judge's family, who resides in the judge's household. See Sections 3E(1) and 4D(5).

"Nonpublic information" denotes information that, by law, is not available to the public. Nonpublic information may include but is not limited to: information that is sealed by statute or court order, impounded or communicated in camera; and information offered in grand jury proceedings, presentencing reports, dependency cases or psychiatric reports. See Section 3B(11).

"Periodic part-time judge." A periodic part-time judge is a judge who serves or expects to serve repeatedly on a part-time basis but under a separate appointment for each limited period of service or for each matter, See Application Section D.

"Political organization" denotes a political party or other group, the principal purpose of which is to further the election or appointment of candidates to political office. See Sections 5A(1), 5B(2) and 5C(1).

"Pro tempore part-time judge." A pro tempore part-time judge is a judge who serves or expects to serve once or only sporadically on a part-time basis under a separate appointment for each period of service or for each case heard. See Application Section E.

"Public election." This term includes primary and general elections; it includes partisan elections, nonpartisan, elections and retention elections. See Section 5C.

"Require." The rules prescribing that a judge "require" certain conduct of others are, like all of the rules in this Code, rules of reason. The use of the term "require" in that context means a judge is to exercise reasonable direction and control over the conduct of those persons subject to the judge's direction and control. See Sections 3B(3), 3B(4), 3B(5), 3B(6), 3B(9) and 3C(2).

"Third degree of relationship." The following persons are relatives within the third degree of relationship: great-grandparent, grandparent, parent, uncle, aunt, brother, sister, child, grandchild, great-grandchild, nephew or niece. See Section 3E(1)(d).

CANON 1

A JUDGE SHALL UPHOLD THE INTEGRITY AND INDEPENDENCE OF THE JUDICIARY

A. An independent and honorable judiciary is indispensable to justice in our society. A judge should participate in establishing, maintaining and enforcing high standards of conduct, and shall personally observe those standards so that the integrity and independence of the judiciary will be preserved. The provisions of this Code are to be construed and applied to further that objective.

Commentary:

Deference to the judgments and rulings of courts depends upon public confidence in the integrity and independence of judges. The integrity and independence of judges depends in turn upon their acting without fear or favor. Although judges should be independent, they must comply with the law, including the provisions of this Code. Public confidence in the impartiality of the judiciary is maintained by the adherence of each judge to this responsibility. Conversely, violation of this Code diminishes public confidence in the judiciary and thereby does injury to the system of government under law.

CANON 2

A JUDGE SHALL AVOID IMPROPRIETY AND THE APPEARANCE OF IMPROPRIETY IN ALL OF THE JUDGE'S ACTIVITIES

A. A judge shall respect and comply with the law* and shall act at all times in a manner that promotes public confidence in the integrity and impartiality of the judiciary.

Commentary:

Public confidence in the judiciary is eroded by irresponsible or improper conduct by judges. A judge must avoid all impropriety and appearance of impropriety. A judge must expect to be the subject of constant public scrutiny. A judge must therefore accept restrictions on the judge's conduct that might be viewed as burdensome by the ordinary citizen and should do so freely and willingly.

The prohibition against behaving with, impropriety or the appearance of impropriety applies to both the professional and personal conduct of a judge. Because it is not practicable to list all prohibited acts, the proscription is necessarily cast in general terms that extend to conduct by judges that is harmful although not specifically mentioned in the Code. Actual improprieties under this standard include violations of law, court rules or other specific provisions of this Code. The test for appearance of impropriety is whether the conduct would create in reasonable minds a perception that the judge's ability to carry out judicial responsibilities with integrity, impartiality and competence is impaired.

See also Commentary under Section 2C.

B. A judge shall not allow family, social, political or other relationships to influence the judge's judicial conduct or judgment. A judge shall not lend the prestige of judicial office to advance the private interests of the judge or others; nor shall a judge convey or permit others to convey the impression that they are in a special position to influence the judge. A judge shall not testify voluntarily as a character witness.

Commentary:

Maintaining the prestige of judicial office is essential to a system of government in which the judiciary functions independently of the executive and legislative branches. Respect for the judicial office facilitates the orderly conduct of legitimate judicial functions. judges should distinguish between proper and improper use of the prestige of office in all of their activities, For example, it would be improper for a judge to allude to his or her judgeship to gain a personal advantage such as deferential treatment when stopped by a police officer for a traffic offense. Similarly, judicial letterhead must not be used for conducting a judge's personal business.

A judge must avoid lending the prestige of judicial office for the advancement of the private interests of others, For example, a judge must not use the judge's judicial position to gain advantage in a civil suit involving a member of the judge's family. In contracts for publication of a judge's writings, a judge should retain control over the advertising to avoid exploitation of the judge's office. As to the acceptance of awards, see Section 4D(5)(a) and Commentary.

Although a judge should be sensitive to possible abuse of the prestige of office, a judge may, based on the judge's personal knowledge, serve as a reference or provide a letter of recommendation. However, a judge must not initiate the communication of information to a sentencing judge or a probation or corrections officer but may provide to such persons information for the record in response to a formal request.

Judges may participate in the process of judicial selection by cooperating with appointing authorities and screening committees seeking names for consideration, and by responding to official inquiries concerning a person being considered for a judgeship. See also Canon 5 regarding use of a judge's name in political activities.

A judge must not testify voluntarily as a character witness because to do so may lend the prestige of the judicial office in support of the party for whom the judge testifies, Moreover, when a judge testifies as a witness, a lawyer who regularly appears before the judge may be placed in the awkward position of cross-examining the judge. A judge may, however, testify when properly summoned. Except in unusual circumstances where the demands of justice require, a judge should discourage a party from requiring the judge to testify as a character witness.

C. A judge shall not hold membership in any organization that practices invidious discrimination on the basis of race, sex, religion or national origin.

Commentary:

Membership of a judge in an organization that practices invidious discrimination gives rise to perceptions that the judge's impartiality is impaired. Section 2C refers to the current practices of the organization. Whether an organization practices invidious discrimination is often a complex question to which judges should be sensitive. The answer cannot be determined from a mere examination of an organization's current membership rolls but rather depends on how the organization selects members and other relevant factors, such as that the organization is dedicated to the preservation of religious, ethnic or cultural values of legitimate common interest to its members, or that it is in fact and effect an intimate, purely private organization whose membership limitations could not be constitutionally prohibited, Absent such factors, an organization is generally said to discriminate invidiously if it arbitrarily excludes from membership on the basis of race, religion, sex or national origin persons who would otherwise be admitted to membership. *See New York State Club Ass'n. Inc. v. City of New York,* 108 S. Ct. 2225, 101 L. Ed. 2d 1 (1988); *Board of Directors of Rotary International v. Rotary Club of Duarte,* 481 U.S. 537, 107 S. Ct. 1940, 95 L. Ed. 2d 474(1987); *Roberts v. United States Jaycees,* 468 U.S. 609, 104 S. Ct. 3244, 82 L. Ed. 2d 462 (1984).

Although Section 2C relates only to membership in organizations that invidiously discriminate on the basis of race, sex, religion or national origin, a judge's membership in an organization that engages in any discriminatory membership practices prohibited by the law of the jurisdiction also violates Canon 2 and Section 2A and gives the appearance of impropriety. In addition, it would be a violation of Canon 2 and Section 2A for a judge to arrange a meeting at a club -that the judge knows practices invidious discrimination on the basis of race, sex, religion or national origin in its membership or other policies, or for the judge to regularly use such a club. Moreover, public manifestation by a judge of the judge's knowing approval of invidious discrimination on any basis gives the appearance of impropriety under Canon 2 and diminishes public confidence in the integrity and impartiality of the judiciary, in violation of Section 2A.

When a person who is a judge on the date this Code becomes effective [in the jurisdiction in which the person is a judge][1] learns that an organization to which the judge belongs

---

1. The language within the brackets should be deleted when the jurisdiction adopts this provision.

engages in invidious discrimination that would preclude membership under Section 2C or under Canon 2 and Section 2A, the judge is permitted, in lieu of resigning, to make immediate efforts to have the organization discontinue its invidiously discriminatory practices, but is required to suspend participation in any other activities of the organization, If the organization fads to discontinue its invidiously discriminatory practices as promptly as possible (and in all events within a year of the judge's first learning of the practices), the judge is required to resign immediately from the organization.

CANON 3[2]

A JUDGE SHALL PERFORM THE DUTIES OF JUDICIAL OFFICE IMPARTIALLY AND DILIGENTLY

A. **Judicial Duties in General.** The judicial duties of a judge take precedence over all the judge's other activities. The judge's judicial duties include all the duties of the judge's office prescribed by law.* In the performance of these duties, the following standards apply.

B. **Adjudicative Responsibilities.**

(1) A judge shall hear and decide matters assigned to the judge except those in which disqualification is required.

(2) A judge shall be faithful to the law* and maintain professional competence in it. A judge shall not be swayed by partisan interests, public clamor or fear of criticism.

(3) A judge shall require* order and decorum in proceedings before the judge.

(4) A judge shall be patient, dignified and courteous to litigants, jurors, witnesses, lawyers and others with whom the judge deals in an official capacity, and shall require* similar conduct of lawyers, and of staff, court officials and others subject to the judge's direction and control.

Commentary:

The duty to bear all proceedings fairly and with patience is not inconsistent with the duty to dispose promptly of the business of the court. judges can be efficient and businesslike while being patient and deliberate.

(5) **A judge shall perform judicial duties without bias or prejudice. A judge shall not, in the performance of judicial duties, by words or conduct manifest bias or prejudice, including but not limited to bias or prejudice based upon race, sex, religion, national origin, disability, age, sexual orientation or socioeconomic status, and shall not permit staff, court officials and others subject to the judge's direction and control to do so.**

Commentary:

A judge must refrain from speech, gestures or other conduct that could reasonably be perceived as sexual harassment and must require the same standard of conduct of others subject to the judge's direction and control.

A judge must perform judicial duties impartially and fairly. A judge who manifests bias on any basis in a proceeding impairs the fairness of the proceeding and brings the judiciary into disrepute. Facial expression and body language, in addition to oral communication, can give to parties or lawyers in the proceeding, jurors, the media and others an appearance of judicial bias. A judge must be alert to avoid behavior that may be perceived as prejudicial.

(6) **A judge shall require* lawyers in proceedings before the judge to refrain from manifesting, by words or conduct, bias or prejudice based upon race, sex, religion, national origin, disability, age, sexual orientation or socioeconomic status, against parties, witnesses, counsel or others. This Section 3B(6) does not preclude legitimate advocacy when race, sex, religion, national origin, disability, age, sexual orientation or socioeconomic status, or other similar factors, are issues in the proceeding.**

---

2. Amended August 10, 1999, American Bar Association House of Delegates, Atlanta, Georgia, per Report 123.

ABA Model Code of Judicial Conduct

(7) A judge shall accord to every person who has a legal interest in a proceeding, or that person's lawyer, the right to be heard according to law*. A judge shall not initiate, permit, or consider ex parte communications, or consider other communications made to the judge outside the presence of the parties concerning a pending or impending proceeding except that:

    (a) Where circumstances require, ex parte communications for scheduling, administrative purposes or emergencies that do not deal with substantive matters or issues on the merits are authorized; provided:

        (i) the judge reasonably believes that no party will gain a procedural or tactical advantage as a result of the ex parte communication, and

        (ii) the judge makes provision promptly to notify all other parties of the substance of the ex parte communication and allows an opportunity to respond.

    (b) A judge may obtain the advice of a disinterested expert on the law* applicable to a proceeding before the judge if the judge gives notice to the parties of the person consulted and the substance of the advice, and affords the parties reasonable opportunity to respond.

    (c) A judge may consult with court personnel* whose function is to aid the judge in carrying out the judge's adjudicative responsibilities or with other judges.

    (d) A judge may, with the consent of the parties, confer separately with the parties and their lawyers in an effort to mediate or settle matters pending before the judge.

    (e) A judge may initiate or consider any ex parte communications when expressly authorized by law* to do so.

Commentary:

The proscription against communications concerning a proceeding includes communications from lawyers, law teachers, and other persons who are not participants in the proceeding, except to the limited extent permitted.

To the extent reasonably possible, all parties or their lawyers shall be included in communications with a judge.

Whenever presence of a party or notice to a party is required by Section 3B(7), it is the party's lawyer, or if the party is unrepresented the party, who is to be present or to whom notice is to be given.

An appropriate and often desirable procedure for a court to obtain the advice of a disinterested expert on legal issues is to invite the expert to file a brief amicus curiae.

Certain ex parte communication is approved by Section 3B(7) to facilitate scheduling and other administrative purposes and to accommodate emergencies. In general, however, a judge must discourage ex parte communication and allow it only if all the criteria stated in Section 3B(7) are clearly met. A judge must disclose to all parties all ex parte communications described in Sections 3B(7)(a) and 3B(7)(b) regarding a proceeding pending or impending before the judge.

A judge must not independently investigate facts in a case and must consider only the evidence presented.

A judge may request a party to submit proposed findings of fact and conclusions of law, so long as the other parties are apprised of the request and are given an opportunity to respond to the proposed findings and conclusions.

A judge must make reasonable efforts, including the provision of appropriate supervision, to ensure that Section 3B(7) is not violated through law clerks or other personnel on the judge's staff.

If communication between the trial judge and the appellate court with respect to a proceeding is permitted, a copy of any written communication or the substance of any oral communication should be provided to all parties.

(8) A judge shall dispose of all judicial matters promptly, efficiently and fairly.

Commentary:

In disposing of matters promptly, efficiently and fairly, a judge must demonstrate due regard for the rights of the parties to be heard and to have issues resolved without unnecessary cost or delay. Containing costs while preserving fundamental rights of parties also protects the interests of witnesses and the general public. A judge should monitor and supervise cases so as to reduce or eliminate dilatory practices, avoidable delays and unnecessary costs. A judge should encourage and seek to facilitate settlement, but parties should not feel coerced into surrendering the right to have their controversy resolved by the courts.

Prompt disposition of the court's business requires a judge to devote adequate time to judicial duties, to be punctual in attending court and expeditions in determining matters under submission, and to insist that court officials, litigants and their lawyers cooperate with the judge to that end.

(9) A judge shall not, while a proceeding is pending or impending in any court, make any public comment that might reasonably he expected to affect its outcome or impair its fairness or make any nonpublic comment that might substantially interfere with a fair trial or hearing. The judge shall require* similar abstention on the part of court personnel* subject to the judge's direction and control. This Section does not prohibit judges from making public statements in the course of their official duties or from explaining for public information the procedures of the court. This Section does not apply to proceedings in which the judge is a litigant in a personal capacity.

Commentary:

The requirement that judges abstain from public comment regarding a pending or impending proceeding continues during any appellate process and until final disposition. This Section does not prohibit a judge from commenting on proceedings in which the judge is a litigant in a personal capacity, but in cases such as a writ of mandamus where the judge is a litigant in an official capacity, the judge must not comment publicly. The conduct of lawyers relating to trial publicity is governed by [Rule 3.6 of the ABA Model Rules of Professional Conduct]. (Each jurisdiction should substitute an appropriate reference to its rule.)

(10) A judge shall not commend or criticize jurors for their verdict other than in a court order or opinion in a proceeding, but may express appreciation to jurors for their service to the judicial system and the community.

Commentary:

Commending or criticizing jurors for their verdict may imply a judicial expectation in future cases and may impair a juror's ability to be fair and impartial in a subsequent case.

(11) A judge shall not disclose or use, for any purpose unrelated to judicial duties, nonpublic information* acquired in a judicial capacity.

C. Administrative Responsibilities.

(1) A judge shall diligently discharge the judge's administrative responsibilities without bias or prejudice and maintain professional competence in judicial administration, and should cooperate with other judges and court officials in the administration of court business.

(2) A judge shall require* staff, court officials and others subject to the judge's direction and control to observe the standards of fidelity and diligence that apply to the judge and to refrain from manifesting bias or prejudice in the performance of their official duties.

(3) A judge with supervisory authority for the judicial performance of other judges shall take reasonable measures to assure the prompt disposition of matters before them and the proper performance of their other judicial responsibilities.

(4) A judge shall not make unnecessary appointments. A judge shall exercise the power of appointment impartially and on the basis of merit. A judge shall avoid nepotism and favoritism. A judge shall not approve compensation of appointees beyond the fair value of services rendered.

Commentary:

Appointees of a judge include assigned counsel, officials such as referees, commissioners, special masters, receivers and guardians and personnel such as clerks, secretaries and bailiffs.

ABA Model Code of Judicial Conduct

Consent by the parties to an appointment or an award of compensation does not relieve the judge of the obligation prescribed by Section 3C(4).

(5) A judge shall not appoint a lawyer to a position if the judge either knows that the lawyer has contributed more than [$] within the prior [ ] years to the judge's election campaign,[3] or learns of such a contribution by means of a timely motion by a party or other person properly interested in the matter, unless

    (a) the position is substantially uncompensated;

    (b) the lawyer has been selected in rotation from a list of qualified and available lawyers compiled without regard to their having made political contributions; or

    (c) the judge or another presiding or administrative judge affirmatively finds that no other lawyer is willing, competent and able to accept the position.

D. **Disciplinary Responsibilities.**

(1) A judge who receives information indicating a substantial likelihood that another judge has committed a violation of this Code should take appropriate action. A judge having knowledge* that another judge has committed a violation of this Code that raises a substantial question as to the other judge's fitness for office shall inform the appropriate authority.*

(2) A judge who receives information indicating a substantial likelihood that a lawyer has committed a violation of the Rules of Professional Conduct [substitute correct title if the applicable rules of lawyer conduct have a different title] should take appropriate action. A judge having knowledge* that a lawyer has committed a violation of the Rules of Professional Conduct [substitute correct title if the applicable rules of lawyer conduct have a different tide] that raises a substantial question as to the lawyer's honesty, trustworthiness or fitness as a lawyer in other respects shall inform the appropriate authority.*

(3) Acts of a judge, in the discharge of disciplinary responsibilities, required or permitted by Sections 3D(1) and 3D(2) are part of a judge's judicial duties and shall be absolutely privileged, and no civil action predicated thereon may be instituted against the judge.

Commentary:

Appropriate action may include direct communication with the judge or lawyer who has committed the violation, other direct action if available, and reporting the violation to the appropriate authority or other agency or body.

E. **Disqualification**

(1) A judge shall disqualify himself or herself in a proceeding in which the judge's impartiality might reasonably be questioned, including but not limited to instances where:

Commentary:

Under this rule, a judge is disqualified whenever the judge's impartiality might reasonably be questioned, regardless whether any of the specific rules in Section 3E(1) apply. For example, if a judge were in the process of negotiating for employment with a law firm, the judge would be disqualified from any matters in which that law firm appeared, unless the disqualification was waived by the parties after disclosure by the judge.

A judge should disclose on the record information that the judge believes the parties or their lawyers might consider relevant to the question of disqualification, even if the judge believes there is no real basis for disqualification.

By decisional law, the rule of necessity may override the rule of disqualification. For example, a judge might be required to participate in judicial review of a judicial salary statute, or might be the only judge available in a matter requiring immediate judicial action, such as a bearing on probable cause or a temporary restraining order. In the latter case, the judge must disclose on the record the basis for possible disqualification and

---

3. This provision is meant to be applicable wherever judges are subject to public election; specific amount and time limitations, to be determined based on circumstances within the jurisdiction, should be inserted in the brackets.

use reasonable efforts to transfer the matter to another judge as soon as practicable.

    (a) **"the judge has a personal bias or prejudice concerning a party or a party's lawyer, or personal knowledge* of disputed evidentiary facts concerning the proceeding;**

    (b) **the judge served as a lawyer in the matter in controversy, or a lawyer with whom the judge previously practiced law served during such association as a lawyer concerning the matter, or the judge has been a material witness concerning it;**

Commentary:

A lawyer in a government agency does not ordinarily have an association with other lawyers employed by that agency within the meaning of Section 3E(1)(b); a judge formerly employed by a government agency, however, should disqualify himself or herself in a proceeding if the judge's impartiality might reasonably be questioned because of such association.

    (c) **the judge knows* that he or she, individually or as a fiduciary, or the judge's spouse, parent or child wherever residing, or any other member of the judge's family residing in the judge's household,* has an economic interest* in the subject matter in controversy or in a party to the proceeding or has any other more than de minimis* interest that could be substantially affected by the proceeding;**

    (d) **the judge or the judge's spouse, or a person within the third degree of relationship* to either of them, or the spouse of such a person:**

        (i) **is a party to the proceeding, or an officer, director or trustee of a party;**

        (ii) **is acting as a lawyer in the proceeding;**

        (iii) **is known* by the judge to have a more than de minimis* interest that could be substantially affected by the proceeding;**

        (iv) **is to the judge's knowledge* likely to be a material witness in the proceeding.**

    (e) **the judge knows or learns by means of a timely motion that a party or a party's lawyer has within the previous [ ] year[s] made aggregate* contributions to the judge's campaign in an amount that is greater than [[[$] for an individual or [$] for an entity]]] [[is reasonable and appropriate for an individual or an entity]].[4]**

Commentary:

The fact that a lawyer in a proceeding is affiliated with a law firm with which a relative of the judge is affiliated does not of itself disqualify the judge. Under appropriate circumstances, the fact that "the judge's impartiality might reasonably be questioned" under Section 3E(1), or that the relative is known by the judge to have an interest in the law firm that could be "substantially affected by the outcome of the proceeding" tinder Section 3E(1)(d)(iii) may require the judge's disqualification.

    (2) **A judge shall keep informed about the judge's personal and fiduciary* economic interests,* and make a reasonable effort to keep informed about the personal economic interests of the judge's spouse and minor children residing in the judge's household.**

    F. **Remittal of Disqualification. A judge disqualified by the terms of Section 3E may disclose on the record the basis of the judge's disqualification and may ask the parties and their lawyers to consider, out of the presence of the judge, whether to waive disqualification. If following disclosure of any basis for disqualification other than personal bias or prejudice concerning a**

---

4. This provision is meant to be applicable wherever judges are subject to public election. Jurisdictions that adopt specific dollar limits on contributions in section 5C(3) should adopt the same limits in section 3E(1)(e). Where specific dollar amounts determined by local circumstances are not used, the "reasonable and appropriate" language should be used.

party, the parties and lawyers, without participation by the judge, all agree that the judge should not be disqualified, and the judge is then willing to participate, the judge may participate in the proceeding. The agreement shall be incorporated in the record of the proceeding.

Commentary:

A remittal procedure provides the parties an opportunity to proceed without delay if they wish to waive the disqualification. To assure that consideration of the question of remittal is made independently of the judge, a judge must not solicit, seek or hear comment on possible remittal or waiver of the disqualification unless the lawyers jointly propose remittal after consultation as provided in the rule. A party may act through counsel if counsel represents on the record that the party has been consulted and consents. As a practical matter, a judge may wish to have all parties and their lawyers sign the remittal agreement.

CANON 4

A JUDGE SHALL SO CONDUCT THE JUDGE'S EXTRA JUDICIAL ACTIVITIES AS TO MINIMIZE THE RISK OF CONFLICT WITH JUDICIAL OBLIGATIONS

A. Extra-judicial Activities in General. A judge shall conduct all of the judge's extra-judicial activities so that they do not:

(1) cast reasonable doubt on the judge's capacity to act impartially as a judge;

(2) demean the judicial office; or

(3) interfere with the proper performance of judicial duties.

Commentary:

Complete separation of a judge from extra-judicial activities is neither possible nor wise; a judge should not become isolated from the community in which the judge lives.

Expressions of bias or prejudice by a judge, even outside the judge's judicial activities, may cast reasonable doubt on the judge's capacity to act impartially as a judge. Expressions which may do so include jokes or other remarks demeaning individuals on the basis of their race, sex, religion, national origin, disability, age, sexual orientation or socioeconomic status, See Section 2C and accompanying Commentary.

B. Avocational Activities. A judge may speak, write, lecture, teach and participate in other extra-judicial activities concerning the law,* the legal system, the administration of justice and non-legal subjects, subject to the requirements of this Code.

Commentary:

As a judicial officer and person specially learned in the law, a judge is in a unique position to contribute to the improvement of the law, the legal system, and the administration of justice, including revision of substantive and procedural law and improvement of criminal and juvenile justice. To the extent that time permits, a judge is encouraged to do so, either independently or through a bar association, judicial conference or other organization dedicated to the improvement of the law. judges may participate in efforts to promote the fair administration of justice, the independence of the judiciary and the integrity of the legal profession and may express opposition to the persecution of lawyers and judges in other countries because of their professional activities.

In this and other Sections of Canon 4, the phrase "subject to the requirements of this Code" is used, notably in connection with a judge's governmental, civic or charitable activities. This phrase is included to remind judges that the use of permissive language in various Sections of the Code does not relieve a judge from the other requirements of the Code that apply to the specific conduct.

C. Governmental, Civic or Charitable Activities.

(1) A judge shall not appear at a public hearing before, or otherwise consult with, an executive or legislative body or official except on matters concerning the law,* the legal system or the administration of justice or except when

acting pro se in a matter involving the judge or the judge's interests.

Commentary:

See Section 2B regarding the obligation to avoid improper influence.

(2) A judge shall not accept appointment to a governmental committee or commission or other governmental position that is concerned with issues of fact or policy on matters other than the improvement of the law,* the legal system or the administration of justice. A judge may, however, represent a country, state or locality on ceremonial occasions or in connection with historical, educational or cultural activities.

Commentary:

Section 4C(2) prohibits a judge from accepting any governmental position except one relating to the law, legal system or administration of justice as authorized by Section 4C(3). The appropriateness of accepting extra-judicial assignments must be assessed in light of the demands on judicial resources created by crowded dockets and the need to protect the courts from involvement in extra-judicial matters that may prove to be controversial. judges should not accept governmental appointments that are likely to interfere with the effectiveness and independence of the judiciary.

Section 4C(2) does not govern a judge's service in a nongovernmental position. See Section 4C(3) permitting service by a judge with organizations devoted to the improvement of the law, the legal system or the administration of justice and with educational, religious, charitable, fraternal or civic organizations not conducted for profit. For example, service on the board of a public educational institution, unless it were a law school, would be prohibited under Section 4C(2), but service on the board of a public law school or any private educational institution would generally be permitted under Section 4C(3).

(3) A judge may serve as an officer, director, trustee or non-legal advisor of an organization or governmental agency devoted to the improvement of the law,* the legal system or the administration of justice or of an educational, religious, charitable, fraternal or civic organization not conducted for profit, subject to the following limitations and the other requirements of this Code.

Commentary:

Section 4C(3) does not apply to a judge's service in a governmental position unconnected with the improvement of the law, the legal system or the administration of justice; see Section 4C(2).

See Commentary to Section 4B regarding use of the phrase "subject to the following limitations and the other requirements of this Code." As an example of the meaning of the phrase, a judge permitted by Section 4C(3) to serve on the board of a fraternal institution may be prohibited from such service by Sections 2C or 4A if the institution practices invidious discrimination or if service on the board otherwise casts reasonable doubt on the judge's capacity to act impartially as a judge.

Service by a judge on behalf of a civic or charitable organization may be governed by other provisions of Canon 4 in addition to Section 4C. For example, a judge is prohibited by Section 4G from serving as a legal advisor to a civic or charitable organization.

> **(a) A judge shall not serve as an officer, director, trustee or non-legal advisor if it is likely that the organization**
>
> **(i) will be engaged in proceedings that would ordinarily come before the judge, or**
>
> **(ii) will be engaged frequently in adversary proceedings in the court of which the judge is a member or in any court subject to the appellate jurisdiction of the court of which the judge is a member.**

Commentary:

The changing nature of some organizations and of their relationship to the law makes it necessary for a judge regularly to reexamine the activities of each organization with which the judge is

ABA Model Code of Judicial Conduct

affiliated to determine if it is proper for the judge to continue the affiliation. For example, in many jurisdictions charitable hospitals are now more frequently in court than in the past. Similarly, the boards of some legal aid organizations now make policy decisions that may have political significance or imply commitment to causes that may come before the courts for adjudication.

(b) A judge as an officer, director, trustee or non-legal advisor, or as a member or otherwise:

(i) may assist such an organization in planning fund-raising and may participate in the management and investment of the organization's funds, but shall not personally participate in the solicitation of funds or other fund-raising activities, except that a judge may solicit funds from other judges over whom the judge does not exercise supervisory or appellate authority;

(ii) may make recommendations to public and private fund-granting organizations on projects and programs concerning the law,* the legal system or the administration of justice;

(iii) shall not personally participate in membership solicitation if the solicitation might reasonably be perceived as coercive or, except as permitted in Section 4C(3)(b)(i), if the membership solicitation is essentially a fund-raising mechanism;

(iv) shall not use or permit the use of the prestige of judicial office for fund-raising or membership solicitation.

Commentary:

A judge may solicit membership or endorse or encourage membership efforts for an organization devoted to the improvement of the law, the legal system or the administration of justice or a nonprofit educational, religious, charitable, fraternal or civic organization as long as the solicitation cannot reasonably be perceived as coercive and is not essentially a fund-raising mechanism. Solicitation of funds for an organization and solicitation of memberships similarly involve the danger that the person solicited will feel obligated to respond favorably to the solicitor if the solicitor is in a position of influence or control. A judge must not engage in direct, individual solicitation of funds or memberships in person, in writing or by telephone except in the following cases: 1) a judge may solicit for funds or memberships other judges over whom the judge does not exercise supervisory or appellate authority, 2) a judge may solicit other persons for membership in the organizations described above if neither those persons nor persons with whom they are affiliated are likely ever to appear before the court on which the judge serves and 3) a judge who is an officer of such an organization may send a general membership solicitation mailing over the judge's signature.

Use of an organization letterhead for fund-raising or membership solicitation does not violate Section 4C(3)(b) provided the letterhead lists only the judge's name and office or other position in the organization, and, if comparable designations are listed for other persons, the judge's judicial designation. In addition, a judge must also make reasonable efforts to ensure that the judge's staff, court officials and others subject to the judge's direction and control do not solicit funds on the judge's behalf for any purpose, charitable or otherwise.

A judge must not be a speaker or guest of honor at an organization's fund-raising event, but mere attendance at such an event is permissible if otherwise consistent with this Code.

D. Financial Activities.

(1) A judge shall not engage in financial and business dealings that:

(a) may reasonably be perceived to exploit the judge's judicial position, or

(b) involve the judge in frequent transactions or continuing business

relationships with those lawyers or other persons likely to come before the court on which the judge serves.

Commentary:

The Time for Compliance provision of this Code (Application, Section F) postpones the time for compliance with certain provisions of this Section in some cases.

When a judge acquires in a judicial capacity information, such as material contained in filings with the court, that is not yet generally known, the judge must not use the information for private gain. See Section 2B; see also Section 3B(11).

A judge must avoid financial and business dealings that involve the judge in frequent transactions or continuing business relationships with persons likely to come either before the judge personally or before other judges on the judge's court. In addition, a judge should discourage members of the judge's family from engaging in dealings that would reasonably appear to exploit the judge's judicial position. This rule is necessary to avoid creating an appearance of exploitation of office or favoritism and to minimize the potential for disqualification. With respect to affiliation of relatives of judge with law firms appearing before the judge, see Commentary to Section 3E(1) relating to disqualification.

Participation by a judge in financial and business dealings is subject to the general prohibitions in Section 4A against activities that tend to reflect adversely on impartiality, demean the judicial office, or interfere with the proper performance of judicial duties. Such participation is also subject to the general prohibition in Canon 2 against activities involving impropriety or the appearance of impropriety and the prohibition in Section 2B against the misuse of the prestige of judicial office. In addition, a judge must maintain high standards of conduct in all of the judge's activities, as set forth in Canon 1. See Commentary for Section 4B regarding use of the phrase "subject to the requirements of this Code."

(2) A judge may, subject to the requirements of this Code, hold and manage investments of the judge and members of the judge's family,* including real estate, and engage in other remunerative activity.

Commentary:

This Section provides that, subject to the requirements of this Code, a judge may hold and manage investments owned solely by the judge, investments owned solely by a member or members of the judge's family, and investments owned jointly by the judge and members of the judge's family.

(3) A judge shall not serve as an officer, director, manager, general partner, advisor or employee of any business entity except that a judge may, subject to the requirements of this Code, manage and participate in:

    (a) a business closely held by the judge or members of the judge's family,* or

    (b) a business entity primarily engaged in investment of the financial resources of the judge or members of the judge's family.*

Commentary:

Subject to the requirements of this Code, a judge may participate in a business that is closely held either by the judge alone, by members of the judge's family, or by the judge and members of the judge's family.

Although participation by a judge in a closely-held family business might otherwise be permitted by Section 4D(3), a judge may be prohibited from participation by other provisions of this Code when, for example, the business entity frequently appears before the judge's court or the participation requires significant time away from judicial duties. Similarly, a judge must avoid participating in a closely-held family business if the judge's participation would involve misuse of the prestige of judicial office.

(4) A judge shall manage the judge's investments and other financial interests to minimize the number of cases in which the judge is disqualified. As soon as the judge can do so without serious financial detriment, the judge shall divest himself or herself of investments

ABA Model Code of Judicial Conduct

and other financial interests that might require frequent disqualification.

(5) A judge shall not accept, and shall urge members of the judge's family residing in the judge's household* not to accept, a gift, bequest, favor or loan from anyone except for:

Commentary:

Section 4D(5) does not apply to contributions to a judge's campaign for judicial office, a matter governed by Canon 5.

Because a gift, bequest, favor or loan to a member of the judge's family residing in the judge's household might be viewed as intended to influence the judge, a judge must inform those family members of the relevant ethical constraints upon the judge in this regard and discourage those family members from violating them. A judge cannot, however, reasonably be expected to know or control all of the financial or business activities of all family members residing in the judge's household.

> (a) a gift incident to a public testimonial, books, tapes and other resource materials supplied by publishers on a complimentary basis for official use, or an invitation to the judge and the judge's spouse or guest to attend a bar-related function or an activity devoted to the improvement of the law,* the legal system or the administration of justice;

Commentary:

Acceptance of an invitation to a law-related function is governed by Section 4D(5)(a); acceptance of an invitation paid for by an individual lawyer or group of lawyers is governed by Section 4D(5)(h).

A judge may accept a public testimonial or a gift incident thereto only if the donor organization is not an organization whose members comprise or frequently represent the same side in litigation, and the testimonial and gift are otherwise in compliance with other provisions of this Code. See Sections 4A(1) and 2B.

> (b) a gift, award or benefit incident to the business, profession or other separate activity of a spouse or other family member of a judge residing in the judge's household, including gifts, awards and benefits for the use of both the spouse or other family member and the judge (as spouse or family member), provided the gift, award or benefit could not reasonably be perceived as intended to influence the judge in the performance of judicial duties;
>
> (c) ordinary social hospitality;
>
> (d) a gift from a relative or friend, for a special occasion, such as a wedding, anniversary or birthday, if the gift is fairly commensurate with the occasion and the relationship;

Commentary:

A gift to a judge, or to a member of the judge's family living in the judge's household, that is excessive in value raises questions about the judge's impartiality and the integrity of the judicial office and might require disqualification of the judge where disqualification would not otherwise be required. See, however, Section 4D(5)(e).

> (e) a gift, bequest, favor or loan from a relative or close personal friend whose appearance or interest in a case would in any event require disqualification under Section 3E;
>
> (f) a loan from a lending institution in its regular course of business on the same terms generally available to persons who are not judges;
>
> (g) a scholarship or fellowship awarded on the same terms and based on the same criteria applied to other applicants; or
>
> (h) any other gift, bequest, favor or loan, only if: the donor is not a party or other person who has come or is likely to come or. whose interests have come or are likely to come before the judge; and, if its value exceeds $150.00, the judge reports it in the same manner as the judge reports compensation in Section 4H.

Commentary:

Section 4D(5)(h) prohibits judges from accepting gifts, favors, bequests or loans from lawyers or their firms if they have come or are likely to come before the judge; it also prohibits gifts, favors, bequests or loans from clients of lawyers or their firms when the clients' interests have come or are likely to come before the judge.

E. Fiduciary Activities.

(1) A judge shall not serve as executor, administrator or other personal representative, trustee, guardian, attorney in fact or other fiduciary,* except for the estate, trust or person of a member of the judge's family,* and then only if such service will not interfere with the proper performance of judicial duties.

(2) A judge shall not serve is a fiduciary* if it is likely that the judge as a fiduciary will be engaged in proceedings that would ordinarily come before the judge, or if the estate, trust or ward becomes involved in adversary proceedings in the court on which the judge serves or one under its appellate jurisdiction.

(3) The same restrictions on financial activities that apply to a judge personally also apply to the judge while acting in a fiduciary* capacity.

Commentary:

The Time for Compliance provision of this Code (Application, Section F) postpones the time for compliance with certain provisions of this Section in some cases.

The restrictions imposed by this Canon may conflict with the judge's obligation as a fiduciary. For example, a judge should resign as trustee if detriment to the trust would result from divestiture of holdings the retention of which would place the judge in violation of Section 4D(4).

F. Service as Arbitrator or Mediator. A judge shall not act as an arbitrator or mediator or otherwise perform judicial functions in a private capacity unless expressly authorized by law.*

Commentary:

Section 4F does not prohibit a judge from participating in arbitration, mediation or settlement conferences performed as part of judicial duties.

G. Practice of Law. A judge shall not practice law. Notwithstanding this prohibition, a judge may act pro se and may, without compensation, give legal advice to and draft or review documents for a member of the judge's family.*

Commentary:

This prohibition refers to the practice of law in a representative capacity and not in a pro se capacity. A judge may act for himself or herself in all legal matters, including matters involving litigation and matters involving appearances before or other dealings with legislative and other governmental bodies. However, in so doing, a judge must not abuse the prestige of office to advance the interests of the judge or the judge's family. See Section 2(B).

The Code allows a judge to give legal advice to and draft legal documents for members of the judge's family, so long as the judge receives no compensation. A judge must not, however, act as an advocate or negotiator for a member of the judge's family in a legal matter.

*****

Canon 6, new in the 1972 Code, reflected concerns about conflicts of interest and appearances of impropriety arising from compensation for off-the-bench activities. Since 1972, however, reporting requirements that are much more comprehensive with respect to what must be reported and with whom reports must be filed have been adopted by many jurisdictions. The Committee believes that although reports of compensation for extra-judicial activities should be required, reporting requirements preferably should be developed to suit the respective jurisdictions, not simply adopted as set forth in a national model code of judicial conduct, Because of the Committee's concern that deletion of this Canon might lead to the misconception that reporting compensation for extra-judicial activities is no longer important, the substance of Canon 6 is carried forward as Section 4H in this Code for adoption in those jurisdictions that do not have other reporting requirements, In jurisdictions that have separately established reporting requirements, Section 4H(2) (Public Reporting) may be deleted and the caption for Section 4H modified appropriately.

*****

H. Compensation, Reimbursement and Reporting.

(1) Compensation and Reimbursement. A judge may receive compensation and reimbursement of expenses for the extra-judicial activities permitted by this Code, if the source of such payments does not give the appearance of influencing the judge's performance of judicial duties or otherwise give the appearance of impropriety.

> (a) Compensation shall not exceed a reasonable amount nor shall it exceed what a person who is not a judge would receive for the same activity.
>
> (b) Expense reimbursement shall be limited to the actual cost of travel, food and lodging reasonably incurred by the judge and, where appropriate to the occasion, by the judge's spouse or guest. Any payment in excess of such an amount is compensation.

(2) Public Reports. A judge shall report the date, place and nature of any activity for which the judge received compensation, and the name of the payor and the amount of compensation so received. Compensation or income of a spouse attributed to the judge by operation of a community property law is not extra-judicial compensation to the judge. The judge's report shall be made at least annually and shall be filed as a public document in the office of the clerk of the court on which the judge serves or other office designated by law.*

Commentary:

See Section 4D(5) regarding reporting of gifts, bequests and loans.

The Code does not prohibit a judge from accepting honoraria or speaking fees provided that the compensation is reasonable and commensurate with the task performed. A judge should ensure, however, that no conflicts are created by the arrangement. A judge must not appear to trade on the judicial position for personal advantage. Nor should a judge spend significant time away from court duties to meet speaking or writing commitments for compensation. In addition, the source of the payment must not raise any question of undue influence or the judge's ability or willingness to be impartial.

I. Disclosure of a judge's income, debts, investments or other assets is required only to the extent provided in this Canon and in Sections 3E and 3F, or as otherwise required by law.*

Commentary:

Section 3E requires a judge to disqualify himself or herself in any proceeding in which the judge has an economic interest. See "economic interest" as explained in the Terminology Section. Section 4D requires a judge to refrain from engaging in business and from financial activities that might interfere with the impartial performance of judicial duties; Section 4H requires a judge to report all compensation the judge received for activities outside judicial office. A judge has the rights of any other citizen, including the right to privacy of the judge's financial affairs, except to the extent that limitations established by law are required to safeguard the proper performance of the judge's duties.

ABA Model Code of Judicial Conduct

CANON 5[5,6]

A JUDGE OR JUDICIAL CANDIDATE SHALL REFRAIN FROM INAPPROPRIATE POLITICAL ACTIVITY

A. All judges and Candidates

(1) Except as authorized in Sections 5B(2), 5C(1) and 5C(3), a judge or a candidate* for election or appointment to judicial office shall not: (a) act as a leader or hold an office in a political organization,* (b) publicly endorse or publicly oppose another candidate for public office; (c) make speeches on behalf of a political organization; (d) attend political gatherings; or (e) solicit funds for, pay an assessment to or make a contribution to a political, organization or candidate, or purchase tickets for political party dinners or other functions.

Commentary:

A judge or candidate for judicial office retains the right to participate in the political process as a voter.

Where false information concerning a judicial candidate is made public, a judgeor another judicial candidate having knowledge of the facts is not prohibited bySection 5A(1) from making the facts public.

Section 5A(1)(a) does not prohibit a candidate for elective judicial office from retaining during candidacy a public office such as county prosecutor, which is not "an office in a political organization."

Section 5A(1)(b) does not prohibit a judge or judicial candidate from privately expressing his or her views on judicial candidates or other candidates for public office.

A candidate does not publicly endorse another candidate for public office by having that candidate's name on the same ticket.

(2) A judge shall resign from judicial office upon becoming a candidate* for a non-judicial office either in a primary or in a general election, except that the judge may continue to hold judicial office while being a candidate for election to or serving as a delegate in a state constitutional convention if the judge is otherwise permitted by law* to do so.

(3) A candidate* for a judicial office:

(a) **shall maintain the dignity appropriate to judicial office and act in a manner consistent with the integrity and independence of the judiciary, and shall encourage members of the candidate's family* to adhere to the same standards of political conduct in support of the candidate as apply to the candidate;**

---

5. Introductory Note to Canon 5: There is wide variation in the methods of judicial selection use, both among jurisdictions and within the jurisdictions themselves, In a given state, judges may be selected by one method initially, retained by a different method, and selected by still another method to fill interim vacancies.

According to figures compiled in 1987 by the National Center for State Courts, 32 states and the District of Columbia use a merit selection method (in which an executive such as a governor appoints a judge from a group of nominees selected by a judicial nominating commission) to select judges in the state either initially or to fill an interim vacancy. Of those 33 jurisdictions, a merit selection method is used in 18 jurisdictions to choose judges of courts of last resort, in 13 jurisdictions to choose judges of intermediate appellate courts, in 12 jurisdictions to choose judges of general jurisdiction courts and in 5 jurisdictions to choose judges of limited jurisdiction courts.

Methods of judicial selection other than merit selection include nonpartisan election (10 states use it for initial selection at all court levels, another 10 states use it for initial selection for at least one court level) and partisan election (8 states use it for initial selection at all court levels, another 7 states use it for initial selection for at least one level). In a small minority of the states, judicial selection methods include executive or legislative appointment (without nomination of a group of potential appointees by a judicial nominating commission) and court selection. In addition, the federal judicial system utilizes an executive appointment method. See State Court Organization 1987 (National Center for State Courts, 1988).

6. Amended August 6, 1997, American Bar Association House of Delegates, San Francisco, California, per Report No. 112, and August 10, 1999, American Bar Association House of Delegates, Atlanta, Georgia, per Report No. 123.

Commentary:

Although a judicial candidate must encourage members of his or her family to adhere to the same standards of political conduct in support of the candidate that apply to the candidate, family members are free to participate in other political activity.

    (b) shall prohibit employees and officials who serve at the pleasure of the candidate,* and shall discourage other employees and officials subject to the candidate's direction and control from doing on the candidate's behalf what the candidate is prohibited from doing under the Sections of this Canon;

    (c) except to the extent permitted by Section 5C(2), shall not authorize or knowingly* permit any other person to do for the candidate* what the candidate is prohibited from doing under the Sections of this Canon;

    (d) shall not:

        (i) make pledges or promises of conduct in office other than the faithful and impartial performance of the duties of the office;

        (ii) make statements that commit or appear to commit the candidate with respect to cases, controversies or issues that are likely to come before the court; or

        (iii) knowingly* misrepresent the identity, qualifications, present position or other fact concerning the candidate or an opponent;

Commentary:

Section 5A(3)(d) prohibits a candidate for judicial office from making statements that appear to commit the candidate regarding cases, controversies or issues likely to come before the court. As a corollary, a candidate should emphasize in any public statement the candidate's duty to uphold the law regardless of his or her personal views. See also Section 3B(9), the general rule on public comment by judges. Section 5A(3)(d) does not prohibit a candidate from making pledges or promises respecting improvements in court administration. Nor does this Section prohibit an incumbent judge from making private statements to other judges or court personnel in the performance of judicial duties. This Section applies to any statement made in the process of securing judicial office, such as statements to commissions charged with judicial selection and tenure and legislative bodies confirming appointment. See also Rule 8.2 of the ABA Model Rules of Professional Conduct.

    (e) may respond to personal attacks or attacks on the candidate's record as long as the response does not violate Section 5A(3)(d).

B. Candidates Seeking Appointment to Judicial or Other Governmental Office.

    (1) A candidate* for appointment to judicial office or a judge seeking other governmental office shall not solicit or accept funds, personally or through a committee or otherwise, to support his or her candidacy.

    (2) A candidate* for appointment to judicial office or a judge seeking other governmental office shall not engage in any political activity to secure the appointment except that:

        (a) such persons may:

            (i) communicate with the appointing authority, including any selection or nominating commission or other agency designated to screen candidates;

            (ii) seek support or endorsement for the appointment from organizations that regularly make recommendations for reappointment or appointment to the office, and from individuals to the extent requested or required by those specified in Section 5B(2)(a); and

            (iii) provide to those specified in Sections 5B(2)(a)(i) and 5B(2)(a)(ii) information as to his or her qualifications for the office;

(b) a non-judge candidate* for appointment to judicial office may, in addition, unless otherwise prohibited by law*:

(i) retain an office in a political organization*,

(ii) attend political gatherings, and

(iii) continue to pay ordinary assessments and ordinary contributions to a political organization or candidate and purchase tickets for political party dinners or other functions.

Commentary:

Section 5B(2) provides a limited exception to the restrictions imposed by, Sections 5A(1) and 5D. Under Section 5B(2), candidates seeking reappointment to the same judicial office or appointment to another judicial office or other governmental office may apply for the appointment and seek appropriate support.

Although under Section 5B(2) non-judge candidates seeking appointment to judicial office are permitted during candidacy to retain office in a political organization, attend political gatherings and pay ordinary dues and assessments, they remain subject to other provisions of this Code during candidacy. See Sections 5B(1), 5B(2)(a), 5E and Application Section.

C. **Judges and Candidates Subject to Public Election.**

(1) A judge or a candidate* subject to public election* may, except as prohibited by law*:

(a) at any time

(i) purchase tickets for and attend political gatherings;

(ii) identify himself or herself as a member of a political party; and

(iii) contribute to a political organization*;

(b) when a candidate for election

(i) speak to gatherings on his or her own behalf;

(ii) appear in newspaper, television and other media advertisements supporting his or her candidacy;

(iii) distribute pamphlets and other promotional campaign literature supporting his or her candidacy; and

(iv) publicly endorse or publicly oppose other candidates for the same judicial office in a public election in which the judge or judicial candidate is running.

Commentary:

Section 5C(1) permits judges subject to election at any time to be involved in limited political activity. Section 5D, applicable solely to incumbent judges, would otherwise bar this activity.

(2) A candidate* shall not personally solicit or accept campaign contributions or personally solicit publicly stated support. A candidate may, however, establish committees of responsible persons to conduct campaigns for the candidate through media advertisements, brochures, mailings, candidate forums and other means not prohibited by law. Such committees may solicit and accept reasonable campaign contributions, manage the expenditure of funds for the candidate's campaign and obtain public statements of support for his or her candidacy. Such committees are not prohibited from soliciting and accepting reasonable campaign contributions and public support from lawyers. A candidate's committees may solicit contributions and public support for the candidate's campaign no earlier than [one year] before an election and no later than [90] days after the last election in which the candidate participates during the election year. A candidate shall not use or permit the use of campaign contributions for the private benefit of the candidate or others.

ABA Model Code of Judicial Conduct

Commentary:

There is legitimate concern about a judge's impartiality when parties whose interests may come before a judge, or the lawyer who represent such parties, are known to have made contributions to the election campaigns of judicial candidates, This is among the reasons that merit selection of judges is a preferable manner in which to select the judiciary. Notwithstanding that preference, Section 5C(2) recognizes that in many jurisdictions judicial candidates must raise funds to support their candidacies for election to judicial office. It therefore permits a candidate, other than a candidate for appointment, to establish campaign committees to solicit and accept public support and reasonable financial contributions, In order to guard against the possibility that conflicts of interest will arise, the candidate must instruct his or her campaign committees at the start of the campaign to solicit or accept only contributions that are reasonable and appropriate under the circumstances. Though not prohibited, campaign contributions of which a judge has knowledge, made by lawyers or others who appear before the judge, may, by virtue of their size or source, raise questions about a judge's impartiality and be cause for disqualification as provided under Section 3E.

Campaign committees established under Section 5C(2) should manage campaign finances responsibly, avoiding deficits that might necessitate post-election fund-raising, to the extent possible. Such committees must at all times comply with applicable statutory provisions governing their conduct,

Section 5C(2) does not prohibit a candidate from initiating an evaluation by a judicial selection commission or bar association, or, subject to the requirements of this Code from responding to a request for information from any organization.

(3) A candidate shall instruct his or her campaign committee(s) at the start of the campaign not to accept campaign contributions for any election that exceed, in the aggregate,* $[ ] from an individual or $[ ] from an entity. This limitation is in addition to the limitations provided in Section 5C(2).[7]

(4) In addition to complying with all applicable statutory requirements for disclosure of campaign contributions, campaign committees established by a candidate shall file with [ ][8] a report stating the name, address, occupation and employer of each person who has made campaign contributions to the committee whose value in the aggregate* exceed [$].[9] The report must be filed within [ ][10] days following the election.

(5) Except as prohibited by law*, a candidate* for judicial office in a public election* may permit the candidate's name: (a) to be listed on election materials along with the names of other candidates for elective public office, and (b) to appear in promotions of the ticket.

Commentary:

Section 5C(3) provides a limited exception to the restrictions imposed by Section 5A(1).

D. Incumbent judges. A judge shall not engage in any political activity except (i) as authorized under any other Section of this Code, (ii) on behalf of measures to improve the law,* the legal system or the administration of justice, or (iii) as expressly authorized by law.

---

7. Jurisdictions wishing to adopt campaign contribution limits that are lower than generally applicable campaign finance regulations provide should adopt this provision, inserting appropriate dollar amounts where brackets appear.

8. Each jurisdiction should identify an appropriate depository for the information required under this provision, giving consideration to the public's need for convenient and timely access to the information. Electronic filing is to be preferred.

9. Jurisdictions wishing to adopt campaign contribution disclosure levels lower than those set in generally applicable campaign finance regulations should adopt this provision, inserting appropriate dollar amounts where brackets appear.

10. A time period chosen by the adopting jurisdiction should appear in the bracketed space.

Commentary:

Neither Section 5D nor any other section of the Code prohibits a judge in the exercise of administrative functions from engaging in planning and other official activities with members of the executive and legislative branches of government. With respect to a judge's activity on behalf of measures to improve the law, the legal system and the administration of justice, see Commentary to Section 4B and Section 4C(1) and its Commentary.

E. Applicability. Canon 5 generally applies to all incumbent judges and judicial candidates.* A successful candidate, whether or not an incumbent, is subject to judicial discipline for his or her campaign conduct; an unsuccessful candidate who is a lawyer is subject to lawyer discipline for his or her campaign conduct. A lawyer who is a candidate for judicial office is subject to [Rule 8.2(b) of the ABA Model Rules of Professional Conduct]. (An adopting jurisdiction should substitute a reference to its applicable rule.)

APPLICATION OF THE CODE OF JUDICIAL CONDUCT

A. Anyone, whether or not a lawyer, who is an officer of a judicial system[11] and who performs judicial functions, including an officer such as a magistrate, court commissioner, special master or referee, is a judge within the meaning of this Code. All judges shall comply with this Code except as provided below.

Commentary:

The four categories of judicial service in other than a full-time capacity are necessarily defined in general terms because of the widely varying forms of judicial service. For the purposes of this Section, as long as a retired judge is subject to recall the judge is considered to "perform judicial functions." The determination of which category and, accordingly, which specific Code provisions apply to an individual judicial officer, depend upon the facts of the particular judicial service.

B. Retired judge Subject to Recall. A retired judge subject to recall who by law is not permitted to practice law is not required to comply:

(1) except while serving as a judge, with Section 4F; and

(2) at any time with Section 4E.

C. Continuing Part-time judge. A continuing part-time judge*:

(1) is not required to comply

   (a) except while serving as a judge, with Section 3B(9); and

   (b) at any time with Sections 4C (2), 4D (3), 4E (1), 4F, 4G, 4H, 5A (1), 5B(2) and 5D.

(2) shall not practice law in the court on which the judge serves or in any court subject to the appellate jurisdiction of the court on which the judge serves, and shall not act as a lawyer in a proceeding in which the judge has served as a judge or in any other proceeding related thereto.

Commentary:

When a person who has been a continuing part-time judge is no longer a continuing part-time judge, including a retired judge no longer subject to recall, that person may act as a lawyer in a proceeding in which he or she has served as a judge or in any other proceeding related thereto only with the express consent of all parties pursuant to [Rule 1. 12 (a) of the ABA Model Rules of Professional Conduct]. (An adopting jurisdiction should substitute a reference to its applicable rule).

---

11. Applicability of this Code to administrative law judges should be determined by each adopting jurisdiction. Administrative law judges generally are affiliated with the executive branch of government rather than the judicial branch and each adopting jurisdiction should consider the unique characteristics of particular administrative law judge positions in adopting and adapting the Code for administrative law judges, See, e.g., Model Code of Judicial Conduct for Federal Administrative Law judges, endorsed by the National Conference of Administrative Law judges in February 1989.

D. Periodic Part-time judge. A periodic part-time judge:*

(1) is not required to comply

(a) except while serving as a judge, with Section 3B(9);

(b) at any time, with Sections 4C(2), 4C(3)(a), 4D(1)(b), 4D(3), 4D(4), 4D(5), 4E, 4F, 4G, 4H, 5A(1), 5B(2) and 5D.

(2) shall not practice law in the court on which the judge serves or in any court subject to the appellate jurisdiction of the court on which the judge serves, and shall not act as a lawyer in a proceeding in which the judge has served as a judge or in any other proceeding related thereto.

Commentary:

When a person who has been a periodic part-time judge is no longer a periodic part-time judge (no longer accepts appointments), that person may act as a lawyer in a proceeding in which he or she has served as a judge or in any other proceeding related thereto only with the express consent of all parties pursuant to [Rule 1.12 (a) of the ABA Model Rules of Professional Conduct]. (An adopting jurisdiction should substitute a reference to its applicable rule.)

E. Pro Tempore Part-time judge. A pro tempore part-time judge*:

(1) is not required to comply

(a) except while serving as a judge, with Sections 2A, 2B, 3B(9) and 4C(1);

(b) at any time with Sections 2C, 4C(2), 4C(3) (a), 4C(3) (b), 4D(1) (b), 4D(3), 4D(4), 4D(5), 4E, 4F, 4G, 4H, 5A(1), 5A(2), 5B(2) and 5D.

(2) A person who has been a pro tempore part-time judge* shall not act as a lawyer in a proceeding in which the judge has served as a judge or in any other proceeding related thereto except as otherwise permitted by [Rule 1.12(a) of the ABA Model Rules of Professional Conduct]. (An adopting jurisdiction should substitute a reference to its applicable rule.)

F. Time for Compliance. A person to whom this Code becomes applicable shall comply immediately with all provisions of this Code except Sections 4D(2), 4D(3) and 4E and shall comply with these Sections as soon as reasonably possible and shall do so in any event within the period of one year.

Commentary:

If serving as a fiduciary when selected as judge, a new judge may, notwithstanding the prohibitions in Section 4E, continue to serve as fiduciary but only for that period of time necessary to avoid serious adverse consequences to the beneficiary of the fiduciary relationship and in no event longer than one year. Similarly, if engaged at the time of judicial selection in a business activity, a new judge may, notwithstanding the prohibitions in Section 4D(3), continue in that activity for a reasonable period but in no event longer than one year.

ABA MODEL CODE OF PROFESSIONAL RESPONSIBILITY

PREAMBLE AND PRELIMINARY STATEMENT

Preamble[1]

The continued existence of a free and democratic society depends upon recognition of the concept that justice is based upon the rule of law grounded in respect for the dignity of the individual and his capacity through reason for enlightened self-government.[2] Law so grounded makes justice possible, for only through such law does the dignity of the individual attain respect and protection. Without it, individual rights become subject to unrestrained power, respect for law is destroyed, and rational self-government is impossible.

Lawyers, as guardians of the law, play a vital role in the preservation of society. The fulfillment of this role requires an understanding by lawyers of their relationship with and function in our legal system.[3] A consequent obligation of lawyers is to maintain the highest standards of ethical conduct.

In fulfilling his professional responsibilities, a lawyer necessarily assumes various roles that require the performance of many difficult tasks. Not every situation which he may encounter can be foreseen,[4] but fundamental ethical principles are always present to guide him. Within the framework of these principles, a lawyer must with courage and foresight be able and ready to shape the body of the law to the ever-changing relationships of society.[5]

The Model Code of Professional Responsibility points the way to the aspiring and provides standards by which to judge the transgressor. Each lawyer must find within his own conscience the touchstone against which to test the extent to which his actions should rise above minimum standards. But in the last analysis it is the desire for the respect and confidence of the members of his profession and of the society which he serves that should provide to a lawyer the incentive for the highest possible degree of ethical conduct. The possible loss of that respect and confidence is the ultimate sanction. So long as its practitioners are guided by these principles, the law will continue to be a noble profession. This is its greatness and its strength, which permit of no compromise.

Preliminary Statement

In furtherance of the principles stated in the Preamble, the American Bar Association has promulgated this Model Code of Professional Responsibility, consisting of three separate but interrelated parts: Canons, Ethical Considerations, and Disciplinary Rules.[6] The Model Code is designed to be adopted by appropriate agencies both as an inspirational guide to the members of the profession and as a basis for disciplinary action when the conduct of a lawyer falls below the required minimum standards stated in the Disciplinary Rules.

Obviously the Canons, Ethical Considerations, and Disciplinary Rules cannot apply to non-lawyers; however, they do define the type of ethical conduct that the public has a right to expect not only of lawyers but also of their non-professional employees and associates in all matters pertaining to professional employment. A lawyer should ultimately be responsible for the conduct of his employees and associates in the course of the professional representation of the client.

The Canons are statements of axiomatic norms, expressing in general terms the standards of professional conduct expected of lawyers in their relationships with the public, with the legal system, and with the legal profession. They embody the general concepts from which the Ethical Consideration and the Disciplinary Rules are derived.

The Ethical Considerations are aspirational in character and represent the objectives toward which every member of the profession should strive. They constitute a body of principles upon which the lawyer can rely for guidance in many specific situations.[7]

The Disciplinary Rules, unlike the Ethical Considerations, are mandatory in character. The Disciplinary Rules state the minimum level of conduct below which no lawyer can fall without being subject to disciplinary action. Within the framework of fair trial,[8] the Disciplinary Rules should be uniformly applied to all lawyers,[9] regardless of the nature of their professional activities.[10] The Model Code makes no attempt to prescribe either disciplinary procedures or penalties[11] for violation of a Disciplinary Rule,[12] nor does it undertake to define standards for civil liability of lawyers for professional conduct. The severity of judgment against one found guilty of violating a Disciplinary Rule should be determined by the character of the offense and the attendant circumstances.[13] An enforcing agency, in applying the Disciplinary Rules, may find interpretive guidance in the basic principles embodied in the Canons and in the objectives reflected in the Ethical Considerations.

NOTES

1. The footnotes are intended merely to enable the reader to relate the provisions of this Model Code to the ABA Canons of Professional Ethics adopted in 1908, as amended, the Opinions of the ABA Committee on Professional Ethics, and a limited number of other sources; they are not intended to be an annotation of the views taken by the ABA Special Committee on Evaluation of Ethical Standards. Footnotes citing ABA Canons refer to the ABA Canons of Professional Ethics, adopted in 1908, as amended.

2. *Cf.* ABA Canons, Preamble.

3. "[T]he lawyer stands today in special need of a clear understanding of his obligations and of the vital connection between these obligations and the role his profession plays in society." *Professional Responsibility: Report of the Joint Conference*, 44 A.B.A.J. 1159, 1160 (1958).

4. "No general statement of the responsibilities of the legal profession can encompass all the situations in which the lawyer may be placed. Each position held by him makes its own peculiar demands. These demands the lawyer must clarify for himself in the light of the particular role in which he serves." *Professional Responsibility: Report of the Joint Conference*, 44 A.B.A.J. 1159, 1218 (1958).

5. "The law and its institutions change as social conditions change. They must change if they are to preserve, much less advance, the political and social values from which they derive their purposes and their life. This is true of the most important of legal institutions, the profession of law. The profession, too, must change when conditions change in order to preserve and advance the social values that are its reasons for being." Cheatham, *Availability of Legal Services: The Responsibility of the Individual Lawyer and the Organized Bar,* 12 U.C.L.A. L. Rev. 438, 440 (1965).

6. The Supreme Court of Wisconsin adopted a Code of Judicial Ethics in 1967. "The code is divided into standards and rules, the standards being statements of what the general desirable level of conduct should be, the rules being particular canons, the violation of which shall subject an individual judge to sanctions." In re Promulgation of a Code of Judicial Ethics, 36 Wis. 2d 252, 255, 153 N.W. 2d 873, 874 (1967).

The portion of the Wisconsin Code of Judicial Ethics entitled "Standards" states that "[t]he following standards set forth the significant qualities of the ideal judge. . . ." *Id.*, 36 Wis.2d at 256, 153 N.W. 2d at 875. The portion entitled "Rules" states that "[t]he court promulgates the following rules because the requirements of judicial conduct embodied therein are of sufficient gravity to warrant sanctions if they are not obeyed. . . ." *Id.*, 36 Wis.2d at 259, 153 N.W. 2d at 876.

7. "Under the conditions of modern practice it is peculiarly necessary that the lawyer should understand, not merely the established standards of professional conduct, but the reasons underlying these standards. Today the lawyer plays a changing and increasingly varied role. In many developing fields the precise contribution of the legal profession is as yet undefined." *Professional Responsibility: Report of the Joint Conference*, 44 A.B.A.J. 1159 (1958).

"A true sense of professional responsibility must derive from an understanding of the reasons that lie back of specific restraints, such as those embodied in the Canons. The grounds for the lawyer's peculiar obligations are to be found in the nature of his calling. The lawyer who seeks a clear understanding of his duties will be led to reflect on the special services his profession renders to society and the services it might render if its full capacities were realized. When the lawyer fully understands the nature of his office, he will then discern what restraints are necessary to keep that office wholesome and effective." *Id.*

8. "Disbarment, designed to protect the public, is a punishment or penalty imposed on the lawyer. . . .

He is accordingly entitled to procedural due process, which includes fair notice of the charge." In re Ruffalo, 390 U.S. 544, 550, 20 L. Ed. 2d 117, 122 88 S. Ct. 1222, 1226 (1968), *rehearing denied,* 391 U.S. 961, 20 L. Ed. 2d 874, 88 S. Ct. 1833 (1968).

"A State cannot exclude a person from the practice of law or from any other occupation in a manner or for reasons that contravene the Due Process or Equal Protection Clause of the Fourteenth Amendment. . . . A State can require high standards of qualification . . . but any qualification must have a rational connection with the applicant's fitness or capacity to practice law." Schware v. Bd. of Bar Examiners, 353 U.S. 232, 239, 1 L. Ed. 2d 796, 801-02, 77 S. Ct. 752, 756 (1957).

"[A]n accused lawyer may expect that he will not be condemned out of a capricious self-righteousness or denied the essentials of a fair hearing." Kingsland v. Dorsey, 338 U.S. 318, 320, 94 L. Ed. 123, 126, 70 S. Ct. 123, 124-25 (1949).

"The attorney and counsellor being, by the solemn judicial act of the court, clothed with his office, does not hold it as a matter of grace and favor. The right which it confers upon him to appear for suitors, and to argue causes, is something more than a mere indulgence, revocable at the pleasure of the court, or at the command of the legislature. It is a right of which he can only be deprived by the judgment of the court, for moral or professional delinquency." Ex parte Garland, 71 U.S. (4 Wall.) 333, 378-79, 18 L. Ed. 366, 370 (1866).

See generally Comment, *Procedural Due Process and Character Hearings for Bar Applicants*, 15 STAN. L. REV. 500 (1963).

9. "The canons of professional ethics must be enforced by the Courts and must be respected by members of the Bar if we are to maintain public confidence in the integrity and impartiality of the administration of justice." In re Meeker, 76 N. M. 354, 357, 414 P.2d 862, 864 (1966), *appeal dismissed,* 385 U.S. 449 (1967).

10. See ABA CANON 45.

11. "Other than serving as a model or derivative source, the American Bar Association Model Code of Professional Responsibility plays no part in the disciplinary proceeding, except as a guide for consideration in adoption of local applicable rules for the regulation of conduct on the part of legal practitioners." ABA COMM. ON PROFESSIONAL ETHICS, INFORMAL OPINION NO. 1420 (1978) [hereinafter each Formal Opinion is cited as *"ABA Opinion"*]. For the purposes and intended effect of the American Bar Association Model Code of Professional Responsibility and of the opinions of the Standing Committee on Ethics and Professional Responsibility, see Informal Opinion No. 1420.

"There is generally no prescribed discipline for any particular type of improper conduct. The disciplinary measures taken are discretionary with the courts, which may disbar, suspend, or merely censure the attorney as the nature of the offense and past indicia of character may warrant." Note, 43 CORNELL L.Q. 489, 495 (1958).

12. The Model Code seeks only to specify conduct for which a lawyer should be disciplined by courts and governmental agencies which have adopted it. Recommendations as to the procedures to be used in disciplinary actions are within the jurisdiction of the American Bar Association Standing Committee on Professional Discipline.

13. "The severity of the judgment of this court should be in proportion to the gravity of the offenses, the moral turpitude involved, and the extent that the defendant's acts and conduct affect his professional qualifications to practice law." Louisiana State Bar Ass'n v. Steiner, 204 La. 1073, 1092-93, 16 So. 2d 843, 850 (1944) (Higgins, J., concurring in decree).

"Certainly an erring lawyer who has been disciplined and who having paid the penalty has given satisfactory evidence of repentance and has been rehabilitated and restored to his place at the bar by the court which knows him best ought not to have what amounts to an order of permanent disbarment entered against him by a federal court solely on the basis of an earlier criminal record and without regard to his subsequent rehabilitation and present good character. . . . We think, therefore, that the district court should reconsider the appellant's application for admission and grant it unless the court finds it to be a fact that the appellant is not presently of good moral or professional character." In re Dreier, 258 F.2d 68, 69-70 (3d Cir. 1958).

CANON 1

A Lawyer Should Assist in Maintaining the Integrity and Competence of the Legal Profession

ETHICAL CONSIDERATIONS

EC 1-1 A basic tenet of the professional responsibility of lawyers is that every person in our society should have ready access to the independent professional services of a lawyer of integrity and competence. Maintaining the integrity and improving the competence of the bar to meet the highest standards is the ethical responsibility of every lawyer.

EC 1-2 The public should be protected from those who are not qualified to be lawyers by reason of a deficiency in education[1] or moral standards[2] or of other relevant factors[3] but who nevertheless seek to practice law. To assure the maintenance of high moral and educational standards of the legal profession, lawyers should affirmatively assist courts and other appropriate bodies in promulgating, enforcing, and improving requirements for admission to the bar.[4] In like manner, the bar has a positive obligation to aid in the continued improvement of all phases of pre-admission and post-admission legal education.

EC 1-3 Before recommending an applicant for admission, a lawyer should satisfy himself that the applicant is of good moral character. Although a lawyer should not become a self-appointed investigator or judge of applicants for admission, he should report to proper officials all unfavorable information he possesses relating to the character or other qualifications of an applicant.[5]

EC 1-4 The integrity of the profession can be maintained only if conduct of lawyers in violation of the Disciplinary Rules is brought to the attention of the proper officials. A lawyer should reveal voluntarily to those officials all unprivileged knowledge of conduct of lawyers which he believes clearly to be in violation of the Disciplinary Rules.[6] A lawyer should, upon request serve on and assist committees and boards having responsibility for the administration of the Disciplinary Rules.[7]

EC 1-5 A lawyer should maintain high standards of professional conduct and should encourage fellow lawyers to do likewise. He should be temperate and dignified, and he should refrain from all illegal and morally reprehensible conduct.[8] Because of his position in society, even minor violations of law by a lawyer may tend to lessen public confidence in the legal profession. Obedience to law exemplifies respect for law. To lawyers especially, respect for the law should be more than a platitude.

EC 1-6 An applicant for admission to the bar or a lawyer may be unqualified, temporarily or permanently, for other than moral and educational reasons, such as mental or emotional instability. Lawyers should be diligent in taking steps to see that during a period of disqualification such person is not granted a license or, if licensed, is not permitted to practice.[9] In like manner, when the disqualification has terminated, members of the bar should assist such person in being licensed, or, if licensed, in being restored to his full right to practice.

DISCIPLINARY RULES

DR 1-101 Maintaining Integrity and Competence of the Legal Profession.
(A) A lawyer is subject to discipline if he has made a materially false statement in, or if he has deliberately failed to disclose a material fact requested in connection with, his application for admission to the bar.[10]
(B) A lawyer shall not further the application for admission to the bar of another person known by him to be unqualified in respect to character, education, or other relevant attribute.[11]

DR 1-102 Misconduct.
(A) A lawyer shall not:
    (1) Violate a Disciplinary Rule.

(2) Circumvent a Disciplinary Rule through actions of another.[12]
(3) Engage in illegal conduct involving moral turpitude.[13]
(4) Engage in conduct involving dishonesty, fraud, deceit, or misrepresentation.
(5) Engage in conduct that is prejudicial to the administration of justice.
(6) Engage in any other conduct that adversely reflects on his fitness to practice law.[14]

DR 1-103 Disclosure of Information to Authorities.
(A) A lawyer possessing unprivileged knowledge of a violation of DR 1-102 shall report such knowledge to a tribunal or other authority empowered to investigate or act upon such violation.[15]
(B) A lawyer possessing unprivileged knowledge or evidence concerning another lawyer or a judge shall reveal fully such knowledge or evidence upon proper request of a tribunal or other authority empowered to investigate or act upon the conduct of lawyers or judges.[16]

NOTES

1. "[W]e cannot conclude that all educational restrictions [on bar admission] are unlawful. We assume that few would deny that a grammar school education requirement, before taking the bar examination, was reasonable. Or that an applicant had to be able to read or write. Once we conclude that *some* restriction is proper, then it becomes a matter of degree—the problem of drawing the line.

. . . .

"We conclude the fundamental question here is whether Rule IV, Section 6 of the Rules Pertaining to Admission of Applicants to the State Bar of Arizona is 'arbitrary, capricious and unreasonable.' We conclude an educational requirement of graduation from an accredited law school is not." Hackin v. Lockwood, 361 F.2d 499, 503-4 (9th Cir. 1966), *cert. denied,* 385 U.S. 960, 17 L. Ed.2d 305, 87 S. Ct. 396 (1966).

2. "Every state in the United States, as a prerequisite for admission to the practice of law, requires that applicants possess 'good moral character.' Although the requirement is of judicial origin, it is now embodied in legislation in most states." Comment, *Procedural Due Process and Character Hearings for Bar Applicants,* 15 STAN. L. REV. 500 (1963).

"Good character in the members of the bar is essential to the preservation of the integrity of the courts. The duty and power of the court to guard its portals against intrusion by men and women who are mentally and morally dishonest, unfit because of bad character, evidenced by their course of conduct, to participate in the administrative law, would seem to be unquestioned in the matter of preservation of judicial dignity and integrity." In re Monaghan, 126 Vt. 53, 222 A.2d 665, 670 (1966).

"Fundamentally, the question involved in both situations [*i.e.* admission and disciplinary proceedings] is the same—is the applicant for admission or the attorney sought to be disciplined a fit and proper person to be permitted to practice law, and that usually turns upon whether he has committed or is likely to continue to commit acts of moral turpitude. At the time of oral argument the attorney for respondent frankly conceded that the test for admission and for discipline is and should be the same. We agree with this concession." Hallinan v. Comm. of Bar Examiners, 65 Cal.2d 447, 453, 421 P.2d 76, 81, 55 Cal.Rptr. 228, 233 (1966).

3. "Proceedings to gain admission to the bar are for the purpose of protecting the public and the courts from the ministrations of persons unfit to practice the profession. Attorneys are officers of the court appointed to assist the court in the administration of justice. Into their hands are committed the property, the liberty and sometimes the lives of their clients. This commitment demands a high degree of intelligence, knowledge of the law, respect for its function in society, sound and faithful judgment and, above all else, integrity of character in private and professional conduct." In re Monaghan, 126 Vt. 53, 222 A.2d 665, 676 (1966) (Holden, C.J., dissenting).

4. "A bar composed of lawyers of good moral character is a worthy objective but it is unnecessary to sacrifice vital freedoms in order to obtain that goal. It is also important both to society and the bar itself that lawyers be unintimidated—free to think, speak, and act as members of an Independent Bar." Konigsberg v. State Bar, 353 U.S. 252, 273, 1 L. Ed. 2d 810, 825, 77 S. Ct. 722, 733 (1957).

5. *See* ABA CANON 29.

6. ABA CANON 28 designates certain conduct as unprofessional and then states that: "A duty to the public and to the profession devolves upon every member of the Bar having knowledge of such

practices upon the part of any practitioner immediately to inform thereof, to the end that the offender may be disbarred." ABA Canon 29 states a broader admonition: "Lawyers should expose without fear or favor before the proper tribunals corrupt or dishonest conduct in the profession."

7. "It is the obligation of the organized Bar and the individual lawyer to give unstinted cooperation and assistance to the highest court of the state in discharging its function and duty with respect to discipline and in purging the profession of the unworthy." *Report of the Special Committee on Disciplinary Procedures*, 80 A.B.A. Rep. 463, 470 (1955).

8. *Cf.* ABA Canon 32.

9. "We decline, on the present record, to disbar Mr. Sherman or to reprimand him—not because we condone his actions, but because, as heretofore indicated, we are concerned with whether he is mentally responsible for what he has done.

"The logic of the situation would seem to dictate the conclusion that, if he was mentally responsible for the conduct we have outlined, he should be disbarred; and, if he was not mentally responsible, he should not be permitted to practice law.

"However, the flaw in the logic is that he may have been mentally irresponsible [at the time of his offensive conduct] . . . , and, yet, have sufficiently improved in the almost two and one-half years intervening to be able to capably and competently represent his clients. . . .

. . . .

"We would make clear that we are satisfied that a case has been made against Mr. Sherman, warranting a refusal to permit him to further practice law in this state unless he can establish his mental irresponsibility at the time of the offenses charged. The burden of proof is upon him.

"If he establishes such mental irresponsibility, the burden is then upon him to establish his present capability to practice law." In re Sherman, 58 Wash. 2d 1, 6-7, 354 P.2d 888, 890 (1960), *cert. denied*, 371 U.S. 951, 9 L. Ed. 2d 499, 83 S. Ct. 506 (1963).

10. "This Court has the inherent power to revoke a license to practice law in this State, where such license was issued by this Court, and its issuance was procured by the fraudulent concealment, or by the false and fraudulent representation by the applicant of a fact which was manifestly material to the issuance of the license." North Carolina ex rel. Attorney General v. Gorson, 209 N.C. 320, 326, 183 S.E. 392, 395 (1936), *cert. denied*, 298 U.S. 662, 80 L. Ed. 1387, 56 S. Ct. 752 (1936).

See also Application of Patterson, 318 P.2d 907, 913 (Or. 1957), *cert. denied*, 356 U.S. 947, 2 L. Ed. 2d 822, 78 S. Ct. 795 (1958).

11. *See* ABA Canon 29.

12. In *ABA Opinion* 95 (1933), which held that a municipal attorney could not permit police officers to interview persons with claims against the municipality when the attorney knew the claimants to be represented by counsel, the Committee on Professional Ethics said:

"The law officer is, of course, responsible for the acts of those in his department who are under his supervision and control. *Opinion 85. In re Robinson*, 136 N.Y.S. 548 (affirmed 209 N. Y. 354-1912) held that it was a matter of disbarment for an attorney to adopt a general course of approving the unethical conduct of employees of his client, even though he did not actively participate therein.

"'. . . The attorney should not advise or sanction acts by his client which he himself should not do.' *Opinion 75.*"

13. "The most obvious non-professional ground for disbarment is conviction for a felony. Most states make conviction for a felony grounds for automatic disbarment. Some of these states, including New York, make disbarment mandatory upon conviction for *any* felony, while others require disbarment only for those felonies which involve moral turpitude. There are strong arguments that some felonies, such as involuntary manslaughter, reflect neither on an attorney's fitness, trustworthiness, nor competence and, therefore, should not be grounds for disbarment, but most states tend to disregard these arguments and, following the common law rule, make disbarment mandatory on conviction for any felony." Note, 43 Cornell L.Q. 489, 490 (1958).

"Some states treat conviction for misdemeanors as grounds for automatic disbarment. . . . However, the vast majority, accepting the common law rule, require that the misdemeanor involve moral turpitude. While the definition of moral turpitude may prove difficult, it seems only proper that those minor offenses which do not affect the attorney's fitness to continue in the profession should not be grounds for disbarment. A good example is an assault and battery conviction which would not involve moral turpitude unless done with malice and deliberation." *Id.* at 491.

"The term 'moral turpitude' has been used in the law for centuries. It has been the subject of many decisions by the courts but has never been clearly defined because of the nature of the term. Perhaps the best general definition of the term 'moral turpitude' is that it imparts an act of baseness, vileness or depravity in the duties which one person owes to another or to society in general, which is contrary to the usual, accepted and customary rule of right and duty which a person should follow. 58 C.J.S. at page

1201. Although offenses against revenue laws have been held to be crimes of moral turpitude, it has also been held that the attempt to evade the payment of taxes due to the government or any subdivision thereof, while wrong and unlawful, does not involve moral turpitude. 58 C.J.S. at page 1205." Comm. on Legal Ethics v. Scheer, 149 W. Va. 721, 726-27, 143 S.E.2d. 141, 145 (1965).

"The right and power to discipline an attorney, as one of its officers, is inherent in the court. . . . This power is not limited to those instances of misconduct wherein he has been employed, or has acted, in a professional capacity; but, on the contrary, this power may be exercised where his misconduct outside the scope of his professional relations shows him to be an unfit person to practice law." In re Wilson, 391 S.W.2d 914, 917-18 (Mo. 1965).

14. "It is a fair characterization of the lawyer's responsibility in our society that he stands 'as a shield,' to quote Devlin, J., in defense of right and to ward off wrong. From a profession charged with these responsibilities there must be exacted those qualities of truth-speaking, of a high sense of honor, of granite discretion, of the strictest observance of fiduciary responsibility, that have, throughout the centuries, been compendiously described as 'moral character.' " Schware v. Bd. of Bar Examiners, 353 U.S. 232, 247 1 L. Ed. 2d 796, 806, 77 S. Ct. 752, 761 (1957) (Frankfurter, J., concurring).

"Particularly applicable here is Rule 4.47 providing that 'A lawyer should always maintain his integrity; and shall not willfully commit any act against the interest of the public; nor shall he violate his duty to the courts or his clients; *nor shall he, by any misconduct, commit any offense against the laws of Missouri or the United States of America, which amounts to a crime involving acts done by him contrary to justice, honesty, modesty or good morals;* nor shall he be guilty of any other misconduct whereby, for the protection of the public and those charged with the administration of justice, he should no longer be entrusted with the duties and responsibilities belonging to the office of an attorney.' " In re Wilson, 391, S.W.2d 914, 917 (Mo. 1965).

15. *See* ABA Canon 29; *cf.* ABA Canon 28.

16. *Cf.* ABA Canons 28 and 29.

CANON 2

A Lawyer Should Assist the Legal Profession in Fulfilling Its Duty to Make Legal Counsel Available

ETHICAL CONSIDERATIONS

EC 2-1 The need of members of the public for legal services[1] is met only if they recognize their legal problems, appreciate the importance of seeking assistance,[2] and are able to obtain the services of acceptable legal counsel.[3] Hence, important functions of the legal profession are to educate laymen to recognize their problems, to facilitate the process of intelligent selection of lawyers, and to assist in making legal services fully available.[4]

Recognition of Legal Problems

EC 2-2 The legal profession should assist laypersons to recognize legal problems because such problems may not be self-revealing and often are not timely noticed. Therefore, lawyers should encourage and participate in educational and public relations programs concerning our legal system with particular reference to legal problems that frequently arise. Preparation of advertisements and professional articles for lay publications[5] and participation in seminars, lectures, and civic programs should be motivated by a desire to educate the public to an awareness of legal needs and to provide information relevant to the selection of the most appropriate counsel rather than to obtain publicity for particular lawyers. The problems of advertising on television require special consideration, due to the style, cost, and transitory nature of such media. If the interests of laypersons in receiving relevant lawyer advertising are not adequately served by print media and radio advertising, and if adequate safeguards to protect the public can reasonably be formulated, television advertising may serve a public interest.

EC 2-3 Whether a lawyer acts properly in volunteering in-person advice to a layperson to seek legal services depends upon the circumstances.[6]

The giving of advice that one should take legal action could well be in fulfillment of the duty of the legal profession to assist laypersons in recognizing legal problems.[7] The advice is proper only if motivated by a desire to protect one who does not recognize that he may have legal problems or who is ignorant of his legal rights or obligations. It is improper if motivated by a desire to obtain personal benefit, secure personal publicity, or cause legal action to be taken merely to harass or injure another. A lawyer should not initiate an in-person contact with a non-client, personally or through a representative, for the purpose of being retained to represent him for compensation.

EC 2-4 Since motivation is subjective and often difficult to judge, the motives of a lawyer who volunteers in-person advice likely to produce legal controversy may well be suspect if he receives professional employment or other benefits as a result.[8] A lawyer who volunteers in-person advice that one should obtain the services of a lawyer generally should not himself accept employment, compensation, or other benefit in connection with that matter. However, it is not improper for a lawyer to volunteer such advice and render resulting legal services to close friends, relatives, former clients (in regard to matters germane to former employment), and regular clients.[9]

EC 2-5 A lawyer who writes or speaks for the purpose of educating members of the public to recognize their legal problems should carefully refrain from giving or appearing to give a general solution applicable to all apparently similar individual problems,[10] since slight changes in fact situations may require a material variance in the applicable advice; otherwise, the public may be misled and misadvised. Talks and writings by lawyers for laypersons should caution them not to attempt to solve individual problems upon the basis of the information contained therein.[11]

Selection of a Lawyer

EC 2-6 Formerly a potential client usually knew the reputations of local lawyers for competency and integrity and therefore could select a practitioner in whom he had confidence. This traditional selection process worked well because it was initiated by the client and the choice was an informed one.

EC 2-7 Changed conditions, however, have seriously restricted the effectiveness of the traditional selection process. Often the reputations of lawyers are not sufficiently known to enable laypersons to make intelligent choices.[12] The law has become increasingly complex and specialized. Few lawyers are willing and competent to deal with every kind of legal matter, and many laypersons have difficulty in determining the competence of lawyers to render different types of legal services. The selection of legal counsel is particularly difficult for transients, persons moving into new areas, persons of limited education or means, and others who have little or no contact with lawyers.[13] Lack of information about the availability of lawyers, the qualifications of particular lawyers, and the expense of legal representation leads laypersons to avoid seeking legal advice.

EC 2-8 Selection of a lawyer by a layperson should be made on an informed basis. Advice and recommendation of third parties—relatives, friends, acquaintances, business associates, or other lawyers—and disclosure of relevant information about the lawyer and his practice may be helpful. A layperson is best served if the recommendation is disinterested and informed. In order that the recommendation be disinterested, a lawyer should not seek to influence another to recommend his employment. A lawyer should not compensate another person for recommending him, for influencing a prospective client to employ him, or to encourage future recommendations.[14] Advertisements and public communications, whether in law lists, telephone directories, newspapers, other forms of print media, television or radio, should be formulated to convey only information that is necessary to make an appropriate selection. Such information includes: (1) office information, such as, name, including name of law firm and names of professional associates; addresses; telephone numbers; credit card acceptability; fluency in foreign languages; and office hours; (2) relevant biographical information; (3) description of the practice, but only by using designations and definitions authorized by [the agency having jurisdiction of the subject under state law], for example, one or more fields of law in which the lawyer or law firm practices; a statement that practice is limited to one or more fields of law; and/or a statement that the lawyer or law firm specializes in a particular field of law practice, but only by using designations, definitions and standards authorized by [the agency having jurisdiction of the subject under state law]; and (4) permitted fee information. Self-laudation should be avoided.

Selection of a Lawyer: Lawyer Advertising

EC 2-9 The lack of sophistication on the part of many members of the public concerning legal services, the importance of the interests affected by the choice of a lawyer and prior experience with unrestricted lawyer advertising, require that special care be taken by lawyers to avoid misleading the public and to assure that the information set forth in any advertising is relevant to the selection of a lawyer. The lawyer must be mindful that the benefits of lawyer advertising depend upon its reliability and accuracy. Examples of information in lawyer advertising that would be deceptive include misstatements of fact, suggestions that the ingenuity or prior record of a lawyer rather than the justice of the claim are the principal factors likely to determine the result, inclusion of information irrelevant to selecting a lawyer, and representations concerning the quality of service, which cannot be measured or verified. Since lawyer advertising is calculated and not spontaneous, reasonable regulation of lawyer advertising designed to foster compliance with appropriate standards serves the public interest without impeding the flow of useful, meaningful, and relevant information to the public.

EC 2-10 A lawyer should ensure that the information contained in any advertising which the lawyer publishes, broadcasts or causes to be published or broadcast is relevant, is disseminated in an objective and understandable fashion, and would facilitate the prospective client's ability to compare the qualifications of the lawyers available to represent him. A lawyer should strive to communicate such information without undue emphasis upon style and advertising stratagems which serve to hinder rather than to facilitate intelligent selection of counsel. Because technological change is a recurrent feature of communications forms, and because perceptions of what is relevant in lawyer selection may change, lawyer advertising regulations should not be cast in rigid, unchangeable terms. Machinery is therefore available to advertisers and consumers for prompt consideration of proposals to change the rules governing lawyer advertising. The determination of any request for such change should depend upon whether the proposal is necessary in light of existing Code provisions, whether the proposal accords with standards of accuracy, reliability and truthfulness, and whether the proposal would facilitate informed selection of lawyers by potential consumers of legal services. Representatives of lawyers and consumers should be heard in addition to the applicant concerning any proposed change. Any change which is approved should be promulgated in the form of an amendment to the Code so that all lawyers practicing in the jurisdiction may avail themselves of its provisions.

EC 2-11 The name under which a lawyer conducts his practice may be a factor in the selection process.[15] The use of a trade name or an assumed name could mislead laypersons concerning the identity, responsibility, and status of those practicing thereunder.[16] Accordingly, a lawyer in private practice should practice only under a designation containing his own name, the name of a lawyer employing him, the name of one or more of the lawyers practicing in a partnership, or, if permitted by law, the name of a professional legal corporation, which should be clearly designated as such. For many years some law firms have used a firm name retaining one or more names of deceased or retired partners and such practice is not improper if the firm is a bona fide successor of a firm in which the deceased or retired person was a member, if the use of the name is authorized by law or by contract, and if the public is not misled thereby.[17] However, the name of a partner who withdraws from a firm but continues to practice law should be omitted from the firm name in order to avoid misleading the public.

EC 2-12 A lawyer occupying a judicial, legislative, or public executive or administrative position who has the right to practice law concurrently may allow his name to remain in the name of the firm if he actively continues to practice law as a member thereof. Otherwise, his name should be removed from the firm name,[18] and he should not be identified as a past or present member of

Model Code of Professional Responsibility

the firm; and he should not hold himself out as being a practicing lawyer.

EC 2-13 In order to avoid the possibility of misleading persons with whom he deals, a lawyer should be scrupulous in the representation of his professional status.[19] He should not hold himself out as being a partner or associate of a law firm if he is not one in fact,[20] and thus should not hold himself out as a partner or associate if he only shares offices with another lawyer.[21]

EC 2-14 In some instances a lawyer confines his practice to a particular field of law.[22] In the absence of state controls to insure the existence of special competence, a lawyer should not be permitted to hold himself out as a specialist or as having official recognition as a specialist, other than in the fields of admiralty, trademark, and patent law where a holding out as a specialist historically has been permitted. A lawyer may, however, indicate in permitted advertising, if it is factual, a limitation of his practice or one or more particular areas or fields of law in which he practices using designations and definitions authorized for that purpose by [the state agency having jurisdiction]. A lawyer practicing in a jurisdiction which certifies specialists must also be careful not to confuse laypersons as to his status. If a lawyer discloses areas of law in which he practices or to which he limits his practice, but is not certified in [the jurisdiction], he, and the designation authorized in [the jurisdiction], should avoid any implication that he is in fact certified.

EC 2-15 The legal profession has developed lawyer referral systems designed to aid individuals who are able to pay fees but need assistance in locating lawyers competent to handle their particular problems. Use of a lawyer referral system enables a layman to avoid an uninformed selection of a lawyer because such a system makes possible the employment of competent lawyers who have indicated an interest in the subject matter involved. Lawyers should support the principle of lawyer referral systems and should encourage the evolution of other ethical plans which aid in the selection of qualified counsel.

Financial Ability to Employ Counsel: Generally

EC 2-16 The legal profession cannot remain a viable force in fulfilling its role in our society unless its members receive adequate compensation for services rendered, and reasonable fees[23] should be charged in appropriate cases to clients able to pay them. Nevertheless, persons unable to pay all or a portion of a reasonable fee should be able to obtain necessary legal services,[24] and lawyers should support and participate in ethical activities designed to achieve that objective.[25]

Financial Ability to Employ Counsel: Persons Able to Pay Reasonable Fees

EC 2-17 The determination of a proper fee requires consideration of the interests of both client and lawyer.[26] A lawyer should not charge more than a reasonable fee,[27] for excessive cost of legal service would deter laymen from utilizing the legal system in protection of their rights. Furthermore, an excessive charge abuses the professional relationship between lawyer and client. On the other hand, adequate compensation is necessary in order to enable the lawyer to serve his client effectively and to preserve the integrity and independence of the profession.[28]

EC 2-18 The determination of the reasonableness of a fee requires consideration of all relevant circumstances,[29] including those stated in the Disciplinary Rules. The fees of a lawyer will vary according to many factors, including the time required, his experience, ability, and reputation, the nature of the employment, the responsibility involved, and the results obtained. It is a commendable and long-standing tradition of the bar that special consideration is given in the fixing of any fee for services rendered a brother lawyer or a member of his immediate family.

EC 2-19 As soon as feasible after a lawyer has been employed, it is desirable that he reach a clear agreement with his client as to the basis of the fee charges to be made. Such a course will not only prevent later misunderstanding but will also work for good relations between the lawyer and the client. It is usually beneficial to reduce to writing the understanding of the parties regarding the fee, particularly when it is contingent. A lawyer should be mindful that many persons who desire to employ him may have had little or no experience with fee charges of lawyers, and for this reason he should explain fully to such persons the reasons for the particular fee arrangement he proposes.

EC 2-20 Contingent fee arrangements[30] in civil cases have long been commonly accepted in the United States in proceedings to enforce claims. The historical bases of their acceptance are that (1) they often, and in a variety of circumstances, provide the only practical means by which one having a claim against another can economically afford, finance, and obtain the services of a competent lawyer to prosecute his claim, and (2) a successful prosecution of the claim produces a *res* out of which the fee can be paid.[31] Although a lawyer generally should decline to accept employment on a contingent fee basis by one who is able to pay a reasonable fixed fee, it is not necessarily improper for a lawyer, where justified by the particular circumstances of a case, to enter into a contingent fee contract in a civil case with any client who, after being fully informed of all relevant factors, desires that arrangement. Because of the human relationships involved and the unique character of the proceedings, contingent fee arrangements in domestic relation cases are rarely justified. In administrative agency proceedings contingent fee contracts should be governed by the same consideration as in other civil cases. Public policy properly condemns contingent fee arrangements in criminal cases, largely on the ground that legal services in criminal cases do not produce a *res* with which to pay the fee.

EC 2-21 A lawyer should not accept compensation or any thing of value incident to his employment or services from one other than his client without the knowledge and consent of his client after full disclosure.[32]

EC 2-22 Without the consent of his client, a lawyer should not associate in a particular matter another lawyer outside his firm. A fee may properly be divided between lawyers[33] properly associated if the division is in proportion to the services performed and the responsibility assumed by each lawyer[34] and if the total fee is reasonable.

EC 2-23 A lawyer should be zealous in his efforts to avoid controversies over fees with clients[35] and should attempt to resolve amicably any differences on the subject.[36] He should not sue a client for a fee unless necessary to prevent fraud or gross imposition by the client.[37]

Financial Ability to Employ Counsel: Persons Unable to Pay Reasonable Fees

EC 2-24 A layman whose financial ability is not sufficient to permit payment of any fee cannot obtain legal services, other than in cases where a contingent fee is appropriate, unless the services are provided for him. Even a person of moderate means may be unable to pay a reasonable fee which is large because of the complexity, novelty, or difficulty of the problem or similar factors.[38]

EC 2-25 Historically, the need for legal services of those unable to pay reasonable fees has been met in part by lawyers who donated their services or accepted court appointments on behalf of such individuals. The basic responsibility for providing legal services for those unable to pay ultimately rests upon the individual lawyer, and personal involvement in the problems of the disadvantaged can be one of the most rewarding experiences in the life of a lawyer. Every lawyer, regardless of professional prominence or professional workload, should find time to participate in serving the disadvantaged. The rendition of free legal services to those unable to pay reasonable fees continues to be an obligation of each lawyer, but the efforts of individual lawyers are often not enough to meet the need.[39] Thus it has been necessary for the profession to institute additional programs to provide legal services.[40] Accordingly, legal aid offices,[41] lawyer referral services, and other related programs have been developed, and others will be developed, by the profession.[42] Every lawyer should support all proper efforts to meet this need for legal services.[43]

Acceptance and Retention of Employment

EC 2-26 A lawyer is under no obligation to act as adviser or advocate for every person who may wish to become his client; but in furtherance of the objective of the bar to make legal services fully available, a lawyer should not lightly decline proffered employment. The fulfillment of this objective requires acceptance by a lawyer of his share of tendered employment which may be unattractive both to him and the bar generally.[44]

EC 2-27 History is replete with instances of distinguished and sacrificial services by lawyers who have represented unpopular clients and causes. Regardless of his personal feelings, a lawyer should not decline representation because a client or a cause is unpopular or community reaction is adverse.[45]

EC 2-28 The personal preference of a lawyer to avoid adversary alignment against judges, other lawyers,[46] public officials, or influential members of the community does not justify his rejection of tendered employment.

EC 2-29 When a lawyer is appointed by a court or requested by a bar association to undertake representation of a person unable to obtain counsel, whether for financial or other reasons, he should not seek to be excused from undertaking the representation except for compelling reasons.[47] Compelling reasons do not include such factors as the repugnance of the subject matter of the proceeding, the identity[48] or position of a person involved in the case, the belief of the lawyer that the defendant in a criminal proceeding is guilty,[49] or the belief of the lawyer regarding the merits of the civil case.[50]

EC 2-30 Employment should not be accepted by a lawyer when he is unable to render competent service[51] or when he knows or it is obvious that the person seeking to employ him desires to institute or maintain an action merely for the purpose of harassing or maliciously injuring another.[52] Likewise, a lawyer should decline employment if the intensity of his personal feeling, as distinguished from a community attitude, may impair his effective representation of a prospective client. If a lawyer knows a client has previously obtained counsel, he should not accept employment in the matter unless the other counsel approves[53] or withdraws, or the client terminates the prior employment.[54]

EC 2-31 Full availability of legal counsel requires both that persons be able to obtain counsel and that lawyers who undertake representation complete the work involved. Trial counsel for a convicted defendant should continue to represent his client by advising whether to take an appeal and, if the appeal is prosecuted, by representing him through the appeal unless new counsel is substituted or withdrawal is permitted by the appropriate court.

EC 2-32 A decision by a lawyer to withdraw should be made only on the basis of compelling circumstances,[55] and in a matter pending before a tribunal he must comply with the rules of the tribunal regarding withdrawal. A lawyer should not withdraw without considering carefully and endeavoring to minimize the possible adverse effect on the rights of his client and the possibility of prejudice to his client[56] as a result of his withdrawal. Even when he justifiably withdraws, a lawyer should protect the welfare of his client by giving due notice of his withdrawal,[57] suggesting employment of other counsel, delivering to the client all papers and property to which the client is entitled, cooperating with counsel subsequently employed, and otherwise endeavoring to minimize the possibility of harm. Further, he should refund to the client any compensation not earned during the employment.[58]

EC 2-33 As a part of the legal profession's commitment to the principle that high quality legal services should be available to all, attorneys are encouraged to cooperate with qualified legal assistance organizations providing prepaid legal services. Such participation should at all times be in accordance with the basic tenets of the profession: independence, integrity, competence and devotion to the interests of individual clients. An attorney so participating should make certain that his relationship with a qualified legal assistance organization in no way interferes with his independent, professional representation of the interests of the individual client. An attorney should avoid situations in which officials of the organization who are not lawyers attempt to direct attorneys concerning the manner in which legal services are performed for individual members, and should also avoid situations in which considerations of economy are given undue weight in determining the attorneys employed by an organization or the legal services to be performed for the member or beneficiary rather than competence and quality of service. An attorney interested in maintaining the historic traditions of the profession and preserving the function of a lawyer as a trusted and independent advisor to individual members of society should carefully assess such factors when accepting employment by, or otherwise participating in, a particular qualified legal assistance organization, and while so participating should adhere to the highest professional standards of effort and competence.

DISCIPLINARY RULES

DR 2-101 Publicity.

(A) A lawyer shall not, on behalf of himself, his partner, associate or any other lawyer affiliated with him or his firm, use or participate in the use of any form of public communication containing a false, fraudulent, misleading, deceptive, self-laudatory or unfair statement or claim.

(B) In order to facilitate the process of informed selection of a lawyer by potential consumers of legal services, a lawyer may publish or broadcast, subject to DR 2-103, the following information in print media distributed or over television or radio broadcast in the geographic area or areas in which the lawyer resides or maintains offices or in which a significant part of the lawyer's clientele resides, provided that the information disclosed by the lawyer in such publication or broadcast complies with DR 2-101(A), and is presented in a dignified manner:

   (1) Name, including name of law firm and names of professional associates; addresses and telephone numbers;
   (2) One or more fields of law in which the lawyer or law firm practices, a statement that practice is limited to one or more fields of law, or a statement that the lawyer or law firm specializes in a particular field of law practice, to the extent authorized under DR 2-105;
   (3) Date and place of birth;
   (4) Date and place of admission to the bar of state and federal courts;
   (5) Schools attended, with dates of graduation, degrees and other scholastic distinctions;
   (6) Public or quasi-public offices;
   (7) Military service;
   (8) Legal authorships;
   (9) Legal teaching positions;
   (10) Memberships, offices, and committee assignments, in bar associations;
   (11) Membership and offices in legal fraternities and legal societies;
   (12) Technical and professional licenses;
   (13) Memberships in scientific, technical and professional associations and societies;
   (14) Foreign language ability;
   (15) Names and addresses of bank references;
   (16) With their written consent, names of clients regularly represented;
   (17) Prepaid or group legal services programs in which the lawyer participates;
   (18) Whether credit cards or other credit arrangements are accepted;
   (19) Office and telephone answering service hours;
   (20) Fee for an initial consultation;
   (21) Availability upon request of a written schedule of fees and/or an estimate of the fee to be charged for specific services;
   (22) Contingent fee rates subject to DR 2-106(C), provided that the statement discloses whether percentages are computed before or after deduction of costs;
   (23) Range of fees for services, provided that the statement discloses that the specific fee within the range which will be charged will vary depending upon the particular matter to be handled for each client and the client is entitled without obligation to an estimate of the fee within the range likely to be charged, in print size equivalent to the largest print used in setting forth the fee information;
   (24) Hourly rate, provided that the statement discloses that the total fee charged will depend upon the number of hours which must be devoted to the particular matter to be handled for each client and the client is entitled to without obligation an estimate of the fee likely to be charged, in print size at least equivalent to the largest print used in setting forth the fee information;
   (25) Fixed fees for specific legal services,* the description of which would not be misunderstood or be deceptive, provided that the statement discloses that the quoted fee will be available only to clients whose matters fall into the services described and that the client is entitled without obligation to a specific estimate of the fee likely to be charged in print size at least equivalent to the largest print used in setting forth the fee information.

(C) Any person desiring to expand the information authorized for disclosure in DR 2-101(B), or to provide for its dissemination through other forums may apply to [the agency having jurisdiction under state law]. Any such application shall be served upon [the agencies having jurisdiction under state law over the regulation of the legal profession and consumer matters] who shall be heard, together with the applicant, on the issue of whether the proposal is necessary in light of the existing provisions of the Code, accords with standards of accuracy, reliability and truthfulness, and would facilitate the process of informed selection of lawyers by potential consumers of legal services. The relief granted in response to any such application shall be promulgated as an amendment to DR 2-101(B), universally applicable to all lawyers.**

*The agency having jurisdiction under state law may desire to issue appropriate guidelines defining "specific legal services."

**The agency having jurisdiction under state law should establish orderly and expeditious procedures for ruling on such applications.

(D) If the advertisement is communicated to the public over television or radio, it shall be prerecorded, approved for broadcast by the lawyer, and a recording of the actual transmission shall be retained by the lawyer.

(E) If a lawyer advertises a fee for a service, the lawyer must render that service for no more than the fee advertised.

(F) Unless otherwise specified in the advertisement if a lawyer publishes any fee information authorized under DR 2-101(B) in a publication that is published more frequently than one time per month, the lawyer shall be bound by any representation made therein for a period of not less than 30 days after such publication. If a lawyer publishes any fee information authorized under DR 2-101(B) in a publication that is published once a month or less frequently, he shall be bound by any representation made therein until the publication of the succeeding issue. If a lawyer publishes any fee information authorized under DR 2-101(B) in a publication which has no fixed date for publication of a succeeding issue, the lawyer shall be bound by any representation made therein for a reasonable period of time after publication but in no event less than one year.

(G) Unless otherwise specified, if a lawyer broadcasts any fee information authorized under DR 2-101(B), the lawyer shall be bound by any representation made therein for a period of not less than 30 days after such broadcast.

(H) This rule does not prohibit limited and dignified identification of a lawyer as a lawyer as well as by name:
 (1) In political advertisements when his professional status is germane to the political campaign or to a political issue.
 (2) In public notices when the name and profession of a lawyer are required or authorized by law or are reasonably pertinent for a purpose other than the attraction of potential clients.
 (3) In routine reports and announcements of a bona fide business, civic, professional, or political organization in which he serves as a director or officer.
 (4) In and on legal documents prepared by him.
 (5) In and on legal textbooks, treatises, and other legal publications, and in dignified advertisements thereof.

(I) A lawyer shall not compensate or give any thing of value to representatives of the press, radio, television, or other communication medium in anticipation of or in return for professional publicity in a news item.

DR 2-102 Professional Notices, Letterheads and Offices.

(A) A lawyer or law firm shall not use or participate in the use of professional cards, professional announcement cards, office signs, letterheads, or similar professional notices or devices, except that the following may be used if they are in dignified form:
 (1) A professional card of a lawyer identifying him by name and as a lawyer, and giving his addresses, telephone numbers, the name of his law firm, and any information permitted under DR 2-105. A professional card of a law firm may also give the names of members and associates. Such cards may be used for identification.
 (2) A brief professional announcement card stating new or changed associations or addresses, change of firm name, or similar matters pertaining to the professional offices of a lawyer or law firm, which may be mailed to lawyers, clients, former clients, personal friends, and relatives.[59]

It shall not state biographical data except to the extent reasonably necessary to identify the lawyer or to explain the change in his association, but it may state the immediate past position of the lawyer.[60] It may give the names and dates of predecessor firms in a continuing line of succession. It shall not state the nature of the practice except as permitted under DR 2-105.[61]

(3) A sign on or near the door of the office and in the building directory identifying the law office. The sign shall not state the nature of the practice, except as permitted under DR 2-105.

(4) A letterhead of a lawyer identifying him by name and as a lawyer, and giving his addresses, telephone numbers, the name of his law firm, associates and any information permitted under DR 2-105. A letterhead of a law firm may also give the names of members and associates,[62] and names and dates relating to deceased and retired members.[63] A lawyer may be designated "Of Counsel" on a letterhead if he has a continuing relationship with a lawyer or law firm, other than as a partner or associate. A lawyer or law firm may be designated as "General Counsel" or by similar professional reference on stationery of a client if he or the firm devotes a substantial amount of professional time in the representation of that client.[64] The letterhead of a law firm may give the names and dates of predecessor firms in a continuing line of succession.

(B) A lawyer in private practice shall not practice under a trade name, a name that is misleading as to the identity of the lawyer or lawyers practicing under such name, or a firm name containing names other than those of one or more of the lawyers in the firm, except that the name of a professional corporation or professional association may contain "P.C." or "P.A." or similar symbols indicating the nature of the organization, and if otherwise lawful a firm may use as, or continue to include in, its name the name or names of one or more deceased or retired members of the firm or of a predecessor firm in a continuing line of succession.[65] A lawyer who assumes a judicial, legislative, or public executive or administrative post or office shall not permit his name to remain in the name of a law firm or to be used in professional notices of the firm during any significant period in which he is not actively and regularly practicing law as a member of the firm,[66] and during such period other members of the firm shall not use his name in the firm name or in professional notices of the firm.[67]

(C) A lawyer shall not hold himself out as having a partnership with one or more other lawyers or professional corporations unless they are in fact partners.[68]

(D) A partnership shall not be formed or continued between or among lawyers licensed in different jurisdictions unless all enumerations of the members and associates of the firm on its letterhead and in other permissible listings make clear the jurisdictional limitations on those members and associates of the firm not licensed to practice in all listed jurisdictions;[69] however, the same firm name may be used in each jurisdiction.

(E) Nothing contained herein shall prohibit a lawyer from using or permitting the use of, in connection with his name, an earned degree or title derived therefrom indicating his training in the law.

DR 2-103 Recommendation of Professional Employment.[70]

(A) A lawyer shall not, except as authorized in DR 2-101(B), recommend employment as a private practitioner,[71] of himself, his partner, or associate to a layperson who has not sought his advice regarding employment of a lawyer.[72]

(B) A lawyer shall not compensate or give anything of value to a person or organization to recommend or secure his employment[73] by a client, or as a reward for having made a recommendation resulting in his employment[74] by a client, except that he may pay the usual and reasonable fees or dues charged by any of the organizations listed in DR 2-103(D).

(C) A lawyer shall not request a person or organization to recommend or promote the use of his services or those of his partner or associate, or any other lawyer affiliated with him or his firm, as a private practitioner,[75] except as authorized in DR 2-101, and except that

(1) He may request referrals from a lawyer referral service operated, sponsored, or

approved by a bar association and may pay its fees incident thereto.[76]

(2) He may cooperate with the legal service activities of any of the offices or organizations enumerated in DR 2-103(D)(1) through (4) and may perform legal services for those to whom he was recommended by it to do such work if:

  (a) The person to whom the recommendation is made is a member or beneficiary of such office or organization; and

  (b) The lawyer remains free to exercise his independent professional judgment on behalf of his client.

(D) A lawyer or his partner or associate or any other lawyer affiliated with him or his firm may be recommended, employed or paid by, or may cooperate with, one of the following offices or organizations that promote the use of his services or those of his partner or associate or any other lawyer affiliated with him or his firm if there is no interference with the exercise of independent professional judgment in behalf of his client:

(1) A legal aid office or public defender office:

  (a) Operated or sponsored by a duly accredited law school.

  (b) Operated or sponsored by a bona fide nonprofit community organization.

  (c) Operated or sponsored by a governmental agency.

  (d) Operated, sponsored, or approved by a bar association.[77]

(2) A military legal assistance office.

(3) A lawyer referral service operated, sponsored, or approved by a bar association.

(4) Any bona fide organization that recommends, furnishes or pays for legal services to its members or beneficiaries[78] provided the following conditions are satisfied:

  (a) Such organization, including any affiliate, is so organized and operated that no profit is derived by it from the rendition of legal services by lawyers, and that, if the organization is organized for profit, the legal services are not rendered by lawyers employed, directed, supervised or selected by it except in connection with matters where such organization bears ultimate liability of its member or beneficiary.

  (b) Neither the lawyer, nor his partner, nor associate, nor any other lawyer affiliated with him or his firm, nor any non-lawyer, shall have initiated or promoted such organization for the primary purpose of providing financial or other benefit to such lawyer, partner, associate or affiliated lawyer.

  (c) Such organization is not operated for the purpose of procuring legal work or financial benefit for any lawyer as a private practitioner outside of the legal services program of the organization.

  (d) The member or beneficiary to whom the legal services are furnished, and not such organization, is recognized as the client of the lawyer in the matter.

  (e) Any member or beneficiary who is entitled to have legal services furnished or paid for by the organization may, if such member or beneficiary so desires, select counsel other than that furnished, selected or approved by the organization for the particular matter involved; and the legal service plan of such organization provides appropriate relief for any member or beneficiary who asserts a claim that representation by counsel furnished, selected or approved would be unethical, improper or inadequate under the circumstances of the matter involved and the plan provides an appropriate procedure for seeking such relief.

  (f) The lawyer does not know or have cause to know that such organization is in violation of applicable laws, rules of court and other legal requirements that govern its legal service operations.

  (g) Such organization has filed with the appropriate disciplinary authority at least annually a report with respect to its legal service plan, if any, showing its terms, its schedule of benefits, its subscription charges, agreements with counsel, and financial results of its legal service activities or, if it has failed to do so, the lawyer does not know or have cause to know of such failure.

(E) A lawyer shall not accept employment when he knows or it is obvious that the person who seeks his services does so as a result of conduct prohibited under this Disciplinary Rule.

DR 2-104 Suggestion of Need of Legal Services.[79,80]

(A) A lawyer who has given in-person unsolicited advice to a layperson that he should obtain counsel or take legal action shall not accept employment resulting from that advice,[81] except that:

(1) A lawyer may accept employment by a close friend, relative, former client (if the advice is germane to the former employment), or one whom the lawyer reasonably believes to be a client.[82]

(2) A lawyer may accept employment that results from his participation in activities designed to educate laypersons to recognize legal problems to make intelligent selection of counsel, or to utilize available legal services if such activities are conducted or sponsored by a qualified legal assistance organization.

(3) A lawyer who is recommended, furnished or paid by a qualified legal assistance organization enumerated in DR 2-103 (D)(1) through (4) may represent a member or beneficiary thereof, to the extent and under the conditions prescribed therein.

(4) Without affecting his right to accept employment, a lawyer may speak publicly or write for publication on legal topics[83] so long as he does not emphasize his own professional experience or reputation and does not undertake to give individual advice.

(5) If success in asserting rights or defenses of his client in litigation in the nature of a class action is dependent upon the joinder of others, a lawyer may accept, but shall not seek, employment from those contacted for the purpose of obtaining their joinder.[84]

DR 2-105 Limitation of Practice.[85]

(A) A lawyer shall not hold himself out publicly as a specialist, as practicing in certain areas of law or as limiting his practice permitted under DR 2-101(B), except as follows:

(1) A lawyer admitted to practice before the United States Patent and Trademark Office may use the designation "Patents," "Patent Attorney," "Patent Lawyer," or "Registered Patent Attorney" or any combination of those terms, on his letterhead and office sign.

(2) A lawyer who publicly discloses fields of law in which the lawyer or the law firm practices or states that his practice is limited to one or more fields of law shall do so by using designations and definitions authorized and approved by [the agency having jurisdiction of the subject under state law].

(3) A lawyer who is certified as a specialist in a particular field of law or law practice by [the authority having jurisdiction under state law over the subject of specialization by lawyers] may hold himself out as such, but only in accordance with the rules prescribed by that authority.[86]

DR 2-106 Fees for Legal Services.[87]

(A) A lawyer shall not enter into an agreement for, charge, or collect an illegal or clearly excessive fee.[88]

(B) A fee is clearly excessive when, after a review of the facts, a lawyer of ordinary prudence would be left with a definite and firm conviction that the fee is in excess of a reasonable fee. Factors to be considered as guides in determining the reasonableness of a fee include the following:

(1) The time and labor required, the novelty and difficulty of the questions involved and the skill requisite to perform the legal service properly.

(2) The likelihood, if apparent to the client, that the acceptance of the particular employment will preclude other employment by the lawyer.

(3) The fee customarily charged in the locality for similar legal services.

(4) The amount involved and the results obtained.

(5) The time limitations imposed by the client or by the circumstances.

(6) The nature and length of the professional relationship with the client.
(7) The experience, reputation, and ability of the lawyer or lawyers performing the services.
(8) Whether the fee is fixed or contingent.[89]

(C) A lawyer shall not enter into an arrangement for, charge, or collect a contingent fee for representing a defendant in a criminal case.[90]

DR 2-107 Division of Fees Among Lawyers.
(A) A lawyer shall not divide a fee for legal services with another lawyer who is not a partner in or associate of his law firm or law office, unless:
(1) The client consents to employment of the other lawyer after a full disclosure that a division of fees will be made.
(2) The division is made in proportion to the services performed and responsibility assumed by each.[91]
(3) The total fee of the lawyers does not clearly exceed reasonable compensation for all legal services they rendered the client.[92]

(B) This Disciplinary Rule does not prohibit payment to a former partner or associate pursuant to a separation or retirement agreement.

DR 2-108 Agreements Restricting the Practice of a Lawyer.
(A) A lawyer shall not be a party to or participate in a partnership or employment agreement with another lawyer that restricts the right of a lawyer to practice law after the termination of a relationship created by the agreement, except as a condition to payment of retirement benefits.[93]
(B) In connection with the settlement of a controversy or suit, a lawyer shall not enter into an agreement that restricts his right to practice law.

DR 2-109 Acceptance of Employment.
(A) A lawyer shall not accept employment on behalf of a person if he knows or it is obvious that such person wishes to:
(1) Bring a legal action, conduct a defense, or assert a position in litigation, or otherwise have steps taken for him, merely for the purpose of harassing or maliciously injuring any person.[94]
(2) Present a claim or defense in litigation that is not warranted under existing law, unless it can be supported by good faith argument for an extension, modification, or reversal of existing law.

DR 2-110 Withdrawal from Employment.[95]
(A) In general.
(1) If permission for withdrawal from employment is required by the rules of a tribunal, a lawyer shall not withdraw from employment in a proceeding before that tribunal without its permission.
(2) In any event, a lawyer shall not withdraw from employment until he has taken reasonable steps to avoid foreseeable prejudice to the rights of his client, including giving due notice to his client, allowing time for employment of other counsel, delivering to the client all papers and property to which the client is entitled, and complying with applicable laws and rules.
(3) A lawyer who withdraws from employment shall refund promptly any part of a fee paid in advance that has not been earned.

(B) Mandatory withdrawal.
A lawyer representing a client before a tribunal, with its permission if required by its rules, shall withdraw from employment, and a lawyer representing a client in other matters shall withdraw from employment if:
(1) He knows or it is obvious that his client is bringing the legal action, conducting the defense, or asserting a position in the litigation, or is otherwise having steps taken for him, merely for the purpose of harassing or maliciously injuring any person.
(2) He knows or it is obvious that his continued employment will result in violation of a Disciplinary Rule.[96]
(3) His mental or physical condition renders it unreasonably difficult for him to carry out the employment effectively.
(4) He is discharged by his client.

(C) Permissive withdrawal.[97]
If DR 2-110(B) is not applicable, a lawyer may not request permission to withdraw in matters pending before a tribunal, and may not withdraw in other matters, unless such request or such withdrawal is because:

(1) His client:
   (a) Insists upon presenting a claim or defense that is not warranted under existing law and cannot be supported by good faith argument for an extension, modification, or reversal of existing law.[98]
   (b) Personally seeks to pursue an illegal course of conduct.
   (c) Insists that the lawyer pursue a course of conduct that is illegal or that is prohibited under the Disciplinary Rules.
   (d) By other conduct renders it unreasonably difficult for the lawyer to carry out his employment effectively.
   (e) Insists, in a matter not pending before a tribunal, that the lawyer engage in conduct that is contrary to the judgment and advice of the lawyer but not prohibited under the Disciplinary Rules.
   (f) Deliberately disregards an agreement or obligation to the lawyer as to expenses or fees.
(2) His continued employment is likely to result in a violation of a Disciplinary Rule.
(3) His inability to work with co-counsel indicates that the best interests of the client likely will be served by withdrawal.
(4) His mental or physical condition renders it difficult for him to carry out the employment effectively.
(5) His client knowingly and freely assents to termination of his employment.
(6) He believes in good faith, in a proceeding pending before a tribunal, that the tribunal will find the existence of other good cause for withdrawal.

NOTES

1. "Men have need for more than a system of law; they have need for a system of law which functions, and that means they have need for lawyers." Cheatham, *The Lawyer's Role and Surroundings*, 25 Rocky Mt. L. Rev. 405 (1953).

2. "Law is not self-applying; men must apply and utilize it in concrete cases. But the ordinary man is incapable. He cannot know the principles of law or the rules guiding the machinery of law administration; he does not know how to formulate his desires with precision and to put them into writing; he is ineffective in the presentation of his claims." *Id.*

3. "This need [to provide legal services] was recognized by . . . Mr. [Lewis F.] Powell [Jr., President, American Bar Association, 1963-64], who said: 'Looking at contemporary America realistically, we must admit that despite all our efforts to date (and these have not been insignificant), far too many persons are not able to obtain equal justice under law. This usually results because their poverty or their ignorance has prevented them from obtaining legal counsel.'" Address by E. Clinton Bamberger, Association of American Law Schools 1965 Annual Meeting, Dec. 28, 1965, in Proceedings, Part II, 1965, 61, 63-64 (1965).

"A wide gap separates the need for legal services and its satisfaction, as numerous studies reveal. Looked at from the side of the layman, one reason for the gap is poverty and the consequent inability to pay legal fees. Another set of reasons is ignorance of the need for and the value of legal services, and ignorance of where to find a dependable lawyer. There is fear of the mysterious processes and delays of the law, and there is fear of overreaching and overcharging by lawyers, a fear stimulated by the occasional exposure of shysters." Cheatham, *Availability of Legal Services: The Responsibility of the Individual Lawyer and of the Organized Bar*, 12 U.C.L.A. L. Rev. 438 (1965).

4. "It is not only the right but the duty of the profession as a whole to utilize such methods as may be developed to bring the services of its members to those who need them, so long as this can be done ethically and with dignity." *ABA Opinion* 320 (1968).

"[T]here is a responsibility on the bar to make legal services available to those who need them. The maxim, 'privilege brings responsibilities,' can be expanded to read, exclusive privilege to render public service brings responsibility to assure that the service is available to those in need of it." Cheatham, *Availability of Legal Services: The Responsibility of the Individual Lawyer and of the Organized Bar*, 12 U.C.L.A. L. Rev. 438, 443 (1965).

"The obligation to provide legal services for those actually caught up in litigation carries with it the obligation to make preventive legal advice accessible to all. It is among those unaccustomed to business affairs and fearful of the ways of the law that such advice is often most needed. If it is not received in time, the most valiant and skillful representation in court may come too late." *Professional Responsibility: Report of the Joint Conference,* 44 A.B.A.J. 1159, 1216 (1958).

5. "A lawyer may with propriety write articles for publications in which he gives information upon the law. . . ." ABA CANON 40.

6. *See* ABA CANON 28.

7. This question can assume constitutional dimensions: "We meet at the outset the contention that "solicitation" is wholly outside the area of freedoms protected by the First Amendment. To this contention there are two answers. The first is that a State cannot foreclose the exercise of constitutional rights by mere labels. The second is that abstract discussion is not the only species of communication which the Constitution protects; the First Amendment also protects vigorous advocacy, certainly of lawful ends, against governmental intrusion. . . .

. . . .

"However valid may be Virginia's interest in regulating the traditionally illegal practice of barratry, maintenance and champerty, that interest does not justify the prohibition of the NAACP activities disclosed by this record. Malicious intent was of the essence of the common-law offenses of fomenting or stirring up litigation. And whatever may be or may have been true of suits against governments in other countries, the exercise in our own, as in this case of First Amendment rights to enforce Constitutional rights through litigation, as a matter of law, cannot be deemed malicious." NAACP v. Button, 371 U.S. 415, 429, 439-40, 9 L. Ed. 2d 405, 415-16, 422, 83 S. Ct. 328, 336, 341 (1963).

8. It is disreputable for an attorney to breed litigation by seeking out those who have claims for personal injuries or other grounds of action in order to secure them as clients, or to employ agents or runners, or to reward those who bring or influence the bringing of business to his office. . . . Moreover, it tends quite easily to the institution of baseless litigation and the manufacture of perjured testimony. From early times, this danger has been recognized in the law by the condemnation of the crime of common barratry, or the stirring up of suits or quarrels between individuals at law or otherwise." In re Ades, 6 F.Supp. 467, 474-75 (D. Mary. 1934).

9. "Rule 2.

" §a. . . .

"[A] member of the State Bar shall not solicit professional employment by

"(1) Volunteering counsel or advice except where ties of blood relationship or trust make it appropriate." CAL. BUSINESS AND PROFESSIONS CODE §6076 (West 1962).

10. "*Rule 18* . . . A member of the State Bar shall not advise inquirers or render opinions to them through or in connection with a newspaper, radio or other publicity medium of any kind in respect to their specific legal problems, whether or not such attorney shall be compensated for his services." CAL. BUSINESS AND PROFESSIONS CODE §6076 (West 1962).

11. "In any case where a member might well apply the advice given in the opinion to his individual affairs, the lawyer rendering the opinion [concerning problems common to members of an association and distributed to the members through a periodic bulletin] should specifically state that this opinion should not be relied on by any member as a basis for handling his individual affairs, but that in every case he should consult his counsel. In the publication of the opinion the association should make a similar statement." *ABA Opinion* 273 (1946).

12. "A group of recent interrelated changes bears directly on the availability of legal services. . . . [One] change is the constantly accelerating urbanization of the country and the decline of personal and neighborhood knowledge of whom to retain as a professional man." Cheatham, *Availability of Legal Services: The Responsibility of the Individual Lawyer and of the Organized Bar,* 12 U.C.L.A. L. REV. 438, 440 (1965).

13. *Cf.* Cheatham, *A Lawyer When Needed: Legal Services for the Middle Classes,* 63 COLUM. L. REV. 973, 974 (1963).

14. *See* ABA CANON 28.

15. *Cf. ABA Opinion* 303 (1961).

16. *See* ABA CANON 33.

17. *Id.*

"The continued use of a firm name by one or more surviving partners after the death of a member of the firm whose name is in the firm title is expressly permitted by the Canons of Ethics. The reason for this is that all of the partners have by their joint and several efforts over a period of years contributed to the good will attached to the firm name. In the case of a firm having widespread connections, this good will is disturbed by a change in firm name every time a name partner dies, and that reflects a loss in some degree of the good will to the building up of which the surviving partners have contributed their time, skill and labor through a period of years. To avoid this loss the firm name is continued, and to meet the requirements of the Canon the individuals constituting the firm from time to time are listed." *ABA Opinion* 267 (1945).

"Accepted local custom in New York recognizes that the name of a law firm does not necessarily identify the individual members of the firm, and hence the continued use of a firm name after the death of one or more partners is not a deception and is permissible. . . . The continued use of a deceased partner's name in the firm title is not affected by the fact that another partner withdraws from the firm and his name is dropped, or the name of the new partner is added to the firm name." *Opinion* No. 45, Committee on Professional Ethics, New York State Bar Ass'n, 39 N.Y.St.B.J. 455 (1967).

Cf. ABA Opinion 258 (1943).

18. *Cf.* ABA Canon 33 and *ABA Opinion* 315 (1965).

19. *Cf. ABA Opinions* 283 (1950) and 81 (1932).

20. *See ABA Opinion* 316 (1967).

21. "The word 'associates' has a variety of meanings. Principally through custom the word when used on the letterheads of law firms has come to be regarded as describing those who are employees of the firm. Because the word has acquired this special significance in connection with the practice of the law the use of the word to describe lawyer relationships other than employer-employee is likely to be misleading." In re Sussman and Tanner, 241 Ore. 246, 248, 405 P.2d 355, 356 (1965).

According to *ABA Opinion* 310 (1963), use of the term "associates" would be misleading in two situations: (1) where two lawyers are partners and they share both responsibility and liability for the partnership; and (2) where two lawyers practice separately, sharing no responsibility or liability, and only share a suite of offices and some costs.

22. "For a long time, many lawyers have, of necessity, limited their practice to certain branches of law. The increasing complexity of the law and the demand of the public for more expertness on the part of the lawyer has, in the past few years—particularly in the last ten years—brought about specialization on an increasing scale." *Report of the Special Committee on Specialization and Specialized Legal Services*, 79 A.B.A. Rep. 582, 584 (1954).

23. *See* ABA Canon 12.

24. *Cf.* ABA Canon 12.

25. "If there is any fundamental proposition of government on which all would agree, it is that one of the highest goals of society must be to achieve and maintain equality before the law. Yet this ideal remains an empty form of words unless the legal profession is ready to provide adequate representation for those unable to pay the usual fees." *Professional Representation: Report of the Joint Conference*, 44 A.B.A.J. 1159, 1216 (1958).

26. *See* ABA Canon 12.

27. *Cf.* ABA Canon 12.

28. "When members of the Bar are induced to render legal services for inadequate compensation, as a consequence the quality of the service rendered may be lowered, the welfare of the profession injured and the administration of justice made less efficient." *ABA Opinion* 302 (1961).

Cf. ABA Opinion 307 (1962).

29. *See* ABA Canon 12.

30. *See* ABA Canon 13; *see also* Mackinnon, Contingent Fees for Legal Services (1964) (A report of the American Bar Foundation).

"A contract for a reasonable contingent fee where sanctioned by law is permitted by *Canon 13*, but the client must remain responsible to the lawyer for expenses advanced by the latter. 'There is to be no barter of the privilege of prosecuting a cause for gain in exchange for the promise of the attorney to prosecute at his own expense.' (Cardozo, C. J. in Matter of Gilman, 251 N.Y. 265, 270-271.)" *ABA Opinion* 246 (1942).

31. *See* Comment, *Providing Legal Services for the Middle Class in Civil Matters: The Problem, the Duty and a Solution*, 26 U. Pitt. L. Rev. 811, 829 (1965).

32. *See* ABA Canon 38.

"Of course, as . . . [Informal Opinion 679] points out, there must be full disclosure of the arrangement [that an entity other than the client pays the attorney's fee] by the attorney to the client. . . ." *ABA Opinion* 320 (1968).

33. "Only lawyers may share in . . . a division of fees, but . . . it is not necessary that both lawyers be admitted to practice in the same state, so long as the division was based on the division of services or responsibility." *ABA Opinion* 316 (1967).

34. *See* ABA Canon 34.

"We adhere to our previous rulings that where a lawyer merely brings about the employment of another lawyer *but renders no service and assumes no responsibility in the matter,* a division of the latter's fee is improper. *(Opinions 18 and 153).*

"It is assumed that the bar, generally, understands what acts or conduct of a lawyer may constitute 'services' to a client within the intendment of *Canon 12*. Such acts or conduct invariably, if not always, involve 'responsibility' on the part of the lawyer, whether the word 'responsibility' be construed to denote the possible resultant legal or moral liability on the part of the lawyer to the client or to others, or the onus of deciding what should or should not be done in behalf of the client. The word 'services' in *Canon 12* must be construed in this broad sense and may apply to the selection and retainer of associate counsel as well as to other acts or conduct in the client's behalf." *ABA Opinion* 204 (1940).

35. *See* ABA Canon 14.

36. *Cf. ABA Opinion* 320 (1968).

37. *See* ABA Canon 14.

"Ours is a learned profession, not a mere moneygetting trade. . . . Suits to collect fees should be avoided. Only where the circumstances imperatively require, should resort be had to a suit to compel payment. And where a lawyer does resort to a suit to enforce payment of fees which involves a disclosure, he should carefully avoid any disclosure not clearly necessary to obtaining or defending his rights." *ABA Opinion* 250 (1943).

But cf. ABA Opinion 320 (1968).

38. "As a society increases in size, sophistication and technology, the body of laws which is required to control that society also increases in size, scope and complexity. With this growth, the law directly affects more and more facets of individual behavior, creating an expanding need for legal services on the part of the individual members of the society. . . . As legal guidance in social and commercial behavior increasingly becomes necessary, there will come a concurrent demand from the layman that such guidance be made available to him. This demand will not come from those who are able to employ the best legal talent, nor from those who can obtain legal assistance at little or no cost. It will come from the large 'forgotten middle income class,' who can neither afford to pay proportionately large fees nor qualify for ultra-low-cost services. The legal profession must recognize this inevitable demand and consider methods whereby it can be satisfied. If the profession fails to provide such methods, the laity will." Comment, *Providing Legal Services for the Middle Class in Civil Matters: The Problem, the Duty and a Solution,* 26 U. PITT. L. REV. 811, 811-12 (1965).

"The issue is not whether we shall do something or do nothing. The demand for ordinary everyday legal justice is so great and the moral nature of the demand is so strong that the issue has become whether we devise, maintain, and support suitable agencies able to satisfy the demand or, by our own default, force the government to take over the job, supplant us, and ultimately dominate us." Smith, *Legal Service Offices for Persons of Moderate Means,* 1949 WIS. L. REV. 416, 418 (1949).

39. "Lawyers have peculiar responsibilities for the just administration of the law, and these responsibilities include providing advice and representation for needy persons. To a degree not always appreciated by the public at large, the bar has performed these obligations with zeal and devotion. The Committee is persuaded, however, that a system of justice that attempts, in mid-twentieth century America, to meet the needs of the financially incapacitated accused through primary or exclusive reliance on the uncompensated services of counsel will prove unsuccessful and inadequate. . . . A system of adequate representation, therefore, should be structured and financed in a manner reflecting its public importance. . . . We believe that fees for private appointed counsel should be set by the court within maximum limits established by the statute." REPORT OF THE ATT'Y GEN'S COMM. ON POVERTY AND THE ADMINISTRATION OF CRIMINAL JUSTICE 41-43 (1963).

40. "At present this representation [of those unable to pay usual fees] is being supplied in some measure through the spontaneous generosity of individual lawyers, through legal aid societies, and increasingly through the organized efforts of the Bar. If those who stand in need of this service known of its availability and their need is in fact adequately met, the precise mechanism by which this service is provided becomes of secondary importance. It is of great importance, however, that both the impulse to render this service, and the plan for making that impulse effective, should arise within the legal profession itself." *Professional Responsibility: Report of the Joint Conference,* 44 A.B.A.J. 1159, 1216 (1958).

41. "Free legal clinics carried on by the organized bar are not ethically objectionable. On the contrary, they serve a very worthwhile purpose and should be encouraged." *ABA Opinion* 191 (1939).

42. "Whereas the American Bar Association believes that it is a fundamental duty of the bar to see to it that all persons requiring legal advice be able to attain it, irrespective of their economic status . . . .

"Resolved, that the Association approves and sponsors the setting up by state and local bar associations of lawyer referral plans and low-cost legal service methods for the purpose of dealing with cases of persons who might not otherwise have the benefit of legal advice . . . ." *Proceedings of the House of Delegates of the American Bar Association,* Oct. 30, 1946, 71 A.B.A. REP. 103, 109-10 (1946).

43. "The defense of indigent citizens, without compensation, is carried on throughout the country by lawyers representing legal aid societies, not only with the approval, but with the commendation of those acquainted with the work. Not infrequently services are rendered out of sympathy or for other philanthropic reasons, by individual lawyers who do not represent legal aid societies. There is nothing whatever in the Canons to prevent a lawyer from performing such an act, nor should there be." *ABA Opinion* 148 (1935).

44. *But cf.* ABA CANON 31.

45. "One of the highest services the lawyer can render to society is to appear in court on behalf of clients whose causes are in disfavor with the general public." *Professional Responsibility: Report of the Joint Conference,* 44 A.B.A.J. 1159, 1216 (1958).

One author proposes the following proposition to be included in "A Proper Oath for Advocates": "I recognize that it is sometimes difficult for clients with unpopular causes to obtain proper legal representation. I will do all that I can to assure that the client with the unpopular cause is properly represented, and that the lawyer representing such a client receives credit from and support of the bar for handling such a matter." Thode, *The Ethical Standard for the Advocate,* 39 TEXAS L. REV. 575, 592 (1961).

"§6068. . . . It is the duty of an attorney:

. . . .

"(h) Never to reject, for any consideration personal to himself, the cause of the defenseless or the oppressed." CAL. BUSINESS AND PROFESSIONS CODE §6068 (West 1962). Virtually the same language is found in the Oregon statutes at ORE. REV. STATS. Ch. 9 §9.460(8).

See Rostow, *The Lawyer and His Client,* 48 A.B.A.J. 25 and 146 (1962).

46. *See* ABA CANONS 7 and 29.

"We are of the opinion that it is not professionally improper for a lawyer to accept employment to compel another lawyer to honor the just claim of a layman. On the contrary, it is highly proper that he do so. Unfortunately, there appears to be a widespread feeling among laymen that it is difficult, if not impossible, to obtain justice when they have claims against members of the Bar because other lawyers will not accept employment to proceed against them. The honor of the profession, whose members proudly style themselves officers of the court, must surely be sullied if its members bind themselves by custom to refrain from enforcing just claims of laymen against lawyers." *ABA Opinion* 144 (1935).

47. ABA CANON 4 uses a slightly different test, saying, "A lawyer assigned as counsel for an indigent prisoner ought not to ask to be excused for any trivial reason. . . ."

48. *Cf.* ABA CANON 7.

49. *See* ABA CANON 5.

50. Dr. Johnson's reply to Boswell upon being asked what he thought of "supporting a cause which you know to be bad" was: "Sir, you do not know it to be good or bad till the Judge determines it. I have said that you are to state facts fairly; so that your thinking, or what you call knowing, a cause to be bad, must be from reasoning, must be from supposing your arguments to be weak and inconclusive. But, Sir, that is not enough. An argument which does not convince yourself, may convince the Judge to whom you urge it: and if it does convince him, why, then, Sir, you are wrong, and he is right." 2 Boswell, THE LIFE OF JOHNSON 47-48 (Hill ed. 1887).

51. "The lawyer deciding whether to undertake a case must be able to judge objectively whether he is capable of handling it and whether he can assume its burdens without prejudice to previous commitments. . . ." *Professional Responsibility: Report of the Joint Conference,* 44 A.B.A.J. 1158, 1218 (1958).

52. "The lawyer must decline to conduct a civil cause or to make a defense when convinced that it is intended merely to harass or to injure the opposite party or to work oppression or wrong." ABA CANON 30.

53. *See* ABA CANON 7.

54. *Id.*

"From the facts stated we assume that the client has discharged the first attorney and given notice of the discharge. Such being the case, the second attorney may properly accept employment. *Canon 7; Opinions 10, 130, 149." ABA Opinion* 209 (1941).

55. *See* ABA CANON 44.

"I will carefully consider, before taking a case, whether it appears that I can fully represent the client within the framework of law. If the decision is in the affirmative, then it will take extreme circumstances to cause me to decide later that I cannot so represent him." Thode, *The Ethical Standard for the Advocate,* 39 TEXAS L. REV. 575, 592 (1961) (from "A Proper Oath for Advocates").

56. *ABA Opinion* 314 (1965) held that a lawyer should not disassociate himself from a cause when "it is obvious that the very act of disassociation would have the effect of violating *Canon 37.*"

57. ABA CANON 44 enumerates instances in which ". . . the lawyer may be warranted in withdrawing on due notice to the client, allowing him time to employ another lawyer."

58. *See* ABA CANON 44.

59. *See ABA Opinion* 301 (1961).

60. "[I]t has become commonplace for many lawyers to participate in government service; to deny them the right, upon their return to private practice, to refer to their prior employment in a brief and dignified manner, would place an undue limitation upon a large element of our profession. It is entirely proper for a member of the profession to explain his absence from private practice, where such is the primary purpose of the announcement, by a brief and dignified reference to the prior employment.

". . . [A]ny such announcement should be limited to the immediate past connection of the lawyer with the government, made upon his leaving that position to enter private practice." *ABA Opinion* 301 (1961).

61. *See ABA Opinion* 251 (1943).

62. "Those lawyers who are working for an individual lawyer or a law firm may be designated on the letterhead and in other appropriate places as 'associates'." *ABA Opinion* 310 (1963).

63. *See* ABA CANON 33.

64. *But see ABA Opinion* 285 (1951).

65. *See* ABA Canon 33; *cf. ABA Opinions* 318 (1967), 267 (1945), 219 (1941), 208 (1940), 192 (1939), 97 (1933), and 6 (1925).

66. *ABA Opinion* 318 (1967) held, "anything to the contrary in Formal Opinion 315 or in the other opinions cited notwithstanding that: "Where a partner whose name appears in the name of a law firm is elected or appointed to high local, state or federal office, which office he intends to occupy only temporarily, at the end of which time he intends to return to his position with the firm, and provided that he is not precluded by holding such office from engaging in the practice of law and does not in fact sever his relationship with the firm but only takes a leave of absence, and provided that there is no local law, statute or custom to the contrary, his name may be retained in the firm name during his term or terms of office, but only if proper precautions are taken not to mislead the public as to his degree of participation in the firm's affairs."

Cf. ABA Opinion 143 (1935), New York County Opinion 67, and New York City Opinions 36 and 798; *but cf. ABA Opinion* 192 (1939) and Michigan Opinion 164.

67. *Cf.* ABA Canon 33.

68. *See ABA Opinion* 277 (1948); *cf.* ABA Canon 33 and *ABA Opinions* 318 (1967), 126 (1935), 115 (1934), and 106 (1934).

69. *See ABA Opinions* 318 (1967) and 316 (1967); *cf.* ABA Canon 33.

70. *Cf.* ABA Canons 28.

71. "We think it clear that a lawyer's seeking employment in an ordinary law office, or appointment to a civil service position, is not prohibited by . . . [Canon 27]." *ABA Opinion* 197 (1939).

72. "[A] lawyer may not seek from persons not his clients the opportunity to perform . . . a [legal] check-up." ABA *Opinion* 307 (1962).

73. *Cf. ABA Opinion* 78 (1932).

74. " 'No financial connection of any kind between the Brotherhood and any lawyer is permissible. No lawyer can properly pay any amount whatsoever to the Brotherhood or any of its departments, officers or members as compensation, reimbursement of expenses or gratuity in connection with the procurement of a case.' " In re Brotherhood of R. R. Trainmen, 13 Ill. 2d 391, 398, 150 N. E. 2d 163, 167 (1958), *quoted in* In re Ratner, 194 Kan. 362, 372, 399 P.2d 865, 873 (1965).

See ABA Opinion 147 (1935).

75. "This Court has condemned the practice of ambulance chasing through the media of runners and touters. In similar fashion we have with equal emphasis condemned the practice of direct solicitation by a lawyer. We have classified both offenses as serious breaches of the Canons of Ethics demanding severe treatment of the offending lawyer." State v. Dawson, 111 So. 2d 427, 431 (Fla. 1959).

76. "Registrants [of a lawyer referral plan] may be required to contribute to the expense of operating it by a reasonable registration charge or by a reasonable percentage of fees collected by them." *ABA Opinion* 291 (1956).

Cf. ABA Opinion 227 (1941).

77. *Cf. ABA Opinion* 148 (1935).

78. United Mine Workers v. Ill. State Bar Ass'n., 389 U.S. 217, 19 L. Ed. 2d 426, 88 S. Ct. 353 (1967); Brotherhood of R.R. Trainmen v. Virginia, 371 U.S. 1, 12 L. Ed. 2d 89, 84 S. Ct. 1113 (1964); NAACP v. Button, 371 U.S. 415, 9 L. Ed. 2d 405, 83 S. Ct. 328 (1963).

79. "If a bar association has embarked on a program of institutional advertising for an annual legal check-up and provides brochures and reprints, it is not improper to have these available in the lawyer's office for persons to read and take." *ABA Opinion* 307 (1962).

Cf. ABA Opinion 121 (1934).

80. ABA Canon 28.

81. *Cf. ABA Opinions* 229 (1941) and 173 (1937).

82. "It certainly is not improper for a lawyer to advise his regular clients of new statutes, court decisions, and administrative rulings, which may affect the client's interests, provided the communication is strictly limited to such information. . . .

"When such communications go to concerns or individuals other than regular clients of the lawyer, they are thinly disguised advertisements for professional employment, and are obviously improper." *ABA Opinion* 213 (1941).

"It is our opinion that where the lawyer has no reason to believe that he has been supplanted by another lawyer, it is not only his right, but it might even be his duty to advise his client of any change of fact or law which might defeat the client's testamentary purpose as expressed in the will.

"Periodic notices might be sent to the client for whom a lawyer has drawn a will, suggesting that it might be wise for the client to reexamine his will to determine whether or not there has been any change in his situation requiring a modification of his will." *ABA Opinion* 210 (1941).

Cf. ABA Canon 28.

83. *Cf. ABA Opinion* 168 (1937).

84. *But cf. ABA Opinion* 111 (1934).

85. *See* ABA Canon 45; *cf.* ABA Canons 43, and 46.

86. This provision is included to conform to action taken by the ABA House of Delegates at the Mid-Winter Meeting, January, 1969.

87. *See* ABA Canon 12.

88. The charging of a "clearly excessive fee" is a ground for discipline. State ex rel. Nebraska State Bar Ass'n. v. Richards. 165 Neb. 80, 90, 84 N.W.2d 136, 143 (1957).

"An attorney has the right to contract for any fee he chooses so long as it is not excessive (see Opinion 190), and this Committee is not concerned with the amount of such fees unless so excessive as to constitute a misappropriation of the client's funds (see Opinion 27)." ABA Opinion 320 (1968).

Cf. ABA Opinions 209 (1940), 190 (1939), and 27 (1930) and State ex rel. Lee v. Buchanan, 191 So.2d 33 (Fla. 1966).

89. Cf. ABA Canon 13; see generally MacKinnon, Contingent Fees for Legal Services (1964) (A Report of the American Bar Foundation).

90. "Contingent fees, whether in civil or criminal cases, are a special concern of the law. . . .

"In criminal cases, the rule is stricter because of the danger of corrupting justice. The second part of Section 542 of the Restatement [of Contracts] reads; 'A bargain to conduct a criminal case . . . in consideration of a promise of a fee contingent on success is illegal. . . .'" Peyton v. Margiotti, 398 Pa. 86, 156 A.2d 865, 967 (1959).

"The third area of practice in which the use of the contingent fee is generally considered to be prohibited is the prosecution and defense of criminal cases. However, there are so few cases, and these are predominantly old, that it is doubtful that there can be said to be any current law on the subject. . . . In the absence of cases on the validity of contingent fees for defense attorneys, it is necessary to rely on the consensus among commentators that such a fee is void as against public policy. The nature of criminal practice itself makes unlikely the use of contingent fee contracts." MacKinnon, Contingent Fees for Legal Services 52 (1964) (A Report of the American Bar Foundation).

91. See ABA Canon 34 and ABA Opinions 316 (1967) and 294 (1958); see generally ABA Opinions 265 (1945), 204 (1940), 190 (1939), 171 (1937), 153 (1936), 97 (1933), 63 (1932), 28 (130), 27 (1930), and 18 (1930).

92. "*Canon 12* contemplates that a lawyer's fee should not exceed *the value of the services* rendered. . . .

"*Canon 12* applies, whether joint or separate fees are charged [by associate attorneys] . . . ." ABA Opinion 204 (1940).

93. "[A] general covenant restricting an employed lawyer, after leaving the employment, from practicing in the community for a stated period, appears to this Committee to be an unwarranted restriction on the right of a lawyer to choose where he will practice and inconsistent with our professional status. Accordingly, the Committee is of the opinion it would be improper for the employing lawyer to require the covenant and likewise for the employed lawyer to agree to it." ABA Opinion 300 (1961).

94. See ABA Canon 30.

"Rule 13. . . . A member of the State Bar shall not accept employment to prosecute or defend a case solely out of spite, or solely for the purpose of harassing or delaying another. . . ." Cal. Business and Professions Code §6067 (West 1962).

95. Cf. ABA Canon 44.

96. See also Code of Professional Responsibility, DR 5-102 and DR 5-105.

97. Cf. ABA Canon 4.

98. Cf. Anders v. California, 386 U.S. 738, 18 L. Ed. 2d 493, 87 S. Ct. 1396 (1967), *rehearing denied*, 388 U.S. 924, 18 L. Ed. 2d 1377, 87 S. Ct. 2094 (1967).

CANON 3

A Lawyer Should Assist in Preventing the Unauthorized Practice of Law

ETHICAL CONSIDERATIONS

EC 3-1 The prohibition against the practice of law by a layman is grounded in the need of the public for integrity and competence of those who undertake to render legal services. Because of the fiduciary and personal character of the lawyer-client relationship and the inherently complex nature of our legal system, the public can better be assured of the requisite responsibility and competence if the practice of law is confined to those who are subject to the requirements and regulations imposed upon members of the legal profession.

EC 3-2 The sensitive variations in the considerations that bear on legal determinations often make it difficult even for a lawyer to exercise appropriate professional judgment, and it is therefore essential that the personal nature of the relationship of client and lawyer be preserved. Competent professional judgment is the product of a trained familiarity with law and legal processes, a disciplined, analytical approach to legal problems, and a firm ethical commitment.

EC 3-3 A non-lawyer who undertakes to handle legal matters is not governed as to integrity or legal competence by the same rules that govern the conduct of a lawyer. A lawyer is not only subject to that regulation but also is committed to high standards of ethical conduct. The public interest is best served in legal matters by a regulated profession committed to such standards.[1] The Disciplinary Rules protect the public in that they prohibit a lawyer from seeking employment by improper overtures, from acting in cases of divided loyalties, and from submitting to the control of others in the exercise of his judgment. Moreover, a person who entrusts legal matters to a lawyer is protected by the attorney-client privilege and by the duty of the lawyer to hold inviolate the confidences and secrets of his client.

EC 3-4 A layman who seeks legal services often is not in a position to judge whether he will receive proper professional attention. The entrustment of a legal matter may well involve the confidences, the reputation, the property, the freedom, or even the life of the client. Proper protection of members of the public demands that no person be permitted to act in the confidential and demanding capacity of a lawyer unless he is subject to the regulations of the legal profession.

EC 3-5 It is neither necessary nor desirable to attempt the formulation of a single, specific definition of what constitutes the practice of law.[2] Functionally, the practice of law relates to the rendition of services for others that call for the professional judgment of a lawyer. The essence of the professional judgment of the lawyer is his educated ability to relate the general body and philosophy of law to a specific legal problem of a client; and thus, the public interest will be better served if only lawyers are permitted to act in matters involving professional judgment. Where this professional judgment is not involved, non-lawyers, such as court clerks, police officers, abstracters, and many governmental employees, may engage in occupations that require a special knowledge of law in certain areas. But the services of a lawyer are essential in the public interest whenever the exercise of professional legal judgment is required.

EC 3-6 A lawyer often delegates tasks to clerks, secretaries, and other lay persons. Such delegation is proper if the lawyer maintains a direct relationship with his client, supervises the delegated work, and has complete professional responsibility for the work product.[3] This delegation enables a lawyer to render legal service more economically and efficiently.

EC 3-7 The prohibition against a non-lawyer practicing law does not prevent a layman from representing himself, for then he is ordinarily exposing only himself to possible injury. The purpose of the legal profession is to make educated legal representation available to the public; but anyone who does not wish to avail himself of such representation is not required to do so. Even so, the legal profession should help members of the public to recognize legal problems and to understand why it may be unwise for them to act for themselves in matters having legal consequences.

EC 3-8 Since a lawyer should not aid or encourage a layman to practice law, he should not practice law in association with a layman or otherwise share legal fees with a layman.[4] This does not mean, however, that the pecuniary value of the interest of a deceased lawyer in his firm or practice may not be paid to his estate or specified persons such as his widow or heirs.[5] In like manner, profit-sharing retirement plans of a lawyer or law firm which include non-lawyer office employees are not improper.[6] These limited exceptions to the rule against sharing legal fees with laymen are permissible since they do not aid or encourage laymen to practice law.

EC 3-9 Regulation of the practice of law is accomplished principally by the respective states.[7] Authority to engage in the practice of law conferred in any jurisdiction is not per se a grant of the right to practice elsewhere, and it is improper for a lawyer to engage in practice where he is not permitted by law or by court order to do so. However, the demands of business and the mobility of our society pose distinct problems in the regulation of the practice of law by the states.[8] In furtherance of the public interest, the legal profession should discourage regulation that unreasonably imposes territorial limitations upon the right of a lawyer to handle the legal affairs of his client or upon the opportunity of a client to obtain the services of a lawyer of his choice in all matters including the presentation of a contested matter in a tribunal before which the lawyer is not permanently admitted to practice.[9]

DISCIPLINARY RULES

DR 3-101 Aiding Unauthorized Practice of Law.[10]

(A) A lawyer shall not aid a non-lawyer in the unauthorized practice of law.[11]

(B) A lawyer shall not practice law in a jurisdiction where to do so would be in violation of regulations of the profession in that jurisdiction.[12]

DR 3-102 Dividing Legal Fees with a Non-Lawyer.

(A) A lawyer or law firm shall not share legal fees with a non-lawyer,[13] except that:

(1) An agreement by a lawyer with his firm, partner, or associate may provide for the payment of money, over a reasonable period of time after his death, to his estate or to one or more specified persons.[14]

(2) A lawyer who undertakes to complete unfinished legal business of a deceased lawyer may pay to the estate of the deceased lawyer that proportion of the total compensation which fairly represents the services rendered by the deceased lawyer.

(3) A lawyer or law firm may include non-lawyer employees in a compensation or retirement plan, even though the plan is based in whole or in part on a profit sharing arrangement providing such plan does not circumvent another Disciplinary Rule.

DR 3-103 Forming a Partnership with a Non-Lawyer.

(A) A lawyer shall not form a partnership with a non-lawyer if any of the activities of the partnership consist of the practice of law.[16]

NOTES

1. "The condemnation of the unauthorized practice of law is designed to protect the public from legal services by persons unskilled in the law. The prohibition of lay intermediaries is intended to insure the loyalty of the lawyer to the client unimpaired by intervening and possibly conflicting interests." Cheatham, *Availability of Legal Services: The Responsibility of the Individual Lawyer and of the Organized Bar*, 12 U.C.L.A. L. REV. 438, 439 (1965).

2. What constitutes unauthorized practice of the law in a particular jurisdiction is a matter for determination by the courts of that jurisdiction." *ABA Opinion* 198 (1939).

"In the light of the historical development of the lawyer's functions, it is impossible to lay down an exhaustive definition of 'the practice of law' by attempting to enumerate every conceivable act performed by lawyers in the normal course of their work." State Bar of Arizona v. Arizona Land Title & Trust Co., 90 Ariz., 76, 87, 366 P.2d 1, 8-9 (1961), *modified*, 91 Ariz. 293, 371 P.2d 1020 (1962).

3. "A lawyer can employ lay secretaries, lay investigators, lay detectives, lay researchers, accountants, lay scriveners, nonlawyer draftsmen or nonlawyer researchers. In fact, he may employ nonlawyers to do any task for him except counsel clients about law matters, engage directly in the practice of law, appear in court or appear in formal proceedings as part of the judicial process, so long as it is he who takes the work and vouches for it to the client and becomes responsible to the client." *ABA Opinion* 316 (1967).

ABA Opinion 316 (1967) also stated that if a lawyer practices law as part of a law firm which includes lawyers from several states, he may delegate tasks to firm members in other states so long as he "is the person who, on behalf of the firm, vouched for the work of all of the others and, with the client and in the courts, did the legal acts defined by that state as the practice of law."

"A lawyer cannot delegate his professional responsibility to a law student employed in his office. He may avail himself of the assistance of the student in many of the fields of the lawyer's work, such as examination of case law, finding and interviewing witnesses, making collections of claims, examining court records, delivering papers, conveying important messages, and other similar matters. But the student is not permitted, until he is admitted to the Bar, to perform the professional functions of a lawyer, such as conducting court trials, giving professional advice to clients or drawing legal documents for them. The student in all his work must act as agent for the lawyer employing him, who must supervise his work and be responsible for his good conduct." *ABA Opinions* 85 (1932).

4. "No division of fees for legal services is proper, except with another lawyer . . . ." ABA CANON 34. Otherwise, according to *ABA Opinion* 316 (1967), "[t]he Canons of Ethics do not examine into the method by which such persons are remunerated by the lawyer. . . . They may be paid a salary, a per diem charge, a flat fee, a contract price, etc."

See ABA CANONS 33 and 47.

5. "Many partnership agreements provide that the active partners, on the death of any one of them, are to make payments to the estate or to the nominee of a deceased partner on a pre-determined formula. It is only where the effect of such an arrangement is to make the estate or nominee a member of the partnership along with the surviving partners that it is prohibited by *Canon 34*. Where the payments are made in accordance with a pre-existing agreement entered into by the deceased partner during his lifetime and providing for a fixed method for determining their amount based upon the value of services rendered during the partner's lifetime and providing for a fixed period over which the payments are to be made, this is not the case. Under these circumstances, whether the payments are considered to be delayed payment of compensation earned but withheld during the partner's lifetime, or whether they are considered to be an approximation of his interest in matters pending at the time of his death, is immaterial. In either event, as Henry S. Drinker says in his book, LEGAL ETHICS, at page 189: 'It would seem, however, that a reasonable agreement to pay the estate a proportion of the receipts for a reasonable period is a proper practical settlement for the lawyer's services to his retirement or death.' " *ABA Opinion* 308 (1963).

6. *Cf. ABA Opinion* 311 (1964).

7. "That the States have broad power to regulate the practice of law is, of course, beyond question." United Mine Workers v. Ill. State Bar Ass'n, 389 U.S. 217, 222 (1967).

"It is a matter of law, not of ethics, as to where an individual may practice law. Each state has its own rules." *ABA Opinion* 316 (1967).

8. "Much of clients' business crosses state lines. People are mobile, moving from state to state. Many metropolitan areas cross state lines. It is common today to have a single economic and social community involving more than one state. The business of a single client may involve legal problems in several states." *ABA Opinion* 316 (1967).

9. "[W]e reaffirmed the general principle that legal services to New Jersey residents with respect to New Jersey matters may ordinarily be furnished only by New Jersey counsel; but we pointed out that there may be multistate transactions where strict adherence to this thesis would not be in the public interest and that, under the circumstances, it would have been not only more costly to the client but also 'grossly impractical and inefficient' to have had the settlement negotiations conducted by separate lawyers from different states." In re Estate of Waring, 47 N.J. 367, 376, 221 A.2d 193, 197 (1966).

Cf. ABA Opinion 316 (1967).

10. Conduct permitted by the Disciplinary Rules of Canons 2 and 5 does not violate DR 3-101.

11. See ABA CANON 47.

12. It should be noted, however, that a lawyer may engage in conduct, otherwise prohibited by this Disciplinary Rule, where such conduct is authorized by preemptive federal legislation. *See* Sperry v. Florida, 373 U.S. 379, 10 L. ED. 2d 428, 83 S. Ct. 1322 (1963).

13. *See* ABA CANON 34 and *ABA Opinions* 316 (1967), 180 (1938), and 48 (1931).

"The receiving attorney shall not under any guise or form share his fee for legal services with a lay agency, personal or corporate, without prejudice, however, to the right of the lay forwarder to charge and collect from the creditor proper compensation for non-legal services rendered by the law [sic] forwarder which are separate and apart from the services performed by the receiving attorney." *ABA Opinion* 294 (1958).

14. *See ABA Opinion* 309 (1963) and 266 (1945).

15. *Cf. ABA Opinion* 311 (1964).

16. *See* ABA CANON 33; *cf. ABA Opinions* 239 (1942) and 201 (1940).

ABA Opinion 316 (1967) states that lawyers licensed in different jurisdictions may, under certain conditions, enter "into an arrangement for the practice of law" and that a lawyer licensed in State A is not, for such purpose, a layman in State B.

Model Code of Professional Responsibility

CANON 4

A Lawyer Should Preserve the Confidences and Secrets of a Client

ETHICAL CONSIDERATIONS

EC 4-1 Both the fiduciary relationship existing between lawyer and client and the proper functioning of the legal system require the preservation by the lawyer of confidences and secrets of one who has employed or sought to employ him.[1] A client must feel free to discuss whatever he wishes with his lawyer and a lawyer must be equally free to obtain information beyond that volunteered by his client.[2] A lawyer should be fully informed of all the facts of the matter he is handling in order for his client to obtain the full advantage of our legal system. It is for the lawyer in the exercise of his independent professional judgment to separate the relevant and important from the irrelevant and unimportant. The observance of the ethical obligation of a lawyer to hold inviolate the confidences and secrets of his client not only facilitates the full development of facts essential to proper representation of the client but also encourages laymen to seek early legal assistance.

EC 4-2 The obligation to protect confidences and secrets obviously does not preclude a lawyer from revealing information when his client consents after full disclosure,[3] when necessary to perform his professional employment, when permitted by a Disciplinary Rule, or when required by law. Unless the client otherwise directs, a lawyer may disclose the affairs of his client to partners or associates of his firm. It is a matter of common knowledge that the normal operation of a law office exposes confidential professional information to non-lawyer employees of the office, particularly secretaries and those having access to the files; and this obligates a lawyer to exercise care in selecting and training his employees so that the sanctity of all confidences and secrets of his clients may be preserved. If the obligation extends to two or more clients as to the same information, a lawyer should obtain the permission of all before revealing the information. A lawyer must always be sensitive to the rights and wishes of his client and act scrupulously in the making of decisions which may involve the disclosure of information obtained in his professional relationship.[4] Thus, in the absence of consent of his client after full disclosure, a lawyer should not associate another lawyer in the handling of a matter; nor should he, in the absence of consent, seek counsel from another lawyer if there is a reasonable possibility that the identity of the client or his confidences or secrets would be revealed to such lawyer. Both social amenities and professional duty should cause a lawyer to shun indiscreet conversations concerning his clients.

EC 4-3 Unless the client otherwise directs, it is not improper for a lawyer to give limited information from his files to an outside agency necessary for statistical, bookkeeping, accounting, data processing, banking, printing, or other legitimate purposes, provided he exercises due care in the selection of the agency and warns the agency that the information must be kept confidential.

EC 4-4 The attorney-client privilege is more limited than the ethical obligation of a lawyer to guard the confidences and secrets of his client. This ethical precept, unlike the evidentiary privilege, exists without regard to the nature or source of information or the fact that others share the knowledge. A lawyer should endeavor to act in a manner which preserves the evidentiary privilege; for example, he should avoid professional discussions in the presence of persons to whom the privilege does not extend. A lawyer owes an obligation to advise the client of the attorney-client privilege and timely to assert the privilege unless it is waived by the client.

EC 4-5 A lawyer should not use information acquired in the course of the representation of a client to the disadvantage of the client and a lawyer should not use, except with the consent of

Model Code of Professional Responsibility

his client after full disclosure, such information for his own purposes.[5] Likewise, a lawyer should be diligent in his efforts to prevent the misuse of such information by his employees and associates.[6] Care should be exercised by a lawyer to prevent the disclosure of the confidences and secrets of one client to another,[7] and no employment should be accepted that might require such disclosure.

EC 4-6 The obligation of a lawyer to preserve the confidences and secrets of his client continues after the termination of his employment.[8] Thus a lawyer should not attempt to sell a law practice as a going business because, among other reasons, to do so would involve the disclosure of confidences and secrets.[9] A lawyer should also provide for the protection of the confidences and secrets of his client following the termination of the practice of the lawyer, whether termination is due to death, disability, or retirement. For example, a lawyer might provide for the personal papers of the client to be returned to him and for the papers of the lawyer to be delivered to another lawyer or to be destroyed. In determining the method of disposition, the instructions and wishes of the client should be a dominant consideration.

DISCIPLINARY RULES

DR 4-101 Preservation of Confidences and Secrets of a Client.[10]

(A) "Confidence" refers to information protected by the attorney-client privilege under applicable law, and "secret" refers to other information gained in the professional relationship that the client has requested be held inviolate or the disclosure of which would be embarrassing or would be likely to be detrimental to the client.

(B) Except when permitted under DR 4-101 (C), a lawyer shall not knowingly:
  (1) Reveal a confidence or secret of his client.[11]
  (2) Use a confidence or secret of his client to the disadvantage of the client.
  (3) Use a confidence or secret of his client for the advantage of himself[12] or of a third person,[13] unless the client consents after full disclosure.

(C) A lawyer may reveal:
  (1) Confidences or secrets with the consent of the client or clients affected, but only after a full disclosure to them.[14]
  (2) Confidences or secrets when permitted under Disciplinary Rules or required by law or court order.[15]
  (3) The intention of his client to commit a crime[16] and the information necessary to prevent the crime.[17]
  (4) Confidences or secrets necessary to establish or collect his fee[18] or to defend himself or his employees or associates against an accusation of wrongful conduct.[19]

(D) A lawyer shall exercise reasonable care to prevent his employees, associates, and others whose services are utilized by him from disclosing or using confidences or secrets of a client, except that a lawyer may reveal the information allowed by DR 4-101 (C) through an employee.

NOTES

1. *See* ABA Canons 6 and 37 and *ABA Opinion* 287 (1953).

"The reason underlying the rule with respect to confidential communications between attorney and client is well stated in Mechem on Agency, 2d Ed., Vol. 2, §2297, as follows: 'The purposes and necessities of the relation between a client and his attorney require, in many cases, on the part of the client, the fullest and freest disclosures to the attorney of the client's objects, motives and acts. This disclosure is made in the strictest confidence, relying upon the attorney's honor and fidelity. To permit the attorney to reveal to others what is so disclosed, would be not only a gross violation of a sacred trust upon his part, but it would utterly destroy and prevent the usefulness and benefits to be derived from professional assistance. Based upon considerations of public policy, therefore, the law wisely declares that all confidential communications and disclosures, made by a client to his legal adviser for the purpose of obtaining his professional aid or advice, shall be strictly privileged;—that the attorney shall not be permitted, without the consent of his client,—and much less will he be compelled—to reveal or disclose communications made to him under such circumstances.'" *ABA Opinion 250* (1943).

"While it is true that complete revelation of relevant facts should be encouraged for trial purposes, nevertheless an attorney's dealings with his client, if both are sincere, and if the dealings involve more than mere technical matters, should be immune to discovery proceedings. There must be freedom from fear of revealment of matters disclosed to an attorney because of the peculiarly intimate relationship existing." Ellis-Foster Co. v. Union Carbide & Carbon Corp., 159 F.Supp. 917, 919 (D.N.J. 1958).

Cf. ABA Opinions 314 (1965), 274 (1946) and 268 (1945).

2. "While it is the great purpose of law to ascertain the truth, there is the countervailing necessity of insuring the right of every person to freely and fully confer and confide in one having knowledge of the law, and skilled in its practice, in order that the former may have adequate advice and a proper defense. This assistance can be made safely and readily available only when the client is free from the consequences of apprehension of disclosure by reason of the subsequent statements of the skilled lawyer. Baird v. Koerner, 279 F.2d 623, 629-30 (9th Cir. 1960).

Cf. ABA Opinion 150 (1936).

3. "Where . . . [a client] knowingly and after full disclosure participates in a [legal fee] financing plan which requires the furnishing of certain information to the bank, clearly by his conduct he has waived any privilege as to that information." *ABA Opinion 320* (1968).

4. "The lawyer must decide when he takes a case whether it is a suitable one for him to undertake and after this decision is made, he is not justified in turning against his client by exposing injurious evidence entrusted to him. . . . [D]oing something intrinsically regrettable, because the only alternative involves worse consequences, is a necessity in every profession." WILLISTON, LIFE AND LAW 271 (1940).

Cf. ABA Opinions 177 (1938) and 83 (1932).

5. *See* ABA CANON 11.

6. *See* ABA CANON 37.

7. *See* ABA CANONS 6 and 37.

"[A]n attorney must not accept professional employment against a client or a former client which will, or even *may* require him to use confidential information obtained by the attorney in the course of his professional relations with such client regarding the subject matter of the employment . . . ." *ABA Opinion* 165 (1936).

8. *See* ABA CANON 37.

"Confidential communications between an attorney and his client, made because of the relationship and concerning the subject-matter of the attorney's employment, are generally privileged from disclosure without the consent of the client, and this privilege outlasts the attorney's employment. Canon 37." *ABA Opinion* 154 (1936).

9. *Cf. ABA Opinion* 266 (1945).

10. *See* ABA CANON 37; *cf.* ABA CANON 6.

11. "§6068. . . It is the duty of an attorney:

. . . .

"(e) To maintain inviolate the confidence, and at every peril to himself to preserve the secrets, of his client." CAL. BUSINESS AND PROFESSIONS CODE §6068 (West 1962). Virtually the same provision is found in the Oregon statutes. ORE. REV. STATS. ch. 9 §9.460(5).

"Communications between lawyer and client are privileged (WIGMORE ON EVIDENCE, 3d Ed., Vol. 8, §§2290-2329). The modern theory underlying the privilege is subjective and is to give the client freedom of apprehension in consulting his legal adviser *(ibid.,* §2290, p. 548). The privilege applies to communications made in seeking legal advice for any purpose *(ibid.,* §2294, p. 563). The mere circumstance that the advice is given without charge therefor does not nullify the privilege *(ibid.,* §2303)." *ABA Opinion* 216 (1941).

"It is the duty of an attorney to maintain the confidence and preserve inviolate the secrets of his client . . . ." *ABA Opinion* 155 (1936).

12. *See* ABA CANON 11.

"The provision respecting employment is in accord with the general rule announced in the adjudicated cases that a lawyer may not make use of knowledge or information acquired by him through his professional relations with his client, or in the conduct of his client's business, to his own advantage or profit (7 C.J.S., §125, p. 958; Healy v. Gray, 184 Iowa 111, 168 N.W. 222; Baumgardner v. Hudson, D.C. App., 277 F. 552; Goodrum v. Clement, D.C. App., 277 F. 586)." *ABA Opinion* 250 (1943).

13. *See ABA Opinion* 177 (1938).

14. "[A lawyer] may not divulge confidential communications, information, and secrets imparted to him by the client or acquired during their professional relations, unless he is authorized to do so by the client (People v. Gerold, 265 Ill. 448, 107 N.E. 165, 178; Murphy v. Riggs, 238 Mich. 151, 213 N.W. 110, 112; Opinion of this Committee, No. 91)." *ABA Opinion* 202 (1940).

Cf. ABA Opinion 91 (1933).

Model Code of Professional Responsibility

15. "A defendant in a criminal case when admitted to bail is not only regarded as in the custody of his bail, but he is also in the custody of the law, and admission to bail does not deprive the court of its inherent power to deal with the person of the prisoner. Being in lawful custody, the defendant is guilty of an escape when he gains his liberty before he is delivered in due process of law, and is guilty of a separate offense for which he may be punished. In failing to disclose his client's whereabouts as a fugitive under these circumstances the attorney would not only be aiding his client to escape trial on the charge for which he was indicted, but would likewise be aiding him in evading prosecution for the additional offense of escape.

"It is the opinion of the committee that under such circumstances the attorney's knowledge of his client's whereabouts is not privileged, and that he may be disciplined for failing to disclose that information to the proper authorities...." *ABA Opinion* 155 (1936).

"We held in *Opinion* 155 that a communication by a client to his attorney in respect to the future commission of an unlawful act or to a continuing wrong is not privileged from disclosure. Public policy forbids that the relation of attorney and client should be used to conceal wrongdoing on the part of the client.

. . . .

"When an attorney representing a defendant in a criminal case applies on his behalf for probation or suspension of sentence, he represents to the court, by implication at least, that his client will abide by the terms and conditions of the court's order. When that attorney is later advised of a violation of that order, it is his duty to advise his client of the consequences of his act, and endeavor to prevent a continuance of the wrongdoing. If his client thereafter persists in violating the terms and conditions of his probation, it is the duty of the attorney as an officer of the court to advise the proper authorities concerning his client's conduct. Such information, even though coming to the attorney from the client in the course of his professional relations with respect to other matters in which he represents the defendant, is not privileged from disclosure.... *ABA*

See *ABA Opinion* 155 (1936).

16. *ABA Opinion* 314 (1965) indicates that a lawyer must disclose even the confidences of his clients if "the facts in the attorney's possession indicate beyond reasonable doubt that a crime will be committed."

See *ABA Opinions* 155 (1936).

17. See ABA Canon 37 and *ABA Opinion* 202 (1940).

18. *Cf. ABA Opinion* 250 (1943).

19. See ABA Canon 37 and *ABA Opinions* 202 (1940) and 19 (1930).

"[T]he adjudicated cases recognize an exception to the rule [that a lawyer shall not reveal the confidences of his client], where disclosure is necessary to protect the attorney's interests arising out of the relation of attorney and client in which disclosure was made.

"The exception is stated in Mechem on Agency, 2d Ed., Vol. 2, §2313, as follows: 'But the attorney may disclose information received from the client when it becomes necessary for his own protection, as if the client should bring an action against the attorney for negligence or misconduct, and it became necessary for the attorney to show what his instructions were, or what was the nature of the duty which the client expected him to perform. So if it became necessary for the attorney to bring an action against the client, the client's privilege could not prevent the attorney from disclosing what was essential as a means of obtaining or defending his own rights.'

"Mr. Jones, in his Commentaries on Evidence, 2d Ed., Vol. 5, §2165, states the exception thus: 'It has frequently been held that the rule as to privileged communications does not apply when litigation arises between attorney and client to the extent that their communications are relevant to the issue. In such cases, if the disclosure of privileged communications becomes necessary to protect the attorney's rights, he is released from those obligations of secrecy which the law places upon him. He should not, however, disclose more than is necessary for his own protection. It would be a manifest injustice to allow the client to take advantage of the rule of exclusion as to professional confidence to the prejudice of his attorney, or that it should be carried to the extent of depriving the attorney of the means of obtaining or defending his own rights. In such cases the attorney is exempted from the obligations of secrecy.' " *ABA Opinion* 250 (1943).

CANON 5

A Lawyer Should Exercise Independent Professional Judgment on Behalf of a Client

ETHICAL CONSIDERATIONS

EC 5-1 The professional judgment of a lawyer should be exercised, within the bounds of the law, solely for the benefit of his client and free of compromising influences and loyalties.[1] Neither his personal interests, the interests of other clients, nor the desires of third persons should be permitted to dilute his loyalty to his client.

Interests of a Lawyer That May Affect His Judgment

EC 5-2 A lawyer should not accept proffered employment if his personal interests or desires will, or there is a reasonable probability that they will, affect adversely the advice to be given or services to be rendered the prospective client.[2] After accepting employment, a lawyer carefully should refrain from acquiring a property right or assuming a position that would tend to make his judgment less protective of the interests of his client.

EC 5-3 The self-interest of a lawyer resulting from his ownership of property in which his client also has an interest or which may affect property of his client may interfere with the exercise of free judgment on behalf of his client. If such interference would occur with respect to a prospective client, a lawyer should decline employment proffered by him. After accepting employment, a lawyer should not acquire property rights that would adversely affect his professional judgment in the representation of his client. Even if the property interests of a lawyer do not presently interfere with the exercise of his independent judgment, but the likelihood of interference can reasonably be foreseen by him, a lawyer should explain the situation to his client and should decline employment or withdraw unless the client consents to the continuance of the relationship after full disclosure. A lawyer should not seek to persuade his client to permit him to invest in an undertaking of his client nor make improper use of his professional relationship to influence his client to invest in an enterprise in which the lawyer is interested.

EC 5-4 If, in the course of his representation of a client, a lawyer is permitted to receive from his client a beneficial ownership in publication rights relating to the subject matter of the employment, he may be tempted to subordinate the interests of his client to his own anticipated pecuniary gain. For example, a lawyer in a criminal case who obtains from his client television, radio, motion picture, newspaper, magazine, book, or other publication rights with respect to the case may be influenced, consciously or unconsciously, to a course of conduct that will enhance the value of his publication rights to the prejudice of his client. To prevent these potentially differing interests, such arrangements should be scrupulously avoided prior to the termination of all aspects of the matter giving rise to the employment, even though his employment has previously ended.

EC 5-5 A lawyer should not suggest to his client that a gift be made to himself or for his benefit. If a lawyer accepts a gift from his client, he is peculiarly susceptible to the charge that he unduly influenced or over-reached the client. If a client voluntarily offers to make a gift to his lawyer, the lawyer may accept the gift, but before doing so, he should urge that his client secure disinterested advice from an independent, competent person who is cognizant of all the circumstances.[3] Other than in exceptional circumstances, a lawyer should insist that an instrument in which his client desires to name him beneficially be prepared by another lawyer selected by the client.[4]

EC 5-6 A lawyer should not consciously influence a client to name him as executor, trustee, or lawyer in an instrument. In those cases where a client wishes to name his lawyer as such, care should be taken by the lawyer to avoid even the appearance of impropriety.[5]

Model Code of Professional Responsibility

EC 5-7 The possibility of an adverse effect upon the exercise of free judgment by a lawyer on behalf of his client during litigation generally makes it undesirable for the lawyer to acquire a proprietary interest in the cause of his client or otherwise to become financially interested in the outcome of the litigation.[6] However, it is not improper for a lawyer to protect his right to collect a fee for his services by the assertion of legally permissible liens, even though by doing so he may acquire an interest in the outcome of litigation. Although a contingent fee arrangement[7] gives a lawyer a financial interest in the outcome of litigation, a reasonable contingent fee is permissible in civil cases because it may be the only means by which a layman can obtain the services of a lawyer of his choice. But a lawyer, because he is in a better position to evaluate a cause of action, should enter into a contingent fee arrangement only in those instances where the arrangement will be beneficial to the client.

EC 5-8 A financial interest in the outcome of litigation also results if monetary advances are made by the lawyer to his client.[8] Although this assistance generally is not encouraged, there are instances when it is not improper to make loans to a client. For example, the advancing or guaranteeing of payment of the costs and expenses of litigation by a lawyer may be the only way a client can enforce his cause of action,[9] but the ultimate liability for such costs and expenses must be that of the client.

EC 5-9 Occasionally a lawyer is called upon to decide in a particular case whether he will be a witness or an advocate. If a lawyer is both counsel and witness, he becomes more easily impeachable for interest and thus may be a less effective witness. Conversely, the opposing counsel may be handicapped in challenging the credibility of the lawyer when the lawyer also appears as an advocate in the case. An advocate who becomes a witness is in the unseemly and ineffective position of arguing his own credibility. The roles of an advocate and of a witness are inconsistent; the function of an advocate is to advance or argue the cause of another, while that of a witness is to state facts objectively.

EC 5-10 Problems incident to the lawyer-witness relationship arise at different stages; they relate either to whether a lawyer should accept employment or should withdraw from employment.[10] Regardless of when the problem arises, his decision is to be governed by the same basic considerations. It is not objectionable for a lawyer who is a potential witness to be an advocate if it is unlikely that he will be called as a witness because his testimony would be merely cumulative or if his testimony will relate only to an uncontested issue.[11] In the exceptional situation where it will be manifestly unfair to the client for the lawyer to refuse employment or to withdraw when he will likely be a witness on a contested issue, he may serve as advocate even though he may be a witness.[12] In making such decision, he should determine the personal or financial sacrifice of the client that may result from his refusal of employment or withdrawal therefrom, the materiality of his testimony, and the effectiveness of his representation in view of his personal involvement. In weighing these factors, it should be clear that refusal or withdrawal will impose an unreasonable hardship upon the client before the lawyer accepts or continues the employment.[13] Where the question arises, doubts should be resolved in favor of the lawyer testifying and against his becoming or continuing as an advocate.[14]

EC 5-11 A lawyer should not permit his personal interests to influence his advice relative to a suggestion by his client that additional counsel be employed.[15] In like manner, his personal interests should not deter him from suggesting that additional counsel be employed; on the contrary, he should be alert to the desirability of recommending additional counsel when, in his judgment, the proper representation of his client requires it. However, a lawyer should advise his client not to employ additional counsel suggested by the client if the lawyer believes that such employment would be a disservice to the client, and he should disclose the reasons for his belief.

EC 5-12 Inability of co-counsel to agree on a matter vital to the representation of their client requires that their disagreement be submitted by them jointly to their client for his resolution, and the decision of the client shall control the action to be taken.[16]

EC 5-13 A lawyer should not maintain membership in or be influenced by any organization of employees that undertakes to prescribe, direct, or suggest when or how he should fulfill his professional obligations to a person or organization that employs him as a lawyer. Although it is not necessarily improper for a lawyer employed by a corporation or similar entity to be a member of an organization of employees, he should be vigilant to safeguard his fidelity as a lawyer to his employer, free from outside influences.

Interests of Multiple Clients

EC 5-14 Maintaining the independence of professional judgment required of a lawyer precludes his acceptance or continuation of employment that will adversely affect his judgment on behalf of or dilute his loyalty to a client.[17] This problem arises whenever a lawyer is asked to represent two or more clients who may have differing interests, whether such interests be conflicting, inconsistent, diverse, or otherwise discordant.[18]

EC 5-15 If a lawyer is requested to undertake or to continue representation of multiple clients having potentially differing interests, he must weigh carefully the possibility that his judgment may be impaired or his loyalty divided if he accepts or continues the employment. He should resolve all doubts against the propriety of the representation. A lawyer should never represent in litigation multiple clients with differing interests;[19] and there are few situations in which he would be justified in representing in litigation multiple clients with potentially differing interests. If a lawyer accepted such employment and the interests did become actually differing, he would have to withdraw from employment with likelihood of resulting hardship on the clients; and for this reason it is preferable that he refuse the employment initially. On the other hand, there are many instances in which a lawyer may properly serve multiple clients having potentially differing interests in matters not involving litigation. If the interests vary only slightly, it is generally likely that the lawyer will not be subjected to an adverse influence and that he can retain his independent judgment on behalf of each client; and if the interests become differing, withdrawal is less likely to have a disruptive effect upon the causes of his clients.

EC 5-16 In those instances in which a lawyer is justified in representing two or more clients having differing interests, it is nevertheless essential that each client be given the opportunity to evaluate his need for representation free of any potential conflict and to obtain other counsel if he so desires.[20] Thus before a lawyer may represent multiple clients, he should explain fully to each client the implications of the common representation and should accept or continue employment only if the clients consent.[21] If there are present other circumstances that might cause any of the multiple clients to question the undivided loyalty of the lawyer, he should also advise all of the clients of those circumstances.[22]

EC 5-17 Typically recurring situations involving potentially differing interests are those in which a lawyer is asked to represent co-defendants in a criminal case, co-plaintiffs in a personal injury case, an insured and his insurer,[23] and beneficiaries of the estate of a decedent. Whether a lawyer can fairly and adequately protect the interests of multiple clients in these and similar situations depends upon an analysis of each case. In certain circumstances, there may exist little chance of the judgment of the lawyer being adversely affected by the slight possibility that the interests will become actually differing; in other circumstances, the chance of adverse effect upon his judgment is not unlikely.

EC 5-18 A lawyer employed or retained by a corporation or similar entity owes his allegiance to the entity and not to a stockholder, director, officer, employee, representative, or other person connected with the entity. In advising the entity, a lawyer should keep paramount its interests and his professional judgment should not be influenced by the personal desires of any person or organization. Occasionally a lawyer for an entity is requested by a stockholder, director, officer, employee, representative, or other person connected with the entity to represent him in an individual capacity; in such case the lawyer may serve the individual only if the lawyer is convinced that differing interests are not present.

EC 5-19 A lawyer may represent several clients whose interests are not actually or potentially differing. Nevertheless, he should explain any circumstances that might cause a client to question his undivided loyalty.[24] Regardless of the belief of a lawyer that he may properly represent multiple clients, he must defer to a client who holds the contrary belief and withdraw from representation of that client.

EC 5-20 A lawyer is often asked to serve as an impartial arbitrator or mediator in matters which involve present or former clients. He may serve in either capacity if he first discloses such present or former relationships. After a lawyer has undertaken to act as an impartial arbitrator or mediator, he should not thereafter represent in the dispute any of the parties involved.

Desires of Third Persons

EC 5-21 The obligation of a lawyer to exercise professional judgment solely on behalf of his client requires that he disregard the desires of others that might impair his free judgment.[25] The desires of a third person will seldom adversely affect a lawyer unless that person is in a position to exert strong economic, political, or social pressures upon the lawyer. These influences are often subtle, and a lawyer must be alert to their existence. A lawyer subjected to outside pressures should make full disclosure of them to his client;[26] and if he or his client believes that the effectiveness of his representation has been or will be impaired thereby, the lawyer should take proper steps to withdraw from representation of his client.

EC 5-22 Economic, political, or social pressures by third persons are less likely to impinge upon the independent judgment of a lawyer in a matter in which he is compensated directly by his client and his professional work is exclusively with his client. On the other hand, if a lawyer is compensated from a source other than his client, he may feel a sense of responsibility to someone other than his client.

EC 5-23 A person or organization that pays or furnishes lawyers to represent others possesses a potential power to exert strong pressures against the independent judgment of those lawyers. Some employers may be interested in furthering their own economic, political, or social goals without regard to the professional responsibility of the lawyer to his individual client. Others may be far more concerned with establishment or extension of legal principles than in the immediate protection of the rights of the lawyer's individual client. On some occasions, decisions on priority of work may be made by the employer rather than the lawyer with the result that prosecution of work already undertaken for clients is postponed to their detriment. Similarly, an employer may seek, consciously or unconsciously, to further its own economic interests through the action of the lawyers employed by it. Since a lawyer must always be free to exercise his professional judgment without regard to the interests or motives of a third person, the lawyer who is employed by one to represent another must constantly guard against erosion of his professional freedom.[27]

EC 5-24 To assist a lawyer in preserving his professional independence, a number of courses are available to him. For example, a lawyer should not practice with or in the form of a professional legal corporation, even though the corporate form is permitted by law,[28] if any director, officer, or stockholder of it is a non-lawyer. Although a lawyer may be employed by a business corporation with non-lawyers serving as directors or officers, and they necessarily have the right to make decisions of business policy, a lawyer must decline to accept direction of his professional judgment from any layman. Various types of legal aid offices are administered by boards of directors composed of lawyers and laymen. A lawyer should not accept employment from such an organization unless the board sets only broad policies and there is no interference in the relationship of the lawyer and the individual client he serves. Where a lawyer is employed by an organization, a written agreement that defines the relationship between him and the organization and provides for his independence is desirable since it may serve to prevent misunderstanding as to their respective roles. Although other innovations in the means of supplying legal counsel may develop, the responsibility of the lawyer to maintain his professional independence remains constant, and the legal profession must insure that changing circumstances do not result in loss of the professional independence of the lawyer.

Model Code of Professional Responsibility

DISCIPLINARY RULES

DR 5-101 Refusing Employment When the Interests of the Lawyer May Impair His Independent Professional Judgment.

(A) Except with the consent of his client after full disclosure, a lawyer shall not accept employment if the exercise of his professional judgment on behalf of his client will be or reasonably may be affected by his own financial, business, property, or personal interests.[29]

(B) A lawyer shall not accept employment in contemplated or pending litigation if he knows or it is obvious that he or a lawyer in his firm ought to be called as a witness, except that he may undertake the employment and he or a lawyer in his firm may testify:
  (1) If the testimony will relate solely to an uncontested matter.
  (2) If the testimony will relate solely to a matter of formality and there is no reason to believe that substantial evidence will be offered in opposition to the testimony.
  (3) If the testimony will relate solely to the nature and value of legal services rendered in the case by the lawyer or his firm to the client.
  (4) As to any matter, if refusal would work a substantial hardship on the client because of the distinctive value of the lawyer or his firm as counsel in the particular case.

DR 5-102 Withdrawal as Counsel When the Lawyer Becomes a Witness.[30]

(A) If, after undertaking employment in contemplated or pending litigation, a lawyer learns or it is obvious that he or a lawyer in his firm ought to be called as a witness on behalf of his client, he shall withdraw from the conduct of the trial and his firm, if any, shall not continue representation in the trial, except that he may continue the representation and he or a lawyer in his firm may testify in the circumstances enumerated in DR 5-101(B) (1) through (4).

(B) If, after undertaking employment in contemplated or pending litigation a lawyer learns or it is obvious that he or a lawyer in his firm may be called as a witness other than on behalf of his client, he may continue the representation until it is apparent that his testimony is or may be prejudicial to his client.[31]

DR 5-103 Avoiding Acquisition of Interest in Litigation.

(A) A lawyer shall not acquire a proprietary interest in the cause of action or subject matter of litigation he is conducting for a client,[32] except that he may:
  (1) Acquire a lien granted by law to secure his fee or expenses.
  (2) Contract with a client for a reasonable contingent fee in a civil case.[33]

(B) While representing a client in connection with contemplated or pending litigation, a lawyer shall not advance or guarantee financial assistance to his client,[34] except that a lawyer may advance or guarantee the expenses of litigation, including court costs, expenses of investigation, expenses of medical examination, and costs of obtaining and presenting evidence, provided the client remains ultimately liable for such expenses.

DR 5-104 Limiting Business Relations with a Client.

(A) A lawyer shall not enter into a business transaction with a client if they have differing interests therein and if the client expects the lawyer to exercise his professional judgment therein for the protection of the client, unless the client has consented after full disclosure.

(B) Prior to conclusion of all aspects of the matter giving rise to his employment, a lawyer shall not enter into any arrangement or understanding with a client or a prospective client by which he acquires an interest in publication rights with respect to the subject matter of his employment or proposed employment.

DR 5-105 Refusing to Accept or Continue Employment if the Interests of Another Client May Impair the Independent Professional Judgment of the Lawyer.

(A) A lawyer shall decline proffered employment if the exercise of his independent professional judgment in behalf of a client will be or is likely to be adversely affected by the acceptance of the proffered employment,[35] or if it would be likely to involve him in representing differing interests, except to the extent permitted under DR 5-105(C).[36]

Model Code of Professional Responsibility

(B) A lawyer shall not continue multiple employment if the exercise of his independent professional judgment in behalf of a client will be or is likely to be adversely affected by his representation of another client, or if it would be likely to involve him in representing differing interests, except to the extent permitted under DR 5-105(C).[37]

(C) In the situations covered by DR 5-105 (A) and (B), a lawyer may represent multiple clients if it is obvious that he can adequately represent the interest of each and if each consents to the representation after full disclosure of the possible effect of such representation on the exercise of his independent professional judgment on behalf of each.

(D) If a lawyer is required to decline employment or to withdraw from employment under a Disciplinary Rule, no partner, or associate, or any other lawyer affiliated with him or his firm, may accept or continue such employment.

DR 5-106 Settling Similar Claims of Clients.[38]

(A) A lawyer who represents two or more clients shall not make or participate in the making of an aggregate settlement of the claims of or against his clients, unless each client has consented to the settlement after being advised of the existence and nature of all the claims involved in the proposed settlement, of the total amount of the settlement, and of the participation of each person in the settlement.

DR 5-107 Avoiding Influence by Others Than the Client.

(A) Except with the consent of his client after full disclosure, a lawyer shall not:
  (1) Accept compensation for his legal services from one other than his client.
  (2) Accept from one other than his client any thing of value related to his representation of or his employment by his client.[39]

(B) A lawyer shall not permit a person who recommends, employs, or pays him to render legal services for another to direct or regulate his professional judgment in rendering such legal services.[40]

(C) A lawyer shall not practice with or in the form of a professional corporation or association authorized to practice law for a profit, if:
  (1) A non-lawyer owns any interest therein,[41] except that a fiduciary representative of the estate of a lawyer may hold the stock or interest of the lawyer for a reasonable time during administration;
  (2) A non-lawyer is a corporate director or officer thereof;[42] or
  (3) A non-lawyer has the right to direct or control the professional judgment of a lawyer.[43]

NOTES

1. *Cf.* ABA Canon 35.
"[A lawyer's] fiduciary duty is of the highest order and he must not represent interests adverse to those of the client. It is true that because of his professional responsibility and the confidence and trust which his client may legitimately repose in him, he must adhere to a high standard of honesty, integrity and good faith in dealing with his client. He is not permitted to take advantage of his position or superior knowledge to impose upon the client; not to conceal facts or law, nor in any way deceive him without being held responsible therefor." Smoot v. Lund, 13 Utah 2d 168, 172, 369 P.2d 933, 936 (1962).

"When a client engages the services of a lawyer in a given piece of business he is entitled to feel that, until that business is finally disposed of in some manner, he has the undivided loyalty of the one upon whom he looks as his advocate and champion. If, as in this case, he is sued and his home attached by his own attorney, who is representing him in another matter, all feeling of loyalty is necessarily destroyed, and the profession is exposed to the charge that it is interested only in money." Grievance Comm. v. Rattner, 152 Conn. 59, 65, 203 A.2d 82, 84 (1964).

"One of the cardinal principles confronting every attorney in the representation of a client is the requirement of complete loyalty and service in good faith to the best of his ability. In a criminal case the client is entitled to a fair trial, but not a perfect one. These are fundamental requirements of due process under the Fourteenth Amendment. . . . The same principles are applicable in Sixth Amendment cases (not pertinent herein) and suggest that an attorney should have no conflict of interest and that he must devote his full and faithful efforts toward the defense of his client." Johns v. Smyth, 176 F. Supp. 949, 952 (E.D. Va. 1959), *modified,* United States ex rel. Wilkins v. Banmiller, 205 F. Supp. 123, 128 n. 5 (E.D. Pa. 1962), *aff'd,* 325 F.2d 514 (3d Cir. 1963), *cert. denied,* 379 U.S. 847, 13 L.Ed. 2d 51, 85 S.Ct. 87 (1964).

2. "Attorneys must not allow their private interests to conflict with those of their clients. . . . They owe their entire devotion to the interests of their clients." United States v. Anonymous, 215 F. Supp. 111, 113 (E.D. Tenn. 1963).

"[T]he court [below] concluded that a firm may not accept any action against a person whom they are presently representing even though there is no relationship between the two cases. In arriving at this conclusion, the court cites an opinion of the Committee on Professional Ethics of the New York County Lawyers' Association which stated in part: 'While under the circumstances * * * there may be no actual conflict of interest * * * "maintenance of public confidence in the Bar requires an attorney who has accepted representation of a client to decline, while representing such client, any employment from an adverse party in any matter even though wholly unrelated to the original retainer." See Question and Answer No. 350, N.Y. County L. Ass'n, Questions and Answer No. 450 (June 21, 1956).' " Grievance Comm. v. Rattner, 152 Conn. 59, 65, 203 A.2d 82, 84 (1964).

3. "Courts of equity will scrutinize with jealous vigilance transactions between parties occupying fiduciary relations toward each other. . . . A deed will not be held invalid, however, if made by the grantor with full knowledge of its nature and effect, and because of the deliberate, voluntary and intelligent desire of the grantor. . . . Where a fiduciary relation exists, the burden of proof is on the grantee or beneficiary of an instrument executed during the existence of such relationship to show the fairness of the transaction, that it was equitable and just and that it did not proceed from undue influence. . . . The same rule has application where an attorney engages in a transaction with a client during the existence of the relation and is benefited thereby. . . . Conversely, an attorney is not prohibited from dealing with his client or buying his property, and such contracts, if open, fair and honest, when deliberately made, are as valid as contracts between other parties. . . . [I]mportant factors in determining whether a transaction is fair include a showing by the fiduciary (1) that he made a full and frank disclosure of all the relevant information that he had; (2) that the consideration was adequate; and (3) that the principal had independent advice before completing the transaction." McFail v. Braden, 19 Ill. 2d 108, 117-18, 166 N.E. 2d 46, 52 (1960).

4. See State ex rel. Nebraska State Bar Ass'n v. Richards, 165 Neb. 80, 94-95, 84 N.W. 2d 136, 146 (1957).

5. *See* ABA Canon 9.

6. *See* ABA Canon 10.

7. *See* Code of Professional Responsibility, EC 2-20.

8. *See* ABA Canon 42.

9. "*Rule 3a.* . . . A member of the State Bar shall not directly or indirectly pay or agree to pay, or represent or sanction the representation that he will pay, medical, hospital or nursing bills or other personal expenses incurred by or for a client, prospective or existing; provided this rule shall not prohibit a member:

"(1) with the consent of the client, from paying or agreeing to pay to third persons such expenses from funds collected or to be collected for the client; or

(2) after he has been employed, from lending money to his client upon the client's promise in writing to repay such loan; or

(3) from advancing the costs of prosecuting or defending a claim or action. Such costs within the meaning of this subparagraph (3) include all taxable costs or disbursements, costs or investigation and costs of obtaining and presenting evidence." Cal. Business and Professions Code §6076 (West Supp. 1967).

10. "When a lawyer knows, prior to trial, that he will be a necessary witness, except as to merely formal matters such as identification or custody of a document or the like, neither he nor his firm or associates should conduct the trial. If, during the trial, he discovers that the ends of justice require his testimony, he should, from that point on, if feasible and not prejudicial to his client's case, leave further conduct of the trial to other counsel. If circumstances do not permit withdrawal from the conduct of the trial, the lawyer should not argue the credibility of his own testimony." *A Code of Trial Conduct: Promulgated by the American College of Trial Lawyers,* 43 A.B.A.J. 223, 224-25 (1957).

11. *Cf.* Canon 19: "When a lawyer is a witness for his client, except as to merely formal matters, such as the attestation or custody of an instrument and the like, he should leave the trial of the case to other counsel."

12. "It is the general rule that a lawyer may not testify in litigation in which he is an advocate unless circumstances arise which could not be anticipated and it is necessary to prevent a miscarriage of justice. In those rare cases where the testimony of an attorney is needed to protect his client's interests, it is not only proper but mandatory that it be forthcoming." Schwartz v. Wenger, 267 Minn. 40, 43-44, 124 N.W. 2d 489, 492 (1963).

13. "The great weight of authority in this country holds that the attorney who acts as counsel and witness, in behalf of his client, in the same cause on a material matter, not of a merely formal character, and not in an emergency, but having knowledge that he would be required to be a witness in ample time to have secured other counsel and given up his service in the case, violates a highly important provision of the Code of Ethics and a rule of professional conduct, but does not commit a legal error in so testifying, as a result of which a new trial will be granted." Erwin M. Jennings Co. v. DiGenova, 107 Conn. 491, 499, 141A. 866, 869 (1928).

14. "[C]ases may arise, and in practice often do arise, in which there would be a failure of justice should the attorney withhold his testimony. In such a case it would be a vicious professional sentiment which would deprive the client of the benefit of his attorney's testimony." Connolly v. Straw, 53 Wis. 645, 649, 11 N.W. 17, 19 (1881).

But see CANON 19: "Except when essential to the ends of justice, a lawyer should avoid testifying in court in behalf of his client."

15. *Cf.* ABA CANON 7.

16. *See* ABA CANON 7.

17. *See* ABA CANON 6; *cf. ABA Opinions* 261 (1944), 242 (1942), 142 (1935), and 30 (1931).

18. The ABA Canons speak of "conflicting interests" rather than "differing interests" but make no attempt to define such other than the statement in Canon 6: "Within the meaning of this canon, a lawyer represents conflicting interests when, in behalf of one client, it is his duty to contend for that which duty to another client requires him to oppose."

19. "Canon 6 of the Canons of Professional Ethics, adopted by the American Bar Association on September 30, 1937, and by the Pennsylvania Bar Association on January 7, 1938, provides in part that 'It is unprofessional to represent conflicting interests, except by express consent of all concerned given after a full disclosure of the facts. Within the meaning of this Canon, a lawyer represents conflicting interests when, in behalf of one client, it is his duty to contend for that which duty to another client requires him to oppose.' The full disclosure required by this canon contemplates that the possibly adverse effect of the conflict be fully explained by the attorney to the client to be affected and by him thoroughly understood....

"The foregoing canon applies to cases where the circumstances are such that possibly conflicting interests may permissibly be represented by the same attorney. But manifestly, there are instances where the conflicts of interest are so critically adverse as not to admit of one attorney's representing both sides. Such is the situation which this record presents. No one could conscionably contend that the same attorney may represent both the plaintiff and defendant in an adversary action. Yet, that is what is being done in this case." Jedwabny v. Philadelphia Transportation Co., 390 Pa. 231, 235, 135 A.2d 252, 254 (1957), *cert. denied*, 355 U.S. 966, 2 L. Ed. 2d 541, 78 S. Ct. 557 (1958).

20. "Glasser wished the benefit of the undivided assistance of counsel of his own choice. We think that such a desire on the part of an accused should be respected. Irrespective of any conflict of interest, the additional burden of representing another party may conceivably impair counsel's effectiveness.

"To determine the precise degree of prejudice sustained by Glasser as a result of the court's appointment of Stewart as counsel for Kretske is at once difficult and unnecessary. The right to have the assistance of counsel is too fundamental and absolute to allow courts to indulge in nice calculations as to the amount of prejudice arising from its denial." Glasser v. United States, 315 U.S. 60, 75-76, 86 L. Ed. 680, 702 S. Ct. 457, 467 (1942).

21. *See* ABA CANON 6.

22. *Id.*

23. *Cf. ABA Opinion* 282 (1950).

"When counsel, although paid by the casualty company, undertakes to represent the policyholder and files his notice of appearance, he owes to his client, the assured, an undeviating and single allegiance. His fealty embraces the requirement to produce in court all witnesses, fact and expert, who are available and necessary for the proper protection of the rights of his client....

"... The Canons of Professional Ethics make it pellucid that there are not two standards, one applying to counsel privately retained by a client, and the other to counsel paid by an insurance carrier." American Employers Ins. Co. v. Goble Aircraft Specialties, 205 Misc. 1066, 1075, 131 N.Y.S.2d, 393, 401 (1954), *motion to withdraw appeal granted*, 1 App. Div. 2d 1008, 154 N.Y.S.2d 835 (1956).

"[C]ounsel, selected by State Farm to defend Dorothy Walker's suit for $50,000 damages, was apprised by Walker that his earlier version of the accident was untrue and that actually the accident occurred because he lost control of his car in passing a Cadillac just ahead. At that point, Walker's counsel should have refused to participate further in view of the conflict of interest between Walker and State Farm.... Instead he participated in the ensuing deposition of the Walkers, even took an *ex parte* sworn statement from Mr. Walker in order to advise State Farm what action it should take, and later used the statement against Walker in the District Court. This action appears to contravene an Indiana attorney's duty 'at every peril to himself, to preserve the secrets of his client' . . . ." State Farm Mut. Auto Ins. Co. v. Walker, 382 F.2d 548, 552 (1967), *cert. denied,* 389 U.S. 1045, 19 L. Ed. 2d 837, 88 S. Ct. 789 (1968).

24. *See* ABA CANON 6.

25. *See* ABA CANON 35.

"Objection to the intervention of a lay intermediary, who may control litigation or otherwise interfere with the rendering of legal services in a confidential relationship, . . . derives from the element of pecuniary gain. Fearful of dangers thought to arise from that element, the courts of several States have sustained regulations aimed at these activities. We intimate no view one way or the other as to the merits of those decisions with respect to the particular arrangements against which they are directed. It is enough that the superficial resemblance in form between those arrangements and that at bar cannot obscure the vital fact that here the entire arrangement employs constitutionally privileged means of expression to secure constitutionally guaranteed civil rights." NAACP v. Button, 371 U.S. 415, 441-42, 9 L. Ed. 2d 405, 423-24, 83 S. Ct. 328, 342-43 (1963).

26. *Cf.* ABA CANON 38.

27. "Certainly it is true that 'the professional relationship between an attorney and his client is highly personal, involving an intimate appreciation of each individual client's particular problem.' And this Committee does not condone practices which interfere with that relationship. However, the, mere fact the lawyer is actually paid by some entity other than the client does not affect that relationship, so long as the lawyer is selected by and is directly responsible to the client. See Informal Opinions 469 and 679. Of course, as the latter decision points out, there must be full disclosure of the arrangement by the attorney to the client. . . ." *ABA Opinion* 320 (1968).

"[A] third party may pay the cost of legal services as long as control remains in the client and the responsibility of the lawyer is solely to the client. Informal Opinions 469 ad [sic] 679. *See also Opinion* 237." *Id.*

28. *ABA Opinion* 303 (1961) recognized that "[s]tatutory provisions now exist in several states which are designed to make [the practice of law in a form that will be classified as a corporation for federal income tax purposes] legally possible, either as a result of lawyers incorporating or forming associations with various corporate characteristics."

29. *Cf.* ABA CANON 6 and *ABA Opinions* 181 (1938), 104 (1934), 103 (1933), 72 (1932), 50 (1931), 49 (1931), and 33 (1931).

"New York County [Opinion] 203. . . . [A lawyer] should not advise a client to employ an investment company in which he is interested, without informing him of this." DRINKER, LEGAL ETHICS 956 (1953).

"In *Opinions* 72 and 49 this Committee held: The relations of partners in a law firm are such that neither the firm nor any member or associate thereof, may accept any professional employment which any member of the firm cannot properly accept.

"In *Opinion* 16 this Committee held that a member of a law firm could not represent a defendant in a criminal case which was being prosecuted by another member of the firm who was public prosecuting attorney. The Opinion stated that it was clearly unethical for one member of the firm to oppose the interest of the state while another member represented those interests. . . . Since the prosecutor himself could not represent both the public and the defendant, no member of his law firm could either." *ABA Opinion* 296 (1959).

30. *Cf.* ABA CANON 19 and *ABA Opinions* 220 (1941), 185 (1938), 50 (1931), and 33 (1931); *but cf.* Erwin M. Jennings Co. v. DiGenova, 107 Conn. 491, 498-99, 141 A. 866, 868 (1928).

31. "This *Canon* [19] *of Ethics* needs no elaboration to be applied to the facts here. Apparently, the object of this precept is to avoid putting a lawyer in the obviously embarrassing predicament of testifying and then having to argue the credibility and effect of his own testimony. It was not designed to permit a lawyer to call opposing counsel as a witness and thereby disqualify him as counsel." Galarowicz v. Ward, 119 Utah 611, 620, 230 P.2d 576, 580 (1951).

32. ABA CANON 10 and *ABA Opinions* 279 (1949), 246 (1942), and 176 (1938).

33. *See* CODE OF PROFESSIONAL RESPONSIBILITY, DR 2-106(C).

34. *See* ABA CANON 42; *cf. ABA Opinion* 288 (1954).

35. *See* ABA CANON 6; *cf. ABA Opinions* 167 (1937), 60 (1931), and 40 (1931).

36. *ABA Opinion* 247 (1942) held that an attorney could not investigate a night club shooting on behalf of one of the owner's liability insurers, obtaining the cooperation of the owner, and later represent the injured patron in an action against the owner and a different insurance company unless the attorney obtain the "express consent of all concerned given after a full disclosure of the facts," since to do so would be to represent conflicting interests.

See ABA Opinions 247 (1942), 24 (1941), 222 (1941), 218 (1941), 112 (1934), 83 (1932), and 86 (1932).

37. *Cf. ABA Opinions* 231 (1941) and 160 (1936).

38. *Cf. ABA Opinions* 243 (1942) and 235 (1941).

39. *See* ABA CANON 38.

"A lawyer who receives a commission (whether delayed or not) from a title insurance company or guaranty fund for recommending or selling the insurance to his client, or for work done for the client or the company, without either fully disclosing to the client his financial interest in the transaction, or crediting the client's bill with the amount thus received, is guilty of unethical conduct." *ABA Opinion* 304 (1962).

40. *See* ABA Canon 35; *cf. ABA Opinion* 237 (1941).

"When the lay forwarder, as agent for the creditor, forwards a claim to an attorney, the direct relationship of attorney and client shall then exist between the attorney and the creditor, and the forwarder shall not interpose itself as an intermediary to control the activities of the attorney." *ABA Opinion* 294 (1958).

41. "Permanent beneficial and voting rights in the organization set up to practice law, whatever its form, must be restricted to lawyers while the organization is engaged in the practice of law." *ABA Opinion* 303 (1961).

42. "*Canon 33* . . . promulgates underlying principles that must be observed no matter in what form of organization lawyers practice law. Its requirement that no person shall be admitted or held out as a practitioner or member who is not a member of the legal profession duly authorized to practice, and amenable to professional discipline, makes it clear that any centralized management must be in lawyers to avoid a violation of this Canon." *ABA Opinion* 303 (1961).

43. "There is no intervention of any lay agency between lawyer and client when centralized management provided only by lawyers may give guidance or direction to the services being rendered by a lawyer-member of the organization to a client. The language in *Canon 35* that a lawyer should avoid all relations which direct the performance of his duties by or in the interest of an intermediary refers to lay intermediaries and not lawyer intermediaries with whom he is associated in the practice of law." *ABA Opinion* 303 (1961).

CANON 6

A Lawyer Should Represent a Client Competently

ETHICAL CONSIDERATIONS

EC 6-1 Because of his vital role in the legal process, a lawyer should act with competence and proper care in representing clients. He should strive to become and remain proficient in his practice[1] and should accept employment only in matters which he is or intends to become competent to handle.

EC 6-2 A lawyer is aided in attaining and maintaining his competence by keeping abreast of current legal literature and developments, participating in continuing legal education programs,[2] concentrating in particular areas of the law, and by utilizing other available means. He has the additional ethical obligation to assist in improving the legal profession, and he may do so by participating in bar activities intended to advance the quality and standards of members of the profession. Of particular importance is the careful training of his younger associates and the giving of sound guidance to all lawyers who consult him. In short, a lawyer should strive at all levels to aid the legal profession in advancing the highest possible standards of integrity and competence and to meet those standards himself.

EC 6-3 While the licensing of a lawyer is evidence that he has met the standards then prevailing for admission to the bar, a lawyer generally should not accept employment in any area of the law in which he is not qualified.[3] However, he may accept such employment if in good faith he expects to become qualified through study and investigation, as long as such preparation would not result in unreasonable delay or expense to his client. Proper preparation and representation may require the association by the lawyer of professionals in other disciplines. A lawyer offered employment in a matter in which he is not and does not expect to become so qualified should either decline the employment or, with the consent of his client, accept the employment and associate a lawyer who is competent in the matter.[4]

EC 6-4 Having undertaken representation, a lawyer should use proper care to safeguard the interests of his client. If a lawyer has accepted employment in a matter beyond his competence but in which he expected to become competent, he should diligently undertake the work and study necessary to qualify himself. In addition to being qualified to handle a particular matter, his obligation to his client requires him to prepare adequately for and give appropriate attention to his legal work.

EC 6-5 A lawyer should have pride in his professional endeavors. His obligation to act competently calls for higher motivation than that arising from fear of civil liability or disciplinary penalty.

EC 6-6 A lawyer should not seek, by contract or other means, to limit his individual liability to his client for his malpractice. A lawyer who handles the affairs of his client properly has no need to attempt to limit his liability for his professional activities and one who does not handle the affairs of his client properly should not be permitted to do so. A lawyer who is a stockholder in or is associated with a professional legal corporation may, however, limit his liability for malpractice of his associates in the corporation, but only to the extent permitted by law.[5]

DISCIPLINARY RULES

DR 6-101 Failing to Act Competently.
(A) A lawyer shall not:
(1) Handle a legal matter which he knows or should know that he is not competent to handle, without associating with him a lawyer who is competent to handle it.
(2) Handle a legal matter without preparation adequate in the circumstances.
(3) Neglect a legal matter entrusted to him.[6]

DR 6-102 Limiting Liability to Client.
(A) A lawyer shall not attempt to exonerate himself from or limit his liability to his client for his personal malpractice.

NOTES

1. "[W]hen a citizen is faced with the need for a lawyer, he wants, and is entitled to, the best informed counsel he can obtain. Changing times produce changes in our laws and legal procedures. The natural complexities of law require continuing intensive study by a lawyer if he is to render his clients a maximum of efficient service. And, in so doing, he maintains the high standards of the legal profession; and he also increases respect and confidence by the general public." Rochelle & Payne, *The Struggle for Public Understanding*, 25 Texas B.J. 109, 160 (1962).

"We have undergone enormous changes in the last fifty years within the lives of most of the adults living today who may be seeking advice. Most of these changes have been accompanied by changes and developments in the law. . . . Every practicing lawyer encounters these problems and is often perplexed with his own inability to keep up, not only with changes in the law, but also with changes in the lives of his clients and their legal problems.

"To be sure, no client has a right to expect that his lawyer will have all of the answers at the end of his tongue or even in the back of his head at all times. But the client does have the right to expect that the lawyer will have devoted his time and energies to maintaining and improving his competence to know where to look for the answers, to know how to deal with the problems, and to know how to advise to the best of his legal talents and abilities." Levy & Sprague, *Accounting and Law: Is Dual Practice in the Public Interest?*, 52 A.B.A.J. 1110, 1112 (1966).

2. "The whole purpose of continuing legal education, so enthusiastically supported by the ABA, is to make it possible for lawyers to make themselves better lawyers. But there are no nostrums for proficiency in the law; it must come through the hard work of the lawyer himself. To the extent that that work, whether it be in attending institutes or lecture courses, in studying after hours or in the actual day in and day out practice of his profession, can be concentrated within a limited field, the greater the proficiency and expertness that can be developed." *Report of the Special Committee on Specialization and Specialized Legal Education*, 79 A.B.A. Rep. 582, 588 (1954).

3. "If the attorney is not competent to skillfully and properly perform the work, he should not undertake the service." Degen v. Steinbrink, 202 App. Div. 477, 481, 195 N. Y. S. 810, 814 (1922), *aff'd mem.*, 236 N. Y. 669 142 N. E. 328 (1923).

4. *Cf. ABA Opinion* 232 (1941).

5. *See ABA Opinion* 303 (1961); *cf.* Code of Professional Responsibility, EC 2-11.

6. The annual report for 1967-1968 of the Committee on Grievances of the Association of the Bar of the City of New York showed a receipt of 2,232 complaints; of the 828 offenses against clients, 76 involved conversion, 49 involved "overreaching," and 452, or more than half of all such offenses, involved neglect. *Annual Report of the Committee on Grievances of the Association of the Bar of the City of New York,* N.Y.L.J., Sept. 12, 1968, at 4, col. 5.

CANON 7

A Lawyer Should Represent a Client Zealously Within the Bounds of the Law

ETHICAL CONSIDERATIONS

EC 7-1 The duty of a lawyer, both to his client[1] and to the legal system, is to represent his client zealously[2] within the bounds of the law,[3] which includes Disciplinary Rules and enforceable professional regulations.[4] The professional responsibility of a lawyer derives from his membership in a profession which has the duty of assisting members of the public to secure and protect available legal rights and benefits. In our government of laws and not of men, each member of our society is entitled to have his conduct judged and regulated in accordance with the law;[5] to seek any lawful objective[6] through legally permissible means;[7] and to present for adjudication any lawful claim, issue, or defense.

EC 7-2 The bounds of the law in a given case are often difficult to ascertain.[8] The language of legislative enactments and judicial opinions may be uncertain as applied to varying factual situations. The limits and specific meaning of apparently relevant law may be made doubtful by changing or developing constitutional interpretations, inadequately expressed statutes or judicial opinions, and changing public and judicial attitudes. Certainty of law ranges from well-settled rules through areas of conflicting authority to areas without precedent.

EC 7-3 Where the bounds of law are uncertain, the action of a lawyer may depend on whether he is serving as advocate or adviser. A lawyer may serve simultaneously as both advocate and adviser, but the two roles are essentially different.[9] In asserting a position on behalf of his client, an advocate for the most part deals with past conduct and must take the facts as he finds them. By contrast, a lawyer serving as adviser primarily assists his client in determining the course of future conduct and relationships. While serving as advocate, a lawyer should resolve in favor of his client doubts as to the bounds of the law.[10] In serving a client as adviser, a lawyer in appropriate circumstances should give his professional opinion as to what the ultimate decisions of the courts would likely be as to the applicable law.

Duty of the Lawyer to a Client

EC 7-4 The advocate may urge any permissible construction of the law favorable to his client, without regard to his professional opinion as to the likelihood that the construction will ultimately prevail.[11] His conduct is within the bounds of the law, and therefore permissible, if the position taken is supported by the law or is supportable by a good faith argument for an extension, modification, or reversal of the law. However, a lawyer is not justified in asserting a position in litigation that is frivolous.[12]

EC 7-5 A lawyer as adviser furthers the interest of his client by giving his professional opinion as to what he believes would likely be the ultimate decision of the courts on the matter at hand and by informing his client of the practical effect of such decision.[13] He may continue in the representation of his client even though his client has elected to pursue a course of conduct contrary to the advice of the lawyer so long as he does not thereby knowingly assist the client to engage in illegal conduct or to take a frivolous legal position. A lawyer should never encourage or aid his client to commit criminal acts or counsel his client on how to violate the law and avoid punishment therefor.[14]

EC 7-6 Whether the proposed action of a lawyer is within the bounds of the law may be a perplexing question when his client is contemplating a course of conduct having legal consequences that vary according to the client's intent, motive, or desires at the time of the action. Often a lawyer is asked to assist his client in developing evidence relevant to the state of mind of the client at a particular time. He may properly assist his client in the development and preservation of evidence of existing motive, intent, or desire; obviously, he may not do anything furthering the creation or preservation of false evidence. In many cases a lawyer may not be certain as to the state of mind of his client, and in those situations he should resolve reasonable doubts in favor of his client.

EC 7-7 In certain areas of legal representation not affecting the merits of the cause or substantially prejudicing the rights of a client, a lawyer is entitled to make decisions on his own. But otherwise the authority to make decisions is exclusively that of the client and, if made within the framework of the law, such decisions are binding on his lawyer. As typical examples in civil cases, it is for the client to decide whether he will accept a settlement offer or whether he will waive his right to plead an affirmative defense. A defense lawyer in a criminal case has the duty to advise his client fully on whether a particular plea to a charge appears to be desirable and as to the prospects of success on appeal, but it is for the client to decide what plea should be entered and whether an appeal should be taken.[15]

EC 7-8 A lawyer should exert his best efforts to insure that decisions of his client are made only after the client has been informed of relevant considerations. A lawyer ought to initiate this decision-making process if the client does not do so. Advice of a lawyer to his client need not be confined to purely legal considerations.[16] A lawyer should advise his client of the possible effect of each legal alternative.[17] A lawyer should bring to bear upon this decision-making process the fullness of his experience as well as his objective viewpoint.[18] In assisting his client to reach a proper decision, it is often desirable for a lawyer to point out those factors which may lead to a decision that is morally just as well as legally permissible.[19] He may emphasize the possibility of harsh consequences that might result from assertion of legally permissible positions. In the final analysis, however, the lawyer should always remember that the decision whether to forego legally available objectives or methods because of non-legal factors is ultimately for the client and not for himself. In the event that the client in a non-adjudicatory matter insists upon a course of conduct that is contrary to the judgment and advice of the lawyer but not prohibited by Disciplinary Rules, the lawyer may withdraw from the employment.[20]

EC 7-9 In the exercise of his professional judgment on those decisions which are for his determination in the handling of a legal matter,[21] a lawyer should always act in a manner consistent with the best interests of his client.[22] However, when an action in the best interest of his client seems to him to be unjust, he may ask his client for permission to forego such action.[23]

EC 7-10 The duty of a lawyer to represent his client with zeal does not militate against his concurrent obligation to treat with consideration all persons involved in the legal process and to avoid the infliction of needless harm.

EC 7-11 The responsibilities of a lawyer may vary according to the intelligence, experience, mental condition or age of a client, the obligation of a public officer, or the nature of a particular proceeding. Examples include the representation of an illiterate or an incompetent, service as a public prosecutor or other government lawyer, and appearances before administrative and legislative bodies.

EC 7-12 Any mental or physical condition of a client that renders him incapable of making a considered judgment on his own behalf casts additional responsibilities upon his lawyer. Where an incompetent is acting through a guardian or other legal representative, a lawyer must look to such representative for those decisions which are normally the prerogative of the client to make. If a client under disability has no legal representative, his lawyer may be compelled in court proceedings to make decisions on behalf of the client. If the client is capable of understanding the matter in question or of contributing to the advancement of his interests, regardless of whether he is legally disqualified from performing certain acts, the lawyer should obtain from him all possible aid. If the disability of a client and the lack of a legal representative compel the lawyer to make decisions for his client, the lawyer should consider all circumstances then prevailing and act with care to safeguard and advance the interests of his client. But obviously a lawyer cannot perform any act or make any decision which the law requires his client to perform or make, either acting for himself if competent, or by a duly constituted representative if legally incompetent.

EC 7-13 The responsibility of a public prosecutor differs from that of the usual advocate; his duty is to seek justice, not merely to convict.[24] This special duty exists because: (1) the prosecutor represents the sovereign and therefore should use restraint in the discretionary exercise of governmental powers, such as in the selection of cases to prosecute; (2) during trial the prosecutor is not only an advocate but he also may make decisions normally made by an individual client, and those affecting the public interest should be fair to all; and (3) in our system of criminal justice the accused is to be given the benefit of all reasonable doubts. With respect to evidence and witnesses, the prosecutor has responsibilities different from those of a lawyer in private practice: the prosecutor should make timely disclosure to the defense of available evidence, known to him, that tends to negate the guilt of the accused, mitigate the degree of the offense, or reduce the punishment. Further, a prosecutor should not intentionally avoid pursuit of evidence merely because he believes it will damage the prosecutor's case or aid the accused.

EC 7-14 A government lawyer who has discretionary power relative to litigation should refrain from instituting or continuing litigation that is obviously unfair. A government lawyer not having such discretionary power who believes there is lack of merit in a controversy submitted to him should so advise his superiors and recommend the avoidance of unfair litigation. A government lawyer in a civil action or administrative proceeding has the responsibility to seek justice and to develop a full and fair record, and he should not use his position or the economic power of the government to harass parties or to bring about unjust settlements or results.

EC 7-15 The nature and purpose of proceedings before administrative agencies vary widely. The proceedings may be legislative or quasi-judicial, or a combination of both. They may be *ex parte* in character, in which event they may originate either at the instance of the agency or upon motion of an interested party. The scope of an inquiry may be purely investigative or it may be truly adversary looking toward the adjudication of specific rights of a party or of classes of parties. The foregoing are but examples of some of the types of proceedings conducted by administrative agencies. A lawyer appearing before an administrative agency,[25] regardless of the nature of the proceeding it is conducting, has the continuing duty to advance the cause of his client within the bounds of the law.[26] Where the applicable rules of the agency impose specific obligations upon a lawyer, it is his duty to comply therewith, unless the lawyer has a legitimate basis for challenging the validity thereof. In all appearances before administrative agencies, a lawyer should identify himself, his client if identity of his client is not privileged,[27] and the representative nature of his appearance. It is not improper, however, for a lawyer to seek from an agency information available to the public without identifying his client.

EC 7-16 The primary business of a legislative body is to enact laws rather than to adjudicate controversies, although on occasion the activities of a legislative body may take on the characteristics of an adversary proceeding, particularly in investigative and impeachment matters. The role of a lawyer supporting or opposing proposed legislation normally is quite different from his role in representing a person under investigation or on trial by a legislative body. When a lawyer appears in connection with proposed legislation, he seeks to affect the lawmaking process, but when he appears on behalf of a client in investigatory or impeachment proceedings, he is concerned with the protection of the rights of his client. In either event, he should identify himself and his client, if identity of his client is not privileged, and should comply with applicable laws and legislative rules.[28]

EC 7-17 The obligation of loyalty to his client applies only to a lawyer in the discharge of his professional duties and implies no obligation to adopt a personal viewpoint favorable to the interests or desires of his client.[29] While a lawyer must act always with circumspection in order that his conduct will not adversely affect the rights of a client in a matter he is then handling, he may take positions on public issues and espouse legal reforms he favors without regard to the individual views of any client.

EC 7-18 The legal system in its broadest sense functions best when persons in need of legal advice or assistance are represented by their own counsel. For this reason a lawyer should not communicate on the subject matter of the representation of his client with a person he knows to be represented in the matter by a lawyer, unless pursuant to law or rule of court or unless he has the consent of the lawyer for that person.[30] If one is not represented by counsel, a lawyer representing another may have to deal directly with the unrepresented person; in such an instance, a lawyer should not undertake to give advice to the person who is attempting to represent himself,[31] except that he may advise him to obtain a lawyer.

Duty of the Lawyer to the Adversary System of Justice

EC 7-19 Our legal system provides for the adjudication of disputes governed by the rules of substantive, evidentiary, and procedural law. An adversary presentation counters the natural human tendency to judge too swiftly in terms of the familiar that which is not yet fully known;[32] the advocate, by his zealous preparation and presentation of facts and law, enables the tribunal to come to the hearing with an open and neutral mind and to render impartial judgments.[33] The duty of a lawyer to his client and his duty to the legal system are the same: to represent his client zealously within the bounds of the law.[34]

EC 7-20 In order to function properly, our adjudicative process requires an informed, impartial tribunal capable of administering justice promptly and efficiently[35] according to procedures that command public confidence and respect.[36] Not only must there be competent, adverse presentation of evidence and issues, but a tribunal must be aided by rules appropriate to an effective and dignified process. The procedures under which tribunals operate in our adversary system have been prescribed largely by legislative enactments, court rules and decisions, and administrative rules. Through the years certain concepts of proper professional conduct have become rules of law applicable to the adversary adjudicative process. Many of these concepts are the bases for standards of professional conduct set forth in the Disciplinary Rules.

EC 7-21 The civil adjudicative process is primarily designed for the settlement of disputes between parties, while the criminal process is designed for the protection of society as a whole. Threatening to use, or using, the criminal process to coerce adjustment of private civil claims or controversies is a subversion of that process;[37] further, the person against whom the criminal process is so misused may be deterred from asserting his legal rights and thus the usefulness of the civil process in settling private disputes is impaired. As in all cases of abuse of judicial process, the improper use of criminal process tends to diminish public confidence in our legal system.

EC 7-22 Respect for judicial rulings is essential to the proper administration of justice; however, a litigant or his lawyer may, in good faith and within the framework of the law, take steps to test the correctness of a ruling of a tribunal.[38]

EC 7-23 The complexity of law often makes it difficult for a tribunal to be fully informed unless the pertinent law is presented by the lawyers in the cause. A tribunal that is fully informed on the applicable law is better able to make a fair and accurate determination of the matter before it. The adversary system contemplates that each lawyer will present and argue the existing law in the light most favorable to his client.[39] Where a lawyer knows of legal authority in the controlling jurisdiction directly adverse to the position of his client, he should inform the tribunal of its existence unless his adversary has done so; but, having made such disclosure, he may challenge its soundness in whole or in part.[40]

Model Code of Professional Responsibility

EC 7-24 In order to bring about just and informed decisions, evidentiary and procedural rules have been established by tribunals to permit the inclusion of relevant evidence and argument and the exclusion of all other considerations. The expression by a lawyer of his personal opinion as to the justness of a cause, as to the credibility of a witness, as to the culpability of a civil litigant, or as to the guilt or innocence of an accused is not a proper subject for argument to the trier of fact.[41] It is improper as to factual matters because admissible evidence possessed by a lawyer should be presented only as sworn testimony. It is improper as to all other matters because, were the rule otherwise, the silence of a lawyer on a given occasion could be construed unfavorably to his client. However, a lawyer may argue, on his analysis of the evidence, for any position or conclusion with respect to any of the foregoing matters.

EC 7-25 Rules of evidence and procedure are designed to lead to just decisions and are part of the framework of the law. Thus while a lawyer may take steps in good faith and within the framework of the law to test the validity of rules, he is not justified in consciously violating such rules and he should be diligent in his efforts to guard against his unintentional violation of them.[42] As examples, a lawyer should subscribe to or verify only those pleadings that he believes are in compliance with applicable law and rules; a lawyer should not make any prefatory statement before a tribunal in regard to the purported facts of the case on trial unless he believes that his statement will be supported by admissible evidence; a lawyer should not ask a witness a question solely for the purpose of harassing or embarrassing him; and a lawyer should not by subterfuge put before a jury matters which it cannot properly consider.

EC 7-26 The law and Disciplinary Rules prohibit the use of fraudulent, false, or perjured testimony or evidence.[43] A lawyer who knowingly[44] participates in introduction of such testimony or evidence is subject to discipline. A lawyer should, however, present any admissible evidence his client desires to have presented unless he knows, or from facts within his knowledge should know, that such testimony or evidence is false, fraudulent, or perjured.[45]

EC 7-27 Because it interferes with the proper administration of justice, a lawyer should not suppress evidence that he or his client has a legal obligation to reveal or produce. In like manner, a lawyer should not advise or cause a person to secrete himself or to leave the jurisdiction of a tribunal for the purpose of making him unavailable as a witness therein.[46]

EC 7-28 Witnesses should always testify truthfully[47] and should be free from any financial inducements that might tempt them to do otherwise.[48] A lawyer should not pay or agree to pay a non-expert witness an amount in excess of reimbursement for expenses and financial loss incident to his being a witness; however, a lawyer may pay or agree to pay an expert witness a reasonable fee for his services as an expert. But in no event should a lawyer pay or agree to pay a contingent fee to any witness. A lawyer should exercise reasonable diligence to see that his client and lay associates conform to these standards.[49]

EC 7-29 To safeguard the impartiality that is essential to the judicial process, veniremen and jurors should be protected against extraneous influences.[50] When impartiality is present, public confidence in the judicial system is enhanced. There should be no extrajudicial communication with veniremen prior to trial or with jurors during trial by or on behalf of a lawyer connected with the case. Furthermore, a lawyer who is not connected with the case should not communicate with or cause another to communicate with a venireman or a juror about the case. After the trial, communication by a lawyer with jurors is permitted so long as he refrains from asking questions or making comments that tend to harass or embarrass the juror[51] or to influence actions of the juror in future cases. Were a lawyer to be prohibited from communicating after trial with a juror, he could not ascertain if the verdict might be subject to legal challenge, in which event the invalidity of a verdict might go undetected.[52] When an extrajudicial communication by a lawyer with a juror is permitted by law, it should be made considerately and with deference to the personal feelings of the juror.

EC 7-30 Vexatious or harassing investigations of veniremen or jurors seriously impair the effectiveness of our jury system. For this reason, a lawyer or anyone on his behalf who conducts an investigation of veniremen or jurors should act with circumspection and restraint.

EC 7-31 Communications with or investigations of members of families of veniremen or jurors by a lawyer or by anyone on his behalf are subject to the restrictions imposed upon the lawyer with respect to his communications with or investigations of veniremen and jurors.

EC 7-32 Because of his duty to aid in preserving the integrity of the jury system, a lawyer who learns of improper conduct by or towards a venireman, a juror, or a member of the family of either should make a prompt report to the court regarding such conduct.

EC 7-33 A goal of our legal system is that each party shall have his case, criminal or civil, adjudicated by an impartial tribunal. The attainment of this goal may be defeated by dissemination of news or comments which tend to influence judge or jury.[53] Such news or comments may prevent prospective jurors from being impartial at the outset of the trial[54] and may also interfere with the obligation of jurors to base their verdict solely upon the evidence admitted in the trial.[55] The release by a lawyer of out-of-court statements regarding an anticipated or pending trial may improperly affect the impartiality of the tribunal.[56] For these reasons, standards for permissible and prohibited conduct of a lawyer with respect to trial publicity have been established.

EC 7-34 The impartiality of a public servant in our legal system may be impaired by the receipt of gifts or loans. A lawyer,[57] therefore, is never justified in making a gift or a loan to a judge, a hearing officer, or an official or employee of a tribunal except as permitted by Section C(4) of Canon 5 of the Code of Judicial Conduct, but a lawyer may make a contribution to the campaign fund of a candidate for judicial office in conformity with Section B(2) under Canon 7 of the Code of Judicial Conduct.[58]

EC 7-35 All litigants and lawyers should have access to tribunals on an equal basis. Generally, in adversary proceedings a lawyer should not communicate with a judge relative to a matter pending before, or which is to be brought before, a tribunal over which he presides in circumstances which might have the effect or give the appearance of granting undue advantage to one party.[59] For example, a lawyer should not communicate with a tribunal by a writing unless a copy thereof is promptly delivered to opposing counsel or to the adverse party if he is not represented by a lawyer. Ordinarily an oral communication by a lawyer with a judge or hearing officer should be made only upon adequate notice to opposing counsel, or, if there is none, to the opposing party. A lawyer should not condone or lend himself to private importunities by another with a judge or hearing officer on behalf of himself or his client.

EC 7-36 Judicial hearings ought to be conducted through dignified and orderly procedures designed to protect the rights of all parties. Although a lawyer has the duty to represent his client zealously, he should not engage in any conduct that offends the dignity and decorum of proceedings.[60] While maintaining his independence, a lawyer should be respectful, courteous, and above-board in his relations with a judge or hearing officer before whom he appears.[61] He should avoid undue solicitude for the comfort or convenience of judge or jury and should avoid any other conduct calculated to gain special consideration.

EC 7-37 In adversary proceedings, clients are litigants and though ill feeling may exist between clients, such ill feeling should not influence a lawyer in his conduct, attitude, and demeanor towards opposing lawyers.[62] A lawyer should not make unfair or derogatory personal reference to opposing counsel. Haranguing and offensive tactics by lawyers interfere with the orderly administration of justice and have no proper place in our legal system.

EC 7-38 A lawyer should be courteous to opposing counsel and should accede to reasonable requests regarding court proceedings, settings, continuances, waiver of procedural formalities, and similar matters which do not prejudice the rights of his client.[63] He should follow local customs of courtesy or practice, unless he gives timely notice to opposing counsel of his intention not to do so.[64] A lawyer should be punctual in fulfilling all professional commitments.[65]

Model Code of Professional Responsibility

EC 7-39 In the final analysis, proper functioning of the adversary system depends upon cooperation between lawyers and tribunals in utilizing procedures which will preserve the impartiality of tribunals and make their decisional processes prompt and just, without impinging upon the obligation of lawyers to represent their clients zealously within the framework of the law.

DISCIPLINARY RULES

DR 7-101 Representing a Client Zealously.

(A) A lawyer shall not intentionally:[66]
  (1) Fail to seek the lawful objectives of his client through reasonably available means[67] permitted by law and the Disciplinary Rules, except as provided by DR 7-101(B). A lawyer does not violate this Disciplinary Rule, however, by acceding to reasonable requests of opposing counsel which do not prejudice the rights of his client, by being punctual in fulfilling all professional commitments, by avoiding offensive tactics, or by treating with courtesy and consideration all persons involved in the legal process.
  (2) Fail to carry out a contract of employment entered into with a client for professional services, but he may withdraw as permitted under DR 2-110, DR 5-102, and DR 5-105.
  (3) Prejudice or damage his client during the course of the professional relationship,[68] except as required under DR 7-102 (B).

(B) In his representation of a client, a lawyer may:
  (1) Where permissible, exercise his professional judgment to waive or fail to assert a right or position of his client.
  (2) Refuse to aid or participate in conduct that he believes to be unlawful, even though there is some support for an argument that the conduct is legal.

DR 7-102 Representing a Client Within the Bounds of the Law.

(A) In his representation of a client, a lawyer shall not:
  (1) File a suit, assert a position, conduct a defense, delay a trial, or take other action on behalf of his client when he knows or when it is obvious that such action would serve merely to harass or maliciously injure another.[69]
  (2) Knowingly advance a claim or defense that is unwarranted under existing law, except that he may advance such claim or defense if it can be supported by good faith argument for an extension, modification, or reversal of existing law.
  (3) Conceal or knowingly fail to disclose that which he is required by law to reveal.
  (4) Knowingly use perjured testimony or false evidence.[70]
  (5) Knowingly make a false statement of law or fact.
  (6) Participate in the creation or preservation of evidence when he knows or it is obvious that the evidence is false.
  (7) Counsel or assist his client in conduct that the lawyer knows to be illegal or fraudulent.
  (8) Knowingly engage in other illegal conduct or conduct contrary to a Disciplinary Rule.

(B) A lawyer who receives information clearly establishing that:
  (1) His client has, in the course of the representation, perpetrated a fraud upon a person or tribunal shall promptly call upon his client to rectify the same, and if his client refuses or is unable to do so, he shall reveal the fraud to the affected person or tribunal, except when the information is protected as a privileged communication.[71]
  (2) A person other than his client has perpetrated a fraud upon a tribunal shall promptly reveal the fraud to the tribunal.[72]

DR 7-103 Performing the Duty of Public Prosecutor or Other Government Lawyer.[73]

(A) A public prosecutor or other government lawyer shall not institute or cause to be instituted criminal charges when he knows or it is obvious that the charges are not supported by probable cause.

(B) A public prosecutor or other government lawyer in criminal litigation shall make timely disclosure to counsel for the defendant, or to the defendant if he has no counsel, of the existence of evidence, known to the prosecutor or other government lawyer, that tends to negate the guilt of the accused, mitigate the degree of the offense, or reduce the punishment.

DR 7-104 Communicating With One of Adverse Interest.[74]

(A) During the course of his representation of a client a lawyer shall not:
  (1) Communicate or cause another to communicate on the subject of the representation with a party he knows to be represented by a lawyer in that matter unless he has the prior consent of the lawyer representing such other party[75] or is authorized by law to do so.
  (2) Give advice to a person who is not represented by a lawyer, other than the advice to secure counsel,[76] if the interests of such person are or have a reasonable possibility of being in conflict with the interests of his client.[77]

DR 7-105 Threatening Criminal Prosecution.

(A) A lawyer shall not present, participate in presenting, or threaten to present criminal charges solely to obtain an advantage in a civil matter.

DR 7-106 Trial Conduct.

(A) A lawyer shall not disregard or advise his client to disregard a standing rule of a tribunal or a ruling of a tribunal made in the course of a proceeding, but he may take appropriate steps in good faith to test the validity of such rule or ruling.

(B) In presenting a matter to a tribunal, a lawyer shall disclose:[78]
  (1) Legal authority in the controlling jurisdiction known to him to be directly adverse to the position of his client and which is not disclosed by opposing counsel.[79]
  (2) Unless privileged or irrelevant, the identities of the clients he represents and of the persons who employed him.[80]

(C) In appearing in his professional capacity before a tribunal, a lawyer shall not:
  (1) State or allude to any matter that he has no reasonable basis to believe is relevant to the case or that will not be supported by admissible evidence.[81]
  (2) Ask any question that he has no reasonable basis to believe is relevant to the case and that is intended to degrade a witness or other person.[82]
  (3) Assert his personal knowledge of the facts in issue, except when testifying as a witness.
  (4) Assert his personal opinion as to the justness of a cause, as to the credibility of a witness, as to the culpability of a civil litigant, or as to the guilt or innocence of an accused;[83] but he may argue, on his analysis of the evidence, for any position or conclusion with respect to the matters stated herein.
  (5) Fail to comply with known local customs of courtesy or practice of the bar or a particular tribunal without giving to opposing counsel timely notice of his intent not to comply.[84]
  (6) Engage in undignified or discourteous conduct which is degrading to a tribunal.
  (7) Intentionally or habitually violate any established rule of procedure or of evidence.

DR 7-107 Trial Publicity.[85]

(A) A lawyer participating in or associated with the investigation of a criminal matter shall not make or participate in making an extrajudicial statement that a reasonable person would expect to be disseminated by means of public communication and that does more than state without elaboration:
  (1) Information contained in a public record.
  (2) That the investigation is in progress.
  (3) The general scope of the investigation including a description of the offense and, if permitted by law, the identity of the victim.
  (4) A request for assistance in apprehending a suspect or assistance in other matters and the information necessary thereto.
  (5) A warning to the public of any dangers.

(B) A lawyer or law firm associated with the prosecution or defense of a criminal matter shall not, from the time of the filing of a complaint, information, or indictment, the issuance of an arrest warrant, or arrest until the commencement of the trial or disposition without trial, make or participate in making an extrajudicial statement that a reasonable person would expect to be disseminated by

means of public communication and that relates to:
(1) The character, reputation, or prior criminal record (including arrests, indictments, or other charges of crime) of the accused.
(2) The possibility of a plea of guilty to the offense charged or to a lesser offense.
(3) The existence or contents of any confession, admission, or statement given by the accused or his refusal or failure to make a statement.
(4) The performance or results of any examinations or tests or the refusal or failure of the accused to submit to examinations or tests.
(5) The identity, testimony, or credibility of a prospective witness.
(6) Any opinion as to the guilt or innocence of the accused, the evidence, or the merits of the case.

(C) DR 7-107 (B) does not preclude a lawyer during such period from announcing:
(1) The name, age, residence, occupation, and family status of the accused.
(2) If the accused has not been apprehended, any information necessary to aid in his apprehension or to warn the public of any dangers he may present.
(3) A request for assistance in obtaining evidence.
(4) The identity of the victim of the crime.
(5) The fact, time, and place of arrest, resistance, pursuit, and use of weapons.
(6) The identity of investigating and arresting officers or agencies and the length of the investigation.
(7) At the time of seizure, a description of the physical evidence seized, other than a confession, admission, or statement.
(8) The nature, substance, or text of the charge.
(9) Quotations from or references to public records of the court in the case.
(10) The scheduling or result of any step in the judicial proceedings.
(11) That the accused denies the charges made against him.

(D) During the selection of a jury or the trial of a criminal matter, a lawyer or law firm associated with the prosecution or defense of a criminal matter shall not make or participate in making an extra-judicial statement that a reasonable person would expect to be disseminated by means of public communication and that relates to the trial, parties, or issues in the trial or other matters that are reasonably likely to interfere with a fair trial, except that he may quote from or refer without comment to public records of the court in the case.

(E) After the completion of a trial or disposition without trial of a criminal matter and prior to the imposition of sentence, a lawyer or law firm associated with the prosecution or defense shall not make or participate in making an extrajudicial statement that a reasonable person would expect to be disseminated by public communication and that is reasonably likely to affect the imposition of sentence.

(F) The foregoing provisions of DR 7-107 also apply to professional disciplinary proceedings and juvenile disciplinary proceedings when pertinent and consistent with other law applicable to such proceedings.

(G) A lawyer or law firm associated with a civil action shall not during its investigation or litigation make or participate in making an extrajudicial statement, other than a quotation from or reference to public records, that a reasonable person would expect to be disseminated by means of public communication and that relates to:
(1) Evidence regarding the occurrence or transaction involved.
(2) The character, credibility, or criminal record of a party, witness, or prospective witness.
(3) The performance or results of any examinations or tests or the refusal or failure of a party to submit to such.
(4) His opinion as to the merits of the claims or defenses of a party, except as required by law or administrative rule.
(5) Any other matter reasonably likely to interfere with a fair trial of the action.

(H) During the pendency of an administrative proceeding, a lawyer or law firm associated therewith shall not make or participate in making a statement, other than a quotation from or reference to public records, that a reasonable person would expect to be disseminated by means of public communication if it is made

outside the official course of the proceeding and relates to:
(1) Evidence regarding the occurrence or transaction involved.
(2) The character, credibility, or criminal record of a party, witness, or prospective witness.
(3) Physical evidence or the performance or results of any examinations or tests or the refusal or failure of a party to submit to such.
(4) His opinion as to the merits of the claims, defenses, or positions of an interested person.
(5) Any other matter reasonably likely to interfere with a fair hearing.

(I) The foregoing provisions of DR 7-107 do not preclude a lawyer from replying to charges of misconduct publicly made against him or from participating in the proceedings of legislative, administrative, or other investigative bodies.

(J) A lawyer shall exercise reasonable care to prevent his employees and associates from making an extrajudicial statement that he would be prohibited from making under DR 7-107.

DR 7-108 Communication with or Investigation of Jurors.

(A) Before the trial of a case a lawyer connected therewith shall not communicate with or cause another to communicate with anyone he knows to be a member of the venire from which the jury will be selected for the trial of the case.

(B) During the trial of a case:
(1) A lawyer connected therewith shall not communicate with or cause another to communicate with any member of the jury.[86]
(2) A lawyer who is not connected therewith shall not communicate with or cause any other to communicate with a juror concerning the case.

(C) DR 7-108 (A) and (B) do not prohibit a lawyer from communicating with veniremen or jurors in the course of official proceedings.

(D) After discharge of the jury from further consideration of a case with which the lawyer was connected, the lawyer shall not ask questions of or make comments to a member of that jury that are calculated merely to harass or embarrass the juror or to influence his actions in future jury service.[87]

(E) A lawyer shall not conduct or cause, by financial support or otherwise, another to conduct a vexatious or harassing investigation of either a venireman or a juror.

(F) All restrictions imposed by DR 7-108 upon a lawyer also apply to communications with or investigations of members of a family of a venireman or a juror.

(G) A lawyer shall reveal promptly to the court improper conduct by a venireman or a juror, or by another toward a venireman or a juror or a member of his family, of which the lawyer has knowledge.

DR 7-109 Contact with Witnesses.

(A) A lawyer shall not suppress any evidence that he or his client has a legal obligation to reveal or produce.[88]

(B) A lawyer shall not advise or cause a person to secrete himself or to leave the jurisdiction of a tribunal for the purpose of making him unavailable as a witness therein.[89]

(C) A lawyer shall not pay, offer to pay, or acquiesce in the payment of compensation to a witness contingent upon the content of his testimony or the outcome of the case.[90] But a lawyer may advance, guarantee, or acquiesce in the payment of:
(1) Expenses reasonably incurred by a witness in attending or testifying.
(2) Reasonable compensation to a witness for his loss of time in attending or testifying.
(3) A reasonable fee for the professional services of an expert witness.

DR 7-110 Contact with Officials.[91]

(A) A lawyer shall not give or lend any thing of value to a judge, official, or employee of a tribunal except as permitted by Section C(4) of Canon 5 of the Code of Judicial Conduct, but a lawyer may make a contribution to the campaign fund of a candidate for judicial office in conformity with Section B(2) under Canon 7 of the Code of Judicial Conduct.

(B) In an adversary proceeding, a lawyer shall not communicate, or cause another to communicate, as to the merits of the cause with a judge

Model Code of Professional Responsibility

or an official before whom the proceeding is pending, except:
(1) In the course of official proceedings in the cause.
(2) In writing if he promptly delivers a copy of the writing to opposing counsel or to the adverse party if he is not represented by a lawyer.
(3) Orally upon adequate notice to opposing counsel or to the adverse party if he is not represented by a lawyer.
(4) As otherwise authorized by law, or by Section A (4) under Canon 3 of the Code of Judicial Conduct.[92]

NOTES

1. "The right to be heard would be, in many cases, of little avail if it did not comprehend the right to be heard by counsel. Even the intelligent and educated layman has small and sometimes no skill in the science of law." Powell v. Alabama, 287 U.S. 45, 68-69, 77 L. Ed. 158, 170, 53 S. Ct. 55, 64 (1932).

2. *Cf.* ABA Canon 4.

"At times . . . [the tax lawyer] will be wise to discard some arguments and he should exercise discretion to emphasize the arguments which in his judgment are most likely to be persuasive. But this process involves legal judgment rather than moral attitudes. The tax lawyer should put aside private disagreements with Congressional and Treasury policies. His own notions of policy, and his personal view of what the law should be, are irrelevant. The job entrusted to him by his client is to use all his learning and ability to protect his client's rights, not to help in the process of promoting a better tax system. The tax lawyer need not accept his client's economic and social opinions, but the client is paying for technical attention and undivided concentration upon his affairs. He is equally entitled to performance unfettered by his attorney's economic and social predilections." Paul, *The Lawyer as a Tax Adviser,* 25 Rocky Mt. L. Rev. 412, 418 (1953).

3. *See* ABA Canons 15 and 32.

ABA Canon 5, although only speaking of one accused of crime, imposes a similar obligation on the lawyer: "[T]he lawyer is bound, by all fair and honorable means, to present every defense that the law of the land permits, to the end that no person may be deprived of life or liberty, but by due process of law."

"Any persuasion or pressure on the advocate which deters him from planning and carrying out the litigation on the basis of 'what, within the framework of the law, is best for my client's interest?' interferes with the obligation to represent the client fully within the law.

"This obligation, in its fullest sense, is the heart of the adversary process. Each attorney, as an advocate, acts for and seeks that which in his judgment is best for his client, within the bounds authoritatively established. The advocate does not *decide* what is just in this case—he would be usurping the function of the judge and jury—he acts for and seeks for his client that which he is entitled to under the law. He can do no less and properly represent the client." Thode, The *Ethical Standard for the Advocate,* 39 Texas L. Rev. 575, 584 (1961).

"The [Texas public opinion] survey indicates that distrust of the lawyer can be traced directly to certain factors. Foremost of these is a basic misunderstanding of the function of the lawyer as an advocate in an adversary system.

"Lawyers are accused of taking advantage of 'loopholes' and 'technicalities' to win. Persons who make this charge are unaware, or do not understand, that the lawyer is hired to win, and if he does not exercise every legitimate effort in his client's behalf, then he is betraying a sacred trust." Rochelle & Payne, *The Struggle for Public Understanding,* 25 Texas B.J. 109, 159 (1962).

"The importance of the attorney's undivided allegiance and faithful service to one accused of crime, irrespective of the attorney's personal opinion as to the guilt of his client, lies in Canon 5 of the American Bar Association Canon of Ethics.

"The difficulty lies, of course, in ascertaining whether the attorney has been guilty of an error of judgment, such as an election with respect to trial tactics, or has otherwise been actuated by his conscience or belief that his client should be convicted in any event. All too frequently courts are called upon to review actions of defense counsel which are, at the most, errors of judgment, not properly reviewable on habeas corpus unless the trial is a farce and a mockery of justice which requires the court to intervene. . . . But when defense counsel, in a truly adverse proceeding, admits that his conscience would not permit him to adopt certain customary trial procedures, this extends beyond the realm of judgment and strongly suggests an invasion of constitutional rights." Johns v. Smyth, 176 F. Supp. 949, 952 (E.D. Va. 1959), *modified,* United States ex rel. Wilkins v. Banmiller, 205 F.

Supp. 123, 128, n. 5 (E.D. Pa. 1962), *aff'd*, 325 F. 2d 514 (3d Cir. 1963), *cert. denied*, 379 U.S. 847, 13 L. Ed. 2d 51, 85 S. Ct. 87 (1964).

"The adversary system in law administration bears a striking resemblance to the competitive economic system. In each we assume that the individual through partisanship or through self-interest will strive mightily for his side, and that kind of striving we must have. But neither system would be tolerable without restraints and modifications, and at times without outright departures from the system itself. Since the legal profession is entrusted with the system of law administration, a part of its task is to develop in its members appropriate restraints without impairing the values of partisan striving. An accompanying task is to aid in the modification of the adversary system or departure from it in areas to which the system is unsuited." Cheatham, *The Lawyer's Role and Surroundings*, 25 Rocky Mt. L. Rev. 405, 410 (1953).

4. "Rule 4.15 prohibits, in the pursuit of a client's cause, 'any manner of fraud or chicane'; Rule 4.22 requires 'candor and fairness' in the conduct of the lawyer, and forbids the making of knowing misquotations; Rule 4.47 provides that a lawyer 'should always maintain his integrity,' and generally forbids all misconduct injurious to the interests of the public, the courts, or his clients, and acts contrary to 'justice, honesty, modesty or good morals.' Our Commissioner has accurately paraphrased these rules as follows: 'An attorney does not have the duty to do all and whatever he can that may enable him to win his client's cause or to further his client's interest. His duty and efforts in these respects, although they should be prompted by his "entire devotion" to the interest of his client, must be within and not without the bounds of the law.' " In re Wines, 370 S.W.2d 328, 333 (Mo. 1963).

See Note, 38 Texas L. Rev. 107, 110 (1959).

5. "Under our system of government the process of adjudication is surrounded by safeguards evolved from centuries of experience. These safeguards are not designed merely to lend formality and decorum to the trial of causes. They are predicated on the assumption that to secure for any controversy a truly informed and dispassionate decision is a difficult thing, requiring for its achievement a special summoning and organization of human effort and the adoption of measures to exclude the biases and prejudgments that have free play outside the courtroom. All of this goes for naught if the man with an unpopular cause is unable to find a competent lawyer courageous enough to represent him. His chance to have his day in court loses much of its meaning if his case is handicapped from the outset by the very kind of prejudgment our rules of evidence and procedure are intended to prevent." *Professional Responsibility: Report of the Joint Conference*, 44 A.B.A.J. 1159, 1216 (1958).

6. "[I]t is . . . [the tax lawyer's] positive duty to show the client how to avail himself to the full of what the law permits. He is not the keeper of the Congressional conscience." Paul, The *Lawyer as a Tax Adviser*, 25 Rocky Mt. L. Rev. 412, 418 (1953).

7. *See* ABA Canons 15 and 30.

8. "The fact that it desired to evade the law, as it is called, is immaterial, because the very meaning of a line in the law is that you intentionally may go as close to it as you can if you do not pass it . . . . It is a matter of proximity and degree as to which minds will differ . . . ." Justice Holmes, in Superior Oil Co. v. Mississippi, 280 U.S. 390, 395-96, 74 L. Ed. 504, 508, 50 S. Ct. 169, 170 (1930).

9. "Today's lawyers perform two distinct types of functions, and our ethical standards should, but in the main do not, recognize these two functions. Judge Philbrick McCoy recently reported to the American Bar Association the need for a reappraisal of the Canons in light of the new and distinct function of counselor, as distinguished from advocate, which today predominates in the legal profession. . . .

". . . In the first place, any revision of the canons must take into account and speak to this new and now predominant function of the lawyer. . . . It is beyond the scope of this paper to discuss the ethical standards to be applied to the counselor except to state that in my opinion such standards should require a greater recognition and protection for the interest of the public generally than is presently expressed in the canons. Also, the counselor's obligation should extend to requiring him to inform and to impress upon the client a just solution of the problem, considering all interests involved." Thode, *The Ethical Standard for the Advocate*, 39 Texas L. Rev. 575, 578-79 (1961).

"The man who has been called into court to answer for his own actions is entitled to fair hearing. Partisan advocacy plays its essential part in such a hearing, and the lawyer pleading his client's case may properly present it in the most favorable light. A similar resolution of doubts in one direction becomes inappropriate when the lawyer acts as counselor. The reasons that justify and even require partisan advocacy in the trial of a cause do not grant any license to the lawyer to participate as legal advisor in a line of conduct that is immoral, unfair, or of doubtful legality. In saving himself from this unworthy involvement, the lawyer cannot be guided solely by an unreflective inner sense of good faith; he must be at pains to preserve a sufficient detachment from his client's interests so that he remains capable of a sound and objective appraisal of the propriety of what his client proposes to do." *Professional Responsibility: Report of the Joint Conference*, 44 A.B.A.J. 1159, 1161 (1958).

10. "[A] lawyer who is asked to advise his client . . . may freely urge the statement of positions most favorable to the client just as long as there is reasonable basis for those positions." *ABA Opinion* 314 (1965).

11. "The lawyer . . . is not an umpire, but an advocate. He is under no duty to refrain from making every proper argument in support of any legal point because he is not convinced of its inherent soundness. . . . His personal belief in the soundness of his cause or of the authorities supporting it, is irrelevant." *ABA Opinion* 280 (1949).

"Counsel apparently misconceived his role. It was his duty to honorably present his client's contentions in the light most favorable to his client. Instead he presumed to advise the court as to the validity and sufficiency of prisoner's motion, by letter. We therefore conclude that prisoner had no effective assistance of counsel and remand this case to the District Court with instructions to set aside the Judgment, appoint new counsel to represent the prisoner if he makes no objection thereto, and proceed anew." McCartney v. United States, 343 F. 2d 471, 472 (9th Cir. 1965).

12. "Here the court-appointed counsel had the transcript but refused to proceed with the appeal because he found no merit in it. . . . We cannot say that there was a finding of frivolity by either of the California courts or that counsel acted in any greater capacity than merely as *amicus curiae* which was condemned in *Ellis, supra*. Hence California's procedure did not furnish petitioner with counsel acting in the role of an advocate nor did it provide that full consideration and resolution of the matter as is obtained when counsel is acting in that capacity. . . .

"The constitutional requirement of substantial equality and fair process can only be attained where counsel acts in the role of an active advocate in behalf of his client, as opposed to that of *amicus curiae*. The no-merit letter and the procedure it triggers do not reach that dignity. Counsel should, and can with honor and without conflict, be of more assistance to his client and to the court. His role as advocate requires that he support his client's appeal to the best of his ability. Of course, if counsel finds his case to be wholly frivolous, after a conscientious examination of it, he should so advise the court and request permission to withdraw. That request must, however, be accompanied by a brief referring to anything in the record that might arguably support the appeal. A copy of counsel's brief should be furnished the indigent and time allowed him to raise any points that he chooses; the court—not counsel—then proceeds, after a full examination of all the proceedings, to decide whether the case is wholly frivolous. If it so finds it may grant counsel's request to withdraw and dismiss the appeal insofar as federal requirements are concerned, or proceed to a decision on the merits, if state law so requires. On the other hand, if it finds any of the legal points arguable on their merits (and therefore not frivolous) it must, prior to decision, afford the indigent the assistance of counsel to argue the appeal." Anders v. California, 386 U.S. 738, 744. 18 L. Ed. 2d 493, 498, 87 S. Ct. 1396, 1399-1400 (1967), *rehearing denied*, 388 U.S. 924, 18 L. Ed. 2d 1377, 87 S. Ct. 2094 (1967).

See Paul, *The Lawyer As a Tax Adviser*, 25 Rocky Mt. L. Rev. 412, 432 (1953).

13. See ABA Canon 32.

14. "For a lawyer to represent a syndicate notoriously engaged in the violation of the law for the purpose of advising the members how to break the law and at the same time escape it, is manifestly improper. While a lawyer may see to it that anyone accused of crime, no matter how serious and flagrant, has a fair trial, and present all available defenses, he may not co-operate in planning violations of the law. There is a sharp distinction, of course, between advising what can lawfully be done and advising how unlawful acts can be done in a way to avoid conviction. Where a lawyer accepts a retainer from an organization, known to be unlawful, and agrees in advance to defend its members when from time to time they are accused of crime arising out of its unlawful activities, this is equally improper."

"See also *Opinion* 155." *ABA Opinion* 281 (1952).

15. *See* ABA Special Committee on Minimum Standards for the Administration of Criminal Justice, *Standards Relating to Pleas of Guilty* pp. 69-70 (1968).

16. "First of all, a truly great lawyer is a wise counselor to all manner of men in the varied crises of their lives when they most need disinterested advice. Effective counseling necessarily involves a thoroughgoing knowledge of the principles of the law not merely as they appear in the books but as they actually operate in action." Vanderbilt, *The Five Functions of the Lawyer: Service to Clients and the Public*, 40 A.B.A.J. 31 (1954).

17. "A lawyer should endeavor to obtain full knowledge of his client's cause before advising thereon. . . ." ABA Canon 8.

18. "[I]n devising charters of collaborative effort the lawyer often acts where all of the affected parties are present as participants. But the lawyer also performs a similar function in situations where this is not so, as, for example, in planning estates and drafting wills. Here the instrument defining the terms of collaboration may affect persons not present and

often not born. Yet here, too, the good lawyer does not serve merely as a legal conduit for his client's desires, but as a wise counselor, experienced in the art of devising arrangements that will put in workable order the entangled affairs and interests of human beings." *Professional Responsibility: Report of the Joint Conference,* 44 A.B.A.J. 1159, 1162 (1958).

19. *See* ABA Canon 8.

"Vital as is the lawyer's role in adjudication, it should not be thought that it is only as an advocate pleading in open court that he contributes to the administration of the law. The most effective realization of the law's aims often takes place in the attorney's office, where litigation is forestalled by anticipating its outcome, where the lawyer's quiet counsel takes the place of public force. Contrary to popular belief, the compliance with the law thus brought about is not generally lip-serving and narrow, for by reminding him of its long-run costs the lawyer often deters his client from a course of conduct technically permissible under existing law, though inconsistent with its underlying spirit and purpose." *Professional Responsibility: Report of the Joint Conference,* 44 A.B.A.J. 1159, 1161 (1958).

20. "My summation of Judge Sharswood's view of the advocate's duty to the client is that he owes to the client the duty to use all legal means in support of the client's case. However, at the same time Judge Sharswood recognized that many advocates would find this obligation unbearable if applicable without exception. Therefore, the individual lawyer is given the choice of representing his client fully within the bounds set by the law *or of telling his client that he cannot do so*, so that the client may obtain another attorney if he wishes." Thode, *The Ethical Standard for the Advocate*, 39 Texas L. Rev. 575, 582 (1961).

Cf. Code of Professional Responsibility, DR 2-110 (C).

21. *See* ABA Canon 24.

22. Thode, *The Ethical Standard for the Advocate*, 39 Texas L. Rev. 575, 592 (1961).

23. *Cf. ABA Opinions* 253 (1943) and 178 (1938).

24. *See* ABA Canon 5 and Berger v. United States, 295 U.S. 78, 79 L. Ed. 1314, 55 S. Ct. 629 (1935).

"The public prosecutor cannot take as a guide for the conduct of his office the standards of an attorney appearing on behalf of an individual client. The freedom elsewhere wisely granted to a partisan advocate must be severely curtailed if the prosecutor's duties are to be properly discharged. The public prosecutor must recall that he occupies a dual role, being obligated, on the one hand, to furnish that adversary element essential to the informed decision of any controversy, but being possessed, on the other, of important governmental powers that are pledged to the accomplishment of one objective only, that of impartial justice. Where the prosecutor is recreant to the trust implicit in his office, he undermines confidence, not only in his profession, but in government and the very ideal of justice itself." *Professional Responsibility: Report of the Joint Conference,* 44 A.B.A.J. 1159, 1218 (1958).

"The prosecuting attorney is the attorney for the state, and it is his primary duty not to convict but to see that justice is done." *ABA Opinion* 150 (1936).

25. As to appearances before a department of government, Canon 26 provides: "A lawyer openly . . . may render professional services . . . in advocacy of claims before departments of government, upon the same principles of ethics which justify his appearance before the Courts . . . ."

26. "But as an advocate before a service which itself represents the adversary point of view, where his client's case is fairly arguable, a lawyer is under no duty to disclose its weaknesses, any more than he would be to make such a disclosure to a brother lawyer. The limitations within which he must operate are best expressed in Canon 22 . . . ." *ABA Opinion* 314 (1965).

27. See Baird v. Koerner, 279 F.2d 623 (9th Cir. 1960).

28. *See* ABA Canon 26.

29. "Law should be so practiced that the lawyer remains free to make up his own mind how he will vote, what causes he will support, what economic and political philosophy he will espouse. It is one of the glories of the profession that it admits of this freedom. Distinguished examples can be cited of lawyers whose views were at variance from those of their clients, lawyers whose skill and wisdom make them valued advisers to those who had little sympathy with their views as citizens." *Professional Responsibility: Report of the Joint Conference,* 44 A.B.A.J. 1159, 1217 (1958).

"No doubt some tax lawyers feel constrained to abstain from activities on behalf of a better tax system because they think that their clients may object. Clients have no right to object if the tax adviser handles their affairs competently and faithfully and independently of his private views as to tax policy. They buy his expert services, not his private opinions or his silence on issues that gravely affect the public interest." Paul, *The Lawyer as a Tax Adviser*, 25 Rocky Mt. L. Rev. 412, 434 (1953).

30. *See* ABA Canon 9.

31. *Id.*

32. *See Professional Responsibility: Report of the Joint Conference,* 44 A.B.A.J. 1159, 1160 (1958).

33. "Without the participation of someone who can act responsibly for each of the parties, this essential narrowing of the issues [by exchange of written pleadings or stipulations of counsel] becomes impossible. But here again the true significance of

partisan advocacy lies deeper, touching once more the integrity of the adjudicative process itself. It is only through the advocate's participation that the hearing may remain in fact what it purports to be in theory: a public trial of the facts and issues. Each advocate comes to the hearing prepared to present his proofs and arguments, knowing at the same time that his arguments may fail to persuade and that his proof may be rejected as inadequate. . . . The deciding tribunal, on the other hand, comes to the hearing uncommitted. It has not represented to the public that any fact can be proved, that any argument is sound, or that any particular way of stating a litigant's case is the most effective expression of its merits." *Professional Responsibility: Report of the Joint Conference,* 44 A.B.A.J. 1159, 1160-61 (1958).

34. *Cf.* ABA Canons 15 and 32.

35. *Cf.* ABA Canon 21.

36. See *Professional Responsibility: Report of the Joint Conference,* 44 A.B.A.J. 1159, 1216 (1958).

37. "We are of the opinion that the letter in question was improper, and that in writing and sending it respondent was guilty of unprofessional conduct. This court has heretofore expressed its disapproval of using threats of criminal prosecution as a means of forcing settlement of civil claims. . . .

"Respondent has been guilty of a violation of a principle which condemns any confusion of threats of criminal prosecution with the enforcement of civil claims. For this misconduct he should be severely censured." Matter of Gelman, 230 App. Div. 524, 527, N. Y. S. 416, 419 (1930).

38. "An attorney has the duty to protect the interests of his client. He has a right to press legitimate argument and to protest an erroneous ruling." Gallagher v. Municipal Court, 31 Cal. 2d 784, 796, 192 P.2d 905, 913 (1948).

"There must be protection, however, in the far more frequent case of the attorney who stands on his rights and combats the order in good faith and without disrespect believing with good cause that it is void, for it is here that the independence of the bar becomes valuable." Note, 39 Colum. L. Rev. 433, 438 (1939).

39. "Too many do not understand that accomplishment of the layman's abstract ideas of justice is the function of the judge and jury, and that it is the lawyer's sworn duty to portray his client's case in its most favorable light." Rochelle and Payne, *The Struggle for Public Understanding,* 25 Texas B.J. 109, 159 (1962).

40. "We are of the opinion that this Canon requires the lawyer to disclose such decisions [that are adverse to his client's contentions] to the court. He may, of course, after doing so, challenge the soundness of the decisions or present reasons which he believes would warrant the court in not following them in the pending case." ABA *Opinion* 146 (1935).

Cf. ABA *Opinion* 280 (1949) and Thode, *The Ethical Standard for the Advocate,* 39 Texas L. Rev. 575, 585-86 (1961).

41. *See* ABA Canon 15.

"The traditional duty of an advocate is that he honorably uphold the contentions of his client. He should not voluntarily undermine them." Harders v. State of California, 373 F.2d 839, 842 (9th Cir. 1967).

42. *See* ABA Canon 22.

43. *Id.; cf.* ABA Canon 41.

44. *See generally* ABA *Opinion* 287 (1953) as to a lawyer's duty when he unknowingly participates in introducing perjured testimony.

45. "Under any standard of proper ethical conduct an attorney should not sit by silently and permit his client to commit what may have been perjury, and which certainly would mislead the court and the opposing party on a matter vital to the issue under consideration. . . .

. . . .

"Respondent next urges that it was his duty to observe the utmost good faith toward his client, and therefore he could not divulge any confidential information. This duty to the client of course does not extend to the point of authorizing collaboration with him in the commission of fraud." In re Carroll, 244 S.W.2d 474, 474-75 (Ky. 1951).

46. *See* ABA Canon 5; *cf. ABA Opinion* 131 (1935).

47. *Cf.* ABA Canon 39.

48. "The prevalence of perjury is a serious menace to the administration of justice, to prevent which no means have as yet been satisfactorily devised. But there certainly can be no greater incentive to perjury than to allow a party to make payments to its opponents witnesses, under any guise or on any excuse, and at least attorneys who are officers of the court to aid it in the administration of justice, must keep themselves clear of any connection which in the slightest degree tends to induce witnesses to testify in favor of their clients." In re Robinson, 151 App. Div. 589, 600, 136 N.Y.S. 548, 556-57 (1912), *aff'd,* 209 N.Y. 354, 103 N.E. 160 (1913).

49. "It will not do for an attorney who seeks to justify himself against charges of this kind to show that he has escaped criminal responsibility under the Penal Law, nor can he blindly shut his eyes to a system which tends to suborn witnesses, to produce perjured testimony, and to suppress the truth. He has an active affirmative duty to protect the administration of justice from perjury and fraud, and that duty is not performed by allowing his subordinates and assistants to attempt to subvert justice and procure results for his

clients based upon false testimony and perjured witnesses." *Id.*, 151 App. Div. at 592, 136 N.Y.S. at 551.

50. *See* ABA Canon 23.

51. "[I]t is unfair to jurors to permit a disappointed litigant to pick over their private associations in search of something to discredit them and their verdict. And it would be unfair to the public too if jurors should understand that they cannot convict a man of means without risking an inquiry of that kind by paid investigators, with, to boot, the distortions an inquiry of that kind can produce." State v. LaFera, 42 N.J. 97, 107, 199 A.2d 630, 636 (1964).

52. *ABA Opinion* 319 (1968) points out that "[m]any courts today, and the trend is in this direction, allow the testimony of jurors as to all irregularities in and out of the courtroom except those irregularities whose existence can be determined only by exploring the consciousness of a single particular juror, New Jersey v. Kociolek, 20, N.J. 92, 118 A.2d 812 (1955). Model Code of Evidence Rule 301. Certainly as to states in which the testimony and affidavits of jurors may be received in support of or against a motion for new trial, a lawyer, in his obligation to protect his client, must have the tools for ascertaining whether or not grounds for a new trial exist and it is not unethical for him to talk to and question jurors."

53. *Generally see* ABA Advisory Committee on Fair Trial and Free Press, Standards Relating to Fair Trial and Free Press (1966).

"[T]he trial court might well have proscribed extrajudicial statements by any lawyer, party, witness, or court official which divulged prejudicial matters.... See State v. Van Dwyne, 43 N.J. 369, 389, 204 A.2d 841, 852 1964), in which the court interpreted Canon 20 of the American Bar Association's Canons of Professional Ethics to prohibit such statements. Being advised of the great public interest in the case, the mass coverage of the press, and the potential prejudicial impact of publicity, the court could also have requested the appropriate city and county officials to promulgate a regulation with respect to dissemination of information about the case by their employees. In addition, reporters who wrote or broadcast prejudicial stories, could have been warned as to the impropriety of publishing material not introduced in the proceedings.... In this manner, Sheppard's right to a trial free from outside interference would have been given added protection without corresponding curtailment of the news media. Had the judge, the other officers of the court, and the police placed the interest of justice first, the news media would have soon learned to be content with the task of reporting the case as unfolded in the courtroom—not pieced together from extrajudicial statements." Sheppard v. Maxwell, 384 U.S. 333, 361-62, 16 L. Ed. 2d 600, 619-20, 86 S. Ct. 1507, 1521-22 (1966).

"Court proceedings are held for the solemn purpose of endeavoring to ascertain the truth which is the *sine qua non* of a fair trial. Over the centuries Anglo-American courts have devised careful safeguards by rule and otherwise to protect and facilitate the performance of this high function. As a result, at this time those safeguards do not permit the televising and photographing of a criminal trial, save in two States and there only under restrictions. The federal courts prohibit it by specific rule. This is weighty evidence that our concepts of a fair trial do not tolerate such an indulgence. We have always held that the atmosphere essential to the preservation of a fair trial—the most fundamental of all freedoms—must be maintained at all costs." Estes v. State of Texas, 381 U.S. 532, 540, 14 L. Ed. 2d 543, 549, 85 S. Ct. 1628, 1631-32 (1965), *rehearing denied*, 382 U.S. 875, 15 L. Ed. 2d 118, 86 S. Ct. 18 (1965).

54. "Pretrial can create a major problem for the defendant in a criminal case. Indeed, it may be more harmful than publicity during the trial for it may well set the community opinion as to guilt or innocence.... The trial witnesses present at the hearing, as well as the original jury panel, were undoubtedly made aware of the peculiar public importance of the case by the press and television coverage being provided, and by the fact that they themselves were televised live and their pictures rebroadcast on the evening show." *Id.*, 381 U.S. at 536-37, 14 L. Ed. 2d at 546-47, 85 S. Ct. at 1629-30.

55. "The undeviating rule of this Court was expressed by Mr. Justice Holmes over half a century ago in Patterson v. Colorado, 205 U.S. 454, 462 (1907):

> The theory of our system is that the conclusions to be reached in a case will be induced only by evidence and argument in open court, and not by any outside influence, whether of private talk or public print."

Sheppard v. Maxwell, 384 U.S. 333, 351. 16 L. Ed. 2d 600, 614, 86 S. Ct. 1507, 1516 (1966).

"The trial judge has a large discretion in ruling on the issue of prejudice resulting from the reading by jurors of news articles concerning the trial.... Generalizations beyond that statement are not profitable, because each case must turn on its special facts. We have here the exposure of jurors to information of a character which the trial judge ruled was so prejudicial it could not be directly offered as evidence. The prejudice to the defendant is almost certain to be as great when that evidence reaches the jury through news accounts as when it is a part of the prosecution's evidence.... It may indeed be greater for it is then not tempered by protective procedures." Marshall v. United States, 360 U.S. 310, 312-13, 3 L. Ed. 2d 1250, 1252, 79 S. Ct. 1171, 1173 (1959).

"The experienced trial lawyer knows that an adverse public opinion is a tremendous disadvantage to the defense of his client. Although grand jurors conduct their deliberations in secret, they are selected from the body of the public. They are likely to know what the general public knows and to reflect the public attitude. Trials are open to the public, and aroused public opinion respecting the merits of a legal controversy creates a court room atmosphere which, without any vocal expression in the presence of the petit jury, makes itself felt and has its effect upon the action of the petit jury. Our fundamental concepts of justice and our American sense of fair play require that the petit jury shall be composed of persons with fair and impartial minds and without preconceived views as to the merits of the controversy, and that it shall determine the issues presented to it solely upon the evidence adduced at the trial and according to the law given in the instructions of the trial judge.

"While we may doubt that the effect of public opinion would sway or bias the judgment of the trial judge in an equity proceeding, the defendant should not be called upon to run that risk and the trial court should not have his work made more difficult by any dissemination of statements to the public that would be calculated to create a public demand for a particular judgment in a prospective or pending case." *ABA Opinion* 199 (1940).

Cf. Estes v. State of Texas, 381 U.S. 532, 544-45, 144 L. Ed. 2d 543, 551, 85 S. Ct. 1628, 1634 (1965), *rehearing denied*, 381 U.S. 875, 15 L. Ed. 2d 118, 86 S. Ct. 18 (1965).

56. *See* ABA Canon 20.

57. Canon 3 observes that a lawyer "deserves rebuke and denunciation for any device or attempt to gain from a Judge special personal consideration or favor."

See ABA Canon 32.

58. *"Judicial Canon 32* provides:

A judge should not accept any presents or favors from litigants, or from lawyers practicing before him or from others whose interests are likely to be submitted to him for judgment.

The language of this Canon is perhaps broad enough to prohibit campaign contributions by lawyers, practicing before the court upon which the candidate hopes to sit. However, we do not think it was intended to prohibit such contributions when the candidate is obligated, by force of circumstances over which he has no control, to conduct a campaign, the expense of which exceeds that which he should reasonably be expected to personally bear!" *ABA Opinion* 226 (1941).

59. *See* ABA Canons 3 and 32.

60. *Cf.* ABA Canon 18.

61. *See* ABA Canons 1 and 3.

62. *See* ABA Canon 17.

63. *See* ABA Canon 24.

64. *See* ABA Canon 25.

65. *See* ABA Canon 21.

66. *See* ABA Canon 15.

67. *See* ABA Canons 5 and 15; *cf.* ABA Canons 4 and 32.

68. *Cf.* ABA Canon 24.

69. *See* ABA Canon 30.

70. *Cf.* ABA Canons 22 and 29.

71. *See* ABA Canon 41; *cf.* Hinds v. State Bar, 19 Cal. 2d 87, 92-93, 119 P.2d 134, 137 (1941); *but see ABA Opinion* 287 (1953) and Texas Canon 38. *Also see* Code of Professional Responsibility, DR 4-101 (C) (2).

72. *See* Precision Inst. Mfg. Co. v. Automotive M.M. Co., 324 U.S. 806, 89 L. Ed. 1381, 65 S. Ct. 993 (1945).

73. *Cf.* ABA Canon 5.

74. "Rule 12.... A member of the State Bar shall not communicate with a party represented by counsel upon a subject of controversy, in the absence and without the consent of such counsel. This rule shall not apply to communications with a public officer, board, committee or body." Cal. Business and Professions Code §6076 (West 1962).

75. *See* ABA Canon 9; *cf. ABA Opinions* 124 (1934), 108 (1934), 95 (1933), and 75 (1932); *also see* In re Schwabe, 242 Or. 169, 174-75, 408 P.2d 922, 924 (1965).

"It is clear from the earlier opinions of this committee that *Canon 9* is to be construed literally and does not allow a communication with an opposing party, without the consent of his counsel, though the purpose merely be to investigate the facts. *Opinions 117, 55, 66," ABA Opinion* 187 (1938).

76. *Cf. ABA Opinion* 102 (1933).

77. *Cf.* ABA Canon 9 and *ABA Opinion* 58 (1931).

78. *Cf.* Note, 38 Texas L. Rev. 107, 108-09 (1959).

79. "In the brief summary in the 1947 edition of the Committee's decisions (p. 17), *Opinion 146* was thus summarized: *Opinion 146*—A lawyer should disclose to the court a decision directly adverse to his client's case that is unknown to his adversary.

....

"We would not confine the Opinion to 'controlling authorities'—i.e., those decisive of the pending case—but, in accordance with the tests hereafter suggested, would apply it to a decision directly adverse to any proposition of law on which the lawyer expressly relies, which would reasonably be considered important by the judge sitting on the case.

. . . .

". . . The test in every case should be: Is the decision which opposing counsel has overlooked one which the court should clearly consider in deciding the case? Would a reasonable judge properly feel that a lawyer who advanced, as the law, a proposition adverse to the undisclosed decision, was lacking in candor and fairness to him? Might the judge consider himself misled by an implied representation that the lawyer knew of no adverse authority?" *ABA Opinion* 280 (1949).

80. "The authorities are substantially uniform against any privilege as applied to the fact of retainer or identity of the client. The privilege is limited to confidential communications, and a retainer is not a confidential communication, although it cannot come into existence without some communication between the attorney and the—at that stage prospective—client." United States v. Pape, 144 F.2d 778, 782 (2d Cir. 1944), *cert. denied,* 323 U.S. 752, 89 L. Ed. 2d 602, 65 S. Ct. 86 (1944).

"To be sure, there may be circumstances under which the identification of a client may amount to the prejudicial disclosure of a confidential communication, as where the substance of a disclosure has already been revealed but not its source." Colton v. United States, 306 F.2d 633, 637 (2d Cir. 1962).

81. *See* ABA Canon 22; *cf.* ABA Canon 17.

"The rule allowing counsel when addressing the jury the widest latitude in discussing the evidence and presenting the client's theories falls far short of authorizing the statement by counsel of matter not in evidence, or indulging in argument founded on no proof, or demanding verdicts for purposes other than the just settlement of the matters at issue between the litigants, or appealing to prejudice or passion. The rule confining counsel to legitimate argument is not based on etiquette, but on justice. Its violation is not merely an overstepping of the bounds of propriety, but a violation of a party's rights. The jurors must determine the issues upon the evidence. Counsel's address should help them do this, not tend to lead them astray." Cherry Creek Nat. Bank v. Fidelity & Cas. Co., 207 App. Div. 787, 790-91, 202 N.Y.S. 611, 614 (1924).

82. *Cf.* ABA Canon 18.

§6068. . . . It is the duty of an attorney:

. . . .

"(f) To abstain from all offensive personality, and to advance no fact prejudicial to the honor or reputation of a party or witness, unless required by the justice of the cause with which he is charged." Cal. Business and Professions Code §6068 (West 1962).

83. "The record in the case at bar was silent concerning the qualities and character of the deceased. It is especially improper, in addressing the jury in a murder case, for the prosecuting attorney to make reference to his knowledge of the good qualities of the deceased where there is no evidence in the record bearing upon his character. . . . A prosecutor should never inject into his argument evidence not introduced at the trial." People v. Dukes, 12 Ill. 2d 334, 341, 146 N.E.2d 14, 17-18 (1957).

84. "A lawyer should not ignore known customs or practice of the Bar or of a particular Court, even when the law permits, without giving timely notice to the opposing counsel." ABA Canon 25.

85. The provisions of Section (A), (B), (C), and (D) of this Disciplinary Rule incorporate the fair trial-free press standards which apply to lawyers as adopted by the ABA House of Delegates, Feb. 19, 1968, upon the recommendation of the Fair Trial and Free Press Advisory Committee of the ABA Special Committee on Minimum Standards for the Administration of Criminal Justice.

Cf. ABA Canon 20; *see generally* ABA Advisory Committee on Fair Trial and Free Press, Standards Relating to Fair Trial and Free Press (1966).

"From the cases coming here we note that unfair and prejudicial news comment on pending trials has become increasingly prevalent. Due process requires that the accused receive a trial by an impartial jury free from outside influences. Given the pervasiveness of modern communications and the difficulty of effacing prejudicial publicity from the minds of the jurors, the trial courts must take strong measures to ensure that the balance is never weighed against the accused. And appellate tribunals have the duty to make an independent evaluation of the circumstances. Of course, there is nothing that prescribes the press from reporting events that transpire in the courtroom. But where there is a reasonable likelihood that judicial news prior to trial will prevent a fair trial, judge should continue the case until the threat abates, or transfer it to another county not so permeated with publicity. . . . The courts must take such steps by rule and regulation that will protect their processes from prejudicial outside interferences. Neither prosecutors, counsel for defense, the accused, witnesses, court staff nor enforcement officers coming under the jurisdiction of the court should be permitted to frustrate its function. Collaboration between counsel and the press as to information affecting the fairness of a criminal trial is not only subject to regulation, but is highly censurable and worthy of disciplinary measures." Sheppard v. Maxwell, 384 U.S. 333, 362-63, 16 L. Ed. 2d 600, 620, 86 S. Ct. 1507, 1522 (1966).

86. *See* ABA Canon 23.

Model Code of Professional Responsibility

87. "[I]t would be unethical for a lawyer to harass, entice, induce or exert influence on a juror to obtain his testimony." ABA *Opinion* 319 (1968).

88. *See* ABA Canon 5.

89. *Cf.* ABA Canon 5.

"Rule 15. . . . A member of the State Bar shall not advise a person, whose testimony could establish or tend to establish a material fact, to avoid service of process, or secrete himself, or otherwise to make his testimony unavailable." Cal. Business and Professions Code §6076 (West 1962).

90. *See* In re O'Keefe, 49 Mont. 369, 142 P. 638 (1914).

91. *Cf.* ABA Canon 3.

92. "Rule 16. . . . A member of the State Bar shall not, in the absence of opposing counsel, communicate with or argue to a judge or judicial officer except in open court upon the merits of a contested matter pending before such judge or judicial officer; nor shall he, without furnishing opposing counsel with a copy thereof, address a written communication to a judge or judicial officer concerning the merits of a contested matter pending before such judge or judicial officer. This rule shall not apply to ex parte matters." Cal. Business and Professions Code §6076 (West 1962).

CANON 8

A Lawyer Should Assist in Improving the Legal System

ETHICAL CONSIDERATIONS

EC 8-1 Changes in human affairs and imperfections in human institutions make necessary constant efforts to maintain and improve our legal system.¹ This system should function in a manner that commands public respect and fosters the use of legal remedies to achieve redress of grievances. By reason of education and experience, lawyers are especially qualified to recognize deficiencies in the legal system and to initiate corrective measures therein. Thus they should participate in proposing and supporting legislation and programs to improve the system,² without regard to the general interests or desires of clients or former clients.³

EC 8-2 Rules of law are deficient if they are not just, understandable, and responsive to the needs of society. If a lawyer believes that the existence or absence of a rule of law, substantive or procedural, causes or contributes to an unjust result, he should endeavor by lawful means to obtain appropriate changes in the law. He should encourage the simplification of laws and the repeal or amendment of laws that are outmoded.⁴ Likewise, legal procedures should be improved whenever experience indicates a change is needed.

EC 8-3 The fair administration of justice requires the availability of competent lawyers. Members of the public should be educated to recognize the existence of legal problems and the resultant need for legal services, and should be provided methods for intelligent selection of counsel. Those persons unable to pay for legal services should be provided needed services. Clients and lawyers should not be penalized by undue geographical restraints upon representation in legal matters, and the bar should address itself to improvements in licensing, reciprocity, and admission procedures consistent with the needs of modern commerce.

EC 8-4 Whenever a lawyer seeks legislative or administrative changes, he should identify the capacity in which he appears, whether on behalf of himself, a client, or the public.⁵ A lawyer may advocate such changes on behalf of a client even though he does not agree with them. But where a lawyer purports to act on behalf of the public, he should espouse only those changes which he conscientiously believes to be in the public interest.

EC 8-5 Fraudulent, deceptive, or otherwise illegal conduct by a participant in a proceeding before a tribunal or legislative body is inconsistent with fair administration of justice, and it should never be participated in or condoned

by lawyers. Unless constrained by his obligation to preserve the confidences and secrets of his client, a lawyer should reveal to appropriate authorities any knowledge he may have of such improper conduct.

EC 8-6 Judges and administrative officials having adjudicatory powers ought to be persons of integrity, competence, and suitable temperament. Generally, lawyers are qualified, by personal observation or investigation, to evaluate the qualifications of persons seeking or being considered for such public offices, and for this reason they have a special responsibility to aid in the selection of only those who are qualified.[6] It is the duty of lawyers to endeavor to prevent political considerations from outweighing judicial fitness in the selection of judges. Lawyers should protest earnestly against the appointment or election of those who are unsuited for the bench and should strive to have elected[7] or appointed thereto only those who are willing to forego pursuits, whether of a business, political, or other nature, that may interfere with the free and fair consideration of questions presented for adjudication. Adjudicatory officials, not being wholly free to defend themselves, are entitled to receive the support of the bar against unjust criticism.[8] While a lawyer as a citizen has a right to criticize such officials publicly,[9] he should be certain of the merit of his complaint, use appropriate language, and avoid petty criticisms, for unrestrained and intemperate statements tend to lessen public confidence in our legal system.[10] Criticisms motivated by reasons other than a desire to improve the legal system are not justified.

EC 8-7 Since lawyers are a vital part of the legal system, they should be persons of integrity, of professional skill, and of dedication to the improvement of the system. Thus a lawyer should aid in establishing, as well as enforcing, standards of conduct adequate to protect the public by insuring that those who practice law are qualified to do so.

EC 8-8 Lawyers often serve as legislators or as holders of other public offices. This is highly desirable, as lawyers are uniquely qualified to make significant contributions to the improvement of the legal system. A lawyer who is a public officer, whether full or part-time, should not engage in activities in which his personal or professional interests are or foreseeably may be in conflict with his official duties.[11]

EC 8-9 The advancement of our legal system is of vital importance in maintaining the rule of law and in facilitating orderly changes; therefore, lawyers should encourage, and should aid in making, needed changes and improvements.

DISCIPLINARY RULES

DR 8-101 Action as a Public Official.
(A) A lawyer who holds public office shall not:
 (1) Use his public position to obtain, or attempt to obtain, a special advantage in legislative matters for himself or for a client under circumstances where he knows or it is obvious that such action is not in the public interest.
 (2) Use his public position to influence, or attempt to influence, a tribunal to act in favor of himself or of a client.
 (3) Accept any thing of value from any person when the lawyer knows or it is obvious that the offer is for the purpose of influencing his action as a public official.

DR 8-102 Statements Concerning Judges and Other Adjudicatory Officers.[12]
(A) A lawyer shall not knowingly make false statements of fact concerning the qualifications of a candidate for election or appointment to a judicial office.
(B) A lawyer shall not knowingly make false accusations against a judge or other adjudicatory officer.

DR 8-103 Lawyer Candidate for Judicial Office.
(A) A lawyer who is a candidate for judicial office shall comply with the applicable provisions of Canon 7 of the Code of Judicial Conduct.

Model Code of Professional Responsibility

NOTES

1. "... [Another] task of the great lawyer is to do his part individually and as a member of the organized bar to improve his profession, the courts, and the law. As President Theodore Roosevelt aptly put it, 'Every man owes some of his time to the upbuilding of the profession to which he belongs.' Indeed, this obligation is one of the great things which distinguishes a profession from a business. The soundness and the necessity of President Roosevelt's admonition insofar as it relates to the legal profession cannot be doubted. The advances in natural science and technology are so startling and the velocity of change in business and in social life is so great that the law along with the other social sciences, and even human life itself, is in grave danger of being extinguished by new gods of its own invention if it does not awake from its lethargy. Vanderbilt, *The Five Functions of the Lawyer: Service to Clients and the Public*, 40 A.B.A.J. 31, 31-32 (1954).

2. *See* ABA Canon 29; *Cf.* Cheatham, *The Lawyer's Role and Surroundings*, 25 Rocky Mt. L. Rev. 405, 406-07 (1953).

"The lawyer tempted by repose should recall the heavy costs paid by his profession when needed legal reform has to be accomplished through the initiative of public-spirited laymen. Where change must be thrust from without upon an unwilling Bar, the public's least flattering picture of the lawyer seems confirmed. The lawyer concerned for the standing of his profession will, therefore, interest himself actively in the improvement of the law. In doing so he will not only help to maintain confidence in the Bar, but will have the satisfaction of meeting a responsibility inhering in the nature of his calling." *Professional Responsibility: Report of the Joint Conference*, 44 A.B.A.J. 1159, 1217 (1958).

3. *See* Stayton, *Cum Honore Officium*, 19 Tex. B.J. 765, 766 (1956); *Professional Responsibility: Report of the Joint Conference*, 44 A.B.A.J. 1159, 1162 (1958); and Paul, *The Lawyer as a Tax Adviser*, _5 Rocky Mt. L. Rev. 412, 433-34 (1953).

4. "There are few great figures in the history of the Bar who have not concerned themselves with the reform and improvement of the law. The special obligation of the profession with respect to legal reform rests on considerations too obvious to require enumeration. Certainly it is the lawyer who has both the best chance to know when the law is working badly and the special competence to put it in order." *Professional Responsibility: Report of the Joint Conference*, 44 A.B.A.J. 1159, 1217 (1958).

5. "*Rule 14.* ... A member of the State Bar shall not communicate with, or appear before, a public officer, board, committee or body, in his professional capacity, without first disclosing that he is an attorney representing interests that may be affected by action of such officer, board, committee or body." Cal. Business and Professions Code §6076 (West 1962).

6. *See* ABA Canon 2.

"Lawyers are better able than laymen to appraise accurately the qualifications of candidates for judicial office. It is proper that they should make that appraisal known to the voters in a proper and dignified manner. A lawyer may with propriety endorse a candidate for judicial office and seek like endorsement from other lawyers. But the lawyer who endorses a judicial candidate or seeks that endorsement from other lawyers should be actuated by a sincere belief in the superior qualifications of the candidate for judicial service and not by personal or selfish motives; and a lawyer should not use or attempt to use the power or prestige of the judicial office to secure such endorsement. On the other hand, the lawyer whose endorsement is sought, if he believes the candidate lacks the essential qualifications for the office or believes the opposing candidate is better qualified, should have the courage and moral stamina to refuse the request for endorsement." *ABA Opinion* 189 (1938).

7. "[W]e are of the opinion that, whenever a candidate for judicial office merits the endorsement and support of lawyers, the lawyers may make financial contributions toward the campaign if its cost, when reasonably conducted, exceeds that which the candidate would be expected to bear personally." *ABA Opinion* 226 (1941).

8. *See* ABA Canon 1.

9. "Citizens have a right under our constitutional system to criticize governmental officials and agencies. Courts are not, and should not be, immune to such criticism." Konigsberg v. State Bar of California, 353 U.S. 252, 269 (1957).

10. "[E]very lawyer, worthy of respect, realizes that public confidence in our courts is the cornerstone of our governmental structure, and will refrain from unjustified attack on the character of the judges, while recognizing the duty to denounce and expose a corrupt or dishonest judge." Kentucky State Bar Ass'n v. Lewis, 282 S.W. 2d 321, 326 (Ky. 1955).

"We should be the last to deny that Mr. Meeker has the right to uphold the honor of the profession and to expose without fear or favor corrupt or dishonest conduct in the profession, whether the conduct be that of a judge or not.... However, this Canon [29] does not permit one to make charges which are false and untrue and unfounded in fact. When one's fancy leads him to make false charges, attacking the character and integrity of others, he does so at his peril. He should not do so without adequate proof of his charges and he is certainly not authorized to make careless, untruthful and vile charges against his professional brethren." In re Meeker, 76 N. M. 354, 364-65, 414 P.2d 862, 869 (1966), *appeal dismissed,* 385 U.S. 449, 17 L. Ed. 2d 510, 87 S. Ct. 613 (1967).

11. *"Opinions 16, 30, 34, 77, 118* and *134* relate to *Canon 6,* and pass on questions concerning the propriety of the conduct of an attorney who is a public officer, in representing private interests adverse to those of the public body which he represents. The principle applied in those opinions is that an attorney holding public office should avoid all conduct which might lead the layman to conclude that the attorney is utilizing his public position to further his professional success or personal interests." *ABA Opinion* 192 (1939).

"The next question is whether a lawyer-member of a legislative body may appear as counsel or co-counsel at hearings before a zoning board of appeals, or similar tribunal, created by the legislative group of which he is a member. We are of the opinion that he may practice before fact-finding officers, hearing bodies and commissioners, since under our views he may appear as counsel in the courts where his municipality is a party. Decisions made at such hearings are usually subject to administrative review by the courts upon the record there made. It would be inconsistent to say that a lawyer-member of a legislative body could not participate in a hearing at which the record is made, but could appear thereafter when the cause is heard by the courts on administrative review. This is subject to an important exception. He should not appear as counsel where the matter is subject to review by the legislative body of which he is a member. . . . We are of the opinion that where a lawyer does so appear there would be conflict of interests between his duty as an advocate for his client on the one hand and the obligation to his governmental unit on the other." In re Becker, 16 Ill. 2d 488, 494-95, 158 N. E. 2d 753, 756-57 (1959).

Cf. ABA Opinions 186 (1938), 136 (1935), 118 (1934), and 77 (1932).

12. *Cf.* ABA Canons 1 and 2.

CANON 9

A Lawyer Should Avoid Even the Appearance of Professional Impropriety

ETHICAL CONSIDERATIONS

EC 9-1 Continuation of the American concept that we are to be governed by rules of law requires that the people have faith that justice can be obtained through our legal system.[1] A lawyer should promote public confidence in our system and in the legal profession.[2]

EC 9-2 Public confidence in law and lawyers may be eroded by irresponsible or improper conduct of a lawyer. On occasion, ethical conduct of a lawyer may appear to laymen to be unethical. In order to avoid misunderstandings and hence to maintain confidence, a lawyer should fully and promptly inform his client of material developments in the matters being handled for the client. While a lawyer should guard against otherwise proper conduct that has a tendency to diminish public confidence in the legal system or in the legal profession, his duty to clients or to the public should never be subordinate merely because the full discharge of his obligation may be misunderstood or may tend to subject him or the legal profession to criticism. When explicit ethical guidance does not exist, a lawyer should determine his conduct by acting in a manner that promotes public confidence in the integrity and efficiency of the legal system and the legal profession.[3]

EC 9-3 After a lawyer leaves judicial office or other public employment, he should not accept employment in connection with any matter in which he had substantial responsibility prior to his leaving, since to accept employment would give the appearance of impropriety even if none exists.[4]

EC 9-4 Because the very essence of the legal system is to provide procedures by which matters can be presented in an impartial manner so that they may be decided solely upon the merits, any statement or suggestion by a lawyer that he can

Model Code of Professional Responsibility

or would attempt to circumvent those procedures is detrimental to the legal system and tends to undermine public confidence in it.

EC 9-5 Separation of the funds of a client from those of his lawyer not only serves to protect the client but also avoids even the appearance of impropriety, and therefore commingling of such funds should be avoided.

EC 9-6 Every lawyer owes a solemn duty to uphold the integrity and honor of his profession; to encourage respect for the law and for the courts and the judges thereof; to observe the Code of Professional Responsibility; to act as a member of a learned profession, one dedicated to public service; to cooperate with his brother lawyers in supporting the organized bar through the devoting of his time, efforts, and financial support as his professional standing and ability reasonably permit; to conduct himself so as to reflect credit on the legal profession and to inspire the confidence, respect, and trust of his clients and of the public; and to strive to avoid not only professional impropriety but also the appearance of impropriety.[5]

EC 9-7 A lawyer has an obligation to the public to participate in collective efforts of the bar to reimburse persons who have lost money or property as a result of the misappropriation or defalcation of another lawyer, and contribution to a clients' security fund is an acceptable method of meeting this obligation.

DISCIPLINARY RULES

DR 9-101 Avoiding Even the Appearance of Impropriety.[6]

(A) A lawyer shall not accept private employment in a matter upon the merits of which he has acted in a judicial capacity.[7]

(B) A lawyer shall not accept private employment in a matter in which he had substantial responsibility while he was a public employee.[8]

(C) A lawyer shall not state or imply that he is able to influence improperly or upon irrelevant grounds any tribunal, legislative body,[9] or public official.

DR 9-102 Preserving Identity of Funds and Property of a Client.[10]

(A) All funds of clients paid to a lawyer or law firm, other than advances for costs and expenses, shall be deposited in one or more identifiable bank accounts maintained in the state in which the law office is situated and no funds belonging to the lawyer or law firm shall be deposited therein except as follows:

 (1) Funds reasonably sufficient to pay bank charges may be deposited therein.

 (2) Funds belonging in part to a client and in part presently or potentially to the lawyer or law firm must be deposited therein, but the portion belonging to the lawyer or law firm may be withdrawn when due unless the right of the lawyer or law firm to receive it is disputed by the client, in which event the disputed portion shall not be withdrawn until the dispute is finally resolved.

(B) A lawyer shall:

 (1) Promptly notify a client of the receipt of his funds, securities, or other properties.

 (2) Identify and label securities and properties of a client promptly upon receipt and place them in a safe deposit box or other place of safekeeping as soon as practicable.

 (3) Maintain complete records of all funds, securities, and other properties of a client coming into the possession of the lawyer and render appropriate accounts to his client regarding them.

 (4) Promptly pay or deliver to the client as requested by a client the funds, securities, or other properties in the possession of the lawyer which the client is entitled to receive.

NOTES

1. "Integrity is the very breath of justice. Confidence in our law, our courts, and in the administration of justice is our supreme interest. No practice must be permitted to prevail which invites towards the administration of justice a doubt or distrust of its integrity." Erwin M. Jennings Co. v. DiGenova, 107 Conn. 491, 499, 141 A. 866, 868 (1928).

2. "A lawyer should never be reluctant or too proud to answer unjustified criticism of his profession, of himself, or of his brother lawyer. He should guard the reputation of his profession and of his brothers as zealously as he guards his own." Rochelle and Payne, *The Struggle for Public Understanding,* 25 TEXAS B. J. 109, 162 (1962).

3. *See* ABA CANON 29.

4. *See* ABA CANON 36.

5. "As said in Opinion 49, of the Committee on Professional Ethics and Grievances of the American Bar Association, page 134: 'An attorney should not only avoid impropriety but should avoid the appearance of impropriety.'" State ex rel. Nebraska State Bar Ass'n v. Richards, 165 Neb. 80, 93, 84 N.W.2d 136, 145 (1957).

"It would also be preferable that such contribution [to the campaign of a candidate for judicial office] be made to a campaign committee rather than to the candidate personally. In so doing, possible appearances of impropriety would be reduced to a minimum." *ABA Opinion* 226 (1941).

"The lawyer assumes high duties, and has imposed upon him grave responsibilities. He may be the means of much good or much mischief. Interests of vast magnitude are entrusted to him; confidence is reposed in him; life, liberty, character and property should be protected by him. He should guard, with jealous watchfulness, his own reputation, as well as that of his profession." People ex rel. Cutler v. Ford, 54 Ill. 520, 522 (1870), and also quoted in State Board of Law Examiners v. Sheldon, 43 Wyo. 522, 526, 7 P.2d 226, 227 (1932).

See ABA Opinion 150 (1936).

6. *Cf.* CODE OF PROFESSIONAL RESPONSIBILITY, EC 5-6.

7. *See* ABA CANON 36.

"It is the duty of the judge to rule on questions of law and evidence in misdemeanor cases and examinations in felony cases. That duty calls for impartial and uninfluenced judgment, regardless of the effect on those immediately involved or others who may, directly or indirectly, be affected. Discharge of that duty might be greatly interfered with if the judge, in another capacity, were permitted to hold himself out to employment by those who are to be, or who may be, brought to trial in felony cases, even though he did not conduct the examination. His private interests as a lawyer in building up his clientele, his duty as such zealously to espouse the cause of his private clients and to defend against charges of crime brought by law-enforcement agencies of which he is a part, might prevent, or even destroy, that unbiased judicial judgment which is so essential in the administration of justice.

"In our opinion, acceptance of a judgeship with the duties of conducting misdemeanor trials, and examinations in felony cases to determine whether those accused should be bound over for trial in a higher court, ethically bars the judge from acting as attorney for the defendants upon such trial, whether they were examined by him or by some other judge. Such a practice would not only diminish public confidence in the administration of justice in both courts, but would produce serious conflict between the private interests of the judge as a lawyer, and of his clients, and his duties as a judge in adjudicating important phases of criminal processes in other cases. The public and private duties would be incompatible. The prestige of the judicial office would be diverted to private benefit, and the judicial office would be demeaned thereby." *ABA Opinion* 242 (1942).

"A lawyer, who has previously occupied a judicial position or acted in a judicial capacity, should refrain from accepting employment in any matter involving the same facts as were involved in any specific question which he acted upon in a judicial capacity and, for the same reasons, should also refrain from accepting any employment which might reasonably appear to involve the same facts." *ABA Opinion* 49 (1931).

See ABA Opinion 110 (1934).

8. *See* ABA *Opinions* 135 (1935) and 134 (1935); *cf.* ABA CANON 36 and *ABA Opinions* 39 (1931) and 26 (1930). *But see ABA Opinion* 37 (1931).

9. "[A statement by a governmental department or agency with regard to a lawyer resigning from its staff that includes a laudation of his legal ability] carries implications, probably not founded in fact, that the lawyer's acquaintance and previous relations with the personnel of the administrative agencies of the government place him in an advantageous position in practicing before such agencies. So to imply would not only represent what probably is untrue, but would be highly reprehensible." *ABA Opinion* 184 (1938).

10. *See* ABA CANON 11.

"Rule 9. . . . A member of the State Bar shall not commingle the money or other property of a client with his own; and he shall promptly report to the client the

Model Code of Professional Responsibility

receipt by him of all money and other property belonging to such client. Unless the client otherwise directs in writing, he shall promptly deposit his client's funds in a bank or trust company . . . in a bank account separate from his own account and clearly designated as 'Clients' Funds Account' or 'Trust Funds Account' or words of similar import. Unless the client otherwise directs in writing, securities of a client in bearer form shall be kept by the attorney in a safe deposit box at a bank or trust company. . . . which safe deposit box shall be clearly designated as 'Clients' Account' or 'Trust Account' or words of similar import, and be bank or trust company, . . . which safe deposit box CAL. BUSINESS AND PROFESSIONS CODE §6076 (West 1962).

"[C]ommingling is committed when a client's money is intermingled with that of his attorney and its separate identity lost so that it may be used for the attorney's personal expenses or subjected to claims of his creditors. . . . The rule against commingling was adopted to provide against the probability in some cases, the possibility in many cases, and the danger in all cases that such commingling will result in the loss of clients' money." Black v. State Bar, 57 Cal. 2d 219, 225-26, 368 P.2d 118, 122, 18 Cal. Rptr. 518, 522 (1962).

DEFINITIONS*

As used in the Disciplinary Rules of the Model Code of Professional Responsibility:

(1) "Differing interests" include every interest that will adversely affect either the judgment or the loyalty of a lawyer to a client, whether it be a conflicting, inconsistent, diverse, or other interest.

(2) "Law firm" includes a professional legal corporation.

(3) "Person" includes a corporation, an association, a trust, a partnership, and any other organization or legal entity.

(4) "Professional legal corporation" means a corporation, or an association treated as a corporation, authorized by law to practice law for profit.

(5) "State" includes the District of Columbia, Puerto Rico, and other federal territories and possessions.

(6) "Tribunal" includes all courts and all other adjudicatory bodies.

(7) "A Bar association" includes a bar association of specialists as referred to in DR 2-105 (A)(1) or (4).

(8) "Qualified legal assistance organization" means an office or organization of one of the four types listed in DR 2-103(D)(1)-(4), inclusive that meets all the requirements thereof.

---

*"Confidence" and "secret" are defined in DR 4-101(A).

NOTES

Why study with Kaplan PMBR?

The most realistic practice.
Our practice tests represent the difficulty and complexity of the real MBE with questions covering issues that are consistently repeated on the MBE—all administered under realistic testing conditions.

The most complete practice.
Kaplan PMBR teaches essential MBE strategies and techniques, with particular attention paid to the subtle distinctions required to master MBE questions.

The most up-to-date practice.
Kaplan PMBR monitors bar exam trends and updates materials yearly to reflect changing exam emphasis.

The most effective practice.
We teach to the test. All Kaplan PMBR courses use question-based review, or "QBR"—you don't just learn the law, you learn how to apply it through the MBE questions.

Call today to enroll!

MULTISTATE BAR REVIEW

1-800-523-0777 | kaplanpmbr.com